Microsoft® Office 2000 9 in 1 For Dummies

KT-224-404

A Typical Office 2000 Scene

Office 2000 is made up of quite a variety of applications, but the look among them can be eerily similar.

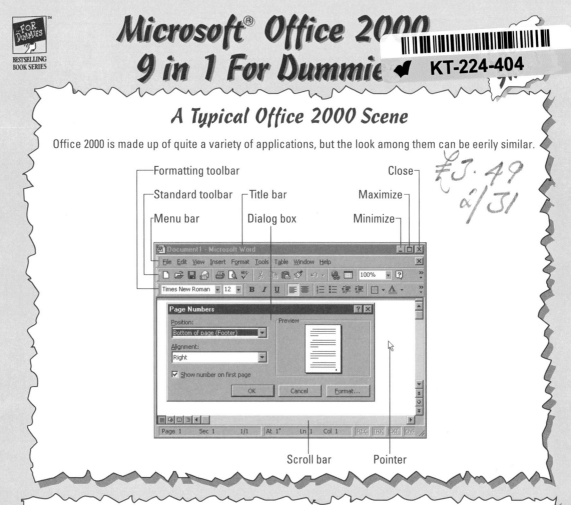

Formatting toolbar

Standard toolbar — Title bar

Menu bar — Dialog box

Close

Maximize

Minimize

£3.49
2/31

Scroll bar — Pointer

Office 2000 Common Commands

Office 2000 applications naturally share many functions. Seeing these buttons over and over again may make you feel right at home. Some of these commands even have keyboard equivalents if you tire of pressing buttons.

Button	Keyboard Equivalent	Action
	Ctrl+N	Opens a new document
	Ctrl+O	Opens an existing document
	Ctrl+S	Saves the open document
	Ctrl+P	Prints the open document
	none	Previews the document before printing
	F7	Checks spelling
	Ctrl+X	Cuts a selection

Button	Keyboard Equivalent	Action
	Ctrl+C	Copies a selection
	Ctrl+V	Pastes a selection
	Ctrl+Shift+C	Copies formatting for you to apply elsewhere
	Ctrl+Z	Undoes an action
	Ctrl+K	Inserts a hyperlink
	F1	Starts the Office Assistant

...For Dummies®: Bestselling Book Series for Beginners

Microsoft® Office 2000 9 in 1 For Dummies®

Cheat Sheet

Office 2000 Survival Glossary

Being productive in Office 2000 isn't so hard, especially if you can figure out some of the lingo. This brief list introduces you to some of the vocabulary that you may encounter often — and need to know.

application: A techie way of saying program (Word 2000 is an application, for example).

check box: A square box (next to an option) inside a dialog box. Click in the box to place a check mark there, thus activating the option. Click again to remove the checkmark.

click: To press the left mouse button once. If you need to click the right mouse button, you are told to "right-click."

clipboard: The place in your system memory where items you cut or copy from one place to another are stored. In most Office 2000 applications, the clipboard now holds 12 items.

default: The built-in setting. In a dialog box, the default setting is the one that an application uses unless you tell it to do something else.

dialog box: A box that appears on-screen and needs more information to complete a task. Fill in the dialog box and click the OK button to give a command.

drop-down list: In a dialog box or on a toolbar, a control (signaled by an upside-down triangle) that you can click to reveal more options.

formatting: The process of changing the appearance of something. For example, in Word you may want to italicize some text. In Excel, you may want to give a column some background color. And so on.

shortcut menu: A menu that appears when you right-click on something. The shortcut menu varies depending on the item that is clicked.

toolbar: An assortment of buttons for performing tasks. Toolbars usually appear at the top of the screen and have little pictures to indicate what they're for.

ToolTip: When you run your mouse pointer over a toolbar button, a little text box pops up with a reminder of what the button is.

Wizard: A series of dialog boxes that assist you in performing an operation.

The Three-Fingered Salute

Ctrl+Alt+Del   Gets you out of a frozen program without your having to quit other open programs or reboot the computer. Also gives you a chance to reboot the computer the preferred way if nothing else can be done.

IDG BOOKS WORLDWIDE

...For Dummies®: Bestselling Book Series for Beginners

TM

References for the Rest of Us! ®

BESTSELLING BOOK SERIES

Are you intimidated and confused by computers? Do you find that traditional manuals are overloaded with technical details you'll never use? Do your friends and family always call you to fix simple problems on their PCs? Then the ...*For Dummies*® computer book series from IDG Books Worldwide is for you.

...*For Dummies* books are written for those frustrated computer users who know they aren't really dumb but find that PC hardware, software, and indeed the unique vocabulary of computing make them feel helpless. ...*For Dummies* books use a lighthearted approach, a down-to-earth style, and even cartoons and humorous icons to dispel computer novices' fears and build their confidence. Lighthearted but not lightweight, these books are a perfect survival guide for anyone forced to use a computer.

Already, millions of satisfied readers agree. They have made ...*For Dummies* books the #1 introductory level computer book series and have written asking for more. So, if you're looking for the most fun and easy way to learn about computers, look to ...*For Dummies* books to give you a helping hand.

IDG
BOOKS
WORLDWIDE

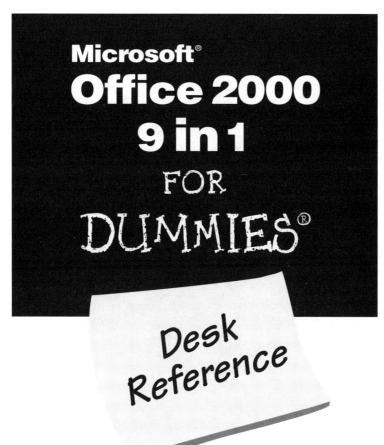

Microsoft®
Office 2000
9 in 1
FOR
DUMMIES®

Desk
Reference

Microsoft® Office 2000 9 in 1 FOR DUMMIES®

Desk Reference

by Greg Harvey, Peter Weverka,
Jim Walkenbach, Alison Barrows,
Bill Dyszel, Camille McCue, Damon Dean,
Jim McCarter, Lee Musick

Edited by Bill Helling

**IDG
BOOKS**
WORLDWIDE

IDG Books Worldwide, Inc.
An International Data Group Company

Foster City, CA ♦ Chicago, IL ♦ Indianapolis, IN ♦ New York, NY

Microsoft® Office 2000 9 in 1 For Dummies® Desk Reference

Published by
IDG Books Worldwide, Inc.
An International Data Group Company
919 E. Hillsdale Blvd.
Suite 400
Foster City, CA 94404
www.idgbooks.com (IDG Books Worldwide Web site)
www.dummies.com (Dummies Press Web site)

Library of Congress Catalog Card No.: 99-61339

ISBN: 0-7645-0333-2

Printed in the United States of America

10 9 8 7 6 5 4 3 2 1

1B/QW/QV/ZZ/IN

Distributed in the United States by IDG Books Worldwide, Inc.

Distributed by CDG Books Canada Inc. for Canada; by Transworld Publishers Limited in the United Kingdom; by IDG Norge Books for Norway; by IDG Sweden Books for Sweden; by IDG Books Australia Publishing Corporation Pty. Ltd. for Australia and New Zealand; by TransQuest Publishers Pte Ltd. for Singapore, Malaysia, Thailand, Indonesia, and Hong Kong; by Gotop Information Inc. for Taiwan; by ICG Muse, Inc. for Japan; by Norma Comunicaciones S.A. for Colombia; by Intersoft for South Africa; by Le Monde en Tique for France; by International Thomson Publishing for Germany, Austria and Switzerland; by Distribuidora Cuspide for Argentina; by Livraria Cultura for Brazil; by Ediciones ZETA S.C.R. Ltda. for Peru; by WS Computer Publishing Corporation, Inc., for the Philippines; by Contemporanea de Ediciones for Venezuela; by Express Computer Distributors for the Caribbean and West Indies; by Micronesia Media Distributor, Inc. for Micronesia; by Grupo Editorial Norma S.A. for Guatemala; by Chips Computadoras S.A. de C.V. for Mexico; by Editorial Norma de Panama S.A. for Panama; by American Bookshops for Finland. Authorized Sales Agent: Anthony Rudkin Associates for the Middle East and North Africa.

For general information on IDG Books Worldwide's books in the U.S., please call our Consumer Customer Service department at 800-762-2974. For reseller information, including discounts and premium sales, please call our Reseller Customer Service department at 800-434-3422.

For information on where to purchase IDG Books Worldwide's books outside the U.S., please contact our International Sales department at 317-596-5530 or fax 317-596-5692.

For consumer information on foreign language translations, please contact our Customer Service department at 1-800-434-3422, fax 317-596-5692, or e-mail rights@idgbooks.com.

For information on licensing foreign or domestic rights, please phone +1-650-655-3109.

For sales inquiries and special prices for bulk quantities, please contact our Sales department at 650-655-3200 or write to the address above.

For information on using IDG Books Worldwide's books in the classroom or for ordering examination copies, please contact our Educational Sales department at 800-434-2086 or fax 317-596-5499.

For press review copies, author interviews, or other publicity information, please contact our Public Relations department at 650-655-3000 or fax 650-655-3299.

For authorization to photocopy items for corporate, personal, or educational use, please contact Copyright Clearance Center, 222 Rosewood Drive, Danvers, MA 01923, or fax 978-750-4470.

 is a registered trademark or trademark under exclusive license to IDG Books Worldwide, Inc. from International Data Group, Inc. in the United States and/or other countries.

ABOUT IDG BOOKS WORLDWIDE

Welcome to the world of IDG Books Worldwide.

IDG Books Worldwide, Inc., is a subsidiary of International Data Group, the world's largest publisher of computer-related information and the leading global provider of information services on information technology. IDG was founded more than 30 years ago by Patrick J. McGovern and now employs more than 9,000 people worldwide. IDG publishes more than 290 computer publications in over 75 countries. More than 90 million people read one or more IDG publications each month.

Launched in 1990, IDG Books Worldwide is today the #1 publisher of best-selling computer books in the United States. We are proud to have received eight awards from the Computer Press Association in recognition of editorial excellence and three from Computer Currents' First Annual Readers' Choice Awards. Our best-selling ...For Dummies® series has more than 50 million copies in print with translations in 31 languages. IDG Books Worldwide, through a joint venture with IDG's Hi-Tech Beijing, became the first U.S. publisher to publish a computer book in the People's Republic of China. In record time, IDG Books Worldwide has become the first choice for millions of readers around the world who want to learn how to better manage their businesses.

Our mission is simple: Every one of our books is designed to bring extra value and skill-building instructions to the reader. Our books are written by experts who understand and care about our readers. The knowledge base of our editorial staff comes from years of experience in publishing, education, and journalism — experience we use to produce books to carry us into the new millennium. In short, we care about books, so we attract the best people. We devote special attention to details such as audience, interior design, use of icons, and illustrations. And because we use an efficient process of authoring, editing, and desktop publishing our books electronically, we can spend more time ensuring superior content and less time on the technicalities of making books.

You can count on our commitment to deliver high-quality books at competitive prices on topics you want to read about. At IDG Books Worldwide, we continue in the IDG tradition of delivering quality for more than 30 years. You'll find no better book on a subject than one from IDG Books Worldwide.

John Kilcullen
Chairman and CEO
IDG Books Worldwide, Inc.

Steven Berkowitz
President and Publisher
IDG Books Worldwide, Inc.

Eighth Annual Computer Press Awards ≥1992

Ninth Annual Computer Press Awards ≥1993

Tenth Annual Computer Press Awards ≥1994

Eleventh Annual Computer Press Awards ≥1995

IDG is the world's leading IT media, research and exposition company. Founded in 1964, IDG had 1997 revenues of $2.05 billion and has more than 9,000 employees worldwide. IDG offers the widest range of media options that reach IT buyers in 75 countries representing 95% of worldwide IT spending. IDG's diverse product and services portfolio spans six key areas including print publishing, online publishing, expositions and conferences, market research, education and training, and global marketing services. More than 90 million people read one or more of IDG's 290 magazines and newspapers, including IDG's leading global brands — Computerworld, PC World, Network World, Macworld and the Channel World family of publications. IDG Books Worldwide is one of the fastest-growing computer book publishers in the world, with more than 700 titles in 36 languages. The "...For Dummies®" series alone has more than 50 million copies in print. IDG offers online users the largest network of technology-specific Web sites around the world through IDG.net (http://www.idg.net), which comprises more than 225 targeted Web sites in 55 countries worldwide. International Data Corporation (IDC) is the world's largest provider of information technology data, analysis and consulting, with research centers in over 41 countries and more than 400 research analysts worldwide. IDG World Expo is a leading producer of more than 168 globally branded conferences and expositions in 35 countries including E3 (Electronic Entertainment Expo), Macworld Expo, ComNet, Windows World Expo, ICE (Internet Commerce Expo), Agenda, DEMO, and Spotlight. IDG's training subsidiary, ExecuTrain, is the world's largest computer training company, with more than 230 locations worldwide and 785 training courses. IDG Marketing Services helps industry-leading IT companies build international brand recognition by developing global integrated marketing programs via IDG's print, online and exposition products worldwide. Further information about the company can be found at www.idg.com.   1/24/99

IDG Books Worldwide, Inc., gratefully acknowledges the contributions of these authors and contributing writers: Greg Harvey, Peter Weverka, John Walkenbach, Alison Barrows, Bill Dyszel, Camille McCue, Damon Dean, Jim McCarter, Lee Musick, Colin Banfield, and Paul Sanna. Bill Helling's developmental and editorial expertise and keen awareness of our readers served to help make this book an invaluable success.

Publisher's Acknowledgments

We're proud of this book; please register your comments through our IDG Books Worldwide Online Registration Form located at http://my2cents.dummies.com.

Some of the people who helped bring this book to market include the following:

Acquisitions, Editorial, and Media Development

Project Editor: Constance Carlisle

Acquisitions Editor: Mike Kelly

Technical Editor(s): Jamey Marcum, Jim McCarter, Allen Wyatt, Bill Karrow, Lee Musick, Kevin McCarter, Julie King

Editorial Manager: Mary Corder

Editorial Assistant: Paul Kuzmic, Beth Parlon, Jamila Pree, Alison Walthall

Special Help

Leah Cameron, Sherry Gomall, Donna Love

Production

Project Coordinator: Regina Snyder

Layout and Graphics: Linda M. Boyer, Angela F. Hunckler, Dave McKelvey, Brent Savage, Janet Seib, M. Anne Sipahimalani, Michael Sullivan, Matthew Brian Torwelle

Proofreaders: Christine Berman, Kelli Botta, Vickie Broyles, Jennifer Mahern, Nancy Price, Marianne Santy, Rebecca Senninger, Ethel M. Winslow, Janet M. Withers

Indexer: Steve Rath

General and Administrative

IDG Books Worldwide, Inc.: John Kilcullen, CEO; Steven Berkowitz, President and Publisher

IDG Books Technology Publishing: Brenda McLaughlin, Senior Vice President and Group Publisher

Dummies Technology Press and Dummies Editorial: Diane Graves Steele, Vice President and Associate Publisher; Mary Bednarek, Director of Acquisitions and Product Development; Kristin A. Cocks, Editorial Director

Dummies Trade Press: Kathleen A. Welton, Vice President and Publisher; Kevin Thornton, Acquisitions Manager

IDG Books Production for Dummies Press: Michael R. Britton, Vice President of Production and Creative Services; Cindy L. Phipps, Manager of Project Coordination, Production Proofreading, and Indexing; Kathie S. Schutte, Supervisor of Page Layout; Shelley Lea, Supervisor of Graphics and Design; Debbie J. Gates, Production Systems Specialist; Robert Springer, Supervisor of Proofreading; Debbie Stailey, Special Projects Coordinator; Tony Augsburger, Supervisor of Reprints and Bluelines

Dummies Packaging and Book Design: Patty Page, Manager, Promotions Marketing

♦

The publisher would like to give special thanks to Patrick J. McGovern, without whom this book would not have been possible.

♦

Contents at a Glance

Cartoons at a Glance

By Rich Tennant

page 7

page 633

page 415

page 487

page 303

page 73

page 203

page 681

page 565

Fax: 978-546-7747 • E-mail: the5wave@tiac.net

Table of Contents

Introduction

*M*icrosoft just won't let up. For your computing convenience, Microsoft has again bundled some of their most useful software products into Microsoft Office 2000. If you're finally getting used to Office 97, don't despair. A lot of what you already know carries over to the new kid on the block. And what if you've never used a Microsoft Office product before and can't tell a Word document from an Excel spreadsheet? Well, you're still in the right place, because this book doesn't start over your head.

Microsoft Office 2000 is a powerful bundle of software, to be sure. You can write a report, make a spreadsheet, design a database, organize a presentation, create a Web page, draw a picture, and much, much more. Office 95 users are surely wondering what the big deal must be, because all these functions have been available for years. Well, Office 2000 goes one step further as Microsoft vows to use Web technology in order to improve collaboration among Office users and to increase your productivity. Are you excited yet? For example, you can save Office documents in HTML file format (as Web documents) so that anyone with a Web browser can view them — but you don't lose your original Office document. Instead, you can "round trip" an Office document saved as HTML back into the original Office program without losing any of your file formats. That isn't enough? How about the promise of applications that are easier to use because of intelligent features and better integration between individual applications?

In fact, some day you may consider Microsoft Office 2000 to be an indispensable part of your personal or business computing — after you stop losing so much time trying to figure it out. Like any powerful tool, this software can do a lot for you if you just know how to use it.

In addition, if you don't already know, all these Office products run under the operating system known as Windows 98 — which is very familiar to users of Windows 95, with a few added wrinkles. If you've never used a Windows operating system before, welcome aboard. You won't be left behind. With just a little help, you can find out how to manage your files and folders within Windows 98 just like the pros. And as an added benefit, the knowledge and experience that you pick up in Windows 98 — or in any of the Office 2000 products — applies to all the other Windows programs, too. What a deal!

About This Book

Microsoft Office 2000 9 in 1 For Dummies Desk Reference is intended to be a reference for all the great things (and maybe a few not-so-great things) that you may need to know when using Windows 98 or any of the Microsoft Office 2000 products: Word, Excel, Access, Outlook, PowerPoint, FrontPage, Publisher, and PhotoDraw. You can go out and buy a different book for Windows 98 and for each of the Office products, but who's going to carry them home for you? (And think of the shelf space you'd need!) *Microsoft Office 2000 9 in 1 For Dummies Desk Reference* doesn't pretend to be a comprehensive reference for every detail of these products. Instead, this book shows you how to get up and running fast so that you have more time to do the things that you really want to do.

Microsoft Office 2000 9 in 1 For Dummies Desk Reference strives to include in one book all the important details you can probably locate in individual books but would really like to have in one source. This is a big book made up of several smaller books — mini-books, so to speak. Whenever one big thing is made up of several smaller things, confusion is always a possibility, right? That's why *Microsoft Office 2000 9 in 1 For Dummies Desk Reference* is designed to have Multiple Access Points (should we call them MAPs?) to help you find what you want. Each mini-book has its own parts page that includes a contents at a glance. Useful running heads (that text you can find at the very top of a page) abound. And who can overlook those handy thumb tabs with mini-book and chapter information? Finally, a small index is at the end of each mini-book (besides the regular index at the end of the entire book).

Who Are You?

Although making too many assumptions about readers is a dangerous thing, it's very possible that you fit into more than just one of the following categories:

✦ You've never used a Windows-based computer but you want to get started in Windows 98 and all those Office 2000 products.

✦ You may have used a Windows-based computer before (probably Windows 95) as well as some Office programs, but you never really got the hang of them before Windows 98 and Office 2000 appeared.

✦ You have no idea what Microsoft Office really is, but you've been told that the software you need to use — Word, Excel, and so on — belongs to this package.

✦ You may have heard about all those power users who can take full advantage of the integrated products from Microsoft Office and you want to join their ranks.

✦ You think that you know everything about Windows and Microsoft Office — and you probably know a lot — but you need a good reference for when your memory fails you (like when your boss asks you to design that new presentation for tomorrow morning or your kid's sixth-grade science project really needs a neat chart).

What this book doesn't assume is that you are a dummy. Unfortunately, the Microsoft products don't operate themselves (just yet), and the way to do things is not always very evident. You don't have time to hunt down a Microsoft Certified System Engineer, and guessing which button to push is not an option that you care for. If you want to help yourself quickly and easily, this is the book for you.

How to Use This Book

You could probably find out a lot by reading this entire book in order from cover to cover as if it were a Tolstoy novel. Resist that urge. You can gain much more by simply going to the part that holds the information you need. That's right; jump around, as necessary, according to your whims and desires. And just try reading a Tolstoy novel that way!

This book acts like a reference so that you can locate what you want to know, get in, and get something done as soon as possible. In this book, you can find concise descriptions introducing important concepts, task-oriented topics to help you realize what you need to do, and step-by-step instructions where necessary to show you the way.

At times, this book presents you with specific ways of performing certain actions. For example, when you must use a menu command, you may see something like this:

File⇨Save

This simply means to use the mouse to open the File menu and then to choose the Save command (you click with the left mouse button on the word File and then move the mouse pointer down to the word Save in the menu that appears). If you look real close, you can see some underlined letters. Those letters are the keyboard hot keys for the command if you don't wish to use the mouse. To use a keyboard hot key, first press the Alt key and then release. Next press the actual letter (in the case of File, it would be F) to open that menu.

At other times, this book may ask you to use specific keyboard shortcuts. These shortcuts are key combinations such as:

Ctrl+X

This means to press and hold down the Ctrl key as you press the X key. Then release both keys together. (No, don't attempt to type a plus sign!)

When you're asked to click or double-click something, this book assumes that your mouse settings have not been changed. In this case, when you're told to click, use the left mouse button. At the times when you need to use the right mouse button, you'll be specifically told to right-click.

How This Book Is Organized

Each of the mini-books contained in *Microsoft Office 2000 9 in 1 For Dummies Desk Reference* can stand alone, if you want. Remember that each has its own contents and index. The first mini-book covers, of course, the operating system under which all the Office products run: Windows 98. After that, the Office mini-books fall into a rough order of popularity among Office users. But you should be jumping around, anyway, according to what you need to do, so the order in which these mini-books have been placed should be judged merely as a publishing convenience and not as a recommendation. Here, then, is a brief description of what you can find in each mini-book:

Windows 98

In this mini-book, you get a brief overview of all the basic features in Windows 98, from taskbars and toolbars to dialog boxes and menus. Find out how to manage your files and folders as well as manipulate your desktop.

Word 2000

Word 2000 is the most powerful word-processing program around! With Word 2000, you can easily create anything as simple as a memo or as complicated as a 1,000-page novel complete with table of contents and an index.

Excel 2000

So you want to get something done with a spreadsheet and make some fancy charts to boot? Let Excel 2000 give you a hand. This mini-book tells you what you need to know to get going fast.

Access 2000

Don't let the mention of databases scare you any longer. With this mini-book, you can uncover the fundamentals of a great database program that does everything for you except for entering the data (that's your job).

Outlook 2000

Who doesn't need e-mail, a time-managing calendar, a tasks list, a contacts organizer, and the like? Outlook 2000 helps you keep up in this fast-paced world, and this book is your entry pass.

PowerPoint 2000

Power Point 2000 allows you to create those great-looking presentations that have always impressed you in the past. This mini-book helps you on your way toward slides and overheads — and why not throw in a graph and a chart while you're at it?

FrontPage 2000

In this mini-book, find out how easy and painless it is to make a Web page. FrontPage 2000 helps you every step of the way, from inserting hyperlinks to adding impressive graphics.

Publisher 2000

If you've ever wanted to produce some of those nice publications turned out by desktop publishing programs, you may be able to take advantage of Publisher 2000. With this program, you can be a desktop publisher, too.

PhotoDraw 2000

PhotoDraw 2000 is a small but powerful tool for creating your own graphics as well as for importing work from scanners and digital cameras. After you have a graphic open in PhotoDraw 2000, you can manipulate it to your heart's content and really make it look like you want.

Appendix A

Because so many tasks are similar among the Office products and the management of Windows 98 stuff applies across the board, this appendix can save you time (and us paper) by showing you the basics, such as starting an Office 2000 application and using the mouse. You can also get some advice on how to use the various help features in Office 2000. By eliminating repeated information, we can reduce your déjà vu experiences.

Appendix B

If you compose that Word document or create that Excel spreadsheet (or any other Office 2000 product), chances are you may want to print it, too. Although some Office applications have very specific printing demands here and there, the general printing routine is pretty much the same for all. Appendix B gets you started printing your creations.

Appendix C

If you create files in Word, Excel, or PowerPoint, let Microsoft Binder help you group these files into, er, binders so that you can keep better track of related documents.

Icons Used in This Book

Icons are peppered throughout this book, but not in any haphazard manner! These icons signal special information.

This is a nice little tip that should save you some time or effort.

Heads up! This icon signals a potential problem or danger for you to avoid.

Just a reminder: This information may be worth keeping in mind.

This icon points out something that you actually may benefit from — if you apply the advice to what you're doing.

Office 2000 is supposed to work well together, but this icon helps to remind us of this capability!

This icon shows you a fast and efficient way to perform a task.

Book I

Windows 98

The 5th Wave   By Rich Tennant

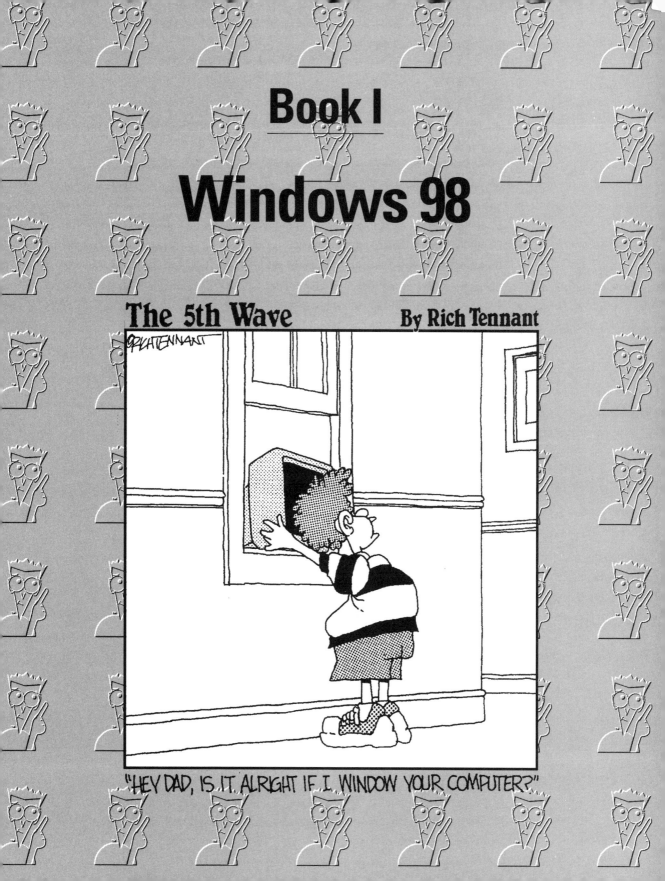

"HEY DAD, IS IT ALRIGHT IF I WINDOW YOUR COMPUTER?"

Contents at a Glance

Chapter 1: Getting to Know the Windows 98 Desktop

In This Chapter

✔ **Becoming comfortable with the Windows desktop**

✔ **Recognizing icons**

✔ **Clicking and opening icons**

✔ **Checking out some standard Windows 98 icons**

1 f you've used Windows 95 before, welcome back to somewhat the same look and feel — with a few added features. If you're jumping up from an earlier version of Windows or if you're a complete novice, you're also in the right place. To get along in the world of Windows 98, you need to feel comfortable with the Windows desktop — the screen where you eventually end up after you start your computer. And what is the most common element that populates the desktop? Those pretty little pictures called icons.

This chapter introduces you to desktop basics and gets you started on working with icons.

Windows Desktop

The Windows desktop is the background against which all the action takes place. The desktop contains the standard Windows icons such as My Computer, Recycle Bin, and the like (explained later in this chapter). In addition, the desktop area holds all the shortcut icons you may create (see Chapter 6 for the lowdown on shortcuts). Finally, the desktop also has the Windows taskbar (which you can read about in Chapter 2). See Figure 1-1 for a typical desktop.

Although working with the Windows desktop isn't a high-maintenance routine, you should know how to manage your desktop and its icons in order to make your life a little easier. (You can find an explanation of icons later in this chapter.) The easiest way to manage your desktop is to use the desktop shortcut menu. You open this menu by right-clicking any open area of the desktop (off the taskbar and any icons) as shown in Figure 1-2. The shortcut menu contains the following commands, which enable you to customize the look and feel of the Windows 98 desktop.

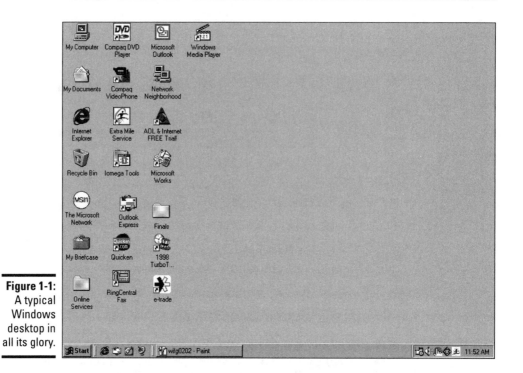

Figure 1-1:
A typical
Windows
desktop in
all its glory.

✦ **Active Desktop:** Turns the Active Desktop off and on with the View As Web Page command; opens the Display Properties dialog box with the Customize My Desktop command; or updates Active Desktop items with the Update Now command. See Chapter 8 for information on the Active Desktop.

✦ **Arrange Icons:** Enables you to arrange the desktop icons by Name, by Type, by Size, or by Date, or you can use Auto Arrange to let Windows 98 decide how to arrange them.

✦ **Line up Icons:** Arranges the icons (by name, in alphabetical order) in neat columns and rows on the desktop.

✦ **Refresh:** Updates icons and Active Desktop items displayed on the desktop.

✦ **Paste:** Creates a shortcut to whatever document you're currently working on and pastes its icon onto the desktop. You can read about shortcuts in Chapter 6.

✦ **Paste Shortcut:** Pastes whatever shortcut you've cut or copied to the Clipboard.

✦ **New:** Creates an empty folder, a file of a particular type (such as an Excel file or Word document), or a new shortcut. You can read about all this stuff in Chapter 6.

✦ **Properties:** Opens the Display Properties dialog box, where you can change display stuff, like the video settings and windows color combinations.

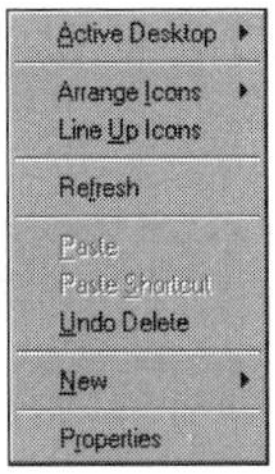

**Getting to Know the
Windows 98
Desktop**

Figure 1-2:
The
desktop
shortcut
menu is
only a
right-click
away.

> Active Desktop ▸
> Arrange Icons ▸
> Line Up Icons
> Refresh
> Paste
> Paste Shortcut
> Undo Delete
> New ▸
> Properties

Icons

Icons are the small pictures identifying the type of object (be it a disk drive, folder, file, or some other such thing) that you're dealing with in Windows 98. You run into icons everywhere you turn — they're all over the desktop, and the Internet Explorer 5, My Computer, and Windows Explorer windows are lousy with them.

Windows 98 gives you a number of new ways to modify the appearance of the icons as well as to determine the order in which they appear on the desktop or within their window (a job that Windows 98 usually does all by itself). See Chapter 3 for details.

It takes all types of icons

The icons that you encounter in Windows 98 fall into one of the following types:

✦ **Disk icons:** Represent the various drives on your computer or drives that are currently connected to your computer.

✦ **File icons:** Represent the different types of documents used by Windows and produced by the programs that you run on your computer.

✦ **Folder icons:** Represent the various directories that you have on your computer.

✦ **Windows component icons:** Represent the various modules that are running on your computer, such as the desktop, My Computer, Internet Explorer, and the Recycle Bin.

✦ **Program icons:** Represent the various executable programs that you have installed on your computer.

✦ **Shortcut icons:** Point to files, folders, Windows components, or executable programs that are located elsewhere on the computer.

Icons are made for clicking

All the icons that you meet in Windows 98 are made for clicking with the mouse — you know, that little white handheld gizmo that came with your computer. Table 1-1 shows the various mouse-click techniques that you employ on the icons you encounter in Windows 98.

Table 1-1	Clicking Icons
Name	*Mouse Action*
Click	Point the mouse pointer at the object and then press and quickly release the primary mouse button. The primary mouse button, whether you're right-or left-handed, is the one closest to your thumb.
Double-click	Press and release the primary mouse two times in rapid succession.
Right-click	Also known as a secondary mouse click, right-click means to press and release the button that is not designated as your primary mouse button. This action often brings up context menus and other goodies.
Drag-and-drop	First point to an object with the mouse pointer; then click and hold down the primary mouse button as you move the mouse to drag the object to a new position on-screen. Finally, let go of the mouse button to drop the object into its new position. This action is quite useful when rearranging icons or moving files to the Recycle Bin.

Selecting and Opening Icons

Traditionally, *graphical user interfaces* (known affectionately as GUIs) such as Windows, use the following mouse-click scheme to differentiate between selecting and opening the icon:

✦ Single-click the icon to select it (indicated on the screen by highlighting the icon).

✦ Double-click the icon to open its object (see "It takes all types of icons" earlier in this section for details on the different types of Windows objects).

Pages on the World Wide Web, however, typically use a slightly different mouse-click scheme to differentiate between selecting and following (the equivalent of opening) hyperlinks, which can be attached to graphics or text on the page:

✦ Move the mouse pointer over the hyperlink to select it (indicated by the mouse pointer changing to the hand icon).

✦ Click (don't double-click) the hyperlink to follow the link. (Normally, following the link means to jump to another section of the page or to open a completely different Web page.)

With the addition of the Active Desktop to Windows 98 (see Chapter 8 for full details) and its stated goal of marrying the Web to the Windows interface, you now have a choice between selecting and opening Windows icons the normal GUI way (single- and double-click) or the normal Web way (point at and click).

When Windows 98 is first installed on your computer, the traditional GUI single- and double-click scheme is in effect. If you want to switch over and experiment with the Web point-and-click system, you can do so at any time by making a few simple modifications to the Folders Options (see Chapter 8 for the fine points of putting this new system into effect).

Selecting More Than One Icon at a Time

The time may come when you need to select more than one icon at a time, especially when these icons represent files and folders. For example, you may wish to drag a bunch of files from one folder to another or carry out a group delete without performing the same action for each icon.

First, you need to know which method you are using to select icons as explained in the preceding section. Next, you need to know if the icons are *contiguous* or *noncontiguous,* which affects how you select more than one icon. So if you know which method you're using to select icons and whether these icons are contiguous or noncontiguous, the rest is simple!

Selecting contiguous icons

Contiguous simply means that the icons are listed next to each other. Actually seeing what icons are next to each other is a lot easier when you view the icons in a window in list form (see Chapter 3).

1. **Select the first icon in a group (either at the top or bottom of the list, which is a whole lot easier to see when the icons are in list form).**

2. **Hold down the Shift key and select the last icon in your group.**

   All the icons in between the two files you have selected become your "selection," as shown in Figure 1-3.

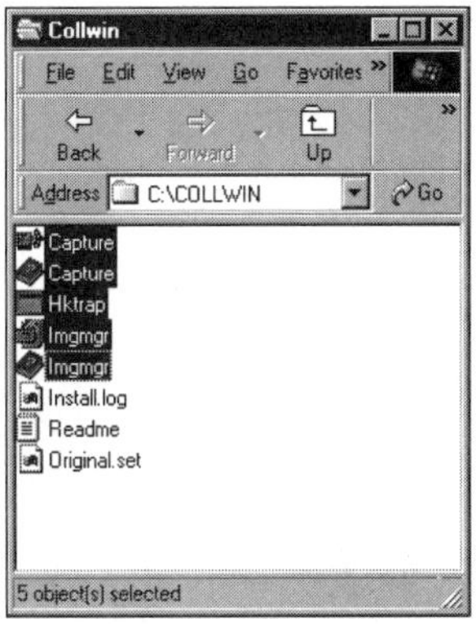

Figure 1-3: Selecting contiguous icons (if what you want is grouped together).

Selecting noncontiguous icons

Noncontiguous simply means that the icons are *not* all listed next to each other.

1. **Select the first icon (select any icon; you have to start somewhere!).**

2. **Hold down the Ctrl key and select each and every icon that you want.**

   All the icons that you select remain selected (as shown in Figure 1-4). If you slip up and select a file you don't want, simply deselect it — which is simply a matter of re-selecting it while still holding down the Ctrl key.

Figure 1-4:
Selecting
non-
contiguous
icons (if
what you
want is
scattered
here and
there).

Lasso them icons

Have you ever seen how easily some of those cowboys and cowgirls in a rodeo can lasso a runaway steer? Well, you can do sort of the same thing with your icons without having to whoop and holler — and your icons never try to run away from you. To select icons by lassoing, simply click outside the icons and, while holding down the mouse button, drag through the icons that you want to select. As you drag, you can see an ever-expanding rectangle that indicates your area of selection.

The icons you select become highlighted. When you let go of the mouse button, the icons remain selected. If you accidentally select an icon that you don't want, simply deselect it by clicking on it with the Ctrl button held down or point to it with the Ctrl button held down (depending on if your selection method is traditional or Web-based, as explained in the section "Selecting and Opening Icons" earlier in this chapter).

Standard Desktop Icons

After you install Windows 98, you notice that the desktop is littered with a few icons that allow you to perform some essential tasks. This section gives a brief overview of some standard desktop icons that every Windows user deals with at some time or another. Double-clicking an icon (or single-clicking, depending on your setup) opens the window, file, or folder (or whatever the icon represents!). You can also right-click an icon and select Open from the pop-up menu that appears.

My Computer

My Computer

My Computer gives you quick access to all the major *local* components of your computer system. When you first open the My Computer window, it displays all the local drives attached to your computer, along with folders for your printers, Control Panel utilities, Dial-Up Networking connections, and regularly scheduled tasks (see Figure 1-5).

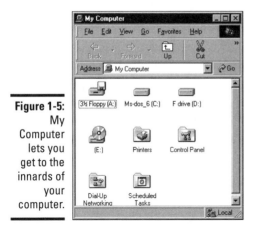

Figure 1-5:
My
Computer
lets you
get to the
innards of
your
computer.

Network Neighborhood

The Network Neighborhood gives you an overview of all the workgroups, computers, and shared resources on your Local Area Network (LAN). As a permanent resident on the desktop, whether you're on a LAN or not, you can open it and get a graphic view of the workgroups set up on your network and the resources that are networked together.

Figure 1-6 shows the icons in the Network Neighborhood window that represent an entire network and its separate workgroups.

Recycle Bin

Recycle Bin

The Recycle Bin is the trash can for Windows 98. Don't be confused by the "recycle" name; you're not going to put things in there to be reused. Anything you delete in Windows goes into the Recycle Bin and stays there until you either

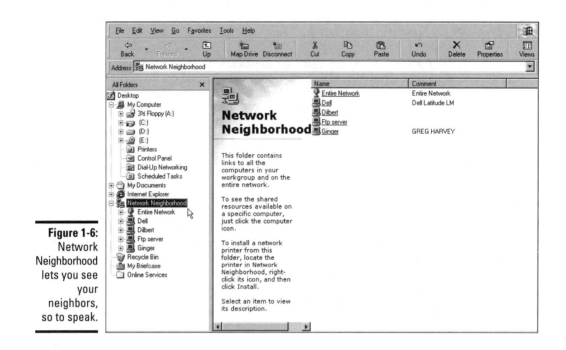

Figure 1-6:
Network
Neighborhood
lets you see
your
neighbors,
so to speak.

retrieve the deleted item or empty the Recycle Bin. The only thing that you gain when you empty the Recycle Bin is the space that the deleted items took up. (See Chapter 7 for how to use the Recycle Bin.)

My Briefcase

My Briefcase

My Briefcase enables you to synchronize versions of files from different computers or disks so that you don't drive yourself crazy trying to figure out which version of the file isn't as up-to-date as the other one.

Online Services

Microsoft has been kind enough to offer easy-access wizards for signing up with some of the largest Internet service providers (ISPs) in the country.

Online
Services

In the Online Services folder (which you open with the Online Services shortcut that appears on the desktop when you install Windows 98), you find icons that enable you to jump right online — assuming you have a modem — and set up an account with any of several companies (including the Microsoft Network).

Inbox

If you've installed Microsoft Exchange, the Inbox icon takes up residence on your desktop. With the Inbox you can access electronic mail systems, fax software, and the like.

Chapter 2: Getting Started (And Stopped) in Windows 98

In This Chapter

✔ Using the taskbar

✔ Customizing the taskbar for your needs

✔ Launching and switching between programs

✔ Shutting down Windows 98

A journey of 1,000 miles begins with the first step, or so the saying goes, and one of the best first steps in Windows 98 can usually be found at the bottom of the desktop screen. Customarily, this area is where the taskbar lurks, and from here you can begin your computer journey. This chapter shows you how to get things going and how to make the taskbar fit your computing needs. You also find out how to end any odyssey so that Windows 98 continues to welcome you warmly on your future journeys.

Taskbar Basics

The taskbar forms the base of the Windows 98 desktop. Running along the bottom the complete width of the screen, the taskbar is divided into three sections: the Start button with the accompanying Start pop-up menu at the far left; buttons for open toolbars and windows in the center area; and, at the far right, the status area with icons showing the current status of computer components, programs, and processes that are running in the background. Figure 2-1 shows you a typical taskbar.

When you open a window or program on the Windows desktop, Windows adds a button representing that window or program to the center section of the taskbar. Clicking one of the window or program buttons brings its window, which is temporarily hidden behind others, to the very front, so you can use the taskbar buttons to quickly switch between the programs you're running in the open windows.

Start menu

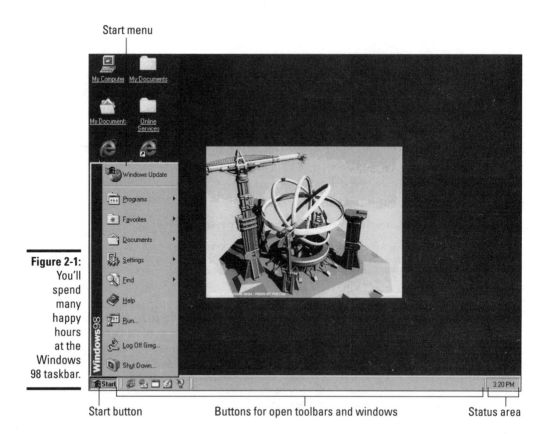

Figure 2-1:
You'll
spend
many
happy
hours
at the
Windows
98 taskbar.

Start button   Buttons for open toolbars and windows   Status area

Starting off with the Start menu

The Start button that opens the Start menu always appears as the first button on the taskbar. The Start menu is the most basic pull-down menu in Windows 98, containing almost all the commands you'll ever need to use. To open the Start menu (shown in Figure 2-2), simply click the Start button in the lower-left corner of the taskbar or press Ctrl+Esc.

Table 2-1 lists the commands you encounter on the Start menu (running from bottom to top). To select a command on the Start menu, just navigate to it with the mouse pointer and click.

Table 2-1	Start Menu Commands
Command	*What It Does*
Shut Down	Opens the Shut Down Windows dialog box, where you can either shut off the computer, restart the computer, restart the computer in MS-DOS mode, or put the computer on Standby, a kind of "sleep" mode that consumes less power if you leave your computer on for extended periods of time.
Log Off	On a Local Area Network (LAN), enables you to log off the current user so that you can then log on as yourself.

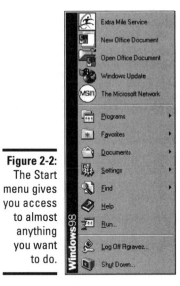

Figure 2-2:
The Start
menu gives
you access
to almost
anything
you want
to do.

Command	*What It Does*
Run	Opens the Run dialog box, where you enter the pathname of the file, folder, program, or Internet resource that you want Windows to locate and open.
Help	Opens Windows Help, an online help database that also includes Web elements, so you can jump to the Internet for even more help.
Find	Opens a submenu with the following options: Files or Folders, to find particular files on local or networked disk drives; Computer, to find a particular computer on your network; On the Internet, to find a Web site on the Internet; On the Microsoft Network, to search for something or someone on the Microsoft Network (available only if you subscribe to MSN); or People, to find a particular person or business in one of the online directories.
Settings	Opens a submenu with the following options: Control Panel, to open the Control Panel window; Printers, to open the Printers window; Taskbar & Start Menu, to open the Taskbar Properties dialog box, where you can modify the appearance of the Start menu and the taskbar; Folders & Icons, to open the Folder Option dialog box; Active Desktop, for activating, customizing, and updating the Active Desktop; and finally, Windows Update, to connect to a page on the Microsoft Web site, where you can download updates to Windows 98.
Documents	Opens a submenu containing shortcuts to all your most recently opened files. You can purge this list from time to time by using the Taskbar Properties dialog box.
Favorites	Enables you to access the items designated as your favorite files, folders, Web channels, or Web pages.

(continued)

Table 2-1 *(continued)*

Command	What It Does
Programs	Opens a submenu containing all the programs installed on your computer at the time you installed Windows 98 as well as Windows Explorer. You can control which programs appear on the Programs continuation menu by adding folders to or removing folders from the Programs folder.
Windows Update	Connects you to the Microsoft Web site, which then checks your computer system to see if your version of Windows 98 needs updating, and, if you allow, automatically downloads and installs the new updated components.
Open Office Document	If you have Microsoft Office installed on your computer (and who doesn't?), you can use this command to display the Open Office Document dialog box, where you can search the particular Office document (such as Word, Excel, PowerPoint, or Access) you want to open.
New Office Document	If you have Microsoft Office installed on your computer, you can use this command to open a new Office document using one of many different types of templates available (Word, Web page, Excel, PowerPoint, Binder, or Access).

Taskbar toolbars for every taste

A new feature in Windows 98 enables you to add various toolbars, such as the Address, Quick Launch, and Desktop toolbars, to the center section of the taskbar. You can then use their buttons to accomplish routine tasks in Windows. See Chapter 4 for details on displaying and using these different toolbars.

Status, anyone?

The status area contains icons that indicate the current status of various physical components, such as a printer attached to a desktop computer, as well as the status of various programs or processes that run in the background, such as a virus-scanning program or the video display settings you're using.

To identify an icon that appears in the status area, position the mouse pointer over it until its ToolTip appears. To change the status of an icon, right-click it to display its pop-up menu, and then click the appropriate menu option.

Note: You can customize your taskbar so that it removes the clock, shows smaller icons, hides itself, and so on. You can also fool around with your Start menu. Click the Start button and choose S̲ettings⇨T̲askbar & Start Menu to get started. See *Windows 98 For Dummies* by Andy Rathbone (from IDG Books Worldwide, Inc.) for all the gory details.

Starting Your Programs

In Windows 98, you can open the programs that you've installed on your hard drive in any one of the following three ways:

✦ **Select the program on the Programs menu, which you open from the Start menu:** See "Starting off with the Start Menu" earlier in this chapter for information about the Start menu.

✦ **Open a shortcut to the program or to a document you open regularly:** See Chapter 6 for information about creating shortcuts for opening a program or a file that in turn opens its associated program.

✦ **Open a file created with the program:** See Chapter 6 for information about opening a program by opening its file.

Switching between Programs

The Windows 98 taskbar makes switching between programs as easy as clicking the button representing the program's window. (Open folders are also represented on the taskbar.) To activate a program (or access an open folder) and bring its window to the top of your screen display, click the appropriate button on the taskbar.

Alt+Tab your way between stuff on the taskbar

After you begin to open a few programs and folders, you may notice that your taskbar gets pretty full and that you can't actually read much of the descriptions. If you like to play games, you can take a chance and guess which button belongs to which folder or which file is running under which program. If you want to greatly increase your odds of choosing the right button, press Alt+Tab, but keep holding down the Alt key. A dialog box appears, with icons for each program and folder window and a description of the icon. When you release both the Alt and Tab keys, Windows activates the window for whatever program or folder icon is selected (indicated by the blue box surrounding the icon). To change the selection, tap on the Tab key as you continue to hold down the Alt key.

Shutting Down Windows 98

Windows 98 includes a shut-down procedure that you should follow before you turn off your machine. To shut down Windows 98 so that you can safely shut off your computer and get on with your life, follow these steps:

1. **Click the Start button and then choose Shut Down from the Start menu to open the Shut Down Windows dialog box shown in Figure 2-3.**

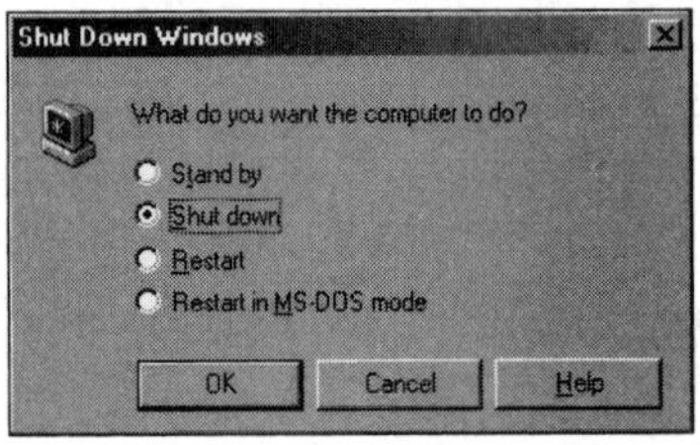

Figure 2-3: Shutting down Windows 98 the correct way.

2. **To completely shut down Windows and power down your computer, make sure that the Shut Down radio button is selected and then click the OK button or press Enter.**

In addition to the Shut Down option, you can select from these options in the Shut Down Windows dialog box:

✦ **Standby:** Choose this radio button when you want to put your computer into a deep sleep. This mode powers down the computer but maintains the state of your desktop.

✦ **Restart:** Choose this radio button when you need to restart the computer (which you often have to do after installing a new piece of hardware or software, for example). You can also use this option in the unlikely event that Windows 98 becomes so screwed up that you need to restart the whole shebang (when, for example, all the colors on the desktop get messed up and go all magenta and green on you).

✦ **Restart in MS-DOS mode:** Choose this radio button when you are inexplicably possessed by a need to type some DOS command or to take one last look at that ugly old DOS prompt.

Chapter 3: Working with Windows (Within Windows)

In This Chapter

✔ **Working with those on-screen windows**

✔ **Manipulating windows**

✔ **Making Windows display icons the way you want**

✔ **Using Windows Explorer**

✔ **Exploring Explorer bars**

This chapter dispenses helpful information for the Windows newbie and seasoned pro alike. If you're just starting out with the Windows operating system or if you need a refresher on its fundamentals, you've come to the right place. A lot of this knowledge also applies to the programs that you use with Windows (and can read about in the rest of this book). This just may be your lucky day!

Windows (The On-Screen Type)

Windows, whether they are the windows you see when you open a system window such as My Computer or a window from a program such as Word, contain various combinations of controls and features that you use to modify the window and, in the case of program windows, navigate a program. Figure 3-1 gives you an idea of a typical window.

The following list describes the features and controls found on all your typical windows:

✦ **Title bar:** Identifies the program or file in the opened window; also houses the Control menu, which appears when you click the program icon on the left side of the Title bar.

✦ **Menu bar:** Contains the pull-down menus with commands specific to a program (see "Messing around with a menu bar for a window" in Chapter 5).

✦ **Minimize button:** Shrinks the window down to a button on the taskbar.

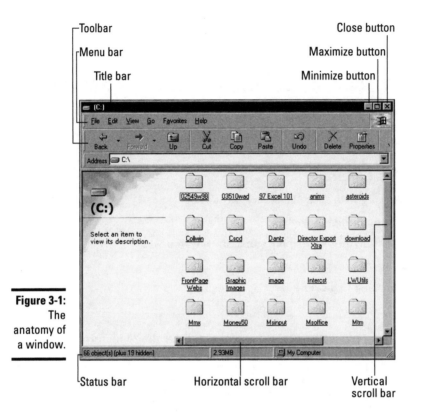

Figure 3-1:
The anatomy of a window.

Toolbar

Menu bar

Title bar

Close button

Maximize button

Minimize button

Status bar

Horizontal scroll bar

Vertical scroll bar

✦ **Maximize button:** Zooms the window up to full size; to restore a maximized window to its former size, click the Restore button that replaces the Maximize button.

✦ **Close button:** Closes the window and exits any program running in it.

✦ **Toolbars:** If the window is equipped with other toolbars, these extra toolbars are usually located below the menu bar.

✦ **Vertical scroll bar:** Enables you to vertically scroll new parts of the window into view with the up and down arrows or by dragging the scroll button.

✦ **Horizontal scroll bar:** Enables you to horizontally scroll new parts of the window into view with the right and left arrows or by dragging the scroll button.

✦ **Status bar:** Gives you different sorts of information about the current state of the program.

Here are some basic tips on dealing with the windows you encounter in Windows 98:

✦ A window must be active before you can select any of its commands or use any of its features. To activate a window, click anywhere on it. The active window is immediately placed on top of the desktop and its title bar becomes highlighted.

✦ You can change the size of a window by dragging its borders with the mouse or by using the Size command (see "Moving and Resizing Windows" later in this chapter).

✦ To move a window on the desktop, position the mouse pointer somewhere on the window's title bar and drag the outline to the new location with the mouse.

✦ If the window contains a toolbar and you don't have a clue as to what the tool does, point to the tool button, and Windows displays a ToolTip with the tool's name.

See Chapter 5 for the lowdown on this special type of window.

Moving and Resizing Windows

You can move windows around the desktop and resize them from full-screen (called *maximized*) all the way down to wee buttons on the taskbar (called *minimized*) at your convenience. To move a window, follow these steps:

1. **If necessary, restore the window to an in-between size, either by clicking the Restore Window button if the window is maximized or by clicking its taskbar button if the window is minimized.**

2. **Position the mouse pointer over the window's title bar.**

3. **Drag the outline of the window to its new location on the desktop.**

4. **Release the mouse button to drop the window in its new location on the desktop.**

To maximize a window, you have two methods to choose from:

✦ Click the Maximize button on the window's title bar if the window is displayed at less than full size. (The Maximize button is located in the middle of the three buttons on the right side of the title bar.) Otherwise, click the window's taskbar button if the window is minimized.

✦ Choose Maximize from the window's Control menu (which you open by clicking the program's icon in the far left of the window's title bar).

Remember that after you maximize a window, you can restore the window to its original size by doing one of these two things:

✦ Click the Restore button on the window's title bar. (The Restore button is located in the middle of the three buttons on the right side of the title bar.)

✦ Choose Restore from the window's Control menu (which you open by clicking the program's icon in the far left of the window's title bar).

To minimize a window to just a button on the taskbar, you can do either of the following:

✦ Click the Minimize button on the window's title bar. (The Minimize button is the one with the minus sign, located on the left of the three buttons on the right side of the title bar.)

✦ Choose Minimize from the window's Control menu (which you open by clicking the program's icon in the far left of the window's title bar).

In addition to using the automatic sizing controls, you can manually size a window (assuming that it's not currently minimized or maximized) by dragging any of its sides or corners. You can always tell when Windows 98 will allow you to move one or more of the sides of a window by dragging, because the mouse pointer changes from the standard pointer to a double-headed arrow.

Arranging and Sizing Icons in a Window

When browsing local files in any browsing window, you can modify the size of the icons used to represent files and folders as well as determine how much (if any) information about them is displayed.

To change the way icons appear in any of these windows, choose from the following commands on the window's View pull-down menu. Note that the same menu options appear when you right-click in the window to display its shortcut menu:

✦ **Large Icons (the default):** Displays the largest version of the folder and file icons, with their names below.

✦ **Small Icons:** Displays a smaller version of the folder and file icons, with their names on the right side of the icons.

✦ **List:** Uses the same icons as the Small Icons option except that the icons with their folders and filenames are arranged in a single column along the left side of the window.

✦ **Details:** Adds columns of additional information (like a description, or the file type, file size, and so on) to the arrangement used when you select the List option.

Figure 3-2 demonstrates the different ways that a window can display your icons.

 Switch to the Small Icons viewing option when you need to see as much of the window's contents as possible. Switch to the Details viewing option when you need to get as much information as possible about the files and folders in a window.

After you decide how file and folder icons appear in a window, you can also choose how they are arranged. Choose View⇨Arrange Icons and select from the following options on the Arrange Icons submenu:

✦ **by Name:** Sort icons alphabetically by name.

✦ **by Type:** Sort icons by file type.

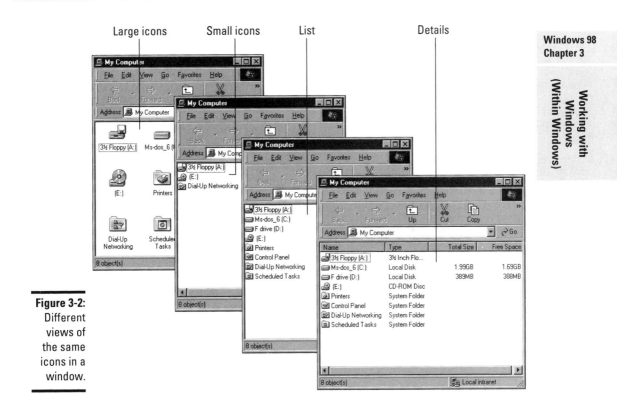

Large icons   Small icons   List   Details

Figure 3-2:
Different
views of
the same
icons in a
window.

+ **by Size:** Sort icons by size, from smallest to largest.

+ **by Date:** Sort icons by date, from oldest to most recent.

+ **Auto Arrange:** Let Windows sort icons by the default setting (which happens to be by type).

When you point to a menu command, the status bar at the bottom of the window displays a description of what that command does.

These methods of arranging icons in windows are pretty old hat to most Windows users. To give your window icons a complete make-over courtesy of Web integration in Windows 98, see Chapter 8.

Windows Explorer

The Windows Explorer enables you to view the contents of any part of your computer system. As with the My Computer and Internet Explorer 5 windows, you can then use the Windows Explorer to open files (and their associated application programs), start programs, or even open Web pages on the Internet or your company's intranet.

The Windows Explorer, however, is most useful when you need to move or copy files to different disks on your computer — or even to networked drives, if you're on a network. See Chapter 7 for details on how to do this.

To open the Windows Explorer, click the Start button and then choose Programs⇨Windows Explorer. Windows opens an Exploring window (which you see in the Figure 3-3) for your disk drive (C:) that is divided into these two panes:

✦ The All Folders pane on the left shows an outline view of all the components on your computer system.

✦ The Contents area on the right displays the folders and files in whatever component is currently selected in the All Folders pane (also shown on the Address bar at the top of the window).

To select a new part of your system to view in the Contents area pane, simply click the icon for that component in the All Folders pane. An icon in the All Folders pane, with a plus sign connected to it, indicates a sublevel within that icon.

When you click a plus sign, Windows expands the outline, showing all the subfolders within the next level. Note also that when you click the plus sign, it turns to a minus sign, and the next level in the item's hierarchy is displayed. Clicking the minus sign collapses the sublevel to which it is attached, thus condensing the outline. Glance at Figure 3-4 for a quick demonstration.

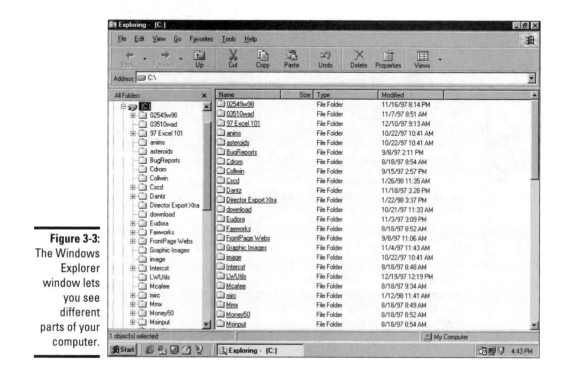

Figure 3-3: The Windows Explorer window lets you see different parts of your computer.

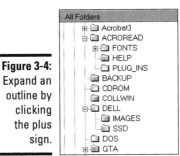

Figure 3-4:
Expand an
outline by
clicking
the plus
sign.

Sometimes, the expanded folder/subfolder outline in the All Folders pane (or the icon arrangements in the Contents pane) becomes too large to view in its entirety given the current Explorer window size. When this happens, vertical and horizontal scroll bars appear as needed, to help you navigate your way through the lists of folders and system components.

Explorer Bars

Explorer bars are a nifty new feature added to Internet Explorer 5, My Computer, and Windows Explorer windows. When you open an Explorer bar in one of these windows, the Explorer bar splits the window into two panes, one on the left and one on the right. The Explorer bar appears in the left pane, and the object or objects that you decide to explore appear in the pane on the right (as suitably shown in Figure 3-5).

Windows 98 offers several different types of Explorer bars (most of which are Internet related). To display a particular Explorer bar, choose View➪Explorer Bar on the window's pull-down menu and then select one of the following commands from the submenu that appears:

✦ **Search:** Opens or closes the Search Explorer bar, where you can select one of the available Web search engines (such as Yahoo!).

✦ **Favorites:** Opens or closes the Favorites Explorer bar, which contains a list of hyperlinks to your favorite Web sites, folders, and files.

✦ **History:** Opens or closes the History Explorer bar, which contains a chronological list of hyperlinks to Web sites you've recently visited and the folders and files that you've recently opened.

✦ **Channels:** Opens or closes the Channel Explorer bar, which contains a list of channel buttons, including one for the Channel Guide, one for each of the channel categories (Lifestyle and Travel, Entertainment, Business, Sports, and News and Technology), along with each channel to which you subscribe.

✦ **None:** Closes whatever Explorer bar is currently open in the window.

✦ **All Files:** (Windows Explorer only.) Opens or closes the All Files pane in the Windows Explorer. When the All Files pane is open (as it normally is), you can open any of the objects that make up your computer system.

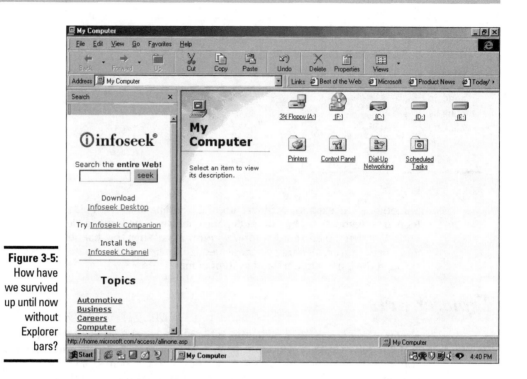

Figure 3-5:
How have we survived up until now without Explorer bars?

Accessibility for everyone

The Accessibility folder located at the very top of the Accessories menu contains two utilities that make it easier for people with less-than-perfect physical dexterity to operate a computer. (Click the Start button on the Windows taskbar, choose Programs⇨Accessories⇨Accessibility.) In the Accessibility folder you find:

- **Accessibility Settings Wizard:** Steps you through configuration settings that determine the smallest size of fonts and other items that appear on-screen.

- **Microsoft Magnifier:** Makes the screen more readable for the visually impaired. The magnifier creates a separate window that displays a magnified image of a portion of your screen. When you open the utility, the dialog box shown in the figure enables you to determine the necessary degree of magnification; you also use the dialog box to turn the feature on and off.

Chapter 4: Dealing with Toolbars

oolbars contain the buttons and menus that you love to click and pull at in Windows 98. Different types of toolbars (each with its own group of buttons) can appear within the various windows, such as My Computer, Windows Explorer, and Internet Explorer 5, as well as on the taskbar on the Windows 98 desktop. No matter where you place them, toolbars become a means to get things done *your* way.

Toolbars

When you first display toolbars in a window, they appear docked one on top of the other in neat little rows at the top of the window. When you first display toolbars on the taskbar, they appear one after the other on the taskbar, often scrunching up the buttons representing the various windows open on the desktop.

To display a certain type of toolbar in a window like My Computer, Windows Explorer, or Internet Explorer 5, choose View➪Toolbars and then select one of the following commands on the cascading menu that appears:

✦ **Standard Buttons:** Displays or hides the Standard Buttons toolbar. The particular buttons that appear on this toolbar depend on whether you are browsing local files and folders or Web pages on the Internet or the corporate intranet.

✦ **Address:** Displays or hides the Address bar. The Address bar contains a text box in which you can enter the URL of the Web page you want to visit or the pathname of the folders you want to browse.

✦ **Links:** Displays or hides the Links bar. The Links bar contains buttons with links to favorite Web pages.

✦ **Text Labels:** Displays or hides text labels under the icons on the Standard Buttons bar. Note that if you choose not to display the text labels, ToolTips appear when you roll over the Standard Buttons bar with the mouse pointer.

Figure 4-1 shows you a window with all the toolbars displayed.

Address toolbar

Standard buttons toolbar

Links toolbar

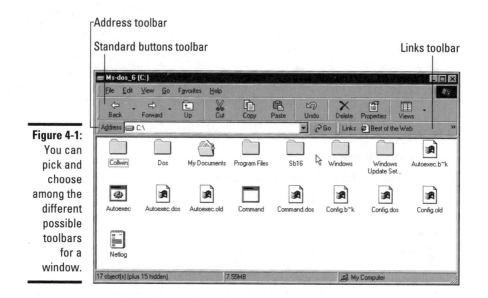

Figure 4-1:
You can
pick and
choose
among the
different
possible
toolbars
for a
window.

Standing up to the Standard Buttons Toolbar

The Standard Buttons toolbar (also known simply as the *toolbar*) is the main toolbar that appears in the My Computer, Windows Explorer, and Internet Explorer 5 windows. It is also the most chameleon-like toolbar, because its buttons change to suit the particular type of browsing you are doing. When you browse local files and folders on your computer, the Standard Buttons toolbar contains the following buttons:

+ **Back:** Returns to the previously browsed folder or Web page.

+ **Forward:** Returns to the folder or Web page that you browsed right before using the Back button to return to the current page.

+ **Up:** Moves up one level in the directory structure.

+ **Cut:** Moves the currently selected files or folders to the Clipboard.

+ **Copy:** Copies the currently selected files or folders to the Clipboard.

+ **Paste:** Places files or folders that have been moved or copied into the Clipboard to the current folder.

+ **Undo:** Eliminates your latest change (blunder?).

+ **Delete:** Gets rid of the files or folders you've selected (see "Deleting Junk" in Chapter 7 for details).

✦ **Properties:** Get properties information about the disks, files, or folders you've selected (see "Owning up to properties dialog boxes" in Chapter 5 for details).

✦ **View:** Click repeatedly to rotate through the icon view options or use the attached pull-down menu to select a different icon view for the current window.

When you browse a Web page, whether it's a local HTML document on your hard drive or one located on a Web server somewhere in cyberspace, the Back and Forward buttons that you see when browsing local folders and files are then joined by the following new buttons:

✦ **Stop:** Immediately halts the downloading of a Web page that is just taking far too long to come in.

✦ **Refresh:** Refreshes the display of the current Web page (which sometimes helps when the contents of the page appear jumbled or incomplete).

✦ **Home:** Displays the Web page designated as the start page. This Web page appears each time you launch Internet Explorer 5 and connect to the Internet.

✦ **Search:** Displays the Search Explorer bar for searching the Internet.

✦ **Favorites:** Displays the Favorites Explorer bar for revisiting favorite Web pages that you've bookmarked.

✦ **History:** Displays the History Explorer bar for revisiting Web pages that you've visited within the last few days or weeks.

✦ **Channels:** Displays the Channels Explorer bar for subscribing to or opening favorite Web channels.

✦ **Fullscreen:** Displays the current Web page at full-screen size, retaining just the buttons (with no text) on the Standard Buttons toolbar.

✦ **Mail:** Displays a pop-up menu of e-mail options, including Read Mail, New Message, Send a Link, Send Page, and Read News.

✦ **Print:** Sends the current Web page to your printer.

✦ **Edit:** Opens the current Web page in the Notepad text editor (exposing the *raw* HTML tags).

Displaying Toolbars on Your Taskbar

In addition to using toolbars with windows, you can also place toolbars on your Windows 98 taskbar in order to customize — or complicate — your computing style. (Read all about the taskbar in Chapter 2.) To display a certain type of toolbar on the taskbar, right-click the taskbar (making sure that you don't click the Start button or any of the other buttons that currently appear on the taskbar), select Toolbars on the context menu, and choose Address, Links, Desktop, Quick Launch, or New Toolbar from the cascading menu that appears.

Taking advantage of the Address bar

You can use the Address bar to search or browse Web pages on the Internet or your corporate intranet or to browse folders and files on local or networked disk drives. Just click the Address bar to insert the cursor into its text, type in the URL of the Web page or the pathname of the folder you want to browse, and then press the Enter key.

Address ⊑ C:\

Latching onto the Links toolbar

The buttons on the Links toolbar (more often than not called simply the *Links bar*) are hyperlinks that open favorite Web pages. When you first start using Windows 98, the Links bar contains only buttons with links to Web pages on the Microsoft Web site. These buttons include Best of the Web, Microsoft, Product News, Today's Links, and Web Gallery.

Start | Links | Best of the Web | Microsoft | Product News | 5:01 PM

You can, if you want, add to the Links toolbar. To add a button with a link to a preferred Web page, folder, or file, you simply drag its icon to the place on the Links bar where you want it to appear (this icon appears on the Address bar in front of the Web page URL or folder or file pathname).

To delete a button that you no longer want on the Links bar, right-click the button and then choose the Delete command on the button's shortcut menu.

Dealing with the Desktop toolbar

The Desktop toolbar contains buttons for all the icons that appear on the Windows 98 desktop. These buttons include ones for the standard Desktop icons, such as My Computer, Internet Explorer 5, and Recycle Bin, as well as those for the program, folder, and file shortcuts that you create (see Chapter 6 for more information on shortcuts).

Start | Desktop | My Computer | Internet Explor | 10:59 PM

Calling on the Quick Launch toolbar

The Quick Launch toolbar adds a group of buttons to the Windows taskbar that you can use to start commonly used modules to get back to the desktop. These buttons, shown here, include:

**Windows 98
Chapter 4**

**Dealing with
Toolbars**

◆ **Launch Internet Explorer Browser:** Starts Internet Explorer 5 for browsing Web pages.

◆ **Launch Outlook Express:** Starts Outlook Express for sending and receiving e-mail and messages from the newsgroups to which you have subscribed.

◆ **Launch TV Viewer:** Starts the Microsoft TV channel guide for getting the latest information on the current TV programming in your local area. Note that this button appears on the Quick Launch toolbar *only* if your computer is equipped with a TV tuner card *and* you have installed the Microsoft guide software.

◆ **Show Desktop:** Minimizes all open windows in order to obtain immediate access to the Windows Desktop and all the Windows icons and Active Desktop items it contains.

◆ **View Channels:** Starts the Active Channel viewer for subscribing to, updating, and browsing particular Web channels.

In addition to these standard buttons, you can add your own custom buttons to the Quick Launch toolbar by dragging the shortcuts to your favorite program or its executable file from the desktop to the Quick Launch toolbar. Follow these steps:

1. **Open the folder that contains the executable file that starts the program or that contains a shortcut to this executable file.**

2. **Drag the program's file icon or shortcut icon to the desired position on the Quick Launch toolbar and then release the mouse button.**

   A button for the program appears at the position of the I-beam in the Quick Launch toolbar.

 You can delete any of the buttons from the Quick Launch toolbar by right-clicking the button, choosing the Delete command on the shortcut menu, and then choosing the Yes button in the alert box that asks you to confirm the deletion.

New Toolbar

The New Toolbar option opens the New Toolbar dialog box, where you can make the items in a particular folder into buttons on a new custom toolbar. In the New Toolbar dialog box, select the folder whose contents is to be used in creating the new toolbar by opening its folder in the New Toolbar list box.

As soon as you close the New Toolbar dialog box, Windows adds the new toolbar, with buttons for each shortcut and icon, to the taskbar. Note that Windows gives the new toolbar the same name as that of the folder you selected, which is automatically displayed along with the names of the buttons.

All custom toolbars that you create last only during your current work session. In other words, whenever you close a custom toolbar or restart your computer, the toolbar is automatically erased and you must re-create it.

Customizing the Appearance of a Toolbar

You can customize the appearance of each toolbar that you display in Windows 98 by changing its position on the desktop (or, in the case of toolbars, its position on the taskbar) or its order at the top of its windows (in the case of the My Computer, Windows Explorer, or Internet Explorer 5 windows). You can also customize a toolbar by modifying its size and the amount of descriptive information that is displayed along with the icons.

When repositioning or resizing a toolbar, keep the following things in mind:

✦ To change the position or length of a toolbar, you drag the toolbar by its sizing handle (the double vertical bar that appears at the very beginning of the toolbar) as soon as the mouse pointer assumes the shape of a double-headed arrow.

Sizing handle

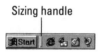

✦ When repositioning a toolbar on the Windows taskbar, you can undock the toolbar and locate it somewhere on the Windows desktop. Just drag its sizing handle up and off the taskbar, releasing the mouse button when the pointer reaches the desired position on the desktop, where it then appears in its own toolbar window complete with Close box. You can also dock the toolbar at the top, far left, or far right of the screen by dragging it to the top edge, left edge, or right edge of the screen before you release the mouse button.

✦ To change which row a toolbar occupies at the top of the My Computer, Windows Explorer, or Internet Explorer 5 window, drag the toolbar's sizing handle up or down until the toolbar jumps to its own row or a row occupied by another toolbar.

Button, button, who's got the button?

If you don't use a button regularly (and maybe after you've created several new buttons), trying to remember what each button on a toolbar is for can be a difficult task. If this is the case, remember that you can identify each of the buttons on the toolbars that appear on the taskbar or at the top of the My Computer, Windows Explorer, or Internet Explorer 5 windows by displaying the button's ToolTip. To display a button's ToolTip, you simply hover the mouse pointer over the button's icon until the comment box containing the button's text label appears.

If you insist on having some text always appear with each button, you can display the names of the buttons by right-clicking somewhere on the toolbar (making sure not to click the button itself) and choose the Show Text command on the toolbar's shortcut menu. Perform the same action, by the way, to have the text removed (the command toggles back and forth).

Chapter 5: Dialog Boxes and Menus

In This Chapter

🖊 **Working with dialog boxes**

🖊 **Managing your pull-down menus**

🖊 **Using context and Control menus**

*I*f you enjoy checking off little boxes, filling in blanks, clicking buttons, tugging on sliders, and this sort of thing, you'll certainly love dealing with the dialog boxes that Windows 98 — and any Windows program — throws at you. In any event, dialog boxes give you some exercise in responsibility because *you* make the choices. And if you have a taste for reading little menus that precede even the most mundane action, you invested your money wisely. The Windows 98 dialog boxes and menus are your gateway to getting productive.

Dialog Boxes

A *dialog box* is a special type of window that enables you to specify a bunch of settings at the same time. Most dialog boxes appear as a result of selecting a menu command from either a pull-down menu or a context (shortcut) menu. You can always tell when choosing a command will open a dialog box, because the command name is followed by an ellipsis (that's Greek for three dots in a row).

At the top of each dialog box you find a title bar that contains the name of the dialog box. You can reposition the dialog box on the screen by dragging it by its title bar (and nowhere else). You can't, however, resize a dialog box, which is the major difference between a dialog box and a window.

Dialog boxes also contain any number of buttons and boxes that you use to make your selections known to Windows 98 or the particular Windows program you have open. Figure 5-1 points out the various boxes and buttons you encounter in dialog boxes. Table 5-1 tells you how to use the boxes and buttons.

Tabs

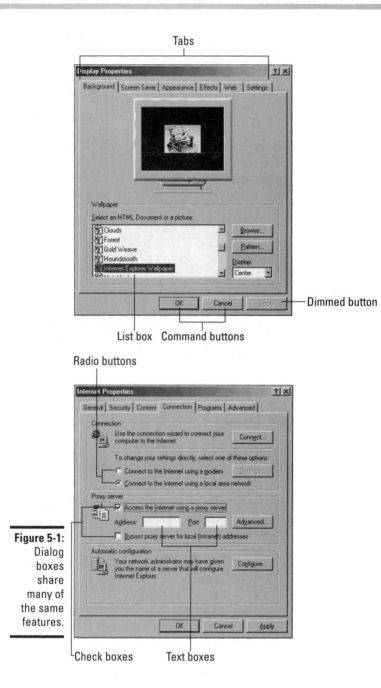

Dimmed button

List box Command buttons

Radio buttons

Figure 5-1:
Dialog
boxes
share
many of
the same
features.

Check boxes   Text boxes

Table 5-1	Common Dialog Box Elements
Parts of a Dialog Box	*What You Do with Them*
Check box	Used with items that enable you to choose more than one option. Selected options appear with a check mark inside the box, while the current check box option appears with a faint, dotted line around the option name.
Command button	Used to initiate an action, such as putting the options you select into effect by clicking the OK button.
Dimmed button	If the command name is dimmed, the button is temporarily out of commission — until you select another prerequisite option.
Drop-down list box	Looks like a text box with a down-arrow button right next door. Click the arrow button to open a list box of possible choices. If there are more choices than will fit in the box, use the scroll bar on the right to display more choices.
List box	Displays an alphabetical list of all choices for an item. Use the scroll bar on the right to display new choices. The current choice is highlighted in the list.
Radio button	Used with items when you can choose only one of several options. The selected option appears with a dot in the middle of the radio button and a faint, dotted line around the option name.
Slider	Lets you change a value (such as the sound playback volume or mouse speed) by dragging the slider back and forth (usually between Low and High, marked at each end).
Spinner button	Lets you select a new number in an accompanying edit box without having to actually type in that box. Clicking the up-arrow spinner button increases the value by one, and clicking the down-arrow spinner button decreases it by one.
Tab	Lets you select a new page of options in the same dialog box, complete with their own buttons and boxes.
Text (edit) box	Shows you the current setting and enables you to edit it or type in a whole new setting. If the text inside the box is selected, anything you type replaces the highlighted text. You can also delete text by pressing the Delete or Backspace key.

Note that if the name on a command button is followed by an ellipsis (. . .), clicking the button displays another dialog box. However, if the name of a command button is followed by two greater-than symbols (>>), choosing the button expands the current dialog box to display more choices.

After you use these various buttons and boxes to make changes to the current settings controlled by the dialog box, you can close the dialog box and put the new settings into effect by choosing the OK button.

 If you want to close the dialog box without making *any* changes to the current settings, press the Esc key or click the Close button of the dialog box.

Menu Management

Menus provide the means for Windows to organize and display the command choices you have at any given time, as well as the means for you to indicate your particular command choice. Windows 98 relies mainly on three types of command menus (each of which is described in the following sections).

The following are a few general guidelines that apply when using these types of menus:

✦ If you see a right-facing arrowhead (>) to the right of an option on a menu, another menu containing more options appears when you highlight (or select) that option.

✦ If you see an ellipsis (. . .) at the end of an option in a menu, a dialog box appears when you select that option (see "Dialog Boxes" earlier in this chapter).

✦ If you don't see any kind of symbol next to a menu option, the selected option is carried out immediately.

Tugging on the old pull-down menus

Pull-down menus are the primary means for making your wishes known in Windows 98. Although most commands on pull-down menus live up to their name and appear below the menu, some (like the Start menu), actually display their options above the menu name when you open them. Within windows, the pull-down menus are located on their own menu bar right below the title bar (as shown in Figure 5-2).

You have two main methods to open pull-down menus and select commands:

✦ **Using the mouse:** Point to the pull-down menu (an "embossed" button appears) and then click the menu name on the menu bar to open the menu. Move the mouse pointer through the menu to highlight the desired command and then click to select the menu command.

✦ **Using the Alt key:** Hold down the Alt key as you type the command letter in the menu name (that is, the underlined letter) to open the pull-down menu. Type the command letter of the menu item to select the command.

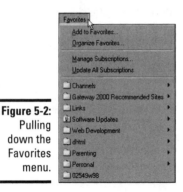

Figure 5-2:
Pulling
down the
Favorites
menu.

REAL WORLD

Your typical menu bar for a window

If you begin to notice some similarity between menu bars, you're not imagining things. The menu bar in Windows 98 modules (such as My Computer, Windows Explorer, and Internet Explorer 5) contain the pull-down menus that you use to perform all kinds of routine tasks:

✔ **File:** Does file-type stuff, such as renaming or deleting files and folders or creating shortcuts to them.

✔ **Edit**: Does editing-type stuff, such as cutting, copying, or pasting files or folders.

✔ **View:** Does show-and-tell stuff, such as displaying or hiding particular toolbars or

parts of the window and changing the way file and folder icons appear in their windows.

✔ **Go:** Does navigation-type stuff, such as going forward and backward through the folders or Web pages you just viewed, or going to Internet Explorer's home page.

✔ **Favorites:** Add to, open, or organize the folders, files, Web pages, and Web channels that you bookmark or subscribe to.

✔ **Help:** Consult particular help topics that direct you in how to use Windows 98.

To open the Start menu on the Windows taskbar with the keyboard, press Ctrl+Esc.

Getting acclimated to context menus

Context (also known as *shortcut*) *menus* are pull-down menus that are attached to particular objects in Windows, such as the desktop icons or even the desktop itself. These menus contain commands directly related to the object to which they are attached. To open a context menu, simply right-click the object with the mouse.

In Figure 5-3, you see the context menu associated with the hard disk icon in the My Computer window. To open this context menu on the lower right of the hard disk (C:) icon, simply right-click the icon.

After you open a context menu, you can use any of the pull-down menu methods described in "Tugging on the old pull-down menus" to choose its commands.

Context menus attached to program, folder, and file icons on the desktop or in a window usually contain varying assortments of the following commands:

✦ **Open:** Opens the object.

✦ **Create Shortcut:** Creates a shortcut for the selected object.

✦ **Properties:** Gives the lowdown on the selected object.

✦ **View:** Changes the size of the icons in a window and the order in which the window's icons are displayed.

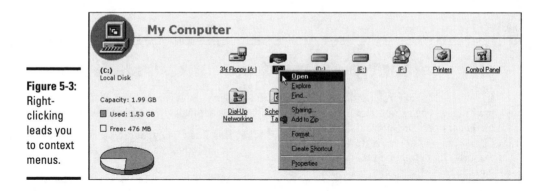

Figure 5-3:
Right-
clicking
leads you
to context
menus.

+ **Explore:** Opens the selected object and shows its contents in the Windows Explorer.

+ **Cut or Copy:** Cuts or copies the object to the Clipboard so that the object can be moved or copied to another place on your system or network.

+ **Delete:** Deletes the object by putting it into the Recycle Bin.

+ **Rename:** Changes the name of the selected object.

+ **Send To:** Sends a copy of the object to an e-mail recipient, a specific floppy drive, My Documents folder, or creates a shortcut to it on the desktop.

Using the Control menu

The Control menu is a standard pull-down menu attached to all the windows that you'll ever open in Windows 98. To open the Control menu, click the little icon to the immediate left of the window's name in the upper-left corner of the window's title bar.

If you double-click this icon instead of single-clicking it, Windows closes the window and quits any application program that happens to be running in it. If you have an unsaved document open in the program whose window you just closed, Windows 98 displays an alert dialog box that gives you a chance to save it before shutting down the shop.

Almost every Control menu you run into has these same old tired commands on it, as Table 5-2 proves.

Owning up to properties dialog boxes

A *properties dialog box* appears when you select an object's icon and then choose the Properties command (either from the File pull-down menu or from the object's context menu, which you open by right-clicking its icon).

When you open the properties dialog box for a particular object (such as a program, folder, or file icon), the dialog box gives you information about that object's current settings. Most of the time, there's not much you can or want to do with the properties for a particular Windows object. Depending on the object, you may have zero chance of changing any of its settings. In those situations where Windows 98 does let you fool around with the property settings, please be very careful not to screw up your computer by foolishly selecting some incompatible setting that you had no business changing.

Table 5-2	Control Menu Commands
Common Menu Commands	*What They Do*
Restore	Restores a maximized or minimized window to an in-between size that you can easily change
Move	Moves the window to a new location on the desktop
Size	Enables you to resize the window by moving its left, right, top, or bottom side
Minimize	Shrinks the window all the way down to a button on the taskbar at the bottom of the screen
Maximize	Zooms the window to full size so that it fills up the entire screen
Close (Alt+F4)	Closes the window, thus automatically exiting the program running in it

A menu for keeping up-to-date

The Windows Update command on the Start menu provides an almost completely automated method for keeping your Windows 98 operating system software up-to-date. As soon as you choose the Windows Update command on the Start menu, Windows puts you online and connects you to the Windows Update Web page on the Microsoft Web site. To have your computer checked out to see if you are in need of some updated Windows components, follow these steps:

1. **On the Windows Update Web page, click the Update Wizard hyperlink and click the Yes button if a Security Alert dialog box appears.**

2. **After the information in the Web page redraws, click the Update Wizard hyperlink to have your computer checked for out-of-date software components.**

   When you click the Update hyperlink, the Welcome To Microsoft Windows Update Wizard Web page opens, and the Update Wizard checks your computer for needed updates. After checking your system, a list of possible updates appears in the Available Updates list box.

3. **To have the Update Wizard install a particular update, click its name in the Available Updates list box to display a description of the update in the Description list box, then click the Install hyperlink that appears above both of these list boxes.**

   After you click the Install button, the Update Wizard downloads and installs the updated files for the component you selected.

4. **Repeat Step 3 until you have installed all of the available updates that you want added to your system.**

5. **Click the Close box in the upper-right corner of the Welcome To Microsoft Windows Update Wizard Web page and the Windows Update Web page to close both Web pages in their browser windows.**

You can remove an update and restore your computer to its previous state by choosing Update Windows on the Windows Start menu and then clicking the Restore hyperlink in the Windows Update Web page on the Microsoft Web site.

Chapter 6: The Lowdown on Files and Folders

In This Chapter

- ✔ Getting to know about files
- ✔ Using folders
- ✔ Opening files and folders
- ✔ Creating shortcuts to files and folders

*I*f you work with any Windows-based program (such as Word, Excel, and so on) for more than a few minutes, you're probably already starting a collection of files that you'll soon lose track of. This is not good. What if you need to finish your Letter to the Editor or redo the presentation that you're giving the next morning? Without a little file-savvy, you could be in trouble. So why not just stick related files in appropriately named folders.

This chapter introduces you to files and folders in general and tells you how to deal with their basics. Chapter 7 then gives you some more ideas on how to manage them.

Files

Files contain all the precious data that you create with those sophisticated (and expensive) Windows-based programs. Files occupy a certain amount of space (rated in kilobytes [K], which is Greek for thousands of bytes) on a particular disk, be it your hard drive or a removable floppy disk. For example, if you write a letter to your brother in Microsoft Word 2000 and then save the document to your hard drive, you've just created a file.

Naming files

Each filename in Windows consists of two parts: a main filename and a file extension. The file extension, which identifies the type of file and what program created it, consists of a maximum of three characters that are automatically assigned by the creating agent or program. Typically, these file extensions are not displayed in the lists of filenames that you see (for information on how to display the file extensions, see Chapter 8).

Whereas the creating program normally assigns the file extension, Windows 98 enables you to call the main part of the filename whatever the heck you want, up to a maximum of 255 characters (including spaces!). Keep in mind, however, that all pre-Windows 95 programs, and even some that run on Windows 98, do not support long filenames. These programs allow a maximum of only eight characters, with no spaces.

Identifying files with their icons

In Windows 98, files are assigned special icons along with their filenames. These icons help you quickly identify the type of file. Table 6-1 shows some example of these icons.

Table 6-1	Icons Associated with Certain Files
File Icon	*File Type and Program That Opens It*
	Program file that will install an application on your computer
	Word document that will open in Word for Windows
	Excel workbook that will open in Excel for Window
	Text file that will open in Notepad utility
	HTML document that will open in Internet Explorer 5
	Unidentified generic file that will open the Open With dialog box, which asks you to identify a program that can open the file

See Chapter 1 for more on the care and feeding of icons.

Folders

Folders are the data containers in Windows 98. You can recognize folder icons because they actually look like those nice manila folders that you never seem to have enough of. Well, don't worry. In Windows, you have access to an endless supply of folders. (And to prevent any confusion while increasing your boredom, folders in Windows always have the little tab on the left side.) Folders can contain files or other folders or a combination of files and folders (see Figure 6-1). Like files, folders occupy a certain amount of space (rated in kilobytes [K], indicating the size of the data files it holds) on a particular disk, be it your hard drive or a removable floppy disk.

Knowing all about your files

Keep in mind that you can get lots of good information on a file — such as which program created it, how big it is, when it was created and last revised, and so on. Choose the Properties command on the file's shortcut menu. (Right-click an icon to bring up the shortcut menu.)

Figure 6-1:
This open folder contains files as well as other folders.

Windows 98 dramatically alters the way you view and navigate through folders on the desktop. The new Folder Options feature enables you to configure folders with attributes normally found in a Web browser, like Internet Explorer. (See Chapter 8 for details.)

To find out more about the ins and outs of folders in Windows 98, see Chapter 7.

Opening Files and Folders

The most common way to open a file or folder is to open its icon in one of the three browsing windows (My Computer, Windows Explorer, or Internet Explorer 5). How you open the file or folder icon after you have it displayed in a browsing window depends on the Active Desktop setting that your computer uses:

✦ Double-click the icon when you've set up the Active Desktop with the so-called "classic" setting.

+ Single-click the icon when you've set up the Active Desktop so that icons act and look like hyperlinks (so-called Web style). See Chapter 8 for information on changing between Web style and classic style.

Remember that you can also open a file or folder by right-clicking its icon and then choosing the Open command at the top of its shortcut menu.

Shortcuts

Shortcuts make it possible to open an object, such as a favorite document, folder, program, or Web page, directly from the desktop of the computer — even when you have absolutely no idea how deep the object is buried on your computer or where it may be in cyberspace. The following list gives the basic lowdown on shortcuts:

+ Shortcuts can be located anywhere on your computer, but keep them right out in the open on the desktop so that you can get at them easily.

+ When you create a shortcut for an object, Windows creates an icon for it with a name like "Shortcut to such and such." You can rename the shortcut to whatever name suits you, just as you can rename any file or folder in Windows (see Chapter 7).

+ You can always tell a shortcut icon from the regular icon because the shortcut icon contains a little box with a curved arrow pointing up to the right.

The path to your files and folders

Sure, you can physically see your file or folder right there on the screen! Nevertheless, that file or folder has a unique path leading directly to it. If you're still enamored of the old DOS way of doing things and can type with more than just two fingers, you can often just as easily use a path (such as in an address bar) to get to something.

The location of a folder (known in tech talk as the folder's *directory path*) is identified by the letter of the drive that holds its disk, the other folder or folders within which it's embedded, and a unique name. The following is an example of a Workstuff folder's directory path, which indicates that Workstuff is a subfolder within the My Documents folder on drive C:

```
C:\My Documents\Workstuff
```

The location of a file (its *pathname*) is identified by the letter of the drive that holds its disk, the folder or subfolders within which it's embedded, and a unique filename. A typical pathname could look like this:

```
C:\MyDocuments\Workstuff\invoice15.xls
```

This pathname is shorthand to indicate that a file named "invoice 15.xls" is located in a folder named "Workstuff," which is itself located in a folder called "My Documents," which is, in turn, located on drive C (the hard drive) of your computer.

To create a shortcut for a folder, file, or other type of local object on the Windows 98 desktop, follow these steps:

1. **Select the icon for the object for which you want to create a shortcut.**

2. **Choose File⇨Create Shortcut or choose Create Shortcut from the object's shortcut menu.**

3. **If Windows displays the error message** Unable to create a short-cut here. Do you want the shortcut placed on the desk-top?, **choose Yes. If Windows doesn't give you this error message, it places the new shortcut in the currently open window. If you want the shortcut on the desktop, where you have constant access to it, drag the shortcut's icon to any place on the desktop and release the mouse button.**

You mess up a shortcut if you move the object to which it refers to a new place on your computer, because Windows still looks for it (unsuccessfully) in the old location. If you do mess up a shortcut by moving the object it refers to, you have to trash the shortcut and then re-create it or move the original file back to its location.

A special folder: Control Panel

The Control Panel in Windows 98 is the place to go when you need to make changes to various settings of your computer system. To open the Control Panel window, click the Start button on the taskbar and then choose Settings⇨Control Panel on the Start menu. (Or open the My Computer window from the Windows desktop and then open the Control Panel folder icon found there.)

✔ The 32 bit ODBC (Open DataBase Connectivity) Properties dialog box enables you to mess around with the data source drivers used in Windows 98.

✔ The Accessibility Properties dialog box allows you to change a number of keyboard, sound, display, and mouse settings that can make using the computer easier if you have less-than-perfect physical dexterity.

✔ The Add New Hardware Properties dialog box opens to a wizard that walks you through the installation of new hardware.

✔ The Add/Remove Programs Properties dialog box enables you to install or uninstall programs on your computer.

✔ The Date/Time Properties dialog box is where you reset the current date and time.

✔ The Display Properties dialog box enables you to customize just about every parameter that affects the way your computer is displayed on a monitor.

✔ The Find Fast Properties dialog box enables you to create and update various indexes that greatly speed up file searches using specific text or phrases that you perform in Windows 98 or with a Microsoft Office program.

✔ The Fonts dialog box shows you all the fonts installed on your computer, as well as installs any new fonts you may get your hands on.

(continued)

(continued)

✔ The Game Controllers dialog box is where you add and configure the killer joystick or game pad you bought.

✔ The Infrared Monitor dialog box enables you to keep track of your computer's infrared activity.

✔ The Internet Properties dialog box enables you to configure all aspects of your Web-browsing experience.

✔ The Keyboard Properties dialog box adjusts the rate at which characters are repeated when you hold down a key, adjust the cursor blink rate, selects a country and language layout for the keyboard, and changes the type of keyboard.

✔ The Microsoft Workgroup Postoffice Admin wizard is what your network administrator uses to create or administer a post office location for sending and receiving messages on your LAN.

✔ The Modems Properties dialog box tells you what modems are installed on your computer, as well as gives you a place to change their dialing properties.

✔ The Mouse Properties dialog box lets you change all kinds of mouse settings, such as setting a right-handed or left-handed button configuration, and so on.

✔ The Multimedia Properties dialog box enables you to mess with all sorts of multimedia settings, such as change the playback or recording volume level, the preferred device for recording, and so on.

✔ The Network dialog box lets your network administrator administer the LAN to his or her heart's content.

✔ The Passwords Properties dialog box enables the network administrator for your LAN to add or change the password required to use various services on your computer system — and other fun stuff.

✔ The PC Card (PCMCIA) Properties dialog box (laptop computers only) enables you to see all the PC cards that you have inserted into the slots in your laptop computer.

✔ The Power Management Properties dialog box (laptop computers only) is where you create individual power schemes for your computer.

✔ The Printers dialog box shows you all the printers that are currently installed for use on your computer and enables you to add a new printer.

✔ The QuickFinder Manager dialog box lets you create, edit, delete, or update a Fast Search.

✔ The Regional Settings Properties dialog box enables you to change the formatting for numbers, currency, dates, and times to suit schemes preferred by countries other than the U.S.

✔ The Sounds Properties dialog box is where you select various sound files to be played when certain events take.

✔ The System Properties dialog box enables you to get system information about your computer, as well as fool around with a lot of settings, such as optimizing the file systems.

✔ The Dialing Properties dialog box is where you configure modem dialing settings when you make calls from different locations.

✔ The User Settings dialog box enables you to set up a personal profile that makes preferred desktop settings available to each person who works on the same computer.

Chapter 7: File and Folder Management

In This Chapter

✔ Creating files and folders

✔ Selecting, copying, and moving files and folders

✔ Finding files and folders

✔ Renaming files and folders

✔ Deleting unwanted files and folders

*Y*ou don't need a degree from Harvard Business School to manage your files and folders in Windows 98. In fact, if you can click a mouse or punch a keyboard, you're pretty much qualified as an expert file and folder manager. You don't even need to worry about filling out those mid-year performance reviews as most managers do. Your files and folders are simple to boss around because they do whatever you tell them to do. How much easier can managing be? This chapter shows you the best ways to create, select, move, copy, paste, find, rename, and delete files and folders.

Creating New Files and Folders

You create empty folders to hold your files and empty files to hold new documents of a particular type, right within Windows 98.

To create an empty folder, follow these steps:

1. **Open the folder inside a browsing window in which the new folder is to appear.**

2. **Choose File⇨New⇨Folder from the menu bar or New⇨Folder on the window's shortcut menu.**

3. **Replace the temporary folder name (New Folder) by typing a name of your choosing and pressing Enter.**

To create an empty file of a certain type, follow these steps:

1. **Open the window and the folder where the new file is required.**

2. **Choose File⇨New from the menu bar or New on the window's shortcut menu.**

3. **Choose the type of file you want to create (such as Microsoft PowerPoint Presentation, Microsoft Excel Worksheet, Microsoft Word Document, Microsoft Access Database, Wave Sound, Text Document, or Briefcase, and so on) from the New submenu.**

4. **Replace the temporary file name (such as New Microsoft Word Document) by typing a name of your choosing and pressing Enter.**

Create a new folder when you need to have a new place to store your files and other folders. Create an empty file in a particular folder before you put something in it. Create lots of empty files and folders with the name "Income 1990-1999" to confuse the IRS long enough for you to get to the Bahamas.

Selecting Files and Folders

If you want to perform many actions on files and folders, you need to know how to select them. Because files and folders are represented by icons, jump back to Chapter 1 for all the details.

Copying (And Moving) Files and Folders

Copying and moving files and folders in Windows 98 is accomplished by using the two universal methods described in this section — drag-and-drop and copy/cut-and-paste.

Drag 'em up, drop 'em down

The art of drag-and-drop is simplicity itself. To copy files with drag-and-drop, follow these steps:

1. **Open the window that contains the items to be copied, as well as the window with the folder or disk to which you want to copy the items.**

2. **Select all the items to be copied (see Chapter 1 for details on selecting).**

3. **Hold down the Ctrl key as you drag the selected items to the folder to which you want to copy them (you'll notice the appearance of a plus sign next to the pointer).**

4. **When the destination folder icon is selected (that is, highlighted), drop the selected items by releasing the mouse button.**

The flavors of copy-and-paste

The copy and paste commands, like many of the everyday tasks in Windows 98, can be performed by either selecting commands on the menu bar or by using keyboard combination shortcuts. To copy files with copy-and-paste, using either method, follow these steps:

1. **Open a browsing window that holds the items to be copied.**

2. **Select all the items to be copied (see Chapter 1 for the details) and then choose Edit⇨Copy, or press Ctrl+C.**

3. **Open a browsing window that holds the folder or disk where the copied items are to appear.**

4. **Open the folder or disk to hold the copied items and then choose Edit⇨Paste, or press Ctrl+V.**

Use drag-and-drop to copy when you have both the folder with the items to be copied and the destination folder or disk displayed on the desktop (as when using the Windows Explorer). Use copy-and-paste to copy when you can't easily display both the folder with the items to be copied and the destination folder or disk together on the desktop.

Move over folders and files

You can move files and folders in the Windows Explorer by using either the drag-and-drop or the cut-and-paste method. To move an object using drag-and-drop, follow these steps:

1. **Open a browsing window that contains the folders and files that you want to move. If you're just moving some files in a folder, be sure to open that folder in the window.**

2. **Open a browsing window that displays the icon for the folder or disk to which the files and folders you're about to select in the first folder (described in Step 1) will be moved.**

3. **Select in the first window all the files and folders that you want to move.**

4. **Drag the selected files and folders from the first window to the window that contains the destination folder or disk (the one where the files are to be moved).**

5. **As soon as you select the icon of the destination folder or disk (indicated by a highlighted name), release the mouse button to move the files into that folder or disk.**

When you drag files or folders from one disk to another, Windows 98 automatically copies the files and folders rather than moving them (meaning that you must still delete them from their original disk if you need the space).

Why copy and drag when you can send?

If all you want to do is back up some files from your hard drive to a floppy disk in drive A or B, you can do so with the Send To command. After selecting the files to copy, just open the shortcut menu attached to one of the file icons by right-clicking the icon. Then choose the correct floppy drive, such as 3¹/₂ Floppy (A) on the Send To menu. Oh, and one thing more: Don't forget to insert a diskette, preferably already formatted and ready to go, before you start this little operation.

You can also send a file or folder to a folder with the Send To command. Just place a shortcut to that folder in your SendTo folder (located itself in the Windows folder on your C: drive — just look in My Computer). When you right-click an icon for a file or folder, you can see the shortcut to your folder on the menu.

Drag-and-drop moving from folder to folder is great because it's really fast. This method does have a major drawback, however: It's pretty easy to drop your file icons into the wrong folder. Instead of having a cow when you open up what you thought was the destination folder and find that your files are gone, you can locate them by using the Find Files or Folders command (see "Finding Files and Folders" later in this chapter).

Moving files and folders via cut-and-paste ensures that the lost files scenario just described won't happen, though it's much clunkier than the elegant drag-and-drop method. To move files and folders with cut-and-paste, use these steps:

1. **Open a window that displays all the files and folders you want to move.**

2. **Select all the files and folders you want to move (see Chapter 1 for info on selecting).**

3. **Choose Edit⇨Cut, or press Ctrl+X, to cut the selected files and place them on the Clipboard.**

4. **Open a window that contains the destination folder or disk (the one to which you want to move the selected files or folders).**

5. **Choose Edit⇨Paste in the window where the selected stuff is to be moved, or press Ctrl+V, to insert the files into the folder or disk.**

Use the drag-and-drop method when on the desktop you can see both the files and folders to be moved and the folder to which you are moving them. Switch to the cut-and-paste method when you cannot see both.

Windows automatically moves files when you drag their file icons from one folder to another on the same disk and copies files (indicated by the appearance of a plus sign next to the pointer) when you drag their icons from one disk to another.

When using the cut and paste commands to move files or folders, you don't have to keep open the first window in which they were originally located after you cut them. Just be sure that you paste the cut files or folders in a location before you choose Edit⇨Copy or Edit⇨Cut again in Windows 98.

Finding Files and Folders

The Find feature enables you to quickly locate all those misplaced files and folders that you're just sure are hiding somewhere on your hard drive. To open the Find window to search for a file or folder, follow these steps:

1. **Click the Start button on the taskbar and then choose Find⇨Files or Folders on the Start menu.**

This action opens the Find: All Files window.

2. **Enter the search conditions and where to look in the appropriate tabs of the Find: All Files window (Name & Location, Date, and Advanced).**

3. **Click the Find Now button to start the search.**

When Windows 98 completes a search, it expands the Find dialog box to display in a list box all the files that meet your search conditions (as shown in Figure 7-1). This list box shows the name, location, size, type, and the date the file was last modified.

The Find dialog box contains three tabs (Name & Location, Date, and Advanced), with various options with which you set the search conditions to use for your search. On the tabs in the Find dialog box, you find the options listed in Table 7-1.

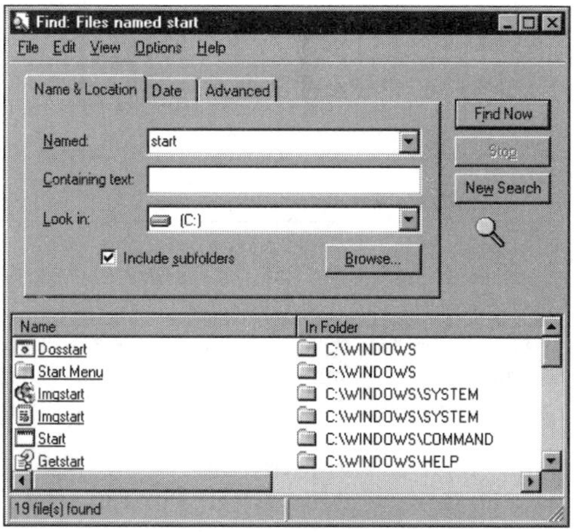

Figure 7-1:
The Find
dialog box
in action.

Table 7-1	Find Dialog Box Options
Name & Location Tab Options	**What They Do**
Named	Enter all or part of the file or folder name you're looking for in this edit box. Don't worry about capitalization. Windows remembers the stuff you enter in this edit box so that you can reselect search text in the drop-down list box.
Containing text	Use this edit box to specify a string of characters, a word, or a phrase that should be contained within the files you're looking for.
Look in	Use this drop-down list box or the Browse button to select the drive where you want to conduct the search.
Include subfolders	Normally, Windows searches all the folders within the folders on the disk specified in the Look In edit box. If you're pretty sure that the files and folders you want won't be found any deeper than in the first level of folders, remove the check mark from this check box.
All files	Normally, Windows automatically selects this radio button and searches all files in the location specified in the Look In text box on the Name & Location tab.
Find all files	Select this radio button and its Created, Modified, or Last accessed options from the drop-down list to find files or folders created, modified, or accessed between certain dates or within the last few days or months (see the following options).
Between and	Select this radio button and enter the two dates between which the files or folders must have been created, edited, or accessed. The two dates you enter in the between text boxes are included in the search.
During the previous month(s)	Select this radio button and enter the number of months in the text box during which files and folders were created, modified, or accessed.
During the previous days	Select this radio button and enter the number of days in the text box during which files and folders were created, modified, or accessed.
Advanced Tab Options	**What They Do**
Of type	Use this drop-down list box to specify a particular type of file to search for (rather than All Files and Folders, which is the default).
Size is	Select the At least or At most option in the drop-down list box and enter the number of kilobytes (KB) that the size of the files to be searched must have attained or not exceeded.

Keep in mind that you don't have to know the name of the file to use the Find feature, because Windows 98 can search for specific text in a file if you use the Containing text box on the Name & Location tab of the Find dialog box.

Renaming Files and Folders

You can rename file and folder icons directly in Windows 98 by typing over or editing the existing file or folder name as outlined in these steps:

1. **Right-click the file or folder icon and select Rename on its shortcut menu.**

2. **Type the new name that you want to give the folder (up to 255 characters) or edit the existing name (use the Delete key to remove characters and the → or ← key to move the cursor without deleting characters).**

3. **After you finish editing the file or folder name, press the Enter key to complete the renaming procedure.**

When the file or folder name is selected for editing, typing anything entirely replaces the current name. If you want to edit the file or folder name rather than replace it, you need to click the insertion point at the place in the name that needs editing before you begin typing.

Deleting Junk

Because the whole purpose of working on computers is to create junk, you need to know how to get rid of unneeded files and folders to free up space on your hard drive. To delete files or folders, follow these steps:

1. **In one of the three browsing windows, open the folder that holds the files or folders to be deleted.**

2. **Select all the files and folders to be deleted (see Chapter 1 for the lowdown on selecting items).**

3. **Choose File⇨Delete on the menu bar or press the Delete key.**

You may find dragging the selected items to the Recycle Bin easier. Use the method you prefer.

4. **Choose the Yes button in the Confirm File Delete dialog box that asks if you want to send the selected file or files to the Recycle Bin.**

Windows 98 puts all items that you delete in the Recycle Bin. To get rid of all the items in the Recycle Bin, open the Recycle Bin and choose File⇨Empty Recycle Bin. Click the Yes button or press Enter in the Confirm File Delete or Confirm Multiple File Delete dialog box that asks if you want to delete the selected file or files. Be aware, however, that there's no turning back from this step. Figure 7-2 shows an open Recycle Bin.

Use the following tips to work efficiently with the Recycle Bin:

✦ **To retrieve stuff from the Recycle Bin:** Open the Recycle Bin and then drag the icons for the files and folders you want to save out of the Recycle Bin and drop them in the desired location. You can also choose File⇨Restore from the Recycle Bin window menu bar.

✦ **To empty the Recycle Bin:** Open the Recycle Bin and choose File⇨Empty Recycle Bin from the Recycle Bin window menu bar. You can also empty it by right-clicking the Recycle Bin icon and choosing Empty Recycle Bin from the icon's context menu.

Figure 7-2:
You can usually find some good things if you rummage through the trash.

Doing DOS stuff

For those Windows users who are tired of looking at icons of files and folders and find themselves longing for the good old days when they used DOS to get things done on a computer, Windows 98 enables you to open a window with the DOS prompt so that you can type away your nostalgia. Everything you need to know about using DOS:

✔ To open a window to DOS within Windows 98 in an MS-DOS Prompt window, click the Start button on the taskbar and then choose Programs⇨MS-DOS Prompt.

✔ To restart your computer in DOS mode (heaven forbid!) rather than in Windows 98, click the Start button on the taskbar and then choose Shut Down on the Start menu to open the Shut Down Windows

dialog box. Select the Restart in MS-DOS Mode radio button in the Shut Down Windows dialog box and then click the OK button.

✔ To return to Windows 98 after restarting in MS-DOS mode, type **exit** at the DOS prompt and then press Enter. To close the MS-DOS Prompt window, you can either type **exit** and press Enter or you can click the window's Close box.

Note: Don't fool around with DOS commands unless you are really sure of what you're doing. If you ever get a DOS window open and then get cold feet, just click the Close button in the MS-DOS Prompt window to close it and get back to Windows 98 where you belong.

Chapter 8: Getting Involved with the Active Desktop

In This Chapter

↙ Taking charge of your Active Desktop

↙ Browsing folders the Windows 98 way

↙ Changing the way you deal with folders

*G*oing from Windows 3.1 to Windows 95 was a big jump for most people. (And if you didn't have to make that leap, just imagine going from an old black-and-white antenna-based TV to a color set with a 100-channel cable connection: lots more to look at and get confused over — but very pretty pictures!)

Fortunately, going from Windows 95 to Windows 98 doesn't have to be that big of a jump. Yes, you can actually keep things pretty much like what you had in Windows 95 — if you want to. However, for the adventurous, Windows 98 enables you to tinker with the way you view and work with files and folders on your computer. It's the Microsoft way of introducing us to the future of computing (according to Microsoft). In any case, the new ways do have some advantages, so why don't you just come along and enjoy the ride. You may even have fun!

The Active Desktop

The Active Desktop is the amazing new set of features that initiates the Microsoft grand plan for building "true" Web integration into the Windows operating environment. The Windows 98 desktop consists of three layers, each of which lies on top of the other.

+ The top layer contains the Windows 98 desktop icons, including standard shortcuts to items such as My Computer and the Network Neighborhood, as well as custom shortcuts to your favorite programs and folders.

+ The middle layer contains all displayed Active Desktop items, such as the Internet Explorer Channel Bar, along with other Active Desktop items that you subscribe to.

+ The bottom layer contains the desktop wallpaper, which can be an HTML document or a BMP, GIF, or JPEG graphics file.

You can turn the "active" aspect of the Windows 98 desktop on and off at will by turning on and off the Web Page view. When you turn the Web Page view off, Windows hides the middle layer, which contains all the Active Desktop items (such as the Internet Explorer Channel Bar, as well as any other items to which you subscribe). In addition, if you have made an HTML document into the desktop wallpaper, turning off the Active Desktop also hides the document on the bottom layer. The result is that only the top layer, which has the regular Windows desktop icons, is visible.

Figure 8-1 shows the desktop of a computer with the Web Page view turned on. In this figure, you can see the whole shebang: the Windows desktop icons on the left, the Active Desktop items (including the MSNBC weather map, Corbis tripscope, the 3D Java clock, and, of course, the Internet Explorer Channel bar) spreading out from the center toward the right, and, at the top, the Microsoft Windows 98 logo, which is part of the HTML document that is designated as the desktop wallpaper.

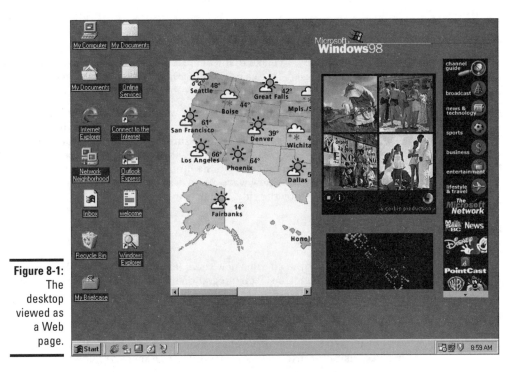

Figure 8-1:
The
desktop
viewed as
a Web
page.

Turning the Desktop Web Page View On and Off

As is often the case, Microsoft gives you a couple of ways to turn the desktop Web Page view on and off:

✦ Right-click somewhere on the desktop (outside of a desktop icon or Active Desktop item) and choose Active Desktop⇨View as Web Page on the shortcut menu.

✦ Click the Start button on the taskbar and then choose Settings⇨ Active Desktop⇨View as Web Page on the Start menu.

The Windows desktop is not the only Windows element that you can view as a Web page. In fact, any window in Windows 98 (My Computer, Windows Explorer, Control Panel, and so on) can be viewed as a Web page (they didn't call it "Web integration" for nothing). For more on working with Web Page views for folders viewed in the browsing windows, see "Browsing folders with Web Page view turned on" later in this chapter.

Browsing Folders on a Local Disk

You can use any of the three Windows 98 browsing windows (My Computer, Windows Explorer, or Internet Explorer 5) to browse the contents of the drives attached to your computer. These disks can be in local drives, such as your floppy drive (A:), hard drive (C:), or CD-ROM drive (D:). If your computer is on a Local Area Network (LAN), these disks can be disks on remote drives to which you have access, such as a network E:, F:, or G: drive. Browsing folders with My Computer and Windows Explorer is much more direct (because these windows both sport icons for the drives attached to your computer) and thus discussed in this section.

Browsing folders with Web Page view turned on

Windows 98 supports a new folder view called Web Page view. When you turn this view on (by choosing View⇨as Web Page) in one of the browsing windows, vital statistics appear in an info panel on the left side of the window each time you select a particular file or folder icon. These statistics include the folder or file name, the last date modified, and, in the case of files, the file type and size in kilobytes. Moreover, when you select an application file, like a Microsoft Word or Excel document, the name of the person who authored the document also appears in the info panel, and when you select a graphics file whose format Windows 98 can decipher or an HTML document, a thumbnail of the image or page appears as well.

Figure 8-2 shows the Windows 98 Explorer after selecting the Graphic Images folder in the All Folders pane, turning on Web Page view, and selecting a file containing a GIF graphic image in the contents pane. Note that in addition to vital statistics (file name, type, last date modified, and size), a thumbnail preview of the graphic appears in the info panel in the contents pane.

Browsing folders with thumbnail view turned on

When browsing folders that contain numerous graphics or Web pages (for example, the pages that you are developing for your own Web site on the Internet), you can add a thumbnail view to the folder's properties and then use this thumbnail view to display the contents of graphic files and Web pages as thumbnail images.

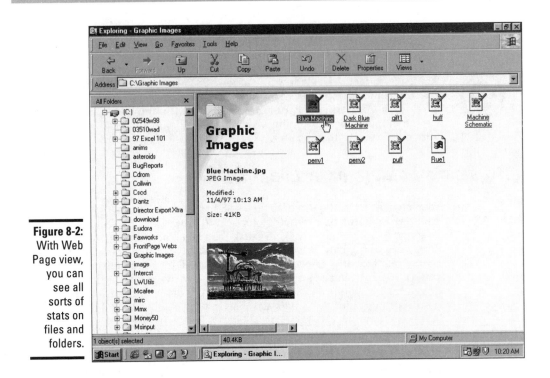

Figure 8-2:
With Web
Page view,
you can
see all
sorts of
stats on
files and
folders.

Before you can use the thumbnail view when browsing the contents of a folder, you must add the thumbnail view to the folder's properties, as follows:

1. **Open one of the three browsing windows (My Computer, Windows Explorer, or Internet Explorer 5) and then open the drive and folder that contains the folder to which you want to add the thumbnail view.**

2. **Right-click the folder's icon and choose Properties from the shortcut menu to open the Properties dialog box for that folder.**

3. **Click the Enable Thumbnail View check box on the General tab of the folder's Properties dialog box and then click OK.**

After you enable the thumbnail view for the folder, you can turn it on by taking these steps:

1. **Open the folder for which you enabled the thumbnail view in the My Computer, Windows Explorer, or Internet Explorer 4 window.**

2. **Choose View➪Thumbnails or click the drop-down button attached to the Views button on the Standard Buttons bar and then choose Thumbnails from its pop-up menu. (Figure 8-3 shows you what a folder looks like with thumbnail view enabled.)**

To turn off the thumbnail view for a folder, just select another view (such as Large Icons or List) on the View pull-down menu or the Views button pop-up menu. (You don't have to go to the trouble of disabling the thumbnail view in the folder's Properties dialog box.)

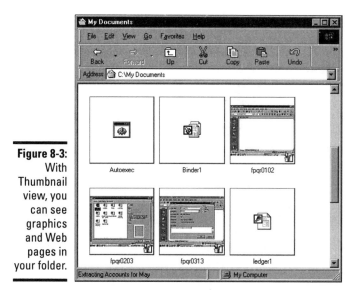

Figure 8-3:
With
Thumbnail
view, you
can see
graphics
and Web
pages in
your folder.

The Web Page view and Thumbnail view are mutually exclusive. When the Web Page view is on and you choose Thumbnails from the View pull-down menu or the Views button pop-up menu, Windows automatically turns off the as Web Page setting. Likewise, if you are using Thumbnail view and then choose as Web Page from the View pull-down menu or the Views button pop-up menu, Windows turns off the Thumbnails setting.

Changing the Folder Options for Windows 98

You can use the Folder Options dialog box to modify the default Active Desktop and Web Page view setting, Folder Options also lets you change how you select and open folder and file icons, what file information appears in the browsing windows, and which programs are associated with what file types.

You can open the Folder Options dialog box in one of two ways:

✦ Choose View⇨Folder Options from the pull-down menus in any of the three browsing windows (My Computer, Windows Explorer, or Internet Explorer 5).

✦ Click the Start button on the Windows taskbar and then choose Settings⇨Folders & Icons from the Start menu.

Changing the way you select and open icons

The General tab of the Folder Options dialog box, shown in Figure 8-4, is where you change the Active Desktop and Web Page view default settings, and also where you change the way you select and open desktop and windows icons with the mouse. The General tab contains the following three style options:

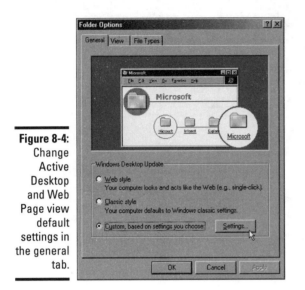

Figure 8-4:
Change
Active
Desktop
and Web
Page view
default
settings in
the general
tab.

✦ **Web style:** Enables all Web-related content on the Active Desktop, enables the Web Page view for all folders with HTML content, and makes all your folders and icons look and act like hyperlinks on a Web page, so that you only have to point to them to select them and then single-click to open them.

✦ **Classic style:** Disables all Web-related content on the Active Desktop, disables the Web Page view for all folders with HTML content, and makes all your folders and icons look and act like they did on the "classic" Windows 95 desktop, so that you need to click to select them and double-click to open them.

✦ **Custom, based on settings you choose:** Enables you to select a blend of the classic and Web style features for a truly personalized setup. Click the Settings button to the immediate right of this radio button to open the Custom Settings dialog box and then choose the settings to customize, as described in the following paragraphs.

When you open the Custom Settings dialog box (which you see in Figure 8-5) by choosing the Custom, Based On Settings You Choose radio button and then clicking the Settings button, you can customize Folder Option settings in the following four areas:

✦ **Active Desktop:** Choose the Enable All Web-Related Content on My Desktop radio button to activate the Active Desktop so that all Active Desktop items and any HTML document used as wallpaper appear on the Windows desktop (see "The Active Desktop" earlier in this chapter). Choose the Use Windows Classic Desktop radio button to turn off the Active Desktop so that all desktop items and any HTML wallpaper disappear.

✦ **Browse folder as follows:** Choose the Open Each Folder in the Same Window radio button to have the contents of each subfolder you open in My Computer replace the contents of the folder in which it resides. Choose the Open Each Folder in Its Own Window radio button to have the contents displayed in a separate, new My Computer window.

✦ **View Web Content in Folders:** Choose the For All Folders with HTML content radio button to have Web Page views turned on for all folders that have them. Choose the Only for Folders Where I Select "as Web Page" (View Menu) radio button to have Web Page views for folders appear only when you choose View⇨as Web Page.

✦ **Click Items As Follows:** Choose the Single-Click to Open Item (Point to Select) radio button to select and open folder and file icons as though they were hyperlinks. Choose Double-Click to Open an Item (Single-Click to Select) to select and open them in the classic single- and double-click manner. When you select the Single-Click to Open Item (Point to Select) radio button, you have a choice between the Underline Icon Titles Consistent with My Browser Settings radio button and the Underline Icon Titles Only When I Point at Them radio button. Choose the former radio button when you want the titles normally to appear underlined (making them appear like hyperlinks on a Web page). Choose the latter radio button when you want this hyperlink effect to appear when you position the mouse pointer somewhere on the associated icon.

Figure 8-5:
Customize
your folder
options in
the Custom
Settings
dialog box.

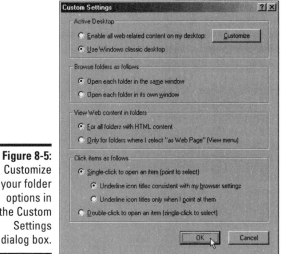

Customizing your desktop

The Display Properties dialog box, which you open via the Display Control Panel in Windows 98, has many new features that allow you to customize nearly every aspect of the way the Windows desktop is displayed on your computer. When you open the Display icon in the Control Panel, you see the Display Properties dialog box. Use the seven tabs in that dialog box to change the following display settings:

✔ **Background tab:** Select a graphics image or HTML (Web page) document to change the pattern or wallpaper used by the desktop. (You change the color of the desktop with the Appearance tab, described in this list.)

✔ **Screen Saver tab:** Select and configure a screen saver and set the interval after which it kicks in. If you have one of those new energy-saving monitors, you can set the interval after which the monitor goes to lower-power standby or shuts off. (If you have such a monitor but Windows 98 isn't using its energy-saving features, first choose the Advanced button on the Settings tab. Then check the Monitor is Energy Star Compliant check box on the Monitor tab of the Display Type dialog box.)

✔ **Appearance tab:** Change the color scheme used by various parts of a window and the color of the desktop. If you change the appearance of an item that uses a font (such as the Icon Title, Inactive Title Bar, or ToolTip), you can change the font and its color, size, and attributes as well.

✔ **Effects tab:** Assign new icons to desktop icons (or restore to the default), select large icons for the desktop and all windows, and choose to display icons in all possible colors. You can also browse to select an icon from another icon file.

✔ **Web tab:** List the channels that you are currently subscribed to as well as the available Active Desktop items. Use the check boxes to select the item to appear on the desktop when using the View as Web Page option for the desktop. This tab also enables you to go to the Folder Options dialog box for further customizations.

✔ **Settings tab:** Change the color palette (meaning the number of colors, such as 16, 256, or even — with some really fancy cards and monitors — millions) used by Windows 98, and resize the desktop area (the higher the number of pixels you select, the smaller the items and fonts appear on the desktop, although making them smaller does allow you to cram more stuff on-screen). You can also use this tab to specify the kind of monitor you have if Windows 98 did not pick up on the monitor type when you first installed it or if you add a new monitor after Windows 98 was installed.

Index

Contents at a Glance

Chapter 1: Word 101

In This Chapter

↙ **Discovering the Word 2000 screen**

↙ **Opening an existing document**

↙ **Navigating in Word**

↙ **Working on more than one document at a time**

↙ **Working in more than one place in a document at a time**

↙ **Zooming in and zooming out**

*I*f you've been around word processors for a while, you probably know a lot of this stuff already. In case you need a refresher, however, don't jump ahead too soon. And in case you've never even touched a word processor before, you've come to the right place. This chapter gets you going by explaining some basic word-processing functions such as opening a document, moving about in a document, zooming in on a document, and the like. So what's a document you say? Well, indeed, you've come to the right place.

What All That Stuff On-Screen Is

Seeing the Word 2000 screen for the first time is sort of like trying to find your way through Tokyo's busy Ikebukuro subway station. Just check out Figure 1-1. It's intimidating. But once you start using Word, you quickly find out what everything is. In the meantime, Table 1-1 gives you some shorthand descriptions.

Table 1-1	The Word 2000 Screen
Part of Screen	*What It Is*
Title bar	At the top of the screen, the title bar tells you the name of the document you're working on.
Control menu	Click here to pull down a menu with options for minimizing, maximizing, moving, and closing the window.
Minimize, Restore, Close buttons	These three magic buttons make it very easy to shrink, enlarge, and close the window you are working in.
Menu bar	The list of menu options, from File to Help, that you choose from to give commands.

(continued)

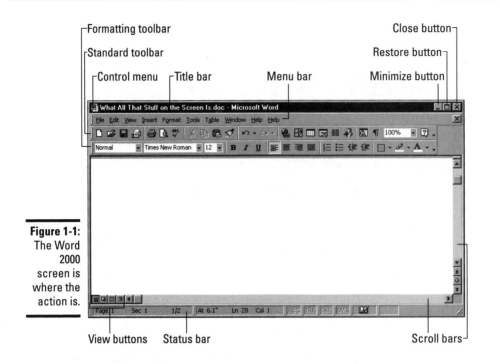

Formatting toolbar — Close button
Standard toolbar — Restore button
Control menu — Title bar — Menu bar — Minimize button

Figure 1-1:
The Word
2000
screen is
where the
action is.

View buttons   Status bar   Scroll bars

Part of Screen	What It Is
Standard toolbar	Offers buttons that you click to execute commands.
Formatting toolbar	Offers formatting buttons and pull-down lists for changing the appearance or layout of text.
Scroll bars	The scroll bars help you get from place to place in a document.
View buttons	Click one of these to change your view of a document.
Status bar	The status bar gives you basic information about where you are and what you're doing in a document. It tells you what page and what section you're in, the total number of pages in the document, and where the insertion point is on the page.

Table 1-1 *(continued)*

What Is a Document?

Document is just a fancy word for a letter, report, announcement, or proclamation that you create with Word.

When you first start Word, you see a document with the generic name "Document1." But if you already have a document on-screen and you want to start a new one, click the New Blank Document button. A brand-new document opens with the generic name "Document2" in the title bar. (The *title bar* is the stripe across the top of the computer screen.) It's called "Document 2" because it's the second one you're working on. The document keeps that name, Document2, until you save it and give it a name of your own.

Opening a Document

Before you can start working on a document that has been created and named, you have to open it. And because finding the file you want to open can sometimes be difficult, Word offers several amenities to help you locate files and quickly open them. (Chapter 2 gives you all you need to know in order to save a new document that you create.)

The conventional way to open a document

Following is the conventional method of opening a document:

1. **Choose File⇨Open, press Ctrl+O, or click the Open button.**

2. **Find the folder that holds the file you want to open. To do that, try using these nifty tools (shown in Figure 1-2):**

Back button

Double-click to see folder's contents ⌐Up One Level button

Click to choose a new drive or folder   View button

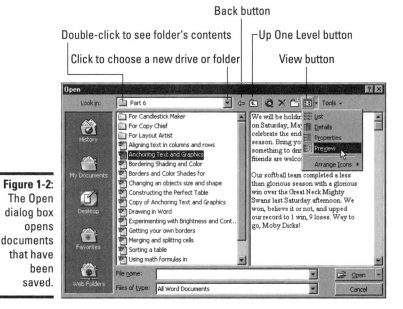

Figure 1-2:
The Open
dialog box
opens
documents
that have
been
saved.

- **Look in drop-down menu:** Click the down arrow to open the Look in drop-down menu, and then click on a drive letter or folder to see its contents.

- **Back button:** If you stray too far in your search, click the Back button to see the folder you looked at previously.

- **Up One Level button:** Click the Up One Level button to climb up the hierarchy of folders on your computer system.

• **Views button and menu:** Click the Views down arrow and choose an option to examine the contents of a folder more closely. The List option on the menu lists file names, the Details option tells how large files are and when they were last modified, the Properties option provides details about the file selected in the dialog box, and the Preview option shows the file. You can also click the Views button to cycle through the choices on the menu.

• **Folders:** Double-click a folder to place its name in the Look in box and see its contents.

3. **When you've found the folder and it is listed in the Look in box, click the name of the file you want to open.**

4. **Either double-click on the file you selected or click the Open button.**

Using dialog boxes and making menu choices is explained in the Windows 98 portion of this book. The basic concepts are the same!

Speed techniques for opening documents

Rooting around in the Open dialog box to find a document is a bother, so Word offers handy buttons that you can click to find and open documents. See Table 1-2.

Table 1-2	Buttons for Finding and Opening Documents
Click This Button	*To See*
History	The last three dozen documents and folders that you opened. Double-click a document to reopen it; double-click a folder to see its contents.
My Documents	The contents of the My Documents folder. Double-click a document to open it. The My Documents folder is a good place to keep documents you are currently working on. When you're done with a current document, you can move it to a different folder for safe-keeping.
Favorites	The Favorites folder with its shortcuts to files and folders that you go to often. Double-click a shortcut icon to open a document or folder. To create a shortcut to a document and place it in the Favorites folder, find and click the document in the Open dialog box, click the Tools down arrow, and choose Add to Favorites. (To remove a shortcut icon, click it and then click the Delete button. By doing so, you delete the shortcut, not the document or folder itself.)

If you want to open a document you worked on recently, it may be on the File menu. Check it out. Open the File menu and see if the document you want to open is one of the four listed at the bottom of the menu. If it is, click its name or press its number (1 through 4). To list more than four files at the bottom of the menu, choose Tools⇨Options, click the General tab in the Options dialog box, and enter a number higher than 4 in the Recently Used File List scroll box.

Opening a New Document

You can start a new document whenever the mood strikes you, and you have a choice of three easy ways:

+ Press the New button

+ Press Ctrl+N

+ Choose File⇨New

If you opt for File⇨New, you see dialog box with tabs and icons for creating documents from templates. A template is a ready-made layout you can use for formatting a document. By choosing a template for creating the new document, you don't have to do the formatting yourself. However, if you want to do the formatting, double-click the Blank Document icon or click OK to open a new document.

Moving Around in Documents

Documents have a habit of getting longer and longer, and as they do that it takes more effort to move around in them. Here are some shortcuts for getting here and there in documents.

Keys for getting around quickly

One of the fastest ways to go from place to place is to press keys and key combinations:

Key to Press	Where It Takes You
PgUp	Up the length of one screen
PgDn	Down the length of one screen
Ctrl+PgUp	To the previous page in the document
Ctrl+PgDn	To the next page in the document
Ctrl+Home	To the top of the document
Ctrl+End	To the bottom of the document

If pressing Ctrl+PgUp or Ctrl+PgDn doesn't get you to the top or bottom of a page, it's because you clicked the Select Browse Object button at the bottom of the vertical scrollbar, so Word goes to the next bookmark, comment, heading, or whatever. Click the Select Browse Object button and choose Browse by Page to make these key combinations work again.

Zipping around with the scroll bar

You can also use the scroll bar to get around in documents. The *scroll bar* is the vertical stripe along the right side of the screen that resembles an elevator shaft. Here's how to move around with the scroll bar:

✦ To move through a document quickly, grab the elevator (called the *scroll box*) and drag it up or down. As you scroll, a box appears with the page number and the names of headings on the pages you scroll past (provided you assigned Word styles to those headings).

✦ To move line by line up or down, click the up or down arrow at the top or bottom of the scroll bar.

✦ To move screen by screen, click anywhere on the scroll bar except on the arrows or the elevator.

By the way, the scroll bar on the bottom of the screen is for moving from side to side.

Understanding How Paragraphs Work

Back in English class, your teacher taught you that a paragraph is a part of a longer composition that presents one idea or, in the case of dialogue, presents the words of one speaker. Your teacher was right, too, but for word processing purposes, a paragraph is a lot less than that. In word processing, a paragraph is simply what you put on-screen before you press the Enter key.

For instance, a heading is a paragraph. So is a graphic. If you press Enter on a blank line to go to the next line, the blank line is considered a paragraph. If you type **Dear John** at the top of a letter and press Enter, "Dear John" is a paragraph.

It's important to know this because paragraphs have a lot to do with formatting. If you choose the Format⇨Paragraph command and monkey around with the paragraph formatting, all your changes affect everything in the paragraph that the cursor is in. To make format changes to a whole paragraph, all you have to do is place the cursor there. You don't have to select the paragraph. And if you want to make format changes to several paragraphs in a row, all you have to do is select those paragraphs first.

Working on Many Documents at Once

In Word, you can work on more than one document at the same time (as shown in Figure 1-3). You can even work in two different places in the same document (the next section in this chapter tells how).

When you open a new document, a new button is placed on the taskbar. To go from one document to another, click its taskbar button. You can also open the Window menu and click the name of a document to see it on-screen. And if you want to see all open documents at once, choose Window⇨Arrange All. To go from one document to the next, either click in a new window pane or press Ctrl+F6.

To focus on one window when several are open, click the Minimize button of the window panes you don't want to see anymore. By doing so, you remove the other documents from the screen. Click the Restore button (the one in the middle with a square on it) to enlarge the window you want to work on to full-screen size.

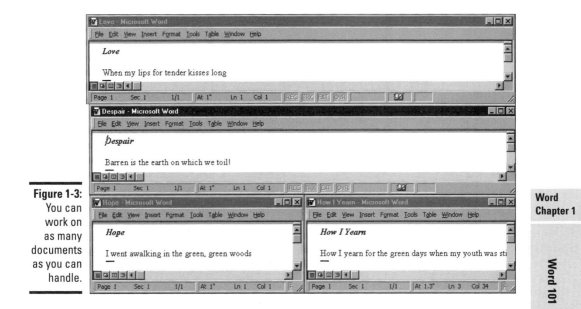

Figure 1-3:
You can
work on
as many
documents
as you can
handle.

To see a window you minimized, either open the Window menu again and choose it from the menu or click a taskbar button.

Working in Two Places in the Same Document

You can open a window on two different places at once in a document. One reason you might do this: You are writing a long report and want the introduction to support the conclusion, and you also want the conclusion to fulfill all promises made by the introduction. That's difficult to do sometimes, but you can make it easier by opening the document to both places and writing the conclusion and introduction at the same time.

You can use two methods to open the same document to two different places: opening a second window on the document or splitting the screen.

Opening a second window

To open a second window on a document, choose Window⇨New Window. Immediately, a second window opens up and you see the start of your document.

✦ If you select the Window menu, you see that it now lists two versions of your document, number 1 and number 2 (the numbers appear after the file name). Choose number 1 to go back to where you were before. You can also click a taskbar button to go from window to window.

✦ You can move around in either window as you please. When you make changes in either window, you make them to the same document. Choose the File⇨Save command in either window and you save all the changes you made in both windows. The important thing to remember here is that you are working on a single document, not two documents.

[X] ✦ When you want to close either window, just click its Close button. You go
back to the other window, and only one version of your document appears
on the Window menu.

Splitting the screen

Splitting a window means to divide it into north and south halves. To do that,
choose Window⇨Split. A gray line appears on-screen. Roll the mouse down until
the gray line is where you want the split to be, and click. You get two screens
split down the middle, as shown in Figure 1-4.

Now you have two windows and two sets of scroll bars along the right side of
the screen.

✦ Use the scroll bars to move up or down on either side of the split, or press
PgUp or PgDn, or press arrow keys. Click the other side if you want to move
the cursor there.

✦ When you tire of this schizophrenic arrangement, choose Window⇨
Remove Split or drag the gray line to the top or bottom of the screen.

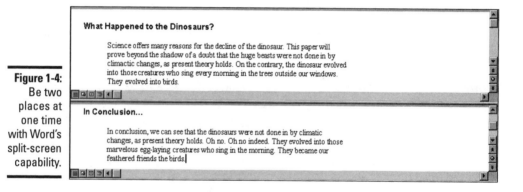

Figure 1-4:
Be two
places at
one time
with Word's
split-screen
capability.

You can also split a screen by moving the mouse cursor to the top of the scroll
bar on the right. Move it just above the arrow. When it turns into a funny shape,
something like a German cross, click and drag the gray line down the screen.
When you release the mouse button, you have a split screen. To quickly
"unsplit" a screen, double-click on the line that splits the screen in two.

Zooming In, Zooming Out

Eyes were not meant to stare at computer screens all day, which makes the
Zoom command all the more valuable. Use this command freely and often to
enlarge or shrink the text on your screen and preserve your eyes for important
things, like gazing at the horizon. Give this command in one of two ways:

◆ Click the down arrow in the Zoom box on the Standard toolbar (the box on the right side that shows a number followed by a percent sign) and choose a magnification percentage from the drop-down list. (See Figure 1-5.)

◆ Click inside the Zoom box, type a percentage of your own, and press Enter.

Sometimes it pays to shrink the text way down to see how pages are laid out. For instance, after you lay out a table, shrink it down to see how it looks from a bird's-eye view.

Enter or choose a zoom percentage here

Figure 1-5:
Now you
can
choose
a size for
any eyes.

Going to a specific item in your document

Sure, you can move around your document by hitting some keys or using the scroll bar, but if you know exactly where you want to go, Word provides as easy way to get there.

1. **Choose Edit⇨Go To, or simply double-click the page number box in the lower-left of the screen.**

2. **From the Go To tab of the Find and Replace dialog box that appears, select the type of item you want to go directly to.**

You can choose to go to a specific page, a section, a line, a bookmark, and many more things that you may never dream of putting into your Word document!

3. **To go to a specific item, type the name or number of the item (depending on what you selected) in the Enter box, and then click Go To.**

To zip along to the next or previous item of the same type, leave the Enter box empty and then click Next or Previous.

Chapter 2: Saving, Naming, Deleting, and Exiting

In This Chapter

- ✔ **Saving a document**
- ✔ **Renaming a document**
- ✔ **Closing a document**
- ✔ **Deleting a document**
- ✔ **Exiting Word 2000**

So you're working right along on your word-processing document, spending precious time and effort composing and fine-tuning a document whose value is inestimable. Maybe you've been sitting there for hours. Your thoughts have been so unique that you are sure you'd never be able to repeat them. Thank goodness you are using Word 2000 to give your creativity some tangible form. Suddenly your computer freezes. Have you saved your document? Oh no! Well, your creativity has suddenly become very intangible again. That hurts.

This scenario could happen to you (as it has happened to many others before you). This chapter wants to help you avoid such losses by showing you how to save and name your documents so that you can have them forever — or for at least a very long time. Along the way, you also find out how to delete a document just in case you really want to lose something forever.

Saving a Document for the First Time

After you open a new document and work on it, you need to save it. As part of saving a document for the first time, Word opens a dialog box and invites you to give the document a name. So the first time you save, you do three things at once — you save your work, choose which folder to save the document in, and name your document.

1. **Choose File⇨Save, press Ctrl+S, or click the Save button.**
2. **In the Save As dialog box that appears (shown in Figure 2-1), find and select the folder that you want to save the file in.**

Save As
Save in:
Birds of the World
Tools
History
My Documents
Desktop
Favorites
Web Folders
Name
Size
Type
Modified
African Lovebird 11 KB Microsoft Word ... 9/7/95 9:09 AM
Blackburnian Warbler 11 KB Microsoft Word ... 9/7/95 9:11 AM
Black-Capped Chickadee 14 KB Microsoft Word ... 9/15/98 12:26 PM
Great Bird of Paradise 14 KB Microsoft Word ... 8/5/98 5:37 PM
Lady Amherst Pheasant 11 KB Microsoft Word ... 9/7/95 9:18 AM
Leadbeater's Cockatoo 11 KB Microsoft Word ... 9/7/95 9:10 AM
Painted Bunting 11 KB Microsoft Word ... 9/7/95 9:13 AM
Ruby-Throated Hummingbird 11 KB Microsoft Word ... 9/7/95 9:14 AM
Scissor-Tailed Flycather 11 KB Microsoft Word ... 9/7/95 9:15 AM
White-Breasted Nuthatch 11 KB Microsoft Word ... 9/7/95 9:12 AM
Yellow-Tailed Galoot 11 KB Microsoft Word ... 9/7/95 9:09 AM
File name:
Yellow-Bellied Sapsucker
Save as type:
Word Document
Save
Cancel

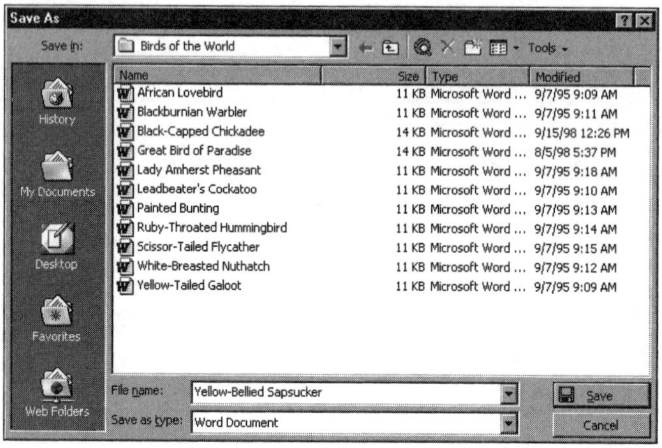

Figure 2-1: The Save As dialog box is your ticket to successful saving.

3. **Word suggests a name in the File Name box (the name comes from the first line in the document). If that name isn't suitable, enter another. Be sure to enter one you will remember later.**
4. **Click the Save button.**

INTEGRATION

Document names can be 255 characters long and can include all characters and numbers except these: / ? : * " < > |. They can even include spaces. This applies to all Office 2000 applications, so getting into a consistent naming scheme for all your Office creations is a good habit. For example, you no longer have to name your Sales Report as **salesrpt** (forget those old DOS restrictions!). Heck, you can now rear back and name it **Sales Report.**

Saving a Document under a New Name

If you want to make a second copy of a document, you can do so by saving the first copy under a new name or by making a copy. Either way you end up with two copies of the same file.

1. **Choose File⇨Save As.**
2. **Find and select a folder to save the newly named document in.**
3. **Give the document a new name in the File Name text box.**
4. **If you're also changing the type of file this is, click the Save as Type drop-down menu and choose the file type.**
5. **Click the Save button.**

To save a copy of a document, open it as you normally would, but click the down arrow next to the Open button in the Open dialog box and choose Open as Copy from the drop-down menu. The new document is given the same name as the old, except the words "Copy of" appear in front of its name.

Saving a Document You've Been Working On

It behooves you to save your documents from time to time as you work on them. (No, *behooves* is not computer jargon. The word just means that you should.) When you save a document, Word takes the work you've done since the last time you saved your document and stores the work safely on the hard disk. You can save a document in three different ways:

+ Choose File➪Save

+ Click the Save button

+ Press Ctrl+S

Save early and often. Make it a habit to click the Save button whenever you leave your desk, take a phone call, or let the cat out. If you don't save your work and there is a power outage or somebody trips over the computer's power cord, you lose all the work you did since the last time you saved your document.

Saving Versions of Documents

In a lengthy document like a manual or a report that requires many drafts, saving different drafts can be helpful. That way, if you want to retrieve something that got dropped from an earlier draft, you can do so. One way to save drafts of a document is to save drafts under different names, but why do that when you can rely on the Versions command on the File menu?

Follow these steps to save different versions of a document as it evolves into a masterpiece:

1. **Choose File➪Versions. The Versions in dialog box (shown in Figure 2-2), which lists past versions of the document that you saved, appears.**

2. **Click the Save Now button.**

3. **In the Save Version dialog box, write a descriptive comment about this version of the document and click OK.**

4. **Click Close in the Versions in dialog box.**

Figure 2-2:
Keep track
of various
versions
of your
document
with the
Save
Version
dialog box.

Versions in Technics Manual	? ☒

New versions

[Save Now...]   ☐ Automatically

Existing versions

Date and time	Saved by	Comments
7/6/98 11:01 AM	Peter Weverka	Second draft reviewe
6/17/98 10:56 AM	Peter Weverka	Second draft
5/28/98 10:55 AM	Peter Weverka	First draft reviewed b
5/1/98 10:55 AM	Peter Weverka	First draft

Save Version	? ☒

Date and time: 8/6/98 11:01 AM
Saved by: Peter Weverka

Comments on version:

Third draft with Big Cheese comments

[OK]   [Cancel]

[Open]   [Delete]   [View Comments...]   [Close]

To review an earlier version of a document, choose File⇨Versions to open the Versions In dialog box, read comments to find the version you want to open, select the versions, and click the Open button. The earlier version appears in its own window next to the up-to-date version. You can tell which version you are dealing with by glancing at the title bar, which lists the date that the earlier version was saved.

Select a version and click the Delete button in the Versions in dialog box to erase a version; click the View Comments button to read its description. The Versions in dialog box also offers a check box for saving a version of the document each time you close it, but I don't recommend saving versions automatically. When you do so, you don't get the opportunity to describe the document, which makes it very hard to tell which draft is which when you want to revisit a draft you worked on before.

Renaming a document

Perhaps you named your last Word file as **Interplay of Light and Color in French Renaissance Poetry**. But you really wanted to call it **Letter to Mom**. If the name you gave to a document suddenly seems inappropriate or downright meaningless, you can rename it. Here's how:

1. **Choose File⇨Open, press Ctrl+O, or click the Open button.**

2. **In the Open dialog box, find the folder that holds the file you want to rename.**

3. **Click the file you want to rename.**

4. **Click the Tools button and choose Rename from the drop-down menu.**

5. **The old name is highlighted. Enter a new name in its place.**

6. **Press the Enter key.**

Closing a Document

☒ Click the Close Window button or choose File⇨Close to close a document when you're done working on it. The Close Window button is located in the upper-right corner of the screen, right below its identical twin, the Close button.

If you try to close a document and you've made changes to it that you haven't saved yet, a dialog box similar to the one in Figure 2-3 asks if you want to save your changes:

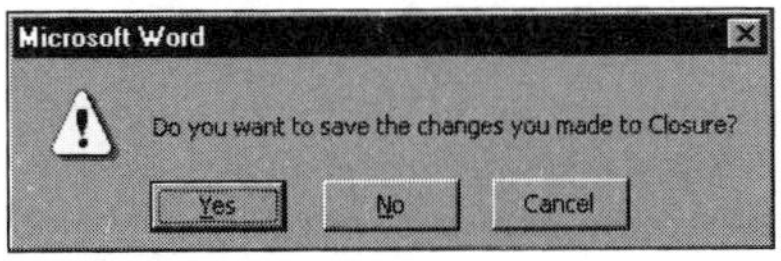

Figure 2-3: The Close dialog box lets you close gracefully.

> **Microsoft Word** ☒
>
> ⚠ Do you want to save the changes you made to Closure?
>
> [Yes]   [No]   [Cancel]

Click Yes unless you're abandoning the document because you want to start all over. In that case, click No.

Deleting a Word Document

Deleting documents is really the duty of the Windows operating system, but you can delete a document without leaving Word by following these steps:

1. **Choose File⇨Open as if you were opening a document, not deleting one.**

2. **In the Open dialog box, find the document you want to delete.**

3. **Either click the Delete button at the top of the dialog box or press the Delete key. You can also right-click and choose Delete from the shortcut menu. (See Figure 2-4.)**

4. **When Word asks if you really want to go through with it and send the file to the Recycle Bin, click Yes.**

5. **Click Cancel or press Esc to remove the Open dialog box.**

If you regret deleting a file, you can resuscitate it. On the Windows desktop, double-click the Recycle Bin icon. The Recycle Bin opens with a list of the files you deleted. Click the one you regret deleting and choose File⇨Restore.

Delete button

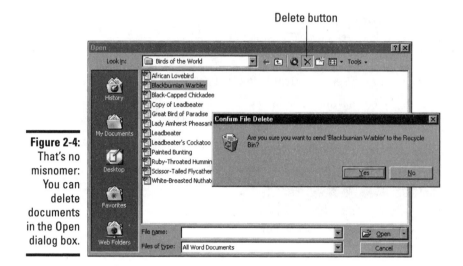

Figure 2-4:
That's no
misnomer:
You can
delete
documents
in the Open
dialog box.

Exiting Word 2000

When it's time to say good-bye to Word, save and close all your documents.
Then do one of the following:

+ Choose File⊅Exit.

🗙 + Click the Close button (the X) on the right side of the title bar.

+ Press Alt+F4.

If perchance you forgot to save and close a document, you see the Do you
want to save the changes? dialog box. Click Yes.

Chapter 3: Changing the Look of Your Document

In This Chapter

- ✔ Customizing your screen
- ✔ Placing headers and footers
- ✔ Numbering pages
- ✔ Breaking a line or a page
- ✔ Hyphenating
- ✔ Spacing lines
- ✔ Inserting symbols
- ✔ Putting a border around a page

Don't just sit down and start pounding away at the keyboard! You can do a number of things before you get started in order to make your word-processing chore go a lot more smoothly. Start by getting the screen to look how you want it. Next, decide on how you want your pages to be numbered, whether you need footers, where you want a page to break, and so on. Have you even given a thought to automatic hyphenating? Probably not.

This chapter preps you so that you can think of these things now rather than later — when you need to be getting down to some serious work.

Changing the Look of the Screen

The Word window is cluttered, to say the least, but you can do something about that with options on the View menu:

- ✦ To remove a toolbar, choose View⇨Toolbars. In the submenu, check marks appear beside the toolbars currently showing. Click a toolbar name to remove the check mark and remove the toolbar from the screen as well. You can also remove a toolbar by right-clicking it or the menu bar and then clicking the name of the toolbar you want to remove on the shortcut menu.

✦ Choose View➪Ruler to get rid of or display the ruler.

✦ Choose View➪Full Screen if you want to get rid of everything except the text you're working on. When you choose Full Screen, everything gets stripped away — buttons, menus, scroll bars and all. Only a single button called Close Full Screen remains. Click it or press Esc when you want the buttons, menus, and so on to come back. As Figure 3-1 shows, you can give commands from the menus on the menu bar in Full Screen View by moving the pointer to the top of the screen to make the menu bar appear. Of course, you can also press shortcut key combinations and right-click to see shortcut menus.

Click to get Word back

Figure 3-1:
Now you
can see
more of
your
creation.

Putting Headers and Footers on Pages

A *header* is a little description that appears along the top of a page so the reader knows what's what. Usually, headers include the page number and a title. A *footer* is the same thing as a header, except it appears along the bottom of the page, as befits its name. To put a header or a footer in a document, follow these steps:

1. **Choose View➪Header and Footer. (See Figure 3-2.)**

 2. **Type your header in the box, or if you want a footer, click the Switch between Header and Footer button and type your footer.**

3. **Click the Close button.**

 While you're typing away in the Header or Footer box, you can call on most of the commands on the Standard and Formatting toolbars. You can change the text's font and font size, click an alignment button, and paste text from the Clipboard.

You can also take advantage of the buttons on the Header and Footer toolbar, as listed in Table 3-1.

Figure 3-2:
A header
can
provide
timely
information
for your
document.

Table 3-1	Header and Footer Buttons
Button	*What It Does*
Insert AutoText ▾	Opens a drop-down menu with options for inserting information about the document, including when it was last saved and printed, and who created it.
	Inserts the page number.
	Inserts the number of pages in the entire document.
	Opens the Page Number Format dialog box so you can choose a format for the page number in the header of footer.
	These buttons insert the date the document is printed and the time it is printed into the header or footer.
	Opens the Layout tab of the Page Setup dialog box so that you can tell Word that you want a different header and footer on the first page of the document, or that you want different headers and footers on odd and even pages (you may use this feature if you're printing on both sides of the page).
	Shows the text on the page so that you can see what the header or footer looks like in relation to the text.
	Tells Word that you don't want this header or footer to be the same as same as the header or footer in the previous section of the document. When this button is pressed down, the header or footer is the same as the header or footer in the previous section of the document and the Header or Footer box reads, "Same as Previous." To enter a different header or footer for a section, click this button and enter the header or footer. To change headers or footers, you must divide a document into sections.
	Switches between the header and the footer.
	Shows the header or footer in the previous and next sections of a document that has more than one section.

**Word
Chapter 3**

**Changing the Look
of Your Document**

Removing headers and footers is as easy as falling off a turnip truck:

 1. **Click View⇨Header and Footer or double-click the header or footer in Print Layout View.**

2. **Select the header or footer.**

3. **Press the Delete key.**

To remove the header and footer from the first page of either a document or a section, choose File⇨Page Setup (or click the Page Setup button on the Header and Footer toolbar). In the Page Setup dialog box, click the Layout tab, click the Different First Page check box, and click OK.

Numbering the Pages

Word numbers the pages of a document automatically, which is great, but if your document has a title page and table of contents and you want to start numbering pages on the fifth page, or if your document has more than one section, page numbers can turn into a sticky business.

The first thing to ask yourself is whether you've included headers or footers in your document. If you have, go to "Putting Headers and Footers on Pages," earlier in this chapter. It explains how to put page numbers in a header or footer.

Meantime, use the Insert⇨Page Numbers command to put plain old page numbers on the pages of a document:

1. **Choose Insert⇨Page Numbers to open the Page Numbers dialog box. (See Figure 3-3.)**

2. **In the Position and Alignment boxes, choose where you want the page number to appear. The lovely Preview box on the right shows where your page number will go.**

3. **Click to remove the check mark from the Show Number on First Page box if you're working on a letter or other type of document that usually doesn't have a number on page 1.**

4. **Click OK.**

⌐Select the position of the page number here.

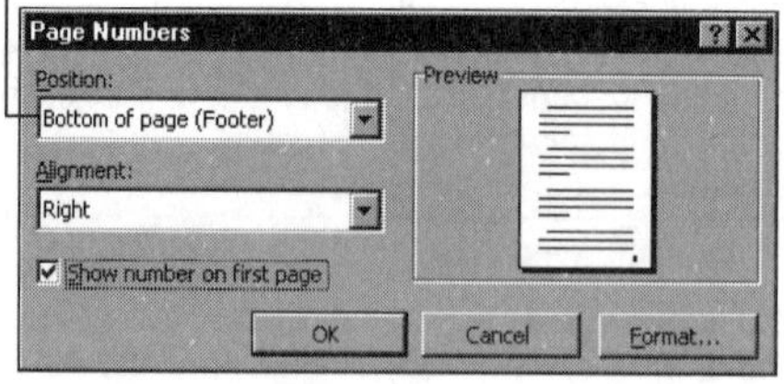

Figure 3-3:
The Page
Numbers
dialog box.

Page Numbers	? X
Position:	Preview
Bottom of page (Footer) ▼	
Alignment:	
Right ▼	
☑ Show number on first page	
OK Cancel Format...	

If you want to get fancy, realize that it's easier to do that in headers and footers than it is in the Page Numbers dialog box. Follow the first three steps in the preceding list and click the Format button. Then, in the Page Number Format dialog box (shown in Figure 3-4), choose an option:

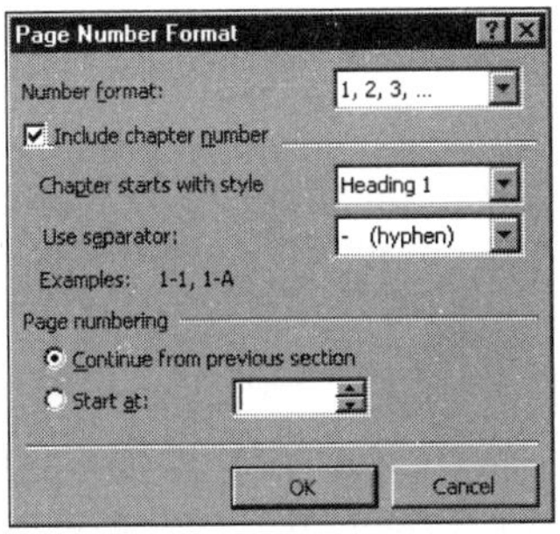

Figure 3-4:
The Page
Number
Format
dialog box.

◆ **Number Format:** Choose a new way to number the pages if you want to. (Notice the *i, ii, iii* choice. That's how the start of books, this one included, is numbered.)

◆ **Include Chapter Number:** Click this check box if you want to start numbering pages anew at the beginning of each chapter. Pages in Chapter 1, for example, are numbered 1-1, 1-2, and so on, and pages in Chapter 2 are numbered 2-1, 2-2, and so forth.

◆ **Chapter Starts with Style:** If necessary, choose a heading style from the drop-down list to tell Word where new chapters begin. Chapter titles are usually tagged with the Heading 1 style, but if your chapters begin with another style, choose that style from the list.

◆ **Use Separator:** From the list, tell Word how you want to separate the chapter number from the page number. Choose the hyphen (1-1), period (1.1), colon (1:1), or one of the dashes (1—1).

◆ **Page Numbering:** This is the one that matters if you've divided your document into sections. Either start numbering the pages anew and enter a new page number to start at (probably 1), or else number pages where the previous section left off.

After you finish, click OK twice to number the pages and get back to your document.

To get rid of the page numbers if you don't like them, follow these steps:

1. **Either choose View➪Header and Footer or double-click the page number in Print Layout view.**

2. **Click the Switch Between Header and Footer button, if necessary, to get to the footer.**

3. **Select the page number by clicking on it, and then press the Delete key.**

You may have to click the number a couple of times to select it properly. You know the number is selected when black squares appear around it.

Breaking a Line

You can break a line in the middle, before it reaches the right margin, without starting a new paragraph. To do that, press Shift+Enter. By pressing Shift+Enter, you can fix problems in the way Word breaks lines. When words are squeezed into narrow columns, it often pays to break lines to remove ugly white spaces.

Figure 3-5 shows two identical paragraphs. To make the lines break better, press Shift+Enter before the word *in* in the first line of the paragraph on the left. Press Shift+Enter again in the second-to-last line before the word *annual*. As you can see, the paragraph on the right fits in the column better and is easier to read.

Figure 3-5: Break your lines for a nicer look.

"A computer in every home and a chicken in every pot is our goal," stated Rupert T. Verguenza, President and CEO of the New Technics Corporation International at the annual shareholder meeting this week.	"A computer in every home and a chicken in every pot is our goal," stated Rupert T. Verguenza, President and CEO of the New Technics Corporation International at the annual shareholder meeting this week.

Breaking a Page

Word gives you another page so you can keep going when you fill up one page. But what if you're impatient and want to start a new page right away? Whatever you do, *don't* press Enter over and over until you fill up the page. Instead, create a page break by doing either of the following:

+ Press Ctrl+Enter.

+ Choose Insert⇨Break, click Page Break, and click OK.

In Normal View, you know when you've inserted a page break because you see the words Page Break and two dotted lines instead of a single dotted line at the end of the page. In Print Layout view, you can't tell where you inserted a page break. To delete a page break, switch to Normal View, click the words Page Break, and press the Delete key. Change views by clicking the View buttons in the lower-left corner of the screen.

Dashes

You can spot the work of an amateur because amateurs always use a hyphen when they ought to use an em dash and en dash. An em dash looks like a hyphen but is wider — it's as wide as the letter m. The last sentence has an em dash in it. Did you notice?

An *en dash* is the width of the letter *n*. Use en dashes to show inclusive numbers or time periods, like so: pp. 45–50, Aug.–Sept. 1998, Exodus 16:11–16:18. An en dash is a little bit longer than a hyphen.

To place em or en dashes in your documents and impress your local typesetter or editor, not to mention your readers:

1. **Choose Insert⇨Symbol.**

2. **Click the Special Characters tab in the Symbol dialog box.**

3. **Choose Em Dash or En Dash.**

4. **Click Insert and then click the Close button.**

Another way to create an em dash is by typing two hyphens in a row. Word turns them into a single em dash. You can also press Alt+Ctrl+- (the minus sign key on the numeric keypad) to enter an em dash, or Ctrl+- (on the numeric keypad) to enter an en dash.

Hyphenating a Document

The first thing you should know about hyphenating the words in a document is that you may not need to do it. Text that hasn't been hyphenated is sometimes easier to read. The text in this book has what typesetters call a *ragged right margin,* which makes for very few hyphenated words. Hyphenate only when text is trapped in columns or in other narrow places or when you want a very formal-looking document.

You can hyphenate text as you enter it, but you may want to wait until you've written everything so you can concentrate on the words themselves. Then after you're done with the writing, you can either have Word hyphenate the document automatically or you can do it yourself.

Hyphenating a document automatically

To hyphenate a document automatically:

1. **Choose Tools⇨Language⇨Hyphenation (appears, as shown in Figure 3-6).**

Hyphenation	? X
☑ Automatically hyphenate document	
☑ Hyphenate words in CAPS	
Hyphenation zone:	0.25"
Limit consecutive hyphens to:	2
OK	Cancel	Manual...

2. **Click Automatically Hyphenate Document to let Word do the job.**

3. **Click Hyphenate Words in CAPS to remove the check mark if you don't care to hyphenate words in uppercase.**

4. **If the text isn't justified — that is, if it's "ragged right" — you can play with the Hyphenation Zone setting.**

Words that fall in the Zone are hyphenated, so a large zone means a less ragged margin but more ugly hyphens, and a small zone means fewer ugly hyphens but a more ragged right margin.

5. **More than two consecutive hyphens in a row on the right margin looks bad, so enter 2 in the Limit Consecutive Hyphens To box.**

6. **Click OK.**

Hyphenating a document manually

The other way to hyphenate is to see where Word wants to put hyphens and "Yea" or "Nay" them one at a time:

1. **Select the part of the document you want to hyphenate, or else place the cursor where you want hyphens to start appearing.**

2. **Choose Tools⇨Language⇨Hyphenation.**

3. **Click the Manual button. Word displays a box with some hyphenation choices in it (as shown in Figure 3-7).**

   The cursor blinks on the spot where Word suggests putting a hyphen.

4. **Click Yes or No to accept or reject Word's suggestion.**

5. **Keep accepting or rejecting Word's suggestions.**

   A box appears to tell you when Word has finished hyphenating. To quit hyphenating yourself, click the Cancel button in the Manual Hyphenation dialog box.

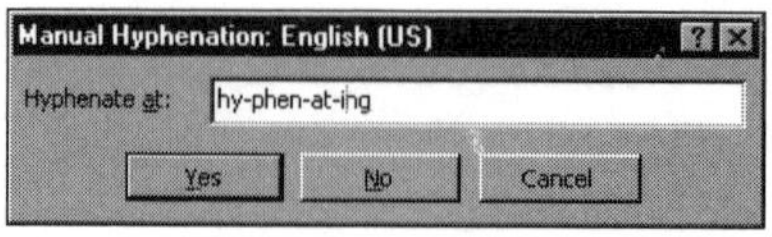

Figure 3-7:
Manual
hyphenation
gives you
complete
control.

Manual Hyphenation: English (US)	? ☒
Hyphenate at: hy-phen-at-ing	
Yes	No	Cancel

A fast way to insert a manual hyphen is to put the cursor where you want the hyphen to go and press Ctrl+hyphen. Press Ctrl+hyphen when there is a big gap in the right margin and a word is crying out to be hyphenated.

By pressing Ctrl+hyphen, you tell Word to make the hyphen appear only if the word breaks at the end of a line. Do not insert a hyphen simply by pressing the hyphen key, because the hyphen will stay there even if the word appears in the middle a line and doesn't need to be broken in half.

Unhyphenating and other hyphenation tasks

More hyphenation esoterica:

✦ To "unhyphenate" a document you hyphenated automatically, choose Tools➪Language➪Hyphenation, remove the check from the Automatically Hyphenate Document box, and click OK. To remove manual hyphens, delete or backspace over them.

✦ To prevent a paragraph from being hyphenated, choose Format➪Paragraph, click the Line and Page Breaks tab, and put a check mark in the Don't Hyphenate box. If you can't hyphenate a paragraph, it is probably because this box was checked unintentionally.

✦ To prevent a paragraph from being hyphenated, choose Format➪ Paragraph➪Line and Page Breaks tab, and click the Don't Hyphenate box to put a check mark in it. (If you can't hyphenate a paragraph, it is probably because this box was checked unintentionally.)

✦ To hyphenate a single paragraph in the middle of a document — maybe because it's a long quotation or some other thing that needs to stand out — select the paragraph and hyphenate it manually by clicking the Manual button in the Hyphenation dialog box.

Word Chapter 3

Changing the Look of Your Document

Spacing Lines

To change the spacing between lines, select the lines whose spacing you want to change or simply put the cursor in a paragraph if you're changing the line spacing in a single paragraph. (If you're just starting a document, you're ready to go.) Choose Format➪Paragraph and select an option in the Line Spacing drop-down list in the paragraph dialog box (see Figure 3-8).

✦ **Single, 1.5 Lines, Double:** These three options are quite up front about what they do, and self-explanatory, too.

✦ **At Least:** Choose this one if you want Word to adjust for tall symbols or other unusual text. Word adjusts the lines but makes sure there is, at minimum, the number of points you enter in the At box between each line.

✦ **Exactly:** Choose this one and enter a number in the At box if you want a specific amount of space between lines.

✦ **Multiple:** Choose this one and put a number in the At box to get triple-, quadruple-, quintuple-, or any other-spaced lines.

You can get a sneak preview of what your lines look like by glancing at the Preview box. Click OK when you've made your choice.

To quickly single-space text, select it and press Ctrl+1. To quickly double-space text, select the text and press Ctrl+2.

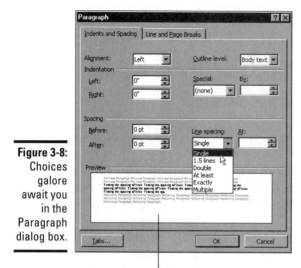

Figure 3-8:
Choices
galore
await you
in the
Paragraph
dialog box.

Watch this box!

Symbols and Special Characters

You can decorate your documents with all kinds of symbols and special characters — a death's head, a smiley face, the Yen symbol. To insert a symbol, click where you want it to go and do the following:

1. **Choose Insert⇨Symbol. The Symbol dialog box opens, shown in Figure 3-9.**

2. **Click the Font drop-down list to choose a symbol set.**

3. **When you choose some fonts, a Subset drop-down menu appears. Choose a subset name from the list — Latin-1, for example — to help locate the symbol you are looking for.**

4. **Click a symbol.**

   When you do so, you see a bigger picture of it on-screen.

5. **Click Insert.**

The symbol you choose is placed in your document, but the Symbol dialog box stays open so that you can select another symbol. Select another one, or click Close or press Esc when you are done.

You can choose special characters and unusual punctuation from the Special Characters tab of the Symbol dialog box.

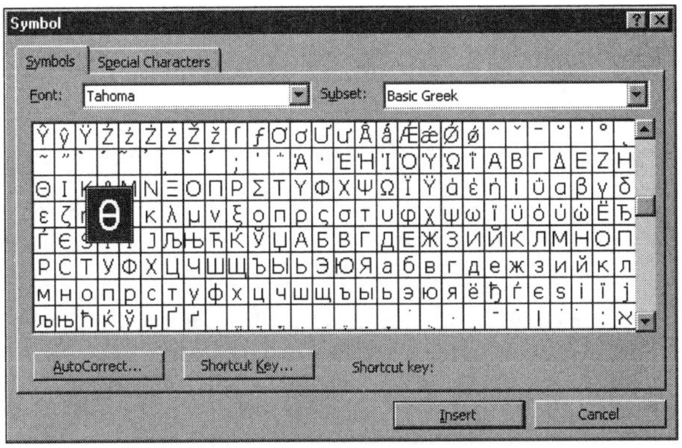

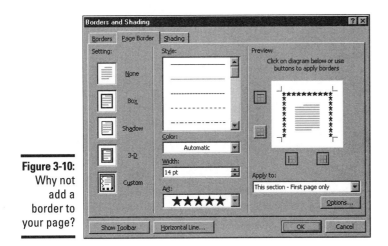

Figure 3-9:
Give your
text
symbolic
meaning!

Decorating a Page with a Border

Word offers a means of decorating title pages, certificates, menus, and similar
documents with a page border. Besides lines, you can decorate the sides of a
page with stars, pieces of cake, and other artwork. If you want to place a border
around a page in the middle of the document, you must create a section break
where the page is. Here's how to put borders around a page:

1. **Place the cursor on the first page of a document if you want to put a
   border around only the first page.**

2. **Choose Format⇨Borders and Shading.**

3. **Click the Page Border tab (see Figure 3-10).**

Figure 3-10:
Why not
add a
border to
your page?

4. **Under Setting, choose which kind of border you want.**

   The Custom setting is for putting borders on one, two, or three sides of the page, not four. Use the None setting to remove borders.

5. **Under Style, scroll down the list and choose a line for the borders.**

   You will find interesting choices at the bottom of the menu. Be sure to look in the Preview window to see what your choices in this dialog box add up to.

6. **Click the Color drop-down menu and choose a color for the borderlines if you want a color border and you have a color printer.**

7. **If you chose artwork for the borders, use the Width drop-down list to tell Word how wide the lines or artwork should be.**

8. **Click the Art drop-down list and choose a symbol, illustration, star, piece of cake, or other artwork, if that is what you want for the borders.**

   You will find some amusing choices on this long list, including ice cream cones, bats, and umbrellas.

9. **Use the four buttons in the Preview window to tell Word on which sides of the page you want borders.**

   Click these buttons to remove or add borders, as you wish.

10. **Under Apply To, tell Word which page or pages in the document get borders.**

11. **Click the Options button and fill in the Border and Shading Options dialog box if you want to get specific about how close the borders can come to the edge of the page or pages.**

12. **Click OK.**

Chapter 4: Editing Made Easy

In This Chapter

✔ **Selecting text**

✔ **Deleting text and undoing mistakes**

✔ **Finding and replacing text**

✔ **Using the thesaurus**

✔ **Spell checking and grammar checking**

✔ **Lowercasing and uppercasing**

1f you've always wanted to find, cut, paste, and replace text like those high-paid editors who helped to put this book together (ha!), this is the chapter for you. If you know a few simple routines, you can save yourself lots of time, especially if you never paid much attention in that high school typing class (who needs to know how to type?). As a bonus, this chapter reveals the secrets of spell-checking and grammar-checking your documents. Who needs editors when you can do all this stuff yourself?

Selecting Text in Speedy Ways

To move text or copy it from one place to another, you have to select it first. You can also erase a great gob of text merely by selecting it and pressing the Delete key. So it pays to know how to select text. Table 4-1 gives some shortcuts for doing it.

Table 4-1	Selecting Shortcuts
To Select This	*Do This*
A word	Double-click the word.
A line	Click in the left margin next to the line.
Some lines	Drag the mouse over the lines or drag the mouse pointer down the left margin.
A paragraph	Double-click in the left margin next to the paragraph.
A mess of text	Click at the start of the text, hold down the Shift key, and click at the end of the text.

(continued)

Table 4-1 *(continued)*

To Select This	Do This
A gob of text	Put the cursor where you want to start selecting, press F8 or double-click EXT (it stands for Extend) on the status bar, and press an arrow key, drag the mouse, or click at the end of the selection.
Yet more text	If you select text and realize you want to select yet more text, double-click EXT on the status bar and start dragging the mouse or pressing arrow keys.
A document	Hold down the Ctrl key and click in the left margin, or triple-click in the left margin, or choose Edit➪Select All, or press Ctrl+A.

If you have a bunch of highlighted text on-screen and you want it to go away but it won't (because you pressed F8 or double-clicked EXT to select it), double-click EXT again.

After you press F8 or double-click EXT, all the keyboard shortcuts for moving the cursor also work for selecting text. For example, press F8 and press Ctrl+Home to select everything from the cursor to the top of the document. Double-click EXT and press End to select to the end of the line.

Deleting Text

To delete a bunch of text at once, select the text you want to delete and press the Delete key or choose Edit➪Clear.

By the way, you can do two things at once by selecting text and then starting to type. The letters you type immediately take the place of and delete the text you selected.

Undoing a Mistake

Fortunately for you, all is not lost if you make a big blunder in Word, because the program has a marvelous little tool called the Undo command.

This command "remembers" your last 99 editorial changes and puts them on the Undo drop-down menu. As long as you catch your error before you do five or six new things, you can "undo" your mistake. Try one of these undo techniques:

✦ **Choose Edit➪Undo.** This command changes names, depending on what you did last. Usually, it says Undo Typing, but if you move text, for example, it says Undo Move. Anyhow, select this command to undo your most recent action.

✦ **Click the Undo button to undo your most recent change.** If you made your error and went on to do something else before you caught it, click the down arrow next to the Undo button. You see a menu of your last five actions (shown in Figure 4-1). Click the one you want to undo or, if it isn't on the list, click the down-arrow on the scroll bar until you find the error, and then click on it. However, if you do this, you also undo all the actions on the Undo menu above the one you're undoing. For example, if you undo the 98th action on the list, you also undo the 97 before it.

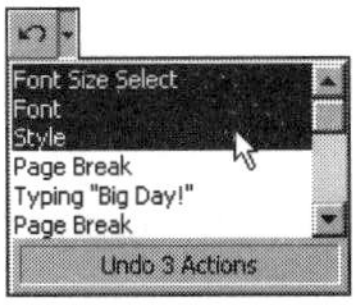

Figure 4-1:
Word does
not easily
forget your
mistakes.

Finding and Replacing Text and Formats

The Edit⇨Replace command is a very powerful tool indeed. If you're writing a Russian novel, and decide on page 816 to change the main character's last name from Oblonsky to Oblomov, you can change it on all 816 pages with the Edit⇨Replace command in about a half a minute.

To replace words, phrases, or formats throughout a document:

1. **Choose Edit⇨Replace, or press Ctrl+H.**

The Find and Replace dialog box appears, as shown in Figure 4-2.

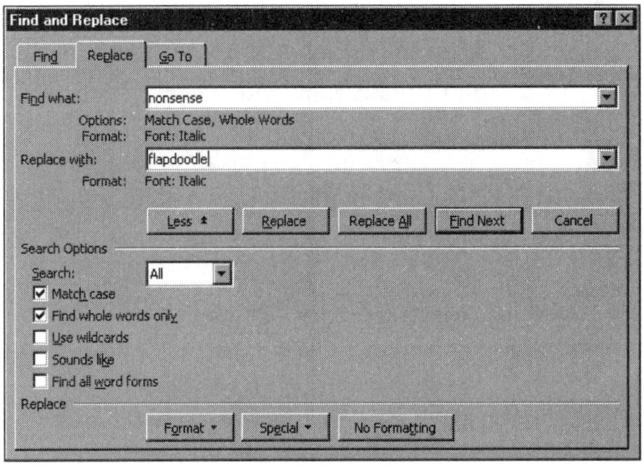

Figure 4-2:
Word
seeks and
replaces
as per your
instructions.

2. **Fill in the Find What box just as you would if you were searching for text or formats, and be sure to click the Find Whole Words Only check box if you want to replace one word with another.**

3. **In the Replace With box, enter the text that will replace what is in the Find What box. If you're replacing a format, enter the format.**

4. **Either replace everything at once or do it one at a time:**

• Click Replace All to make all replacements in an instant.

• Click Find Next and then either click Replace to make the replacement or Find Next to bypass it.

REAL WORLD

Too many errors to keep track of?

What if you commit a monstrous error or innumerable errors but can't correct it with the Undo command? You can try closing your document without saving the changes you made to it. As long as you didn't save your document after you made the errors, the errors won't be in your document when you open it again — but neither will the changes you want to keep.

Word tells you when you're finished.

WARNING!

The Edit⇨Replace command is very powerful. *Always* save your document before you use this command. Then, if you replace text that you shouldn't have replaced, you can close your document without saving it, open your document again, and get your original document back.

Finding Text and More

You can search for a word in a document, and even for fonts, special characters, and formats. Here's how:

1. **Choose Edit⇨Find, press Ctrl+F, or click the Select Browse Object button in the lower-right corner of the screen and choose Find. The Find and Replace dialog box appears (in Figure 4-3, the More button is clicked so you can see all the Find options).**

2. **Enter the word, phrase, or format that you're looking for in the Find What dialog box.**

3. **Click the Find Next button if you are looking for a simple word or phrase. Otherwise, click the More button to conduct a sophisticated search before you click Find Next.**

If the thing you're looking for can be found, Word highlights it in the document. To find the next instance of the thing you're looking for, click Find Next again. You can also close the dialog box and click either the Previous Find/Go To or Next Find/Go To button at the bottom of the scroll bar to the right of the screen (or press Ctrl+Page Up or Ctrl+Page Down) to go to the previous or next instance of the thing you are looking for.

By clicking the More button in the Find and Replace dialog box, you can get very selective about what to search for and how to search for it:

✦ **Search:** Click the down arrow and choose All, Up, or Down to search the whole document, search from the cursor position upward, or search from the cursor position downward, respectively.

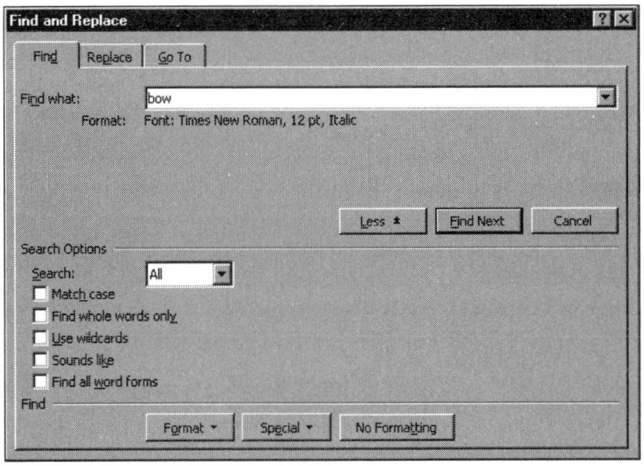

Figure 4-3:
The find
and
replace
options.

✦ **Match Case:** Searches for words with upper- and lowercase letters that exactly match those in the Find What box. With this box selected, a search for *bow* finds that word, but not *Bow* or *BOW*.

✦ **Find Whole Words Only:** Normally, a search for *bow* yields *elbow, bowler, bow-wow,* and all other words with the letters *b-o-w* (in that order). Click this option and you only get *bow*.

✦ **Use Wildcards:** Click here if you intend to use wildcards in searches.

✦ **Sounds Like:** Looks for words that sound like the one in the Find what box. A search for *bow* with this option selected finds *beau,* for example.

✦ **Find All Word Forms:** Takes into account verb endings and plurals. With this option clicked, you get *bows, bowing,* and *bowed,* as well as *bow*.

To search for words, paragraphs, tab settings, and styles, among other things, that are formatted a certain way, click the Format button and choose an option from the menu. You see the familiar dialog box you used in the first place to format the text. In the Find dialog box shown in this book, you find Font chosen from the Format menu and the Font dialog box completed in order to search for the word "bow" in Times Roman, 12-point, italicized font.

Click the Special button to look for format characters, manual page breaks, and other unusual stuff.

That No Formatting button is there so you can clear all the formatting from the Find What box. After you've found something, you can give Word instructions for replacing it by clicking the Replace tab. To find out about that, you have to read "Finding and Replacing Text and Formats," also in this chapter.

After you click the More button to get at the sophisticated search options, the button changes its name to Less. In this instance, More is Less. Click the Less button to shrink the dialog box and get more room to work on-screen.

The Thesaurus's Role in Finding the Right Word

If you can't seem to find the right word: if the word is on the tip of your tongue but you can't quite remember it; you can always give the Thesaurus a shot. To find synonyms (words that have the same or a similar meaning) for a word in your document, start by right-clicking the word and choosing Synonyms from the shortcut menu. With luck, the synonym you are looking for appears on the submenu and all you have to do is click to enter the synonym in your document. Usually, however, finding a good synonym is a journey, not a Sunday stroll. Follow these steps to search for a synonym:

1. **Place the cursor in the word.**

2. **Choose Tools⊅Language⊅Thesaurus, or press Shift+F7.**

3. **Begin your quest for the right word.**

4. **When you find it, click it in the list of words in the Replace with Synonym box and then click the Replace button. (Take a glance at Figure 4-4.)**

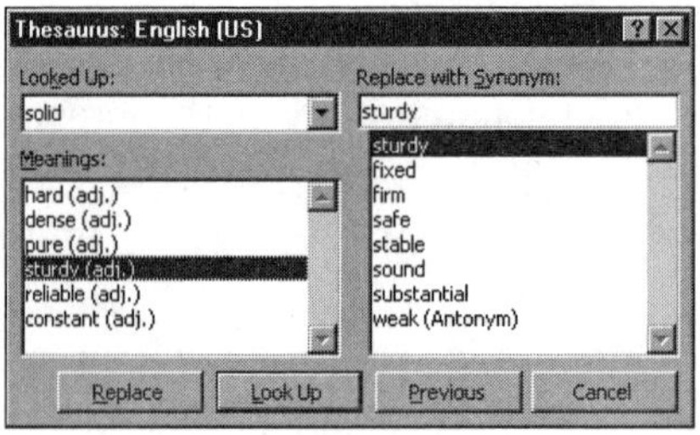

Figure 4-4:
Using a
thesaurus
has never
been
easier.

![Thesaurus dialog box: Thesaurus: English (US). Looked Up: solid. Meanings: hard (adj.), dense (adj.), pure (adj.), sturdy (adj.), reliable (adj.), constant (adj.). Replace with Synonym: sturdy. List: sturdy, fixed, firm, safe, stable, sound, substantial, weak (Antonym). Buttons: Replace, Look Up, Previous, Cancel.]

Spell-Checking (And Grammar-Checking) a Document

As you must have noticed by now, red wiggly lines appear under words that are misspelled, and green wiggly lines appear under words and sentences that Word thinks are grammatically incorrect. Correct spelling and grammar errors by right-clicking them and choosing an option from the shortcut menu. If the red or green lines annoy you, you can remove them from the screen. Choose Tools⊅Options, click the Spelling & Grammar tab, and click to remove the check marks from Check Spelling as You Type or Check Grammar as You Type options.

That's the one-at-a-time method for correcting misspelled words and grammatical errors. You can also go the whole hog and spell- or grammar-check an entire document or text selection by starting in one of these ways:

✦ Choose Tools⊅Spelling and Grammar

✦ Press F7

✦ Click the Spelling and Grammar button

The Spelling and Grammar dialog box appears, as shown in Figure 4-5. Spelling errors appear in red type in this dialog box. Grammatical errors are colored green.

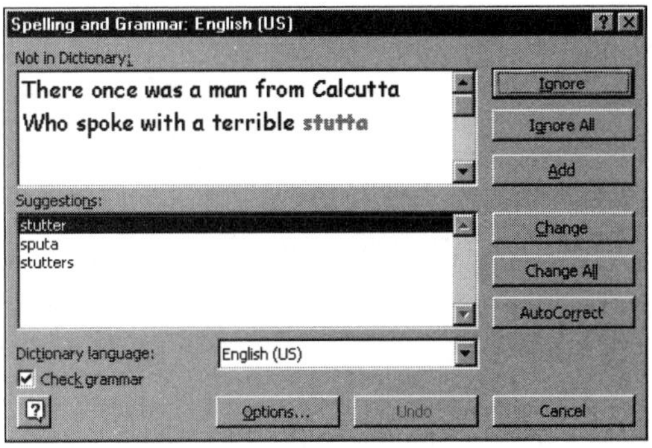

Word
Chapter 4

Editing Made Easy

Figure 4-5: Now you have one less excuse for making a spelling mistake!

Correcting misspellings

Here are your options for handling red spelling errors:

+ **Not in Dictionary:** Shows the word that is spelled incorrectly in context. You can click the scroll arrows in this box to see preceding or following text.

+ **Suggestions:** Provides a list of words to use in place of the misspelling. Click the word that you want to replace the misspelled one.

+ **Ignore:** Ignores the misspelling, but stops on it again if it appears later in the document.

+ **Ignore All:** Ignores the misspelling wherever it appears in the document. Not only that, it ignores it in all your other open documents.

+ **Add:** Adds the word in the Not in Dictionary box to the words in the dictionary that Microsoft Word deems correct. Click this button the first time that the Spell Checker stops on your last name to add your last name to the spelling dictionary.

+ **Change:** Click this button to insert the word in the Suggestions box in your document in place of the misspelled word.

+ **Delete:** The Delete button appears where the Change button is when the Spell Checker finds two words in a row ("the the," for example). Click the Delete button to remove the second word.

+ **Change All:** Changes not only this misspelling to the word in the Suggestions box, but all identical misspellings in the document.

+ **AutoCorrect:** Adds the suggested spelling correction to the list of words that are corrected automatically as you type them.

+ **Undo:** Goes back to the last misspelling you corrected and gives you a chance to repent and try again.

But I know that my spelling is correct!

Suppose you have a bunch of computer code or French language text that you would like the Spell Checker to either ignore or check against its French dictionary instead of its English one. If not, Word will think you a much worse speller than you actually are. To tell the Spell Checker how to handle text like that, select the text, choose Tools⇔Language⇔Set Language. In the Language dialog box, choose a new language for your words to be spell-checked against, or else click the Do Not Check Spelling or Grammar check box.

You can click outside the Spelling dialog box and fool around in your document, in which case the Ignore button changes names and becomes Resume. Click the Resume button to start the Spell Checker again.

You probably shouldn't trust your smell-checker, because it can't catch all misspelled words. If you mean to type **middle** but type **fiddle** instead, the Spell Checker won't catch the error because *fiddle* is a legitimate word. The moral is: If you're working on an important document, proofread it carefully. Don't rely on the Spell Checker to catch all your smelling errors.

Fixing grammar errors

Word's Grammar Checker is theoretically able to correct grammatical mistakes in a document. However, a machine can't tell what's good writing and what isn't. Period. Use it with caution.

Anyhow, grammar errors appear in green in the top of the Spelling and Grammar dialog box, as shown Figure 4-6.

Click the following buttons to fix errors with the robo-grammarian:

✦ **Suggestions**: Lists ways to correct the error. Click the correction you want to make.

✦ **Ignore:** Lets the error stand in your document.

✦ **Ignore Rule:** Ignores this grammatical error and all other grammatical errors of this type in this document and all open documents.

✦ **Next Sentence:** Ignores the error and takes you to the next sentence in the text.

✦ **Change:** Replaces the error with what is in the Suggestions box.

✦ **Undo:** Reverses your most recent correction.

If you have confidence in your grammatical abilities, click the Check Grammar check box to remove the check mark and keep so-called grammatical errors from being flagged.

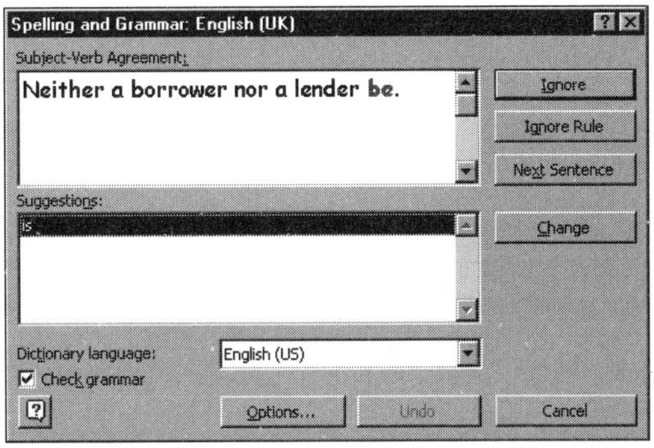

Figure 4-6:
Shakespeare
would not
make it
beyond his
first page
in the
Grammar
Checker!

Spelling and Grammar: English (UK)

Subject-Verb Agreement:

Neither a borrower nor a lender be.

Ignore
Ignore Rule
Next Sentence

Suggestions:

Change

Dictionary language: English (US)

☑ Check grammar

Options... | Undo | Cancel

Changing lowercase to UPPERCASE, UPPERCASE to lowercase

What do you do if you look at your screen and discover to your dismay that you entered characters IN THE WRONG CASE! It happens. And sometimes Word does mysterious things to letters at the start of sentences and capital letters in the middle of words. What can you do about that?

You can fix uppercase and lowercase problems in two ways.

The fastest way is to select the text you entered incorrectly and press Shift+F3. Keep pressing Shift+F3 until the text looks right. Shift+F3 changes the characters to all lowercase, to Initial Capitals, to ALL UPPERCASE, and back to all lowercase again.

The other way is to select the text, choose Format⇨Change Case, and click an option in the Change Case dialog box:

✦ **Sentence case:** Makes the text look like this.

✦ **lowercase:** makes the text look like this.

✦ **UPPERCASE:** MAKES THE TEXT LOOK LIKE THIS.

✦ **Title Case:** Makes The Text Look Like This.

✦ **tOGGLE cASE:** mAKES THE TEXT LOOK LIKE THIS, AND i WOULD CHOOSE THIS OPTION IF i ACCIDENTALLY TYPED LOTS OF TEXT WITH CAPS LOCK ON.

Microsoft Word is very presumptuous about how it thinks capital letters should be used. You've probably noticed that already. You can't type a lowercase letter after a period. You can't enter a newfangled company name like QUestData because Word refuses to let two capital letters in a row stand. You can't enter lowercase computer code at the start of a line without Word capitalizing the first letter.

Chapter 5: Basic Formatting

In This Chapter

✔ **Bolding, italicizing, and underlining**

✔ **Centering, justifying, and aligning**

✔ **Changing fonts and colors**

✔ **Creating numbered and bulleted lists**

✔ **Indenting and setting margins**

✔ **Using your tabs**

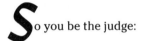o you be the judge:

```
Bob, I really need you to help me with the Henderson contracts, the
school board proposal, and the review of Johnson's 1999 Fiduciary
Returns. If you don't help, we'll all be in big trouble when the boss
gets back.
```

Bob, I *really* need you to help me with

- **the Henderson contracts**
- **the school board proposal**
- **the review of Johnson's 1999 *Fiduciary Returns***

If you don't help, we'll all be in BIG trouble when the boss gets back.

If you think that the first sample is easier to read, just go ahead and skip on to another chapter. If you like the idea of formatting your documents to make them more effective, you've opened up to the right page. This chapter shows you how to squeeze some nice looking text out of any ordinary document.

Adding Bold, Italic, Underline, and Other Effects

Embellishing text with **boldface,** *italics,* <u>underlines,</u> and other font styles and text effects is easy. You can do it with the Formatting toolbar or by way of the Format⇨Font command. First the Formatting toolbar:

- ✦ **Boldface:** Click the Bold button (or press Ctrl+B) and start typing. If you've already entered the text, select the text first and then click Bold or press Ctrl+B. Bold text is often used in headings.

- ✦ **Italics:** Click the Italic button (or press Ctrl+I). Select the text first if you've already entered it. Italics are used to show emphasis and also for foreign words such as *voilà, gung hay fat choy,* and *Que magnifico!*

- ✦ **Underline:** Click the Underline button (or press Ctrl+U). Select the text first and then click the button if you've already typed the text. You can also get double underlines with the Format⇨Font command.

The second way to get boldface, italicized, and underline text is to choose Format⇨Font or right-click text and choose Font from the shortcut menu. When the Font dialog box appears (see Figure 5-1), choose options from the Font Style scroll list.

Choose underline options   Choose font styles

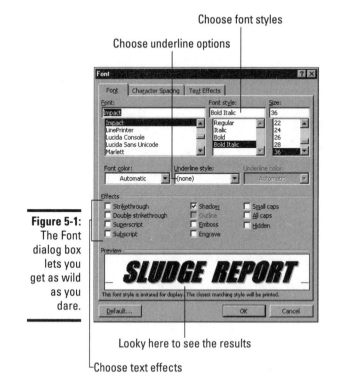

Figure 5-1:
The Font
dialog box
lets you
get as wild
as you
dare.

Looky here to see the results

Choose text effects

The Font dialog box offers many other options for embellishing text. By choosing combinations of font styles and text effects, you can create interesting but sometimes unreadable letters and words. It's easy to overdo it with text effects. Use them sparingly. When it comes to text effects, a little goes a long way.

Centering, Justifying, and Aligning Text

All you have to do to align text in a new way is select the text and either click an Alignment button on the Formatting toolbar or press a keyboard shortcut as shown in Table 5-1.

Table 5-1		Alignment Buttons	
Button	*Button Name*	*Keyboard Shortcut*	*What It Does*
≣	Align Left	Ctrl+L	Lines up text along the left margin or left side of columns.
≣	Center	Ctrl+E	Centers text, leaving space on both sides.
≣	Align Right	Ctrl+R	Lines up text along the right margin or right side of columns.
≣	Justify	Ctrl+J	Lines up text on both the left and right margins or sides of columns.

Changing the Font of Text

Font is the catchall name for type style and type size. When you change fonts, you choose another style of type or change the size of the letters. Word offers a whole bunch of different fonts. You can see their names by clicking the down arrow next to the Font drop-down list and scrolling down the list. Fonts with *TT* beside their names are *TrueType fonts*. These fonts look the same on-screen as they do when printed on paper.

To change the font:

1. **Select the text or place the cursor where you want the font to change.**

2. **Click the down arrow on the Font drop-down list.**

You see the names of fonts, each one dressed up and looking exactly like itself. Word puts all the fonts you've used so far in the document at the top of the Font drop-down list to make it easier for you to find the fonts you use most often.

3. **Scroll down the list of fonts, if necessary (some are shown in Figure 5-2).**

4. **Click a font name.**

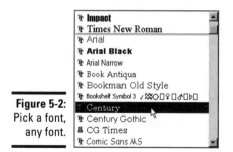

Figure 5-2:
Pick a font,
any font.

To change the size of letters:

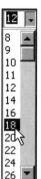

1. **Select the letters or place the cursor where you want the larger or smaller letters to start appearing.**

2. **Click the down arrow on the Font Size drop-down list.**

3. **Scroll down the list if you want a large font.**

4. **Click a point size — 8, 12, 36, 48, and so on.**

You can also change font sizes quickly by selecting the text and pressing Ctrl+Shift+< or Ctrl+Shift+>, or by clicking in the Font Size drop-down list, entering a point size yourself, and pressing Enter. To change fonts and fonts sizes at the same time, choose Format⇨Font and make your choices in the Font dialog box.

Type is measured in *points*. A point is $1/72$ of an inch. The larger the point size, the larger the letters. Business and love letters usually use 10- or 12-point type. For headings, choose a larger point size. In this book, first-level main headings are 18 points high and are set in the Cascade Script font. The text you are reading is Cheltenham 9-point font. Just thought you wanted to know.

Coloring Text

If you're lucky enough to own or have access to a color printer, you can print text in different colors. And even if you don't own a color printer, you can change the color of text on-screen. You may do that to call attention to parts of a document or Web page, for example. Word offers 40 colors, plus white, black, and four gray shades.

1. **Select the text.**

2. **Click the down arrow beside the Font Color button and click a color, black, white, or one of the four gray shades. (See Figure 5-3.)**

Figure 5-3:
If only this figure were in color... you could see your color choices.

After you choose a color, the Font Color button changes color and becomes the color you chose. To apply the same color again, click the Font Color button without having to open the drop-down list. You can also apply colors by way of the Font Color menu in the Font dialog box. To get there, choose Format⇨Font.

To remove the color from text, select it, click the Font Color drop-down list, and choose Automatic.

Fast Formatting with the Format Painter

The fastest way to format a document is with the Format Painter. You can use this tool to make sure that the headings, lists, text paragraphs, and whatnot in your document are formatted the same way. To use the Format Painter, follow these steps:

1. **Click on the text whose formats you want to apply throughout your document.**

For example, if your document is a report with first-, second-, and third-level heads, format a first-level head so that it looks just right and click it.

2. **Double-click the Format Painter button. The mouse pointer changes into a paint brush icon.**

3. **Find the text you want to copy the format to, click the mouse button, and roll the mouse pointer over it as though you were selecting it.**

After you're done, the text takes on the new formats.

4. **Keep going. Find every place in your document that you can copy this format to and baste it with the Format Painter. You can click the scroll bar and use keyboard commands to move through your document.**

5. **Click the Format Painter button when you're done.**

Creating Numbered and Bulleted Lists

Numbered lists are invaluable in manuals and books like this one that present a lot of step-by-step procedures. Use bulleted lists when you want to present alternatives to the reader. A *bullet* is a black filled-in circle or other character.

Simple numbered and bulleted lists

The fastest, cleanest, and most honest way to create a numbered or bulleted list is to enter the text without any concern for numbers or bullets. Just press Enter at the end of each step or bulleted entry. After you're done, select the list and click the Numbering or Bullets button on the Formatting toolbar.

Another way to create a numbered list is to type the number 1, type a period, press the spacebar, type the first entry in the list, and press Enter to get to the next line and type the second entry. As soon as you press Enter, Word inserts the number 2 and formats the list for you. Keep typing list entries, and Word keeps right on numbering and formatting the list.

Ending and continuing lists

To end a numbered or bulleted list and tell Word that you want to go back to writing normal paragraphs, get to the Bullets and Numbering dialog box either by choosing Format⇨Bullets and Numbering or by right-clicking and choosing Bullets and Numbering from the shortcut menu (see Figure 5-4). In the dialog box, click the Numbered or Bulleted tab (if necessary), select None, and then click OK.

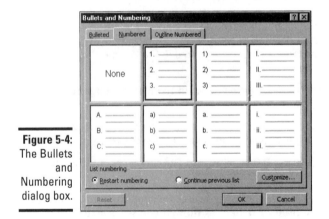

Figure 5-4:
The Bullets
and
Numbering
dialog box.

Suppose that you want a numbered list to pick up where a list you entered earlier ended. In other words, suppose that you ended a four-step list a couple of paragraphs back and now you want the list to resume at Step 5. In that case, click the Numbering button to start numbering again, open the Bullets and Numbering dialog box, and click the Continue Previous List option button. The list will pick up where the previous numbered list in the document left off.

Also in the Bullets and Numbering dialog box is an option for starting a list anew. Choose Restart Numbering when Word insists on starting a list with a number other than 1 or when you want to break off one list and start another.

Indenting Paragraphs and First Lines

An *indent* is the distance between a margin and the text, not the left side of the page and the text. Word offers a handful of different ways to change the indentation of paragraphs.

The fastest way is to use the Increase Indent and Decrease Indent buttons on the Formatting toolbar to move the paragraph away from or toward the left margin:

1. **Click in the paragraph whose indentation you want to change. If you want to change more than one paragraph, select them.**

2. **Click one of these buttons as many times as necessary to indent the text:**

   - **Increase Indent:** Indents the paragraph from the left margin by one tab stop. (You can also press Ctrl+M.)

   - **Decrease Indent:** Moves the paragraph back toward the left margin by one tab stop. (You can also press Ctrl+Shift+M.)

You can also change indentations by using the ruler to "eyeball it." This technique requires some dexterity with the mouse, but it allows you to see precisely where paragraphs and the first lines of paragraphs are indented.

1. **Choose <u>V</u>iew⇨<u>R</u>uler, if necessary, to put the ruler on-screen (see Figure 5-5).**

2. **Select the paragraph or paragraphs whose indentation you want to change.**

3. **Slide the indent markers with the mouse:**

   - **First-line indent marker:** Drag the down-pointing arrow on the ruler to indent the first line of the paragraph only.

   - **Left indent marker:** This one, on the bottom-left side of the ruler, comes in two parts. Drag the arrow that points up (called the hanging indent marker), but not the box underneath it, to move the left margin independently of the first-line indentation. To move the left indentation *and* the first-line indentation relative to the left margin, slide the box. Doing so moves everything on the left side of the ruler.

   - **Right indent marker:** Drag this one to move the right side of the paragraph away from the right margin.

Word Chapter 5

Basic Formatting

Figure 5-5: The lowdown on the Word ruler.

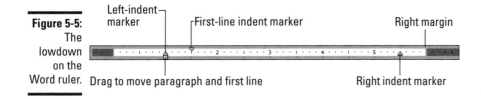

Left-indent marker — First-line indent marker — Right margin

Drag to move paragraph and first line — Right indent marker

If you're not one for "eyeballing it," you can use the Format⇨Paragraph command to indent paragraphs:

1. **Choose Format⇨Paragraph or double-click the Left or Right indent marker on the ruler. (See Figure 5-6.)**

2. **Make your selections in the Indentation area.**

3. **Click OK.**

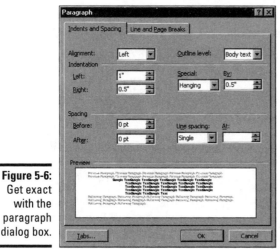

Figure 5-6:
Get exact
with the
paragraph
dialog box.

The Indentation options are self-explanatory. As you experiment, watch the Preview box — it shows exactly what your choices will do to the paragraph. In the Special drop-down list, you can choose First Line to indent the first line from the left margin or Hanging to create a *hanging indent,* an indent in which the second and subsequent lines in the paragraph are indented farther from the left margin than the first line. Enter a measurement in the By box to say how far you want these indents to travel. Did you notice that Alignment drop-down list in the upper-left corner? You can even align paragraphs from this dialog box.

Setting Up and Changing the Margins

Margins are the empty spaces along the left, right, top, and bottom sides of a page. Headers and footers are printed in the top and bottom margins, respectively.

Don't confuse margins with indents. Text is indented from the margin, not from the edge of the page. If you want to change how far a paragraph is indented, use the ruler or the Format⇨Paragraph command and change its indentation.

To change the margin settings:

1. **Place the cursor where you want to change margins if you are changing margins in the middle of a document. Otherwise, to change the margins in the entire document, it doesn't matter where you place the cursor.**

2. **Choose File⇨Page Setup to get the Page Setup dialog box.**

3. **Choose the settings on the Margins tab and watch the Preview box to see what your choices do:**

- **Top, Bottom, Left, Right, Inside, Outside:** Set the top, bottom, left and right, or inside and outside, margins. (You see the Inside and Outside settings if you click the Mirror Margins check box.)

- **Gutter:** Allows extra space on the inside margin for documents that will be bound. Click the up arrow to see what binding looks like as it eats into the left side of the page and alters the left margin.

- **Header:** Increases or decreases the amount of space allowed for headers at the top of the page.

- **Footer:** Increases or decreases the amount of space allowed for footers.

- **Apply To:** Choose Whole Document to apply your settings to the entire document, This Section to apply them to a section, or This Point Forward to change margins for the rest of a document. When you choose This Point Forward, Word creates a new section.

- **Mirror Margins:** Click this check box if you want to print on both sides of the paper and you intend to bind your document. That way, you can set the inside margin, the margin on sides of pages where the binding is, and the outside margin, the margin on the sides of pages that is not affected by binding.

- **2 Pages Per Sheet:** For printing pamphlets and other types of documents in which the pages are half the usual size and are cut in half after printing. When you click this check box, the Top margin becomes the Outside margin, the area in the middle of the page that may need to be larger so the page can be cut, and the Bottom margin becomes the Inside margin, the area away from the dividing line that doesn't have to be as large.

- **Gutter Position:** Click the Top option button if you intend to bind documents from the top, not the left side of pages.

4. **Click OK.**

If you don't care for Word's default margin settings, make your own in the Page Setup dialog box and click the Default button. Henceforth, new documents that you open will have *your* margin settings. (See Figure 5-7.)

Word Chapter 5

Basic Formatting

Working with the ruler

The ruler along the top of the screen is there to help you change and identify margins, tab settings, and indents, as well as place graphics and text boxes. (If you don't see it, choose View⇨Ruler.) In Print Layout View, a similar ruler is along the left side of the screen.

You can change the unit of measurement that is shown on the rulers. Choose Tools⇨Options, click the General tab, and choose Inches, Centimeters, Millimeters, Points, or Picas from the Measurement Units drop-down list.

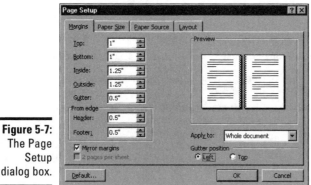

Figure 5-7:
The Page
Setup
dialog box.

You can change the top and bottom margins with the horizontal ruler in Print Layout View. Simply drag the margin bar up or down.

Working with Tabs

A *tab stop* is a point on the ruler around which or against which text is formatted. When you press the Tab key, you advance the text cursor by one tab stop. Tab stops are set at half-inch intervals on the ruler, but you can change that if you want to. Figure 5-8 shows some different kinds of tabs.

You can also change the type of tab. By default, tabs are left-aligned, which means that when you enter letters after you press the Tab key, the letters move toward the right in the same way that they move toward the right when text is left-aligned. However, Word also offers right, center, decimal, and bar tabs. Notice the symbols on the ruler — they tell you what type of tab you are dealing with.

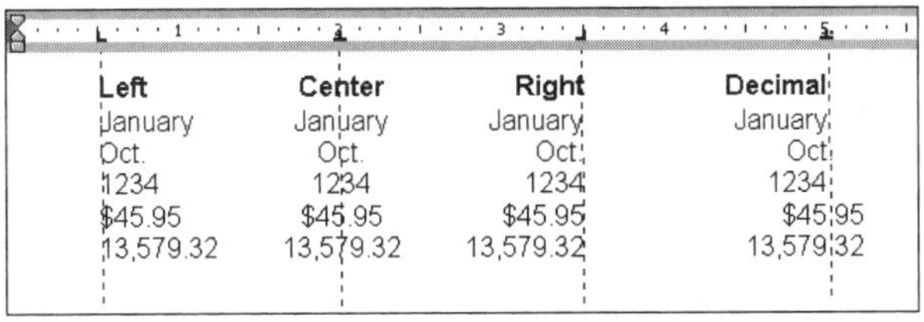

	Left	Center	Right	Decimal
	January	January	January	January
	Oct.	Oct.	Oct.	Oct
	1234	1234	1234	1234
	$45.95	$45.95	$45.95	$45.95
	13,579.32	13,579.32	13,579.32	13,579.32

Figure 5-8:
Tabbing as
it should
be done.

To change tabs or change where tabs appear on the ruler:

1. Click in the box on the left side of the ruler to get different tab settings. As you click, the symbols change, as shown:

Symbol	Tab Type
⌞	Left-aligned tab
⊥	Center-aligned tab
⌟	Right-aligned tab
⊥	Decimal tab
❙	Bar tab

2. When you come to the symbol that represents the type of tab you want (keep clicking), click at the place on the ruler where you want to put a tab stop. You can click as many times as you want and enter more than one kind of tab.

You can move a tab on the ruler simply by dragging it to a new location. Text that has been aligned with the tab moves as well, if you select it first. To remove a tab, drag it off the ruler. When you remove a tab, the text to which it was aligned is aligned to the next tab stop on the ruler.

You can also make tab settings with the Tabs dialog box:

1. Place the cursor where you want your new tab settings to take effect. Or else select the text to which you want to apply your new tabs.

2. Choose Format⇨Tabs. You see the Tabs dialog box, as shown in Figure 5-9.

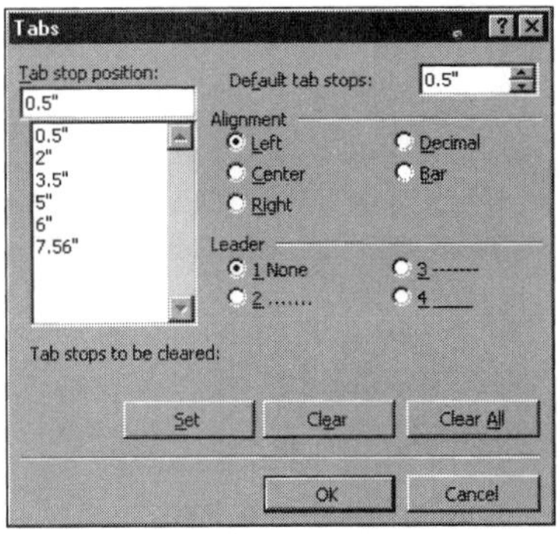

Figure 5-9:
The Tabs
dialog box.

3. **Enter a position for the first new tab in the Tab Stop Position box.**

4. **Choose an Alignment option. The Bar option places a vertical bar, or straight line, at the tab stop position.**

You can place numbers inside the bar tabs, for example, to help line them up, although doing so is utterly ridiculous when you can do that far more easily in a table.

5. **Choose a leader, if you want one. For example, if you choose 2, Word places periods in the document whenever you press Tab at this setting.**

A *leader* is a series of identical characters. Leaders are often found in tables of contents — they are the periods between the table of contents entry and the page number it refers to.

6. **Click the Set button.**

7. **Repeat Steps 3 through 6 for the next tab setting and all other tab settings. If you change your mind about a setting, select it in the Tab Stop Position scroll box and click Clear. Click Clear All if you change your mind in a big way and want to start all over.**

8. **Click OK.**

¶ Sometimes it is hard to tell where tabs were put in the text. To find out, click the Show/Hide ¶ button to see the formatting characters, including the arrows that show where the Tab key was pressed.

Chapter 6: Advanced Formatting

In This Chapter

✔ **Applying styles**

✔ **Creating and modifying styles**

✔ **Using a drop cap**

✔ **Dividing a document into sections**

✔ **Making newspaper-like columns**

Sometimes if you go that extra yard (.91 m), people will sit up and take notice. Why not find out how to give your documents that extra little push so that they stand out from the rest? If you know how to bold, italicize, underline, and all that other stuff explained in Chapter 5, you are qualified to undertake advanced formatting. But even if you haven't glanced at Chapter 5 and have no idea of what is going on, this chapter still helps you master some neat techniques to make your documents look better.

Applying Styles for Consistent Formatting

If you want to do any serious work whatsoever in Word 2000, you need to know about styles. A *style* is a collection of formats that have been bundled under one name. Instead of visiting many different dialog boxes to reformat a paragraph, you can choose a style from the Style menu — and the paragraph is reformatted instantaneously. If you modify a style, Word instantly modifies all paragraphs in your document that were assigned the given style.

What's more, many Word features rely on styles. For example, before you can see the Document Map, organize a document with an outline, or generate a table of contents, you must have assigned heading styles to the headings in your document. Turning a Word document into a Web page is easy if you thoughtfully assigned styles to the different parts of the document.

By using styles, you make sure that the different parts of a document are consistent with one another and that your document has a professional look.

Applying a style to text and paragraphs

Open the Style menu on the Formatting toolbar to see which styles are available in the document you are working on. A simple document created by clicking the New Blank Document button or pressing Ctrl+N has but a few basic styles, but documents like the one shown in Figure 6-1 that were created with a template come with many styles.

To tell which style has been assigned to a paragraph, click the paragraph and glance at the style name in the Style drop-down list. Names on the Style drop-down list give a hint of what the styles do to paragraphs and text. Each name is formatted to look like a style, and the box to the right of each name tells how the style aligns text, the font size of the text, and whether the style is a paragraph or character style. *Paragraph styles,* which are marked by the paragraph symbol on the Style drop-down list, determine the formatting of entire paragraphs. Create and use *character styles* as a means of changing fonts and type sizes quickly in Word. Character styles are marked with an underlined *a*.

By now you must be itching to apply a style. Follow these steps:

1. **Click the paragraph you want to apply the style to, or, to apply a style to several paragraphs, select all or part of them. If you're applying a character style, select the letters whose formatting you want to change.**

2. **Click the down arrow on the Style drop-down list to see the list of styles.**

3. **Click a style name.**

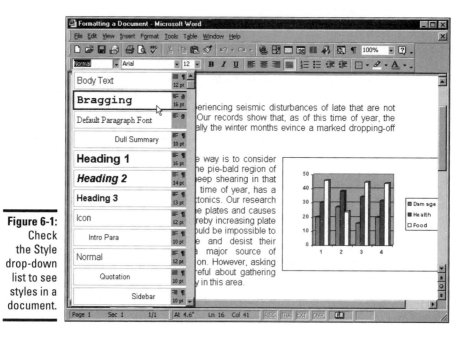

Figure 6-1: Check the Style drop-down list to see styles in a document.

Creating a new style

You can create new styles and add them to the Style menu in two ways: with the Format⇨Style command and directly from the screen. First, the directly-from-the-screen method, which you can use to create paragraph styles.

1. **Click a paragraph whose formatting you would like to turn into a style and apply to other paragraphs in your document.**

   Remember, a heading is also a paragraph as far as Word is concerned, so if you're creating a style for a heading, click the heading.

2. **Click in the Style drop-down list and type a name for the style. Choose a meaningful name that you will remember.**

3. **Press the Enter key.**

When you create a new style from scratch with the Format⇨Style command, it takes a bit longer, but you can be very precise about the style and its formatting.

1. **Choose Format⇨Style.**

2. **Click the New button in the Style dialog box.**

3. **Fill in the New Style dialog box, shown in Figure 6-2.**

   As you do so, keep your eyes on the Preview box. It shows you what your new style will look like in a document.

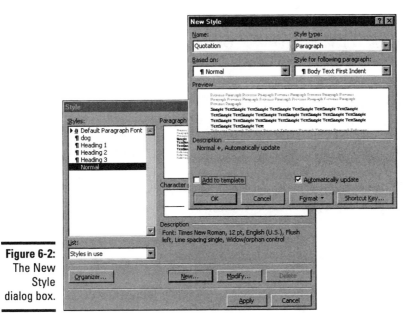

Figure 6-2:
The New
Style
dialog box.

- **Name:** Enter a name for the style. The name you enter will appear on the Style menu.

- **Style Type:** Click the down arrow and choose Character if you're creating a style for characters rather than paragraphs.

- **Based On:** If your new style is similar to one that is already on the menu, click here and choose the style to get a head start on creating the new one. Be warned, however, that if you or someone else changes the Based On style, your new style will inherit those changes and be altered as well.

- **Style for Following Paragraph:** Choose a style from the drop-down list if the style you're creating is always followed by an existing style. For example, a new style called "Chapter Title" might always be followed by a style called "Chapter Intro Paragraph."

- **Add to Template:** Adds the style to the document's template so that other documents based on the template you are using can also make use of the new style.

- **Automatically Update:** With this box checked, all paragraphs in the document that were assigned the style are altered each time you change a single paragraph that was assigned the style.

- **Format:** This is the important one. Click the button and make a formatting choice. Word takes you to dialog boxes so that you can create the style.

- **Shortcut Key:** Opens a dialog box so that you can apply the new style simply by pressing a shortcut key combination.

4. **Click OK to close the New Style dialog box.**

5. **Click Apply to format the paragraph.**

Modifying a style

What if you decide at the end of an 80-page document that all 35 introductory paragraphs to which you've assigned the "Intro Para" style look funny? If you clicked the Automatically Update check box in the New Style dialog box when you created the style, all you have to do is alter a paragraph to which you assigned the Intro Para style to alter all 35 introductory paragraphs. However, if you decided against updating styles automatically, you can still change the introductory paragraphs throughout your document. Follow these steps to modify a style that isn't updated automatically:

1. **Click on any paragraph or group of characters to which you've assigned the style you want to change.**

2. **Reformat the paragraph or characters.**

3. **Click in the Style box on the Formatting toolbar. When you do so, you click the name of the style you are modifying.**

4. **Press Enter.**

The Modify Style dialog box appears (as seen in Figure 6-3).

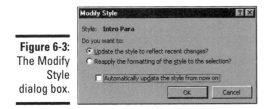

5. **Click the Update the Style to Reflect Recent Changes? radio button.**

While you're here, you might also click the Automatically Update the Style from Now On check box to update the style automatically from now on. (If you change your mind about modifying the style, click the Reapply the Formatting of the Style to the Selection? radio button.)

6. **Click OK.**

If you've devised a tortuously complicated style and want to change it, use the Modify Style dialog box. Choose Format⇨Style and click the Modify button in the Style dialog box. If the Modify Style dialog box looks familiar, that's because it is identical to the New Style dialog box you used to create the style in the first place. Change the settings, click OK, and click Apply to apply the new style throughout your document.

Dropping In a Drop Cap

A *drop cap* is a large capital letter that "drops" into the text. Drop caps appear at the start of chapters in antiquated books, but you can find other uses for them. In Figure 6-4, a drop cap marks the "A" side of a list of songs on a homemade reggae tape.

To create a drop cap:

1. **Click anywhere in the paragraph whose first letter you want to "drop."**

2. **Choose Format⇨Drop Cap.**

3. **In the Drop Cap dialog box, choose which kind of drop cap you want by clicking a box.**

The None setting is for removing a drop cap.

4. **Choose a font from the Font drop-down list.**

Choose one that's different from the text in the paragraph. You can come back to this dialog box and get a different font later, if you wish.

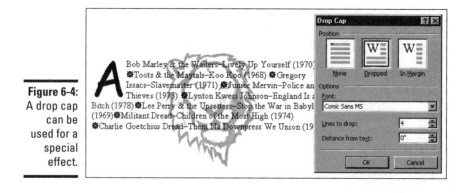

Figure 6-4:
A drop cap
can be
used for a
special
effect.

5. **In the Lines to Drop scroll box, choose how many text lines the letter should "drop on."**

6. **Keep the 0 setting in the Distance from Text box unless you're dropping an *I, 1,* or other skinny letter or number.**

7. **Click OK.**

You see your drop cap in Print Layout View. The drop cap appears in a text frame. To change the size of the drop cap, you can tug and pull at the sides of the box (by dragging the handles with the mouse). However, you're better off choosing Format⇨Drop Cap again and playing with the settings in the Drop Cap dialog box.

Dividing a Document into Sections

Every document has at least one *section.* That's why "Sec 1" appears on the left side of the status bar at the bottom of the screen. When you want to change page numbering schemes, headers and footers, margin sizes, and page layouts, you have to create a section break to start a new section. Word creates one for you when you create newspaper-style columns or change the size of margins. To create a new section:

1. **Click where you want to insert a section break.**

2. **Choose Insert⇨Break to get to the Break dialog box, as shown in Figure 6-5.**

3. **Under Section Break Types, tell Word which kind of section break you want.**

   All four Section break options create a new section, but they do so in different ways:

   • **Next Page:** Inserts a page break as well as a section break so that the new section can start at the top of a new page (the next one). Select this option to start a new chapter, for example.

Juggling your columns

Sometimes it is easier to create columns by creating a table or by using tabs instead, especially when the columns refer to one another. In a two-column résumé, for example, the left-hand column often lists job titles ("Facsimile Engineer") whose descriptions are found directly across the page in the right-hand column ("I Xeroxed stuff all day long"). Creating a two-column résumé with Word's Format⇨Columns command would be futile because making the columns line up is impossible. Each time you add something to the left-hand column, everything "snakes" — it gets bumped down in the left-hand column and the right-hand column as well.

- **Continuous:** Inserts a section break in the middle of a page. Select this option, for example, if you want to introduce newspaper-style columns in the middle of a page.

- **Even Page:** Starts the new section on the next even page. This option is good for two-sided documents where the headers on the left- and right-hand pages are different.

- **Odd Page:** Starts the new section on the next odd page. You might choose this option if you have a book in which chapters start on odd pages. (By convention, that's where they start.)

4. **Click OK.**

In Normal View, you can tell where a section ends because `Section Break` and a double dotted line appear on-screen. The only way to tell where a section ends in Print Layout View is to glance at the "Sec" listing on the status bar or click the Show/Hide ¶ button. To delete a section break, make sure that you are in Normal View, click the dotted line, and press the Delete key.

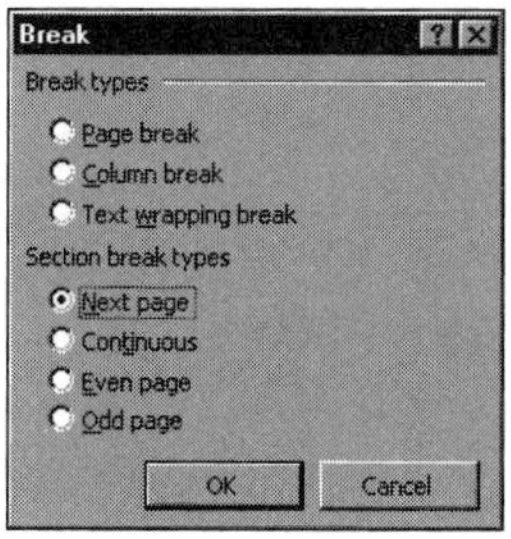

Figure 6-5:
The Break
dialog box.

Putting Newspaper-Style Columns in a Document

Columns look great in newsletters and similar documents. And you can pack a lot of words in columns. With columns, you can present more than one document on a single page so that readers have a choice of what they read.

Before you put text in newspaper-style columns, write it. Take care of the spelling, grammar, and everything else first because making text changes to words after they've been arranged in columns is hard.

You have two ways to create columns: with the Columns button on the toolbar and with the Format⇨Columns command. Format⇨Columns gives you considerably more leeway because the Columns button lets you create only columns of equal width. To use the Columns button:

1. **Select the text to be put in columns or simply place the cursor in the document to "columnize" all the text.**

2. **Click the Columns button on the toolbar.**

A menu drops down so that you can choose how many columns you want.

3. **Click and drag to choose from one to six columns.**

Word creates a new section if you selected text before you columnized it, and you see your columns in Print Layout View. Very likely, they don't look so good. It's hard to get it right the first time. You can drag the column border bars on the ruler to widen or narrow the columns:

Drag to change column width.

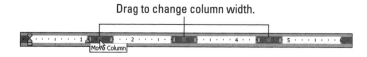

However, it's much easier to choose Format⇨Columns and play with options in the Columns dialog box. If you want to start all over, or if you want to start from the beginning with the Columns dialog box, here's how:

1. **Select the text to be put in columns, or put the cursor in the section to be put in columns, or place the cursor at a position in the document where columns are to start appearing.**

2. **Choose Format⇨Columns.**

3. **Choose options from the Columns dialog box, shown in Figure 6-6.**

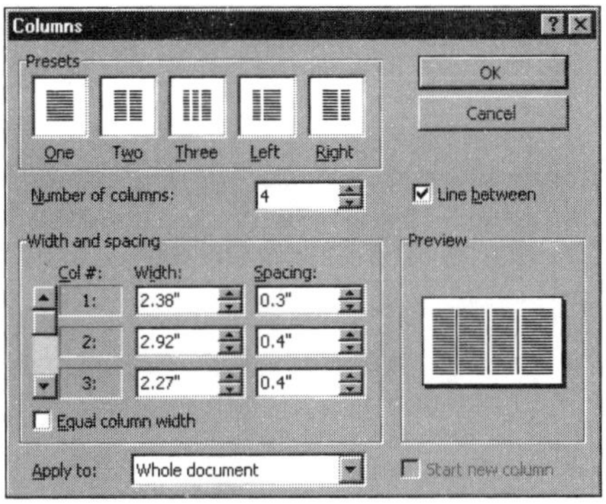

Figure 6-6:
The
Columns
dialog box
will get you
started on
your nice
layout.

As you do so, keep your eye on the Preview box in the lower-right corner:

- **Presets:** Click a box to choose a preset number of columns. Notice that, in some of the boxes, the columns aren't of equal width. Choose One if you want to remove columns from a document.

- **Number of Columns:** If you want more than three columns, enter a number here.

- **Line Between:** Click this box to put lines between columns.

- **Col #:** If your document has more than three columns, a scroll bar appears to the left of the Col # boxes. Scroll to the column you want to work with.

- **Width:** If you click the Equal Column Width box to remove the check mark, you can make columns of unequal width. Change the width of each column by using the Width boxes.

- **Spacing:** Determines how much blank space appears to the right of the column.

- **Equal Column Width:** Click this box to remove the check mark if you want columns of various widths.

- **Apply To:** Choose which part of the document you want to "columnize" — selected text, the section the cursor is in, this point forward in your document, or the whole document.

- **Start New Column:** This box is for putting empty space in a column, perhaps to insert a text box or picture. Place the cursor where you want the empty space to begin, open the Columns dialog box, click this check box, and choose This Point Forward from the Apply To drop-down list. Text below the cursor moves to the next column.

4. Click OK.

Faster ways to "break" a column in the middle and move text to the next column are to press Ctrl+Shift+Enter or choose Insert➪Break and click the Column Break radio button.

As you format your multicolumn newsletter or incendiary pamphlet, click the Print Preview button early and often. The best way to see what a multicolumn document really looks like is to see it on the Print Preview screen.

Chapter 7: Envelopes, Labels, and Form Letters

In This Chapter

✔ **Addressing envelopes**

✔ **Making labels**

✔ **Creating form letters**

*I*f you have ever wanted to know how Publisher's Clearinghouse and Ed McMahon could churn out millions of personalized letters and blanket the entire country, this chapter helps you understand how easy it is. And you can do it, too! Word 2000 lends itself to making mundane tasks easier, so you really have no excuse for not letting it help you with your correspondence. Word 2000 can do everything except come up with the money-making schemes!

Printing Addresses on Envelopes

You don't have to address envelopes by hand, although it's often easier to do it that way. Here's how to print addresses and return addresses on envelopes:

1. **Open the document that holds the letter you want to send, and select the name and address of the person you want to send the letter to.**

2. **Choose Tools⇨Envelopes and Labels.**

   The Envelopes and Labels dialog box appears (shown in Figure 7-1) with the address you selected in the Delivery Address box. Your name and address should appear in the Return Address box. (If it isn't there, see the Tip at the end of this section to find out how to put it there.)

3. **Change the Delivery Address or Return Address, if necessary.**

4. **Click the Omit check box if you don't want your return address to appear on the envelope.**

5. **Click the Print button.**

Note: See Appendix A for the full scoop on how to print in Word or in any Office 2000 application. The basics are the same for all applications, so getting comfortable with one application prepares you for doing some tasks in the others.

Two commands on the Envelopes tab tell Word how your printer handles envelopes and what size your envelopes are.

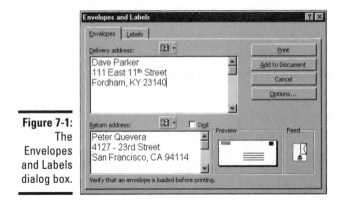

Figure 7-1:
The
Envelopes
and Labels
dialog box.

Click the envelope icon below the word "Feed" to choose the right technique for feeding envelopes to your printer. Click one of the Feed Method boxes, click the Face Up or Face Down option button, and pull down the Feed From menu to tell Word which printer tray the envelope is in or how you intend to stick the envelope in your printer (see Figure 7-2). Click OK after you're done.

After you've fed the envelope to your printer, click the envelope icon below the word "Preview" — that's right, click the icon — to tell Word what size your envelopes are and choose other settings:

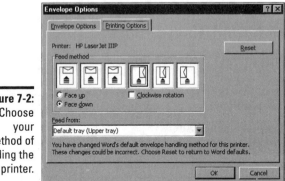

Figure 7-2:
Choose
your
method of
feeding the
printer.

+ **Envelope Size:** Pull down the menu and select the right size.

+ **Delivery Point Bar Code:** Click here to put bar codes on the envelope and help the United States Postal Service deliver the letter faster.

+ **FIM-A Courtesy Reply Mail:** Click here to put Facing Identification Marks on the envelope. These marks, which tell letter-processing machines at the post office whether the envelope is face up, also aid the speedy delivery of mail.

+ **Delivery Address:** Change the font of the delivery address and the address's position. Change the From Left and From Top settings to slide the address up or down on the envelope.

✦ **Return Address:** Ditto for the return address.

To make your name and return address appear automatically in the Return Address box, choose Tools➪Options, click the User Information tab, and enter your name and address in the Mailing Address box.

Printing Labels

You can print pages of labels in Word, and single labels, too. Needless to say, printing labels makes mass mailing and bulk mailing much easier. Before you start printing labels, however, note what size and what brand your labels are. You are asked about label sizes when you print labels.

Printing labels one at a time

To print mailing labels, follow these steps:

1. **Open the document that contains the address of the label you want to print, and select the address.**

2. **Choose Tools➪Envelopes and Labels.**

3. **Click the Labels tab (shown in Figure 7-3). The address appears in the Address box. If the name or address is wrong, now's the time to fix it. If you're printing labels with your return address on them, click the Use Return Address box or enter your return address.**

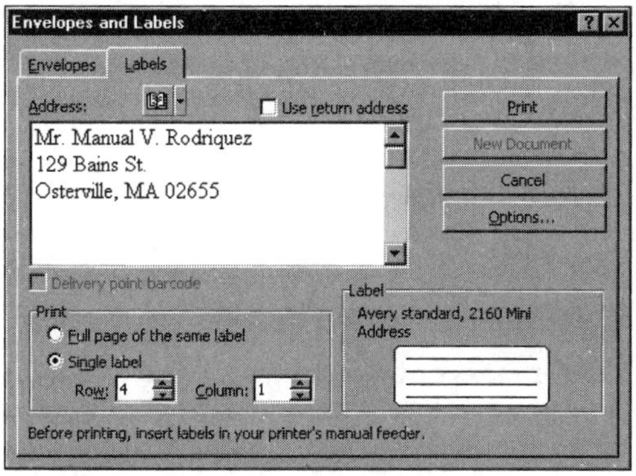

Figure 7-3:
The
Envelopes
and Labels
dialog box
with the
Labels tab
chosen.

4. **Either click the Options button or click the label icon in the Label box (see Figure 7-4).**

5. **In the Printer Information area, click either Dot Matrix or Laser and Ink Jet to say which kind of printer you have. Then pull down the Tray drop-down list and click the option that describes how you will feed the labels to your printer.**

6. **Click the Label Products drop-down list and choose the brand or type of labels that you have.**

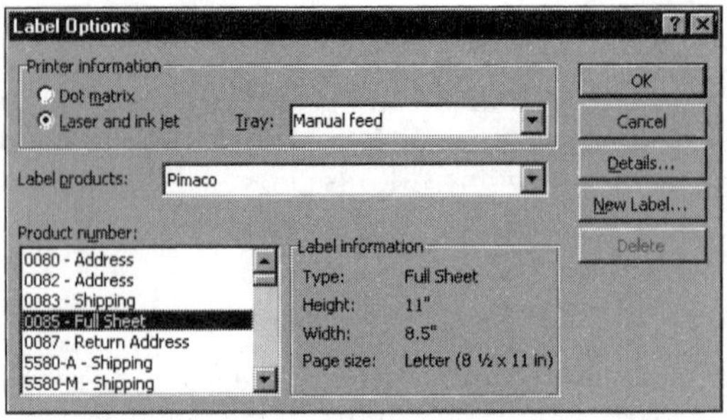

Figure 7-4:
The Label
Options
dialog box
is where
you really
need to
know your
label type.

If your brand is not on the list, you can choose Other (found at the bottom of the list), click the Details button, and describe your labels in the extremely confusing Address Information dialog box. A better way, however, is to measure your labels and see whether you can find a label of the same size by experimenting with Label Products option and Product Number combinations.

7. **In the Product Number box, click the product number listed on the box your labels came in. Look in the Label Information box on the right to make sure that the Height, Width, and Page Size measurements match those of the labels you have.**

8. **Click OK to go back to the Envelopes and Labels dialog box.**

9. **Choose a Print option:**

   • **Full Page of the Same Label:** Click this box if you want to print a pageful of the same label. Likely, you'd choose this option to print a pageful of your own return addresses. Click the New Document button after you make this choice. Word creates a new document with a pageful of labels. Save and print this document.

   • **Single Label:** Click this box to print one label. Then enter the row and column where the label is and click the Print button.

Printing labels for mass mailings

To print a mess of labels for mass or bulk mailings, Word offers the Mail Merge Helper. The best way to use this nifty tool is to create a table (or a database table if you are adept with Access 2000 or another database program) with the label addresses. See also Chapter 10, "Constructing the Perfect Table," to find out how to create tables. After you have created the addresses table, save it as a file and make sure that nothing is in the file except the table itself. You can use your addresses table over and over again for printing labels and for form letters as well.

To use the Mail Merge Helper to create a file of address labels:

1. **Open a new document and choose Tools➪Mail Merge. The Mail Merge Helper opens.**

2. **Click the Create button and then click Mailing Labels in the drop-down list.**

3. In the message box, click <u>A</u>ctive Window to add the labels to the new document that you just opened.

4. Under Step 2 in the Mail Merge Helper, click <u>G</u>et Data to see the menu of choices for getting the mailing label addresses, and choose <u>O</u>pen Data Source from the menu.

With this option, you get the names and addresses from a mailing list table that you or somebody else has already created and saved in a file.

5. In the Open Data Source dialog box, find the document that holds the table with your addresses, select it, and click the <u>O</u>pen button.

6. In the message box that appears, click the <u>S</u>et Up Main Document button.

7. Choose options in the Label Options dialog box.

This is where you tell Word what size the labels are. Click OK when you're done. The Create Labels dialog box appears. (See Figure 7-5.)

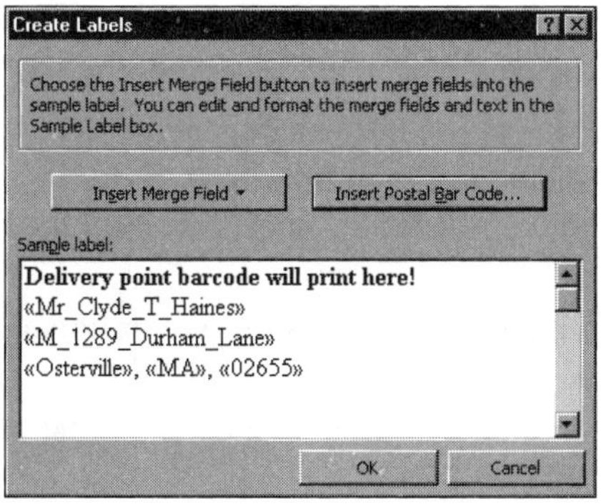

Figure 7-5:
Making
labels will
allow you
to perform
mass
mailings
with ease.

Create Labels

Choose the Insert Merge Field button to insert merge fields into the sample label. You can edit and format the merge fields and text in the Sample Label box.

[Insert Merge Field ▾]   [Insert Postal <u>B</u>ar Code...]

Sample label:

Delivery point barcode will print here!
«Mr_Clyde_T_Haines»
«M_1289_Durham_Lane»
«Osterville», «MA», «02655»

[OK]   [Cancel]

---

8. In this dialog box, you create the sample label that Word will use as a model for all the labels on the list. To do that, place the cursor in the Sample Label box where you want the addressee's name to go, click In<u>s</u>ert Merge Field, and choose the name from the top of the drop-down list.

It appears in the Sample Label box.

9. Press Enter to go to the next line in the Sample Label box, click In<u>s</u>ert Merge Field again, and enter the next line in the address, probably the street number and street name. Press Enter again.

10. Insert the city name, state, and zip code. Enter a comma and a space after the city name, and another space after the state.

Whatever you do, don't erase the angle brackets (<<>>) or press Enter inside them. The brackets are there to mark off the parts of the address.

11. **You can enter a postal bar code with the Insert Postal Bar Code button and drop-down list. In the Insert Postal Bar Code dialog box, choose the sample zip code from the drop-down list.**

12. **Click OK.**

13. **Back in the Mail Merge Helper, click the Merge button. You see the Merge dialog box (shown in Figure 7-6).**

Figure 7-6:
The Merge
dialog box
is your
last step
to mass
mailing.

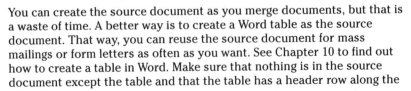

Ms. Gladys Yee
1293 Durham Lane
Osterville, MA 02655

Ms. Esther Harmony
2601 Estner Rd.
Osterville, MA 02655

Ms. Melinda Sings
2789 Estner Rd.
Osterville, MA 02655

Mr. Rupert S. Stickenmud
119 Scutter Lane
Osterville, MA 02655

14. **Make sure that the Don't Print Blank Lines When Data Fields Are Empty box is checked. This prevents blank lines from appearing in your labels.**

15. **Click the Merge button.**

If you want, you can choose a new font for the labels by pressing Ctrl+A to select the document and then choosing a new font from the Font drop-down list.

16. **Choose File⇨Save, press Ctrl+S, or click the Save button and save your label file under a new name in the Save As dialog box.**

17. **Now that your labels are on disk, put a blank sheet of labels in the printer and print your new labels.**

Churning Out Form Letters

Thanks to the miracle of computing, you can churn out form letters in the privacy of your home or office, just like the big companies do. To create form letters, you complete three steps:

1. **Create the *main document,* the document with the actual text of the letter.**

2. **Create the *source document,* the document with the names, addresses, and any other text that differs from letter to letter.**

You can create the source document as you merge documents, but that is a waste of time. A better way is to create a Word table as the source document. That way, you can reuse the source document for mass mailings or form letters as often as you want. See Chapter 10 to find out how to create a table in Word. Make sure that nothing is in the source document except the table and that the table has a header row along the top that labels the information below it. For example, a table of names and addresses would have a header row with these labels: Name, Street, City, State, and Zip.

3. Merge the two documents to generate the form letters.

Before you generate the form letter, write a first draft. That way, you will know precisely what information varies from recipient to recipient — the names and addresses, for example — before you start generating the letter. Your Word table must contain all the variable information that you will add to the main document when you merge the documents and generate the form letters.

Figure 7-7 shows the first draft of the letter (the main document) and the table with information for the form letter (the source document). Variable information is in boldface:

Name
Street
City, State Zip

Dear **Name**,

It was a pleasure serving you last **season**. May your holidays be joyful and loving.

Sincerely,
The Lighthouse Staff

Name	Street	City	State	Zip	Season
Mr. Clyde T. Haines	1289 Durham Lane	Osterville	MA	02655	Summer
Ms. Gladys Yee	1293 Durham Lane	Osterville	MA	02655	Summer
Ms. Esther Harmony	2601 Estner Rd.	Osterville	MA	02655	Fall
Ms. Melinda Sings	2789 Estner Rd.	Osterville	MA	02655	Spring
Mr. Rupert S. Stickenmud	119 Scutter Lane	Osterville	MA	02655	Fall
Ms. Martha Hines	1263 Tick Park	Osterville	MA	02655	Summer

Figure 7-7:
The main
and the
source
documents.

Follow these steps to generate form letters:

1. **Open the main document, the one with the text of the letter, if it is not already open.**

2. **Choose Tools⇨Mail Merge. The Mail Merge Helper dialog box appears.**

3. **Click the Create button and choose Form Letters from the drop-down list.**

4. **A message box asks if you want to create the form letters in the active document or in a new document. Click the Active Window button.**

5. **Under Step 2 in the Mail Merge Helper, click Get Data and choose Open Data Source from the drop-down list.**

6. **In the Open Data Source dialog box, locate the source document with your addresses and other variable information, select the document, and click the Open button.**

7. **In the message box that appears, click the Edit <u>M</u>ain Document button.**

Back in the main document, the Mail Merge toolbar appears along the top of the screen. On the toolbar's Insert Merge Field drop-down list are the names of each column from the source table whose data you will put in the form letter.

8. **One by one, go to each piece of variable information in the table, erase it if necessary, and choose a field from the Insert Merge Field drop-down list.**

Field names appear in brackets in the letter after you insert them. Make sure that the punctuation and spacing around the field names are correct. For example, a comma should go after "Dear <<Name>>."

9. **Click the <u>M</u>erge button on the Mail Merge toolbar to start merging the main document and source document. You see the Merge dialog box.**

10. **Make a choice on the Me<u>r</u>ge To drop-down list and then click the <u>M</u>erge button to merge the fill-in-the-blanks in the main document with the information from the source document:**

• **New Document:** Creates a new document with all the form letters in it. A document like this can be very long if the source document includes many records (rows with information in them). After you click the Merge button, your new document appears on-screen. Save it and then print the form letters.

• **Printer:** Prints the form letters without saving them in a document. This option saves disk space because the merged letters are not saved on disk. After you click the Merge button, you see the Print dialog box. Make sure that your printer is on and click OK to print the form letters.

Figure 7-8 shows a form letter after the main document and source document were merged. Notice how smoothly the information in the first row of the source table fits into the form letter.

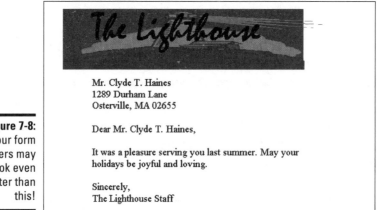

Mr. Clyde T. Haines
1289 Durham Lane
Osterville, MA 02655

Dear Mr. Clyde T. Haines,

It was a pleasure serving you last summer. May your holidays be joyful and loving.

Sincerely,
The Lighthouse Staff

Figure 7-8:
Your form
letters may
look even
better than
this!

Chapter 8: Making Your Work Go Faster

In This Chapter

↙ **Changing menus and keyboard shortcuts**

↙ **Rearranging toolbars to your liking**

↙ **Correcting typos as you type**

↙ **Repeating actions**

↙ **Moving around in your document**

↙ **Inserting text and graphics automatically**

*F*aster, faster, faster! Work faster!

Does this sound familiar? If you can't seem to work smarter, you can always try to work faster. Word 2000 has ways to help you save time here and there. You can correct typos as you type, repeat actions, navigate quickly, insert text automatically, and perform many other time-saving tasks. Who needs to work smarter when they can take advantage of what Word 2000 has to offer?

Customizing Word 2000

You can make Word 2000 work your way by putting the menu commands in different places, inventing your own keyboard shortcuts for executing commands, and even creating your own toolbars. Read on to find out how to change the menu commands and designate your own keyboard shortcuts. Changing the menus around is well worth your while if you are a speed demon who likes to get work done fast.

Changing the menu commands

You can decide for yourself which menu commands appear on which menus. You can also add macros, fonts, AutoText entries, and styles to menus. Doing so is easy, and if you make a mistake, going back to the original menus is easy, too.

The quickest (but scariest) way to remove a command from a menu is to press Ctrl+Alt+hyphen. When the cursor changes into an ominous black bar, simply select the menu command that you want to remove. Press Esc, by the way, if you decide after you press Ctrl+Alt+hyphen that you don't want to remove menu commands.

A more precise way to remove menu commands or alter the menus is to use the Commands tab of the Customize dialog box:

1. **Choose Tools⇨Customize.**

2. **Click the Commands tab (as shown in Figure 8-1).**

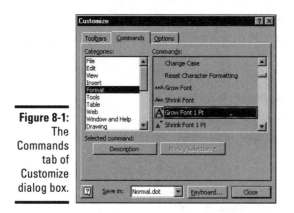

Figure 8-1:
The
Commands
tab of
Customize
dialog box.

3. **If you want the menu changes you make to be made to a template other than Normal.dot or the template you are working in, choose the template in the Save In drop-down list.**

4. **In the Categories list, select the menu you want to change.**

If you're adding a macro, font, AutoText entry, or style to a menu, scroll to the bottom of the Categories list and select it. The commands that are on the menu you chose appear in the Commands list on the right.

5. **Choose the command you're changing in the Commands list.**

You can click the Description button to read a description of the command if you aren't quite sure what it does.

6. **What you do next depends on whether you want to remove a command from a menu, add a command to a menu, or change its position on a menu. Changing menu commands requires moving the pointer out of the Customize dialog box and clicking menus on the menu bar.**

- **Removing:** To remove a menu command, move the pointer over the menu that holds the command you want to remove and click gently. That's right — click the menu name as you normally would if you were pulling it down to choose one of its commands. When the menu appears, click the menu command you want to remove, and drag it off the menu. You see a gray rectangle above the pointer and an *X* below it. Release the mouse button after you have dragged the menu command away from the menu.

- **Adding:** To add a menu command to a menu, drag it from the Commands list in the Customize dialog box to the menu itself. As you do this, you see a gray rectangle above the pointer and a plus sign below it. Move the pointer over the menu to which you want to add the command. The menu appears. Gently drag the pointer down the menu to the spot where you want the command to be listed. A black line appears on the menu to show where your command will go. When the command is in the right spot, release the mouse button.

- **Changing position:** To change the position of a command on a menu, move the pointer out of the Customize dialog box and gently click on the menu whose command you want to move. Then drag the pointer up or down the list of commands. A black line shows where the command will move when you release the mouse button. When the black line is in the right spot, let up on the mouse button.

7. **Click Close.**

If you wish that you hadn't messed with the menus and want to repent, choose Tools⇨Customize, click the Commands tab, move the pointer out of the dialog box and right-click on the name of the menu whose commands you fooled with, and choose Reset from the shortcut menu.

Changing the keyboard shortcuts

If you don't like Word's keyboard shortcuts, you can change them and invent keyboard shortcuts of your own. You can also assign keyboard shortcuts to symbols, macros, fonts, AutoText entries, and styles.

1. **Choose Tools⇨Customize.**

2. **Click the Keyboard button. You see the Customize Keyboard dialog box (shown in Figure 8-2).**

3. **To make the changes to a template other than Normal.dot or the template you are working in, choose a template in the Save Changes In drop-down list.**

4. **In the Categories list, choose the menu with the command to which you want to assign the keyboard shortcut.**

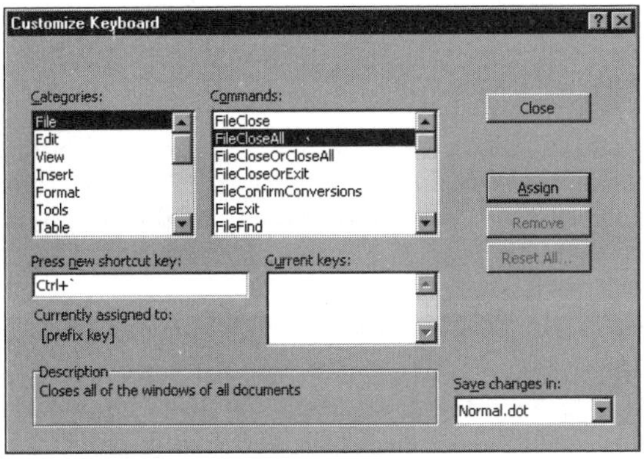

Figure 8-2:
The
Customize
Keyboard
dialog box.

> **Customize Keyboard**
>
> Categories:
> File
> Edit
> View
> Insert
> Format
> Tools
> Table
>
> Commands:
> FileClose
> FileCloseAll
> FileCloseOrCloseAll
> FileCloseOrExit
> FileConfirmConversions
> FileExit
> FileFind
>
> Close
> Assign
> Remove
> Reset All...
>
> Press new shortcut key:
> Ctrl+`
>
> Current keys:
>
> Currently assigned to:
> [prefix key]
>
> Description
> Closes all of the windows of all documents
>
> Save changes in:
> Normal.dot

Keeping track of all those buttons

To find out what a button on a toolbar does, choose Help⇨What's This? (or press Shift+F1) and click a toolbar button. A description of the button appears on-screen. You can also move the mouse pointer over a button to read a one- or two-word description. If you're not seeing the descriptions, choose Tools⇨Customize, click the Options tab of the Customize dialog box, and click the Show ScreenTips on Toolbars check box.

At the bottom of the list are the Macro, Font, AutoText, Style, and Common symbols categories.

5. **Choose the command name, macro, font, AutoText entry, style, or symbol name in the C̲ommands list.**

6. **Click in the Press N̲ew Shortcut Key box and type the keyboard short-cut. Press the actual keys. For example, if the shortcut is Ctrl+~, press the Ctrl key and the ~ key — don't type out C-t-r-l-+-~.**

   If you try to assign a shortcut that is already assigned, the words Currently assigned to and a command name appear below the Press New Shortcut Key box. You can override the preassigned keyboard assignment by entering a keyboard assignment of your own.

7. **Click the A̲ssign button.**

8. **After you're done, click the Close button.**

9. **Click Close in the Customize dialog box.**

To delete a keyboard shortcut, display it in the Current Keys box, click it to select it, and click the Remove button.

You can always get the old keyboard shortcuts back by choosing the Reset All button in the Customize Keyboard dialog box. Click Yes when Word asks whether you really want the old keyboard shortcuts back.

Rearranging the Toolbars

To make working with toolbars easier, you can drag them around on-screen. You can remove buttons from toolbars and replace them with buttons of your own choosing. You can even create your own toolbars and invent new toolbar buttons.

Displaying other toolbars

Two toolbars appear at the top of the Word window: the Standard toolbar and the Formatting toolbar. To place new toolbars in the window, right-click a toolbar and click the toolbar's name on the shortcut menu. You can also choose

View⇨Toolbars and click a name on the submenu. What's more, you can display the Drawing toolbar or Tables and Borders toolbar by clicking their buttons on the Standard toolbar.

After a toolbar is on-screen, try dragging it into the window and repositioning it or changing its shape:

✦ To unanchor a toolbar that is stuck to the top or bottom of the Word window, move the mouse pointer over the slider on the left side of the toolbar and, when you see the four-headed arrow, click and drag the toolbar onto the screen.

✦ To move a toolbar on-screen, drag its title bar.

✦ To change a toolbar's shape, place the mouse on a border. When you see the two headed arrow, drag the border until the toolbar is the shape you want.

Figure 8-3 shows all the Word toolbars on the shortcut menu. They have been dragged into the window and reshaped.

TIP

To remove a toolbar that you've dragged into the window, click its Close button (the *X* in the upper-right corner), or choose View⇨Toolbars and click its name on the submenu. Double-click its title bar to move it back to its rightful place at the top or bottom of the window.

Occasionally when you click a down arrow and open a drop-down list, you see a line along the top of the list. When you see that line, you can turn the list into a *floating toolbar,* a menu that you can move around on-screen like the Font Color floating toolbar shown in Figure 8-4. To do so, click and drag the line. You can

Word Chapter 8

Making Your Work Go Faster

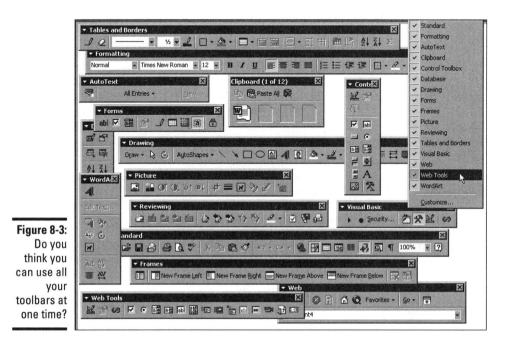

Figure 8-3: Do you think you can use all your toolbars at one time?

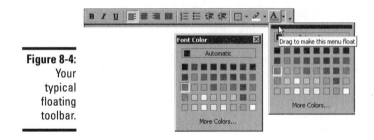

Figure 8-4:
Your
typical
floating
toolbar.

drag a floating toolbar anywhere you want on-screen. Floating toolbars are convenient when you want to try out different commands. Instead of having to open a menu and choose a command, you simply click different buttons on the floating toolbar until you discover the right choice.

Choosing which buttons appear on toolbars

You may never do some of the tasks that the buttons on the Standard and Formatting toolbars were put there to help you do. If you're not using a button, you can take it off the toolbar and replace it with a button that you do use. Adding buttons to and removing buttons from toolbars are easy, and if you make a mistake, getting the original toolbars back is easy, too. If you don't have Microsoft Excel, for example, you can chuck the Insert Microsoft Excel Worksheet button on the Standard toolbar and put a button that you do use in its place.

The fastest way to change the buttons on a toolbar is to click the toolbar arrow on the right side of a toolbar, but you can also go to the Customize dialog box to do a more thorough job. First, the toolbar arrow method:

1. **Put the toolbar whose buttons you want to change on-screen. To do so, choose View⇨Toolbar and click the toolbar's name.**

2. **Click the tiny arrow on the right side of the toolbar, the one directly to the right of the rightmost button.**

3. **Choose Add or Remove buttons, the only choice on the drop-down list.**

A menu appears with the names of buttons now on the toolbar. If you are dealing with the Standard or Formatting toolbar, a handful of extra buttons appears at the bottom of the list. (See Figure 8-5.)

4. **Click the check boxes next to button names to add or remove buttons from the toolbar.**

A check mark next to a button means that it appears on the toolbar.

To get the officially certified Microsoft toolbar that came with the program, click the toolbar arrow, choose Add or Remove buttons, and choose Reset Toolbar at the bottom of the buttons list.

So much for the toolbar arrow method. To do a more thorough job of customizing toolbars, to rearrange the buttons on a toolbar, or to bring buttons from distant toolbars to rest on the toolbar of your choice, follow these steps:

1. **Put the toolbar that you want to customize on-screen.**

2. Choose Tools⇨Customize, or right-click a toolbar and choose Customize from the shortcut menu.

The Customize dialog box appears (and can be gawked at in Figure 8-6).

Check or uncheck buttons to add or remove them

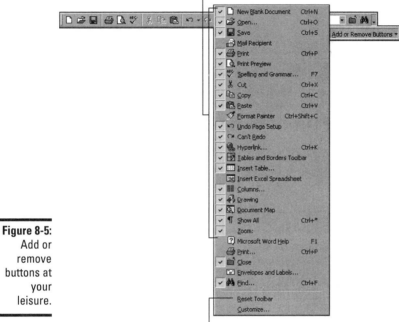

Figure 8-5:
Add or
remove
buttons at
your
leisure.

Click to get the original toolbar back

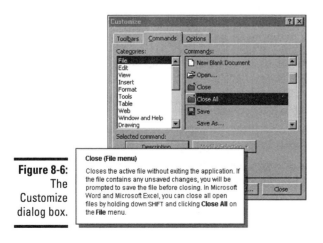

Figure 8-6:
The
Customize
dialog box.

Close (File menu)

Closes the active file without exiting the application. If the file contains any unsaved changes, you will be prompted to save the file before closing. In Microsoft Word and Microsoft Excel, you can close all open files by holding down SHIFT and clicking **Close All** on the **File** menu.

3. **Click the Commands tab.**

The Categories list in this dialog box lists all the menus and several of the toolbars. At the bottom of the list are the styles, macros, AutoText entries, and fonts that are available in the template you're using. You can find every command in Word in this dialog box by clicking an item in the Categories box and then scrolling in the Commands box. If you aren't sure what a button does, click it in the Commands box and then click the Description button.

4. **Remove or add a button from the toolbar you displayed in Step 1. To do so, you move the pointer outside the Customize dialog box and click toolbars at the screen:**

- **Removing:** To remove a button from a toolbar, simply drag it off the toolbar. As you drag, a gray rectangle appears above the pointer, and an *X* appears below it. Release the mouse button, and the toolbar button disappears.

- **Adding:** To add a button, find it in the Customize dialog box by clicking categories and scrolling in the Commands box. When you have found the button, gently drag it out of the Customize dialog box and place it on the toolbar where you want it to appear. As you do so, a gray rectangle appears above the cursor. A plus sign appears below it when you move the button onto the toolbar.

5. **While the Customize dialog box is open, you can drag buttons to new locations on toolbars.**

6. **If you want your new toolbar arrangement to appear only in certain templates, click the Save In drop-down list and choose the template.**

7. **Click Close.**

You can also move buttons between toolbars by dragging them from toolbar to toolbar while the Customize dialog box is open. To copy buttons from one toolbar to another, hold down the Ctrl key as you drag the buttons.

If you make a boo-boo and wish that you hadn't fooled with the buttons on the toolbar, choose Tools⇨Customize or right-click a toolbar and choose Customize to get to the Customize dialog box. From there, click the Toolbars tab, click the toolbar whose buttons you fooled with, and click the Reset button. Click OK in the Reset Toolbar dialog box.

Creating your own toolbar

You can also create a new toolbar with your favorite buttons on it. If you want, you can even create toolbar buttons for styles, fonts, AutoText entries, and macros.

1. **Choose Tools⇨Customize, or right-click a toolbar and choose Customize from the shortcut menu to see the Customize dialog box.**

2. **Click the Toolbars tab.**

3. **Click the New button.**

The New Toolbar dialog box appears (shown in Figure 8-7).

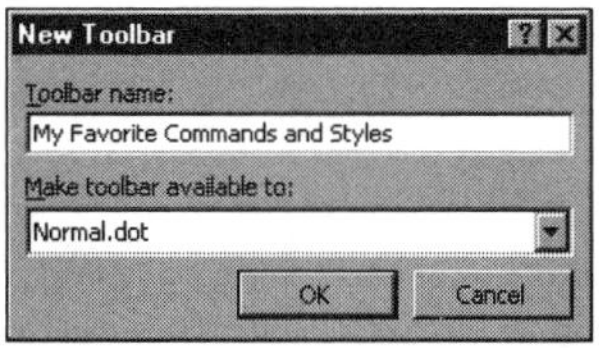

Figure 8-7:
The New
Toolbar
dialog box.

New Toolbar	? X
Toolbar name:	
My Favorite Commands and Styles	
Make toolbar available to:	
Normal.dot	
OK	Cancel

4. **Type a name for your toolbar in the Toolbar Name box.**

The name you type here will appear on the View➪Toolbars submenu.

5. **If necessary, choose a template in the Make Toolbar Available To drop-down list.**

6. **Click OK. A tiny toolbar with the name you entered appears on the screen.**

7. **Double-click the title bar of your new toolbar to move it to the top of the screen.**

8. **Click the Commands tab in the Customize dialog box.**

9. **In the Categories box, find and click the category in which the command, style, font, macro, or AutoText entry you want to put on a toolbar is found.**

10. **To add a button, drag an item from the Commands box right onto your new toolbar.**

11. **After you've added all the buttons, drag them where you want them to stand on the toolbar.**

12. **If you've added styles or fonts, you may want to shorten their names to make them fit better on the toolbar. To do that, right-click the button whose name you want to shorten and enter a new name in the Name text box.**

13. **When your toolbar is just-so, click Close.**

You can always delete a toolbar you made yourself. Choose Tools➪Customize, or right-click a toolbar and choose Customize to get to the Customize dialog box. Then click the Toolbars tab, click the toolbar you want to extinguish (self-made toolbars are at the bottom of the list), and click the Delete button. Click OK when Word asks if you really want to go through with it.

Correcting Typos on the Fly

Unless you or someone else has messed with the AutoCorrect settings, the invisible hand of Word corrects certain typos as you enter them. Try misspelling *weird* by typing *wierd* to see what happens. Try entering two hyphens (- -) and you get an em dash (—). You can have Word correct the typos that you make often, and with a little cunning, you can even use the AutoCorrect feature to enter long company names and hard-to-spell names on the fly.

To change the settings and make AutoCorrect work for you, choose Tools⇨AutoCorrect. The AutoCorrect dialog box appears (see Figure 8-8).

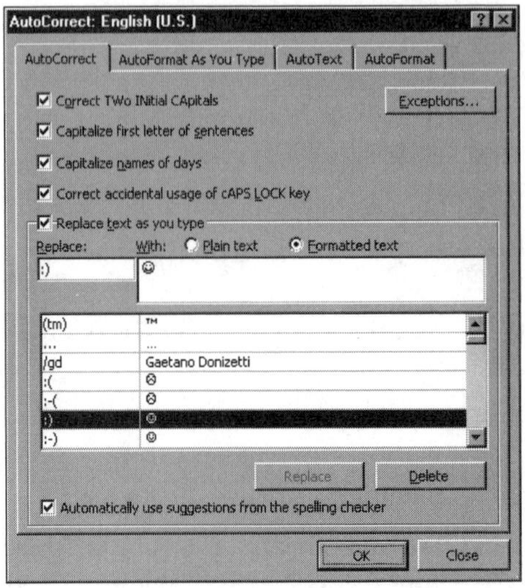

Figure 8-8:
The
AutoCorrect
dialog box.

AutoCorrect: English (U.S.)

AutoCorrect | AutoFormat As You Type | AutoText | AutoFormat

☑ Correct TWo INitial CApitals   Exceptions...
☑ Capitalize first letter of sentences
☑ Capitalize names of days
☑ Correct accidental usage of cAPS LOCK key
☑ Replace text as you type
Replace: With: ○ Plain text   ⦿ Formatted text
:)   ☺

(tm)   ™
...   ...
/gd   Gaetano Donizetti
:(☹
:-(☹
:)   ☺
:-)   ☺

            Replace   Delete

☑ Automatically use suggestions from the spelling checker

            OK   Close

+ Remove the check marks from the AutoCorrect features that you don't want. For example, if you enter a lot of computer code in your manuscripts, you don't necessarily want the first letter of sentences to be capitalized automatically, so you should click the Capitalize First Letter of Sentences check box to deselect it.

+ If you want, remove the check mark from the Replace Text as You Type box to keep Word's invisible hand from correcting idiosyncrasies in capitalization and spelling as you enter them.

+ Scroll through the list and take a look at the words that are "autocorrected." If you don't want a word on the list to be corrected, select it and click Delete.

+ If a word that you often misspell isn't on the list, you can add it to the list and have Word correct it automatically. Enter the misspelling in the Replace box, enter the right spelling in the With box, and click the Add button.

+ If you don't like one of the replacement words, select the word on the list, enter a new replacement word in the With box, and click the Replace button.

The Spelling dialog box has an AutoCorrect option. Choose it when you're spell-checking a document to add the word you're correcting to the list of words that are "autocorrected." The AutoCorrect choice also appears on the shortcut menu when you right-click a misspelled word. Choose AutoCorrect on the shortcut menu and choose a correct spelling to add the misspelling to the family of words that get corrected automatically.

Repeating an Action — and Quicker This Time

The Edit menu has a command called Repeat that you can choose to repeat your last action, and it can be a mighty time-saver. The command changes names, depending on what you did last.

For example, if you just changed a heading style, the command is called Edit⇨Repeat Style. To change another heading in the same way, move the cursor to the heading and choose Edit⇨Repeat Style (or press F4 or Ctrl+Y) instead of going to the trouble of clicking the Style menu and choosing a heading style from the drop-down list.

If you had to type "I will not talk in class" a hundred times, all you would have to do is write it once and choose Edit⇨Repeat Typing (or press F4 or Ctrl+Y) 99 times.

 Similar to the Edit⇨Repeat command is the Redo button. It "redoes" the commands you "undid" with the Undo menu or Undo button. If you've "undone" a bunch of commands and regret having done so, pull down the Redo menu by clicking its down arrow and choose the commands you thoughtlessly "undid" the first time around.

Going Here, Going There in Documents

Word offers three very speedy techniques for jumping around in documents: the Select Browse Object button, the Edit⇨Go To command, and the document map.

"Browsing" around a document

A really fast way to move around quickly is to click the Select Browse Object button in the lower-right corner of the screen. When you click this button, Word presents ten "Browse by" icons (see Figure 8-9).

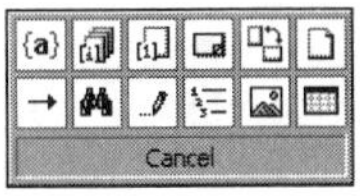

Figure 8-9:
Choose your method of browsing.

Cancel

Select the icon that represents the element you want to go to, and Word takes you there immediately. For example, click the Browse by Heading icon to get to the next heading in your document (provided that you assigned a heading style to the heading). After you have selected a "Browse by" icon, the navigator buttons — the double-arrows directly above and below the Select Browse Object button — turn blue. Click a blue navigator button to get to the next example or the previous example of the element you chose. For example, if you selected the Browse by Heading icon, all you have to do is click blue navigator buttons to get from heading to heading backwards or forwards in a document.

Going there fast

Another fast way to go from place to place in a document is to use the Edit⇨ Go To command. Choose this command or press Ctrl+G to see the Go To tab of the Find and Replace dialog box (see Figure 8-10).

Figure 8-10:
The Find
and
Replace
dialog box
with the Go
To tab
selected.

Find and Replace

| Find | Replace | Go To |

Go to what:

Bookmark
Comment
Footnote
Endnote
Field
Table
Graphic

Enter footnote number:

29

Enter + and − to move relative to the current location. Example: +4 will move forward four items.

Previous   Go To   Close

The Go to What menu in this dialog box lists everything that can conceivably be numbered in a Word document, and other things, too. Everything that you can get to with the Select Browse Object button, as well as lines, equations, and objects, can be reached by way of the Go To tab. Click a menu item and enter a number or choose an item from the drop-down list to go elsewhere.

Click the Previous button to go back to the footnote, endnote, comment, line, or whatever you just came from. You can press + or − and enter numbers to go backward or forward by one or several numbered items at once.

Hopping from place to place

Yet another way to hop from place to place is by turning on the document map. To do so, click the Document Map button or choose View⇨Document Map (as shown in Figure 8-11). Everything in the document that hasn't been assigned the Normal style — headings, captions, and so on — appears along the left side of the screen.

By placing the pointer on the text that doesn't fit on-screen, you can read it. Click the heading, caption, or whatever that you want to go to, and Word takes you there in the twinkling of an eye. Right-click the document map and choose a heading level option from the shortcut menu to tell Word which headings to display in the map. To put away the document map and see only the document on-screen, click the Document Map button again.

Figure 8-11:
View your
document's
structure at
a glance.

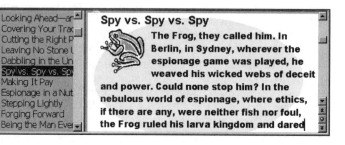

Looking Ahead—ar
Covering Your Trac
Cutting the Right P
Leaving No Stone l
Dabbling in the Un
Spy vs. Spy vs. Spy
Making It Pay
Espionage in a Nut
Stepping Lightly
Forging Forward
Being the Man Ever

Spy vs. Spy vs. Spy

The Frog, they called him. In Berlin, in Sydney, wherever the espionage game was played, he weaved his wicked webs of deceit and power. Could none stop him? In the nebulous world of espionage, where ethics, if there are any, were neither fish nor foul, the Frog ruled his larva kingdom and dared

Bookmarks for hopping around

Instead of pressing PgUp or PgDn or clicking the scrollbar to thrash around in a long document, you can use bookmarks. All you do is put a bookmark in an important spot in your document that you'll return to many times.

1. **Click where you want the bookmark to go.**

2. **Choose Insert⇨Bookmark (or press Ctrl+Shift+F5) to go to the Bookmark dialog box, shown in Figure 8-12.**

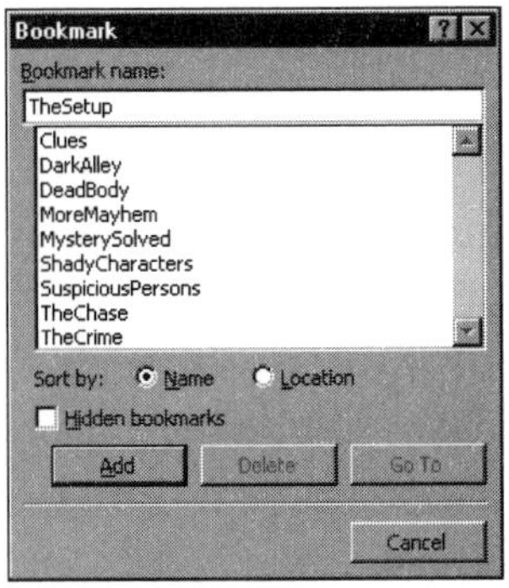

Figure 8-12:
The
Bookmark
dialog box.

3. **Type a descriptive name in the Bookmark Name box.**

You cannot include spaces in bookmark names.

4. **Click the Add button.**

To go to a bookmark:

1. **Choose Insert⇨Bookmark (or press Ctrl+Shift+F5).**

2. **Double-click the bookmark or select it and click the Go To button.**

3. **Click Cancel or press Esc.**

You can arrange bookmarks in the list in alphabetical order or by location in the document by choosing Name or Location at the bottom of the Bookmark dialog box. Click the Hidden bookmarks check box to see cross-references in the Bookmark Name box, although hidden bookmarks appear as code and don't tell you much about what they are or where they are in the document.

To delete a bookmark, select it in the Bookmark dialog box and click the Delete button.

Entering Graphics and Text Quickly

Put the text and graphics that you often use on the Insert⇨AutoText list. That way, you can enter the text or graphics simply by clicking a few menu commands or by choosing names from a toolbar. Addresses, letterheads, and company logos are ideal candidates for the AutoText list because they take so long to enter.

Creating your own AutoText entries

Follow these steps to create an AutoText entry:

1. **Type the text or import the graphic.**

2. **Select the text or graphic.**

3. **Choose Insert⇨AutoText⇨New or press Alt+F3.**

   The Create AutoText dialog box appears (as shown in Figure 8-13).

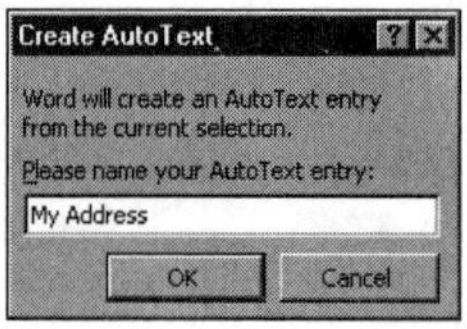

Figure 8-13:
The Create
AutoText
dialog box.

4. **Type a name for the text or graphic in the text box and click OK.**

Inserting an AutoText entry

The fastest way to insert an AutoText entry is to place the cursor where you want it to go and start typing the entry's name. Midway through, a bubble appears with the entire entry. Press Enter at that point to insert the whole thing.

Another speedy way to insert AutoText entries is to type the entry's name and then press F3.

AutoText entries that you create yourself appear on the Normal submenu. Follow these steps to insert one of your own AutoText entries or one that comes with Word:

1. **Place the cursor where you want the text or graphic to appear.**

2. **Choose Insert⇨AutoText⇨Normal and select an entry, or choose an entry from one of the submenus below Normal.**

To delete an AutoText entry, choose Insert⇨AutoText⇨AutoText to open the AutoCorrect dialog box, click the AutoText tab, click the entry that you want to delete, and click the Delete button.

Those yellow AutoText bubbles can be very annoying. They pop up in the oddest places. Try typing the name of a month, for example, to see what happens. To keep the bubbles from appearing, choose Insert⇨AutoText⇨ AutoText and click to remove the check mark from the Show AutoComplete Tip for AutoText and Dates check box.

Chapter 9: Getting Really Organized

*I*f you are working on a document that is more than one page long, you may notice that keeping track of your document's structure begins to become a bit more difficult. And if you are composing your masterpiece novel or your Ph.D. dissertation on *The Guardians in the 'Roman de la Rose' of Guillaume do Lorris and Jean de Meun,* you soon discover that you can use some serious help with organization!

Word 2000 not only outlines your work for you, it can also make it possible for you to work on long documents — and even on a group of documents — without you losing your place or giving up in frustration.

Outlines for Organizing Your Work

Outline view is a great way to see at a glance how your document is organized and whether you need to organize it differently. To take advantage of this feature, you must have used the Style menu to assign heading levels to the headings in your document. (See Chapter 6 for info on applying styles.) In Outline view, you can see all the headings in your document. If a section is in the wrong place, you can move it simply by dragging an icon or by pressing one of the buttons on the Outline toolbar.

To see a document in Outline view, choose View⇨Outline or click the Outline View button in the lower-left corner of the screen. Figure 9-1 is a sample document in Outline view with the All button selected to show all the headings and the normal text in paragraphs.

To change how much of a document you see in Outline view:

◆ **Headings:** Click a Show Heading button (1 through 7) to see different heading levels.

◆ **All:** Click the All button to see the whole show.

◆ **Headings in one section:** If you want to see the headings and text in only one section of a document, choose that section by clicking the plus sign beside it and then click the Expand button. Click the Collapse button after you're done.

◆ **Normal text:** Click the Show First Line Only button to see only the first line in each paragraph. First lines are followed by an ellipsis (. . .) so that you know that more text follows.

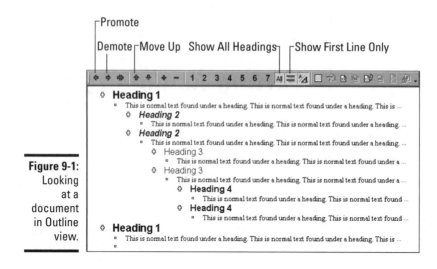

Figure 9-1:
Looking
at a
document
in Outline
view.

Notice the plus icons and square icons next to the headings and the text. A plus icon means that the heading has subtext under it. For example, headings almost always have plus icons because text comes after them, but body text has a square icon because it is lowest on the Outline totem pole.

To select text in Outline view, click either the plus sign or the square icon. To select more than one section, Shift+click its icon. After the text has been selected, you can do the following tasks:

+ **Promote a head:** Click the Promote button to move a heading up the ladder. For example, you can promote a Heading 2 to a Heading 1.

+ **Demote a head:** Click the Demote button to bust down a Heading 1 to a Heading 2, for example. When you promote or demote a head or section, you do the same to all the subtext beneath it.

+ **Make a head into normal text:** Click the Demote to Body Text button to make a heading into text.

+ **Move a section:** To move a section up or down in the document, click the Move Up or Move Down button. You can also drag the plus sign or square icon to a new location. If you want to move the subordinate text and headings along with the section, click the Collapse button to tuck all the subtext into the heading before you move it.

Linking Documents to Make Your Work Easier

You can save a lot of time and effort by connecting two documents so that changes made to the first are made automatically to the second. This process is called *linking*. If a table in a memo you're working on happens to be useful in an annual report as well, you can link the documents, and updates to the table in the memo will show up in the annual report as well. Word offers two kinds of links, automatic and manual:

✦ With an *automatic link,* changes made to the original document are made in the linked document as well each time you reopen the linked document. Text is displayed in full in your document if the link is automatic.

✦ With a *manual link,* you have to tell Word to update the link. Manual links are represented in the text by an icon. The text or graphic in the original file doesn't appear in your document.

Creating a link

Before you create a link between documents, ask yourself whether either document is likely to be moved out of the folder where it is now. Links are broken when documents are moved. Although you can reestablish a link, doing so is a chore. The better strategy is to plan ahead and link only documents that are not going to be moved to different folders. Follow these steps to create an automatic link between documents:

Word
Chapter 9

Getting Really
Organized

1. **Open the document with the text you want to link.**

2. **Select the text and copy it to the Clipboard by clicking the Copy button, pressing Ctrl+C, or choosing Edit⇨Copy.**

3. **Switch to the document where the linked text is to be pasted and put the cursor where you want the text to go.**

4. **Choose Edit⇨Paste Special.**

   The Paste Special dialog box appears (see Figure 9-2).

5. **Click the Paste Link radio button.**

6. **Under As, choose Formatted Text (RTF) or Unformatted Text; otherwise, if the thing being linked is not text, choose another option.**

7. **Click OK.**

Figure 9-2:
Get ready
to link with
the Paste
Special
dialog box.

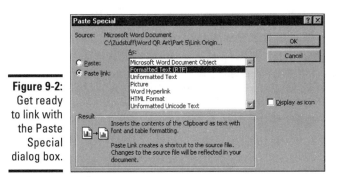

Updating, breaking, and changing links

With an automatic link, changes made to the original document are made to the linked document whenever the linked document is reopened. With manual links, however, you have to tell Word to update the link. To update a link — and do other things besides — go to the Links dialog box:

1. **Choose Edit⇨Links.**

2. **In the Links dialog box (shown in Figure 9-3), select the link you want to update.**

Be sure to look at the Source File listing at the bottom of the dialog box to make sure that you're updating the right link.

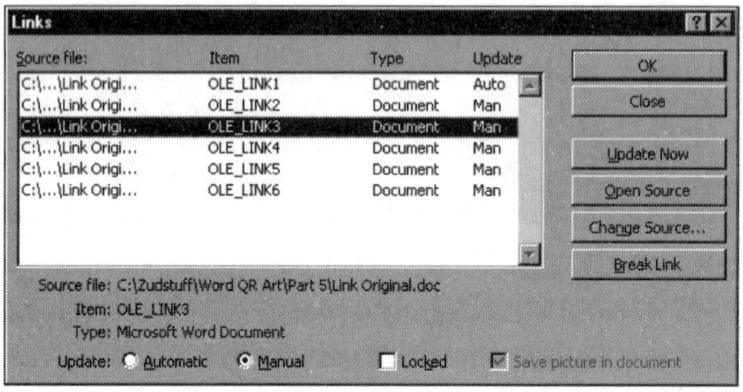

Source file:	Item	Type	Update	
C:\...\Link Origi...	OLE_LINK1	Document	Auto	OK
C:\...\Link Origi...	OLE_LINK2	Document	Man	Close
C:\...\Link Origi...	OLE_LINK3	Document	Man	
C:\...\Link Origi...	OLE_LINK4	Document	Man	Update Now
C:\...\Link Origi...	OLE_LINK5	Document	Man	Open Source
C:\...\Link Origi...	OLE_LINK6	Document	Man	Change Source...
				Break Link

Source file: C:\2udstuff\Word QR Art\Part 5\Link Original.doc
Item: OLE_LINK3
Type: Microsoft Word Document
Update: ○ Automatic ● Manual   ☐ Locked ☑ Save picture in document

Figure 9-3:
Telling
Word to
update a
link.

3. **Click the Update Now button.**

4. **Click OK.**

You can update several links at the same time by Ctrl+clicking the links before you click the Update Now button.

The Links dialog box offers several more buttons and check boxes for handling links:

✦ **Open Source:** Opens the original document so that you can make changes to text.

✦ **Change Source:** If you move the original document to another folder, Word doesn't know where to look for the document that contains the original text. Click this button to open the Change Source dialog box. Then find the original document and click Open. The link is re-established.

✦ **Break Link:** Severs the tie between the original document and the document with the link in it. Once you click this button, the link is broken, and you can't get it back.

✦ **Automatic:** Click this option button to change the link to an automatic link.

✦ **Manual:** Click to change the link to a manual link.

✦ **Locked:** Makes it so that updates to the original document don't affect the linked document. Choose this option instead of Break Link if you want to break the link but still be able to go to the original document if you have to.

✦ **Save Picture in Document:** Saves a graphic in your document instead of a link to the graphic. Uncheck this check box to a store a link to the graphic.

Suppose that you're in the linked document and you realize that you need to change the original text. If the link is a manual one, all you have to do is double-click the Microsoft Word Document icon to get to the original text. With an automatic link, choose Edit⇨Linked Document Object⇨Open Link, or right-click and choose Linked Document Object⇨Open Link from the shortcut menu.

To make sure that all links are updated before you print documents, choose Tools⇨Options, click the Print tab, and click the Update Links check box.

Chapter 10: Constructing the Perfect Table

In This Chapter

- ✓ Creating and modifying a table
- ✓ Sorting and reordering a table
- ✓ Formatting a table
- ✓ Repeating headers across pages
- ✓ Merging and splitting cells
- ✓ Using math formulas

The time will come when you need to put text into little boxes that are organized into columns and row. Yes, we're talking about tables here. As everyone who has ever worked on one knows, tables are a chore. Getting all the columns to fit, making columns and rows the right width and height, and editing text in a table is not easy. So problematic are tables that Word 2000 has devoted an entire menu to constructing them: the Table menu. Fortunately for you, the commands on this menu make formatting and working with tables easy.

This chapter explains how to create tables, enter text into tables, change the number and size of columns and rows, sort tables, and format tables.

Constructing the Perfect Table

Like so much else in Computerland, tables have their own jargon. A *cell* is the box that is formed where a row and column intersect. Each cell holds one data item. The *header row* is the name of the labels along the top row that explain what is in the columns below. *Borders* are the lines in the table. The *gridlines* are the gray lines that show where the columns and rows are. Gridlines are not printed — they appear to help you format your table. (Choose Table⇨Show Gridlines or Table⇨ Hide Gridlines to display or hide them.) Word prints only the borders when you print a table. A sample table is shown in Figure 10-1.

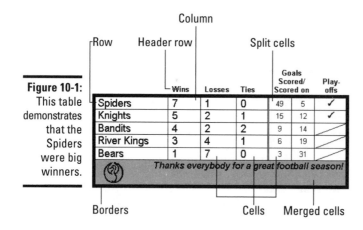

Figure 10-1:
This table
demonstrates
that the
Spiders
were big
winners.

Creating a table

Word offers no less than four ways to create the cells and rows for a table: the Insert Table button, the Draw Table button, the Table⇔Insert⇔Table command, and the Table⇔Convert⇔Text to Table command.

The fastest way to create a table is to click the Insert Table button on the Standard toolbar:

1. **Place the cursor where you want the table to go.**

2. **Click the Insert Table button, drag out the menu to the number of rows and columns you want, and let go of the mouse button.**

That's easy enough. Another easy way is to make like your computer is a scratch pad and draw a table. This is the way to create a table if you want rows and columns of different widths and heights.

1. **To draw a table, choose Table⇔Draw Table or click the Draw Table button on the Tables and Borders toolbar.**

Choose a thick line from the Line Weight menu on the toolbar to see the lines better as you draw them. The pointer changes into a pencil. By the way, you can click the Tables and Borders button on the Standard toolbar to display the Tables and Border toolbar.

2. **Start drawing.**

As you drag the pencil on-screen, you get columns and rows.

3. **If you make a mistake, click the Eraser button on the Tables and Border toolbar.**

   The pointer changes into an eraser. Drag it over the parts of the table you regret drawing.

4. **After you're finished drawing the table, click the Draw Table button to put the pencil away.**

Here's another way to create a table:

1. **Place the cursor where you want the table to be.**

2. **Choose Table⇨Insert⇨Table. The Insert Table dialog box appears.**

3. **In the Number of Columns box, enter the number of columns you want.**

4. **In the Number of Rows box, enter the number of rows you want.**

5. **Under AutoFit Behavior, you can enter a measurement in the Fixed Column Width text box to make all columns the same width. (The Auto setting creates columns of equal width and stretches the table so that it fits across the page between the left and right margin.)**

6. **Click the AutoFormat button to open a dialog box from which you can choose one of Word's table formats.**

7. **Click OK.**

The fourth way to create a table is to convert text that you've already entered. This is the way to go if you've created a list and you don't want to go to the trouble of re-entering the text all over again for the new table. To convert text into a table:

1. **Either press Tab or enter a comma in the list where you want columns to be divided.**

   For example, if you are turning an address list into a table, put each name and address on one line and press Tab or enter a comma after the first name, the last name, the street address, the city, the state, and the zip code. For this feature to work, each name and address — each line — must have the same number of tab spaces or commas in it.

2. **Start a new paragraph — press Enter, that is — where you want each row to end.**

3. **Select the text you want to turn in a table.**

4. **Choose Table⇨Convert⇨Text to Table.**

5. **Under Separate Text At in the Convert Text to Table dialog box, choose Tabs or Commas to tell Word how the columns are separated.**

6. **Choose an AutoFit Behavior option, if you want.**

7. **Click OK.**

In this illustration, five tab stops were entered on each line in an address list. Below the list is the table that was created from the address list.

Word Chapter 10

Constructing the Perfect Table

Roger Wilco	1227 Jersey St.	San Francisco	CA	94114	415/555-3424
Dane Bergard	2234 Pax St.	Pacifica	CA	93303	415/555-2341
J.S. Minnow	10 Taylor St.	Daly City	CA	94404	415/555-9843

Roger Wilco	1227 Jersey St.	San Francisco	CA	94114	415/555-3424
Dane Bergard	2234 Pax St.	Pacifica	CA	93303	415/555-2341
J.S. Minnow	10 Taylor St.	Daly City	CA	94404	415/555-9843

Entering text and numbers in a table

After you've created the table, you can start entering text. All you have to do is click in a cell and start typing. If you need to add a row at the bottom of the table to enter more text, place the cursor in the last column of the last row and press the Tab key.

Changing the layout of a table

Very likely, you created too many or too few rows or columns for your table. Some columns are probably too wide, and others may be too narrow. If that is the case, you have to change the layout of the table by deleting, inserting, and changing the size of columns and rows. (Putting borders around tables and embellishing them in other ways is explained later in this chapter.)

Modifying Different Parts of a Table

Before you can fool with cells, rows, or columns, you have to select them:

✦ **Cells:** To select a cell, click in it. You can select several cells at once by dragging the cursor over them.

✦ **Rows:** Place the cursor in the left margin and click to select one row, or click and drag to select several rows. You can also select rows by placing the cursor in the row you want to select and then choosing the Table⇨Select⇨Row command. To select several rows, select cells in the rows and then choose Table⇨Select⇨Row command.

✦ **Columns:** To select a column, move the cursor to the top of the column. When the cursor changes into a fat down-pointing arrow, click once. You can click and drag to select several columns. The other way to select a column is to click anywhere in the column and choose Table⇨Select⇨Column. To select several columns with this command, select cells in the columns before giving the Select command.

✦ **A table:** To select a table, click in the table and choose Table⇨Select⇨Table; hold down the Alt key and double-click; or press Alt+5 (the 5 on the numeric keypad, not the one on the keyboard).

Inserting and deleting columns and rows

Here's the lowdown on inserting and deleting columns and rows:

✦ **Inserting columns:** To insert a blank column, select the column to the right of where you want the new column to go. If you want to insert two or more columns, select the number of columns you want to add. Then right-click and choose Insert Columns, or choose Table⇨Insert⇨Columns to the Left (or Columns to the Right).

✦ **Deleting columns:** To delete columns, select them. Then choose Table⇨ Delete⇨Columns, or right-click and choose Delete Columns. (Pressing the Delete key deletes the data in the column.)

✦ **Inserting rows:** To insert a blank row, select the row below which you want the new one to appear. If you want to insert more than one row, select more than one. Then right-click and choose Insert Rows, or choose Table⇨Insert⇨ Rows Above (or Rows Below). You can also insert a row at the end of a table by moving the cursor into the last cell in the last row and pressing Tab.

✦ **Deleting rows:** To delete rows, select them and choose Table⇨Delete⇨Rows, or right-click and choose Delete Rows from the shortcut menu. (Pressing the Delete key deletes the data in the row.)

Moving columns and rows

Because there is no elegant way to move a column or row, you should move only one at a time. If you try to move several at once, you open a can of worms that is best left unopened. To move a column or row:

1. **Select the column or row you want to move.**

2. **Right-click in the selection and choose Cut from the shortcut menu. The column or row disappears to the Clipboard.**

3. **Move the column or row:**

• **Column:** Click in the topmost cell in the column to the right of where you want to move the column. In other words, to make what is now column 4 column 2, cut column 4 and click in the topmost cell of column 2. Then right-click and choose Paste Columns from the shortcut menu.

• **Row:** Move the cursor into the first column of the row below which you want to move your row. In other words, if you're placing the row between what are now rows 6 and 7, put the cursor in row 7. Then right-click and choose Paste Rows from the shortcut menu.

Resizing columns and rows

The fastest way to adjust the width of columns and the height of rows is to "eyeball it." To make a column wider or narrower, move the cursor onto a gridline or border. When the cursor changes into a double-headed arrow, start dragging. Tug and pull, tug and pull until the column is the right width or the row is the right height. You can also slide the column bars on the ruler or the rows bars on the vertical ruler (if you're in Print Layout View) to change the width of columns and height of rows.

Word
Chapter 10

Constructing the
Perfect Table

Because resizing columns and rows can be problematic, Word offers these commands on the Table➪AutoFit submenu for adjusting the width and height of rows and columns:

+ **AutoFit to Contents:** Makes each column wide enough to accommodate its widest entry.

+ **AutoFit to Window:** Stretches the table so that it fits across the page between the left and right margin.

+ **Fixed Column Width**: Fixes the column widths at their current settings.

+ **Distribute Rows Evenly:** Makes all rows the same height as the tallest row. You can also click the Distribute Rows Evenly button on the Tables and Borders toolbar. Select rows before giving this command to make the command affect only the rows you selected.

+ **Distribute Columns Evenly:** Makes all columns the same width. You can also click the Distribute Columns Evenly button. Select columns before giving this command if you want to change the size of a few rows, not all the rows in the table.

Aligning text in columns and rows

The easiest way to align text in the columns or cells is to rely on the Align Left, Center, Align Right, and Justify buttons on the Standard toolbar. Select a cell, a column, or columns and click one of those buttons to align the text in a column the same way.

Sorting, or Reordering, a Table

The fastest way to rearrange the rows in a table is to use the Table➪Sort command or click one of the Sort buttons on the Tables and Borders toolbar. *Sorting* means to rearrange all the rows in a table on the basis of data in one column. For example, the first table shown in Figure 10-2 is arranged, or sorted, on the fifth column, "Total Votes." This column has been sorted in *descending* order from most to fewest votes. The second table has been sorted on the first column. It is sorted by the candidates' names in *ascending* order alphabetically. Both tables present the same information, but the information has been sorted in different ways.

	1st Ward	2nd Ward	3rd Ward	Total Votes
Muñoz	2,567	7,399	10,420	20,386
Wilson	3,113	9,907	4,872	17,892
Teel	67	211	89	367
Greenstein	12	2	113	127

	1st Ward	2nd Ward	3rd Ward	Total Votes
Greenstein	12	2	113	127
Muñoz	2,567	7,399	10,420	20,386
Teel	67	211	89	367
Wilson	3,113	9,907	4,872	17,892

Figure 10-2: Two tables sorted differently.

The difference between ascending and descending sorts is as follows:

+ Ascending arranges text from A to Z, numbers from smallest to largest, and dates from the oldest in time to the most recent.

+ Descending arranges text from Z to A, numbers from largest to smallest, and dates from most recent to the oldest in time.

When you rearrange a table by sorting it, Word rearranges the formatting as well as the data. Do your sorting before you format the table.

For simple sorts, select the column that is to be the basis of the sort and click the Sort Descending button on the Tables and Borders toolbar for a descending sort or the Sort Ascending button for an ascending sort. You can also select a column and choose Table➪Sort, click the Ascending or Descending radio button in the Sort dialog box, and click OK.

Dressing Up Your Table

After you enter the text, put the rows and columns in place, and make them the right size, the fun begins. Now you can dress up your table and make it look snazzy.

Almost everything you can do to a document you can do to a table by selecting parts of it and choosing menu commands or clicking buttons. You can change text fonts, align data in the cells in different ways, and even import a graphic into a cell. You can also play with the borders that divide the rows and columns and "shade" columns, rows, and cells by filling them with gray shades or a black background. Read on to find out how to do these tricks and also how to center a table or align it with the right page margin.

Formatting a table with Word's AutoFormats

The fastest way to get a good-looking table is to let Word do the work for you:

1. **Click your table.**

2. **Choose Table➪Table AutoFormat. The Table AutoFormat dialog box appears, as shown in Figure 10-3.**

3. **Rummage through the Formats menu until you find a table to your liking.**

You can see what tables look like in the Preview box.

4. **Check and uncheck the Formats to Apply and Apply Special Formats To check boxes.**

As you do so, watch the Preview box to see what your choices do.

5. **When you have the right table format, click OK.**

Getting your own borders, shading, and color

Instead of relying on Word's Table➪Table AutoFormat command, you can draw borders yourself and shade or give color to different parts of a table as well. Doing so by means of the Tables and Borders toolbar is easier than you might think.

Watch this box!

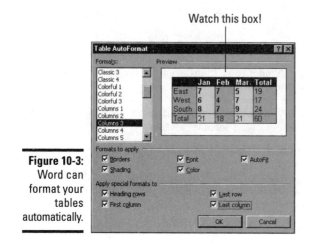

Figure 10-3:
Word can
format your
tables
automatically.

Click the Tables and Borders button on the Standard toolbar to display the Tables and Borders toolbar (see Figure 10-4) and then follow these steps to decorate a table with borders, shading, and color.

1. **Select the part of the table that you want to decorate.**

For example, to put a border along the top or bottom of a row, select the row; to shade two columns, select them.

Borders menu ─┐ ┌─Border Color button

Line Weight menu ─┐   Borders button   Shading Color menu

Line Style menu   Shading Color button

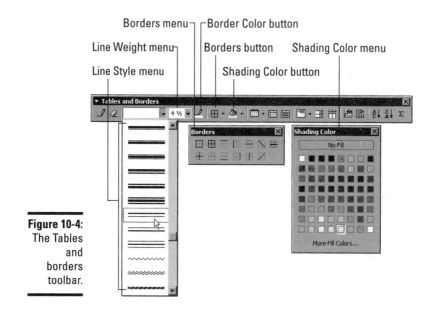

Figure 10-4:
The Tables
and
borders
toolbar.

2. **Use the tools on the Tables and Borders toolbar to decorate your table:**

- **Choosing lines for borders:** Click the down arrow beside the Line Style button and choose a line, dashed line, double line, or wiggly line for the border. (Choose No Border if you don't want a border or you are removing one that is already there.) Then click the down arrow beside the Line Weight button to choose a line width for the border.

- **Choosing line colors:** Click the Border Color button and click one of the color boxes on the menu. Use the Automatic choice to remove colors and gray shades.

- **Drawing the border lines:** Click the down arrow beside the Border button and choose one of the border buttons on the menu. (Click No Border to remove borders.) For example, click the Top Border button to put a border along the top of the part of the table you selected in Step 1; click the Inside Border button to put the border on the interior lines of the part of the table you selected.

- **Shading or giving a color background to table cells:** Click the down arrow on the Shading Color menu and click one of the color or gray-shade buttons.

After you make a choice from a menu on the Tables and Borders toolbar, the choice you made appears on the button that is used to open the menu. Choose Blue on the Shading Color menu, for example, and the Shading Color button turns blue. If the choice you want to make from a menu happens to be the last choice you made, you can click the button instead of opening the menu. To make a blue background show in a table, for example, you can simply click the Shading Color button as long as the Shading Color button is blue.

Constructing the Perfect Table

Merging and Splitting Cells and Tables

The cells in the second row in this small table have been merged to create one large cell. Where the first and third row have six cells, the second has only one.

1993	1994	1995	1996	1997	1998
Sammy Sosa's Homeruns					
19	27	44	39	53	64

To merge cells in a table:

1. **Select the cells you want to merge.**

2. **Choose Table⇨Merge Cells or click the Merge Cells button on the Tables and Borders toolbar.**

In the same vein, you can split a cell into two or more cells:

1. **Click in the cell you want to split.**

2. Choose Table⇨Split Cells or click the Split Cells button on the Tables and Borders toolbars.

3. In the Split Cells dialog box, declare how many cells you want to split the cell into and click OK.

Still in the same vein, you can split a table as well:

1. Place the cursor in what you want to be the first row of the new table.

2. Choose Table⇨Split Table.

Using Math Formulas in Tables

No, you don't have to add the figures in columns and rows yourself; Word gladly does that for you. Word can perform other mathematical calculations as well.

To total the figures in a column or row, place the cursor in the cell that is to hold the total and click the AutoSum button on the Tables and Borders toolbar.

The AutoSum button, however, is only good for adding figures. To perform other mathematical calculations and tell Word how to format sums and products:

1. Put the cursor in the cell that will hold the sum or product of the cells above, below, to the right, or to the left.

2. Choose Table⇨Formula.

The Formula dialog box appears (shown in Figure 10-5).

3. In its wisdom, Word makes a very educated guess about what you want the formula to do and places a formula in the Formula box. If this isn't the formula you want, delete everything except the equal sign in the Formula box, click the down arrow in the Paste Function box, and choose another formula. You may have to type left, right, above, or below in the parentheses beside the formula to tell Word where the figures that you want it to compute are.

4. In the Number Format box, click the down arrow and choose a format for your number.

5. Click OK.

Units Sold	Price Unit ($)	Total Sale
13	178.12	$2,315.56
15	179.33	$2,689.95
93	178.00	$16,554.00
31	671.13	
24	411.12	
9	69.13	
11	79.40	
$ 196.00	$1,766.23	

Formula   ? ✕

Formula:
| =PRODUCT(left) |

Number format:
| $#,##0.00;($#,##0.00) | ▼ |

Paste function: Paste bookmark:
| | ▼ | | | ▼ |

[OK] [Cancel]

Figure 10-5: The Formula dialog box.

Repeating header rows on subsequent pages

Your new table sure looks great — until you turn to the next page and can no longer see the column headings and can't tell which figures are your earnings and which figures are your debts. Making sure that the header row appears on a new page if the table breaks across pages is absolutely essential. Without a header row, readers can't tell what the information in a table is or means. To make the header row (or rows) repeat on the top of each new page, place the cursor in the header row (or select the header rows if you have more than one) and choose Table⇨Heading Rows Repeat. By the way, heading rows appear only in Print Layout view, so don't worry if you're in Normal view and you can't see them.

Word does not calculate blank cells in formulas. Enter a **0** in blank cells if you want them to be included in calculations. You can copy functions from one cell to another to save yourself the trouble of opening the Formula dialog box.

Chapter 11: Drawing and Inserting Things into Your Document

In This Chapter

↙ **Drawing lines and shapes**

↙ **Inserting pictures and graphics**

*Y*ou thought that you were just going to type plain old text and make some nice looking memos and reports in Word 2000, didn't you? Think again! Word 2000 is more than just the most expensive typewriter that you have ever purchased. Why not put that money to good use and take advantage of the desktop publishing capabilities in Word? With a little effort, you can go from memos and reports to neat newsletters and fancy brochures. (Or you can at least have the nicest looking memos and reports around!)

This chapter shows you how you can insert pictures, borders, charts, and anything else you can think of into documents that are sure to impress your friends and neighbors — unless you slip up and reveal to them just how easy it is.

Drawing Lines and Shapes

The Drawing toolbar offers many opportunities for decorating documents and Web pages with lines, lines with arrows on the end, shapes such as ovals and rectangles, and what Word calls *autoshapes* — stars, banners, and various other artistic tidbits. You can even create shadow backgrounds and 3-D effects for shapes. Figure 11-1 shows some of the things you can do with the buttons and menus on the Drawing toolbar.

Follow these steps to draw lines and shapes:

> Draw ▾

1. **Display the Drawing toolbar. To do so, click the Drawing button on the Standard toolbar, or right-click a toolbar and choose Drawing from the shortcut menu.**

2. **Click the appropriate button on the Drawing toolbar and then drag the pointer across the screen to draw the line or shape.**

See Chapter 12 to find out how to shrink or enlarge lines and shapes, move them, fill them with color, and change the width of lines on their borders.

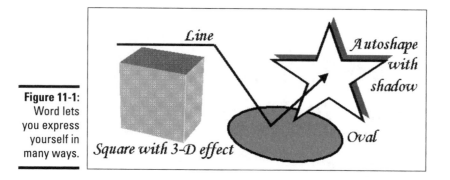
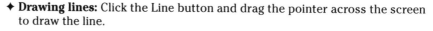

Figure 11-1:
Word lets
you express
yourself in
many ways.

Here are the specifics of drawing lines and shapes:

✦ **Drawing lines:** Click the Line button and drag the pointer across the screen to draw the line.

✦ **Drawing arrows on lines:** Start by clicking the Line or Arrow button and drawing a line. To choose an arrow style of your own, select the line by clicking it, click the Arrow Style button, and choose a style from the pop-up menu. Choose More Arrows from the pop-up menu to go to the Format AutoShape dialog box and select different arrows or different-size arrows for either side of the line.

✦ **Drawing rectangles and ovals:** Click the Rectangle or Oval button and drag the cursor across the screen to draw the rectangle or oval. Hold down the Shift key as you drag to draw a square or circle.

✦ **Drawing an autoshape:** Click the AutoShapes button, move the pointer over a submenu, and click a shape. Then drag the cursor across the screen to draw it. A yellow diamond appears beside some autoshapes so that you can adjust their appearance. Drag the yellow diamond to make the autoshape look just right. The AutoShapes submenus offer many different shapes.

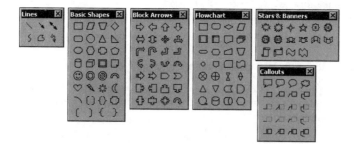

✦ **Putting shadows and three-dimensional effects on shapes:** Click a shape, click the Shadow or 3-D button, and choose shadow style or 3-D effect from the pop-up menu. Choose No Shadow or No 3-D to remove shadows and third dimensions.

Inserting Pictures and Graphics into Documents

If you keep clip art on your computer, and as long as the Word 2000 CD is sitting in your CD-ROM drive, you have a golden opportunity to embellish your documents with art created by genuine artists. You don't have to tell anyone where this art came from, either, as long as you are a good liar.

This entry explains how to insert a clip art image, change its resolutions, and crop it. See Chapter 12 to find out how to move and change the size and shape of a clip art image, put borders and color shades on it, or wrap text around it.

Inserting a clip art image

Before you insert a clip art image, make sure that the Word 2000 CD is loaded in your computer. Word gets images from the CD. Then follow these steps to insert a clip art image:

1. **Click in the paragraph that you want the image to be attached to.**

As the paragraph moves from page to page during editing, so will your image, so choose a paragraph carefully.

2. **Click the Insert Clip Art button on the Drawing toolbar or choose Insert⇨Picture⇨Clip Art.**

You see the Insert ClipArt dialog box, as shown in Figure 11-2.

3. **Find the clip art image that you want to insert.**

In the course of your search, you can click the Back or Forward button to retrace your steps or return to images you saw before.

**Word
Chapter 11**

**Drawing and
Inserting Things into
Your Document**

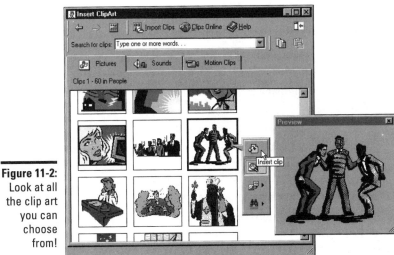

Figure 11-2:
Look at all
the clip art
you can
choose
from!

- **Search by keyword:** In the Search for Clips text box, type a word that describes what kind of clip art you want, and press Enter. You can choose a keyword from the drop-down list if you are re-enacting a keyword search that you made earlier.

- **Scroll to a category and select it:** Scroll through the category list and click a category that piques your interest. Click the All Categories button (or press Alt+Home) to see all the categories again if that proves necessary.

- **Scrounge images from the Internet:** Click the Clips Online button and follow the directions to go to the Microsoft Clip Gallery Live site. When you get there, either enter a keyword for the search or search by category from the Browse drop-down list. To download an image to your computer, check it off, click it, and then click its larger preview image. The image appears in the Insert ClipArt dialog box. Images scrounged from the Internet are kept in the Downloaded Clips category of the Insert ClipArt dialog box.

4. **When you find the image you want, click it.**

   A callout menu appears. You can click the Preview Clip button on the callout menu to get a better look at your images.

5. **Click the Insert Clip button to place the image in your document.**

You can insert a graphic by clicking the Insert Picture button on the Picture toolbar or by choosing Insert⇨Picture⇨From File and, in the Insert Picture dialog box, finding and double-clicking the name of the graphic file whose image you want to insert.

Experimenting with brightness, contrast, and appearance

After you insert an image, you can alter it a bit by experimenting with its brightness and contrast or by turning it into a grayscale or black-and-white image. Here's how:

1. **Click the image to select it.**

   You know that an image is selected when its square selection handles appear.

2. **Display the Picture toolbar and experiment with the different buttons:**

   - **Image Control:** Click the Image Control button and choose Grayscale to see the image in shades of gray, Black & White to see the *film noir* version, or Watermark to see a bleached-out image.

   - **More Contrast and Less Contrast:** These buttons either heighten or mute line and color distinctions.

   - **More Brightness and Less Brightness:** These buttons either lighten or darken the image.

To get the original picture back if you experiment too enthusiastically, either click the Reset Picture button on the Picture toolbar or click the Image Control button and choose Automatic.

You can also experiment with clip art images by clicking the Format Picture button on the Picture toolbar or by choosing Format⇨Picture. On the Picture tab of the Format Picture dialog box, choose an option from the Color menu or use the Brightness and Contrast sliders to alter your image. However, you can't see how good an artist you are until you click OK and view your image on-screen.

Cropping off part of a graphic

You can *crop* — that is, cut off parts of — a graphic, but not very elegantly. To do that, select a graphic and click the Crop button on the Picture toolbar. The pointer changes into an odd shape with two intersecting triangles on it. Move the pointer to a selection handle and start dragging. The dotted line tells you what part of a graphic you are cutting off. Sorry, you can crop off only the sides of a graphic. You can't cut a circle out of the middle, for example, proving once again that the computer will never replace that ancient and noble device, the scissors.

Working with text boxes

Put text in a text box when you want it to stand out on the page. Text boxes can be shaded, filled with color, and given borders. What's more, you can move one around at will on the page until it lands in the right place. To put a text box in a document, follow these steps:

1. **Choose Insert⇨Text Box.**

   The pointer turns into a cross.

2. **Click and drag to draw the text box.**

   Lines show you how big it will be when you release the mouse button.

3. **Release the mouse button.**

After you've inserted the text box, you can type text in it and call on all the formatting techniques in Word to boldface it, align it, or do what you will with it. You can still change the text box, too, even after you place it. Simply click on the text box in order to edit its text. Clicking a text box also makes its handles appear. Grab onto one of its handles and pull in any direction to change the size of the box.

Note: On the Text Box toolbar is a little toy called the Change Text Direction button. Click a text box and click this button to make the text in the text box change orientation.

Hello, this is a *text box* into which I am typing, uh, text. You can format text in a text box *any* way you want. So why not give a text box a try **today**?

Chapter 12: Doing Some Desktop Publishing

In This Chapter
- ✓ Handling inserted objects
- ✓ Creating text boxes
- ✓ Using WordArt
- ✓ Using borders and colors on objects

*A*fter you insert clip art or a chart in a document, don't think that you have to be satisfied with your handiwork. For you creative types, your job has just begun. Now you can expertly maneuver, manipulate, and even mess up your page layout just like those desktop publishers do day in and day out.

Handling Objects on Pages

After you place a clip art image, graphic, text box, line, shape, autoshape, or WordArt image in a document, it ceases being what it was before and becomes a mere object, at least as far as Word is concerned. That's good news, however, because the techniques for manipulating objects are the same. To move, reshape, draw borders around, fill in, lock in place, overlap, or wrap text around an object, use the techniques described on the following pages.

Selecting objects

Before you can do anything to an object, you have to select it. To do so, click the object. You can tell when an object has been selected because square *selection handles* appear on the sides and corners (in lines, only two selection handles appear, one on either side of the line). To select more than one object at the same time, hold down the Shift key and click the objects.

 When objects overlap, sometimes selecting one of them is difficult. To select an object that is stuck among other objects, click the Select Objects button on the Drawing toolbar and then click the object.

Moving and resizing graphics, text boxes, and other objects

Moving an object on a page is easy enough. All you have to do is click the graphic, text box, shape, or whatever, wait till you see the four-headed arrow, and click. Next, drag the pointer where you want the object to be on the page. Dotted lines show where you are moving the object. When the object is in the right position, release the mouse button. If you are moving a text box, place the pointer on the perimeter of the box to see the four-headed arrow.

If you can't move an object, it's because Word thinks that it is an inline image and shouldn't be moved. On the Picture toolbar, click the Text Wrapping button and click any button on the pop-up menu except Edit Wrap Points. See "Wrapping text around a text box, graphic, or other object" later in this chapter if you need to know how text wrapping works.

How you change an object's size depends on whether you want to keep its proportions:

✦ **Changing size but not proportions:** To change the size of an object but keep its proportions, click the object and move the cursor to one of the selection handles on the *corners*. The cursor changes into a double-headed arrow. Click and start dragging. Dotted lines show how you are changing the size of the frame. When it's the right size, release the mouse button.

✦ **Changing size and proportions:** To change both the size of an object *and* its proportions, move the cursor to a selection handle on the *side*. When the cursor changes into a double-headed arrow, click and start dragging. Dotted lines show how the object is being changed. When it is the size and shape you want, release the mouse button.

Figure 12-1 shows the same graphic at three different sizes. The original graphic is on the left. For the middle graphic, a corner selection handle was pulled to enlarge it but keep its proportions. For the one on the right, a selection handle on the side was pulled to enlarge it and change its proportions.

Figure 12-1:
A graphic manipulated by pulling on it.

If you want to get very specific about how big an object is, go to the Size tab of the Format dialog box. To do that, right-click the object, choose Format, and click the Size tab. Then enter measurements in the Height and Width boxes. Go this route if you want to make text boxes or graphics the same size, for example.

Locking objects in place

Suppose that you want an object such as a text box, WordArt image, or clip art image to stay in the same place. Normally, what is in the middle of page 1 is pushed to the bottom of the page or to page 2 when you insert paragraphs at the start of a document. What if you want the paragraph or graphic to stay put, come hell or high water? In that case, you can *lock* it to the page. After you lock it, text flows around your image or text box, but the image or text box stays put. Follow these steps to lock an object in place:

1. **Move the object to the position on the page where you want it to remain at all times.**

2. **Right-click or select the object, choose F̲ormat, and then choose the last command on the format menu. (The command is named after the kind of object you are working with.)**

3. **Click the Layout tab in the Format dialog box.**

4. **On the Layout tab, choose any Wrapping Style option; however, you can't choose I̲n Line with Text if the I̲n Line with Text option is selected.**

See "Wrapping text around a text box, graphic, or other object" later in this chapter to find out about text wrapping.

5. **Click the A̲dvanced button.**

6. **In the Advanced Layout dialog box (shown in Figure 12-2), click the Picture Position tab.**

7. **Click the Absolute Po̲sition option button under Vertical.**

8. **Click the L̲ock Anchor check box.**

9. **Click the M̲ove Object with Text check box to remove the check mark.**

As soon as you do so, the Absolute Position Below setting under Vertical changes to Page.

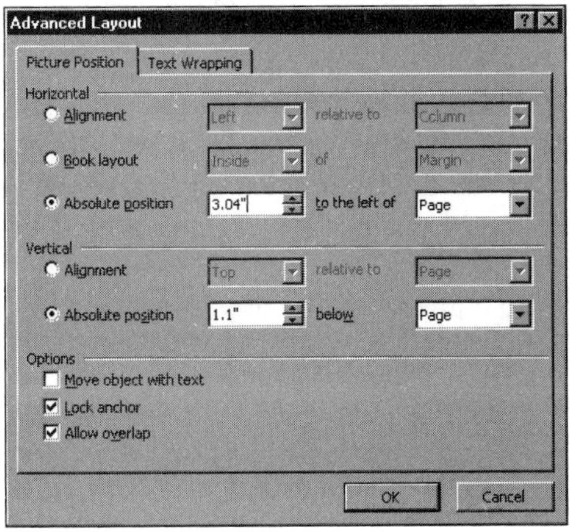

Figure 12-2:
The
Advanced
Layout
dialog box.

10. **Under Horizontal, choose Page from the Absolute Position To the Left Of drop-down list.**

Now the object is locked, horizontally and vertically, to the page, and Word knows to keep it at its current position on the page and *not* move it in the document when text is inserted before it. For now, don't worry about the To the Left Of and Below settings. In Step 12, you will drag the object on the page exactly where you want it to be.

11. **Click OK in the Advanced Layout dialog box and OK again in the Format dialog box. Back in your document, your object may have slid to a different position.**

12. **Drag the object where you want it to be on the page.**

To tell whether an object has been locked in place, click the Show/Hide ¶ button and look for the picture of an anchor and a tiny padlock in the left margin of the document.

Handling objects that overlap

Chances are, objects like the ones in Figure 12-3 overlap when more than one appears on the same page. And when objects are placed beside text, do you want the text to appear in front of the objects, or do you want the objects to cover up the text?

Figure 12-3:
Overlapping
objects.

Word offers special Order commands for determining how objects overlap with one another and with text. However, before you know anything about the Order commands, you need to know about *layers,* also known as *drawing layers.* From top to bottom, text and objects can appear on these layers:

✦ **Foreground layer:** Objects on this layer cover up objects on the text layer and background layer. Only objects, not text, can appear on the foreground layer. When you insert a new object in a document, it appears on the foreground layer.

✦ **Text layer:** The text you type appears on this layer. No objects can appear on this layer. Text on this layer is covered by objects on the foreground layer but covers objects on the background layer.

✦ **Background layer:** Only objects can appear on this layer. Objects on the background layer are covered by objects on the foreground layer and by text.

Follow these steps to tell Word whether an object should overlap text or overlap other objects:

1. **Click the object to select it.**

2. **Click the D̲raw button on the Drawing toolbar, choose O̲rder, and choose a Send or Bring command on the Order menu; or right-click, choose O̲rder, and choose a submenu command.**

The commands on the Order submenu do the following:

✦ **Bring to Front:** When objects are on the same layer, either the foreground or background, moves the object in front of all others on the layer.

✦ **Send to Back:** When objects are on the same layer, moves the object behind all others on the layer.

✦ **Bring Forward:** When three or more objects are on the same layer, either foreground or background, moves the object higher in the stack of objects.

✦ **Send Backward:** When three or more objects are on the same layer, moves the object lower in the stack so that more objects overlap the object you selected.

✦ **Bring in Front of Text:** Moves the object from the background layer to the foreground layer, where it appears in front of text.

✦ **Send Behind Text:** Moves the object from the foreground layer to the background layer, where it appears behind text.

Working with Text Boxes

Put text in a text box when you want it to stand out on the page. Text boxes like the one shown in Figure 12-4 can be shaded, filled with color, and given borders. What's more, you can move one around at will on the page until it lands in the right place. You can even use text boxes as columns and make text jump from one text box to the next in a document — a nice feature, for example, when you want a newsletter article on page 1 to be continued on page 2. Instead of cutting and pasting text from page 1 to page 2, Word moves the text for you as the column on page 1 fills up.

See "Handling Objects on Pages" earlier in this chapter to find out how to change the size of a text box, change its borders, fill it with color, and move it on-screen.

Word
Chapter 12

Doing Some Desktop Publishing

Figure 12-4:
You can
use text
boxes for
neat
effects.

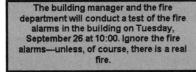

The building manager and the fire department will conduct a test of the fire alarms in the building on Tuesday, September 26 at 10:00. Ignore the fire alarms—unless, of course, there is a real fire.

Inserting a text box

To put a text box in a document, follow these steps:

1. Choose Insert⊅Text Box or click the Text Box button on the Drawing toolbar. The pointer turns into a cross.

2. Click and drag to draw the text box. Lines show you how big it will be when you release the mouse button.

3. Release the mouse button.

After you insert the text box, you can type text in it and call on all the formatting techniques in Word to boldface it, align it, or do what you will with it.

Changing the direction of the text

On the Text Box toolbar is a little toy called the Change Text Direction button. Click a text box and click this button to make the text in the text box change orientation. In Figure 12-5, you can see what happens when you click the Change Text Direction button.

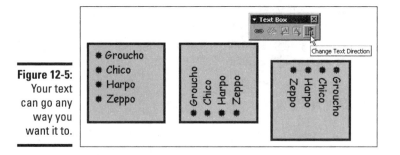

Figure 12-5: Your text can go any way you want it to.

Wrapping text around a text box, graphic, or other object

Word gives you lots of interesting opportunities to wrap text around text boxes, graphics, and other objects in a document. By playing with the different ways to wrap text, you can create very sophisticated layouts. When you wrap text, you pick a wrapping style and the side of the object around which to wrap the text. Figure 12-6 demonstrates several of the wrapping styles and directions that text can be wrapped.

The fastest way to wrap text is to click the object around which text is to be wrapped, click the Text Wrapping button on the Picture toolbar, and choose an option from the drop-down list.

Wrapped text looks best when it is justified and hyphenated. That way, text can get closer to the object that is being wrapped.

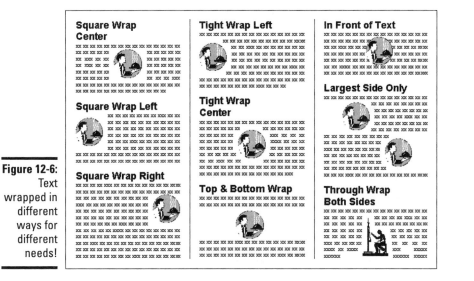

Figure 12-6:
Text
wrapped in
different
ways for
different
needs!

To wrap text around an object:

1. **Select the object by clicking it.**

2. **Right-click and choose Format, or else choose Format on the menu bar and then choose the last option on the Format menu. (The option is named after the kind of object you are dealing with.)**

3. **Click the Layout tab in the Format Picture dialog box (shown in Figure 12-7).**

4. **Click a box under Wrapping Style to tell Word how you want the text to behave when it reaches the graphic or text box.**

The In Line with Text option keeps text from wrapping around objects.

5. **Under Horizontal Alignment, tell Word where you want the object to be in relation to the text.**

For example, click the Left radio button to make the object stand to the left side of text as it flows down the page.

If you want text to wrap to the largest side or to both sides without the object being centered, click the Other radio button and then click the Advanced button. In the Advanced Layout dialog box, click the Text Wrapping tab, choose either the Both Sides or Largest Only radio button, and click OK. The Text Wrapping tab also offers choices for telling Word how close text can come to the object as it wraps around it.

6. **Click OK.**

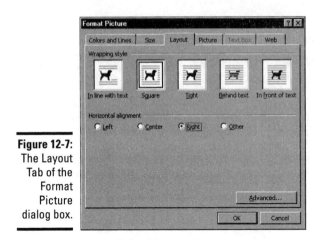

Figure 12-7:
The Layout
Tab of the
Format
Picture
dialog box.

WordArt for Embellishing Documents

You can bend, spindle, and mutilate text with a feature called WordArt. This feature was inspired by old superhero comics, in which words and images that may have come from the WordArt Gallery appeared whenever Batman, Spiderman, and Wonder Woman brawled with the criminal element.

To create a WordArt image, put the cursor roughly where you want the image to go and do the following:

1. Choose Insert⇨Picture⇨WordArt or click the Insert WordArt button on the Drawing toolbar.

You see the WordArt Gallery, as shown in Figure 12-8.

2. Click the image that strikes your fancy and then click OK.

3. In the Edit WordArt Text dialog box, type a word or words of your own.

4. Choose a new font from the Font menu or change the size of letters with the Size menu, and click OK.

The image arrives on-screen with its selection handles showing. To really bend the word or words out of shape, click and drag the yellow diamond on the image. To change the wording, click Edit Text on the WordArt toolbar to reopen the Edit WordArt Text dialog box. To choose a new WordArt image, click the WordArt Gallery button. To change the shape of a WordArt image, click the WordArt Shape button on the WordArt toolbar and choose a shape from the pop-up menu.

See "Handling Objects on Pages" earlier in this chapter if you need advice for moving, resizing, or otherwise manipulating WordArt images.

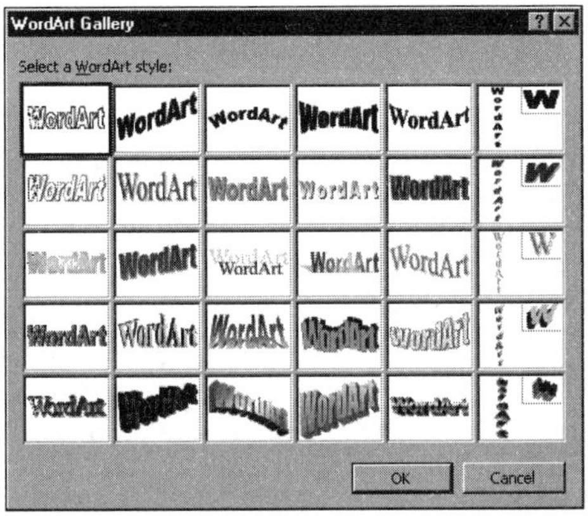

Figure 12-8: The WordArt Gallery dialog box awaits your choices.

Borders and Color Shades for Graphics and Text Boxes

By putting borders around graphics, text boxes, shapes, and other objects, and by putting interesting gray shades and colors behind them as well, you can amuse yourself on a rainy afternoon. And you can sometimes create fanciful artwork. The text boxes and graphics in Figure 12-9 were created by a 7-year-old with help from his father. This part of the book explains how to put borders and gray shades on objects.

Putting borders on objects

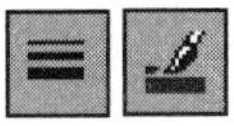

The fastest way to put a border around an object is to select it, click the Line Style button on the Picture or Drawing toolbar, and choose a line from the pop-up menu. To change the color of borders, click the down arrow beside the Line Color button on the Drawing toolbar and then choose a color from the pop-up menu.

To get fancy with borders, click the object and do the following:

1. **Right-click the object and choose Format from the shortcut menu, or else choose Format on the menu bar and then choose the bottom-most command on the Format menu.**

2. **Click the Colors and Lines tab in the Format dialog box.**

3. **Under Line, click the Color drop-down list and choose a color. (Black is the first choice in the box.) Click the No Line option to remove borders from an object.**

Figure 12-9: Have a 7-year-old help you with your graphics.

4. Click the <u>D</u>ashed down arrow and choose a dashed or dotted line, if you want.

5. Click the <u>S</u>tyle down arrow and tell Word what kind of line you want.

6. Click arrows in the <u>W</u>eight box or enter a number yourself to tell Word how wide or narrow to make the borderlines.

7. Click OK.

Filling an object with a color or gray shade

The fast way to "fill" a graphic or text box is to select it, click the down arrow beside the Fill Color button on the Drawing toolbar, and choose a color or gray shade. By clicking Fill Effects at the bottom of the menu, you can get to interesting gray shades and textures.

Or, if you are the kind who likes dialog boxes, select the thing you are filling and either right-click and choose Format, or else choose Format on the menu bar and then choose the bottom-most command on the Format menu — Picture, Object, Text Box, or AutoShape. Then click the Colors and Lines tab in the Format dialog box, click the Color drop-down list, and make a choice. Experiment with the Semitransparent check box if you want a soupy, fainter-looking color.

Chapter 13: Web Publishing

In This Chapter

- ✔ Creating a Web page
- ✔ Choosing a background and theme
- ✔ Hyperlinking your Web page

*E*veryone wants to get on the Web, and why should you be any different? In the past, you were probably prevented from making Web documents because you didn't have the time to learn how to do all that HTML (what Web pages are written in) and other techno stuff needed in order to make a splash on the Web. Hesitate no more! If you can create a simple Word document, you can let Word 2000 take care of all the other chores.

This chapter helps you to discover how Word 2000 can help you make your own Web site and create those nifty Web pages that you once thought were beyond your grasp.

Creating Your Own Web Pages and Sites

In the future, everyone will be famous for 15 minutes, and everyone will have a Web page. Looking toward the future, Word offers commands for creating a Web page from scratch, for turning a Word document into a Web page, and even for creating a *Web site,* a collection of hyperlinked Web pages.

If you create your Web page with the Web Page Wizard, you very likely will be asked where you want to place the items shown in Figure 13-1: the title, frame, and hyperlinks. Fold down the corner of this page in case you have to come back here and see precisely what you are being asked about.

Word offers three different ways to create Web pages. You can turn a Word document that you already created into a Web page; you can create a Web page from a template; or you can use the Web Page Wizard to create a Web page or even an entire Web site.

Before you create a Web page or Web site, however, you need to create a new folder in which to store it. You need the new folder because Word creates special subfolders when you create a Web page and places the subfolders in whatever folder the Web page you create is located in. The special subfolders hold support files that make displaying the Web page possible. If you disregard this advice and

Title

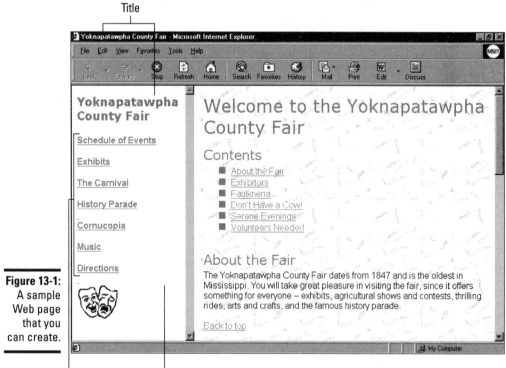

Figure 13-1:
A sample
Web page
that you
can create.

Hyperlinks   Vertical frame

don't put your Web page in its own folder, you will have a hard time figuring out which files and subfolders are needed to display your Web page. When the time comes to ship your Web page files and folders to an ISP (Internet service provider) or to your network administrator so that your Web pages can be displayed on the Internet or the company network, you will not know which files and folders to send.

Converting Word documents to Web pages

A Web browser such as Internet Explorer or Netscape Navigator cannot "see" images and text or display them on a computer screen unless the images and text have been tagged with *hypertext markup language* (HTML) codes. Fortunately for you and for the teeming multitudes who will admire your Web pages, Word has made the dreary task of entering HTML codes very easy: Word can do it for you. It can code a document and do a good job of it, as long as you thoughtfully assign styles to the different parts of the document. When Word converts a document to HTML, it converts styles to HTML codes.

However, not all Word styles can be converted to HTML codes. Text effects, drop caps, text boxes and autoshapes, margins, page borders, footnotes and endnotes, and columns are not on speaking terms with HTML. And to convert Word documents to Web pages, Microsoft Internet Explorer must have been installed on your computer.

To turn a Word document into a Web page:

1. **Open the document to be converted to an HTML document.**

2. **Choose File⇨Save as Web Page.**

3. **In the Save As dialog box, find the folder that will hold your HTML file and enter a name in the File Name box.**

4. **Click the Change Title button and, in the Set Page Title dialog box, enter a descriptive name for your Web page and click OK.**

   The name you enter appears in the title bar of the Web browser when your Web page is shown online.

5. **Click the Save button. Word gives the file the *.htm* extension. When next you see the file, it appears in Web Layout View.**

Creating a Web page from a template

You can save a lot of time by creating Web pages from templates. Instead of doing the layout work yourself, you can let Word do it for you. After you have created a new folder to hold your Web page, follow these steps to create a Web page from a template:

1. **Choose File⇨New to open the New dialog box.**

2. **Click the Web Pages tab. You see several template icons. Click a couple of icons and look in the Preview box to get a glimpse of the Web pages you can create.**

3. **Click the template you want and click OK.**

You get a generic Web page with sample text and perhaps a placeholder graphic. Your job now, if you choose to accept it, is to replace the generic text with your own words. You can call on all the formatting commands in Word, import clip art, and do what you will to make this Web page a lively one.

Creating a Web site with the Web Page Wizard

To create a Web site, a bunch of linked Web pages on the same topic, you can use the Web Page Wizard. Use the Wizard to create Web pages from scratch and also to make Web pages that you already created part of a Web site. Before you create your Web site, create a new folder to store it in. Then follow these steps to create your Web site:

1. **Choose File⇨New.**

2. **Click the Web Pages tab in the New dialog box.**

3. **Double-click the Web Page Wizard icon. After a moment, you see the first Web Page Wizard dialog box. To create your Web site, you visit each Wizard dialog box — Title and Location, Navigation, Add Pages, Organize Pages, and Visual Theme — and tell Word what you want to appear on your Web site.**

4. **Click the Next button to go from page to page in the Web Page Wizard dialog box, answer the questions, and click the Finish button when you are done.**

If you change your mind while you are giving birth to your Web site, click a page name or the Back button to return to a page you visited before.

Answer the questions on these pages in the Web Page Wizard dialog box:

✦ **Title and Location:** Enter a title for the Web site and choose the folder you will store it in — the folder you created before you began developing your Web site. The title you enter appears prominently at the top of the table of contents page and in the title bar of the Web browser with which others view your site, so choose a title carefully. Click the Browse button, locate and select the folder in the Copy dialog box, and click the Open button.

✦ **Navigation:** For the *home page,* the first page that visitors see when they come to your site, choose the kind of frame you want, Vertical Frame or Horizontal Frame, or choose Separate Page for displaying only hyperlinks on the home page. This dialog box is for choosing how visitors to your site will go from page to page. As the dialog box shows, Vertical Frame places hyperlinks on the left side, Horizontal Frame places them along the top, and Separate Page places them in the middle of the home page.

✦ **Add Pages:** How many pages does your Web site need? Most Web site developers believe that no page should be so long that you have to scroll to get to the bottom. Better to divide the material across several pages.

To add a page, click the Add New Blank Page button. To include a page that you already created in the site, click the Add Existing File button, find and select the page in the Open dialog box, and click the Open button. To get a page from a template, click the Add Template Page button, choose a template in the Web Page Templates dialog box, and click OK.

✦ **Organize Pages:** If necessary, change the position of the Web pages by clicking a page and then clicking the Move Up or Move Down button.

The page at the top of the list is your home page. In navigation frames, hyperlinks to pages 2, 3, and so on appear one below the other on the left side of the screen if you choose a vertical frame, or to the right of one another along the top of the page if you choose a horizontal frame.

✦ **Visual Theme:** This is where you decide what your Web site will look like. Click the Add a Visual Theme option button, click the Browse Themes button, choose a theme for your Web pages from the Theme dialog box, and click OK.

After you are done creating your shell of a Web site, start entering text. Go to it. The hyperlinks and design are already set up for you. Now, as they say in the business, you have to "provide the content." Visit the various pages in your Web site and enter the text and graphics.

Choosing Backgrounds and Themes for Web Pages

To decorate your Web page, you can give it a background color or what Microsoft calls a "theme" — a coordinated design with different colors assigned to headings, text, bulleted lists, and hyperlinks. You are hereby encouraged to experiment with backgrounds and themes until you hit paydirt and fashion a lively design.

To select a background color, choose Format⇨Background and select a color from the Color menu, or else click the Fill Effects option and choose a background from the Fill Effects dialog box. The Texture tab offers some neat backgrounds that are highly suitable for Web pages. To remove a background, choose Format⇨Background and click the No Fill option.

Follow these steps to choose a theme:

**Word
Chapter 13**

Web Publishing

1. **Choose Format⇨Theme.**

You see the Theme dialog box, as shown in Figure 13-2.

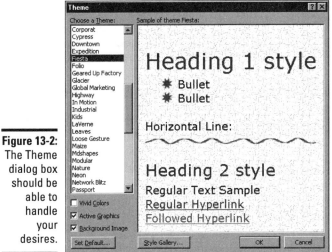

Figure 13-2:
The Theme
dialog box
should be
able to
handle
your
desires.

2. **In the Choose a Theme list, click a few names until you see a theme you like.**

The Sample of Theme box shows what the themes look like.

3. **Check and uncheck the Vivid Colors, Active Graphics, and Background Image check boxes in the lower-left corner of the dialog box and watch what happens in the Sample of Theme box.**

4. **Click OK.**

REAL WORLD

Seeing your Web page in a browser

When you start making Web pages, you may soon realize that you have a very important task to do before you even think about putting your page on the Web for all to see. If you don't preview your page before it gets on the Web, you may find yourself in an embarrassing position! Save yourself the pain. Choose File➪Web Page Preview to see what your Web page looks like to someone viewing it with a Web browser. The Microsoft Web browser, Internet Explorer, opens, and you see your Web page in all its glory. A Web page as seen in Web Layout view in Word and the same page in Internet Explorer look remarkably alike.

Hyperlinking Your Web Page to Other Pages

A *hyperlink* is an electronic shortcut from one Web page to another on the Internet, from one place to another in the same Web site, or from one place to another on the same Web page. You can always tell when the pointer has moved over a hyperlink because it changes into a gloved hand with a pointing finger. And when the pointer is over a hyperlink, a box appears with either the name of the link or its address.

If you want to link your Web page to a page on the Internet, go to the page and jot down its address. You can find the address by looking in your browser's Address bar (right-click the main menu and choose Address Bar from the shortcut menu to see the Address bar in Internet Explorer). Word offers a couple techniques for entering Web addresses without typing them in, but those techniques fall in the "more trouble than its worth" category.

Word makes it very easy to create a link to a different place on the same Web page if the place happens to be a heading. If you want to link to a graphic or a place in the text, create a bookmark there. Follow these steps to create a hyperlink on your Web page:

1. **Select the text or graphic that will comprise the link. In other words, drag the pointer over the word or words that will form the hyperlink. If a graphic will comprise the hyperlink, click to select it.**

2. **Choose Insert➪Hyperlink, press Ctrl+K, or right-click and choose Hyperlink.**

   You see the Insert Hyperlink dialog box, as shown in Figure 13-3.

3. **Click the ScreenTip button and, in the Set Hyperlink ScreenTip dialog box, enter a brief two-or-three word description of the hyperlink and click OK.**

   When visitors to your site move their mouse pointers over the link, they will see the description you enter. If you don't enter a ScreenTip description, visitors merely see the address of or path to the hyperlink destination.

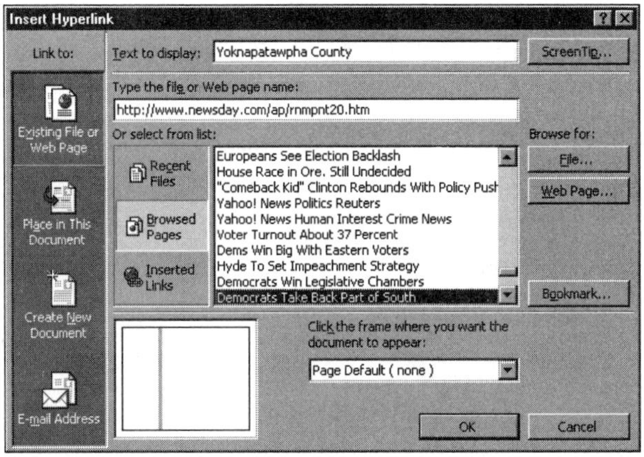

Figure 13-3:
The Insert
Hyperlink
dialog box.

4. Create the link to a Web page on the Internet, another page on your Web site, or a place on the same page.

If you've previously linked to the place you want to link to, simply click the Inserted Link button and choose the link from the list.

- **The Internet:** Click the Existing File or Web Page button. Then type the address of the site you want to link to in the Type the File or Web Page Name text box; click the Browsed Pages button, scroll the list of sites, and click a site name (the names come from the list of sites that Internet Explorer keeps in the History folder); or click the Web Page button, go on the Internet, and find the page you want to link to to make its name appear in the Type the File or Web Page Name text box.

- **Another page on the site:** Click the Existing File or Web Page button. Then click the File button, find and select the page in the Link to File dialog box, and click OK. You can also click the Recent Files button and search through the exhaustive list of the million files you opened and try to find the page there.

- **Place on the same page:** Click the Place in This Document button. Then click the plus signs next to the Headings and the Bookmarks label to see the headings and bookmarks on the page, find the one you want to link to, and click it.

5. Click OK to close the Insert Hyperlink dialog box.

After you create a hyperlink, be sure to test it. If the link takes you to an address on the Internet, clicking the link starts the Internet Explorer browser. You soon see the page whose address you entered in the Insert Hyperlink dialog box. If the link is inside your Web site, you see the Web toolbar after you click your hyperlink. Click the Back button on the toolbar to return from whence you came.

If the hyperlink doesn't work, right-click it and choose Hyperlink⇨Edit Hyperlink. You see the Edit Hyperlink dialog box, which offers the same options as the Insert Hyperlink dialog box. Very likely, your hyperlink doesn't work because you entered it incorrectly or you linked to a page on the Internet that no longer exists. Either edit your hyperlink or re-enter it.

To remove a hyperlink, right-click it and choose Hyperlink⇨Remove Hyperlink.

Index

Book III

Excel 2000

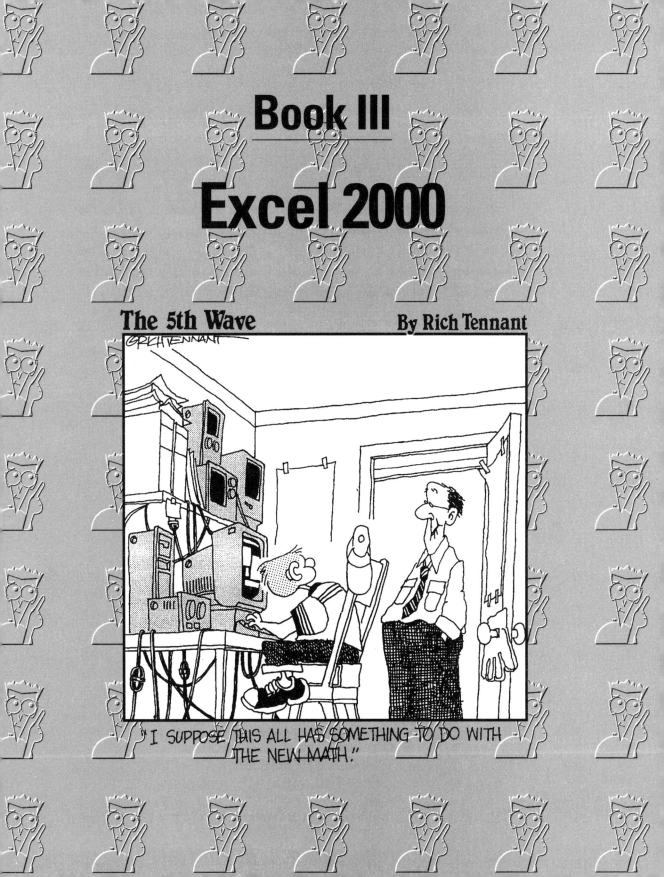

The 5th Wave   By Rich Tennant

"I SUPPOSE THIS ALL HAS SOMETHING TO DO WITH THE NEW MATH."

Contents at a Glance

Chapter 1: Getting to Know Excel 2000

In This Chapter

✔ Getting acquainted with the Excel 2000 screen

✔ Mastering cells and ranges

✔ Navigating in Excel

*M*icrosoft Excel 2000 may not be the only spreadsheet program around, but it may be the only one you'll ever need. You can use Excel on many different levels. But most users find out what the program can really do after it gets going. Excel is a user-friendly program — especially for those who are comfortable getting right in and clicking things. However, some parts of Excel can seem intimidating (especially when you just want to do something simple but don't know where to start).

This chapter serves as an initiation into the basics of Excel so that you can jump into the rest without fear.

Acquainting Yourself with the Excel Screen

Figure 1-1 shows a typical Excel screen, with some of the important parts pointed out. This terminology rears its ugly head throughout this book, so pay attention.

Excel behind the Scenes

A *spreadsheet program* is essentially a highly interactive environment that lets you work with numbers and text in a large grid of cells. Excel also creates graphs and maps from numbers stored in a worksheet and works with database information stored in a record and field format.

Workbooks, worksheets, and chart sheets

Excel files are known as *workbooks*. A single workbook can store as many sheets as will fit into memory, and these sheets are stacked like the pages in a notebook. Sheets can be either *worksheets* (a normal spreadsheet-type sheet) or *chart sheets* (a special sheet that holds a single chart).

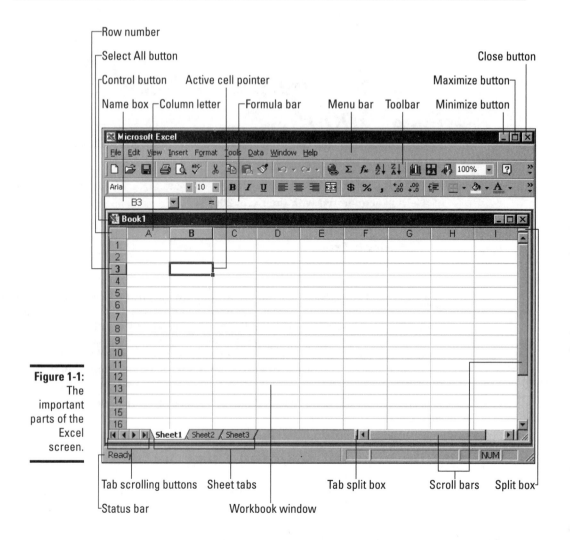

Figure 1-1:
The
important
parts of the
Excel
screen.

Most of the time, you work with worksheets — each of which has exactly 65,536 rows and 256 columns. Rows are numbered from 1 to 65,536, and columns are labeled with letters. Column 1 is A, column 26 is Z, column 27 is AA, column 52 is AZ, column 53 is BA, and so on up to column 256 (which is IV).

Cells — and what you can put in them

The intersection of a row and column is called a *cell.* A quick calculation with Excel tells me that this works out to 16,777,216 cells — which should be enough for most people. Cells have *addresses,* which are based on the row and column that they are in. The upper left cell in a worksheet is called A1, and the cell way down at the bottom is called IV65536. Cell K9 (also known as the dog cell) is the intersection of the eleventh column and the ninth row.

REAL WORLD

Selecting noncontiguous cells as a range (huh?)

The selected *range* is usually a group of contiguous cells, but it doesn't have to be. Sometimes you may want to select a bunch of different cells here and there as a range. If you hold down the Ctrl key while you click a cell (or click and drag through some cells), you can select more than one group of cells.

	A	B	C	D
1	Smith	456		
2	Spencer	432		
3	Hammill	654		
4	Caitherner	231		
5	Clapp	479		
6	Starnes	709		
7	Stewart	578		
8				
9				
10				

A cell in Excel can hold a number, some text, a formula, or nothing at all. You already know what numbers and text are, but you may be a bit fuzzy on the concept of a formula. A *formula* is a special way to tell Excel to perform a calculation using information stored in other cells. For example, you can insert a formula that tells Excel to add up the values in the first 10 cells in column A and to display the result in the cell that contains the formula.

Formulas can use normal arithmetic operators such as + (plus), – (minus), * (multiply), and / (divide). They can also use special built-in functions that let you do powerful things without much effort on your part. For example, Excel has functions that add up a range of values, calculate square roots, compute loan payments, and even tell you the time of day.

When you create a chart from numbers stored in a worksheet, you can put the chart directly on the worksheet or in a special chart sheet in the workbook. When you're working with a chart, some of Excel's menus change so that they are appropriate for chart-type operations.

If your worksheet contains geographic data, you can create maps from the data. Maps reside on a worksheet (there's no such thing as a map sheet).

The active cell and ranges

In Excel, one of the cells in a worksheet is always the *active cell*. The active cell is the one that's selected and it displays with a thicker border. Its contents appear in the *formula bar*. You can also select a group (or range) of cells by clicking and dragging the mouse over them. When you issue a command that does something to a cell or a range of cells, that something will be done to the active cell or to the selected range of cells.

Navigational techniques

With more than 16 million cells in a worksheet, you need ways to move to specific cells. Fortunately, Excel provides you with many techniques to move around a worksheet. As always, you can use either your mouse or the keyboard on your navigational journeys. The Table 1-1 lists the keystrokes that allow you to move through a worksheet.

Table 1-1	Moving around in Excel
Keys	*Action*
Up arrow	Moves the active cell up one row
Down arrow	Moves the active cell down one row
Left arrow	Moves the active cell one column to the left
Right arrow	Moves the active cell one column to the right
PgUp	Moves the active cell up one screen
PgDn	Moves the active cell down one screen
Alt+PgDn	Moves the active cell right one screen
Alt+PgUp	Moves the active cell left one screen
Ctrl+Backspace	Scrolls to display the active cell
Up arrow*	Scrolls the screen up one row (active cell does not change)
Down arrow*	Scrolls the screen down one row (active cell does not change)
Left arrow*	Scrolls the screen left one column (active cell does not change)
Right arrow*	Scrolls the screen right one column (active cell does not change)

* With Scroll Lock on

The actions for some of the keys in the preceding table may be different, depending on the transition options you've set. Select the Tools⇨Options command and then click the Transition tab in the Options dialog box. If the Transition Navigation Keys option is checked, the navigation keys correspond to those used in older versions of Lotus 1-2-3. Generally, it's better to use the standard Excel navigation keys than those for 1-2-3.

If you need basic help with dialog boxes, menus, icons, and the like, be sure to check out Chapter 1 of Windows 98 in this very book.

Chapter 2: Working with Workbook Files

In This Chapter

✔ Creating a workbook file

✔ Saving and closing a workbook file

✔ Using a workbook template

✔ Finding a workbook file

✔ Getting rid of a workbook file

✔ Guarding a workbook file from changes

✔ Viewing two different parts of a worksheet at one time

An Excel 2000 file is called a workbook. A workbook is made up of one or more worksheets. And that's about the extent of it, right? Well, this brief introduction is only the beginning. To get something done in Excel, you have to know how to deal with workbooks: creating, saving, closing, and so on.

If you can start Excel, you're ready to begin working with workbooks (see Chapter 3 for the details on worksheets). This chapter shows you how to handle your workbooks so that your real work (the stuff you put into a workbook) remains safe and sound — and usable.

Creating an Empty Workbook File

When you start Excel, it automatically creates a new (empty) workbook called Book1. If you're starting a new project from scratch, you can use this blank workbook. You can create another blank workbook in any of three ways:

✦ Click the New button on the Standard toolbar.

✦ Press Ctrl+N.

✦ Select File➪New and double-click the Workbook icon in the General tab of the New dialog box.

Any of these methods creates a blank default workbook.

Opening a Workbook File

If you have a workbook file already created that you want to open, Excel makes this task easy for you.

1. **Choose File⇨Open to bring up the Open dialog box (shown in Figure 2-1).**

You can also click the Open button on the Standard toolbar.

2. **Specify the folder that contains the file.**

3. **Select the workbook file and click Open or double-click the filename.**

You can select more than one file in the Open dialog box. The trick is to hold down the Ctrl key while you click the filenames. After you select all of the files you want, click Open.

Excel 2000 comes with a new "Web browser-style" Open dialog box. On the left-hand side of the dialog box is a vertical toolbar for quick access to commonly used folders. The blue arrow in the toolbar functions like a browser's back button. In the dialog box's toolbar, clicking the arrow takes you back to folders viewed previously.

Saving a Workbook File

When you save a workbook for the first time, Excel displays its Save As dialog box. When you save the same workbook anytime after that, Excel overwrites the previous copy of the file.

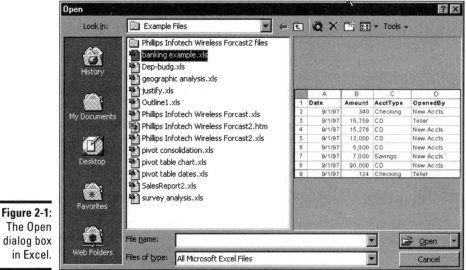

Figure 2-1:
The Open
dialog box
in Excel.

REAL WORLD

Opening an Excel workbook for dialog box-challenged users

If you don't like rummaging through dialog boxes every time you want to open something, you can take advantage of other ways to open a workbook file:

✔ Double-click the workbook icon in any folder window. If Excel is not running, it starts automatically. Or you can drag a workbook icon into the Excel window to load the workbook.

✔ If you already have Excel running, open the File menu. Excel provides a list of files you've worked with recently at the bottom of the menu. If the file you want appears in this list, you can choose it directly from the menu.

To save the active workbook to disk, follow these steps:

1. **Choose the File⇨Save command.**

If the file has not yet been saved, Excel prompts you for a name using its Save As dialog box (see Figure 2-2).

You may prefer to use any of the following methods to save:

- Click the Save button on the Standard toolbar

- Press the Ctrl+S shortcut key combination

- Press the Shift+F12 shortcut key combination

2. **Select the folder that will hold the file.**

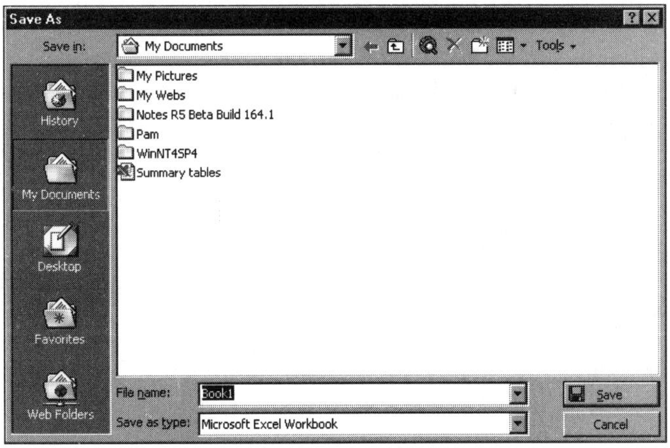

**Excel
Chapter 2**

**Working with
Workbook Files**

Figure 2-2:
The Save
As dialog
box lets
you name
and place
your file.

3. **Enter a name in the File name box. (A filename can consist of as many as 255 characters, including spaces.)**

4. **Click Save.**

You should save your work at a time interval that corresponds to the maximum amount of time that you're willing to lose. For example, if you don't mind losing an hour's work, save your file every hour. Most people save at more frequent intervals.

Sometimes, you may want to keep multiple versions of your work by saving each successive version under a different name. No problem!

1. **Use File⇨Save As to display the Save As dialog box.**

2. **Select the folder in which to store the workbook.**

3. **Enter a new filename in the File name box.**

4. **Click Save.**

A new copy is created with a different name, but the original version of the file remains intact.

Closing a Workbook

After you're finished using a workbook, use any of these methods to close it and free up the memory it uses. (If you haven't saved it since the last time you made any change, you are prompted to do so!)

✦ Use the File⇨Close command.

[X] ✦ Click the Close button in the workbook's title bar (or on the menu bar if the workbook is maximized).

✦ Double-click the Control button in the workbook's title bar (or on the menu bar if the workbook is maximized).

✦ Press Ctrl+F4.

✦ Press Ctrl+W.

To close all open workbooks, press the Shift key and choose the File⇨Close All command (this command only appears when you hold down the Shift key while you click the File menu). Excel closes each workbook, prompting you for each unsaved workbook.

Using a Workbook Template

A *workbook template* is a normal workbook that is used as the basis for other workbooks. A workbook template can use any of Excel's features such as charts, formulas, and macros. Normally, you set up a template so that you can enter some values and get immediate results. Excel includes several templates, and you can create your own.

1. **Choose the File⇨Save As command.**

2. **Select Template from the drop-down list box labeled Save as type.**

3. **Save the template in your Templates folder (or a subfolder within the Templates folder).**

If you don't want to create your own templates but like the idea of ready-made workbooks, why not let good 'ol Excel help you? The Spreadsheet Solutions templates distributed with Excel are nicely formatted and relatively easy to customize.

To create a workbook from a template, follow these steps:

1. **Select the File⇨New command.**

2. **In the New dialog box that appears, select the template that you want.**

The New dialog box has several tabs. Clicking a tab displays additional templates.

3. **Click OK to open a copy of the template.**

Finding a Workbook File

It's not uncommon to "lose" a file. Fortunately, Excel makes it fairly easy to locate files. The searching all takes place from the Open dialog box. You can search for files based on the name of the file, type of the file, text contained in the file, properties associated with the file, or time frame when the file was last modified. And if you can't use any of these factors to help the search, that file may really be lost!

Excel
Chapter 2

Working with
Workbook Files

1. **Select File⇨Open (or press Ctrl+O) to display the Open dialog box (as shown in Figure 2-1).**

2. **Specify the search scope in the Look in field.**

The search scope can be very broad (My Computer) or quite narrow (a single folder).

3. **Select Tools⇨Find in the Open dialog box.**

4. **Determine how you want to search and fill in the appropriate field(s) at the bottom of the dialog box.**

If you aren't sure of the exact filename, use wildcard characters to specify an approximate match. Use a question mark (?) as a placeholder for a single character and an asterisk (*) as a placeholder for any number of characters.

5. **To start the search, click the Find Now button.**

Excel eventually displays a list of files that match your criteria (or not!).

Deleting a Workbook File

When you no longer need a workbook file, you may want to delete it from your disk to free up space and reduce the number of files displayed in the Open dialog box. You can delete files using standard Windows techniques, or you can delete files directly from Excel.

1. **Use either the File⇨Open command or the File⇨Save As command to bring up a dialog box with a list of filenames (see Figure 2-3).**

2. **Right-click a filename and choose Delete from the shortcut menu.**

Depending on how your system is set up, you may have to confirm this action.

If your system is set up to use the Recycle Bin, you may be able to recover a file that you delete accidentally. Before you empty the Recycle Bin, open it up and drag out any items you wish to save.

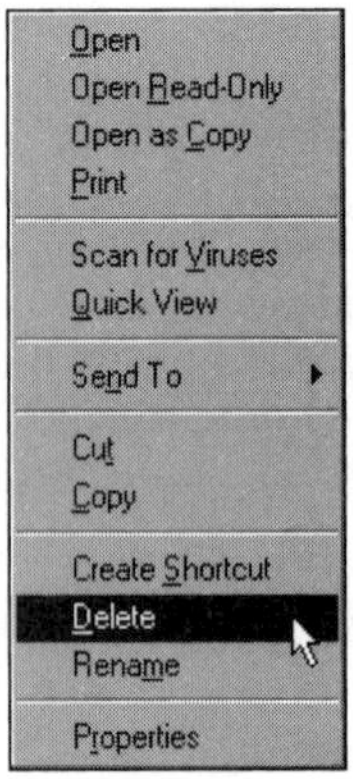

Figure 2-3:
You can
delete a
file from
the Open
dialog box.

> Open
> Open Read-Only
> Open as Copy
> Print
>
> Scan for Viruses
> Quick View
>
> Send To ▶
>
> Cut
> Copy
>
> Create Shortcut
> Delete
> Rename
>
> Properties

Creating Multiple Windows (Views) for a Workbook

Sometimes, you may like to view two different parts of a worksheet at once. Or you may want to see more than one sheet in the same workbook. You can accomplish either of these actions by displaying your workbook in one or more additional windows.

To create a new view of the active workbook choose Window⇨New Window. Excel displays a new window for the active workbook. To help you keep track of the windows, Excel appends a colon and a number to each window.

Chapter 3: Working with the Worksheets in Your Workbook

In This Chapter

✔ **Adding and arranging worksheets**

✔ **Managing your worksheets**

✔ **Navigating in a worksheet**

✔ **Moving a worksheet**

✔ **Deleting a worksheet**

*I*f you look at an Excel 2000 workbook, you may notice that it's composed of one or more worksheets, each with its own little tab at the bottom of the workbook window. These tabs make worksheets look like upside-down folders (you know, those manila folders that fit neatly into a drawer, and whose tabs make them easy to find even if the folders are all stacked into tight rows). The similarity stops there, however, because worksheets are much more useful than a bunch of upside-down manila folders. Worksheets are the holders of the cells (explained in Chapter 1) into which you place your valuable, hard-earned data. Just try putting some valuable things into upside-down manila folders in your file cabinet!

In this chapter you find out about fundamental worksheet management.

Working with Worksheets

A workbook can consist of any number of *worksheets*. To activate a different sheet, just click its tab (see Figure 3-1). If the tab for the sheet that you want to activate is not visible, use the tab scrolling buttons to scroll the sheet tabs.

You also can use these shortcut keys to activate a different sheet:

✦ **Ctrl+PgUp:** Activates the previous sheet, if there is one.

✦ **Ctrl+PgDn:** Activates the next sheet, if there is one.

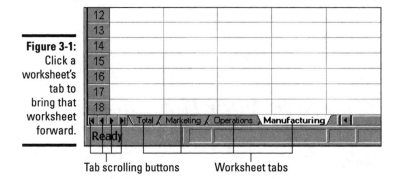

Figure 3-1:
Click a
worksheet's
tab to
bring that
worksheet
forward.

Tab scrolling buttons   Worksheet tabs

Adding a new worksheet

What? Three worksheets aren't enough for you! Fortunately, you can add a new worksheet to a workbook in several ways:

✦ Select the Insert➪Worksheet command.

✦ Right-click on a sheet tab, choose Insert from the shortcut menu, and select sheet from the Insert dialog box.

✦ Press Shift+F11.

Excel inserts a new worksheet before the active worksheet; the new worksheet then becomes the active worksheet.

Changing a sheet's name

Worksheets, by default, are named Sheet1, Sheet2, and so on. Providing more meaningful names helps you identify a particular sheet. To change a sheet's name, use any of these methods:

✦ Choose the Format➪Sheet➪Rename command.

✦ Either double-click or right-click on the sheet tab and choose the Rename command from the shortcut menu.the sheet tab.

Any of these methods selects the text in the tab. Just type the new sheet name directly on the tab.

Sheet names can be up to 31 characters. Spaces are allowed, but the following characters are not: [ ] (square brackets); : (colon); / (slash);\ (backslash); ? (question mark); and * (asterisk). Your computer may catch on fire if you try to name your worksheet something like ?*?\ : /*]?[

Keep in mind that the name you give is displayed on the sheet tab; a longer name results in a wider tab. Therefore, if you use lengthy sheet names, you can see fewer sheet tabs without scrolling.

Manipulating Your Worksheets

That's right. You need to be manipulative with your worksheets. Show them who's boss.

Copying a worksheet

You can make an exact copy of a worksheet — and put it either in its original workbook or in a different workbook — in one of two ways:

♦ Select the Edit⇨Move or Copy Sheet command. Select the location for the copy and make sure that the check box labeled Create a Copy is checked. Click OK to make the copy.

♦ Click the sheet tab, press Ctrl, and drag it to its desired location. When you drag, the mouse pointer changes to a small sheet with a plus sign on it.

If necessary, Excel changes the name of the copied sheet to make it unique within the workbook. For example, if you copy a sheet named Sheet1 to a workbook that already has a sheet named Sheet1, Excel changes the name to Sheet1 (2). To change the name of a sheet see "Changing a sheet's name," earlier in this chapter.

Creating and using named views

Excel lets you name various *views* of your worksheet and to switch quickly among these named views. A view includes settings for window size and position, frozen panes or titles, outlining, zoom factor, the active cell, print area, and many of the settings in the Options dialog box. A view can also include hidden print settings and hidden rows and columns.

To create a named view, follow these steps:

1. **Set up the worksheet the way you want it to appear.**

2. **Select the View⇨Custom Views command.**

3. **In the Custom Views dialog box, click the Add button and then enter a descriptive name for the view.**

To display a view that you've named, select the View⇨Custom Views command, select the view from the list, and click the Show button. (See Figure 3-2).

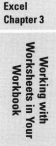

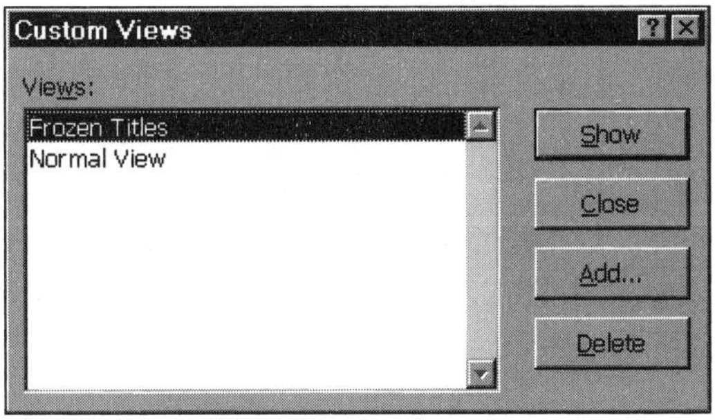

Excel Chapter 3

Working with Worksheets in Your Workbook

Figure 3-2:
Go quickly
to a named
view from
the Custom
Views
dialog box.

Custom Views

Views:

Frozen Titles
Normal View

Show

Close

Add...

Delete

Using full screen view

If you would like to see as much information as possible, Excel offers a full screen view. Choose the View⇨Full Screen command, and Excel maximizes its window and removes all elements except the menu bar.

Zooming worksheets

Normally, everything you see in Excel is at 100 percent size. You can change the *zoom percentage* from 10 percent (very tiny) to 400 percent (huge). Using a small zoom percentage can help you get a bird's-eye view of your worksheet to see how it's laid out. Zooming in is useful if your eyesight isn't quite what it used to be and you have trouble deciphering those 8-point sales figures.

If you have a Microsoft IntelliMouse, or equivalent device, you can zoom out on a worksheet by pressing Ctrl while you move the mouse wheel. Make sure the Zoom on roll with IntelliMouse option is selected in the Options dialog box (select the Tools⇨Options command and click the General tab).

The easiest way to change the zoom factor of the active worksheet is to use the Zoom control on the Standard toolbar. Just click on the arrow and select the desired zoom factor from the list. Your screen transforms immediately. (You can also choose View⇨Zoom to bring up the Zoom dialog box, or type a number directly into the Zoom box on the Standard toolbar.)

The Selection option in the toolbar Zoom control drop-down list zooms the worksheet to display only the selected cells. This option is useful if you want to view only a particular range. For finer control over the zoom factor you can click the Zoom control, enter a zoom factor directly, and press Enter.

Freezing row or column titles

Many worksheets (such as budgets) are set up with row and column headings. When you scroll through such a worksheet, it's very easy to get lost when the row and column headings scroll out of view. Excel provides a handy solution: freezing rows and/or columns.

1. **Move the cell pointer to the cell below the row that you want to freeze and to the right of the column that you want to freeze.**

   For example, to freeze row 1 and column A, move the cell pointer to cell B2.

2. **Select the Window⇨Freeze Panes command.**

Excel inserts dark lines to indicate the frozen rows and columns. These frozen rows and columns remain visible as you scroll throughout the worksheet. To remove the frozen rows or columns, select the Window⇨Unfreeze Panes command.

Splitting panes

Splitting a window into two or four panes lets you view multiple parts of the same worksheet — as long as you think your mind can handle it.

✦ The Window⇨Split command splits the active worksheet into two or four separate panes.

✦ The split occurs at the location of the cell pointer.

✦ You can use the mouse to drag the pane and resize it.

✦ To remove the split panes, choose <u>W</u>indow⇨Remove <u>S</u>plit.

A faster way to split and unsplit panes is to drag either the vertical or horizontal split bar, shown in the Figure 3-3. To remove split panes using the mouse, drag the pane separator all the way to the edge of the window or just double-click it.

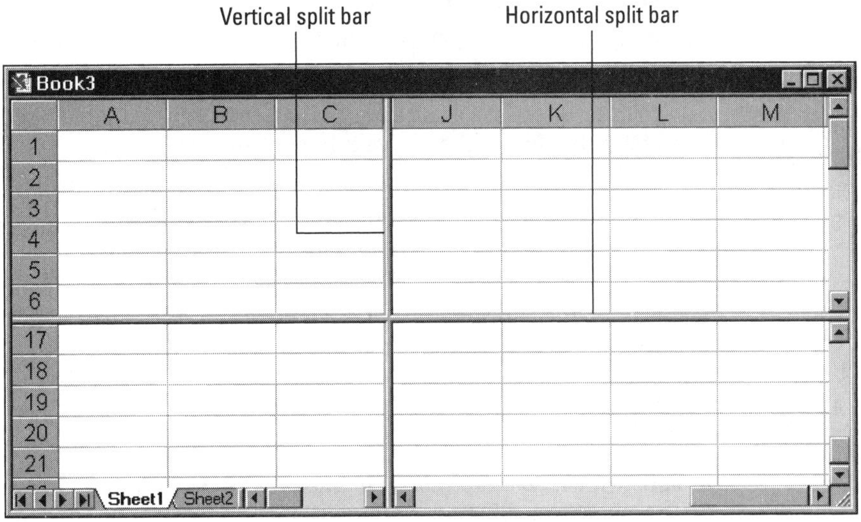

Vertical split bar   Horizontal split bar

Figure 3-3:
Now you can look at four different parts of your worksheet at one time.

Moving and resizing windows

To move a window, first make sure that it is not maximized. If it is maximized, click its Restore button (shown in the margin). Move the window by clicking and dragging its title bar with your mouse. Note that the window can extend off-screen in any direction, if you like.

To resize a window, click and drag any of its borders until it's the size you want it to be. When you position the mouse pointer on a window's border, the mouse pointer changes shape (into a double arrow) to let you know that you can then click and drag. To resize a window horizontally and vertically at the same time, click and drag any of its corners.

Moving Around in a Worksheet

Navigating through a worksheet with a mouse works just as you would expect. Just click a cell and it becomes the active cell. If the cell that you want to activate is not visible in the workbook window, you can use the scroll bars to scroll the window in any direction.

✦ To scroll one cell, click one of the arrows on the scroll bar.

✦ To scroll by a complete screen, click either side of the scroll bar's elevator button (the large center button).

✦ To scroll faster, drag the elevator button. And away you go!

✦ To scroll a long distance vertically, hold down the Shift key while dragging the elevator button.

Notice that only the active workbook window has scroll bars. When you activate a different window, the scroll bars appear.

When you drag the scroll bar's thumb, a small box appears that tells you which row or column you will scroll to when you release your finger from the mouse.

Using the scroll bars doesn't change the active cell. It simply scrolls the worksheet. To change the active cell, you must click on a new cell after scrolling.

Your mouse may be equipped with a small wheel (Microsoft's IntelliMouse is an example). If you have such a mouse, you can spin the wheel to scroll vertically. If this doesn't work, select Tools⇨Options, click the General tab, and remove the check mark from Zoom on roll with IntelliMouse.

See Chapter 1 in this mini-book for some info on moving around by using the keyboard.

Moving a Sheet

Sometimes, you want to rearrange the order of worksheets in a workbook — or move a sheet to a different workbook.

First, select the sheet that you want to move by clicking the sheet tab. You also can move multiple sheets at once by selecting them: Press Ctrl while you click the sheet tabs that you want to move.

You can move a selected worksheet(s) in one of two ways:

✦ Select the Edit⇨Move or Copy Sheet command. The Move or Copy dialog box pops up asking you to select the workbook and the new location (see Figure 3-4).

✦ Click the sheet tab and drag it to its desired location (either in the same workbook or in a different workbook). When you drag, the mouse pointer changes to a small sheet, and a small arrow guides you. To move a worksheet to a different workbook, both workbooks must be open.

Dragging is usually the easiest method, but if the workbook has many sheets, you may prefer to use the Move or Copy dialog box.

If you move a worksheet to a workbook that already has a sheet with the same name, Excel changes the name to make it unique. For example, if you move a sheet named Sheet1 to a workbook that already has a sheet named Sheet1, Excel changes the name to Sheet1 (2). To change the name of a sheet, see "Changing a sheet's name," earlier in this chapter.

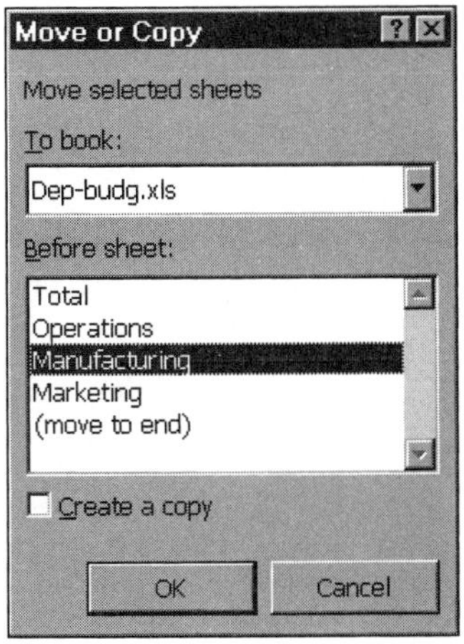

Figure 3-4:
The Move
or Copy
dialog box
lets you,
well, move
or copy.

Deleting a Worksheet

You can delete a worksheet in one of two ways:

♦ Activate the sheet and select the Edit⇨Delete Sheet command.

♦ Right-click on the sheet tab and choose the Delete command from the shortcut menu.

In either case, Excel asks you to confirm the fact that you want to delete the sheet. Every workbook must have at least one sheet so, if you try to delete the only sheet, Excel complains.

To select multiple sheets to delete, press Ctrl while clicking the sheet tabs that you want to delete. To select a group of contiguous sheets, click the first sheet tab, press Shift, and then click the last sheet tab.

When you delete a worksheet, it's gone for good. This is one of the few operations in Excel that can't be undone. You may want to save a workbook before deleting worksheets. Then, if you inadvertently delete a worksheet, you can revert to the saved version.

**Excel
Chapter 3**

**Working with
Worksheets in Your
Workbook**

Chapter 4: Entering Worksheet Data

In This Chapter

☞ **Placing your data into worksheets**

☞ **Entering formulas into worksheets**

☞ **Putting fractions into worksheets**

*W*ith all those pretty horizontal and vertical lines, worksheets sure look impressive. And with those official-looking row and column indicators, worksheets seem to be saying, "Hey, I'm important. You'd better take me seriously."

A worksheet is only as good as the data you put into it, however. Whether that data be Grandma's Secret Recipes or June 1999 Mid-West Sales Figures, a worksheet needs data to find fulfillment. This chapter reveals how to enter all sorts of data — from simple text to complex formulas — into your worksheets.

Entering Data into a Worksheet

Each worksheet in a workbook is made up of cells, and a cell can hold any of four types of data:

✦ A value (including a date or a time)

✦ Text

✦ A logical value (TRUE or FALSE)

✦ A formula, which returns a value, text, or a logical value

Entering text into cells

To enter text (rather than a value or a formula) into a cell, follow these steps:

1. **Move the cell pointer to the appropriate cell (this makes it the active cell).**

2. **Type the text.**

3. **Press Enter or any of the direction keys.**

In Excel, a cell can hold as many as 32,767 characters. (But who would want to put that much text into a cell?)

If you enter text that's longer than its column's current width, one of two things happens:

✦ If the cells to the immediate right are blank, Excel displays the text in its entirety, spilling the entry into adjacent cells.

✦ If an adjacent cell is not blank, Excel displays as much of the text as possible. (The full text is contained in the cell; it's just not displayed.)

In either case, you can always see the text that you're typing because it appears in the formula bar as well as in the cell.

If you need to display a long text entry that's adjacent to a cell with an entry, you can edit your text to make it shorter, increase the width of the column, or wrap the text within the cell so that it occupies more than one line.

If you have lengthy text in a cell, you can force Excel to display it in multiple lines within the cell. Use Alt+Enter to start a new line in a cell. When you add this line break, Excel automatically changes the cell's format to Wrap Text.

Entering values into cells

Enter a numeric value into a cell is just like entering text.

1. **Move the cell pointer to the appropriate cell.**

2. **Enter the value.**

3. **Press Enter or any of the direction keys.**

The value displays in the cell, and it also appears in the Excel formula bar. You can also include a decimal point, dollar sign, plus sign, minus sign, and comma. If you precede a value with a minus sign or enclose it in parentheses, Excel considers the value to be a negative number.

Sometimes the value isn't displayed exactly as you enter it. Excel may convert very large numbers to scientific notation. The formula bar always displays the value that you originally enter. If you make the column wider, the number displays as you entered it.

Entering the current date or time into a cell

If you need to date-stamp or time-stamp your worksheet, Excel provides two shortcut keys that do this for you (which is a lot easier than having to dig out your calendar or look at your watch — provided that your computer has the correct date and time entered).

✦ **Current date:** Ctrl+; (semicolon)

✦ **Current time:** Ctrl+Shift+; (semicolon)

Entering dates and times

To Excel, a date or a time is simply a value — but it's formatted to appear as a date or a time.

Excel's system for working with dates uses a serial number system. The earliest date that Excel understands is January 1, 1900 (which has a serial number of 1). January 2, 1900, has a serial number of 2, and so on. This system makes it easy to deal with dates in formulas.

Normally, you don't have to be concerned with the Excel serial number date system. You can simply enter a date in a familiar format, and Excel takes care of the details.

If you plan to use dates in formulas, make sure that the date you enter is actually recognized as a date (that is, a value); otherwise, your formulas will produce incorrect results. Excel is quite smart when it comes to recognizing dates that you enter into a cell, and it recognizes most common date formats. But it's not perfect. For example, Excel interprets the following entries as text, not dates:

✦ June 1 1998

✦ Jun-1 1998

✦ Jun-1/1998

The Year 2000 issue deserves a mention here. Entering 1/1/29 is interpreted by Excel as January 01, 2029. Entering 1/30 is interpreted by Excel as January 30, 1999 (or whatever is the current year). To be safe, enter the year as a four-digit value, and then format it as desired.

Excel works with times by using fractional days. When working with times, you simply extend Excel's date serial number system to include decimals. For example, the date serial number for June 1, 1998, is 35947. Noon (halfway through the day) is represented internally as 35947.5.

The best way to deal with times is to enter the time into a cell in a recognized format. Here are some examples of time formats that Excel recognizes.

Entered into a Cell	Excel's Interpretation
11:30:00 am	11:30 a.m.
11:30:00 AM	11:30 a.m.
11:30 pm	11:30 p.m.
11:30	11:30 a.m.

You also can combine dates and times, as follows.

Entered into a Cell	Excel's Interpretation
6/1/98 11:30	11:30 a.m. on June 1, 1998

Entering the same data into a range of cells

If you need to enter the same data (value, text, or formula) into multiple cells, your first inclination may be to enter it once and then copy it to the remaining cells. Here's a better way:

1. **Select all the cells that you want to contain the data.**

2. **Enter the value, text, or formula into one cell.**

3. Press Ctrl+Enter.

The single entry is inserted into each cell in the selection.

Entering Formulas

A *formula* is a special type of cell entry that returns a result: When you enter a formula into a cell, the cell displays the result of the formula. The formula itself appears in the formula bar (which is just below the toolbars at the top of the Excel window) when the cell is activated.

A formula begins with an equal sign (=) and can consist of any of the following elements:

+ Operators such as + (for addition) and * (for multiplication)

+ Cell references, including addresses such as B4 or C12, as well as named cells and ranges

+ Values and text

+ Worksheet functions (such as SUM)

You can enter a formula into a cell in three ways: manually (typing it in), by pointing to cell references, or with the assistance of the formula palette.

See Chapter 8 for the lowdown on formulas.

Entering formulas manually

Entering a formula manually is not as hard as it sound.

1. Move the cell pointer to the cell that you want to hold the formula.

2. Type an equal sign (=) to signal the fact that the cell contains a formula.

3. Type the formula and press Enter.

As you type, the characters appear in the cell as well as in the formula bar. You can use all the normal editing keys (Delete, Backspace, direction keys, and so on) when entering a formula.

Entering formulas by pointing

The pointing method of entering a formula still involves some manual typing. The advantage is that you don't have to type the cell or range references. Rather, you point to them in the worksheet, which is usually more accurate and less tedious.

The best way to explain this procedure is with an example. To enter the formula **=A1/A2** into cell A3 by the pointing method, just follow these steps:

1. Move the cell pointer to cell A3.

This is where you want the formula (and the result) to go.

2. Type an equal sign (=) to begin the formula.

3. **Press the up arrow twice.**

As you press this key, notice that Excel displays a faint moving border around the cell and that the cell reference appears in cell A3 and in the formula bar.

4. **Type a division sign (/).**

The faint border disappears, and Enter reappears in the status bar at the bottom of the screen.

5. **Press the up arrow once.**

A2 is added to the formula.

6. **Press Enter to end the formula.**

Entering formulas using the formula palette

The *formula palette* helps you create formulas and enter worksheet functions (see Chapter 8 for info on functions).

To use the formula palette to help you create a formula, click the = icon on the formula bar. Excel displays the formula palette directly below the formula bar. Excel displays the formula's result in the formula palette as you create the formula. (See Figure 4-1.)

You can move the formula palette anywhere you like. Just click and drag it to a new location.

When using the formula palette you can enter cell references directly, or you can point to them. To insert a worksheet function, select it from the list in the formula bar.

You can also use the formula palette to edit an existing formula. Activate the cell that contains the formula, and then click the = icon in the formula bar.

Entering Fractions

To enter a fraction into a cell, leave a space between the whole number part and the fractional part. For example, to enter the decimal equivalent of 6 $^7/_8$, follow these steps:

1. **Type** 6.

2. **Type a space.**

3. **Type** 7/8.

4. **Press Enter.**

Excel enters 6.875 into the cell and automatically formats the cell as a fraction.

If there is no whole number part (for example, $^1/_8$), you must enter a zero and a space first, like this: **0 1/8**.

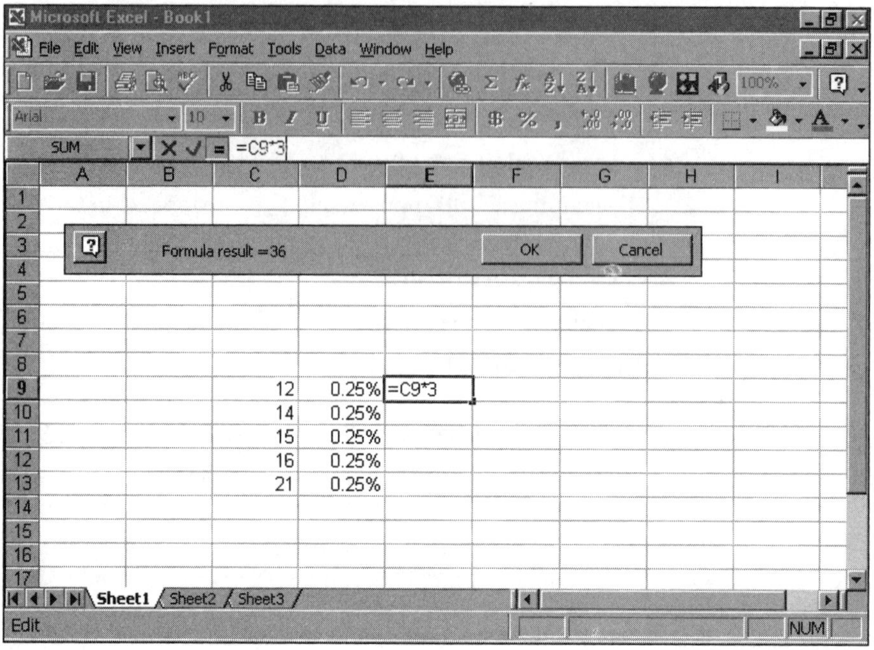

Figure 4-1:
The
formula
palette
helps you
with your
artistic
formulas.

Inserting cells, rows, and columns

The time will come when you need to squeeze more stuff into a section of a worksheet already occupied by other cell entries. Inserting a new cell range is a snap.

1. **Select the cells (both occupied and unoccupied) where you want the new cells to appear.**

2. **Right-click the selection and choose Insert from the shortcut menu or choose Insert⇨Cells to bring up the Insert dialog box.**

   You have a choice of radio buttons to select: Shift Cells Right or Shift Cells Down.

3. **Select the proper choice and then click OK.**

You may notice that you can also choose the options of inserting an entire row or column from the Insert dialog box. Inserting a row or a column is even easier if you simply choose Insert⇨Rows or Insert⇨Columns. Rows are inserted below and columns are inserted to the right of where you have a cell selected. Insert as many rows or columns that you want at a time simply by selecting more than one row or column.

Chapter 5: Editing the Data You Enter

In This Chapter

✔ Fixing your data

✔ Filling in data automatically

✔ Making comments on your data

✔ Searching and replacing your data

✔ Checking your spelling

*I*magine that you're perfect and that you have all the time in the world. You enter your data and you're done. You never need to go back and fix any mistakes. You never have to locate any stray data. You never have to check your spelling (because you were the fifth-grade spelling bee champion of Laura G. Hose Elementary School).

If you don't recognize yourself in the preceding paragraph, don't worry. Excel 2000 makes it simple to enter changes and to correct mistakes. Excel gives you lots of help entering data the easy way and even performing some automated tasks. And Excel makes it a breeze to find and repair data as well as to correct those spelling mistakes that seem to creep into even the most carefully prepared document. You don't need to do everything right the first time when you have Excel on your side. You just need to know a few Excel tips here and there, and this chapter strives to show you how to be productive without having to be perfect.

Basic Cell Editing

If you never have to go back and fix what you enter into a cell, you may as well skip this section. However, if you're curious about what those other error-prone people must do to repair their mistakes, you may enjoy reading some of this advice.

Editing a cell's contents

After you enter information into a cell, you can change it — or edit it. When you want to edit the contents of a cell, you can use one of these ways to get into cell edit mode:

✦ Double-click the cell to edit the cell contents directly in the cell.

✦ Press F2. This enables you to edit the cell contents directly in the cell.

✦ Activate the cell that you want to edit; then click in the formula bar to edit the cell contents in the formula bar.

✦ Activate the cell that you want to edit; then click the = icon in the formula bar to edit the cell contents in the formula bar.

If nothing happens when you double-click a cell, or if pressing F2 puts the cursor in the formula bar instead of the directly in the cell, the in-cell editing feature is turned off. To turn in-cell editing on, follow these steps:

1. **Select the Tools⇨Options command.**

2. **Click the Edit tab.**

3. **Check the check box labeled Edit directly in cell.**

When you're editing a cell that contains a formula, the Function list (located at the extreme left in the formula bar, as shown in Figure 5-1) displays a list of worksheet functions. You can select a function from the list, and Excel provides assistance entering the arguments.

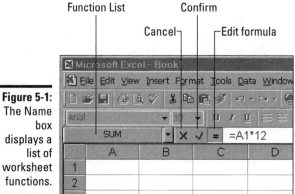

Figure 5-1:
The Name box displays a list of worksheet functions.

When you're editing the contents of a cell, the cursor changes to a vertical bar; you can move the vertical bar by using the direction keys. You can add new characters at the cursor location. Once you're in edit mode, you can use any of the following keys or key combinations to perform your edits:

✦ **Left/right arrow:** Moves the cursor left or right one character, respectively, without deleting any characters.

✦ **Ctrl+left/right arrow:** Moves the cursor one group of characters to the left or right, respectively.

✦ **Shift+left/right arrow:** Selects characters to the left or right of the cursor, respectively.

✦ **Shift+Home:** Selects from the cursor to the first character in the cell.

+ **Shift+End:** Selects from the cursor to the last character in the cell.

+ **Backspace:** Erases the character to the immediate left of the cursor.

+ **Delete:** Erases the character to the right of the cursor or erases all selected characters.

+ **Insert:** Places Excel in OVR (Overwrite) mode. Rather than add characters to the cell, you *overwrite,* or replace, existing characters with new ones, depending on the position of the cursor.

+ **Home:** Moves the cursor to the beginning of the cell entry.

+ **End:** Moves the cursor to the end of the cell entry.

+ **Enter:** Accepts the edited data.

If you change your mind after editing a cell, you can select Edit⇨Undo (or press Ctrl+Z) to restore the cell's previous contents.

You also can use the mouse to select characters while you're editing a cell. Just click and drag the mouse pointer over the characters that you want to select.

Replacing the contents of a cell

To replace the contents of a cell with something else, follow these steps:

1. **Select the cell.**

2. **Make your new entry (it replaces the previous contents).**

Any formatting that you applied to the cell remains.

Erasing data in cells and ranges

To erase the contents of a cell but leave the cell's formatting and cell comments intact, perform the following two steps:

1. **Select the cell or range you want to erase.**

2. **Press Delete.**

For more control over what gets deleted, you can use the Edit⇨Clear command. This menu item leads to a submenu with four additional choices, as shown in Figure 5-2.

All: Clears everything from the cell

Formats: Clears only the formatting and leaves the value, text, or formula

Contents: Clears only the cell's contents and leaves the formatting

Comments: Clears the comment (if one exists) attached to the cell

**Excel
Chapter 5**

**Editing the Data
You Enter**

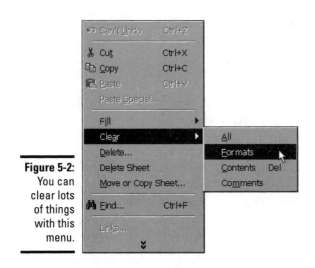

Figure 5-2:
You can
clear lots
of things
with this
menu.

Undoing Changes and Mistakes

One very useful feature in Excel is its multilevel undo. This means that you can reverse your recent actions, one step at a time. For example, if you discover that you accidentally deleted a range of data several minutes ago, you can use the undo feature to "backtrack" through your actions until the deleted range reappears.

Undoing your actions can only be done in a sequential manner. In other words, if you want to undo an action you must also undo all of the actions that you performed after the action that you want to undo. You can undo the past 16 operations that you performed.

To undo an operation, use any of the following techniques:

+ Select the Edit⇨Undo command. The command tells you what you will be undoing.

+ Press Ctrl+Z or Ctrl+Backspace until you arrive at the action that you want to undo.

 + Click the Undo button on the Standard toolbar until you arrive at the action that you want to undo.

+ Click the arrow on the Undo button on the Standard toolbar. This displays a description of your recent actions (see Figure 5-3). Select the actions to undo.

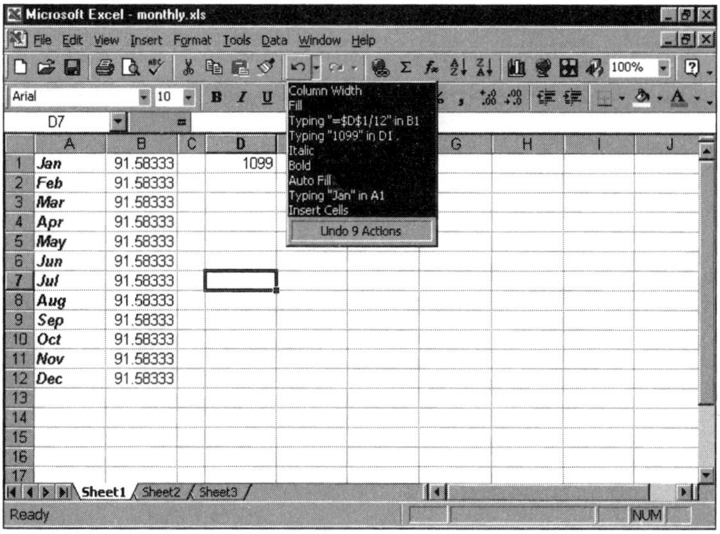

Microsoft Excel - monthly.xls

File Edit View Insert Format Tools Data Window Help

Arial | 10 | B I U

D7 =

	A	B	C	D
1	Jan	91.58333		1099
2	Feb	91.58333		
3	Mar	91.58333		
4	Apr	91.58333		
5	May	91.58333		
6	Jun	91.58333		
7	Jul	91.58333		
8	Aug	91.58333		
9	Sep	91.58333		
10	Oct	91.58333		
11	Nov	91.58333		
12	Dec	91.58333		
13				
14				
15				
16				
17				

Column Width
Fill
Typing "=D1/12" in B1
Typing "1099" in D1
Italic
Bold
Auto Fill
Typing "Jan" in A1
Insert Cells

Undo 9 Actions

Sheet1 / Sheet2 / Sheet3 /

Ready NUM

Figure 5-3:
Look at all
the things
you can
undo!

Using AutoComplete

AutoComplete enables you to type the first few letters of a text entry into a cell, and Excel automatically completes the entry based on other entries that you've already made in the column. AutoComplete works with no effort on your part:

1. **Begin entering text or a value.**

2. **If Excel recognizes your entry, it automatically completes it.**

3. **If Excel guesses correctly, press Enter to accept it. If you want to enter something else, just continue typing and ignore Excel's guess.**

TIP

You also can access this feature by right-clicking the cell and selecting Pick from list. With this method, Excel displays a drop-down list with all of the entries in the current column. Just click the one that you want, and it's entered automatically.

If you don't like this feature, you can turn it off in the Edit panel of the Options dialog box. Remove the check mark from the check box labeled Enable AutoComplete for Cell Values.

Using AutoFill

AutoFill is a handy feature that has several uses (mouse required). AutoFill uses the fill handle — the small square that appears at the bottom-right corner of the selected cell or range. If you right-click and drag a fill handle, Excel displays a shortcut menu of fill options (as shown in Figure 5-4).

Excel
Chapter 5

Editing the Data
You Enter

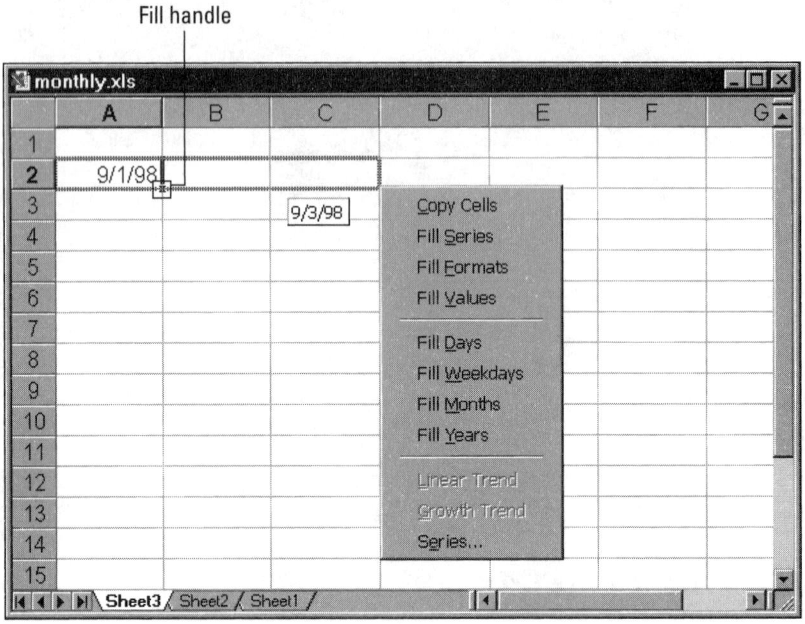

Fill handle

	A	B	C	D	E	F	G
1							
2	9/1/98						
3			9/3/98	Copy Cells			
4				Fill Series			
5				Fill Formats			
6				Fill Values			
7							
8				Fill Days			
9				Fill Weekdays			
10				Fill Months			
11				Fill Years			
12				Linear Trend			
13				Growth Trend			
14				Series...			
15							

monthly.xls

Sheet3 / Sheet2 / Sheet1 /

Figure 5-4:
AutoFill
fills cells to
your order.

If the selected cell or range does not have a fill handle, it means that this feature is turned off. To turn AutoFill on, follow these steps:

1. **Select the Tools⇨Options command.**

2. **Click the Edit tab.**

3. **Check the check box labeled Allow cell drag and drop.**

You cannot use AutoFill when you've made a multiple selection.

Entering a series of incremental values or dates

To use AutoFill to enter a series of incremental values, follow these steps:

1. **Enter at least two values or dates in the series into adjacent cells. These values need not be consecutive.**

2. **Select the cells you used in Step 1.**

3. **Click and drag the fill handle to complete the series in the cells that you select.**

While you drag the fill handle, Excel displays a small box that tells you what it's planning to enter into each cell.

If you drag the fill handle when only one cell is selected, Excel examines the data and determines whether to increment the value or simply copy it. For more control, drag the fill handle while pressing the right mouse button. When you release the button, you get a list of options.

Making a custom list

Are you tired of always retyping the starting lineup of your softball team or the home office's Pacific rim sales staff? Why not teach Excel to recognize these lists? You can make a custom list for anything. Choose Tools➪Options and click the Custom Lists tab. Click the NEW LIST option and enter your list in the box labeled List entries. Click Add to store the list. Your custom list also works with AutoFill.

AutoFill also works in the negative direction. For example, if you use AutoFill by starting with two cells that contain **–20** and **–19**, Excel fills in –18, –17, and so on.

If the values in the cells that you enter do not have equal increments, Excel completes the series by calculating a simple linear regression. This feature is handy for performing simple forecasts. *Note:* Excel calculates a simple linear regression or progression, depending on the direction (negative or positive) of the series.

Entering a series of text

Excel is familiar with some text series (days of the week, month names), and it can complete these series for you automatically. You no longer have to remember such things, thus freeing your mind for more important matters! Here's how to use AutoFill to complete a known series of text:

1. **Enter any of the series into a cell (for example,** Monday **or** February**).**

2. **Click and drag the fill handle to complete the series in the cells that you select.**

Using Automatic Decimal Points

If you're entering lots of numbers with a fixed number of decimal places, you can save some time by letting Excel enter the decimal point (like the feature available on some adding machines).

1. **Select the Tools➪Options command.**

2. **Click the Edit tab.**

3. **Check the check box labeled Fixed decimal and make sure that it's set for the number of decimal places that you want to use.**

Excel now supplies the decimal points for you automatically. For example, if you have it set for two decimal places and you enter **12345** into a cell, Excel interprets it as 123.45 (it adds the decimal point). To restore things to normal, just uncheck the Fixed Decimal check box in the Options dialog box.

Excel Chapter 5

Editing the Data You Enter

Using Cell Comments

The Excel cell comment feature enables you to attach a comment to a cell — useful when you need to document a particular value or to help you remember what a formula does. When you move the mouse pointer over a cell that has a comment, the comment pops up in a small box.

Adding a cell comment

To add a comment to a cell, follow these steps:

1. **Select the cell.**

2. **Choose the Insert⇨Comment command (or press Shift+F2).**

   Excel displays a text box that points to the cell.

3. **Enter the text for the comment into the text box.**

4. **Click any cell when you're finished.**

The cell displays a small red triangle to indicate that the cell contains a comment, as demonstrated in Figure 5-5.

Editing a cell comment

To edit a cell comment, select the cell that contains the comment and then choose the Insert⇨Edit Comment command. Or you can right-click and choose Edit Comment from the shortcut menu.

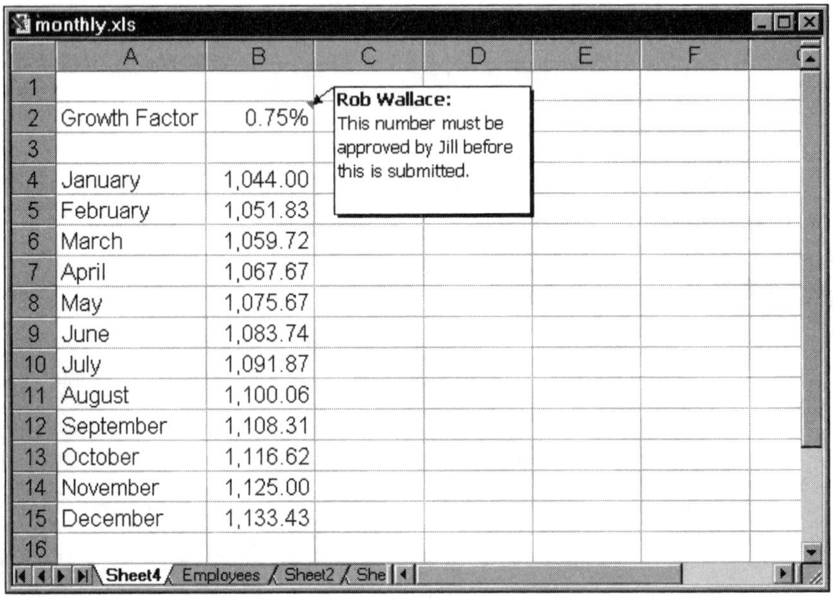

Figure 5-5: Your cells can tell you oh so much with cell comments.

Searching for Data

If your worksheet contains lots of data, you may find it difficult to locate a particular piece of information. A quick way to do so is to let Excel do it for you. Make Excel earn its keep. To locate a particular value or sequence of text, follow these steps:

1. **Select the area of the worksheet that you want to search. If you want to search the entire worksheet, just select a single cell (any cell will do).**

2. **Choose the Edit⇨Find command or press Ctrl+F.**

Excel displays its Find dialog box (see Figure 5-6).

3. **In the Find what box, enter the characters to search for. (If you want to make your search case sensitive, put a check mark in the Match case check box.)**

4. **In the Look in box, specify what to look in: Formulas, Values, or Comments.**

5. **Click the Find Next button.**

Excel selects the cell that contains what you're looking for.

6. **If there is more than one occurrence, repeat Step 5 until you find the cell that you're looking for.**

7. **Click the Close button to end.**

For approximate searches, use *wildcard characters*. An asterisk represents any group of characters in the specified position, and a question mark represents any single character in the specified position. For example, **w*h** represents all text that begins with *w* and ends with *h*. Similarly, **b?n** matches three-letter words such as bin, bun, and ban.

Excel
Chapter 5

Editing the Data
You Enter

Searching and Replacing Data

Sometimes you may need to replace all occurrences of a value or text with something else. Excel makes this task easy to do:

1. **Select the area of the worksheet that you want to search. If you want to search the entire worksheet, just select a single cell (any cell will do).**

2. **Choose the Edit⇨Replace command or press Ctrl+H.**

Excel displays the Replace dialog box.

3. **In the Find what box enter the characters to search for.**

4. **In the Replace with box, enter the characters to replace them.**

5. **Click the Replace All button to have Excel search and replace automatically.**

If you want to verify each replacement, click the Find Next button. Excel pauses when it finds a match. To replace the found text, click Replace. To skip it and find the next match, click the Find Next button again.

6. **Click the Close button when you are finished.**

Spell Checking

Excel has a spell checker that works just like the feature found in word-processing programs. You can access the spell checker using any of these methods:

◆ Select the Tools⇨Spelling command.

 ◆ Click the Spelling button on the Standard toolbar.

◆ Press F7.

The extent of the spell checking depends on what was selected when you accessed the dialog box.

What Is Selected	What Gets Checked
A single cell	The entire worksheet, including cell contents, notes, text in graphic objects and charts, and page headers and footers
A range of cells	Only that range is checked
A group of characters	Only those characters are checked in the formula bar

If Excel encounters a word that isn't in the current dictionary or is misspelled, it offers a list of suggestions you can click to respond to.

Chapter 6: Making Your Work Look Good

In This Chapter

- Formatting cells and ranges automatically

- Formatting cells and ranges the old-fashioned way

- Copying formats for cells and ranges

- Working with numbers

After you enter your data (shown in Chapter 4) and make your various adjustments (as explained in Chapter 5), you can scoot your chair back and admire your work. However, whether you are simply going to view your work onscreen or print a copy of it (see Appendix B for printing help), you may eventually realize that your precious data sure looks boring sitting there in those little cells. Everything appears the same! Why not let yourself get a little creative and make your data more appealing by doing some formatting? Align some text, apply some color, make some backgrounds, change column widths and row heights . . . in brief, let your data express itself. A touch of formatting makes your hard work look really good.

Using AutoFormats

The Excel AutoFormatting feature applies attractive formatting to a table automatically. You hardly have to move a muscle.

1. **Move the cell pointer anywhere within a table that you want to format (Excel determines the table's boundaries automatically).**

2. **Choose the Format➪AutoFormat command.**

    Excel responds with its AutoFormat dialog box (as shown in Figure 6-1).

3. **Select one of the 17 AutoFormats from the list and click OK.**

    Excel formats the table using the selected AutoFormat.

You can't define your own AutoFormats, but you *can* control the type of formatting that is applied. When you click the Options button in the AutoFormat dialog box, the dialog box expands to show six options.

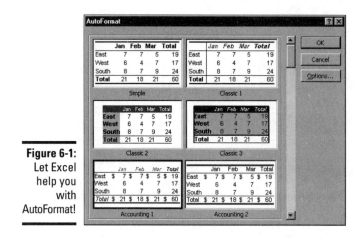

Figure 6-1:
Let Excel
help you
with
AutoFormat!

Initially, the six check boxes are all checked, which means that Excel applies formatting from all six categories. If you want it to skip one or more categories, just uncheck the appropriate boxes by clicking in them before you click OK.

Formatting Cells and Ranges to Your Liking

If AutoFormatting is not for you, realize that you have lots of control over the appearance of information that you enter into a cell. Excel provides three ways to format cells:

✦ **Toolbar buttons:** Common formatting commands are available on toolbar buttons on the Formatting toolbar.

✦ **Shortcut keys:** Some common formats can be applied by pressing shortcut key combinations. For example, Ctrl+B makes the text bold.

✦ **The Format Cells dialog box:** This tabbed dialog box provides all the cell formatting commands. Click one of the six tabs to access a particular panel in the dialog box.

You can bring up the Format Cells dialog box by choosing the Format⇨Cells command or by right-clicking selected cell or range of cells and choose Format Cells from the shortcut menu.

You can format cells before or after you enter information. For example, if you're entering a series of numbers, you can *preformat* the cells so the numbers will appear with commas and the desired number of decimal places.

Aligning cell contents

By default, cell contents appear at the bottom, numbers are right-aligned, text is left-aligned, and logical values are centered in cells.

You can apply the most common horizontal alignment options by selecting the cell or range of cells and using the tools on the Formatting toolbar: Align Left, Center, and Align Right. You can use the following procedure to align cell contents:

1. **Select the cell or range of cells to align.**

2. **Choose the Format⇨Cells command (or press Ctrl+1).**

3. **Click the Alignment tab in the Format Cells dialog box (shown in Figure 6-2).**

4. **Choose the desired horizontal or vertical alignment option from the drop-down lists.**

5. **Click OK.**

Applying background colors and patterns

A cell with some background color or a pattern can really stand out. Changing the background color or pattern used in cells is a breeze.

1. **Select the cell or range that you want to format.**

2. **Choose the Format⇨Cells command (or press Ctrl+1).**

3. **Click the Patterns tab in the Format Cells dialog box.**

4. **Choose a color from the Color section.**

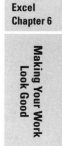

Excel Chapter 6

Making Your Work Look Good

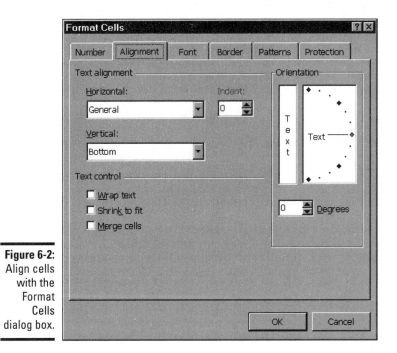

Figure 6-2:
Align cells with the Format Cells dialog box.

5. **To add a pattern, click the Pattern drop-down box and choose a pattern.**

If you like, you can choose a second color for the pattern.

6. **Click OK to apply the color and/or pattern.**

A faster way to change the background color (but not a pattern) is to select the cells and then select a color from the Fill Color tool on the Formatting toolbar.

Applying colors to text

Perhaps you want certain cells to have important text or numbers in a different color. (Red, for example, just begs to be taken notice of.) Following is the fastest way to change the color of text:

1. **Select the cell or range.**

2. **Select a color from the Font Color tool on the Formatting toolbar.**

If you click the down arrow button on the Font Color tool, it expands to show more colors.

You can also change text color in the Font panel of the Format Cells dialog box, if you aren't in a hurry.

Changing column width

You may want to change the width of a column if it's not wide enough to display values fully (you get a series of pound signs like this ####### if your cell entry is too long — and who wants to look at that?). Or you may simply want to space out the cells horizontally. Before changing the width, you can select a number of columns so that the selected columns will all have the same width.

Use any of these methods to change the width of selected columns.

✦ Choose the Format⇨Column⇨Width command and enter a value in the Column Width dialog box.

✦ Drag the right border of the column heading with the mouse until the column is the desired width.

✦ Choose the Format⇨Column⇨AutoFit Selection command. This adjusts the width of the selected column(s) so that the widest entry in the column fits.

✦ Double-click on the right border of a column heading to automatically set the column width to the widest entry in the column.

To change the default width of all columns, use the Format⇨Column⇨Standard Width command. This displays a dialog box into which you enter the new default column width. All columns that haven't been previously adjusted take on the new column width.

Changing row height

Row height is measured in *points* (a standard unit of measurement in the printing trade; 72 points equal one inch). Changing the row height is useful for spacing out rows; it's better to change the row height than to insert empty rows between rows of data. If you want, you can select several rows before using the following techniques to set row height:

✦ Drag the lower row border with the mouse until the row is the desired height.

✦ Choose the Format⇨Row⇨Height command and enter a value (in points) in the Row Height dialog box.

✦ Double-click the bottom border of a row to automatically set the row height to the tallest entry in the row. You also can use the Format⇨Row⇨AutoFit command for this.

Changing fonts and text sizes

The easiest way to change the font or text size for selected cells is to use the Font and Font Size tools on the Formatting toolbar. Just select the cells, click the appropriate tool, and select the font or size from the drop-down list.

You can also use the following technique, which lets you control several other properties of the font from a single dialog box:

1. **Select the cell or range to modify.**

2. **Choose the Format⇨Cells command (or press Ctrl+1).**

3. **Click the Font tab in the Format Cells dialog box (see Figure 6-3).**

4. **Make the desired changes and click OK.**

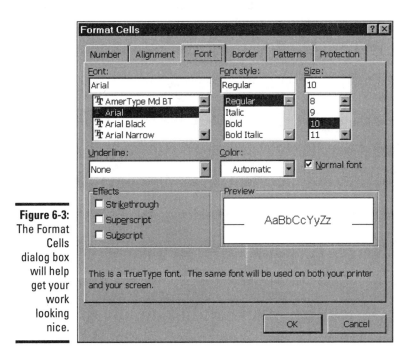

Figure 6-3:
The Format
Cells
dialog box
will help
get your
work
looking
nice.

Changing text direction

Normally, the contents of a cell are displayed horizontally. How traditional! In some cases, you may want to display the text vertically or at an angle for a special effect — or to make it hard for your boss to figure out just where you messed up on last year's sales records.

1. **Select the cell or range to modify.**

2. **Choose the Format➪Cells command (or press Ctrl+1).**

3. **Click the Alignment tab in the Format Cells dialog box.**

4. **Select one of the options in the Orientation section.**

   Adjust the angle by dragging the gauge or specifying an angle (in degrees).

5. **Click OK to apply the formatting to the selection.**

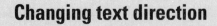

	A	B	C	D	E	F	G	
3		*2nd Q.*	Unit-1	Unit-2	Unit-3			
4		January	132	232	546			
5		February	154	209	566			
6		March	165	312	433			
7								

Bold, italic, underline, and strikethrough!

The easiest way to bold, italicize, underline, or strikethrough text is to select the cell or range and then click the appropriate tool on the Formatting toolbar (for Bold, Italic, or Underline).

Or you can use the following shortcut keys to modify the selected cells.

Format	Shortcut Keys	Toolbar Equivalent
Bold	Ctrl+B	**B**
Italic	Ctrl+I	*I*
Underline	Ctrl+U	U
~~Strikethrough~~	Ctrl+5	

These toolbar buttons and shortcut keys act as a toggle. For example, you can turn bold on and off by repeatedly pressing Ctrl+B (or clicking the Bold tool).

Indenting the contents of a cell

Excel enables you to indent text in a cell. Using this feature is much easier than padding the cell with spaces to indent. Figure 6-4 shows six cells that are indented.

1. **Select the cell or range of cells to indent.**

2. **Choose the Format⇨Cells command (or press Ctrl+1).**

3. **Click the Alignment tab in the Format Cells dialog box.**

4. **Specify the number of spaces to indent in the Indent text box.**

5. **Click OK.**

Indented text is always left-aligned.

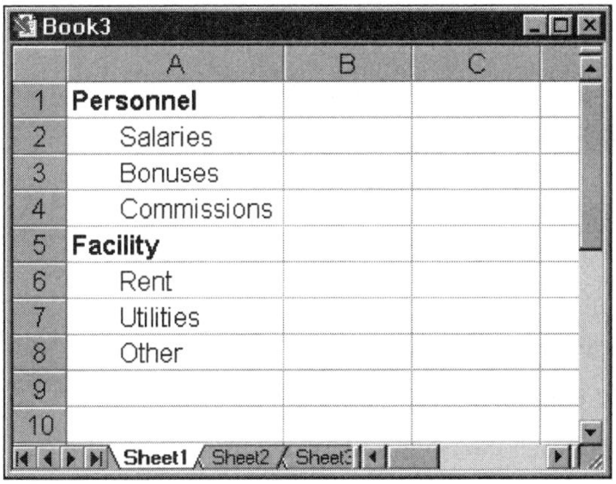

	A	B	C
1	**Personnel**		
2	Salaries		
3	Bonuses		
4	Commissions		
5	**Facility**		
6	Rent		
7	Utilities		
8	Other		
9			
10			

Figure 6-4: Indenting can make your text look more organized.

Excel
Chapter 6

Making Your Work Look Good

Merging cells

Excel offers a helpful feature that allows you to merge cells into a single, larger cell. This feature lets you have cells of unequal sizes. For example, if you have a table that spans six columns, you can merge six cells at the top to form a single larger cell for the table's title. In Figure 6-5, cells C3:E3 are merged horizontally, and cells A5:A8 are merged vertically. To merge a range of cells:

1. **Select the cells to be merged.**

2. **Choose Format⇨Cells (or press Ctrl+1).**

3. **Click the Alignment tab.**

4. **Select the Merge cells checkbox.**

5. **Click OK.**

 You can also merge cells by using the Merge and Center button on the Formatting toolbar. But the only way to "unmerge" cells is to use the Format Cells dialog box and remove the checkmark from the Merge cells checkbox.

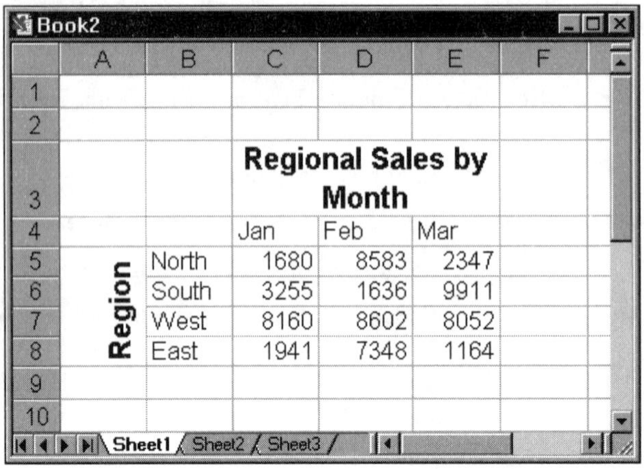

	A	B	C	D	E	F
1						
2						
3			Regional Sales by Month			
4			Jan	Feb	Mar	
5		North	1680	8583	2347	
6		South	3255	1636	9911	
7		West	8160	8602	8052	
8		East	1941	7348	1164	
9						
10						

Figure: 6-5:
Caution!
Merging
cells.

Copying Formats

Instead of redoing all your formats every time you want other cells or ranges to have similar formats, you can use a quick way to copy the formats: Use the Format Painter button on the Standard toolbar.

1. **Select the cell or range that has the formatting attributes that you want to copy.**

2. **Click the Format Painter button.**

Notice that the mouse pointer appears as a miniature paintbrush.

3. **Select (paint) the cells to which you want to apply the formats.**

4. **Release the mouse button, and Excel copies the formats.**

Double-clicking the Format Painter button causes the mouse pointer to remain a paintbrush after you release the mouse button. This lets you paint other areas of the worksheet with the same formats. To exit paint mode, click the Format Painter button again (or press Esc).

Formatting Numbers

Excel is smart enough to perform some number formatting for you automatically. For example, if you enter **9.6%** into a cell, Excel knows that you want to use a percentage format and applies it for you automatically. Similarly, if you use commas to separate thousands (such as **123,456**), or a dollar sign to indicate currency (such as **$123.45**), Excel applies appropriate formatting for you.

Use the Formatting toolbar to quickly apply common number formats. When you click one of these buttons, the active cell takes on the specified number format. Table 6-1 lists these toolbar buttons.

Table 6-1	Number Formats	
Button Name		*Formatting Applied*
Currency Style	$	Adds a dollar sign to the left, separates thousands with a comma, and displays the value with two digits to the right of the decimal point
Percent Style	%	Displays the value as a percentage with no decimal places
Comma Style	,	Separates thousands with a comma and displays the value with two digits to the right of the decimal place
Increase Decimal	+.0 .00	Increases the number of digits to the right of the decimal point by one
Decrease Decimal	.00 +.0	Decreases the number of digits to the right of the decimal point by one

Remember: These five toolbar buttons actually apply predefined *styles* to the selected cells. This is not the same as simply changing the number format.

If none of the predefined number formats fits the bill, you need to use the Format Cells dialog box:

1. **Select the cell or range that contains the values to format.**

2. **Choose the Format⇨Cells command (or press Ctrl+1).**

3. **Click the Number tab.**

4. **Select one of the 12 categories of number formats.**

When you select a category from the list box, the right side of the panel changes to display appropriate options.

5. **Select an option from the right side of the dialog box.**

Options will vary, depending on your category choice. The top of the panel displays a sample of how the active cell will appear with the selected number format.

6. **After you make your choices, click OK to apply the number format to all the selected cells.**

Excel
Chapter 6

Making Your Work
Look Good

Chapter 7: Selecting, Copying, and Moving Your Data

In This Chapter

↙ **Selecting cells and ranges**

↙ **Copying cells and ranges**

↙ **Moving cells and ranges**

*U*nless you type 500 words per minute without mistake, one of the biggest time-savers you need to know is how to copy some data from one place to another, whether it be between places in the same worksheet, between worksheets in the same workbook, or even between worksheets of different workbooks. And if you can copy, you can also move data between places. No more retyping! What a breakthrough in spreadsheet management!

The key to copying and moving data, however, is knowing how to select data. This chapter gives you the lowdown on all these actions. You won't regret opening to this page.

Selecting Cells and Ranges

In Excel, you normally select a cell or range before performing an operation that works with the cell or range. Topics in this section describe how to make various types of cell and range selections.

Selecting a cell

To select a cell (and make it the active cell), use any of the following techniques:

✦ Move the cell pointer to the cell using the arrow keys.

✦ Click the cell with the mouse.

✦ Use the Edit⇨Go To command (or press F5 or Ctrl+G), enter the cell address in the Reference box, and click OK.

The selected cell has a dark border around it, and its address appears in the Name box.

Selecting entire rows and columns

You can select entire rows or columns in several ways:

✦ Click the row or column heading to select a single row or column.

✦ To select multiple adjacent rows or columns, simply click a row or column heading and drag to highlight additional rows or columns.

✦ To select multiple (nonadjacent) rows or columns, press Ctrl while you click the row or column headings that you want.

✦ Press Ctrl+spacebar to select the column of the active cell or the columns of the selected cells.

✦ Press Shift+spacebar to select the row of the active cell or the rows of the selected cells.

✦ Click the Select All button (or Ctrl+Shift+spacebar) to select all rows. Selecting all rows is the same as selecting all columns, which is the same as selecting all cells.

Selecting a range

You can select a range in several ways:

✦ Click the mouse in a cell and drag to highlight the range. If you drag to the end of the screen, the worksheet scrolls.

✦ Move to the first cell of the range. Press F8 and then move the cell pointer with the direction keys to highlight the range. Press F8 again to return the direction keys to normal movement.

✦ Press the Shift key while you use the arrow keys to select a range.

✦ Use the Edit⇨Go To command (or press F5), enter a range's address in the Reference box, and click OK.

When you select a range in Excel 2000, Excel shows the range in the See-Through View. Instead of appearing in reversed video like older versions of Excel, the cells appear as if behind a transparent colored shade. This transparent selection makes it easier to see the true colors and formatting underneath the selection.

Selecting noncontiguous ranges

Most of the time, the ranges that you select will be *contiguous* — a single rectangle of cells. Excel also lets you work with noncontiguous ranges, which consist of two or more ranges (or single cells), not necessarily next to each other (also known as a *multiple selection*), as demonstrated in Figure 7-1.

If you want to apply the same formatting to cells in different areas of your worksheet, one approach is to make a multiple selection. After you select the appropriate cells or ranges, Excel applies the formatting that you choose to all the selected cells. You can select a noncontiguous range in several ways:

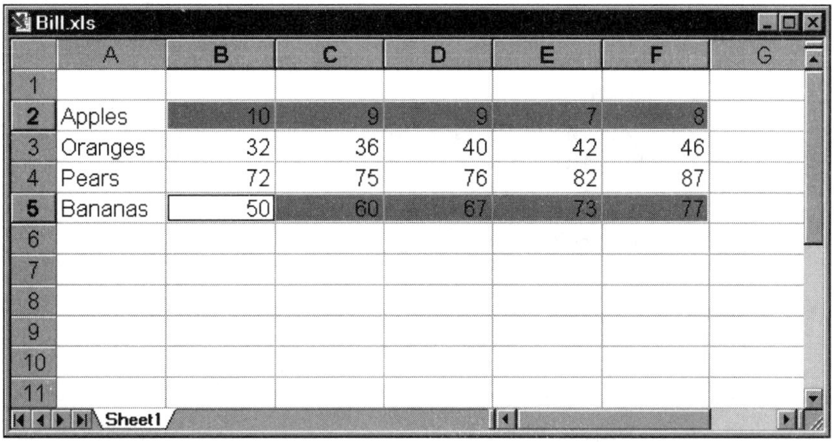

	A	B	C	D	E	F	G
1							
2	Apples	10	9	9	7	8	
3	Oranges	32	36	40	42	46	
4	Pears	72	75	76	82	87	
5	Bananas	50	60	67	73	77	
6							
7							
8							
9							
10							
11							

Figure 7-1:
You can select non-contiguous ranges if need be.

♦ Hold down Ctrl while you click the mouse and drag to highlight the individual cells or ranges.

♦ From the keyboard, select a range by pressing F8 and then use the arrow keys. After selecting the first range, press Shift+F8, move the cell pointer, and press F8 to start selecting another range.

♦ Use the Edit⇨Go To command (or press F5 or Ctrl+G) and enter a range's address in the Reference box. Separate the different ranges with a comma. Click OK, and Excel selects the cells in the ranges that you specified.

Copying Cells and Ranges

Copying cells is a very common spreadsheet operation, and several types of copying are allowed. You can do any of the following:

♦ Copy one cell to another cell.

♦ Copy a cell to a range of cells. The source cell is copied to every cell in the destination range.

♦ Copy a range to another range.

Older versions of Excel use the Windows Clipboard to hold data for copying and pasting. The Windows Clipboard can store only one piece of data at a time. When you copy new data to the Windows Clipboard, it replaces the existing data. Excel 2000 uses the new Office Clipboard, which can store up to 12 data items at one time.

Remember: Copying a cell normally copies the cell contents, its cell comment (if any), and the formatting applied to the original cell. When you copy a cell that contains a formula, the cell references in the copied formulas are changed automatically to be relative to their new location. See Chapter 8 for help with formulas.

Excel
Chapter 7

Selecting, Copying, and Moving Your Data

In general, copying consists of two steps:

1. **Select the cell or range to copy (the source range) and copy it to the Office Clipboard.**

2. **Move the cell pointer to the range that will hold the copy (the destination range) and paste the Clipboard contents.**

You may select more than one cell or range to copy at a time. When you copy the second cell or range to the Office Clipboard, Excel pops up the Clipboard toolbar (see Figure 7-2). From the Clipboard toolbar you can select an item to paste to a new range in your workbook or you can simultaneously paste all of the copied items to the new range.

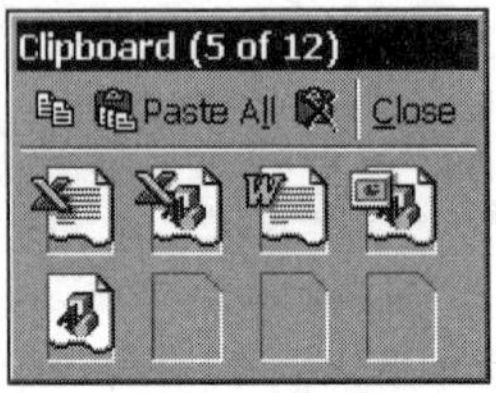

Figure 7-2:
The Clipboard shows five items ready for pasting.

Copying a cell to another cell or a range

To copy the contents of one cell to a range of cells, follow these steps:

1. **Move the cell pointer to the cell to copy.**

2. **Click the Copy button on the Standard toolbar.**

   You can also press Ctrl+C or choose Edit⇨Copy.

3. **Select the cell or range that you want to hold the copy.**

4. **Press Enter.**

> If the range that you're copying to is adjacent to the cell that you're copying from, you can drag the cell's AutoFill handle to copy it to the adjacent range. (The AutoFill handle is that little black square in the lower-right of a cell.)

Copying a range to another range

If you can copy and paste a cell's contents, why not an entire range? You have the power within you. To copy the contents of one range to another range of the same size, follow these steps:

1. **Select the range to copy.**

2. **Click the Copy button on the Standard toolbar (you can also press Ctrl+C or choose the Edit⇨Copy command).**

3. **Select the upper-left cell of the range that you want to hold the copy.**

4. **Press Enter.**

Copying data to another worksheet or workbook

Someday you may want to copy something to another worksheet or even to another workbook. The routine may seem somewhat familiar to you if you've already copied data within the same worksheet.

1. **Select the cell or range to copy.**

2. **Click the Copy button on the Standard toolbar.**

You can also press Ctrl+C or choose the Edit⇨Copy command.

3. **Click the tab of the worksheet that you're copying to.**

If the worksheet is in a different workbook, activate that workbook (you can select the workbook from the Window menu) and then click the tab of the worksheet that you want to hold the copied data.

4. **Select the upper-left cell of the range that you want to hold the copy.**

5. **Press Enter.**

Moving Cells and Ranges

Moving the data in a cell or a range is common. For example, you may need to relocate a range of data to make room for something else. Or you just may have plunked down some data in the wrong place. It happens. Moving works on the same principle as copying (explained earlier in this chapter).

Moving data to a new location in the same worksheet

Here's how to move a cell or range:

1. **Select the cell or range to move.**

2. **Select the Edit⇨Cut command.**

Or you can press Ctrl+X or click the Cut button on the Standard toolbar.

3. **Move the cell pointer to the range that you want to hold the copy (you need only select the upper-left cell).**

4. **Press Enter.**

If the range that you're moving contains formulas that refer to other cells, the references continue to refer to the original cells. You almost always want references to continue to refer to the original cells.

When you move data, make sure that there are enough blank cells to hold it. Excel overwrites existing data without warning.

Remember: If you change your mind after Step 2, press Esc to cancel the operation. If you change your mind after you've already moved the data, choose Edit⇨Undo Paste or press Ctrl+Z.

Moving data to a different worksheet or workbook

If you want to move the contents of a cell or range to a different worksheet or to a different workbook, follow these steps:

1. **Select the cell or range to move.**

2. **Select the Edit⇨Cut command.**

Or you can press Ctrl+X or click the Cut button on the Standard toolbar.

3. **Activate the worksheet that you're moving to. If you're moving the selection to a different workbook, activate that workbook and then activate the worksheet.**

4. **Move the cell pointer to the range that you want to hold the copy (you need only select the upper-left cell).**

5. **Press Enter.**

When you move data, make sure that there are enough blank cells to hold it. Excel overwrites existing data without warning.

Remember: If you change your mind after Step 2, press Esc to cancel the operation. If you change your mind after the data has already been moved, choose the Edit⇨Undo Paste command or press Ctrl+Z.

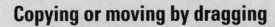

Copying or moving by dragging

If the location that you're copying or moving to isn't too far away (and you want to conserve precious seconds or maybe just impress onlookers), you can drag data from place to place.

1. **Select the cell or range to copy.**

2. **Hold down the Ctrl key if you want to copy data. Don't hold down anything if you want to move data.**

3. **Move the mouse pointer to any of the selection's borders.**

   The mouse pointer turns into an arrow accompanied by a small plus sign (+) if you are copying. If you are moving, the mouse pointer turns into an arrow without anything.

4. **Drag the mouse to the location where you want to copy or move the cell or range.**

5. **Release the mouse button.**

   Your data is either copied or moved as if by magic.

Remember that the key (literally!) to copying or moving by dragging is the Ctrl key.

Chapter 8: Using Formulas and Functions

In This Chapter

✔ Creating your own formulas

✔ Discovering your formula errors

✔ Making absolute and relative cell references

✔ Entering functions

✔ Using the Formula Palette

*Y*ou haven't chosen to work in Excel 2000 just to type your diary into neat little cells or to conduct your business correspondence (and if you have, jump right back to the section of this book covering Word 2000). You're certainly working in Excel in order to manipulate your data — adding, subtracting, multiplying, finding standard deviations (whatever those are), and the like. This chapter introduces you to the wonderful world of formulas — as well as to the Excel built-in functions that you can use to assist you in formula construction and to make your formulas perform some additional calculations.

Using Formulas

You use formulas to perform all sorts of calculations on the data that you enter. When you enter a formula into a cell, the cell displays the result of the formula. You see the formula itself in the formula bar when the cell is activated.

Table 8-1 provides a list of operators that you can use in formulas.

Table 8-1	Formula Operators
Operator	*Name*
+	Addition
−	Subtraction
*	Multiplication

(continued)

Table 8-1 *(continued)*

Operator	Name
/	Division
^	Exponentiation (raised to a power)
&	Concatenation (joins text)
=	Logical comparison (equal to)
>	Logical comparison (greater than)
<	Logical comparison (less than)

Operator precedence is the set of rules that Excel uses to perform its calculations in a formula. Table 8-2 lists the Excel operator precedence. This table shows that exponentiation has the highest precedence (that is, it's performed first), and logical comparisons have the lowest precedence. If two operators have the same precedence, Excel performs the calculations from left to right.

Remember: You can override operator precedence by using parentheses in your formulas.

Table 8-2	**Operator Precedence**	
Symbol	*Operator*	*Precedence*
^	Exponentiation	1
*	Multiplication	2
/	Division	2
+	Addition	3
–	Subtraction	3
&	Concatenation	4
=	Equal to	5
>	Greater than	5
<	Less than	5

Creating a formula is a snap — as long as you remember to begin every formula with an equal sign (=). For example, suppose that you have a column of numbers that you want to add (as shown in Figure 8-1). Cell B4 seems like a good spot to place your total, right? So just follow these steps:

1. **Select the cell where you want to place your formula's results (in this case, cell B4).**

2. **Type your formula:**

   =B1+B2+B3

3. **Press Enter.**

   Your formula disappears from the cell, and the result appears in the cell that you selected. Your formula (if you re-select that cell) appears in the formula bar.

Note: Don't worry about having to redo a formula if you make a change in the data. Excel automatically recalculates the results for you. Now that's service!

If you think that creating a formula is easy, the process gets even easier when you discover how to use functions, which are ready-made formulas. (You can read about functions later in this chapter.)

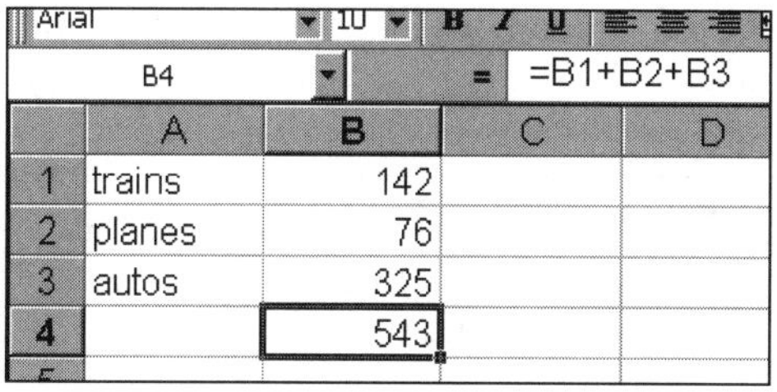

Arial		▼	10	▼	B	I	U	≡	≡	≡	
B4		▼			=	=B1+B2+B3					

Figure 8-1:
Let Excel
do your
calculations
for you.

	A	B	C	D
1	trains	142		
2	planes	76		
3	autos	325		
4		543		

Identifying Formula Errors

Excel flags errors in formulas with a message that begins with a pound sign (#). The message part itself is in all capital letters so that you don't miss it. This occurrence signals that the formula is returning an error value. You have to correct the formula (or correct a cell that is referenced by the formula) to get rid of the error display.

If the entire cell is filled with pound signs, the column isn't wide enough to display the value. Check out Chapter 6 for info on how to widen a column.

Table 8-3 lists the types of error values that may appear in a cell that has a formula.

Table 8-3	Types of Error Values
Error Value	**Explanation**
#DIV/0!	The formula is trying to divide by zero (an operation that's not allowed on this planet). This also occurs when the formula attempts to divide by an empty cell.
#NAME?	The formula uses a name that Excel doesn't recognize. This can happen if you delete a name that's used in the formula or if you have unmatched quotes when using text.
#N/A	The formula is referring (directly or indirectly) to a cell that uses the NA functions to signal the fact that data is not available.
#NULL!	The formula uses an intersection of two ranges that don't intersect.
#NUM!	There is a problem with a value; for example, you specified a negative number where a positive number is expected.
#REF!	The formula refers to a cell that isn't valid. This can happen if the cell has been deleted from the worksheet.
#VALUE!	The formula has a function with an invalid argument, or the formula uses an operand of the wrong type (such as text where a value is expected).

Using Absolute, Relative, and Mixed References

An *absolute reference* uses two dollar signs in its address: one for the column part and one for the row part. When you copy a formula that has an absolute reference, the reference is not adjusted in the copied cell.

Relative references, on the other hand, are adjusted when the formula is copied.

Excel also allows mixed references in which only one of the address's parts is absolute. The following table summarizes all of the possible types of cell references.

Example	Type
A1	Relative reference
A1	Absolute reference
$A1	Mixed reference (column part is absolute)
A$1	Mixed reference (row part is absolute)

To change the type of cell reference in a formula, follow these steps:

1. **Double-click the cell (or press F2) to get into edit mode.**

2. **In the formula bar, move the cursor to a cell reference.**

3. **Press F4 repeatedly to cycle through all possible cell reference types. Stop when the cell reference displays the proper type.**

When a formula refers to cells in a different workbook, the other workbook doesn't need to be open. If the workbook is closed, you must add the complete path to the reference. Here's an example:

```
=A1*'C:\MSOffice\Excel\[Budget For 1999]Sheet1'!A1
```

Using Functions in Your Formulas

Excel provides more than 300 built-in functions that can make your formulas perform powerful feats and save you a great deal of time.

Functions do the following:

✦ Simplify your formulas

✦ Allow formulas to perform calculations that are otherwise impossible

✦ Allow "conditional" execution of formulas — giving them some rudimentary decision-making capability

Table 8-4 shows you a list of some of the most popular functions. Why not all? Remember that Excel has more than 300 ready-made functions for all purposes, from math to engineering, from financial to statistical (and more). Take a look at the Help files in Excel 2000 for an explanation of all the functions. (Did you know that COSH returns the hyperbolic cosine of a number? Most humans don't need to do that, whatever it is — but someone somewhere is very happy that Excel can handle hyperbolic cosines!)

Table 8-4	Common Functions in Excel
Function	*Action*
SUM	The sum of the values
COUNT	The number of items
AVERAGE	The average of the values
MAX	The largest value
MIN	The smallest value
PRODUCT	The product of the values
STDDEV	An estimate of the standard deviation of a population, where the sample is all the data to be summarized
STDDEVP	The standard deviation of a population, where the population is all the data to be summarized
VAR	An estimate of the variance of a population, where the sample is all the data to be summarized
VARP	The variance of a population, where the population is all the data to be summarized

Entering functions manually

If you're familiar with the function that you want to use, you may choose to type the function and its arguments into your formula. Often this is the most efficient method. A function is composed of three elements:

+ The equal sign (=) to indicate that what follows is a formula

+ The function name, such as SUM or AVERAGE, which indicates what operation is to be performed

+ The argument, which indicates the cell addresses of the data that the function will act on — and you can indicate the range of a row or column by inserting a colon (:) between the starting and ending cell addresses, such as A1:A70

If you glance back at "Creating a formula" earlier in this chapter, you can see the simple formula:

=B1+B2+B3

You can more easily express this as a function by typing:

=SUM(B1:B3)

When you enter a function, Excel always converts it to uppercase. It's a good idea to use lowercase when entering functions: If Excel doesn't convert it to uppercase, it means that it doesn't recognize your entry as a function (you probably spelled it incorrectly).

Modifying a range reference used in a function

When you edit a cell that contains a formula, Excel color-codes the references in the formula and places an outline around each cell or range referenced in the formula. The color of the outline corresponds to the color displayed in the formula. Each outlined cell or range also contains a fill handle (a small square in the lower-left corner), as shown in Figure 8-2.

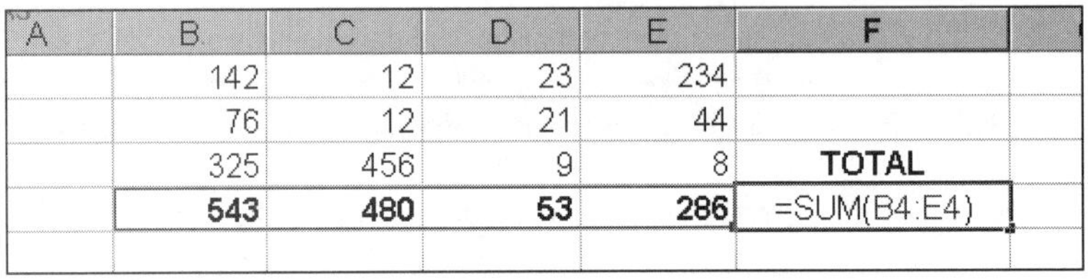

Figure 8-2:
Just
imagine
the pretty
colors you
can see
when you
edit a cell
with a
formula!

A	B	C	D	E	F
	142	12	23	234	
	76	12	21	44	
	325	456	9	8	TOTAL
	543	480	53	286	=SUM(B4:E4)

If your formula contains a function that uses a range argument, you can easily modify the range reference by following these steps:

1. **To begin editing the formula, press F2, double-click the cell, or click the Edit Formula icon (=) in the formula bar.**

2. **Locate the range that the function uses (the range is outlined).**

3. **Drag the fill handle to extend or contract the range. Or, you can click a border of the outlined range and move the outline to a new range. In either case, Excel changes the range reference in the formula.**

4. **Press Enter.**

Using the Formula Palette

The Formula Palette makes it easy to enter a function and its arguments. Using this tool ensures that the function is spelled correctly and has the proper number of arguments in the correct order.

To enter a function using the Formula Palette, select the cell that will contain the function and then use either of these two methods:

✦ Select the Insert⬧Function command (or click the Paste Function button) and select the function from the Paste Function dialog box (shown in Figure 8-3).

✦ Click the Edit Formula icon (=) on the edit line and then select a function from the function list in the Name box. If the function does not appear on the list, select the More Functions option and choose the function from the Paste Function dialog box.

REAL WORLD

Editing formulas and functions

If you make a typo when entering a formula or a function, you can edit your entry just like editing any other entry in Excel.

1. **Select the cell that contains your formula or function.**

2. **Click in the Formula bar and use the left or right arrow key to move your insertion point.**

3. **Use the Delete or Backspace keys to delete characters. You can also block text**

by dragging through it and then replacing the selected characters by simply typing in a new entry.

4. **Press Enter when you're satisfied that you got it right this time.**

If you're in a big hurry to edit that cell, double-click the cell. The insertion point appears inside the cell, and you can undo your damage from there, saving a long trip up to the Formula bar.

Excel displays the Formula Palette directly below the edit line (you can drag it to a new location if it's in your way). The Formula Palette prompts you for each argument of the function you selected. You can enter the arguments manually or (if they are cell references) point to them in the worksheet. The Formula Palette displays the result. When you've specified all of the required arguments, click OK.

◆ You can use the Formula Palette to insert a function into an existing formula. Click the Edit Formula button (=) to bring up the Formula Palette. Then move the cursor to the location where you want to insert the function and choose the function from the function list.

◆ You can use the Formula Palette to edit a function in an existing formula. Click the Edit Formula button (=) to bring up the Formula Palette. Then click the function in the formula. Use the Formula Palette to adjust the function's arguments.

**Excel
Chapter 8**

**Using Formulas
and Functions**

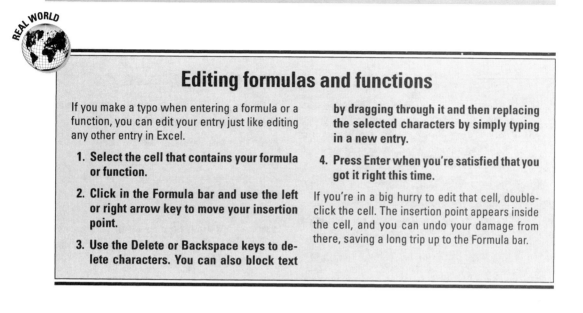

Figure 8-3:
The
Formula
Palette
helps you
enter a
function.

REAL WORLD

Using templates to make your life easier

A *template* is a workbook that's all set up with formulas and ready for you to enter data. Lucky for you, Excel comes with templates for workbooks. To create a workbook from a template, follow these steps:

1. Choose File⇨New to bring up the New dialog box.

2. Select the template that you want (click a tab to display additional templates).

3. Click OK to open a copy of the template.

If you can't find a ready-made template for what you want to do, you can simply create your own. You may be surprised how easy it is!

1. Create a workbook to your liking to serve as a template for your future work.

2. With your workbook open, choose File⇨Save As.

3. In the Save As dialog box that appears, select Template from the drop-down list box labeled Save As Type.

4. Save the template in your Templates folder (or a subfolder within the Templates folder).

Chapter 9: Managing and Analyzing Your Data

In This Chapter

✓ Filtering and sorting lists of data

✓ Making a formula return a desired value

✓ Performing what-if analysis

*Y*ou can stare at your data for hours on end and still gain nothing for your time. Spreadsheet data is often not much good unless you can analyze it. If you're familiar with some of the actions that you can perform on a database, managing and analyzing your data in Excel 2000 is within your grasp. And even if you've never heard of a database, you can still filter and sort lists to your heart's content.

Besides filtering and sorting actions, you can also use this chapter to discover how to observe effects on formulas when you change input values.

If you enjoy this sort of stuff — and who doesn't? — get started on this chapter without delay.

Filtering and Sorting Lists

You can store information of just about any type in a *list.* If you're familiar with the concept of a *database table,* you'll recognize that a list has many similarities:

✦ Columns correspond to fields.

✦ Rows correspond to records.

✦ The first row of the table should have field names that describe the data in each column.

Applying database functions with lists

To create a formula that returns results based on filtered criteria, use the Excel database worksheet functions. For example, you can create a formula that calculates the sum of values in a list that meet certain criteria. Set up a criteria range in your worksheet and then enter a formula such as the following:

```
=DSUM(ListRange,FieldName,Criteria)
```

In this case, *ListRange* refers to the list, *FieldName* refers to the field name cell of the column being summed, and *Criteria* refers to the criteria range.

Table 9-1 describes the database functions.

Table 9-1	Excel Database Functions
Function	*Description*
DAVERAGE	Returns the average of selected database entries
DCOUNT	Counts the cells containing numbers from a specified database and criteria
DCOUNTA	Counts nonblank cells from a specified database and criteria
DGET	Extracts from a database a single record that matches the specified criteria
DMAX	Returns the maximum value from selected database entries
DMIN	Returns the minimum value from selected database entries
DPRODUCT	Multiplies the values in a particular field of records that match the criteria in a database
DSTDEV	Estimates the standard deviation based on a sample of selected database entries
DSTDEVP	Calculates the standard deviation based on the entire population of selected database entries
DSUM	Adds the numbers in the field column of records in the database that match the criteria
DVAR	Estimates variance based on a sample from selected database entries
DVARP	Calculates variance based on the entire population of selected database entries

Here are some examples of text criteria:

Criteria	Effect
>K	Text that begins with L through Z
<>C	All text, except text that begins with C
January	Text that matches January
Sm*	Text that begins with sm
s*s	Text that begins with s and ends with s
s?s	Three-letter text that begins with *s* and ends with *s*

The text comparisons are not case sensitive. For example, si* matches *Simon* as well as *sick*.

Computed criteria filters the list based on one or more calculations and does not use a field header from the list (it uses a new field header). Computed criteria essentially computes a new field for the list so that you must supply new field names in the first row of the criteria range.

Computed criteria is a logical formula (returns True or False) that refers to cells in the first row of data in the list; it does *not* refer to the header row.

Filtering a list with autofiltering

Autofiltering lets you view only certain rows in your list by hiding rows that do not qualify based on criteria you set. To autofilter a list, follow these steps:

1. **Move the cell pointer anywhere within the list.**

2. **Choose the Data⇨Filter⇨AutoFilter command.**

   Excel analyzes your list and then adds drop-down arrows to the field names in the header row, as shown in Figure 9-1.

3. **Click the arrow on one of these drop-down lists.**

   The list expands to show the unique items in that column.

4. **Select an item.**

   Excel hides all rows except those that include the selected item. In other words, the list is filtered by the item that you selected.

After you filter the list, the status bar displays a message that tells you how many rows qualified. In addition, the drop-down arrow changes color to remind you that the list is filtered by a value in that column.

The drop-down list includes five other items:

  ✦ **All:** Displays all items in the column. Use this to remove filtering for a column.

  ✦ **Top 10:** Filters to display the "top 10" items in the list. Actually, you can display any number of the top (or bottom) values.

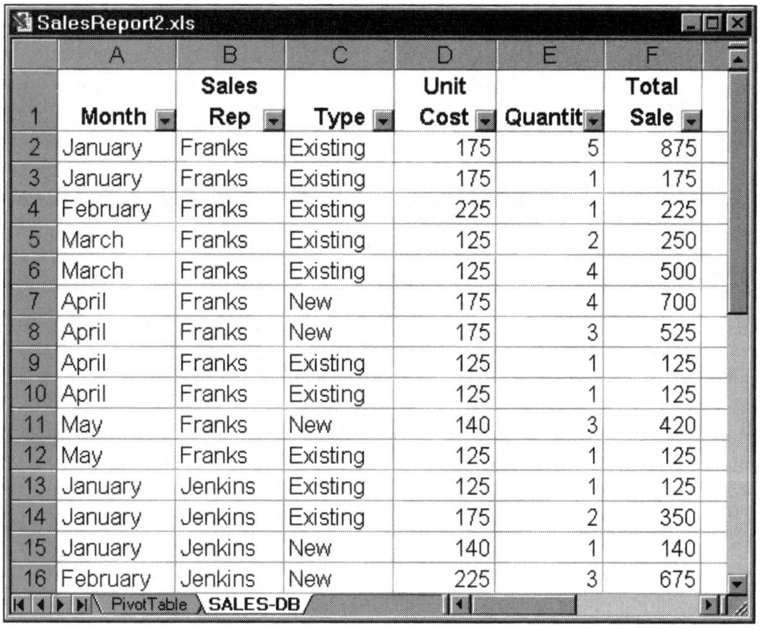

	A	B	C	D	E	F
1	Month	Sales Rep	Type	Unit Cost	Quantity	Total Sale
2	January	Franks	Existing	175	5	875
3	January	Franks	Existing	175	1	175
4	February	Franks	Existing	225	1	225
5	March	Franks	Existing	125	2	250
6	March	Franks	Existing	125	4	500
7	April	Franks	New	175	4	700
8	April	Franks	New	175	3	525
9	April	Franks	Existing	125	1	125
10	April	Franks	Existing	125	1	125
11	May	Franks	New	140	3	420
12	May	Franks	Existing	125	1	125
13	January	Jenkins	Existing	125	1	125
14	January	Jenkins	Existing	175	2	350
15	January	Jenkins	New	140	1	140
16	February	Jenkins	New	225	3	675

Figure 9-1: Autofiltering can hide unqualified rows for your convenience.

+ **Custom:** Lets you filter the list by multiple items.

+ **Blanks:** Filters the list by showing only rows that contain blanks in this column.

+ **NonBlanks:** Filters the list by showing only rows that contain non-blanks in this column.

The Blanks and NonBlanks options will only appear if the list contains at least one blank field

To display the entire list again, select the Data⇨Filter⇨Show All command.

To get out of AutoFilter mode and remove the drop-down arrows from the field names, choose the Data⇨Filter⇨AutoFilter command again.

Filtering a list with custom autofiltering

Normally, autofiltering involves selecting a single value for one or more columns. The list is then filtered by that value. For more flexibility, choose the Custom option in an AutoFilter drop-down list. The Custom AutoFilter dialog box lets you filter in several ways (see Figure 9-2):

+ **Values above or below a specified value:** For example, sales amounts greater than 10,000.

+ **Values within a range:** For example, sales amounts greater than 10,000 AND sales amounts less than 50,000.

+ **Values outside of a range:** For example, sales amounts less than 10,000 or sales amounts greater than 50,000.

+ **Two discrete values:** For example, state equal to New York OR state equal to New Jersey.

+ **Approximate matches:** You can use the * and ? wildcards to filter in many other ways. For example, to display only those customers whose last name begins with a B, use **B***.

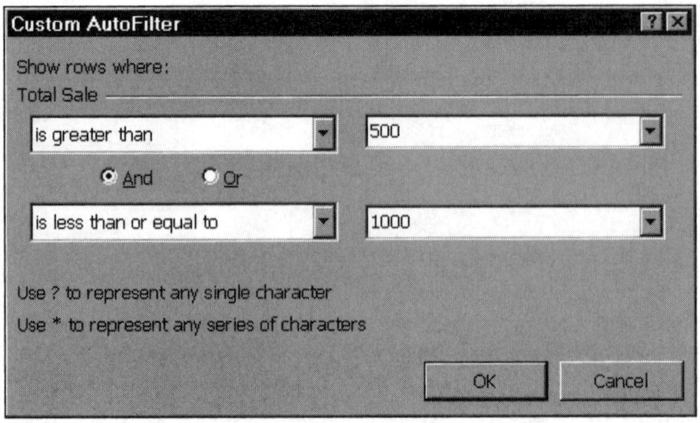

Figure 9-2:
Use the
Custom
AutoFilter
to
customize
your
filtering.

Custom AutoFilter	? X
Show rows where:	
Total Sale	
is greater than ▼	500 ▼
⦿ And ◯ Or	
is less than or equal to ▼	1000 ▼
Use ? to represent any single character	
Use * to represent any series of characters	
	OK Cancel

Custom autofiltering is useful, but it has limitations. For example, if you would like to filter the list to show only three values in a field (such as New York or New Jersey or Connecticut), you can't do it by using autofiltering. Such filtering tasks require the advanced filtering feature.

Performing Advanced Filtering

Before you can use the advanced filtering feature, you must set up a *criteria range* — a range on a worksheet that holds the information Excel uses to filter the list. The criteria range must conform to the following specifications:

✦ The criteria range consists of at least two rows.

✦ The first row contains some or all of the field names from the list.

✦ The other rows consist of filtering criteria.

If you use more than one row below the field names in the criteria range, the criteria in each row are joined with an OR operator.

The entries that you make in a criteria range can be either of the following:

✦ Text or value criteria: The filtering involves comparisons to a value or text, using operators such as equal (=), greater than (>), not equal to (<>), and so on.

✦ Computed criteria: The filtering involves some sort of computation.

Advanced filtering is more flexible than autofiltering, but it takes some up-front work to use it. Advanced filtering provides you with the following capabilities:

✦ You can specify more complex filtering criteria.

✦ You can specify computed filtering criteria.

✦ You can extract a copy of the rows that meet the criteria to another location.

To perform advanced filtering on a list, follow these steps:

1. **Set up a criteria range.**

2. **Choose the Data⇨Filter⇨Advanced Filter command.**

3. **In the Advanced Filter dialog box (shown in Figure 9-3), specify the list range and the criteria range, and make sure to select the option labeled Filter the list, in-place.**

4. **Click OK, and the list is filtered by the criteria that you specified.**

Sorting a list

Sorting a list involves rearranging the rows such that they are in ascending or descending order, based on the values in one or more columns. For example, you may want to sort a list of salespeople alphabetically by last name or by sales region. Or you may want to sort your relatives by how much money they owe you. The fastest way to sort a list is to use the Sort Ascending or Sort Descending buttons on the Standard toolbar:

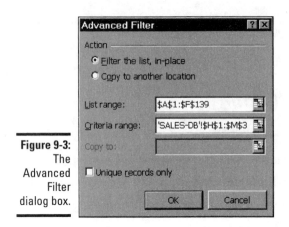

Figure 9-3:
The
Advanced
Filter
dialog box.

1. **Move the cell pointer to the column upon which you want to base the sort.**

2. **Click the Sort Ascending button or the Sort Descending button.**

Excel sorts the list by the current column.

You may need to sort a list by more than one column. For example, you might want to sort by state, by city within the state, and by zip code within the city. To sort a list on multiple columns, use the procedure above for each column that you want to sort. Always start with the "least important" column (for example, zip code) and end with the "most important" column (for example, state).

When you sort a filtered list, only the visible rows are sorted. When you remove the filtering from the list, the list will no longer be sorted.

If the sorted list contains formulas that refer to cells in other rows in the list, the formulas will not be correct after the sorting. If formulas in your list refer to cells outside the list, make sure that the formulas use an absolute cell reference.

Another way to sort a list follows:

1. **Choose the Data⇨Sort command.**

Excel displays the Sort dialog box. (See Figure 9-4.)

2. **Select the first sort field from the drop-down list labeled Sort by and specify Ascending or Descending order.**

3. **Repeat Step 2 for the second and third sort fields (if desired).**

4. **Click Options and select any sort options (described here).**

• **First key sort order:** Lets you specify a custom sort order for the sort.

• **Case sensitive:** Makes the sorting case sensitive so that uppercase letters appear before lowercase letters in an ascending sort. Normally, sorting ignores the case of letters.

• **Orientation:** Lets you sort by columns rather than by rows (the default).

5. **Click OK to return to the Sort dialog box.**

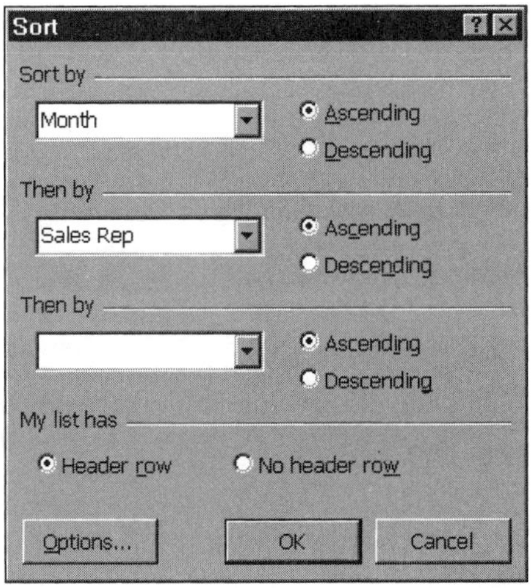

Figure 9-4:
The user-
friendly
Sort dialog
box.

6. **Click OK and the list's rows are rearranged.**

If the Header row option is set, the first row (field names) is not affected by the sort.

Using a custom sort order

Sorting is done either numerically or alphabetically, depending on the data. In some cases, you may want to sort your data in other ways. If your data consists of month names, you probably want them to appear in month order rather than alphabetically. Excel, by default, has four custom lists, and you can define your own. To sort by a custom list, click the Options button in the Sort dialog box; then select the list from the First key sort order drop-down list. Excel custom lists are as follows:

✦ **Abbreviated days:** Sun, Mon, Tue, Wed, Thu, Fri, Sat

✦ **Days:** Sunday, Monday, Tuesday, Wednesday, Thursday, Friday, Saturday

✦ **Abbreviated months:** Jan, Feb, Mar, Apr, May, Jun, Jul, Aug, Sep, Oct, Nov, Dec

✦ **Months:** January, February, March, April, May, June, July, August, September, October, November, December

To create a custom list, follow these steps:

1. **Choose the Tools⇨Options command.**

2. **In the Options dialog box, click the Custom Lists tab.**

3. **Click the NEW LIST option.**

4. **Enter your list in the List entries box.**

5. **Click Add and then click OK to close the Options dialog box.**

Goal Seeking: Making a Formula Return a Desired Value

Excel's goal-seeking feature lets you determine which value an input cell will produce a desired result in a formula cell. And if you can comprehend that, here's the procedure:

1. **Start with a workbook that uses formulas.**

2. **Select the Tools⇨Goal Seek command.**

3. **Complete the Goal Seek dialog box (shown in Figure 9-5) by specifying the formula cell to change, the value to change it to, and the cell to change.**

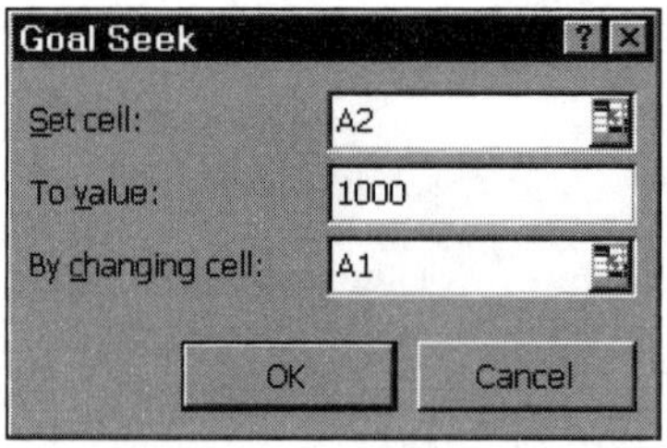

Figure 9-5:
Goal
seeking
with the
Goal Seek
dialog box.

Goal Seek	? X
Set cell:	A2
To value:	1000
By changing cell:	A1
OK	Cancel

4. **Click OK.**

Excel displays the solution.

5. **Click OK to replace the original value with the found value; or click Cancel to restore your worksheet to the form that it was in before you issued the Tools⇨Goal Seek command.**

Excel can't always find a value that produces the result that you're looking for (sometimes a solution just doesn't exist). In such a case, the Goal Seek status box informs you of that fact.

Performing What-If Analysis (Scenarios)

What-if analysis refers to the process of changing one or more input cells and observing the effects on formulas. An *input cell* is a cell that is used by a formula. For example, if a formula calculates a monthly payment amount for a loan, the formula would refer to an input cell that contains the loan amount.

Creating a data table (one-input)

A *one-input data table* displays the results of one or more result formulas for multiple values of a single input cell. For example, if you have a formula that calculates a loan payment, you can create a data table that shows the payment amount for various interest rates. The interest rate cell is the input cell. Boring but useful, as demonstrated in Figure 9-6.

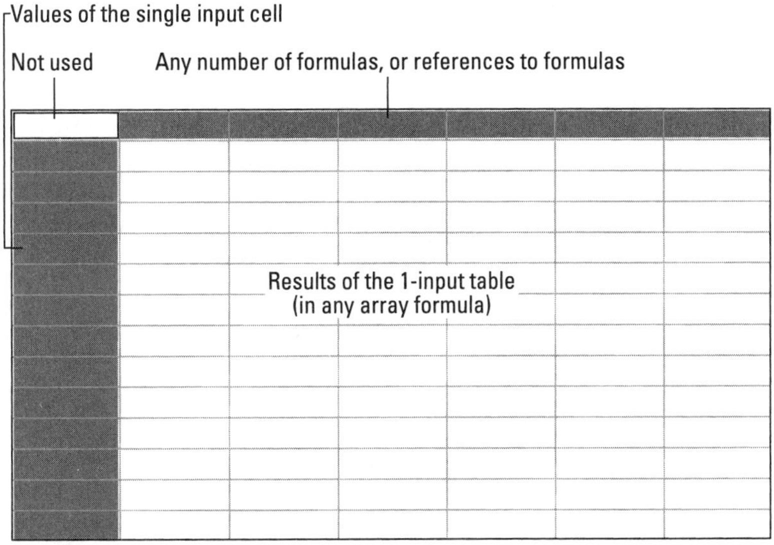

Values of the single input cell

Not used   Any number of formulas, or references to formulas

Results of the 1-input table
(in any array formula)

Figure 9-6:
A one-input data table.

To create the table, follow these steps:

1. **Select the table range.**

2. **Choose the Data⇨Table command.**

3. **Specify the worksheet cell that you're using as the input value.**

If the variables for the input cell are located in a column, use the Column input cell field. If the variables are in a row, use the Row input cell field.

4. **Click OK.**

Excel performs the calculations and fills in the table.

Excel uses an array formula that uses the TABLE function. Therefore, the table will be updated if you change the cell references in the first row or plug in different values in the first column.

Creating a data table (two-input)

A *two-input data table* displays the results of a single formula for various values of *two* input cells (see Figure 9-7). For example, if you have a formula that calculates a loan payment, you can create a data table that shows the payment amount for various interest rates and loan amounts. The interest rate cell and the loan amount cell are the input cells.

Different values of the first input cell

A single formula, or a reference to a formula

Different values of the second input cell

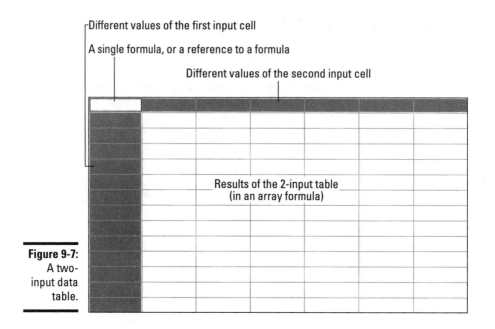

Results of the 2-input table
(in an array formula)

Figure 9-7:
A two-
input data
table.

To create a two-input data table, follow these steps:

1. **Select the table range.**

2. **Choose the Data⇨Table command.**

3. **Specify the cell for the Row input cell.**

4. **Specify the cell for the Column input cell.**

5. **Click OK.**

Excel performs the calculations and fills in the table.

Chapter 10: Taking Advantage of Pivot Tables

In This Chapter

✔ **Making and formatting pivot tables**

✔ **Inserting and removing fields and items in a pivot table**

✔ **Modifying and refreshing a pivot table**

You haven't had any fun in Excel 2000 until you get to use pivot tables. Why, you ask? Well, the name sounds as if you are doing something really complicated, so impressing your family and professional colleagues is very easy:

"Mr. Taylor, I'd like have the McKinley report on your desk by tomorrow morning, but I have to create a pivot table in order to perform a dynamic summary of my data." (**Note:** If you're trying to impress your family, substitute "Mom" or any relevant title for "Mr. Taylor.")

If they only knew the truth. Excel 2000 makes creating and using pivot tables as easy as choosing a few menu options and clicking buttons here and there on some simple dialog boxes. All you have to do is to provide the data.

Pivot Tables

A *pivot table* is a dynamic summary of data contained in a database (contained on a worksheet or in an external file). A pivot table lets you create frequency distributions and cross-tabulations made up of several different data dimensions. In addition, you can display subtotals at any level of detail you desire. Generally speaking, fields in a database table can be one of two types:

✦ *Data:* Contains a value

✦ *Category:* Describes the data

A database table can have any number of data fields and any number of category fields. When you create a pivot table, you usually want to summarize one or more of the data fields. The values in the category fields appear in the pivot table as rows, columns, or pages.

Creating a pivot table

To create a pivot table from a worksheet database, follow these steps:

1. **Move the cell pointer to any cell in the database.**

2. **Choose the Data➪PivotTable and PivotChart Report command.**

   Excel displays the first of three dialog boxes.

3. **Make sure that the options labeled Microsoft Excel List or Database and PivotTable are selected and click Next.**

4. **In the second dialog box, ensure that the database range is specified (Excel automatically identifies the database range) and click Next.**

5. **In the third dialog box, specify the location for the pivot table (a new worksheet or an existing worksheet).**

6. **Click the Options button if desired to specify additional options (see below) and then click Finish.**

7. **Excel 2000 displays on-sheet interactive drop zones and a floating PivotTable Toolbar that includes the field names from your database. Drag the field names from the PivotTable toolbar to the appropriate drop zones.**

   The drop zones are outlined in blue and are labeled for easy identification. (See Figure 10-1.)

Excel includes several options for pivot tables, which are available when you click the Options button in the third step of the PivotTable Wizard (shown in Figure 10-2):

AutoFormat table: Check this box if you want Excel to apply a default AutoFormat to the pivot table. Excel uses the AutoFormat even if you rearrange the table layout.

Subtotal hidden page items: Check this box if you want Excel to include hidden items in the Page fields in the subtotals.

Merge labels: Check this box if you want Excel to merge the cells for outer row and column labels. Doing so may make the table more readable.

Preserve formatting: Check this box if you would like Excel to keep any formatting that you applied when the pivot table is updated.

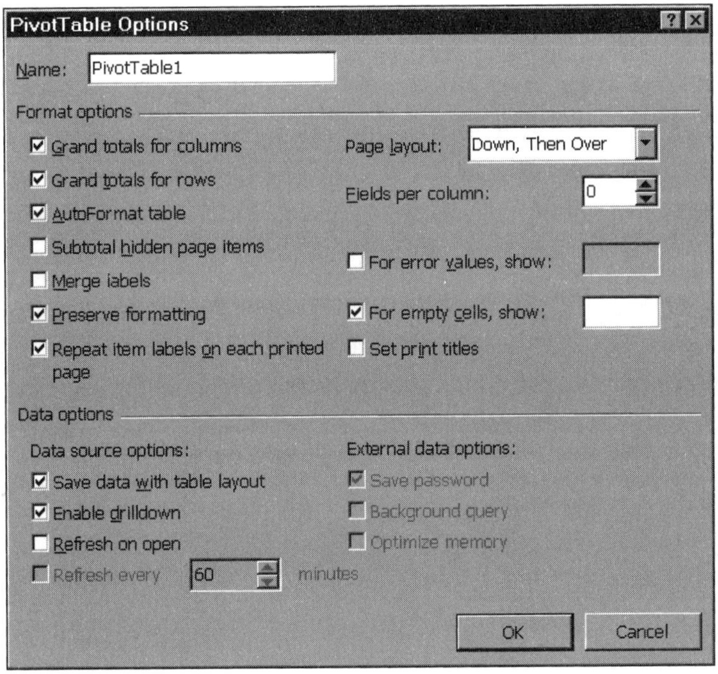

Figure 10-2:
The
imposing
PivotTable
Options
dialog box.

Repeat item labels on each printed page: Check this box if you want Excel to repeat item labels on each page for all rows to the left of the field for which a page break separates a group of items.

Page layout: Specify the order in which you want the page fields to appear.

Fields per column: Specify the number of page fields to show before starting another row of page fields.

For error values, show: You can specify a value to show for pivot table cells that display an error.

For empty cells, show: You can specify a value to show for pivot table cells that are empty.

Set print titles: Check this box if you want Excel to repeat row labels, column labels, and item labels on each page of a PivotTable report. This option is applicable only for PivotTable reports in indented format. Also, Page Setup options used to repeat rows and columns should be cleared.

Save data with table layout: If this option is checked, Excel stores an additional copy of the data (called a *pivot table cache*) to allow it to recalculate the table more quickly when you change the layout. If memory is an issue, keep this option unchecked (updating will be a bit slower).

Enable drilldown: If checked, you can double-click a cell in the pivot table to view details.

Refresh on open: If checked, the pivot table is refreshed whenever you open the workbook.

Refresh every xxxxx minutes: To periodically refresh a report based on external data, check this box and then enter the interval you want in the minutes box. This check box is unavailable for reports based on Excel source data. Minutes can range from 1 to 32767 inclusive.

Save password: If you use an external database that requires a password, this option enables you to store the password as part of the query so you won't have to enter it.

Background query: If checked, Excel runs the external database query in the background while you continue your work.

Optimize memory: This option reduces the amount of memory used when you refresh an external database query.

If the data is in an external database, select the External Data Source option in Step 3 of the preceding list of steps. The data is retrieved using MS Query (a separate application), and you'll be prompted for the data source in the second PivotTable Wizard dialog box.

In Step 7, you can drag as many fields as you want to any of the drop zones, and you don't have to use all the fields. Fields that aren't used don't appear in the pivot table.

Formatting a pivot table

When you create a pivot table, you have an option of applying a default table AutoFormat. After the pivot table is created, you can specify a different AutoFormat. Excel 2000 comes with a new PivotTable AutoFormat feature that provides 22 pivot table AutoFormats. Figure 10-3 shows a few of these formats.

To change or use an AutoFormat after the pivot table is created, select a cell within the pivot table and use any of the these methods:

✦ Choose the Format➪AutoFormat command. This command displays the AutoFormat dialog box with a list of pivot table AutoFormats. This list replaces the standard worksheet AutoFormats.

✦ Right-click anywhere in the pivot table and select Format Report from the shortcut menu.

✦ Choose the PivotTable➪Format Report command on the Pivot Table toolbar.

When Excel creates a pivot table report, it does not retain any special number formatting that you may have applied to your original data. For example, if you apply a currency format to your data and then use that data in the pivot table, the currency formatting is not retained in the pivot table.

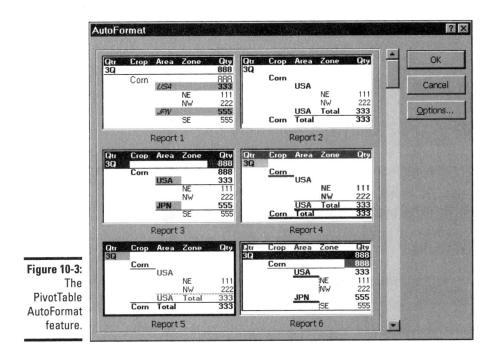

Figure 10-3:
The
PivotTable
AutoFormat
feature.

To change the number format for the data in the pivot table, here's what you need to do:

1. **Select any cell in the pivot table's data area.**

2. **Right-click and choose Fi_e_ld Settings from the shortcut menu.**

Excel displays its PivotTable Field dialog box.

3. **Click the _N_umber button.**

4. **Select the number format that you need.**

Use one of the AutoFormats labeled Report 1, Report 2, Report 3, and so on when you want to display and/or print a report in indented format, similar to the traditional banded or formatted database report. Selecting an indented format changes the layout of your report.

Grouping pivot table items

A handy feature enables you to group specific items in a field of a pivot table. If one of the fields in your database consists of dates, for example, the pivot table displays a separate row or column for every date. You may find it more useful to group the dates into months or quarters and then hide the details. To create a group of items in a pivot table, follow these steps:

1. **Select the cells to be grouped.**

2. Choose the Data⇨Group and Outline⇨Group command.

Excel creates a new field that consists of the selected items.

3. You can change the names of the new field and the items by editing them in the Formula bar.

If the items to be grouped are not next to each other, make a multiple selection by pressing Ctrl and selecting the items that will make up the group.

If the field items consist of values, dates, or times, you can let Excel do the grouping for you. Why should you sweat it? To create groups *automatically*, follow these steps:

1. Select any item in the field (only one).

2. Choose the Data⇨Group and Outline⇨Group command.

Excel displays the Grouping dialog box, shown in Figure 10-4.

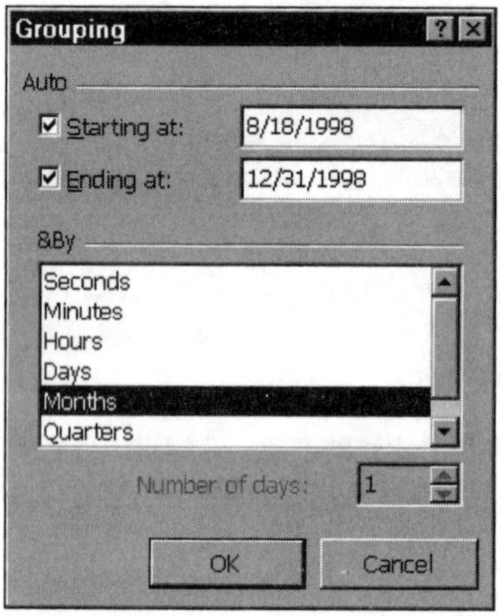

Figure 10-4:
The
Grouping
dialog box
is always
ready to
group.

3. Select the grouping options.

4. Click OK.

Excel creates the groups.

Inserting a new field into a pivot table

To add a new field to a pivot table, follow these steps:

1. Move the cell pointer anywhere within the pivot table.

2. Drag the new field from the PivotTable toolbar to the desired location in the pivot table.

Removing a field from a pivot table

To remove a field from a pivot table (maybe the one you just added!), follow these steps:

1. **Click the field button that you want to remove.**

2. **Drag it away from the pivot table.**

3. **Release the mouse button, and Excel updates the pivot table, removing the field you dragged away.**

Inserting a calculated field into a pivot table

Excel lets you create new calculated fields for a pivot table. For example, if you have a field named TotalSales, you may want to create a calculated field to project sales for another period. The calculation would use the value of TotalSales. Calculated fields must reside in the Data area of the pivot table (you cannot use them in the Page, Row, or Column areas).

To create a calculated field, follow these steps:

1. **Move the cell pointer anywhere within the pivot table.**

2. **Right-click and choose Formulas⇨Calculated Field from the shortcut menu.**

Excel displays the Insert Calculated Field dialog box (see Figure 10-5).

3. **Enter a name for the field and specify the formula. The formula can use other fields and worksheet functions, but it cannot refer to cells or use names.**

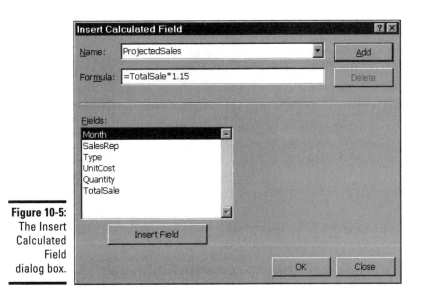

Figure 10-5:
The Insert
Calculated
Field
dialog box.

4. **Click the Add button.**

5. **Repeat Steps 3 and 4 if you want to create additional fields.**

6. **Click OK to close the dialog box.**

After you create the field, it appears in the pivot table.

If you plan on using field names in your calculated field formulas, you should name the fields without spaces.

Inserting a calculated item into a pivot table

Excel enables you to create new calculated items for a pivot table. For example, if you have a field named Months, you can create a calculated item (called Q1, for example) that displays the sum of January, February, and March. Calculated items must reside in the Page, Row, or Column area of a pivot table (you cannot use them in the Data area).

To create a calculated item, follow these steps:

1. **Move the cell pointer to a Row, Column, or Page area of the pivot table.**

The cell pointer cannot be in the Data area.

2. **Right-click and choose For̲mulas⊳Calculated I̲tem from the shortcut menu.**

Excel displays the Insert Calculated Item dialog box, as ably demonstrated in Figure 10-6.

3. **Type a name for the item and specify the formula.**

The formula can use items in other fields and worksheet functions, but it cannot refer to cells or use names.

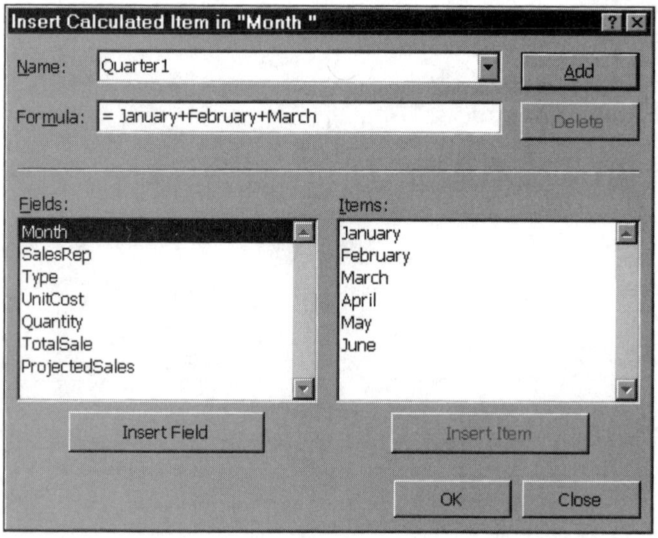

Figure 10-6:
The Insert
Calculated
Item
dialog box.

Insert Calculated Item in "Month "	? ☒
N̲ame: Quarter1 ▾	Add
For̲mula: = January+February+March	Delete

F̲ields:	I̲tems:
Month	January
SalesRep	February
Type	March
UnitCost	April
Quantity	May
TotalSale	June
ProjectedSales	

Insert Field	Insert Item
	OK Close

4. **Click the Add button.**

5. **Repeat Steps 3 and 4 if you want to create additional items.**

6. **Click OK to close the dialog box.**

After you create the item, it appears in the pivot table.

If you plan on using item names in your calculated item formulas, you should name the items without spaces.

Modifying a pivot table's structure

A pivot table displayed in a worksheet includes the field buttons. You can drag any of the field buttons to a new position in the pivot table (this is known as *pivoting*). For example, you can drag a column field to the row position. Excel immediately redisplays the pivot table to reflect your change.

You also can change the order of the row fields or the column fields by dragging the buttons. This affects how the fields are nested and can have a dramatic effect on how the table looks. You can also drag fields from the PivotTable toolbar to modify an existing pivot table's structure.

A pivot table is a special type of range, and (except for formatting) you can't make any changes to it. For example, you can't insert or delete rows, edit results, or move cells. If you attempt to do so, Excel displays an error message. Do you want that to happen?

Refreshing a pivot table

If you change the source data that is used by a pivot table, the pivot table doesn't get updated automatically. Rather, you must *refresh* it manually. To refresh a pivot table, use any of the these methods:

✦ Choose the Data➪Refresh Data command.

✦ Right-click anywhere in the pivot table and select Refresh Data from the shortcut menu.

✦ Click the Refresh button on the Pivot Table toolbar.

If the source database is large, there may be some delay while this recalculation takes place, but for small databases the update is virtually instantaneous.

Excel
Chapter 10

Taking Advantage of
Pivot Tables

Chapter 11: Charting the Excel Way

In This Chapter

🖊 **Creating charts with the Chart Wizard**

🖊 **Doing basic chart maintenance**

🖊 **Changing charts and chart types**

🖊 **Managing chart elements**

🖊 **Viewing more of a 3-D chart**

*W*hen you show your data to someone, wouldn't it be great to put that data into a visual form? Excel 2000 helps you convert data into chart form so that your data is more than an abstract jumble of text and numbers. Of course, you can create many different types of charts, including the standard favorites such as bar, pie, line, and scatter charts.

You can also choose from variants such as column and area charts, or explore chart types such as bubble, cylinder, cone, and pyramid. To get started on a chart, let the Chart Wizard of Excel 2000 get you going.

Using the Chart Wizard

The Chart Wizard consists of a series of four dialog boxes that prompt you for various settings for the chart. By the time you reach the last dialog box, the chart will usually be exactly what you need:

1. **Before you invoke the Chart Wizard, you should select the data that you want to include in the chart. Include in your selection items such as labels and series identifiers.**

The data that you're plotting doesn't have to be contiguous. You can press Ctrl while making a multiple selection.

2. **After selecting the data, invoke the Chart Wizard by clicking the Chart Wizard button on the Standard toolbar. Or you can select the Insert⇨Chart command.**

Excel displays the first Chart Wizard dialog box, as shown in Figure 11-1.

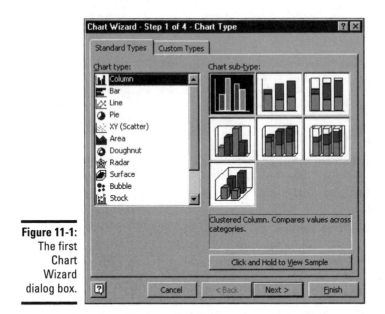

Figure 11-1:
The first
Chart
Wizard
dialog box.

While using the Chart Wizard, you can go back to the previous step by clicking the Back button. Or you can click Finish to end the Chart Wizard. If you end it early, Excel creates the chart using the information you provided up to that point.

Chart Wizard Step 1 of 4

The first step of the Chart Wizard involves selecting the chart type.

1. **Select the chart type.**

To use a standard chart type, make your selection in the Standard Types tab. Then choose one of the chart subtypes.

To get a preview of how your data will look with the selected chart type, use the button below the list of chart subtypes. Click the button, but don't release it.

To use a custom chart type, make your selection in the Custom Types tab.

2. **Click the Next button to move on to the next step.**

Chart Wizard Step 2 of 4

In the second step of the Chart Wizard (see Figure 11-2), you verify (or change) the ranges used in the chart.

1. **Make sure the range displayed in the Data range box is the range you want to use for the chart.**

2. **If the data series are in rows, click the Rows option. If the data series are in columns, select the Columns option.**

The dialog box displays a preview.

3. **If you want to adjust the ranges used for an individual series, click the Series tab and make the changes.**

4. **Click the Next button to move on to the next step.**

Remember: The Row or Column selection in Step 2 is an important choice that has a drastic effect on the look of your chart. Most of the time, Excel guesses the data orientation correctly — but not always.

Chart Wizard Step 3 of 4

The third Chart Wizard dialog box (shown in Figure 11-3) consists of six tabs. Use these tabs to adjust various options for the chart. As you make your selections, the preview chart reflects your choices.

Titles: Enter titles for various parts of the chart.

Axes: Select the type of values to display on the axes.

Gridlines: Specify gridlines, if any.

Legend: Specify whether to display a legend, and its location in the chart.

Data Labels: Specify whether to display data labels (and which type) for the data series.

Data Table: Specify whether to display a table of values used by the chart.

Click Next to move to the final step.

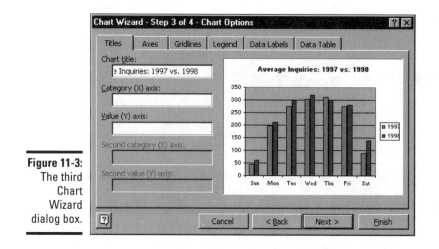

Figure 11-3:
The third
Chart
Wizard
dialog box.

Chart Wizard Step 4 of 4

In Step 4 of the Chart Wizard (shown in Figure 11-4), you specify where you want the chart to display. You can display it as a new chart sheet or as an object in an existing worksheet (you can select the sheet).

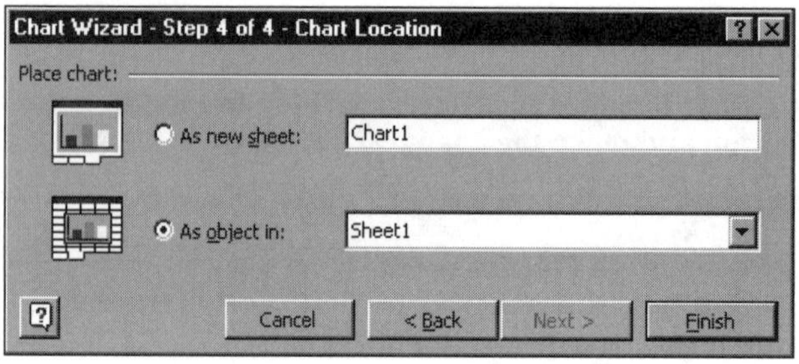

Figure 11-4:
Step 4 of
the Chart
Wizard.

When you click Finish, Excel creates the chart per your specifications.

Charting Basics

After your chart is done, you still can't relax. Now it's time to do all those things that you should have done right earlier!

Before you can do anything with a chart, you must activate it:

✦ To activate a chart on a chart sheet, click the chart sheet's tab.

✦ To activate an embedded chart, click the chart.

Adding a new data series to a chart

You can add a new data series to a chart in several ways:

✦ Select the range to be added and drag it into the chart. When you release the mouse button, Excel updates the chart with the data you dragged into it. This technique works only if the chart is embedded on the worksheet.

✦ Activate the chart and select the Chart➪Add Data command. Excel displays a dialog box that prompts you for the range of data to add to the chart.

✦ Select the range to be added and copy it to the Office Clipboard. Then activate the chart and choose the Edit➪Paste Special command. Excel responds with the Paste Special dialog box. Complete this dialog box to correspond to the data that you selected.

✦ Activate the chart and then click the Chart Wizard tool. You'll get the first Chart Wizard dialog box. Click the Next button to get to the second dialog box. Edit the range reference to include the new data series (or point to the new range in the worksheet). Click Finish and Excel updates the chart with the new data.

Changing a chart's data series

Often, you create a chart that uses a particular range of data, and then you extend the data range by adding new data points in the worksheet. When you add new data to a range, the new data won't be included in the data series. Or you may delete some of the data points in a range that is plotted. If you delete data from a range, the chart displays the deleted data as zero values.

To update the chart to reflect the new data range, follow these steps:

1. **Activate the chart.**

2. **Choose the Chart➪Source Data command.**

3. **In the Source Data dialog box, select the tab labeled Series.**

4. **Select the data series that you want to modify from the list labeled Series.**

5. **Use the range selection boxes to change the data series. You may also need to modify the range used for the Category values.**

6. **Click OK, and the chart is updated with the new data range.**

In Step 4, you could select the Data Range tab of the Source Data dialog box and specify the data range for the entire chart.

When you activate a chart, the ranges used by the chart are outlined in the worksheet. To extend or reduce the range, simply drag the handle on the outline in the worksheet.

A better way to handle data ranges that change is to use named ranges. Simply create names for the data ranges that you use in the chart. Activate the chart, select the data series, and edit the SERIES formula by clicking the formula bar. Replace each range reference with the corresponding range name. If you change the definition for a name, the chart is updated.

Working with chart legends

If you created your chart with the Chart Wizard, you had an option to include a legend (Step 3). If you change your mind, you can easily delete the legend or add one if you need one.

If you didn't include legend text when you originally selected the cells to create the chart, Excel displays *Series 1, Series 2,* and so on in the legend. To add series names, follow these steps:

1. **Activate the chart.**

2. **Choose the Chart⇨Source Data command.**

3. **In the Source Data dialog box, click the Series tab.**

4. **Select a series in the Series box and then enter a name in the Name box.**
For the name, you can use text or a reference to a cell that contains the series name.

5. **Repeat Step 4 for each series that you want to name.**

6. **Click OK and the new names appear in the legend.**

Changing a chart's scale

Adjusting the scale of a value axis can have a dramatic effect on the appearance of the chart. Excel always determines the scale for your charts automatically. You can, however, override the choice Excel makes:

1. **Activate the chart.**

2. **Select the value (Y) axis.**

3. **Choose the Format⇨Selected Axis command (or double-click the axis).**

4. **In the Format Axis dialog box shown in Figure 11-5, click the Scale tab.**

5. **Make the changes and then click OK.**

The dialog box varies slightly depending on which axis is selected. The Scale tab of the Format Axis dialog box offers the following options:

Minimum: Lets you enter a minimum value for the axis. If checked, Excel determines this value automatically.

Maximum: Lets you enter a maximum value for the axis. If checked, Excel determines this value automatically.

Major unit: Lets you enter the number of units between major tick marks. If checked, Excel determines this value automatically.

Minor unit: Lets you enter the number of units between minor tick marks. If checked, Excel determines this value automatically.

Category (X) axis Crosses at: Lets you position the axes at a different location. By default, the axes are positioned at the edge of the plot area. The exact wording of this option varies, depending on which axis you select.

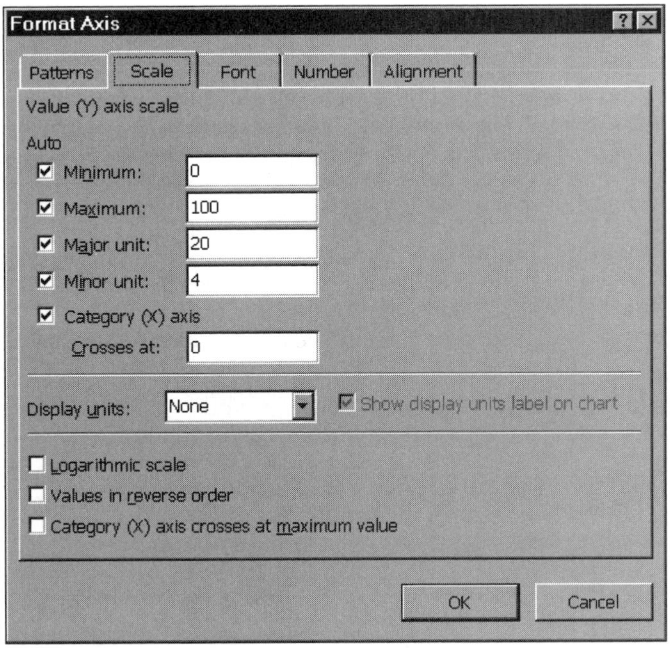

Format Axis

Patterns | Scale | Font | Number | Alignment

Value (Y) axis scale

Auto

☑ Mi_n_imum: `0`

☑ Ma_x_imum: `100`

☑ Ma_j_or unit: `20`

☑ Mi_n_or unit: `4`

☑ Category (X) axis

_C_rosses at: `0`

Display _u_nits: `None` ☑ Show display units label on chart

☐ _L_ogarithmic scale
☐ Values in _r_everse order
☐ Category (X) axis crosses at _m_aximum value

OK | Cancel

Figure 11-5:
The Format
Axis
dialog box.

Display units: Lets you set the display units for large numbers on the axis. Using this option can make numbers displayed on the axis shorter and more readable.

Show display units label on chart: Lets you add a label on the axis that describes the units selected in the Display units drop-down box.

Logarithmic scale: Lets you use a logarithmic scale for the axes. Useful for scientific applications in which the values to be plotted have an extremely large range; a log scale gives you an error message if the scale includes 0 or negative values.

Values in reverse order: Makes the scale values extend in the opposite direction.

***Category (X) axis* crosses at maximum value:** Lets you position the axes at the maximum value of the perpendicular axis (normally, the axis is positioned at the minimum value). The exact wording varies, depending on which axis you select.

Excel
Chapter 11

Charting the
Excel Way

Changing a chart's gridlines

Gridlines can help you determine what the chart series represents numerically. Gridlines simply extend the tick marks on the axes.

To add or remove gridlines, follow these steps:

1. **Activate the chart.**

2. **Choose the _C_hart⇨Chart _O_ptions command.**

3. **Click the Gridlines tab.**

4. **Check or uncheck the check boxes that correspond to the desired gridlines.**

Each axis has two sets of gridlines: major and minor. Major units are the ones displaying a label. Minor units are those in between. If you're working with a 3-D chart, the dialog box has options for three sets of gridlines.

Changing a chart's location

If your chart is embedded on a worksheet, you can click a border and drag it to a new location on the worksheet. To move the embedded chart to a different sheet or to a separate chart sheet, select the chart and choose the Chart⇨Location command. Specify the new location and click OK.

Changing the Chart Type

Excel supports a wide variety of chart types (line charts, column charts, and so on). To change the chart type, follow these steps:

1. **Activate the chart.**

2. **Select the Chart⇨Chart Type command to display the Chart Type dialog box.**

3. **Click the desired chart type.**

You can select from standard chart types (in the Standard tab) or custom chart types (listed in the Custom tab). You see a preview of how your chart will look.

4. **When you're satisfied with the chart's appearance, click OK.**

The chart types displayed in the Custom tab of the Chart Type dialog box are standard chart types that have been modified in one or more ways. Excel comes with a variety of custom chart types, and you can create your own.

Another way to change the chart type is to use the Chart Type tool on the Chart toolbar. This tool displays the major chart types (you cannot select custom chart types).

If you've customized some aspects of your chart, choosing a new chart type may override some or all of the changes you've made. For example, if you add gridlines to the chart and then select a chart type that doesn't use gridlines, your gridlines disappear.

Dealing with Chart Elements

Working with an element in a chart is similar to everything else you do in Excel: First you make a selection (in this case, select a chart part), and then you issue a command to do something with the selection.

After you activate a chart, you can select a chart element in any of three ways:

+ Click the chart element.

+ Press the up-arrow or down-arrow key to cycle through all the elements in the chart. When a data series is selected, you can press the right-arrow or left-arrow key to select individual points in the series.

+ Use the Chart Objects control in the Chart toolbar. This is a drop-down list that contains all of the elements in the chart (as shown in Figure 11-6).

No matter which method you use, the name of the selected item appears in the Name box (at the left of the formula bar). Many of the chart element names include a number that further describes the element. For example, the third point of the first data series is named Series 1 Point 3. You cannot change the names of chart elements, and you cannot select more than one element at a time.

When you move the mouse pointer over a chart element, a chart tip displays the name of the element. If the element is a data point, the chart tip displays the value. To control what appears in these chart tips, use the Tools⇨Options command and click the Chart tab. Make your selection in the Chart tips section of the dialog box.

Modifying a chart element

Most elements in a chart can be modified in several ways. For example, you can change colors, line widths, fonts, and so on. Modifications are made in the Format dialog box (which varies for each type of chart element).

Excel
Chapter 11

Charting the
Excel Way

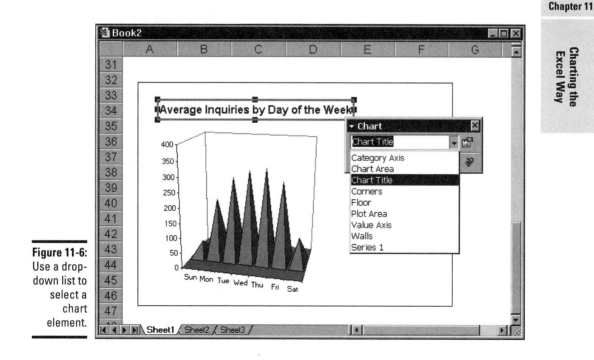

Figure 11-6:
Use a drop-down list to select a chart element.

To modify an element in a chart, follow these steps:

1. **Select the chart element.**

2. **Access the Format dialog box using any of the following techniques:**

- Double-click the item.

- Choose the Format [*Item Name*] command.

- Press Ctrl+1.

- Right-click the item and choose Format [*Item Name*] from the shortcut menu.

3. **Click the tab that corresponds to what you want to do.**

4. **Make the changes.**

5. **Click OK.**

Moving a chart element

Some of the chart parts can be moved (any of the titles, data labels, and the legend). To move a chart element, follow these steps:

1. **Select the chart element you want to move.**

2. **Click the border of the element and drag it to the desired location in the chart.**

Deleting a chart element or data series

You can delete any element in a chart. Heaven knows that you'll change your mind often enough. To delete a chart element, follow these steps:

1. **Select the element or data series to be deleted.**

2. **Press Delete.**

If you delete the last data series in a chart, the chart will be empty.

Rotating 3-D charts

Sure, they're neat to look at, but when you work with 3-D charts, you may find that some data is completely or partially obscured. Drats! How can you convince the big executives at the Annual Sales Meeting that you aren't completely inept? Lucky for you, you can rotate the chart so that it shows the data better:

1. **Activate the 3-D chart.**

2. **Choose the Chart⇨3-D View command.**

3. **In the 3-D View dialog box, make your rotations and perspective changes by clicking the appropriate controls.**

4. **Click OK (or click Apply to see the changes without closing the dialog box).**

Chapter 12: Getting Your Work on the Web

In This Chapter

- Getting ready for the Web
- Saving a Workbook for the Web
- Publishing your data on the Web

*Y*ou could attach your Excel 2000 file to an e-mail and send it to countless innocent people if you wanted the exposure — or the censure! You could also load that new ink cartridge into your printer and print yourself as many copies as you can mail, hand out, tack up, or otherwise distribute to the general public. As you can imagine, however, both these methods of distribution are far from ideal. You have a much better way right now to get your data to the rest of the world: Publish it on the Web.

Why use inefficient and time-consuming ways to get your data to those you want to see it? With Excel 2000, you can save your work in a format that is ready to put on the World Wide Web for all to consume. Although Excel can't set up a Web server or create a Web site, it can make it much easier for you to publish a document that can slip right into an established Web site.

Web Publishing with Excel

Web publishing is the process of placing your Excel data on a Web or intranet server as a Web page. In this process, your Excel data is saved in HTML format. Because your data is in HTML format, users can view your data using their Internet browsers. Excel 97 provided some rudimentary publishing features that were often cumbersome to use. Excel 2000 provides several new features designed to make the publishing process relatively painless.

In Excel 2000, you can publish your data in static or interactive form. If you publish your data in static form, users can only view the data. If you publish your data with interactive functionality, users can work with and manipulate the data within their browsers. Excel 2000 provides three types of interactive functionality:

+ **Spreadsheet functionality:** When you publish your data with spreadsheet functionality, users can enter and calculate data, format, sort, filter, or cut and paste data in the published sheet.

✦ **PivotTable functionality:** When you publish your data with PivotTable functionality, users can change the layout of a pivot table, format, sort, filter, or cut and paste data in the published pivot table.

✦ **Chart functionality:** When you publish your data with Chart functionality, users can make changes to the source data (which is published with the chart) that will automatically update the chart.

Customizing the Way Excel Saves a File for Publishing

Excel 2000 applies default formatting options when saving a file in HTML format. Excel also gives you the ability to modify many of these options. To customize the way that Excel writes an HTML file, follow these steps:

1. **Select the Tools⇨Options command and then click the General tab in the Options dialog box.**

2. **Click the Web Options button.**

The last action displays the Web Options dialog box (shown in Figure 12-1). You can modify the default formatting option settings in any one of the five tabs provided.

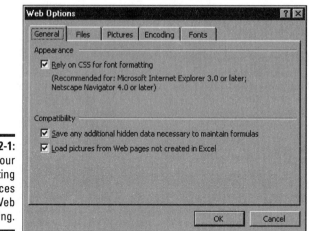

Figure 12-1:
Set up your
formatting
preferences
for Web
publishing.

The following describes the options under the Web Options dialog box tabs.

Rely on CSS for font formatting: You find this option under the **General** tab. Cascading Style Sheets (CSS) is a mechanism that describes how documents are presented on screen or in print. Most current browsers provide support for CSS. If you want to accommodate older Web browsers that do not support CSS, clear this check box.

Save any additional hidden data necessary to maintain formulas: You find this option under the **General** tab. If the data on your worksheet begins in a cell other than the upper-left cell (A1), Excel automatically moves your beginning cell of data into cell A1, when you put the data on a Web page. If you want the empty cells in the upper-left corner of your worksheet to appear blank when you publish or save it as a Web page, clear this check box.

Load pictures from Web pages not created in Excel: You find this option under the **General** tab. In general, select this check box if you want to load graphics from a Web page not created in Excel when you open the Web page in Excel 2000. In particular, if you want to use Web queries created by Excel 97 in Excel 2000, you should clear this check box to avoid possible errors in your worksheet that imported pictures displacing data and formulas can cause. Web queries allow you to set up criteria for importing current data from the Internet or an intranet.

Organize supporting files in a folder: You find this option under the **Files** tab. When you save a Web page, Excel by default stores all supporting files — such as bullets, background textures, and graphics — in a separate subfolder. If you want to save supporting files in the same folder as the Web page, clear this check box.

Use long file names whenever possible: You find this option under the **Files** tab. If you use a long file name to save a Web page to a file server, users with Microsoft Windows 3.1 won't be able to find or open your Web page. To always save files for Web pages with short file names, clear this check box.

Update links on save: You find this option under the **Files** tab. If you move or copy your Web page to a new location without moving the supporting files, the links to graphics — such as photos, bullets, and background textures — may be broken. Select this check box to automatically update the paths to all links when you save Web pages in Excel 2000.

Check if Office is the default editor for Web pages created in Office: You find this option under the **Files** tab. Many Web browsers have a setting that specifies which program to use to edit the current Web page (for example, Word or Notepad). For best results, use the program that you created the Web page in to edit the Web page. Select this check box to override the browser's setting so that the browser will use Excel 2000 to edit pages that were created in Excel 2000.

Download Office Web Components: You find this option under the **Files** tab. To create or use Excel 2000 interactive data on the Web, you must install the Web Components that come with Microsoft Office 2000 Professional or Premium Edition. If you have problems using the interactive features on a Web page after you initially install the Web Components, select this check box. In the Location box, type the path for the server or drive letter for the CD-ROM that contains the installation program for Office 2000.

Rely on VML for displaying graphics in browsers: You find this option under the **Pictures** tab. Check this box if you want your Web pages to download faster. To view graphics in Vector Markup language (VML) format, you must use a browser that supports PNG format, such as Microsoft Internet Explorer 5.0 or later versions.

Allow PNG as an output format: You find this option under the **Pictures** tab. Check this box if you want your workbook to be saved faster, take up less disk space, and download faster. To view graphics in Portable Network Graphics (PNG) format, you must use a browser that supports PNG format, such as Microsoft Internet Explorer 5.0 or later versions.

Target monitor: You find this option under the **Pictures** tab. The screen size you specify for your Web page video resolution can affect the size and layout of images and text on your Web page. Use the Target monitor controls to change the screen and pixel settings to accommodate the intended viewers of your Web page.

Reload the current document as: You find this option under the **Encoding** tab. When you open a Web page that is encoded for a language different from the default language, Excel 2000 tries to determine the language. If Excel displays the wrong characters for that language when you open the page, you can select the language that you think the page in encoded in with the Reload the current document as option.

Save document as: You find this option under the **Encoding** tab. Use this option if you want to specify a language code that Excel should use to save your Web page. This option is mutually exclusive with the Always save Web pages in the default encoding option.

Always save Web pages in the default encoding: You find this option under the **Encoding** tab. Check this check box if you want Excel to always save your Web pages using the default language encoding. This option is mutually exclusive with the Save document as option.

Character Set, Proportional font, Fixed-width font: You find these options under the **Fonts** tab. If the wrong character set or font for a Web page or plain text file is applied when you import a Web page into Excel 2000, the Web page may not display correctly. This option enables you to select the character set and font that you think the page is encoded in. Proportional font is used for normal text. Fixed-width font is used for monospace text.

Most of the Web Option settings apply to the current page and any future pages that you save in Excel 2000.

Publishing Your Worksheet Data to a Web Page

To publish worksheet data to a Web page, follow these simpler than simple steps:

1. **Select the worksheet that contains the data you want to put on a Web page.**

2. **Select the File⇨Save as Web Page command.**

3. **In the Save As dialog box (shown in Figure 12-2), click the Publish button.**

4. **In the Publish as Web Page dialog box (as shown in Figure 12-3), make a selection from the Choose list box. This list box provides three main selections:**

   Previously published items: Use this option to republish your data. See the next section, Republishing your worksheet data to the Web, for use of this option.

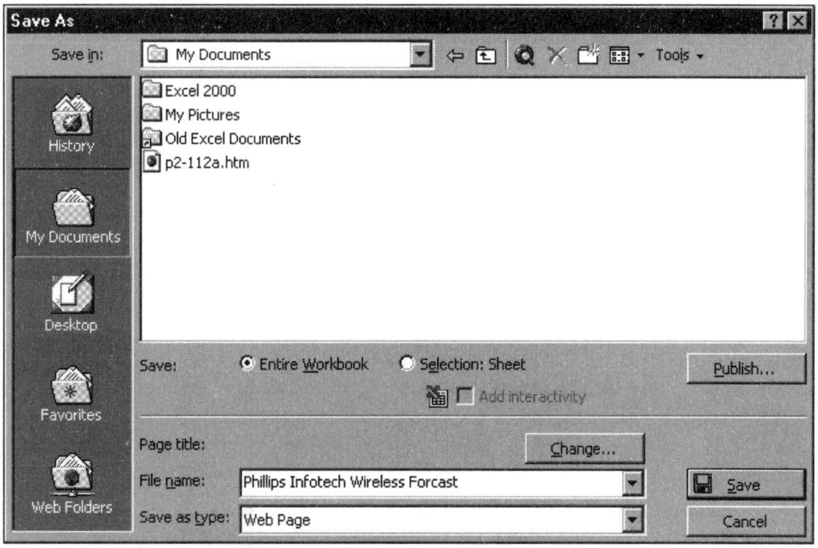

Figure 12-2:
Save your
file as a
Web page.

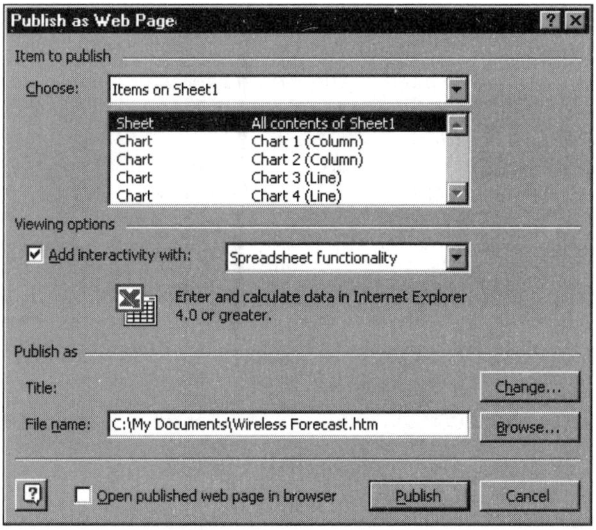

Figure 12-3:
The Publish
as Web
Page
dialog box.

Range of cells: Use this option to publish a range of cells on your worksheet. This option is automatically selected for you if the range is selected prior to Step 2 of this procedure.

Items on *<Sheetname>*: Use this option to publish items on *<Sheetname>*, where *<Sheetname>* is the actual name of the worksheet on which you want to publish the items. This option is automatically selected if you do not select a specific item on *<Sheetname>* prior to Step 2 of this procedure.

5. **In the selection box below the Choose list box, select the range or worksheet item you want to publish.**

   If you selected Items on *<Sheetname>* in Step 4, the selection box may display up to five items, depending on the objects in your worksheet. These items are: Sheet (for example, all data), Chart, PivotTable, AutoFilter, and Print Area.

6. **In the File name box, type the pathname and filename where you want to save your worksheet or worksheet items. Click the Browse button to help you locate the appropriate directory, folder, intranet, or Internet location.**

   You may also check any or all of the following options prior to Step 7:

   • **Add Interactivity with:** Check this box if you want to allow users to manipulate the data after it is published. Select the appropriate functionality (spreadsheet, pivot table, or chart functionality as applicable) from the list box.

   • **Change:** Click this button if you want to add a title for the Web page.

   • **Open published Web page in browser:** Check this box if you want to view the Web page in your browser after you save or publish it.

7. **Click the Publish button.**

Before you put your Web page on the Web server where users will view it, it's a good idea to put the Web page on your hard drive or file server so you can confirm that the page appears and is working properly. Another good idea is to check your Web page in different browsers before publishing it to see how the different browsers affect the format of your document.

If you select the sheet, range, chart, pivot table, autofilter, or print area prior to choosing the File⇨Save as Web Page command, you can skip the Publish as Web page dialog box by clicking the Selection: *<Item>* radio button in the Save As dialog box. *<Item>* may be Sheet, Chart, PivotTable, AutoFilter, Print Area, or a range of cells. All the options in the Publish as Web page dialog box are available to you, except Open published Web page in a browser.

If you select a worksheet that contains a chart and save or publish it with spreadsheet functionality, the chart is not included on the Web page.

You may not be able to view all of the formatting options applied to your document when the file is opened in a Web browser, because Excel embeds additional information describing complex formatting options to the HTML file. Many browsers are unable to interpret this additional information.

Index

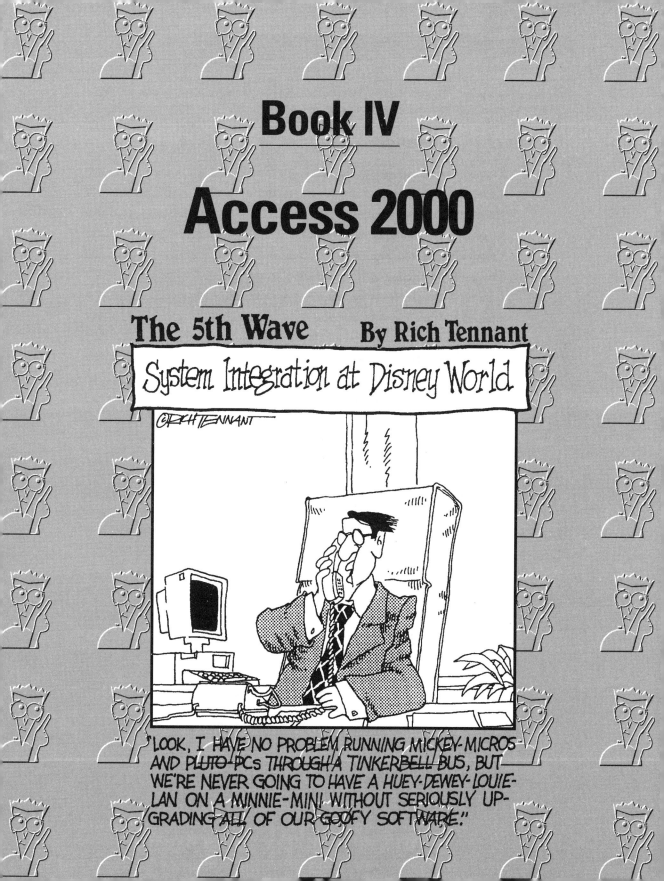

Book IV

Access 2000

The 5th Wave   **By Rich Tennant**

System Integration at Disney World

"LOOK, I HAVE NO PROBLEM RUNNING MICKEY-MICROS AND PLUTO-PCs THROUGH A TINKERBELL BUS, BUT WE'RE NEVER GOING TO HAVE A HUEY-DEWEY-LOUIE-LAN ON A MINNIE-MINI WITHOUT SERIOUSLY UP-GRADING ALL OF OUR GOOFY SOFTWARE."

Contents at a Glance

Chapter 1: Access Basics

In This Chapter

- ✓ Getting acquainted with databases
- ✓ Taking a look at the Access window
- ✓ Opening, saving, and closing a database
- ✓ Working with database wizards
- ✓ Quitting Access

*Y*ou really need to know some things before getting started in Access — not because Access is an impossibly hard program to master, but the demands of database creation can sometimes be more involved than things you do every-day (unless you are a professional database designer, of course). Beginning with a brief explanation of databases in general, this chapter gives you a quick look at opening, saving, and closing an Access database. (By the way, be sure to check out Appendix A for refreshers on how to do basic windows stuff in Access and in all other Office 2000 programs.) Finally, you get introduced to the ideas of Access Wizards (a concept for which you will surely be grateful!) as you also discover how to quit Access the recommended way.

About Databases

A *database* is an organized collection of related data. In a well-built database, you can organize your data so that you see only the data you need to see, in the order you need to see it. In technical terms, a database enables you to *filter* and *sort* data. You can also choose the format in which you want to view your data — a table, for example, or a form.

On the most basic level, databases are organized into records. A *record* is one batch of related information. If you think of your address book as a database, one record is the information about your best friend — her name, address, phone number, and any other information that you have about her in the address book.

Tables store records of data. A table consists of rows and columns. The rows are records, and the columns are fields. A *field* is one category of information that you collect for every record. In a database that stores your address book, the fields may be first name, last name, street address, birthday, and so on. The intersection of a field and a row is a cell. (See Figure 1-1.)

Record   Field   Cell

First Name	Last Name	Street	City	State	Zip
Emma	Rucci	322 Apple Ave.	Norway	ME	04268
Nora	Sweeney	95 Lilly Ave.	Canaan	VT	05903
Edward	Dill	817 Tulip Ave.	Belgrade	ME	04917
Jake	Barrows	9569 Crocus Rd.	South China	ME	04358
Madeline	Molkenbur	15 Hydrangea St.	Poland	ME	04358
Zeke	Mace	456 Iris St.	Jericho	VT	05465
Riley	Newman	76 Peony Rd.	Naples	ME	04055
Figaro	Aronoff	149 Rose Ave.	Lisbon	ME	04250
Fennel	Smith	5 Raspberry St.	Orleans	MA	02653
Seth	Ronn	116 Tuberose Rd.	New Britain	CT	06050
Abby	Aikens	11448 Orchard La.	New Sweden	ME	04762
Farley	Spitzer	26 Meadow La.	Mexico	ME	04257
Jillian	Staiti	48 Cotton Candy Rd.	Belfast	ME	04915
Bjorn	Marik	748 Phlox St.	Jamaica	VT	05343

Customers : Table

Record: 1 of 17

Figure 1-1:
A database
table.

It's important to store each type of information in a separate field. Organizing
your data into many different fields enables you to slice the data any way you
want. For instance, if you decide that having separate fields for first and last
names is a waste of time, you lose out on the option of sorting the database by
either first or last name.

REAL WORLD

Using Access as it was meant to be used

Access is a *relational database,* which means
that one database file can consist of many tables
of *related* data. For example, you may have a table
called Orders that lists orders and includes the
Product Number of each item ordered, and
another table called Products that contains
information about products, which identifies each
product using another Product Number field.
When you tell Access that the two Product
Number fields are related, you provide a link
between the two tables that allows you to ask
your database a question that requires data from
both tables to answer. For instance, you may want
to know who ordered which products
(information stored in the Orders table), and how
much the product costs at wholesale (information
stored in the Products table). The related Product
Number fields allow you to pull the related data
from two tables.

Access Database Objects

An Access database can contain different types of Access *objects:* tables, forms, queries, and reports.

+ Access stores data in *tables.*

+ You use Access *forms* just like paper forms: to enter and display data.

+ You create *queries* to gather the information you need about the data you've entered.

+ Use *reports* to present the information you gather about your data.

Each of these types of objects is covered in a this book.

Opening a Database File

When you start Access by using the Start⇨Programs menu, a dialog box lists databases that you've used recently (see Figure 1-2). To open one of these databases, select it from this initial dialog box (be sure that the Open an Existing File option is selected), and click OK.

You can also open an Access file by double-clicking the file name in Windows Explorer or My Computer, or by choosing the file off of the Start⇨Documents menu. Opening an Access file also starts Access.

If you're already in Access, use the Open dialog box to open a file, or choose a recently used database file from the bottom of the File menu.

Follow these steps to use the Open dialog box to open a database:

1. **Click the Open button (alternatively, choose File⇨Open or press Ctrl+O) to bring up the Open dialog box (shown in Figure 1-3).**

Figure 1-2:
You can begin with a new or an existing file.

```
Open                                                    ? X
Look in:    My Documents              ← ⛗ 🔍 ✕ ⌸ 🎞 ▼  Tools ▾

        Name                      Size  Type           Modified          ▲
        My Pictures                     Folder         9/22/98 10:02 AM
        My Webs                         Folder         1/27/99 9:07 PM
History Samples                         Folder         10/19/98 9:50 PM
        Asset Tracking.mdb        2052 KB Microsoft Access... 3/23/99 11:12 AM
        Billing.mdb               9280 KB Microsoft Access... 3/17/99 10:53 AM
        billing97.mdb              208 KB Microsoft Access... 3/12/99 3:41 PM
My Documents CCRS final 97.mdb     656 KB Microsoft Access... 3/12/99 3:41 PM
        CCRS.mdb                  1164 KB Microsoft Access... 3/24/99 10:26 AM
        CCRS_97.mdb                756 KB Microsoft Access... 12/21/98 11:...
        Clown Supplies.mdb          92 KB Microsoft Access... 12/23/98 1:55 PM
Desktop Consulting customers.mdb   204 KB Microsoft Access... 3/26/99 6:01 PM
        Consulting.mdb            1008 KB Microsoft Access... 3/27/99 1:13 PM
        Consulting_97.mdb          178 KB Microsoft Access... 3/15/99 2:35 PM
        Insurance.mdb              180 KB Microsoft Access... 12/16/99 3:26 PM
Favorites Shower.xls                19 KB Microsoft Excel ... 5/12/97 9:52 AM ▼

        File name:    [                              ▼ ]  📂 Open  ▾
Web Folders Files of type: [Data Files (*.mdb;*.adp;*.mdw;*.mda;*.mde; *.ade;*.tx ▼]  Cancel
```

Figure 1-3:
The Open
dialog box.

2. Select the file you want. (You may need to browse to it.)

Use the icons on the left of the Open dialog box to see different folders —
History displays recently used files, Desktop displays desktop icons,
Favorites displays the contents of the Favorites folder and Web Folders
displays defined Web folders.

3. Click the Open button or simply double-click the filename.

Access opens the database.

Saving a Database File

Access is designed so that many people can use one database — and all at the
same time, if they need to. So, unlike a spreadsheet or word processing program, Access doesn't require you to save the entire file — instead you save
object definitions (such as a table or form definition) one at a time. Access takes
care of saving data as soon as it's entered.

 To save an object definition, make the object active (by clicking its window) and
then click the Save button on the toolbar, or press Ctrl+S, or choose File➪Save.
If you close an object without saving it, Access displays a dialog box asking
whether you want to save the object:

✦ Choose Yes to save the object.

✦ Choose No to close the object without saving changes to the definition.

✦ Choose Cancel to cancel the command and return to the unsaved object.

Closing a Database File

|X| To close a database, simply close the database window by clicking its close (X) button. The database window is the window that has `Name of the database file: Database` in the title bar.

Working with Wizards

Access provides wizards to help you build and use databases. A *wizard* consists of a series of dialog boxes that ask you questions and then creates something (such as a database, a query, or a report) based on your answers. The many wizards in Access 2000 do a variety of tasks, but they all work in a similar way: They present you with screens that ask you questions, such as which tables or fields you want to use and which format you prefer.

Specific wizards are covered in other parts of this book, but the following sections cover the basic techniques you must know in order to use any wizard.

Selecting fields

Many wizards have windows like the one in Figure 1-4, where you choose fields.

To tell Access that you want to use a field, you first have to tell it where to find the field by choosing a table or query from the drop-down list in the Tables/ Queries list box. Access displays the fields from the table or query you choose

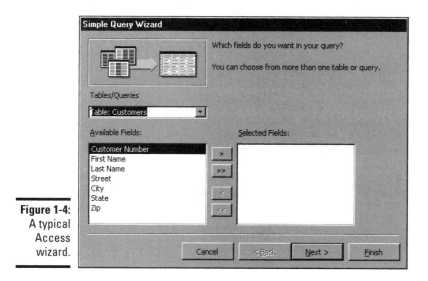

Figure 1-4:
A typical
Access
wizard.

Access
Chapter 1

Access Basics

in the Available Fields list box. Use one of the following methods to tell Access that you want it to use a field:

+ Double-click the field.

 + Select the field and click the single right-facing arrow button.

 To choose all the fields displayed in the Available Fields list box, click the double right-facing arrow.

 If you make a mistake, and want to remove a field from the Selected Fields list box, double-click it, or select it and click the single left-facing arrow button.

 To remove all fields from the Selected Fields list box, click the double left-facing arrow button.

To select fields from other tables or queries, choose another table or query from the Tables/Queries drop-down list and select the additional fields.

Viewing more windows

When you finish answering all the questions on one window of a wizard, you're ready to see the next window. The buttons at the bottom of the wizard enable you to proceed through the questions the wizard asks you:

+ **Cancel:** Exits the wizard without letting the wizard complete its task.

+ **Back:** Displays the previous window of the wizard.

+ **Next:** Displays the next window of the wizard.

+ **Finish:** Tells Access to complete whatever it is that this particular wizard does, using the information it already has, and using the default values on any windows that you skip by clicking the Finish button.

When you get to the last window of a wizard, you see the black and white checkered Finish flag. Access asks you if you want help, and it often asks you to name the object the wizard is creating and choose how you want to view the new object. When you finish with these options, click the Finish button to tell the wizard to complete its task.

Quitting Access 2000

 You quit Access the same way that you quit any other Windows program. Once again, Windows offers a boatload of options. If you have parts of a database open, and you've made changes since the last time you saved the object, Access gives you the option of saving the object before you quit. Following are the most popular ways to close Access:

+ Click the Close button in the top-right corner of the Access window (it looks like an X).

+ Choose File⊃Exit from the Access menu.

Chapter 2: Creating and Navigating a Database

In This Chapter

✓ Creating a database by yourself or with wizards

✓ Getting to know the database window

✓ Using the database toolbars

*U*nless you're lucky enough to have inherited a nice database to work on, you need to know how to create one. Fortunately, you can use a wizard if you don't want to build a database all yourself. After you have all your database objects in place, manipulating them is a breeze. (By the way, you read about database objects — tables, reports, queries, and forms — in later chapters.) This chapter does not guarantee to make you an expert database creator, but it can show you the ins and outs that you can later build on.

Creating a Database

Designing databases is a topic unto itself — this book certainly can't tell you everything you need to know. It can, however, give you some basic guidelines. It is important to give some consideration to the design of your database before you begin entering data into tables. Consider the data you have and how you want to use it — what kinds of queries, forms, and reports do you want to include in your database? What additional needs may crop up later? These questions help you figure out what data you need, and how to break up your data into fields and tables so that you can create the reports, forms, and queries that you will need.

Much of the work of designing a database to meet your needs is in deciding how to break your data into fields and which fields to store in each table; these can make or break your database. Use these guidelines for designing your database:

✦ Split data into its smallest logical parts. Usually this means the smallest unit that you may ever want to use. For instance, give each name at least two fields; first name and last name. This allows you to work with either one or the other for sorting, form letters, and so on.

✦ Use multiple tables so that each table contains information on one topic. For instance, one table may contain order information, while another contains the customer's billing information and shipping address. You can password-protect a table, so it makes sense to put sensitive information in a separate table.

✦ Make sure you know which fields in different tables are related. For instance, the Customer Number field you use in the Orders table connects to the Customer Number in the Customer table containing customer's shipping addresses and billing information.

✦ Avoid repeating data. If a table listing employee information has fields for both department name and department manager you are repeating data. It may make more sense to list a department in the employee table and have a separate table for departments and department managers.

Developing a database

Follow these general steps to develop a database:

1. **Open a new database.**

2. **Create tables.**

3. **Tell Access how your tables are related.**

4. **(Optional) Create forms to make data entry clearer and to display a full record's worth of information at a time.**

5. **Enter your data.**

6. **Create queries to give you the information you need.**

7. **Create reports to transfer the information to paper in a clear format.**

Creating a database from scratch

If Access is closed, Start Access by using the Start button menu (or your favorite method) and, in the introductory dialog box, choose Blank Access Database (see Figure 2-1). Access displays the File New Database dialog box, where you name the new database.

If Access is running, click the New Database button, press Alt+N, or choose File⇨New Database. The New dialog box appears. Click the General tab in the New dialog box, select Blank Database, and then click OK. Access displays the File New Database dialog box.

Access displays the File New Database dialog box, with the File Name setting highlighted. Use this dialog box to give the database a filename by typing the name of the new database into the File Name box. If you want to store the file in a folder other than the one displayed in the Save In box, change the folder. Then click Create.

Access takes a few seconds to create the new database; then it displays the Tables view of the Database window and the Database toolbar.

Access 2000 offers you a several new options on the New dialog box. You can create a new database, but you can also create a Data Access Page, a Project (using an existing database), and a Project using a new database.

Figure 2-1:
Start a
blank
database
here.

Creating a database with a wizard

Using wizards is a great way to get a jumpstart on creating a database. Even if they don't provide exactly what you want, wizards give you a framework to start from. Access 2000 comes with a number of database wizards:

Asset Tracking	Contact Management
Event Management	Expenses
Inventory Control	Ledger
Order Entry	Resource Scheduling
Time and Billing	Service Call Management

Follow these steps to create a database by using a wizard:

1. **Display the New dialog box by choosing Database Wizard in the initial screen when you open Access and clicking OK, choosing File⇨New from the menu, clicking the New File button, or pressing Ctrl+N.**

   Access displays the New dialog box.

2. **Click the Databases tab.**

   A list of wizards appears. The name of the wizard gives you a general idea about what kind of data the wizard is set up to work with.

3. **Click a database name to get a graphical preview of the wizard.**

4. **To open a wizard, double-click the database icon (or name), or click the icon once to select it and then click the OK button.**

   Access displays the File New Database dialog box where you can name the database.

5. **Accept the name in the File name box by pressing Enter, or edit the name and then press Enter.**

   The wizard takes a few moments to set up, and then displays the first window, which shows you some information about the database that you're setting up.

6. **Click Next to display the next window of the wizard.**

   Click the Finish button now to accept the wizard's defaults and create the database.

7. **Use the options on each window of the wizard to customize the database the wizard is creating for you.**

   You may see more than one screen of options. Follow the directions in each screen to determine which options to change. Access allows you to add additional fields, choose a form style, choose a report style, and give the database a name (which will appear in the Access title bar). The last screen gives you a setting to check if you want to view online help about the database.

8. **Click the Finish button to tell the wizard to create the database.**

   Finally, the database opens, displaying the Main Switchboard — a menu of options.

9. **You can work with the database by using the menu, or you can display the familiar Database window by clicking the Database Window button.**

   Redisplay the Main Switchboard by choosing it from the Window menu. You can also view the Switchboard by clicking the Forms button in the Database window and double-clicking Switchboard.

Finding Your Way around a Database

An Access database consists of data and database objects. Tables, reports, forms, and queries are the types of objects that you're most likely to work with. The Database window is the table of contents for all the objects in your database. From the Database window you can access each object in the database (see Figure 2-2).

The Database window has a different look in Access 2000 than in prior versions of the software — object types appear as buttons on the left side of the window rather than as tabs across the top. You may notice the Database window now resembles the Outlook window.

The view for each type of object contains at least two different types of icons — icons for creating a new object of this type, and icons for each defined object of this type in the database. For instance, in addition to the three tables defined in the database, you also see three icons for creating new tables (refer to Figure 2-1). Notice that the icons for the tables and the icons that create new tables are different.

Buttons for each type of object in the database

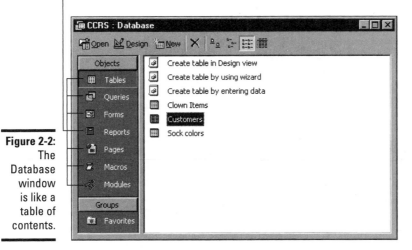

Figure 2-2:
The
Database
window
is like a
table of
contents.

To see all the objects of a certain type, click the appropriate button. To see the names of all the forms in the database, for example, click the Forms button. To open a specific form, click the form name to select it and then click the Open button on the toolbar.

Use any of these ways to view the database window:

✦ Click the Database Window button.

✦ Press F11.

✦ Choose Window from the menu and choose the item at the bottom of the drop-down list that shows Name of Database: Database.

✦ If you can see even part of the Database window, click it to make it the active window.

Use the Database window to see any object in the database, or to create a new object. Click any button in the Objects list to see all the objects of that type. Click the Reports button, for example, to see all the reports in the database. You can then use the Open and Design buttons (or the Preview and Design buttons) in the Database window to view the selected object.

The Database Window Toolbar

The Database window contains buttons useful for copying, printing, and creating objects (see Figure 2-3). If you've seen any Office 2000 application before, most of these buttons will seem familiar to you. Table 2-1 gives the rundown on those buttons.

Figure 2-3:
Useful
database
buttons
abound.

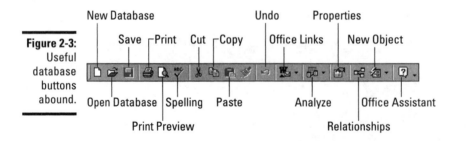

New Database   Undo   Properties
Save ┌Print Cut ┌Copy   Office Links   New Object
Open Database │ Spelling Paste   Analyze   Office Assistant
Print Preview   Relationships

Table 2-1	Toolbar Buttons
Button	*What It Does*
New Database	Creates a new database
Open Database	Opens an existing database (and closes the currently open database)
Print	Prints the selected object
Print Preview	Displays the selected object as it will look when printed
Spelling	Checks the spelling of the selected object
Cut	Deletes the selected object and saves a copy in the Windows Clipboard
Copy	Copies the selected object to the Windows Clipboard
Paste	Pastes the contents of the Windows Clipboard to the Database window
Undo	Undoes the last undoable action
OfficeLinks: Word	Opens another Office 2000 application
Analyze	Runs the Table Analyzer Wizard or another analyzer wizard
Properties	Displays the properties of the selected object
Relationships	Displays the Relationships window
New Object: Autoform	Creates a new object
Office Assistant	Displays the Office Assistant

In addition, the Database window has a secondary toolbar that contains the buttons shown in Figure 2-4. Table 2-2 explains the use of each button.

Table 2-2	More Toolbar Buttons
Button	*What It Does*
Open or Preview	Displays the selected object
Design	Displays the design view of the selected object
New	Displays a dialog box of options for creating a new object of the type currently displayed

Button	What It Does
Delete	Deletes the selected object
Large Icons	Displays objects in the Database window as large icons
Small Icons	Displays objects in the Database window as small icons
List	Displays objects in the Database window in a list
Details	Displays objects in the Database window with details, including a description, last date modified, date created, and type of object

One advantage of using the Details view is that you can see when an object was last modified. You can also sort objects — just click the gray column header to sort by that column. And, if you want to see which table was modified most recently click the Modified column header.

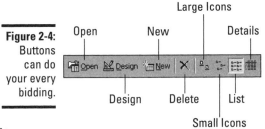

Figure 2-4: Buttons can do your every bidding.

Large Icons

Open   New   Details

Design   Delete   List

Small Icons

Sample databases to play with

Access comes with a number of samples that can help you understand how Access databases work. The Northwind database is the most frequently used sample database. The database is an example of how to track products, suppliers, and sales for a company called Northwind Traders. Playing around with the Northwind database is one way to become familiar with different Access features.

The Northwind database is stored in C:\Program Files\MicrosoftOffice\Office\Samples\Nwind.mdb when it is installed. If it has not been installed, it can be found on your Access 2000 or Office 2000 CD in /. Access provides a shortcut to the Northwind database in the My Documents folder, which is the folder you usually see when you display the Open dialog box.

Access Chapter 2

Creating and Navigating a Database

Chapter 3: Tables: A Home for Your Data

*B*ecause tables hold your data, tables are the fundamental element of any database. If you can create and move around in your tables, the world of databases seems to open up to you. But hold on! You also need to do more than just create tables; you need to be able to link tables so that you can actually do something with your database. And for linking purposes, you must take into account your primary keys. Hey, this topic appears to be getting complicated very fast. It's a good thing for you that Chapter 3 is devoted to getting you comfortably started in table basics.

About Tables

Tables are the basic building block of your database — they store the data. One *table* stores a collection of related data in records and fields. *Fields* define each piece of information about an item, and these related fields are stored in *records*. Most databases have a number of tables. Each table stores a set of related data, and normally each table in the database is related to other tables through the repetition of a common field. You can work with tables in two different views: Datasheet view and Design view.

Working in Datasheet view

A table in Datasheet view looks like a spreadsheet — it stores a collection of similar data in records and fields (see Figure 3-1). The Datasheet view now enables you to see related records in other tables. A plus sign (+) appears to the left of records for which you can display related records from another table. Display a list of tables by viewing the Database window and clicking the Tables button on the left side. To display a table in Datasheet view:

✦ Double-click the name of the table in the Database window.

✦ Select the table in the Database window and click the Open button on the toolbar.

✦ Click the Datasheet View button when the table is in Design view.

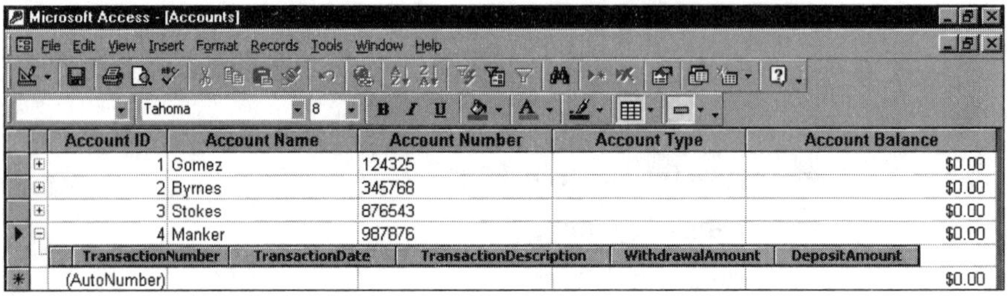

Figure 3-1:
A table in
Datasheet
view.

	Account ID	Account Name	Account Number	Account Type	Account Balance
	1	Gomez	124325		$0.00
	2	Byrnes	345768		$0.00
	3	Stokes	876543		$0.00
	4	Manker	987876		$0.00

TransactionNumber	TransactionDate	TransactionDescription	WithdrawalAmount	DepositAmount
(AutoNumber)				$0.00

Microsoft Access - [Accounts]
File Edit View Insert Format Records Tools Window Help
Tahoma 8 B I U

Working in Design view

Design view gives you ways to specify field properties and refine the table definition (see Figure 3-2). You use Design view to define the type of data stored in a field, define the format of a field, identify the primary key, and enter data validation rules. To display a table in Design view:

✦ Hold down the Ctrl key while you double-click the name of the table in the Database window.

✦ Select the table in the Database window and click the Design button on the toolbar.

✦ Right-click the table name in the Database window and choose Design from the shortcut menu.

 ✦ Click the Design View button when the table is in Datasheet view.

In Design view, each field gets a row, with the field name displayed in the first column, the type of data stored in the field displayed in the second column, and a description of the field displayed in the third column. The bottom half of the Design view window is called the Field Properties pane, and it displays additional options for the selected field (the one with a triangle in the row selector, immediately to the left of the field name).

Adding a New Table to Your Database

You can create a table by several different methods: by using a wizard, by entering data and field names in a datasheet, or by using Design view. This section attempts to get you started.

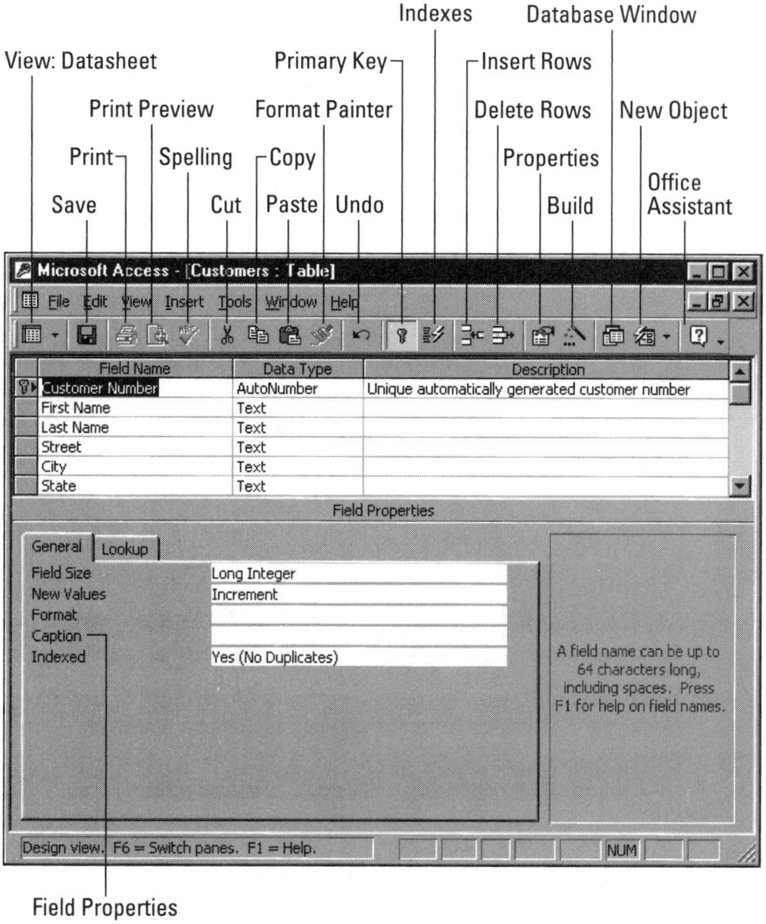

Indexes
Database Window
View: Datasheet
Primary Key
Insert Rows
Print Preview
Format Painter
Delete Rows
New Object
Print
Spelling
Copy
Properties
Office Assistant
Save
Cut
Paste
Undo
Build
Microsoft Access - [Customers : Table]
File Edit View Insert Tools Window Help
Field Name
Data Type
Description
Customer Number
AutoNumber
Unique automatically generated customer number
First Name
Text
Last Name
Text
Street
Text
City
Text
State
Text
Field Properties
General
Lookup
Field Size
Long Integer
New Values
Increment
Format
Caption
Indexed
Yes (No Duplicates)
A field name can be up to 64 characters long, including spaces. Press F1 for help on field names.
Design view. F6 = Switch panes. F1 = Help.
NUM
Field Properties

Figure 3-2: A table in Design view.

FAST TRACK

Creating a table using the Table Wizard

The Table Wizard simplifies the process of creating a table by allowing you to choose from among some common tables and often-used fields.

1. **Begin the table wizard by:**
   - Double-clicking the Create Table by Using Wizard icon in the Table view of the Database window.
   - Choosing Table Wizard from the New Table dialog box. (Display the New Table dialog box by clicking the New button in the Database window when the Table view is displayed.)

   Access displays the first window of the Table Wizard.

2. **If your database is for personal rather than business use, click the Personal radio button in the bottom-left corner to display tables and sample fields commonly used in personal applications.**

3. **Select a table in the Sample Tables list.**

   The field names in the Sample Fields list change to reflect the table you select. (Don't forget to use the scroll bars to see all the options.)

4. **Add fields to the Fields in My New Table list by double-clicking the field name in the Sample Fields list. You can select all the fields in the Sample Fields list by clicking the double-right-arrow button.**

   The selected field(s) appears in the Fields in My New Table list.

5. **If necessary, remove fields from the Fields in My New Table list.**

   To remove one field name, select it and click the left-arrow button to the left of the Fields in My New Table list. To remove all fields (maybe you need to start over!), click the double left-facing arrow that is beneath the left-arrow button.

6. **(Optional) You can rename a field by selecting it in the Fields in My New Table list and clicking the Rename Field button.**

   Access displays the Rename Field dialog box. Type the new name or edit the name displayed in the dialog box, and press Enter.

   Any time after you select the table and fields, you can click Finish to accept the Table Wizard defaults and create the table.

7. **Click Next to display the next Table Wizard window.**

8. **Change the name of the table (if you think it needs a better name) and use the radio buttons to tell Access whether you want it to set a primary key.**

9. **Click Next to display the next window. (This window asks if any fields in the new table are related to any existing tables in the database.)**

10. **If fields in the new table are related to fields in an existing table, select the table and click the Relationships button. (Use the Relationships dialog box to tell Access how the tables are related; then click OK.)**

11. **Click Next to display the last window.**

12. **Click the radio button that describes what you want to do when the table is created.**

13. **Click Finish to create the table.**

Creating a table in Datasheet view

Datasheet view is the most straightforward way to create a table. A datasheet looks like a spreadsheet — you can name your fields and begin entering data. Access figures out the type of data that each field holds.

Creating a table in Datasheet view does not prevent you from using the more advanced settings in Design view. To display Design view at any time, click the Design View button.

Follow these steps to create a table in Datasheet view:

1. **Display the Table view in the Database window and double-click the Create Table by Entering Data icon, or choose Datasheet View from the New Table dialog box.**

Access creates a table called Table1. Across the top of the table are field names: Field1, Field2, and so on.

2. **Enter one record of data (fill in the first row). Move to the next field by pressing Tab or Enter.**

Access displays a pencil icon in the left border of the row to indicate that you are entering or changing data.

3. **Save the table by clicking the Save button, pressing Ctrl+S, or choosing File⇨Save.**

Access displays the Save As dialog box.

4. **Type a new name for the table (assign the table a name that indicates what data is stored in it), and press Enter.**

5. **When Access asks whether you want to define a primary key, choose Yes or No. If you're not sure, choose No — you can go back to the table later to define a primary key, if you need to.**

See also "Identifying Records with a Primary Key Field," later in this chapter.

When you save the table, Access gets rid of any additional columns in the datasheet. You can still add or remove fields, though.

6. **Rename a field by double-clicking the field name, typing a new name, and pressing Enter.**

Assign fields names that reflect the data contained in them. Rename all the fields. Access automatically saves the new field names.

7. **Enter the rest of your data.**

Access automatically saves the data when you move to the next cell.

To move to the beginning of a row, press the Home key. To move to the next line when you've completed a record, press Tab or Enter (this only works after you have saved the table the first time). You can also move to the next row by pressing the ↓ key.

 8. **Close the table by clicking its Close button.**

Creating a table in Design view

Design view is a good place to create your table if you want to use the more advanced settings, called *field properties,* available only in this view. Otherwise, Datasheet view usually works best.

You can only define fields in Design view — you can't enter any data. You have to use the Datasheet view or a form to do that.

To use Design view to create a table, follow these steps:

1. **Click the Table button in the objects list of the Database window and double-click the Create Table in Design View icon or choose Design View from the New Table dialog box.**

   Access displays a Design view for the new, blank table called Table1. The cursor is in the first row, below the Field Name column heading. (See Figure 3-3.)

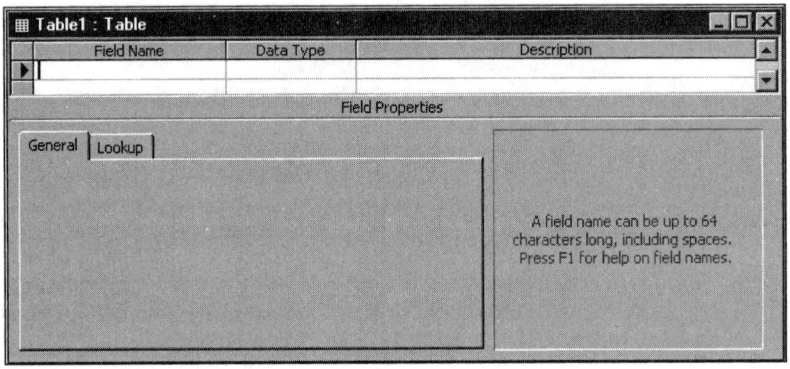

Figure 3-3:
You can
create a
table in
Design
view.

2. **Type the name of the first field; then press Enter or Tab to move to the Data Type column.**

   Access displays the default Data Type, which is Text. As soon as the you establish a data type for a field, Access displays field properties for that type of data in the Field Properties pane of the Design View window.

3. **To view all data types, press F4 (or click the down arrow) to display the drop-down list of data type options.**

4. **Select the appropriate data type for the field (see Figure 3-4).**

   See "Changing Data Types," later in this chapter.

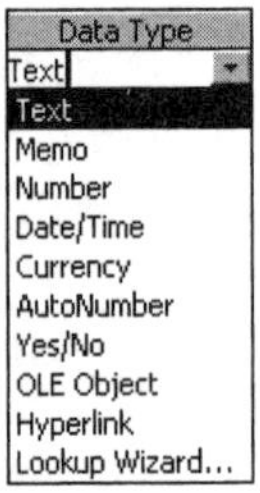

Figure 3-4:
Select the
appropriate
data type.

5. **(Optional) Type a description in the third column (the one labeled Description).**

The description you type appears in the status bar whenever the field is selected. Typing a description can give you and other users a hint about using the field.

6. Define additional fields in the table by repeating Steps 3 through 5.

7. Define a *primary key* (a field that uniquely identifies each record) by putting the cursor in the row with the primary key field and clicking the Primary Key button on the toolbar. Access displays a key to the left of the field name.

See "Identifying Records with a Primary Key Field," later in this chapter.

8. Click the Save button or press Ctrl+S to display the Save As dialog box.

9. Type a new name for the table and then press Enter.

To enter data after you design the table, click the Datasheet View button to display Datasheet view.

Moving Around in a Datasheet

You can move around a datasheet in three ways: with the mouse, with keystrokes, and with the VCR buttons at the bottom of the Datasheet window:

✦ Moving with the mouse: Click the cell in the datasheet where you want the cursor to be. You can also click the vertical and horizontal scroll bars to change the part of the datasheet that is displayed.

✦ Moving with keys: In addition to using arrows, Page Up and Page Down, you can use the keystrokes shown in Table 3-1 to move around a datasheet:

Table 3-1	Moving Around with Keys
Key to Press	*Where It Takes You*
Ctrl+PgUp	Left one screen
Ctrl+PgDn	Right one screen
Tab	Following field
Shift+Tab	Preceding field
Home	First field of the current record
End	Last field of the current record
Ctrl+	First record of the current field
Ctrl+Ø	Last record of the current field
Ctrl+Home	First record of the first field (the top-left corner of the datasheet)
Ctrl+End	Last record of the last field (the bottom-right corner of the datasheet)
F5	Specified record (type a record number and press Enter to go to a specific record)

✦ Moving with VCR buttons: Use the VCR buttons at the bottom of the datasheet to move the cursor (see Figure 3-5). When you know the record number you want, type it in the Record Number box and press Enter.

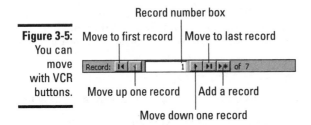

Figure 3-5: You can move with VCR buttons.

Record number box
Move to first record | Move to last record
Move up one record | Add a record
Move down one record

Adding Data to Your Database

The easiest way to put data into a database, or to work with the data already there, is to use Datasheet view. Data can also be added to the database through Forms and Queries. Here's how to add new records to an existing table:

1. **Open the table in Datasheet view.**

The easiest way to open a table is to double-click the table name in the Database window.

2. **Click the New Record button on the toolbar or at the bottom of the Datasheet.**

Access moves the cursor to the last record, which is blank and waiting for input.

3. **Type the appropriate information in the first field.**

4. **Press Enter or Tab after you type data in a cell to move to the next field. You can also click a cell to move the cursor to that cell.**

5. **Enter data in all the fields in the record (as needed) by repeating Steps 3 and 4.**

To enter data for another record, simply press Enter when the cursor is in the last field — Access automatically creates a new record.

Access automatically saves the data in the database file when you move to the next record.

Editing Data in a Datasheet

Edit a value by moving the cursor to the value, pressing F2, or clicking on the value to see a cursor. Delete characters by using the Delete and Backspace keys. Add new characters by typing them.

To replace the contents of a field, select the entire field by clicking at the beginning of the field, holding the mouse button down, and dragging the mouse pointer to the end of the field. Then type the new entry — whatever you type replaces the selected characters.

Changing Data Types

Fields have to have a *type,* which describes the kind of data that can be entered into the field. Common data types are text, numeric, and date/time. Table 3-2 describes each data type.

Table 3-2	Access Datatypes
Data Type	**What It Holds**
Text	The Text type can contain numbers, letters, punctuation, spaces, and special characters (such as #, @, !, %). If you use hyphens or parentheses in phone numbers (and almost everyone does), the phone-number field is defined as a text field. You can't use a number in a text field in calculations (but who wants to add phone numbers?). A text field holds up to 255 characters.
Memo	The Memo type can contain numbers, letters, spaces, and special characters, just like the Text type, but more of them fit in a Memo field than in a Text field — up to 65,535 characters. (You really have to work to fill up this type of field!)
Number	The Number type can contain only numbers. You may use + and – before the number, and a decimal point as long as it is followed by at least one number. You can use Number fields in calculations.
Date/Time	The Date/Time type can hold, well, dates and times. You can do calculations with Date/Time fields.
Currency	The Currency type holds numbers with a currency sign in front of them ($, £, ¥, and so on). You can do calculations with Currency fields. (A font with the new Euro symbol is available from the Microsoft Web site.)
AutoNumber	The AutoNumber type includes numbers unique to each record. Access assigns these numbers starting at 1, and automatically increments subsequent records.
Yes/No	The Yes/No type holds any kind of yes-or-no data. You can set up a Yes/No field to contain other two-word sets, such as True/False, On/Off, and Male/Female, and so on.
OLE Object	The OLE Object type can hold a picture, a sound, or another object created with OLE-compatible software other than Access.
Hyperlink	The Hyperlink type can hold links to World Wide Web addresses (URLs), objects within the database, files, and other kinds of hyperlink addresses.
Lookup Wizard	The Lookup Wizard type runs the Lookup Wizard, which enables you select a table or type a list to display in a drop-down list used for data entry.

If you create your table in Datasheet view and enter data, Access selects a data type based on the entered data. If you enter text, Access makes the data type of the field Text. If you enter numbers with a currency symbol in front, Access sets the data type to Currency. To change the data type Access chooses, use the Data Type setting for the field in Design view. Follow these steps:

1. **Switch to Design view by clicking the Design View button.**

2. **Click the Data Type column of the field whose data type you want to change.**

3. **Display the drop-down list by clicking the down-arrow key or by pressing F4.**

4. **Choose the data type that you want by clicking it.**

You can also cycle through the data types without displaying the drop-down list by double-clicking the Data Type setting.

Relating (Linking) Tables

Most databases consist of a number of tables. Each table contains a number of fields that are related. For instance, one table may contain customer information with fields for names, address, and phone number. Another table may contain customer orders with fields for data ordered and number of items ordered. Yet another table may contain detail information on the order with fields for the item number, description, and price. All the tables contain related data, but Access doesn't know that until you link the tables by defining related fields. For example, a customer number field is used to link the customer information table to the customer order table, which means that the customer number field must appear in both tables. And an order number is used to link the customer order table to the order detail table.

Once tables are linked with related fields, you can create queries and reports that use fields from a number of tables. Telling Access about the relationships between tables is the key to making your relational database useful.

Pick your related fields carefully — make sure that both fields contain exactly the same type of data. Usually, a related field is the primary key in one table and simply information in the other table. A *primary key* is the field that uniquely identifies each record in the table. (See "Identifying Records with a Primary Key Field," later in this chapter, for more information about key fields.)

Related fields must be the same data type, or the link will not work.

Types of relationships

Fields that appear in more than one table can be related in one of four ways. The four types of relationships are:

✦ **One-to-one:** A record in one table has exactly one related record in another table. For example, each record in a table that lists employees by name has exactly one related record in a table that lists employees by employee number, and each employee number refers to only one employee.

✦ **One-to-many:** One record in the first table has many related records in the second table. For example, one table that lists artists may have many related records in another table that lists CDs by artist.

✦ **Many-to-one:** This relationship is identical to one-to-many, except that you look at the relationship from the other side. For example, each record in a table that lists CDs by artist has only one related record in a table that lists artists, but many CDs may have the same artist.

✦ **Many-to-many:** This relationship is the most complicated type. A many-to-many relationship requires a linking table. For example, the item field in a table listing items by the stores that sell them has a many-to-many relationship to the item field in a table listing stores and the items they sell. An item may be sold by many stores, and many stores sell a particular item.

Creating and managing relationships

To define the relationships in your database:

1. **Choose Tools⇨Relationships or click the Relationships button on the toolbar.**

If no relationships are defined in the database, Access displays the Show Table dialog box, where you choose which tables with fields you want to use in relationships. If you already defined relationships in the database, Access displays the Relationships window.

2. **Add tables to the Relationships window by selecting them in the Show Table dialog box and clicking the Add button.**

You can also add a table to the Relationships window by double-clicking the table name. You can select more than one table by selecting the first table and Ctrl+clicking the others. Then click the Add button.

3. **Click the Close button to close the Show Table dialog box. If you need to display it again, click the Show Tables button on the toolbar.**

4. **Pick two related fields. Use the scroll bars to display the fields you want to link. Drag the field from one table and drop it on its related field in the second table.**

If you drag the wrong field, just drop it on the gray background rather than dragging it to a field in a table. Then you're ready to start again.

When you release the mouse button, Access displays the Edit Relationships dialog box that details the nature of the relationship (See Figure 3-6).

5. **Make sure that the table and field names are correct; then click Create to tell Access to create the relationship.**

If a field name is incorrect, you can change it by clicking the name of the field, clicking the arrow to display the drop-down list, and choosing another field name from the same table. If the relationship looks completely wrong, click Cancel and start over.

Access Chapter 3

Tables: A Home for Your Data

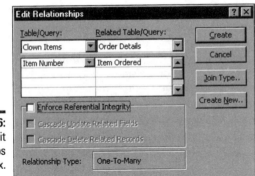

Figure 3-6:
The Edit
Relationships
dialog box.

To reopen the Relationships dialog box after you've closed it, double-click the line joining two fields in the Edit Relationships window.

6. Repeat Steps 3 through 5 to create relationships between other fields.

Access automatically saves the relationships that you create. You can view the relationships in the Relationships window (see Figure 3-7). You can print relationships by selecting File➪Print Relationships from the menu when the Relationships window is active. To delete a relationship, click the line that connects two fields in the Relationships window and press Delete.

Figure 3-7:
You can
view your
table
relationships.

You can move tables around in the Relationships window so that the relationships are easy to understand; just drag the title bar of the table to move it. You can also size a table so that you can see more field names; just drag the border.

Identifying Records with a Primary Key Field

A *primary key* uniquely identifies every record in a table. Most of the time, the primary key is a single field, but it can also be a combination of fields, in which case it is called a *multiple-field primary key*. Examples of a primary key field are Social Security Number, a unique customer number, or some other field that uniquely identifies the record.

Exporting and importing data

You can export an object from an Access database to a file that isn't an Access file — a dBase or Excel file, for example. You can also use this technique to create a static HTML file. To export an object, follow these steps:

1. **Open the database that contains the object.**

2. **Select the object in the Database window.**

3. **Choose File⇨Export, or right-click the object and then choose Export from the shortcut menu.**

4. **In the Export dialog box, select the file type that you want to create using the Save as Type drop-down list.**

5. **Select the file to which you want to save the object by typing the name in the File Name box.**

   You can save to a file that already exists, or you can create a completely new file by typing a new name in the File Name box. If you're creating a non-Access file, type a name for your brand-new file.

6. **Click the Save button.**

   If you're exporting an existing Access file, you see the Export dialog box, where you can rename the object (if you want to) and tell Access whether you want to export all the data or just the object definition (field names, format, and any expressions). When you save a report to HTML, Access

will ask you for the name of the HTML template file. You can find out about HTML template files from the Access help system.

The easiest way to import data is to use the Import Data Wizard. This wizard enables you to see what you're working with and gives you more options than importing or linking with a simple menu command. Open the database that you want to add the imported or linked data to, and follow these steps to import data:

1. **Click New in the Tables tab of the Database window and choose Import Table New Table dialog box.**

2. **In the Import dialog box, use the Files of type drop-down menu to choose the file type that you're importing from.**

   For example, if you're importing data from an Excel file, choose Microsoft Excel (*.xls). Access then displays the Excel files in the current folder.

3. **Navigate the folder structure (if necessary) to find the file that contains the data you want to use and click the file name so that it appears in the File name box on the Import dialog box.**

4. **Click the Import button.**

   The wizard takes over and guides you through the process of choosing the data you want to import. The windows you see depend on the type of file that contains the data you're importing.

You can identify an existing field as the primary key, or you can ask Access to create one. To have Access create a primary key for you, follow these steps:

1. **Close the table.**

   Access asks whether you want to create a primary key.

2. Select Yes.

> Access creates a field called ID in the first column of the table. The field starts at 1 and increases by 1 for each record (it's an AutoNumber field). Access automatically inserts a new number each time you add a new record to the table.

You can also create a primary key in Design view. Click the cursor in the field you want to make the primary key and click the Primary Key button. Access displays the key symbol to the left of the field name.

To make an AutoNumber primary key field, create an AutoNumber field and designate it as the primary key.

To make a *multiple-field primary key,* select the fields in Design view. To select a field, click the row selector — the gray block to the left of the field name. Then Ctrl+click to select fields after you select the first field. When the fields are selected, click the Primary Key button.

Chapter 4: Getting Your Tables Just Right

In This Chapter

- ✓ Getting your columns and rows as you like them
- ✓ Inserting and moving columns
- ✓ Making your datasheets look good
- ✓ Deleting records
- ✓ Saving your table

*A*s smart as Access 2000 seems to be sometimes, it doesn't have a creative side. If Access had its way, everything in every table would look just the same. It doesn't know how wide you want your columns or how high you'd like to see your rows. In addition, it doesn't care that you can add colors and change fonts in your datasheets. Access never even reminds you that you can change how its gridlines look. Although these options are never going to be crucial to the importance of your data, having *some* control over the look and feel of your tables may just help you regain some human dignity. Besides, you are the one who has to look at your tables on screen, and you can make them easier to work with. In addition, you need to know how to delete unwanted records and — goodness forbid if you forget — save your tables.

Changing Column Width

Initially, Access gives all columns in a datasheet the same width. You can change the width one column at a time, or a few columns at once.

To change the width of one column, follow these steps:

1. Move the mouse pointer to the right border of the column and then up to the top of the column, where the field names appear.

The pointer turns into the change-column-width pointer.

2. Click and drag the column border to a new position.

You can change the width of several adjacent columns at the same time using this method — simply select all the columns (click the first column header and drag to the header for the last column that you want to select). Change the width of one of the selected columns. All the selected columns become the same width as the one column whose width you changed.

You can also tell Access to change the column width so that the column is wide enough for the widest data in the column. To size the column to fit the contents, move the mouse pointer so that you see the change-column-width pointer, and double-click.

Changing Row Height

You can change row heights in the same way that you change column widths. Changing row height has a catch, though — when you change the height of one row, the heights of all the other rows in the datasheet change, too. You can wrap text on a datasheet by making the row tall enough to fit multiple lines. (See Figure 4-1.)

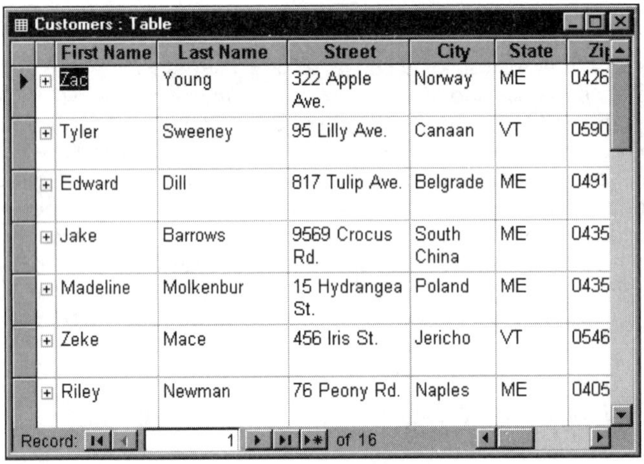

Customers : Table

	First Name	Last Name	Street	City	State	Zip
Zac	Young	322 Apple Ave.	Norway	ME	0426
Tyler	Sweeney	95 Lilly Ave.	Canaan	VT	0590
Edward	Dill	817 Tulip Ave.	Belgrade	ME	0491
Jake	Barrows	9569 Crocus Rd.	South China	ME	0435
Madeline	Molkenbur	15 Hydrangea St.	Poland	ME	0435
Zeke	Mace	456 Iris St.	Jericho	VT	0546
Riley	Newman	76 Peony Rd.	Naples	ME	0405

Record: 1 of 16

Figure 4-1: Rows can be any height that you desire.

Change the height of rows in a datasheet by using one of these methods:

♦ Click and drag between rows in the row selector boxes. (To make a row exactly two lines tall, use the row borders as a guide as you drag the change-row-height pointer.)

♦ Use the Row Height dialog box. Display it by right-clicking a row selector and choosing Row Height. (See Figure 4-2.)

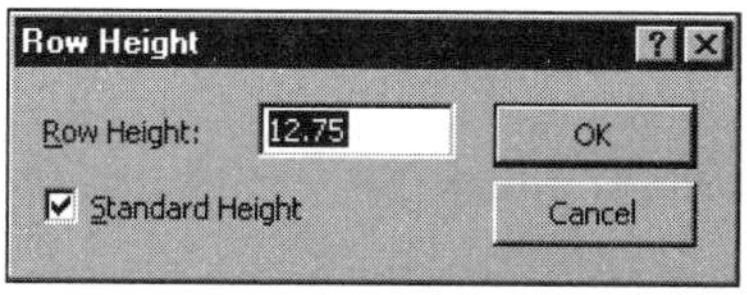

Figure 4-2:
The
diminutive
Row
Height
dialog box.

Row Height	? X
Row Height: `12.75`	OK
☑ Standard Height	Cancel

Inserting a Column/Adding a Field

Inserting a column into a datasheet gives you the space to add a new field to the table. You can add a field to your table using either Datasheet or Design view. To add a column in Datasheet view, follow these steps:

1. Right-click the field name of the column to the right of where you want the new column.

Access selects the column and displays the shortcut menu.

2. Choose Insert Column from the shortcut menu.

To add a field in Design view, follow these steps:

1. Right-click the row selector of the field that will immediately follow the field you're inserting.

Access selects the row and displays the shortcut menu.

2. Choose Insert Rows from the shortcut menu.

Access adds a row. Now you can define your field.

Moving a Column in a Datasheet

Move a column heading (the entire column goes with it) in Datasheet view by dragging it. Follow these steps:

1. Click the field header of the column you want to move to select the column.

2. Click the field name a second time and drag the column to its new position.

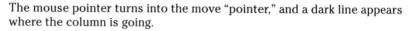

The mouse pointer turns into the move "pointer," and a dark line appears where the column is going.

3. When the dark line is in the position you want the column in, release the mouse button.

**Access
Chapter 4**

**Getting Your Tables
Just Right**

Formatting Datasheets

Although you don't have the flexibility in formatting datasheets that you do with reports and forms, you do have some options. You can change the font, row height, column width, and some other options. To change a datasheet's format, use the Format menu. (A datasheet has to be the active window for you to see this menu.)

Changing the font

You can change the font and font size in your datasheet by using the Font dialog box. You cannot change the font of just one cell, column or row — changing the font changes the whole datasheet. Display the Font dialog box by choosing Format⇨Font. (See Figure 4-3.)

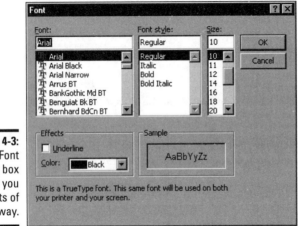

Figure 4-3:
The Font dialog box gives you lots of leeway.

Displaying and removing gridlines

Gridlines are the gray horizontal and vertical lines that separate cells in a datasheet. You can change the color of the gridlines displayed in a datasheet or not display gridlines at all. You can also give cells some special effects, rather than simply separating them with gridlines.

To change gridlines, choose Format⇨Datasheet. Access displays the Datasheet Formatting dialog box.

As you change the settings, the Sample box shows the effect of the changes on the datasheet. Table 4-1 shows what the options on the Datasheet Formatting dialog box do to your datasheet.

Table 4-1	Datasheet Formatting Options
Option	*What It Does*
Horizontal	Displays or hides horizontal gridlines.
Vertical	Displays or hides vertical gridlines.
Cell Effect: Flat, Raised, or Sunken	Displays the cells normally (Flat) or with a three-dimensional effect.
Background Color	Allows you to choose a background color for cells.
Gridline Color	Allows you to choose a gridline color.
Border and Line Styles	Allows you to change the look of the border, horizontal gridline, vertical gridline, and column header underline. Select the line that you want to format in the first box, and choose the line style in the second box.

Deleting Records

To delete a record in a datasheet, follow these steps:

1. **Right-click the row selector of the record that you want to delete.**

2. **Choose Delete Record from the shortcut menu.**

 Alternatively, you can put the cursor anywhere in the row that you want to delete and then click the Delete Record button.

Deleting a record is permanent. When you delete data, you can't get it back — so make sure that you really want to delete it!

Saving a Table

Access automatically saves data entered in a table when you move to the next record. However, you do need to save the table design — the field definitions and formats. To save a table design, follow these steps:

1. **Make sure the table is active.**

If the table is active, the color of its title bar matches the color of the Access title bar. You can click a window to make it active.

2. **Click the Save button, press Ctrl+S, or choose File⇨Save.**

You can also save a table by closing it. If you have made changes in a table since the last time you used it, when you close the table, Access asks whether you want to save it. Remember that the data is saved automatically each time you move to another field. What you need to save is the table design and the datasheet formatting.

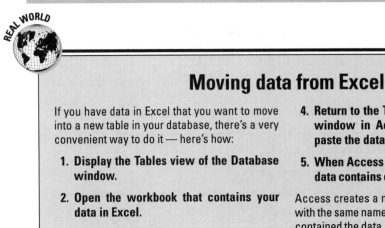

Moving data from Excel

If you have data in Excel that you want to move into a new table in your database, there's a very convenient way to do it — here's how:

1. **Display the Tables view of the Database window.**

2. **Open the workbook that contains your data in Excel.**

   Make sure the first row of data will make adequate field names.

3. **Select the data in Excel and press Ctrl+C to copy the data to the clipboard.**

4. **Return to the Table view of the Database window in Access and press Ctrl+V to paste the data into a new table.**

5. **When Access asks if the first row of your data contains column headings, click Yes.**

Access creates a new table with the Excel data with the same name that the Excel worksheet that contained the data. You may need to rename your table, but wasn't that easy?

Chapter 5: Working with Fields

In This Chapter

- ✔ Copying, naming, and opening fields
- ✔ Changing field names and size
- ✔ Freezing and hiding columns
- ✔ Formatting all types of fields
- ✔ Creating a lookup field

*F*ields are categories of data in your database. Each field holds one kind of data. For example, you may have a field called Birthdays that stores all the birthdays of the people entered in your database. Then you are always prepared to send them a birthday greeting as a cheap advertising gimmick. Or you can have a field called Delinquent Accounts to include all your favorite customers. You can send them a sort of greeting, too. The different categories of data are simply unlimited.

In order to understand better the concept of a field, you may need to visualize one. If you think in terms of a table, fields would be the columns of data, each column having a "heading" to indicate what type of data it holds. No matter which way you think, however, fields are the cornerstone of your database.

Field Management

If you control your fields, you're the master of your database. Basic field management isn't very complicated, however, and Excel 2000 almost makes it an enjoyable task.

Copying a field

You can copy a field. This capability is particularly useful if you are creating several similar fields — rather than defining the data type and properties for each field, you can simply copy a field definition and edit the field as necessary.

You may want to copy a field that you are using to link tables. This ensures that the field has the same properties in both tables, a requirement for related fields.

1. **Display the table in Design view.**

2. **Select the field you want to copy by clicking the row selector.**

3. **Copy the field by clicking the Copy button or choosing Edit⇨Copy.**

4. **Move to a blank row or create a blank row by right-clicking within a row and choosing Insert Rows from the shortcut menu. If you're copying the field to a different table, display that table in Design view and move to a blank row.**

5. **Click the Paste button or choose Edit⇨Paste.**

   Notice that Access copies the field properties as well as the information in the selected row.

6. **Type a new name to rename the copied field.**

   Access has the field name selected, so typing a new name replaces the selected name.

7. **Press Enter to complete the new field.**

8. **Edit the Description, if necessary.**

9. **Save the table.**

You can copy the field again by moving to another blank row and clicking the Paste button.

Naming and renaming fields

The rules for naming Access fields are simple:

+ Start with a letter or a number. (Actually, this isn't a hard and fast rule, but it's good practice.)

+ Don't use more than 64 characters.

Changing the name of a field before you finish designing a table is a hassle-free task. To rename a field, follow these steps:

1. **Double-click the field name.**

   Access selects the entire name.

2. **Type a new name for the field.**

   Alternatively, you can edit the current name by pressing F2 to deselect the name but remain in edit mode. Then press the Backspace and Delete keys to remove unnecessary characters, and type in new characters.

3. **Press Enter to enter the new name, or press Esc to cancel the renaming procedure.**

Setting field size

For Text and Memo fields, use the Field Size option in the Field Properties pane of the table in Design view to limit input in the field to a specific number of characters. For Number data, the Field Size defines the type of number, and tells Access how much space is required to store each value. Table 5-1 gives the Field Size options for numeric data.

Table 5-1	Numeric Data Field Size
Numeric Field Size Settings	*What They Do*
Byte	Allows values from 0 to 255 with no decimal places
Integer	Allows values from -32,768 to 32,767 with no decimal places
Long Integer	Allows values from about negative 2 billion to about positive 2 billion with no decimal places
Double	Allows really huge numbers, both positive and negative, with up to 15 decimal places
Single	Allows not-quite-as-huge numbers, both positive and negative, with up to seven decimal places

If you shorten the field size after entering data, you risk losing data when Access truncates entries longer than the new field size. The default field size for Text data, for example, is 50 characters. If you change the field-size setting to 25, all entries longer than 25 characters are truncated to 25 characters. However, Access will warn you if you are going to lose data as a result of shortening the field length.

Freezing a column in a datasheet

When you're working with a wide datasheet, you may want to freeze one column so that you can move all the way to the right edge of the table and still see that particular field. When you freeze a column, it moves to the left side of the window (no matter where it appeared before) and stays there, even when you scroll or pan all the way to the right.

1. **Right-click the field name to select the column and display the shortcut menu.**

2. **Select Free𝑧e Columns to freeze the selected column.**

To unfreeze a column, choose Format⇨Unfreeze All Columns.

Deleting a column/removing a field

You can delete a field from a table, but you should do so very carefully — a 24-hour waiting period may be in order. When you delete a field (a column in a datasheet), you also irretrievably delete all the data in the field.

1. **Right-click the field name for the column.**

Access selects the column and displays the shortcut menu.

2. **Choose Delete Colum𝑛 from the shortcut menu.**

Access displays a warning box, telling you that you will permanently delete the field and the data in it.

3. **Click Yes to delete the field (or No if you change your mind).**

To delete a field in Design view, follow the same procedure, except right-click the row selector for the field that you want to delete and choose Delete Rows from the shortcut menu.

Access
Chapter 5

Working with Fields

Formatting Fields

When you're working with a table in Design view, you can format various fields by using the Format setting in the Field Properties pane. These options change how the data appears in the table, and may affect how the data appears in queries, forms, and reports.

Formatting Text and Memo fields

When you're dealing with a Text field, the Format options of the Field Properties pane enable you to specify how the text in a field should appear, as well as how many characters may be entered in the field. To format Text and Memo fields, type the characters in Table 5-2 into the Format section of the Field Properties pane.

Table 5-2	Formatting Options for Text and Memo Fields
Formatting for Text	**What You Type**
Display text all uppercase	>
Display text all lowercase	<
Display text left-aligned	!
Specify a color	[*color*] (black, blue, green, cyan, magenta, yellow, and white are the color options)
Specify a certain number of characters	@ (Type @ for each character to be included — including spaces)
Specify that no character is required	&
Display text	**/text**

You can tell Access to add characters such as +, —, $, a comma, parentheses, or a space to the data entered. For example, you may want to enter the following in the Format setting for a phone number:

(@@@)@@@-@@@@

If you then enter ten digits into this field, the numbers appear with parentheses and the hyphen, even though you don't type those extra characters.

You can even format fields to include additional text. Just enclose the text you want to add in quotation marks or precede it with a slash (/).

Formatting Number and Currency fields

Access has common formats for Number and Currency fields built right in — all you have to do is choose the format that you want from the Format drop-down list in the Field Properties pane (see Figure 5-1). Table 5-3 describes the different formats from which you can choose:

Figure 5-1:
Access
has
formats for
Number
and
Currency
fields built
right in.

Field Properties		
General Lookup		
Field Size	Integer	
Format		▼
Decimal Places	General Number	3456.789
Input Mask	Currency	$3,456.79
Caption	Fixed	3456.79
Default Value	Standard	3,456.79
Validation Rule	Percent	123.00%
Validation Text	Scientific	3.46E+03
Required	No	

The display layout for the field. Select a pre-defined format or enter a custom format. Press F1 for help on formats.

Table 5-3	Formatting Options for Number and Currency Fields
Number Format	*How It Works*
Number	Displays numbers without commas and with as many decimal places as the user enters
Currency	Displays numbers with the local currency symbol (determined from the Regional Settings found in the Windows Control Panel), commas as thousands separators, and two decimal places
Fixed	Displays numbers with the number of decimal places specified in the Decimal Places setting (immediately below the Format setting); the default is 2
Standard	Displays numbers with commas as thousands separators and the number of decimal places specified in the Decimal Places property
Percent	Displays numbers as percentages — that is, multiplied by 100 and followed by a percent sign
Scientific	Displays numbers in scientific notation

If the numbers in the field don't seem to be formatted according to the Number Format property, you may need to change the Field Size property. For example, if you have the Field Size property set to Integer or Long Integer, it doesn't matter what value you use in the Decimal Places property, Access insists on displaying the value as an integer — with no decimal places. Try using Single or Double in the Format property instead.

Formatting Date/Time fields

Access has built-in Date/Time formats from which you can choose. To see these formats, display the drop-down list in the Format section of the Field Properties pane (see Figure 5-2).

Next to each format name is an example of how the date and/or time is displayed. If you don't specify a format for a Date/Time field, Access uses the General Date format.

You can create your own Date/Time format if you don't like the ones that Access offers on the drop-down list. To see what characters you can use to create your own Date/Time format, do the following:

1. **Select a Date/Time field in Table Design view.**

Figure 5-2:
The drop-down list in the Format section of the Field Properties pane.

General Date	6/19/94 5:34:23 PM
Long Date	Sunday, June 19, 1994
Medium Date	19-Jun-94
Short Date	6/19/94
Long Time	5:34:23 PM
Medium Time	5:34 PM
Short Time	17:34

2. **Move your cursor to the Format field property — the first option in the Field Properties pane at the bottom of the window.**

3. **Press F1.**

Access displays general help on the Format property.

To see help specific to creating your own Date/Time format, click the Date/Time Data Type link.

Creating a Lookup Field

You can create your own drop-down list in a table to guide others (or yourself) as they enter data. A lookup field provides the user with a list of choices, rather than requiring users to type a value into the datasheet. Lookup fields enable you to keep your database small and the data entered in it accurate and consistent.

The items on the drop-down list can come from a list you type, or from a field in another table. For example, you may want to input the customer number when you know the customer name. Using the Lookup Wizard, you can tell Access to display a drop-down list in the Customer Number field that displays the first and last name as well as the customer number (as shown in Figure 5-3). When a customer is selected, the customer number is put in the table. (It's not as confusing as it sounds!)

Figure 5-3:
Access can display a drop-down list for a field.

		Customer Num	Order Number	Order Date	Ship Date
	⊞	2	1	10/1/98	
▶	⊞	6 ▾	2	10/5/98	
	⊞	6 Madeline Molkenbur		10/6/98	
	⊞	7 Zeke Mace		10/6/98	
	⊞	8 Riley Newman		10/14/98	
	⊞	9 Figaro Aronoff		10/25/98	
	⊞	10 Fennel Smith		11/1/98	
	⊞	11 Seth Ronn		11/3/98	
	⊞	12 Abby Aikens		11/3/98	
	⊞	13 Farley Spitzer		11/15/98	
	⊞	5	12	11/14/98	
	⊞	12	13	11/16/98	
*		0	(AutoNumber)		

Order Summary : Table

Record: ◄◄ ◄ [2] ► ►I ►* of 12

Here's how to use the Lookup Wizard.

1. **Display the table in Design view.**

2. **Display the drop-down list for the Data Type for the field that will contain the drop-down list and select Lookup Wizard.**

3. **Tell the wizard whether the values you want to appear on the field's drop-down list are coming from a field in another table or from a list that you type.**

If the field simply consists of several choices, choose the second option and type the list. But if you want to store more information about those choices (maybe you're entering the name of a customer who bought something, but you also want to store the customer's address and phone number in another table), store the values in a table.

4. **Click Next to display the next window of the Lookup Wizard.**

What you see in the second window depends on the option you choose in the first window:

- If you ask the lookup field to display values from another table, Access asks you about the name of the table.

- If you tell Access that you want to type in the values, you get a table in which you can type the lookup list (see Figure 5-4).

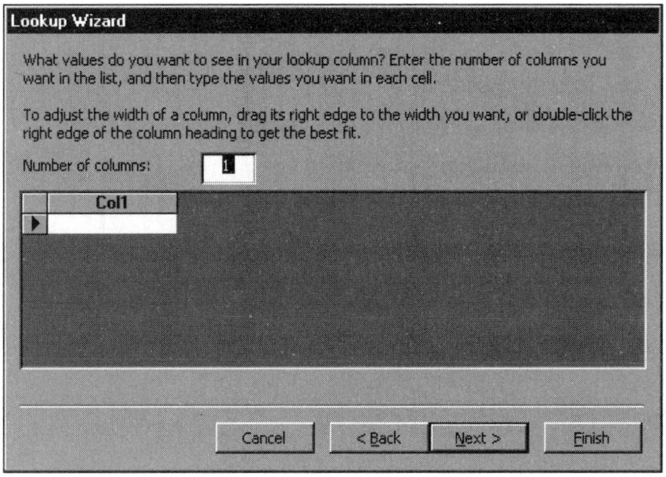

Lookup Wizard

What values do you want to see in your lookup column? Enter the number of columns you want in the list, and then type the values you want in each cell.

To adjust the width of a column, drag its right edge to the width you want, or double-click the right edge of the column heading to get the best fit.

Number of columns: 1

Col1

| Cancel | < Back | Next > | Finish |

Figure 5-4:
You can type the lookup list in the Lookup Wizard.

5. **If you're typing values to choose among, click in the table in the wizard window (which currently has only one cell), and type the first entry in the list. Press Tab — not Enter — to create new cells for additional entries.**

If you want your lookup list to include values stored in a table or query, select the object containing the field with the values you want to choose among. You can choose an existing query by clicking the Queries or Both radio button.

6. **Click Next to display the next window.**

7. **If you typed a list, this screen you see is the last screen of the wizard — skip to Step 12. If you're using a table for the lookup, you have to tell Access which field(s) you want to use by moving field names from the Available Fields list box to the Selected Fields list box.**

   If you pick multiple fields, the information in each field is displayed on the drop-down list. However, only one field's information can be stored, so the next window asks you which field's value you want to store in the new field. For instance, you may display the Customer Number, First Name, and Last Name in the drop-down list, but you can only store one of those values — in the example in the figure, that value is the Customer Number.

8. **Click Next to display the next window.**

   This window shows you a table with the values in the lookup list, and allows you to change the width of the columns. The window also contains a checkbox which, when selected, hides the key field (if you selected the key field). Depending on your application, you may want to display the key field by unselecting the Hide Key Column checkbox.

9. **Change the width of the column if necessary.**

   You can change the width of the column to automatically fit the widest entry by double-clicking the right edge of the field name that appears at the top of the column.

10. **Click Next to display the final window of this wizard.**

11. **Edit the name that Access gives the lookup column, if you want, and then click Finish to create the lookup column.**

12. **Now check out your lookup list by viewing your table in Datasheet view. When you click the field for which you created the lookup list, you see an arrow that indicates that a drop-down list is available. Click the arrow to see options in the list.**

The default setting lets users either choose from the drop-down list or type in a value. To force users to choose from the drop-down list (or enter a value that is on the drop-down list) click the Lookup tab in the Field Properties pane and change the Limit To List setting from No to Yes.

You can add values to an existing lookup list. If you typed values for the lookup list yourself, switch to Design view, click the field with the lookup, and click the Lookup tab in the Field Properties pane. You can add options to the Row Source — separate the values with a semicolon. If the lookup list gets its values from a table, you can add records to the table to see additional choices in the lookup list.

The lookup field is not automatically updated when you add additional items. Refresh the data in the lookup field by pressing F9.

Chapter 6: Manipulating Your Data

*Y*ou don't always want people — or yourself — to enter data willy-nilly into your database. If you know what kind of data you want, Access 2000 can help you set limits on data entry and block unwanted data (to keep the riff-raff out, so to speak). Then after you get all this nice data entered into your database, Access can make it a breeze for you to find and filter your data according to your deep-rooted database needs. And while you're at it, feel free to go ahead and sort that data. This chapter gives you a head start on all these worthy activities.

Finding Data in a Table

To find a record that contains a particular word or value, use the Find and Replace dialog box. To display the Find and Replace dialog box, open a datasheet and do one of the following:

✦ Press Ctrl+F

✦ Choose Edit⇨Find

✦ Click the Find button

To use the Find and Replace dialog box, follow these steps:

1. **In Datasheet view, put the cursor in the field that contains the value you're searching for.**

2. **Display the Find and Replace dialog box**

3. **In the Find What box, type the text or value that you're looking for.**

4. Use the Look In option to determine where to look — in the field your cursor is in, or in the whole table.

5. Use the Match option to determine whether you're looking for part of a field (Any Part of Field); you want an exact match for the whole field (Whole Field); or if you want the field to start with the text in the Find What box (Start of Field).

6. Click Find Next to find the first instance of the value or text in the table.

Access displays the section of the table containing the values in the Find What box.

7. If you do not find what you're looking for, click Find Next until you do.

You can display more options on the Find and Replace dialog box by clicking the More button. Use the settings in the Find and Replace dialog box to find exactly what you're looking for:

✦ **Search:** This option determines the direction in which Access searches. Choose Up, Down, or All. Choose All to find the text or value anywhere in the table — however, Access starts the search at the cursor.

✦ **Match:** Choose Any Part of Field, Whole Field, or Start of Field to tell Access whether the value or text that you typed is in the entire field, at the beginning of the field, or anywhere in the field (which means that the text may start somewhere in the middle of the field).

✦ **Match Case:** When you activate this check box, Access finds only text that matches the case of the text that you type in the Find What box.

✦ **Search Fields As Formatted:** This option matches the contents of the Find What box to the formatted data (the way the data appears in the table, using the format and input mask properties, rather than the way it was entered).

✦ **Replace With:** Use this option on the Replace tab of the Find and Replace dialog box to replace instances of the Find What text with the Replace With text. Replace one instance at a time by clicking the Replace button. Replace all instances by clicking the Replace All button.

Filtering Your Data

Filtering allows you to look at a subset of your table — records that match a particular criteria. (In English, this means that you can create a test for your data to pass, and then look only at the rows in your table that pass your test.) In Access, a criterion for filtering is something like "I want to find all the records with 2 in the Number of Items field." To use more advanced criteria such as "2 or more" or "between 3 and 20," you need to use the Advanced Filter/Sort command or a query.

When filtering doesn't give you the options you need, you probably need to use a query (see Chapters 7 and 8). You can filter in three ways: Filter by Selection, Filter by Form, and Advanced Filter/Sort.

Filtering creates a temporary table containing only those records that fit the criteria you choose. If you want a permanent table that updates as more records are added, you need to create a query.

You can tell when a table is filtered by looking at the bottom of the table — the status bar tells you how many records are in the table and displays "Filtered" in parentheses.

You can't save a filter — if you want to be able to use a filtered table later, you need to create a query that contains the same criterion as your filter.

Filtering by selection

When you have only one criterion for one field that filtered records need to meet, and you can find one record that matches your criterion. To find all the Maine addresses in your address table, for example, you need to find an address that has ME in the State field.

1. **Put the cursor in the record and field that matches the criterion.**

To find all addresses in Maine, for example, you may put the cursor in the State field that contains the abbreviation ME.

2. **Click the Filter by Selection button or choose Records⇨ Filter⇨Filter by Selection.**

Access creates a temporary table consisting of the records that meet the criterion. Access finds records that have identical entries in the selected field (See Figure 6-1).

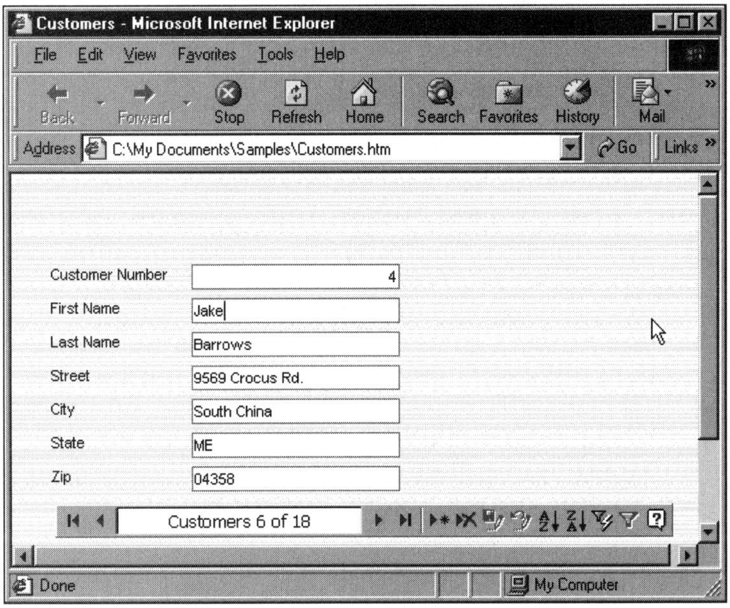

Figure 6-1: This table has been filtered by the State field.

> **Customers - Microsoft Internet Explorer**
> File Edit View Favorites Tools Help
> Back Forward Stop Refresh Home Search Favorites History Mail
> Address: C:\My Documents\Samples\Customers.htm   Go Links
>
> Customer Number   4
> First Name   Jake
> Last Name   Barrows
> Street   9569 Crocus Rd.
> City   South China
> State   ME
> Zip   04358
>
> Customers 6 of 18
> Done   My Computer

350 *Filtering Your Data*

If you haven't narrowed the list down enough, you can filter the filtered table again by using the same technique. You can choose a different field, or even select just one word or part of a field, before clicking the Filter by Selection button.

To see the entire table again, click the Remove Filter button.

You can select particular records that you want to filter out and then choose Records⇨Filter⇨Filter Excluding Selection to exclude the selected records from the table. Use this technique in combination with the Filter by Selection command to see only the records you want to see. To see the entire table, click the Apply Filter button again.

Filtering by form

When you have more than one criterion to match, filter by form. For instance, say that you are looking for orders over $50 that were sent before December 1. The Filter by Form window enables you to pick the values you want the filtered records to have. Unlike the Filter by Selection command, however, Filter by Form allows you to choose more than one value and to choose values to match for more than one field.

When you filter by form, you can use multiple criteria. If you specify more than one criterion on a Filter by Form tab, Access treats the criteria as AND criteria, meaning that a record has to pass *all* the criteria in order to be displayed on the filtered datasheet.

If you use criteria on different tabs (using the OR tab at the bottom of the window to display a clean grid), Access treats the criteria as OR criteria. That means that a record has to meet the criteria on one tab or the other to be included on the filtered datasheet.

Using AND and OR criteria enables you to filter the records using more than one rule or set of rules. For example, you can find addresses from South China, ME, as well as addresses in Vermont by using the OR tab at the bottom of the Filter by Form window.

Follow these steps to filter a datasheet by form:

1. Click the Filter by Form button or choose Records⇨Filter⇨Filter by Form.

Access displays the Filter by Form window, which looks like an empty datasheet with some different buttons in the toolbar, and some different menu choices.

2. Move the cursor to a field you have a criterion for.

A down arrow appears in the field the cursor is in.

3. Click the arrow to see the list of all the values for that field.

4. Click the value that you want the filtered records to match (see Figure 6-2).

If you want the criteria to specify part of the value in the field, type LIKE "*value that you're looking for*". For example, typing LIKE "n" in the Name field finds all records in the Name field containing the letter *n*.

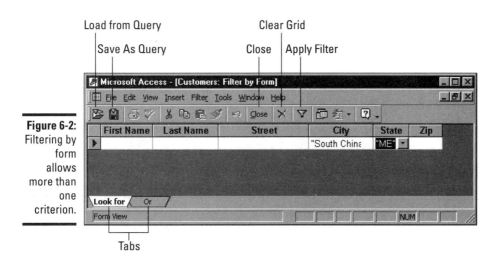

Load from Query   Clear Grid

Save As Query   Close │ Apply Filter

Figure 6-2:
Filtering by
form
allows
more than
one
criterion.

Tabs

5. **If you have criteria for another field that should be applied at the same time as the criterion you set in Step 4 (AND criteria), repeat Steps 3 and 4 for the additional field.**

   For example, if you want to find addresses in San Francisco, CA, set the State field to CA, and the City field to San Francisco.

6. **If you have another set of rules to filter records by, click the Or tab at the bottom of the Filter by Form window.**

   Access displays a blank Filter by Form window. When you set criteria on more than one tab, a record only has to meet all the criteria on any one tab to be displayed on the filtered datasheet.

7. **Choose the criteria on the second tab in the same way that you chose those on the first — click the field, and choose the value that you want to match.**

   For example, if, in addition to all the addresses in San Francisco, you want to see all addresses from Boston, MA, set the State field on the new Filter by Form grid to MA, and the City field to Boston.

   Another Or tab appears, allowing you to continue adding as many sets of OR criteria as you need.

8. **To see the filtered table, click the Apply Filter button.**

Filtering by Advanced Filter/Sort

The easiest kind of query to create is one that filters records in only one table. You perform this simple query by using the Advanced Filter/Sort command. Follow these steps:

1. **Open the table you want to filter in Datasheet view.**

2. **Choose Records⇨Filter⇨Advanced Filter/Sort.**

   Access displays the Filter window, which has two parts, just like the Query Design view.

3. **Click the first field you want to use to filter the table and drag it to the Field row of the first column of the grid in the bottom half of the window.**

   Instead of dragging a field, you can choose a field from the Field drop-down list.

4. **Click the Criteria row in the first column and type the criteria to limit the records you see.**

   For example, if you want to see only items that cost more that $10, put the Cost per Item field in the Field row of the first column, and type >10 in the Criteria row.

5. **Repeat Steps 3 and 4 to add other fields and criteria to the grid.**

6. **(Optional) Choose a field by which to sort the resulting table.**

   Set a sort order by displaying the drop-down list for the Sort row in the column containing the field you want to sort by — choose Ascending or Descending. This option tells Access to sort the table that results from the advanced filter in ascending or descending order, using the field listed in the same column as the sort key.

7. **When you finish creating all the criteria you need, click the Apply Filter button to see the resulting table.**

   Access displays all the fields in the original table, but it filters the records and displays only those that meet the criteria.

You can do several things with the resulting table:

✦ **Save it:** If you want to save your advanced filter, you have to save it in Design view. After you apply the filter, return to Design view by choosing Record⇨Filter⇨Advanced Filter/Sort and click the Save As Query button to save the advanced filter. You can get to the filter after it's saved through the Queries tab of the Database window.

✦ **Filter it:** Use the filter buttons and Record⇨Filter to filter the table even more.

✦ **Print it:** Click the Print button.

✦ **Sort it:** The best way to sort is to use the Sort row in the design grid. But you can use the Sort Ascending or Sort Descending buttons to sort the query-result table by the field that the cursor is in.

✦ **Fix it:** Choose Record⇨Filter⇨Advanced Filter/Sort to display the Design view to fix the criteria or other information in the grid.

✦ **Add data to it:** Add data to the table by clicking the New Record button and typing the data.

✦ **Edit data:** Edit data the same way that you do in the datasheet and press F2.

✦ **Delete records:** You can delete entire records if you want — click the record you want to delete and click the Delete Record button.

✦ **Toggle between the filtered table and the full table:** Click the Apply Filter button. If you're looking at the full table, clicking the Apply Filter button displays the filtered table (according to the last filter that you applied). If you're looking at the filtered table, clicking the Apply Filter button displays the full table.

Sorting a Table

Your data may have been entered randomly, but it doesn't have to stay that way. Use the Sort commands (or buttons) to sort your data.

Before you sort, you have to know what you want to sort by. Do you want the Addresses table in order by last name, for example, or by zip code? When you know which field you want to sort by, sorting is a piece of cake.

You can sort in ascending order or descending order. *Ascending order* means that you start with the smallest number or the letter nearest the beginning of the alphabet, and work up from there. When you sort in ascending order, fields starting with *A* are at the top of the table, and fields starting with *Z* are at the bottom. *Descending order* is the opposite. Follow these steps to sort a table in Datasheet view:

1. **Select the field you want to sort by (sometimes called the *sort key*) by clicking the field name.**

   If you don't select the column (and you don't have to), Access uses the field the cursor is in as the sort key.

2. **Click the Sort Ascending or Sort Descending button, depending on which order you want to sort in.**

Blocking Unwanted Data with an Input Mask

An *input mask* limits the information allowed in a field by specifying what characters can be entered. An input mask is useful when you know the form the data should take — for instance, if an order number has two letters followed by four digits. Phone numbers and zip codes are other examples of fields where input masks are useful.

Input masks are commonly used in tables, but you can also add them to queries and forms where data may be entered. In all cases, you have to add an input mask from the Design view.

You can use an input mask to specify that the first character in a field must be a letter and every character after the first must be a number, for example. You can also use an input mask to add characters to a field — for example, use an input mask to display ten digits as a phone number, with parentheses around the first three digits and a dash after the sixth digit. If the data in a field varies or is not easily described, it's probably not a good candidate for an input mask.

The input mask for the field is in effect when data is being entered into the field in a datasheet or a form.

You can create input masks for text, number, and currency data; other data types don't have the Input Mask field property.

To create an input mask, enter a series of characters in the Input Mask section of the Field Properties pane to tell Access what kind of data to expect. Data that doesn't match the input mask cannot be entered. To block data from a field, first figure out exactly what data you want to allow in a field; then use the characters in the following table to code the data in the Input Mask field property in the table Design view. See Table 6-1.

Table 6-1	Input Mask Possibilities
Input Mask Character	*What It Allows/Requires*
0	Requires a number; + and - not allowed
9	Allows a number; + and - not allowed
#	Allows a space, converts a blank to a space, allows + and -
L	Requires a letter
?	Allows a letter
A	Requires a letter or number
a	Allows a letter or number
C	Allows any character or a space
<	Converts the following characters to lowercase
>	Converts the following characters to uppercase
!	Fills field from right to left, allowing characters on the left side to be optional
\	Displays the character following in the field (\Z appears as Z)
. ,	Displays the decimal placeholder or thousands separator
; : - /	Displays the date separator (the symbol used depends on the setting in the Regional Settings section of the Windows Control Panel)

Chapter 7: Queries: Getting Answers from Your Data

In This Chapter

- ✔ Making queries with Query Wizard
- ✔ Using Query Design view
- ✔ Making a select query
- ✔ Saving a query

*Q*ueries can help you narrow down and find the information you need. So why not just use filtering and sorting (as explained in Chapter 6), you may ask? Well, you're not far off. Queries are nothing more than a heavy-duty way to filter and sort your data. You can use queries to select records from a database and to create summary calculations, for example. Maybe you want to know the people to whom you owe more than $100 but less than $500 (if you just so happen to keep a database on such stuff). Access 2000 helps you with a Query Wizard if you don't want to go it alone. And if you want to get your feet wet, feel free to plunge ahead and create your own queries. This chapter gets you started on creating queries so that you, too, can join the fun.

About Queries

Queries enable you to select specific data from one or more tables. Like tables, queries have two views: Design view and Datasheet view. In the Design view, you tell Access which fields tables you want to see, which tables they come from, and the criteria that have to be true for a record to appear on the resulting datasheet.

Criteria are tests that a record has to pass — for example, you may want to see only records with a value in the Amount field greater than 100. The criterion is that the value in the Amount field must be greater than 100.

In Datasheet view, you see the fields and records Access finds that meet your criteria.

A query doesn't store data — it just pulls data out of tables for you to look at. A query is *dynamic* — as you add to or change your data, the result of the query also changes. When you save your query, you're not saving the table that the query produces — you're just saving the query design so that you can ask the same question again.

Following are some kinds of queries:

✦ **Advanced filter/sort:** The Advanced Filter/Sort feature in Access is the simplest kind of query; it allows you to find and sort information from one table in the database. This option is available from the Datasheet view of a table by choosing Records⇨Filter⇨Advanced Filter/Sort.

✦ **Select:** A select query finds the data you want from one or more tables and displays it in the order in which you want it displayed. A select query can include criteria that tell Access to filter records and display only some of them.

✦ **Total:** These queries are similar to select queries, but they allow you to calculate a sum or some other aggregate (such as an average).

✦ **Action:** Action queries change your data based on some set of criteria. Action queries can delete records, update data, append data from one or more tables to another table, and make a new table.

✦ **Crosstab:** Most tables in Access, including ones generated by queries, have records down the side and field names across the top. Crosstab queries produce tables with the values from one field down the side and values from another field across the top of the table. A crosstab query performs a calculation — it sums, averages, or counts data that is categorized in two ways.

Using a Query Wizard

If you click the New button in the Queries tab of the Database window, you see not one but four wizards to help you build your query. The wizard you use depends on what you want your query to do. Table 7-1 lists the four query wizards and tells when you may find each useful.

Table 7-1	Query Wizards
Query Wizard	*When to Use It*
Simple Query Wizard	Use this wizard to build a select query. If you want to perform summary calculations with the query, the wizard can help you. If you have criteria, however, you still have to enter them in Design view, so the Simple Query Wizard is not a huge improvement over designing the query yourself.
Crosstab Query Wizard	Use this wizard to create a crosstab query.
Find Duplicates Query Wizard	Use this wizard to find duplicate data in the database.
Find Unmatched Query Wizard	Use this wizard to find records with no corresponding records in related tables.

Wizards give you help creating queries, but the queries that they create are just like the ones you create — you can see them in Design or Datasheet view and do anything with them that you might do with any other query of the same type.

Using a query wizard and studying the Design view of the queries that they create is a good way to learn how to use some of the more advanced features of queries. Start a query wizard by following these steps:

1. **Display the Queries view of the Database window.**

2. **Click the New button.**

Access displays the New Query dialog box.

3. **Select the wizard you want to use.**

On the left side of the dialog box, Access displays a brief summary of what the wizard does (see Figure 7-1).

4. **Click OK.**

Access starts the wizard that you chose. That's it!

The following sections give you help getting going with some of the more popular Query Wizards.

Find Duplicates Query Wizard

Use this wizard when you want to find duplicate entries in a field in a table or query. The Find Duplicates Query Wizard can help you find identical records as well as records with the same name and different addresses, for example.

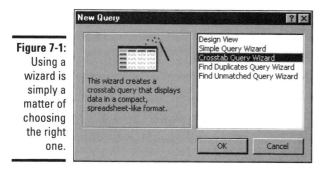

Figure 7-1:
Using a
wizard is
simply a
matter of
choosing
the right
one.

The Find Duplicates Query Wizard needs to know the following things:

✦ The table or query you want it to examine: The wizard displays table names first — if you want to see query names, click the Queries or Both radio button.

✦ The fields in the table or query you picked that may have duplicate information: Select fields that may have duplicate entries and click the right arrow to move them into the Duplicate-value fields list box.

✦ Any additional fields that you want to see in the datasheet produced by the query: Seeing additional fields can be useful if you're editing or deleting duplicated records.

✦ The name of the query.

When you click the Finish button and display the datasheet, you see a list of records. Duplicates are listed in groups. You can edit this datasheet to update your data or to delete unneeded records by editing the datasheet, or by using the query design created by the wizard to create an update or delete query.

Find Unmatched Query Wizard

The Find Unmatched Query Wizard finds records in one table that have no matching records in another, related table. You may store orders in one table and details about customers in another table, for example. If the tables are linked by, say, a Customer Number field, the Unmatched Query Wizard can tell you whether you have any customers listed in the Orders table who aren't listed in the Customers table.

The Find Unmatched Query Wizard needs to know the following things:

+ The table (or query) in which all records should have related records. In the preceding example, this is the Order table where the details of each order are stored. (You should have a related record about each customer.) If you want to choose a query, click the Queries or Both radio button.

+ The name of the table that contains the related records. In the example, this is the Customer table where the details about each customer are stored. If you want to see queries in addition to tables, click the Queries or Both radio button.

+ The names of the related fields. Access makes a guess, especially if there is a field in each table with the same name. (It's a little odd that Access can't figure out the names of the related fields by itself, especially if you've defined relationships, but there it is.)

+ The fields that you want to see in the datasheet resulting from the query.

+ The name for the query.

Using the Simple Query Wizard

The Simple Query Wizard does a great deal of the work of creating a query for you. The most basic query you can create with the Simple Query Wizard pulls together related data from different fields. The Simple Query Wizard is a terrific way to create some summary calculations from your data — such as how much was spent on an order or how many items were ordered.

The Simple Query Wizard gives you the option of creating a *summary* or *detail* query if the fields you choose for the query include both of the following:

+ A field with values

+ A field with repetitions, used to group the values

A *detail query* lists every record that meets your criteria. A *summary query* performs calculations on your data to summarize it. You can sum, average, count the number of values in a field, or find the minimum or maximum value in a field. A summary query creates new calculated fields that you can use in other queries or in reports.

For example, if you have a field that lists the amount spent and a field that lists the dates on which the money was spent, Access can create a summary query for you that sums the amount spent by date.

Follow these steps to use the Simple Query Wizard to create a query:

1. **Create a new query by displaying the Queries tab of the Database Window and clicking New.**

Access displays the New Query dialog box.

2. **Select Simple Query Wizard and click OK.**

Access displays the first window of the query.

3. **Use the Tables/Queries list box to choose the first table or query that you want to use fields from.**

When you select a table or query, fields from that object appear in the Available Fields list box.

4. **Move fields you want to use in the query from the Available Fields list to the Selected Fields list by double-clicking a field name or by selecting the field name and then clicking the right-arrow button.**

5. **If you're using fields from more than one table or query, repeat Steps 3 and 4 to add fields from the additional tables or queries to the Selected Fields list.**

6. **Click Next after selecting all the fields you need for the query.**

Access displays the next window, which asks you if you want a Detail or Summary query. If summary calculations are not possible with the fields you've chosen, Access skips this window. For simple queries you may see the Finish window — skip to Step 11.

7. **Choose the type of query you want: Detail or Summary.**

If you choose a Summary query, click the Summary Options button to display the window where you tell the wizard how to summarize each field (see Figure 7-2).

Use the check boxes to indicate the new fields for Access to create with this query. For example, if you want to add all the values in the Cost per item field, click the Sum check box in the row for the Cost per item field.

Don't overlook the Count check box(es) that may appear in this window — selecting a count check box tells the wizard to create a field that counts the records within each grouping.

8. **Click OK to leave the Summary Options window.**

9. **Click Next to view the next window.**

If you are summarizing data, and if the fields being summarized can be grouped by a Time/Date field, the wizard displays a window where you choose the time interval the records should be grouped by.

**Access
Chapter 7**

**Queries: Getting
Answers from
Your Data**

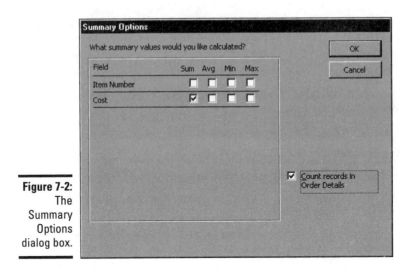

Figure 7-2:
The
Summary
Options
dialog box.

For example, if you choose to sum a field that details check amounts, and check amounts were entered in a record that also contains a field telling the date each check was written, you can choose to display total check amounts by Day, Month, Quarter, or Year. Select the time interval to group by.

10. **Click Next to see the final window.**

11. **Type a name for the query in the box at the top of the window.**

12. **Choose whether you want to Open the query to view information, which shows you the query in Datasheet view, or to Modify the query design, which shows you the query in Design view.**

If you want to see the help screen on working with a query, click the Display Help on Working With the Query check box.

13. **Click Finish to view the query.**

You can't tell the Simple Query Wizard about criteria. If you want to include criteria in your query, open the query created by the wizard in Design view and add the criteria.

Using the Crosstab Query Wizard

A *crosstab query* is a specialized kind of query for displaying summarized data. Instead of creating a table with rows showing record data and columns showing fields, you can use a crosstab query table to use data from one field for the row labels and data from another field for column labels. The result is a more compact, spreadsheet-like presentation of your data.

The Crosstab Query Wizard works only with one table or query. If the fields you want to use in the Crosstab query are not in one table, you have to create a query that combines those fields in one query before you use the Crosstab Query Wizard.

Start the Crosstab Query Wizard by following these steps:

1. **Display the Queries in the Database window.**

   Access displays the names of any queries you have in your database.

2. **Click the New button.**

   Access displays the New Query dialog box.

3. **Select Crosstab Query Wizard and click OK.**

   Access starts the Crosstab Query Wizard.

The Crosstab Query Wizard asks you for the following information:

✦ The table or query you want to use to create the crosstab table

✦ The field you want to use for row headings

✦ The field you want to use for column headings

✦ The field you want to summarize by using the row and column headings

✦ How you want to summarize the field (count the entries, add them together, average them, and so on)

✦ Whether you want Access to sum each row (Access adds a Sum of *Field Name* column to the table to display the result)

About Query Design View

Whichever kind of query you're using, you have to use Query Design view to tell Access about the data you're looking for and where to look for it (see Figure 7-3). Do one of the following to display a query in Design view:

✦ Click the Queries button in the Objects list on the Database window, select the query name, and click the Design button on the toolbar.

✦ Ctrl+double-click the query name in the Queries view of the Database window.

Table 7-2 explains what the buttons on the Query Design View toolbar that are unique to queries do.

Table 7-2		Query Design View Toolbar Buttons
Toolbar Button	*Button Name*	*What It Does*
▦	View	Displays Datasheet view
💾	Save	Saves the query so that you can view the design and the query datasheet again

(continued)

Table 7-2 *(continued)*

Toolbar Button	Button Name	What It Does
↶	Undo	Undo your last undoable action (Many actions cannot be undone, so always keeping a backup is a good idea.)
▦ ▾	Select Query Type	Displays a drop-down list from which you can choose a query type: Select Query, Crosstab Query, Make-Table Query, Update Query, Append Query, or Delete Query
!	Run	Runs the query (For a select query, clicking the Run button does the same thing as clicking the View button. When the query is an action query, the Run button performs the action. Use this button carefully.)
⊞	Show Table	Displays the Show Table dialog box so that you can add tables to the query
Σ	Totals	Displays the Total row in the query grid (Use the total row to tell Access what kind of calculation you want.)
All ▾	Top Values	Limits the result of the query displayed in the datasheet to the number of records or the percentage of records displayed in this option
▤	Properties	Displays properties for the selected field or field list
⚒	Build	Displays the Expression Builder dialog box (This button is "live" only when the cursor is in the Field or Criteria row.)
▤	Database Window	Displays the Database window

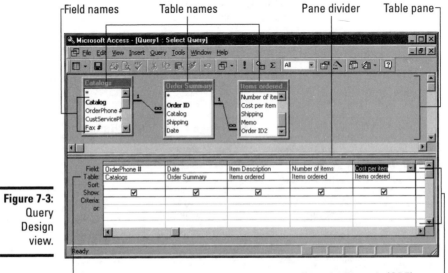

Figure 7-3: Query Design view.

Field names — Table names — Pane divider — Table pane

Tables used in query — Query by Ecample (QBE) pane

The top half of the window displays the tables containing fields that you want to use in the query. Use the bottom half of the window to give Access specifics about the datasheet you want the query to produce — specifically, what fields to display, and how to decide whether to display a record.

Each row in the query grid has a specific purpose. Table 7-3 tells you how to use each of them.

Table 7-3	Query Grid Rows
Query Grid Row	*What It Does*
Field	Provides the name of a field that you want to include in a query
Table	Provides the name of the table that the field comes from (This row is not always visible.)
Total	Performs calculations in your query (This row is not always visible — use the Totals button on the toolbar to display or hide it.)
Sort	Determines the sort order of the datasheet produced by the query
Show	Shows a field (If you want to use a field to determine which records to display on the datasheet, but not actually display the field, remove the check mark from the Show column for the field.)
Criteria	Tells Access the criteria for the field in the same column
Or	Use for additional criteria

Adding a Select Query to the Database

The most frequently used type of query is called a *select query*. A select query displays fields from one or more tables based on criteria that you define. This section demonstrates how to create a select query from scratch.

1. **Display Queries in the Database window.**

2. **Double-click the Create query in Design view icon.**

Access displays Query Design view and the Show Table dialog box.

3. **Select the table(s) that contain fields you want to display in the query datasheet or use to create criteria by selecting the table(s) and then clicking the Add button in the Show Table dialog box.**

If you want to include a field generated by another query, you can add queries to a query by clicking the Queries or Both tab of the Show Table dialog box and double-clicking the query name.

4. **Click the Close button in the Show Table dialog box.**

5. **Select the fields that you want to use in the query table.**

You can drag a field name to the design grid or double-click a field name to move it to the design grid. You can also use the drop-down Field and Table lists in the query grid to select the fields that you want to use.

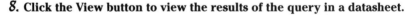

Showing or hiding a field

You include some fields in your query simply so that you can filter or sort based on them. However, chances are that you may not always want to see those fields in your query results. For example, you may want to find all customers who purchased items within the past six months — but you don't necessarily want to see the dates for all these purchases. To exclude a field from showing up in your query results, makes sure that the check box in the Show row is blank. Select the check box again to have the field appear in query results.

6. Type the criteria that you want to use to create the query table.

For example, if you want to see only records with values in the Order Numbers field over 100, type **>100** in the Criteria row of the column that contains the Order Numbers in a Field row. Or, if you want to see only those records whose Author field is Hemingway, type **Hemingway** in the Criteria row for the Author column.

7. Set the Sort and Show options to create your perfect query table.

8. Click the View button to view the results of the query in a datasheet.

9. **Save the query by clicking the Save button in the query's Design or Datasheet view.**

If you're querying just one table, the easiest way to create the query is to select the table in the Database window and then click the New Object: Query button. (Query is not always what the New Object button is set to create — you may have to use the New Object button's drop-down list to choose Query.) Then select Design View in the New Query dialog box. Access displays Query Design view with the table that you selected displayed.

Saving a Query

You don't have to save a query. Often, queries are created on the fly to answer a question. You don't need to clutter your database with queries that you're unlikely to need again.

That said, you can certainly save a query design (but not the query data sheet) when you need to. Use any of the following methods:

+ In Design or Datasheet view, click the Save button or choose File➪Save. If you haven't saved the query yet, Access asks you for a name for the query. Type the name and then click OK.

+ Close the query (clicking the Close button is a popular method). If you've never saved the query, or if you've changed the query design since you last saved it, Access asks whether you want to save the query. If you've never saved the query, give it a name and then click OK; otherwise, click Yes to save the query.

Be sure to give your new query a name that tells you what the query does. That way, you won't have to open one query after another to find the one you're looking for.

If you want to create a query similar to one you already have in your database, select or open the query and choose File➪Save As to save the query with a new name. Then you can keep the original query and make changes to the new copy.

Printing an object

Views that you can print have a Print button in the toolbar. Some views (notably Design views) cannot be printed. In those views, the Print button is grayed out, indicating that you can't click it.

Although you can't print the Design view of a table, query, report, or form, you can print definitions for these objects. Choose Tools⇨Analyze⇨Documenter to open the Documenter dialog box. You can print an object such as a datasheet or a report in three ways:

✔ To print the object currently on your screen without changing any settings, click the Print button.

✔ If you want to change some settings in the Print dialog box before printing the object, choose File⇨Print or press Ctrl+P. Change settings as necessary and click OK to print the object.

✔ To print an object without opening it, select it in the Database window and then click the Print button, or right-click the object and then choose Print from the shortcut menu. Access sends the object straight to the printer. To display the Print dialog box first, select the object, and choose File⇨Print. Change settings as necessary and click OK to print the object.

Note: For information on printing in general for Access or for any other Office 2000 application, see Appendix B.

Chapter 8: More Fun with Queries

In This Chapter

✔ **Sorting queries**

✔ **Inserting fields into a query**

✔ **Correcting queries**

✔ **Attaching tables to queries**

✔ **Limiting the data that queries display**

*Q*ueries are so much fun that this mini-book devotes two entire chapters to them. Well, it may also be true that queries are important enough to require the extra space. In any case, you should realize that you can perhaps do a lot more with queries than you first imagined. For example, you can sort a table produced by a query. You can also correct a query should you somehow make a mistake. And you can use criteria expressions to limit the data that your queries display (do you really need to see a list of all the people named Smith in Tennessee?). Read on for some help with these topics as well as a few more things you may want to do with queries.

Sorting a Query

You can sort a table produced by a query in several ways. The first way is to use the Sort row in the query grid. Use the Sort row to tell Access which field to use to sort the datasheet. To sort by a field, display your query in Design view and follow these steps:

1. **Move the cursor to the Sort row in the column that contains the field according to which you want to sort.**

2. **Display the drop-down list for the Sort row.**

   Access displays the options for sorting: Ascending, Descending, and (not sorted).

3. **Choose Ascending or Descending.**

You can use the Sort row in the query grid to sort by more than one field. You may want to sort the records in the datasheet by last name, for example, but more than one person may have the same last name. You can specify another field (perhaps first name) as the second sort key. If you want, you can specify more than two fields by which to sort.

When you sort using more than one field, Access always works from left to right, first sorting the records by the first field (the primary sort key) that has Ascending or Descending in the Sort row, and then sorting any records with the same primary sort key value by the second sort key.

You can also sort the datasheet that results from the query, using the same technique you use to sort any datasheet: Click the field that you want to sort by and then click the Sort Ascending or Sort Descending button.

Inserting Fields in a Query Grid

You can move a field from the table pane to the query grid in three easy ways:

✦ Double-click the field name. Access moves the field to the first open column in the grid.

✦ Drag the field name from the table pane to the field row of an unused column in the query grid.

✦ Use the drop-down list in the Field row of the query grid to choose the field you want. If you use this method with a multiple-table query, you may find it easier to choose the table name from the drop-down Table list before selecting the field name.

You can put all the field names from one table into the query grid in two ways:

✦ **Put one field name in each column of the grid.** If you have criteria for all the fields, you can put one field name in each column of the query grid in just two steps. Double-click the table name where it appears in the table pane of the Design view to select all the fields in the table. Then drag the selected names to the grid. When you release the mouse button, Access puts one name in each column.

✦ **Put all the field names in one column.** This method is useful if you want to find something that could be in any field or if you have one criterion for all the fields in the table. The asterisk appears above the first field name in each Table window. Drag the asterisk to the grid to tell Access to include all field names in one column. The asterisk is also available as the first choice in the drop-down Field list — it appears as `TableName.*`.

Editing a Query

You can do a few things in a query to edit it — you can move the columns around, delete a column, or delete all the entries in the design grid. To do any of those things, though, you first have to select the column in the grid by clicking the column selector — the gray block at the top of each column in the grid. (See Figure 8-1.) Table 8-1 has some things you may want to do to make your query better.

Column selector

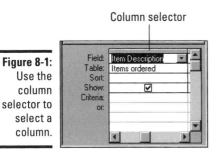

Figure 8-1:
Use the
column
selector to
select a
column.

Table 8-1	Making a Better Query
When You Want to . . .	*Here's What to Do*
Move a column	Click the column selector to select the column, click a second time, and then drag the column to its new position.
Delete a column	Click the column selector to select the column; then press the Delete key to delete the column.
Delete all columns	Choose Edit⇨Clear Grid.
Insert a column	Drag a field from the table pane to the column in the grid where you want to insert it. Access inserts an extra column for the new field.
Change the displayed name	Use a colon between the display name and the actual name of the field in the Field row *(display name: field name).*

Attaching a Table to a Query

In order to use a table's fields in a query, you have to "attach" the table to the query — that is, display the table name in the top half of the Query window.

It's a little odd that to add a table to a query, you use a dialog box called Show Table — but that's how it's done. Display the Show Table dialog box by doing any of the following things:

✦ Right-click the table part of Query Design view and choose Show Table from the shortcut menu

✦ Click the Show Table button

✦ Choose Query⇨Show Table

After you display the Show Table dialog box, you add a table to the table pane of Query Design view by doing either of the following things:

✦ Double-clicking the table name in the Show Table dialog box

✦ Selecting the table and then clicking the Add button

You can also add a query to the table pane if you want to use a field that was created or filtered by a query. Click the appropriate tab at the top of the Show Table dialog box to see all Tables, all Queries, or all tables and queries (both).

When you have added all the tables that you need, click the Close button in the Show Table dialog box to work with the Query window.

To remove a table from a query, press Delete when a field in the table is highlighted. Deleting a table from a query is absurdly easy and can have damaging consequences for your query — when a table is deleted, all the fields from that table are deleted from the query grid. Take care when your fingers get close to the Delete key.

Limiting Records with Criteria Expressions

Criteria enable you to limit the data that the query displays. Although you can use a query to see data from related tables together in one record, the power of queries is that you can filter your data to see only records that meet certain criteria. You use the Criteria and Or rows in the query grid to tell Access exactly which records you want to see.

Access knows how to *query by example* (QBE). In fact, the grid in Design view is sometimes called the QBE grid. QBE makes creating criteria easy. If you tell Access what you're looking for, Access goes out and finds it. For example, if you want to find values equal to 10, the Criteria is simply 10. Access then finds records that match that criteria.

The most common type of criteria are called logical expressions. A *logical expression* gives a yes or no answer. Access shows you the record if the answer is yes, but not if the answer is no. The operators commonly used in logical expressions include <, >, AND, OR, and NOT.

Although we use uppercase to distinguish operators and functions, case does not matter in the query design grid.

Querying by example

If you want to find all the addresses in Virginia, the criterion for the state field is simply the following:

```
Virginia
```

You may want to add another criterion in the next line (OR) to take care of different spellings, as follows:

```
VA
```

Access puts the text in quotes for you. The result of the query is all records that have either *Virginia* or *VA* in the state field.

Using operators in criteria expressions

The simplest way to use the query grid is to simply tell Access what you're looking for by typing a value you want to match in the Criteria row for the field. But often, your criteria are more complicated than "all records with Virginia in the state field." You use operators in your criteria expressions to tell Access about more complex criteria.

Table 8-2 lists the operators that you're likely to use in a criteria expression.

Table 8-2	Operators to Use in a Criteria Expression
Relational Operator	*What It Does*
=	Finds values equal to text, a number, or date/time
< >	Finds values not equal to text, a number, or date/time
<	Finds values less than a given value
< =	Finds values less than or equal to a given value
>	Finds values greater than a given value
> =	Finds values greater than or equal to a given value
BETWEEN	Finds values between or equal to two values
IN	Finds values or text included in a list
LIKE	Finds matches to a pattern

When you type your criteria, you don't have to tell Access that you're looking for Costs<10, for example. When you put <10 in the Criteria row, Access applies the criteria to the field that appears in the Field row of the same column. Table 8-3 shows some examples of criteria that use operators.

Table 8-3	Examples of Criteria That Use Operators
Expressions with Operator	*What the Operator Tells Access to Do*
<10	Finds record with values less than 10
>10	Finds records with values greater than 10
<>10	Finds records with values not equal to 10
>10 AND <20	Finds records with values between 10 and 20
>=10 AND <=20	Finds records with values between 10 and 20, including 10 and 20
BETWEEN 10 AND 20	The same as >=10 AND <=20
IN ("Virginia", "VA")	Finds the values *Virginia* and *VA*
LIKE "A*"	Finds text beginning with the letter A. You can use LIKE with wildcards such as * to tell Access in general terms what you're looking for.

Using AND, OR, and NOT

The most common way to combine expressions that tell Access what you're looking for is to use AND, OR, and NOT in your criteria. These three operators can be a little difficult to figure out unless you aced Logic 101 in college. Here's exactly how they work:

✦ **AND:** Tells Access that a particular record must meet more than one criterion to be shown in the datasheet

✦ **OR:** Tells Access that a particular record must meet only one of several criteria to be shown in the datasheet

✦ **NOT:** Tells Access that a criterion has to be false for the record to be included in the datasheet

You can combine operators in one criterion expression, such as when you are looking for the following:

```
>10 OR <18 NOT 15
```

This expression produces records with the values 11, 12, 13, 14, 16, and 17 (assuming that all values in the field are integers).

Using multiple criteria

When you have criteria for only one field, you can use the OR operator in two different ways:

✦ Type your expressions into the Criteria row separated by OR.

✦ Type the first expression in the Criteria row, and type subsequent expressions using the Or rows in the query grid.

Whichever approach you take, the result is the same — Access displays records in the Datasheet that satisfy one or more of the Criteria expressions.

When you use criteria in multiple fields, Access assumes that you want to find records that meet all the criteria — in other words, that the criteria in each row are considered to be joined by AND statements. If you type criteria on the same row for two fields, a record has to meet both criteria to be displayed on the datasheet.

When you use the Or row, the expressions on each row are treated as though they are joined by AND, but the expressions on different rows are treated as though they are joined by OR. Access first looks at one row of criteria, and finds all the records that meet all the criteria on that row. Then it starts over with the next row of criteria, the Or row, and finds all the records that meet all the criteria on that row. A record only has to meet all the criteria on one row to be displayed in the datasheet.

Using dates, times, text, and values in criteria

Access does its best to recognize the types of data that you use in criteria and encloses elements of the expression between the appropriate characters. You are less likely to create criteria that Access doesn't understand, however, if you use those characters yourself.

Table 8-4 lists types of elements that you may include in a criteria expression and the character to use to make sure that Access knows that the element is text, a date, a time, a number, or a field name.

Table 8-4	Types of Data to Use in Certain Expressions
Use This Type of Data . . .	*In an Expression Like This . . .*
Text	"text"
Date	#1-Feb-97#
Time	#12:00am#
Number	10
Field name	[field name]

You can refer to dates or times by using any allowed format. December 25, 1999, 12/25/99, and 25-Dec-99 are all formats that Access recognizes. You can use AM/PM or 24-hour time.

Chapter 9: Using Aggregate Calculations and Building Expressions

In This Chapter

✔ Creating a calculation that works with a group of data

✔ Adding calculations to queries

*U*sing aggregate calculations and building expressions sure sounds a lot more complicated than such topics as opening your database or giving your database some color. You may be surprised, however, at how simple these complicated-sounding activities really are. When you want to create a calculation that works with a group of data, you need an aggregate calculation. For example, you may want to count the number of orders that come in each day for potatoes on your potato farm, or calculate an average amount for all orders. And when you're creating your database, you shouldn't waste your time dragging out your calculator, doing the math yourself, and then typing in the result. Instead, tell Access 2000 to perform any calculation for you. The work gets done faster, and the result is always up to date — even if you later add, delete, or change records. Your potatoes will never go bad in the barn again!

Calculating Summary Data for a Group of Data

An *aggregate equation* is one that uses a bunch of records to calculate some result. For example, you may want to calculate the total cost of an order, count the number of orders that come in each day, or calculate an average dollar amount for all orders.

When you create an aggregate calculation, you tell Access to *group* data using a particular field. For example, if you want to know the number of orders that come in each day, you need to group the order data by date; that is, using the field that contains the date. If you want to count the number of orders for each item, then you need to group data using the field that contains the item name or number.

The easiest way to create aggregate calculations is to use the Summary option in the Simple Query Wizard (see Chapter 7).

Using the Total row

The Total row in the query grid enables you to aggregate data. To perform a total calculation on your data, you must select one of the options from the drop-down list for each field in the query grid.

Σ The first step in creating a total is displaying the Total row in the query grid by clicking the Totals button. The Totals button appears to be raised when the Total row is not displayed and depressed when the Total row is displayed (you have to move the pointer to the button to see the 3-D effect).

When the Total row is displayed, you must select a setting in the Total row for each field in the query. Table 9-1 lists the choices for the Total row and how each works.

Table 9-1	Total Row Choices
Total Row	**How It Works**
Group By	Groups the values in this field so that like values are in the same group, allowing you to perform calculations on a group
Sum	Calculates the sum (total) of values in the field
Avg	Calculates the average of values in the field (blanks are not included in the calculation)
Min	Finds the minimum value in the field
Max	Finds the maximum value in the field
Count	Counts the entries in the field (does not count blanks)
StDev	Calculates the standard deviation of values in the field
Var	Calculates the variance of values in the field
First	Finds the value in the first record in the field
Last	Finds the value in the last record in the field
Expression	Tells Access that you plan to type your own expression for the calculation
Where	Tells Access to use the field to limit the data included in the total calculation

Aggregating groups of records

To calculate aggregates, you must select one or more fields to group by. In the example, say you want to calculate the total cost of an order, so you group by the fields defined in the Order Summary table that contains one record for each order. (See Figure 9-1.)

The Group By option in the Total row enables you to perform an aggregate calculation on a group of records. The result is a datasheet that has one row for each value in the field (with no repetitions) and a calculated field for the value.

Each field with an aggregate function (Sum, Avg, Min, Max, Count, StDev, Var, First, or Last) in the Total row is displayed as a calculated field in the datasheet that results from the query. (See Figure 9-2.)

Access creates new fields to hold the aggregate calculation. You can use these new fields in reports, forms, and other queries.

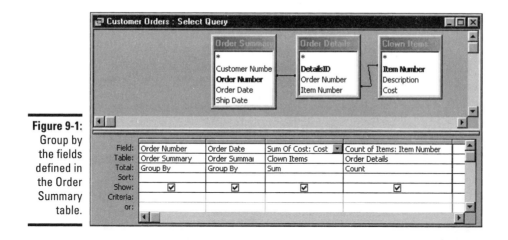

Figure 9-1:
Group by
the fields
defined in
the Order
Summary
table.

Figure 9-2:
Fields are
displayed
as
calculated
fields.

To create an aggregate calculation for grouped records, follow these steps:

1. **Create a new query in Design view.**

2. **From the Show Tables window, choose the tables that you need fields from and add them to the query. Close the Show Tables window.**

3. **Double-click the field you want to group data by to display it in the query grid.**

4. **Choose Group By from the drop-down list in the Total row.**

   If the Total row doesn't appear in the query grid, click the Totals button on the toolbar.

5. **Move the fields that you want to use in aggregate calculations to the query grid.**

6. **Choose the type of calculation that you want for each field from the drop-down list in the Total row.**

Access
Chapter 9

Using Aggregate
Calculations and
Building
Expressions

To perform more than one type of calculation on a field, put the field in more than one column in the query grid and specify a different type of calculation in each Total row.

You can also group by more than one field. If you want aggregate information about people who have the same last name and live at the same address, you can use the Group By setting in both the last name field and the address field.

If you don't use the Group By option for any of the fields in the query grid, the result of any aggregation is the same — the "group" that you aggregate includes all records.

Limiting records to aggregate

You can use the Criteria and the Total rows together to limit the records used in the aggregate calculation or to limit the records displayed after the calculations are performed. You have to be careful, though, to make sure that Access does exactly what you want it to do. Here are some tips on using the Criteria and Total rows in one query.

✦ If you use Criteria in a Group By field, you limit the data that Access uses for the aggregate calculation. In other words, Access first finds the records that meet the criterion and then performs the aggregate calculation on just those records.

✦ If you use Criteria in a field with an aggregate function (Sum, Avg, Min, Max, Count, StDev, Var, First, or Last), Access uses the criteria to limit the result of the calculation. It first does the calculation and then selects the results that meet the criteria for the datasheet.

✦ Use the Where option in the Total row when you want to limit the records used for the calculation by using a field that is not a Group By field. When you use the Where option, you can also use a criterion. The Where option limits the records used for the aggregate calculation to those that pass the criterion for the field — think of it as meaning "Limit the records to Where this criterion is true."

When you use the Where option, you use it only to limit records — Access knows this and turns off the Show check box. In fact, you can't show a field used with the Where option in the Total row. If you want to display a field used with the Where option, use the same field in another column of the query grid with the Group By option in the Total row.

Creating your own expression for an aggregate calculation

You're not limited to the aggregate functions Access provides to perform a calculation in a query — you can write your own expression, instead. To write your own expression for an aggregate calculation, choose Expression in the Total row and type the expression into the Field row of the grid. To create your own expression, follow these steps:

1. **Move your cursor to the Field row of a blank column in the query grid.**

2. **Type the name of the new field that you are creating, followed by a colon.**

3. **Type the expression in the Field row after the colon.**

4. **Select Expression in the Total row of the new field.**

Calculating Fields (Building Expressions)

You can add calculations to queries and reports by typing an expression, sometimes called a *formula,* which tells Access exactly what to calculate. In a query, you put the expression in the Field row of one column of the query grid.

Most expressions include some basic elements, such as field names, values, and operators. Field names must be enclosed in brackets. Following is an example of an expression that calculates profit using fields called "Revenues" and "Expenses":

```
Profit: [Revenues] - [Expenses]
```

The name of the new field appears first, followed by a colon. The names of existing fields are enclosed in square brackets.

You can also use values in an expression, as follows:

```
Retail Cost: [Wholesale Cost] * 1.50
```

You aren't limited to performing calculations with values; you can also perform calculations with dates, times, and text data.

Some types of data must be enclosed between special characters so that Access knows what kind of data it is:

Type of Data in an Expression	How It Should Look
Text	"Massachusetts"
Date/time	#15-jan-97#
Field name	[Cost]

The following are the basic steps to take to add a calculated field to a query:

Access
Chapter 9

1. **In the query grid, click the Field row of a blank column.**

2. **Type the name of the new field, followed by a colon.**

   If you don't give the new field a name, Access names it for you — with something unintelligible, such as Expr1. If you're writing an expression to calculate cost and you want to call the new field Total Cost, type **Item Cost:**.

3. **Type the expression you want Access to calculate.**

   In Figure 9-3, the new field is called Item Cost, and the expression to calculate it follows the colon.

 4. **To see the result, click the View button (see Figure 9-4).**

Using Aggregate
Calculations and
Building
Expressions

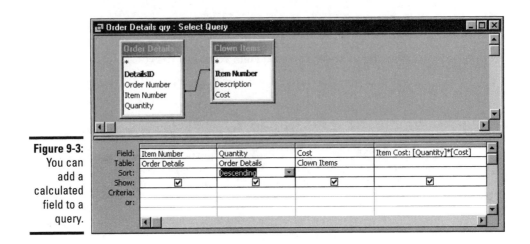

Figure 9-3:
You can
add a
calculated
field to a
query.

After you create the new field, you can use it in other queries and in other calculations.

Figure 9-4:
The results
of adding a
calculated
field to a
query.

You can display a zoom window for your expression that allows you to see the whole expression. To display the contents of cell in a zoom window, position your cursor in the cell and press Shift+F2. (This works in a table, too.)

Using a parameter in an expression

You may want to change the value in a criteria or expression without having to rewrite the expression in Query Design view each time. For instance, you may want to see the names of customers who ordered a particular product. You can do so by creating a parameter query. When you run a parameter query, Access displays the Enter Parameter Value dialog box and tells you the name of the field for which it needs a value.

Enter the value of the field name listed, and click OK to see the datasheet.

You can use this to your advantage — for instance, if you're in retail and want to be able to calculate the markup for a variety of your products, first, make sure you don't name any of your fields Markup, then create an expression that includes [Markup]. Then, each time you run the query, you get the Enter Parameter Value dialog box, and can enter a different markup value.

Using operators in calculations

Access has a slew of operators. The operators that you're most likely to have worked with are the *logical* and *relational* operators, which result in a true or false result. However, Access also has operators that you use in calculations.

Mathematical operators work with numbers. Table 9-2 lists mathematical operators and what they do.

Table 9-2	Mathematical Operators
Mathematical Operator	*What It Does*
*	Multiplies
+	Adds
−	Subtracts
/	Divides
^	Raises to a power

Creating a text field with an expression

Text data are often called a *strings* by technoids. Text/string operators work with text and memo fields. You can add two strings together by using "&," the string operator that concatenates (adds together) strings. Access also has functions that work with strings.

You can use different types of data in an expression that results in a text string; you're not limited to text data. You may want to include a numeric value or a date in a string, for example. Using the "&" operator converts data to a string, so the final result is a string.

Chapter 10: Reporting Results

In This Chapter

✓ Creating a report with AutoReport

✓ Creating a report with the Report Wizard

✓ Creating a report in Design View

✓ Editing objects in a report

✓ Sending a report to another Microsoft application

✓ Sorting records in a report

Compiling exactly the data you're looking for is all fine and good, but making that data look great so that you can print it, pass it around, impress your friends, and send it to your high school business teacher who said that you wouldn't amount to anything is the whole point, right? In Access 2000, spiffy output comes in the form of reports.

Who wouldn't be impressed? Just imagine. You can create a report from one table or query, or from several linked tables and queries. You can even create a report from a filtered table. Nothing can hold you back now.

About Reports

Reports can group information from different tables — for instance, you can display the customer information just once, and list all the items the customer has ordered. You can also use calculations in reports to create totals, subtotals, and other results. You can create invoices with reports, as well as other output that summarizes your data. Thanks to the trusty Label Wizard, reports are also the best way to create mailing labels from the data contained in a database.

You can create a report from one table or query, or from several linked tables and queries. You can even create a report from a filtered table.

Adding a Report with AutoReport

AutoReports are an easy way to create a report out of one table or query. AutoReports don't have the flexibility that regular reports have — you can't create groups with an AutoReport, for example — but they are an excellent way to get your data into a report quickly. You can customize an AutoReport by using the formatting tricks described elsewhere in this chapter.

Access has two kinds of AutoReports: columnar and tabular. A columnar AutoReport prints the field names in a column on the left and the data for the record in a column on the right (as shown in Figure 10-1).

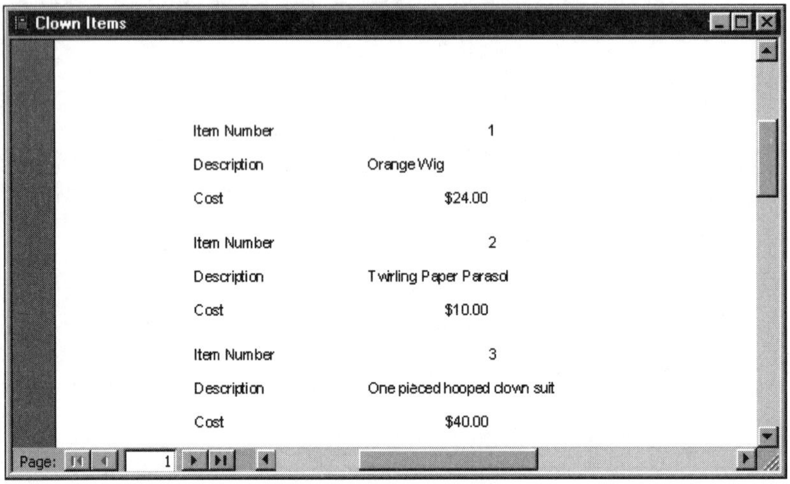

Figure 10-1:
A columnar
report.

A tabular AutoReport looks similar to a datasheet. Data is displayed in columns with field names as the column headers (as shown in Figure 10-2).

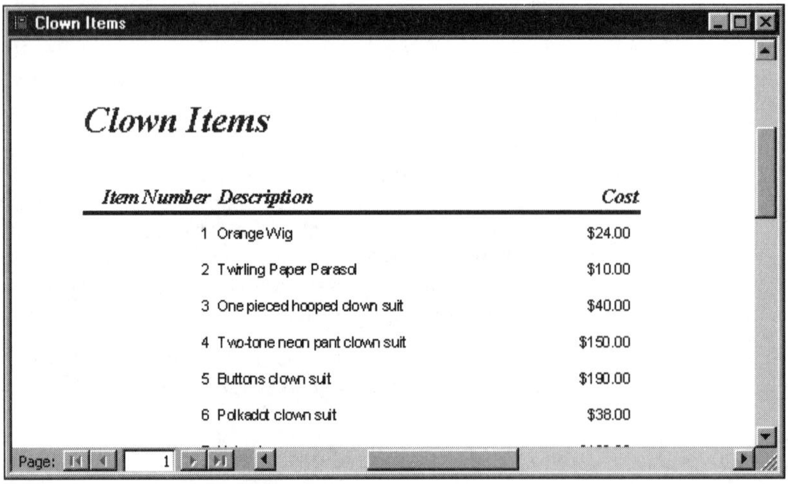

Figure 10-2:
A tabular
report.

To create a columnar AutoReport, follow these steps:

1. **In the Database window, select the table or query that contains the data you want to display in a report.**

2. **Click the arrow next to the New Object button and choose AutoReport from the drop-down list.**

Access creates the report.

Another way to create an AutoReport — and the only way to create a tabular AutoReport — is to click the New button in the Reports tab of the Database window. Access displays the New Report dialog box — choose the type of AutoReport and the table or query that you want it to use; then click OK. Access creates the report.

Adding a Report with the Report Wizard

Using the Report Wizard is the best way to create a report. You may be happy with the resulting report, or you may want to edit the report further, but if you use the Report Wizard, at least you have a report to work with.

One big advantage of using the Report Wizard is that you can choose fields for the report from more than one table or query — you don't have to gather all the data you want in the report into one table or query.

The Report Wizard displays different windows depending on the data and options you select, so don't be surprised if you don't see every window of the wizard. Follow these steps to create a report with the Report Wizard:

1. **Display the Reports view in the Database window and double-click the Create Report by Using Wizard icon.**

Access displays the first Report Wizard window, where you select the fields that you want to use in your report.

You can also start the wizard by displaying the New Report dialog box (click the New button or choose Report from the New Object button drop-down list), selecting Report Wizard, and clicking OK.

2. **From the Tables/Queries list, select the first table or query from which you want to select fields.**

3. **Add the fields you want displayed in the report to the Selected Fields list.**

4. **Repeat Steps 3 and 4 for fields in other tables or queries until all the fields you want to display in the report appear in the Selected Fields list.**

5. **Click the Next button to see the next window of the wizard.**

If the fields you've chosen for your reports are grouped in some way (usually by a many-to-one relationship with another field chosen for the report) you will see the window shown in Figure 10-3, which allows you to choose which table you want to use to group your data.

Double-click a table name to group the data in the report by using that table; then click Next to continue to the next window, which lets you group by individual fields.

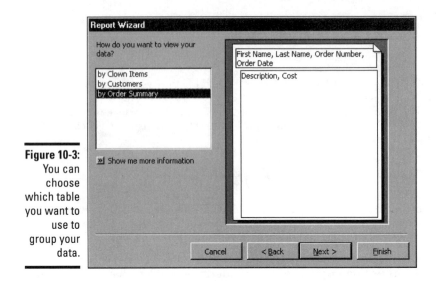

Figure 10-3:
You can
choose
which table
you want to
use to
group your
data.

6. **Add grouping fields if desired by selecting the field and clicking the right-arrow button (>).**

You can change the importance of a field in the grouping hierarchy by selecting the field on the right side of the window and then clicking the up- and down-arrow buttons labeled Priority.

Click the Grouping Options button to display the Grouping Intervals dialog box, where you can specify exactly how to group records using the fields you chose as grouping fields.

The Grouping Intervals dialog box lets you select grouping intervals for each field used to group the report.

Click OK to leave the Grouping Intervals dialog box.

7. **When you finish grouping your data, click the Next button to see options for sorting and summarizing.**

Access automatically sorts the report by the first grouping field.

This window allows you to tell Access how you want to sort the detail section of the report. The detail section is the part of the report that displays the records within each group. You don't have to change anything in this window if you don't need the detail section sorted in any particular order.

If you want to specify a sort order for the detail objects, display the drop-down list of field names next to the box labeled "1." Click the Sort button to change the sort order from ascending (A to Z, 1 to 10) to descending (Z to A, 10 to 1). Click the button again to change the sort order back. You can sort by up to four fields — use the additional boxes to specify additional fields on which to sort. Additional sort fields are used only when the initial sort field is identical for two or more records — then the next sort field is used to determine in what order to display those records.

8. **To display summary calculations, click the Summary Options button.**

Access displays the Summary Options dialog box where you can tell Access to display totals or other calculated summary data in the report. The options displayed in the Summary Options dialog box depend on the data in your report.

9. **Click check boxes to indicate the field(s) you want to summarize and what kind of calculation you want for the summary.**

This dialog box also has options that allow you to show the Summary Only or the Detail and Summary data. If you choose Summary Only, the report displays only the result of the calculation, not the data from the records that were used to calculate the result. If you want to see the data in individual records, choose Detail and Summary data.

Also on this dialog box also is a check box to tell Access to Calculate percent of Total for Sums; Access then calculates the percentage of the total that each group represents.

10. **When you're done with the Summary Options dialog box, click OK; you see the window with sorting options again. Then click <u>N</u>ext in the Report Wizard window to view the next window.**

Access displays the window that allows you to specify how to lay out your report.

11. **Choose the layout that you prefer and the orientation that works best with your report.**

You can preview the layout options by clicking one of the Layout radio buttons. The example box on the left changes to show you what your chosen layout looks like.

12. **Click <u>N</u>ext to see the next window, where you choose the style that you prefer.**

Styles consist of background shadings, fonts, font sizes, and the other formatting used for your report.

13. **Select a style. You can preview each style by clicking it.**

14. **Click the <u>N</u>ext button to view the last window of the wizard.**

15. **Type a new name for the report (if you don't like the name that the Report Wizard has chosen).**

If you want to view the report in Design view, click Modify the Report's Design; otherwise, the Preview the Report radio button is selected, and Access shows you the report in Print Preview. You can also tell Access that you want to see the Help window (which gives you hints on how to customize the report) by clicking the check box titled Display Help on Working with the Report?

16. **Click the <u>F</u>inish button to view your report. Your computer may whir and grind for a minute before your report appears (see Figure 10-4).**

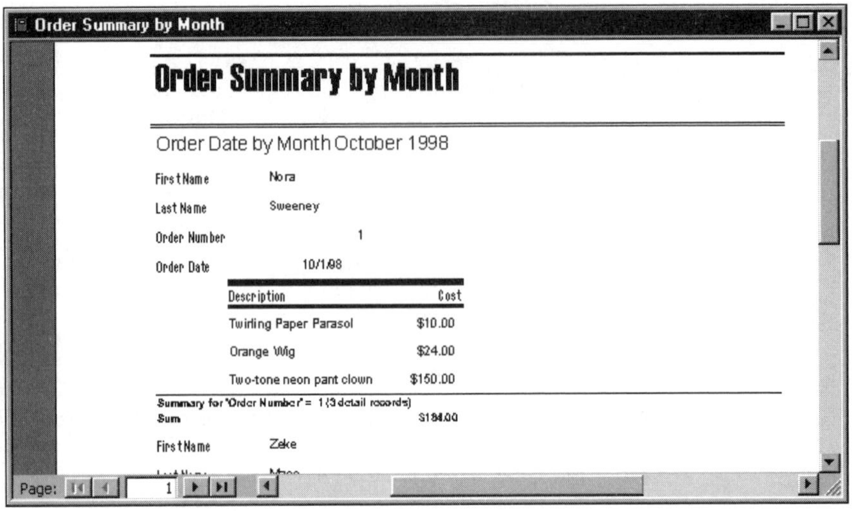

Figure 10-4:
Your report
may just
turn out
nice when
you use a
wizard.

Although the Report Wizard does well setting up groups, it doesn't create a perfect report. Some controls may be the wrong size, and the explanatory text the wizard uses for calculated fields is a little pedantic. Display the report in Design view to fix anything that's wrong with it.

Adding a Report Created in Design View

You may have a personal thing against wizards, or you may just need to know how to create or edit a report in Design View. Whichever is the case, this section covers how to add *controls* that tell Access what to display on the report.

Controls tell Access what you want to see on your report: Text, the contents of a field, and lines are all added to reports by using controls. Follow these general steps to create the report itself:

1. **Display Reports in the Database window by clicking the Reports button in the Objects list.**

2. **Click the New button.**

Access displays the New Report dialog box.

3. **Select Design View (it is probably already selected).**

4. **Select the query or table on which you want to base the report from the drop-down list at the bottom of the dialog box.**

If you want to bind the report to more than one table, the easiest way is to create a query that includes all the fields you want to display in the report.

Binding a report to a query can be very useful — it means that you can create criteria for choosing the records that appear in your report so that Access doesn't include them all. You may want to make a report that includes only clients whose payments are overdue, for example, or you may want a report that includes only the addresses of people whom you're inviting to your wedding.

5. **Click OK.**

Access displays the Report Design view (see Figure 10-5).

6. **Save the report design by clicking the Save button on the toolbar.**

Give the report a name that will help you and others figure out which data it displays. Remember to save your report design often.

After you've created the blank report, you're ready to start adding controls to it, as explained later in this section.

Although it seems like it would be easy to create a report in Design view by double-clicking the Create Report in Design View icon, this method does not allow you to select the table or query you want to base the report on. If you create a report this way, you have to select the table or query that has the data in the Record Source option on the report Properties dialog box.

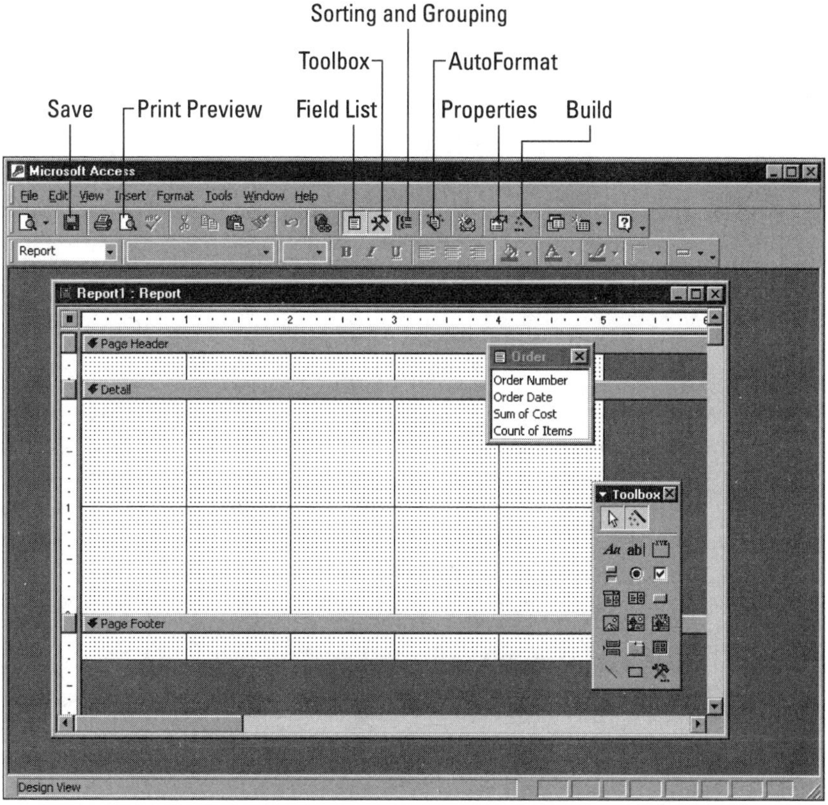

Sorting and Grouping

Toolbox ─ ─ AutoFormat

Save ─ Print Preview   Field List │   Properties   Build

Figure 10-5:
The Report
Design
view.

Using tools in Report Design view

Creating reports is complicated enough that Access gives you a group of new tools to work with in report Design view: the buttons and boxes in the Formatting toolbar and in the Toolbox. Access also displays the grid in the background (to help you align objects in the report), as well as the rulers at the top and left of the design window.

You can choose which of these tools you want to appear by using the View menu when you're in Design view. Items with a check mark appear in the Design window.

 You can also display and close the Toolbox by clicking the Toolbox button on the toolbar. (See Figure 10-6.)

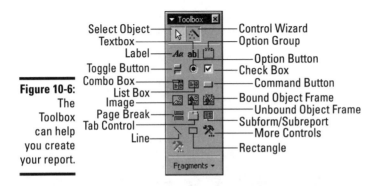

Figure 10-6:
The Toolbox can help you create your report.

Select Object — Control Wizard
Textbox — Option Group
Label — Option Button
Toggle Button — Check Box
Combo Box — Command Button
List Box — Bound Object Frame
Image — Unbound Object Frame
Page Break — Subform/Subreport
Tab Control — More Controls
Line — Rectangle

Each type of object that you may want to add to your report has a different button in the Toolbox — choose the type of object that you want and then click the spot in the report where you want to put the object.

You can move the Toolbox so that it appears along one edge of the Access window instead of floating free. To anchor the Toolbox to an edge, click its title bar and drag the Toolbox to one edge of the screen. A gray outline shows you where the Toolbox will be when you drop it. When the gray outline appears in one row or column against one side of the Access window, release the mouse. You can make the Toolbox free-floating again by clicking and dragging by the top (if the Toolbox is vertical) or the left of the bar. (In fact, you can perform this trick with any toolbar.)

You can also make the Toolbox a different size by clicking and dragging a border. The size you choose affects the number of buttons that appear on each row.

Adding a control

A report is made up of controls that tell Access what to display on the report. To display the contents of a field in a report, you have to create a *bound* control. The control is bound to a field, which tells Access to display the contents of a field in that control.

The people who developed Access knew you would want to add fields to reports frequently. So they made it possible to add a field to a report with a single drag-and-drop procedure, rather than forcing you to use two steps — first creating the control and then telling Access to display the contents of a field in the control.

To add a control that displays the contents of a field to a report, display the report in Design view and follow these steps:

1. **Display the Field List window by clicking the Field List button on the toolbar.**

Access displays a small window that contains the names of the fields available to use on the report. If you didn't bind a table or query to the report in the New Report dialog box, you won't have any fields to view. (See Figure 10-7.)

Figure 10-7:
The Field
List
window.

2. **Drag the field that you want to use in your report from the Field List window to the report design. Drop the field in the place in the report design where you want the contents of the field to appear.**

Access puts a field control and a label control in the report. The label control contains the name of the field, followed by a colon. The field control tells Access to display the contents of the field. You can edit or delete either control.

You can put several fields in the report by Ctrl+clicking to select multiple field names. You can also select consecutive fields by clicking the first field and then Shift+clicking the last field that you want to select. Then drag all the selected fields to the design grid where they appear one under the other. Once in the design grid, you can edit and move the controls.

If you want to get rid of the label that Access adds automatically, or move the label to a different place in the report, select the label and then press Ctrl+X. To display the label in a different position, click the report design where you want the label to appear and then press Ctrl+V. You can move the label by dragging the larger handle that appears on its upper-left corner when you select it.

Adding a line

Remember that what you see in Report Design view is not exactly how the printed report will appear. Not everything you see in Design view prints — for example, those little dots and the vertical and horizontal lines you see in the background of the Design view, as well as the boxes around the objects you put in the report design, are all non-printing elements of the design. To see what the printed report will look like, click the Print Preview button or the View button.

You can put a vertical, horizontal, or diagonal line into a report by adding it to the report design. If you want to create a box to surround an object, you actually want to work with the object's border.

 Insert a line into a report by clicking the Line button in the Toolbox. Then move the mouse pointer into the report design, click where you want the line to begin, and drag to where you want the line to end. A line must begin and end in the same section of the report.

 After you create a line, you can change its color and width by using the Line/Border Color and Line/Border Width buttons in the Formatting toolbar. You can delete the line by selecting it and pressing the Delete (Del) key. You can move the line by clicking it and dragging it to a new position, or by using the Cut and Paste buttons on the toolbar.

Adding a label

If you want to create a text label that isn't attached to a field control, you can do so by using the Label button in the Toolbox. For example, you may want to create a label to display the name of the report. Display the report in Design view and follow these steps to add a label to the report:

 1. **Click the Label button in the Toolbox.**

2. **Click and drag in the report design to create a box the right size and position for your label.**

3. **Type the text that you want to appear in the label.**

4. **Press Enter.**

 If you want more than one line of text in your label box, press Ctrl+Enter to start a new line.

To edit the label, click the text box once to select it; then press F2 to edit the label. Press Enter when the edits are complete, or Esc to cancel the edits you made.

Adding pictures and other objects

You can add a picture to a report in several ways; the method you use depends on how you want to use the picture. A picture can be bound or unbound (in fact, any object on the report can be bound or unbound). An *unbound* object is always the same, such as a logo. A *bound* object is tied to one or more fields and will change for different records. You may store a picture of each person in your address database, for example, and display the appropriate pictures next to the addresses in your report using a bound object. Or you may display your logo on each invoice using an unbound object.

You can link or insert a picture. A *linked* picture is stored in its own file; Access goes out and finds it when necessary. The contents of the linked file may change — Access will simply display the current contents. An *inserted* picture is stored in the Access database.

You can display a picture as an object in the report, or you can display it in the background of the report, like a watermark. If the picture is an object in the report, you can edit the picture by double-clicking it.

The easiest way to insert a picture into a report is to follow these steps:

1. **Display the report in Design view.**

2. **Click the Image button in the Toolbox.**

3. **Click the report where you want the picture to appear.**

    Access displays the Insert Picture dialog box, where you can find the file that contains the picture you want to display on the report.

4. **In the Insert Picture dialog box, navigate your folders until you find the file that you need.**

5. **Select the file and then click OK.**

You can even search the Web for an appropriate picture; just click the Search the Web button in the Insert Picture dialog box to launch Internet Explorer.

You can change the size and position of a picture the same way that you change the size or position of any object in the report.

To link to a picture, follow these steps:

1. **Insert the picture using the previous set of steps.**

2. **Select the picture object in the report.**

3. **Display the properties of the image by clicking the Properties button on the toolbar.**

4. **Change the Picture Type to Linked (use the drop-down list to see the options).**

    The Picture Type option is in the Format and All tabs of the Image Properties dialog box.

You can delete a picture from the report by selecting it and pressing the Delete key.

Editing Objects in a Report

Access
Chapter 10

To edit any part of a report, you first must display the report in Design view, which you can accomplish by taking one of the following actions:

+ Select the report in the Reports tab of the Database window and then click the Design button

+ Click the View: Design button when you preview the report

To edit any object in a report, you first have to select it. Clicking an object is the best way to select it.

You can change the wording of a label by selecting the label control and then clicking the label again or pressing F2. Access displays a pop-up box with a cursor — use Delete and Backspace to delete unneeded characters and type any new characters. Press Enter to put the changes on the report; press Esc to cancel your edits.

Reporting Results

You may also want to use the control's properties to edit it. To display the properties for a control, double-click the control, or select it and click the Properties button on the toolbar. You see different properties depending on the type of control you're working with. Table 10-1 lists the properties that you're likely to find useful.

Table 10-1	The Properties for a Control
Control Property	*What It Does*
Name	Displays the name of the control.
Caption	Displays the contents of a label control.
Control Source	Displays the name of the field bound to (displayed in) the control.
Format	Displays the format option for the control.
Can Grow	Allows the control to grow vertically when the data doesn't fit in the space allotted. When Can Grow is set to No, only the data that fits in the allotted space appears on the report.
Can Shrink	Allows the control to shrink when less space is needed to display the data.

You can delete any object in a report by selecting it and then pressing the Del key.

Sending a report to another application

Microsoft makes it very easy for you to send a report (or a datasheet, for that matter) to another Microsoft application. All you need to do is click the OfficeLinks button, which appears on the Print Preview toolbar. The OfficeLinks default application is Word, but you can select Excel from the drop-down list.

When you click the OfficeLinks button, Access saves your report in the format that you've chosen

(word-processing document or spreadsheet), opens the chosen application, and displays your report. Then you can edit, analyze, or print your report in that application.

You may prefer to use the drag and drop functionality to exchange data with Excel. You can drag Access tables and queries from the database window to Excel. You can also select portions of a datasheet, and drag them to Excel.

Chapter 11: Changing the Look of Your Report

In This Chapter

✔ Deciding where your pages end

✔ Changing borders and colors

✔ Using dates and page numbers

✔ Changing your fonts

✔ Adjusting the report layout

✔ Using AutoFormat

Despite what you may read in Chapter 10, simply creating a nice report is not always the fastest way to impress the lucky recipients of your data. You can do so much more than simply churn out nice reports. Why not try to add a little color to emphasize a point? How about giving some special text a unique font such as Baskerville Old Face? Would you consider adjusting the borders of your report? If you answer yes to the preceding questions, you just may be ready to take advantage of what this chapter wants to show you so that your reports can be the talk of the town.

Inserting Page Breaks in a Report

You can add a page break to a report in Design view. Follow these steps:

1. **Click the Page Break button in the Toolbox.**

2. **Move the pointer to the part of the design where you want the page break and click the mouse button.**

   Access inserts a page break, which looks like a series of dots that are slightly darker than the grid.

Take care where you insert a page break into a report design — you're working with the design, so the break repeats itself. A good place to use a page break is at the end of a section. For example, if you have records grouped by month and you want each month on a separate page, put the page break at the bottom of the Date Footer section in Design view.

Playing with Borders

You can change the appearance of the border surrounding an object not only by changing its color, but also by changing the width and the style of the border. To change the width of the border (that is, the thickness of the line), follow these steps:

1. **Select the object.**

2. **Click the arrow next to the Line/Border Width button.**

Access displays a drop-down list of border-width options. The first option is an invisible border.

3. **Click the border thickness that you want to use. Access changes the border of the selected object to match the border that you select.**

To change the style of the border, use the Special Effects button. Follow these steps:

1. **Select the object.**

2. **Click the arrow next to the Special Effects button.**

Access displays some options (shown in Figure 11-1).

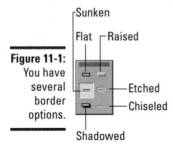

Figure 11-1: You have several border options.

3. **Click the option that you want to use.**

Because the options in the drop-down list don't give you a very good idea of how the option will appear in your report, the best way to see an effect is to try it.

Adding Color to a Report

The Formatting toolbar provides options for adding color to a report. You can change the color of text, backgrounds, and lines by using one of three buttons on the Formatting toolbar. Table 11-1 lists the buttons on the toolbar that control color, what they're called, and how they work.

Table 11-1	Color Control Buttons	
Button	*What It's Called*	*What It Does*
	Fill/Back Color	Changes the color of the background of the selected object or the background of the selected section when no control is selected.
	Font/Fore Color	Changes the color of the text in the selected object.
	Line/Border Color	Changes the color of the border (the box around the object) of the selected object; also changes the color of a selected line.

You use each of these buttons the same way. Follow these steps:

1. **Select the object that you want to work with.**

2. **Click the arrow to the right of the button that changes colors.**

   Access displays a palette of colors.

3. **Click the color that you want to use.**

If you want the object to be invisible or the same color as the general background, choose Transparent from the top of the color grid.

Adding Dates and Page Numbers

Access 2000 is a whiz at many things, including adding dates and page numbers. Access can number the pages of your report or put today's date in a report — all you have to do is ask.

The most sensible place to add the date and page number is in the page header or page footer of the report. The Report Wizard puts both the date and the page number (in the format *Page X of Y*) in the page footer for you.

Inserting the date and/or time

If you want to add the date and/or time yourself, rather than relying on the Report Wizard, display the report in Design view and follow these steps:

1. **Click the section (or** *band***) in which you want the date and/or time to appear.**

2. **Choose Insert➪Date and Time to insert the date, the time, or both.**

   The Date and Time dialog box appears. The Date and Time dialog box provides options for including the date, the time, or both, and allows you to choose the format.

3. **Select Include Date and/or Include Time and then select the format you want.**

   Check the Sample box to see how the date and/or time will appear on your report.

4. **Click OK. Access adds the date and/or time to the section of your report that you selected in Step 1.**

Inserting page numbers

To add page numbers yourself, rather than relying on the Report Wizard, display the report in Design view and follow these steps:

1. **Choose Insert⇨Page Numbers. The Page Numbers dialog box appears.**

   The Page Numbers dialog box gives you several choices about how your page numbers will appear on your report:

   • Format: Select Page N to show only the current page number, or select Page N of M to show both the current page number and the total number of pages.

   • Position: Decide whether the page numbers will appear in the page header or the page footer.

   • Alignment: Click the down-arrow of this list box and choose Center (centers page numbers between the margins), Left (aligns page numbers with the left margin), Right (aligns page numbers with the right margin), Inside (prints page numbers alternately on the right and left sides of facing pages), or Outside (prints page numbers alternately on the left and right sides of facing pages).

   • Show Number on First Page: Deselect (remove the check mark from) this option if you want to hide the page number on the first page of your report (a good way to keep your title page spiffy).

2. **Change the options in the dialog box to suit your purposes.**

3. **Click OK.**

   Access puts the page number in the position you selected (Top of Page or Bottom of Page).

Aligning Report Objects

Access automatically aligns the contents of a bound control — that is, a control that displays the contents of a field: Text is left justified and numbers and dates are right justified within the control. The three alignment buttons on the Formatting toolbar allow you to customize the alignment of the contents of a control.

To change the alignment of the contents of a control, follow these steps:

1. **Select the object.**

2. **Click the appropriate alignment button: Align Left, Center, or Align Right (see Figure 11-2).**

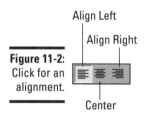

Figure 11-2:
Click for an
alignment.

Align Left

Align Right

Center

Changing Date or Number Formats

To change the format of a date or number in a field control, you need to use the Format property for the control. Follow these steps to display the properties for the control and change the format:

1. **Select the control.**

 2. **Display the control's properties by clicking the Properties button.**

3. **Click the Format option (in the All and the Format tabs).**

4. **Choose the format that you want to use from the drop-down list.**

5. **Close the Properties box.**

Changing Font and Font Size

Changing the font and font size of text in a report is one of the easiest formatting tasks. All you need to do is select the control that contains the text you want to format and choose the font and/or font size you want from the Font and Font Size options on the formatting toolbar. (See Figure 11-3.)

Figure 11-3:
The Font
and Font
Size
options.

Font   Font size

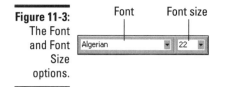

You can make the text bold, italic, and/or underlined by clicking the Bold, Italic, and/or Underline button(s) while the object is selected.

Changing Page Layout

Use the Page Setup dialog box to change the way Access prints your report on the page. Display the Page Setup dialog box by choosing File⇨Page Setup when working with the report in either Design view or Print Preview.

Choosing landscape versus portrait

To choose whether the report should appear in *landscape* (longer than it is tall) or *portrait* (taller than it is long) orientation, follow these steps:

1. **Display the Page Setup dialog box by choosing File⇨Page Setup.**

2. **Click the Page tab at the top of the dialog box.**

3. **Select the Portrait or Landscape radio button.**

4. **Click OK to close the dialog box.**

Adjusting margins

To change the margins for a report, follow these steps:

1. **Display the Page Setup dialog box by choosing File⇨Page Setup.**

2. **Click the Margins tab at the top of the dialog box.**

3. **Change the Top, Bottom, Left, and Right margins as necessary.**

4. **Click OK to close the dialog box.**

Changing the Size of an Object

You can change the size of a control by clicking and dragging the border of the control while you're in Design view. Follow these steps:

1. **Select the object whose size you want to change. Anchors (little black boxes) appear around the selected object.**

2. **Move the mouse pointer to one of the anchors.**

The pointer turns into a two-headed arrow, indicating that you can change the size of the box.

3. **Drag the edge of the box so that the object is the size you want it to be. (See Figure 11-4.)**

Figure 11-4:
Resize your
objects as
you will.

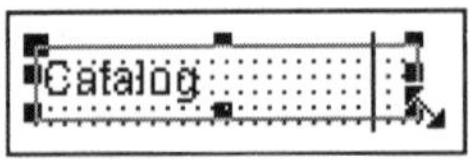

The Format⇨Size menu has additional options that allow you to change the size of an object:

✦ If you just want an object to be just the right size to display its contents, choose Format⇨Size⇨To Fit.

Copying formatting from one control to another

After you go to the effort of prettifying one control, why reinvent the wheel to make another control match it? You can simply copy the formatting from one control to another by using the Format Painter. The Format Painter copies all formatting — colors, fonts, font sizes, border sizes, border styles, and anything else that you can think of. Follow these steps to copy formatting from one control to another.

1. **Select the object that has the formatting you want to copy.**

2. ![] **Click the Format Painter button on the toolbar. If you want to format more than one object, double-click the Format Painter button.**

   The Format Painter button now looks pushed in. When the mouse pointer is on

an object that can be formatted, the pointer has a paintbrush attached to it. When the mouse pointer is on a part of the report that can't be formatted with the Format Painter, the paintbrush has a circle and line over it to indicate that you cannot format there.

3. **Click the object to which you want to copy the formatting. Access copies the formatting. If you used a single click to turn the Format Painter on, the mouse pointer loses its paintbrush. If you double-clicked to turn the Format Painter on, you can click additional objects to format them, too. To turn the Format Painter off, click the Format Painter button.**

✦ If you want several objects to be the same size, select all the objects and then choose Format⇨Size⇨To Tallest, To Shortest, To Widest, or To Narrowest. Access makes all the objects the same size. If you choose To Shortest, for example, Access changes all the objects to the same size as the shortest object that was selected when you chose the menu option.

Moving a Control

You can move a control by dragging it. Follow these steps:

1. **Select the object you want to move.**

   Anchors appear around the selected object.

2. **Move the mouse pointer to the edge of the box.**

   The pointer changes into a hand to indicate that you can move the selected objects.

3. **Click and drag the objects to where you want them (see Figure 11-5).**

Access
Chapter 11

Changing the Look
of Your Report

Figure 11-5:
Move your
controls by
dragging.

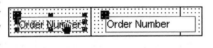

To move just one control when the control is paired (like a label and a field control) click and drag the large handle that appears at the top left corner of the object.

Formatting Reports with AutoFormat

With AutoFormat, you can apply the same predefined formats that you saw in the Report Wizard to your report. You have to tell Access which part of the report you want to format — you can choose the whole report, one section, or even just one control. Here's how to use AutoFormat to format your report:

1. **Display the report in Design view.**

2. **Select the part of the report that you want to format with AutoFormat.**

3. **Click the AutoFormat button.**

Access displays the AutoFormat dialog box.

4. **Choose the format you want from the Report AutoFormats list.**

5. **Click OK to apply the format to the selected part of the report.**

Some additional options appear in the AutoFormat dialog box. If you click the Options button, Access displays check boxes that allow you to choose attributes of AutoFormat: Font, Color, and Border. The default is to apply all three, but you can choose not to apply the fonts, colors, or borders in the AutoFormat to your report by clicking to remove the check mark from the formatting option you don't want Access to apply to your report.

The Customize button displays the Customize AutoFormat dialog box, where you can create and delete AutoFormats. You can create your own format based on the current format of the selection or change the AutoFormat so that it matches the format of the current selection.

Chapter 12: Forms for Displaying and Entering Data

In This Chapter

↗ **Getting to know forms**

↗ **Creating forms with a wizard or by yourself**

↗ **Entering data into forms**

↗ **Putting controls in your forms**

↗ **AutoFormatting your form**

↗ **Using Design View to work on your form**

*T*ables are a great way to store data, but they aren't always great tools when you want to enter data — particularly related data that you want to store in separate tables. That's when you need a form.

Unlike tables, forms display only the fields you want to see. You can create a format that shows all the data for one record on the screen at one time — something that is difficult to do when you have a number of fields in a table. You can also add features such as check boxes and drop-down lists that make entering data easier. And making it easy to enter data into your database should be your life-long ambition.

About Forms

Forms are similar to reports, except that *forms* enable you to input and edit data, not just view and print it. You can easily create a form that enables you to work with linked tables — you can see and enter related data in the same place, and you can see all the fields in one record at the same time, instead of having to scroll across a table. You can also create different forms for different people or groups of people who use a database.

Forms can range from relatively simple to complex. Really extravagant forms can include formatting, calculated fields, and controls (such as check boxes, buttons, and pictures) that make entering data easier. Forms are so similar to reports that many of the features you use to create a form are the same features you use to create a report.

Adding a Form to Your Database

Making a new form is similar to making any new Access object. The easiest way to create a new form is to follow these steps:

1. **Display the Forms view in the Database window.**

2. **Click the New button.**

Access displays the New Form dialog box, which gives you several choices for creating your form (see Figure 12-1).

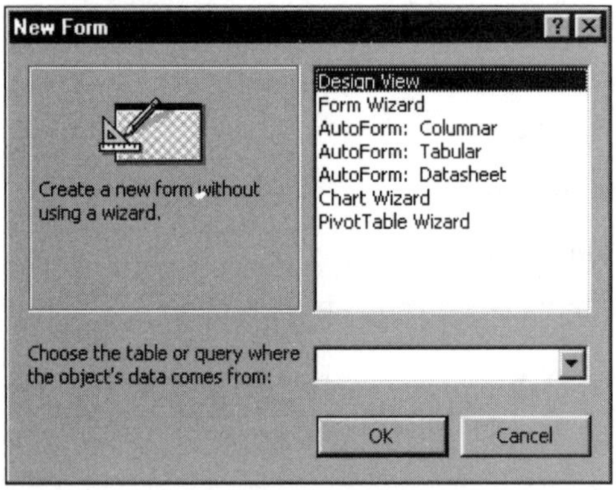

Figure 12-1:
The New
Form
dialog box.

3. **Choose the method you want to use to create the form.**

4. **Select the table or query on which you want to base the form.**

5. **Click OK.**

Table 12-1 describes the choices on the New Form dialog box and tells you when to use each of them.

Table 12-1	Choices on the New Form Dialog Box
Option	*When to Use It*
Design View	When you want to design your own form from scratch, with no help from Access. (Design view is great for putting your own stamp on a form, but getting started with a wizard really helps.)
Form Wizard	When you want help creating a form. The Form Wizard walks you through the creation of a form, enabling you to use fields from multiple tables and queries, to create groups, and to perform calculations for summary fields. The resulting form is bland, but editing an existing form is much easier than creating one from scratch.
AutoForm: Columnar	When you want to create a quick and easy columnar form (the field names go in one column and the data in another) from the table or query you specify.

Option	When to Use It
AutoForm: Tabular	When you want to create a quick and easy tabular form from the table or query that you specify. A tabular form displays data in rows, like a datasheet, but with more room for each row.
AutoForm: Datasheet	When you want to create a datasheet form from the table or query that you specify. These forms look almost exactly like a datasheet. (Tabular AutoForms are similar, but a little spiffier.)
Chart Wizard	When you want to create a form consisting of a chart.
PivotTable Wizard	When you want to create a form with an Excel PivotTable.

You don't have to use the New button in the Forms tab of the Database window to create a new form; you can also use the New Object button. In fact, the default setting for the New Object button is an AutoForm. You can also display the button's drop-down list and choose Form. The AutoForm option creates a Columnar AutoForm from the data in the table or query selected in the Database window.

The quick way to create a form from a table or query is to select the name of the table or query that you want to use in the Database window and then click the New Object button and select Form or AutoForm. Choosing Insert⇨Form or Insert⇨AutoForm also creates a new form.

Adding a Form with the Form Wizard

The Form Wizard is a great way to create a simple or complex form — but especially a complex form. If you want to use fields from multiple tables in your form, the Form Wizard is the way to go. Here's how to create a form using the Form Wizard:

1. **Display the Forms view of the Database window and double-click the Create Form by Using Wizard button.**

    Access displays the first window of the Form Wizard, where you can choose the fields that you want to use in the form.

2. **Use the Tables/Queries drop-down list to choose the first table or query from which you want to use fields.**

3. **Select the fields in the Available Fields list that you want to appear on the form and move them to the Selected Fields list by double-clicking, or by selecting a field and clicking the right-arrow button.**

4. **Repeat Steps 3 and 4 to select fields from other tables or queries.**

5. **When all the fields that you want to display in the form appear in the Selected Fields box, click Next.**

    The Form Wizard displays the next window (see Figure 12-2). If you selected fields from only one table, this window asks you to choose a format for the form — skip right to Step 10. Otherwise, the window asks how you want to group your data.

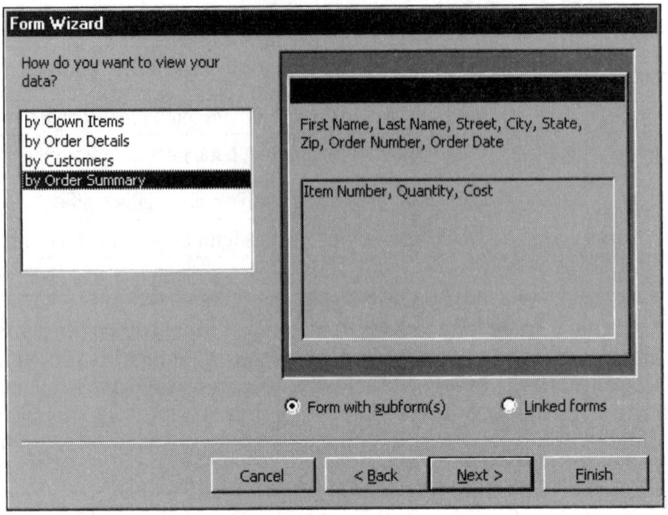

Figure 12-2:
You can
choose a
format for
your form.

6. Choose the organization that you want for your form by double-clicking the table or query by which you want to group records.

Grouping items in a form is similar to grouping fields in a report. In the preceding figure, for example, many items are related to a single order, so grouping the data according to the data in the Order Summary table displays the summary information for the order only once, and then shows all the items ordered (grouped by the catalog from which they were ordered) and the specific information about the order.

7. Choose Form with Subforms(s) or Linked Forms from the radio buttons at the bottom of the window.

If you want to see all the fields on the form at one time, click the Form with Subform(s) radio button. If you click Linked Forms, Access creates a separate form for the detail records. Users can then view this form by clicking a button in the first form. (If you're not sure which option to choose, go for Form with Subforms(s).)

8. Click Next to see the next window.

Access displays a window that enables you to choose the layout for the form or subform, if you're creating one.

9. Choose the layout.

You can click a layout option to see what it looks like. If you're not sure which layout to use, stick with Columnar — it's easy to use and easy to edit. If you're working with grouped fields, this window gives you only two options: Tabular and Datasheet.

10. Click Next to see the next window, which enables you to choose a style for the form.

11. **Choose one of the lovely styles that the Form Wizard offers.**

Click a style to see a sample of a form formatted with that style. None of the styles is gorgeous, so pick one and get on with the real work.

12. **Click Next to see the final window.**

13. **Give the form a name, and decide whether you want to see the form itself (Open the form to view or enter information) or the form Design view (Modify the form's design).**

If you're creating subforms or linked forms, Access enables you to name those items, too (or you can accept the names that Access gives them).

14. **Click Finish to create the form. (See Figure 12-3.)**

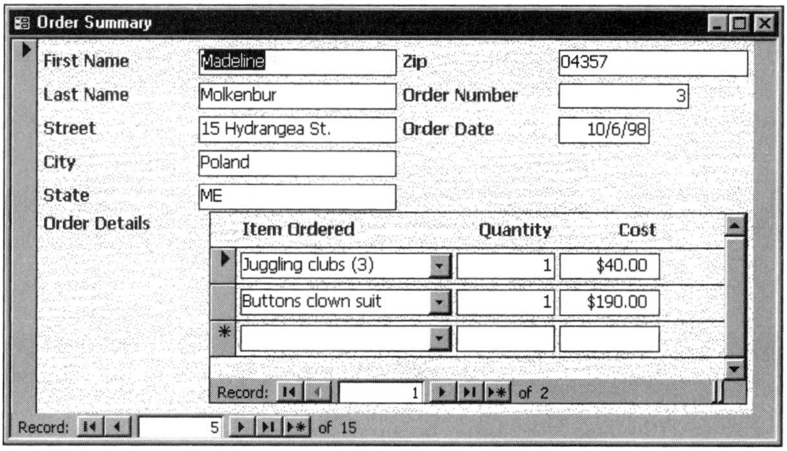

Order Summary			
First Name	Madeline	Zip	04357
Last Name	Molkenbur	Order Number	3
Street	15 Hydrangea St.	Order Date	10/6/98
City	Poland		
State	ME		

Order Details

	Item Ordered	Quantity	Cost
▶	Juggling clubs (3)	1	$40.00
	Buttons clown suit	1	$190.00
*			

Record: ◄◄ ◄ 1 ► ►► ►* of 2

Record: ◄◄ ◄ 5 ► ►► ►* of 15

Figure 12-3:
Oh what forms you can create!

Entering Data through a Form

After you create a form, you want to use it for its intended purpose: viewing and entering data. To use a form that you created, double-click the form name in the Database window — you're now in Form view. The data that a form displays comes directly from tables in the database, and any changes that you make in that data are reflected in the table. When you add data by using a form, the data is added to the table.

In general, you use the same skills to work with a form as you use to work with datasheets. You can use navigation buttons at the bottom of the form or subform to move to different records, and you press the Tab or Enter key to move from one field to another.

Access Chapter 12

Forms for Displaying and Entering Data

Editing and Formatting Forms

The steps for creating, editing, and formatting form controls are identical to performing the same tasks with report controls. However, some formatting tasks are even easier with forms than with reports because they can be done from the Form view without switching to the Design view.

You can do the following formatting in Form view:

+ Change control properties: Right-click the control and choose Properties to display the properties.

+ Change font.

+ Change font size.

+ Change text appearance using the bold, italic, and underline buttons.

The formatting toolbar is normally displayed in Form view (unless you turn it off), and any of the buttons can be used to format the selected control. Note that in Form view there is no visual clue that a control is selected — the selected control is the last one you click. Design view is superior for making wholesale changes because only one control at a time can be selected in Form view, but the new feature makes on-the-fly editing possible in Form view.

AutoFormatting Your Form

You can use AutoFormat to give your form one of the format styles that Access provides. The styles you see in the AutoFormat dialog box are the same ones you see in the Form Wizard.

To format your form, you first have to select what you want to format: the entire form, part of the form, or even just one control. Selecting part of a form in Design view is identical to selecting part of a report in Design view. To use AutoFormat to format your form, follow these steps:

1. **Display the form in Design view.**

2. **Select the part of the form that you want to format with AutoFormat.**

 3. **Click the AutoFormat button in the toolbar.**

Access displays the AutoFormat dialog box.

4. **Select the format that you want to use.**

You can select a format to see an example of how your form looks formatted.

5. **Click OK to apply the format to the part of the form that you selected in Step 2.**

Viewing Your Form in Design View

If you want to work on the design of your form, you can display the form in Design view (as shown in Figure 12-4).

You can display the Design view of a form by doing either of the following things:

✦ Selecting the form in the Forms tab of the Database window and clicking the Design button.

 ✦ Clicking the Design View button when you're working with the form in Form view.

You can also now change control properties without displaying the form in Design view — change properties from the Form view by right-clicking the control and choosing Properties from the shortcut menu.

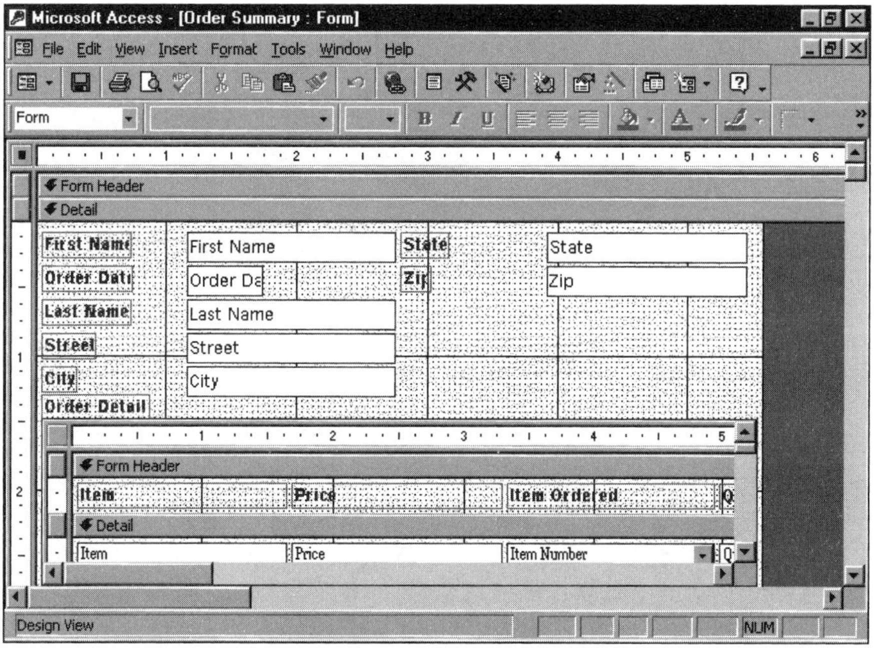

Figure 12-4:
A form
displayed
in Design
view.

**Access
Chapter 12**

**Forms for Displaying
and Entering Data**

Index

Book V

Outlook 2000

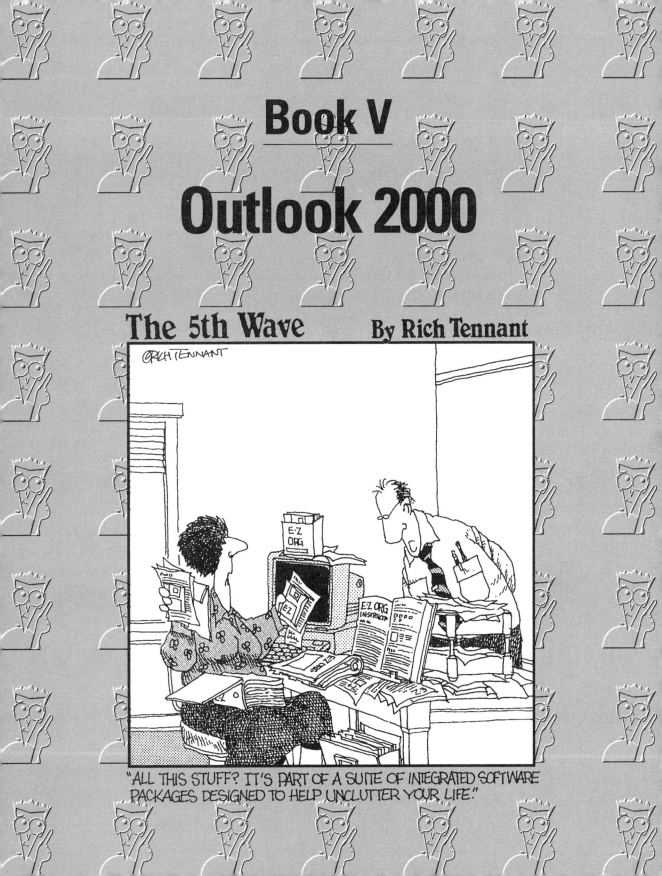

The 5th Wave   By Rich Tennant

"ALL THIS STUFF? IT'S PART OF A SUITE OF INTEGRATED SOFTWARE PACKAGES DESIGNED TO HELP UNCLUTTER YOUR LIFE."

Contents at a Glance

Chapter 1: All About Outlook

In This Chapter

✔ **Getting acquainted with the look of Outlook**

✔ **Customizing the Outlook bar**

✔ **Adding specialized applications**

✔ **Archiving your old work**

*W*hen the hordes of Microsoft programmers put the last touches on Outlook 2000, they surely took a step back in awe of what they had wrought. What most regular people saw as only some fancy e-mail software was actually a "messaging and collaboration client." Microsoft had realized that information was spread out over everywhere: in calendars, in schedulers, in planners, in Rolodexes, in folders, in sticky notes — and in e-mail, of course. So why not create a way within a single product that allows people to share this information? Outlook is the result of this question.

Chapter 1 introduces you to the Outlook interface (how the thing actually appears on screen) and gets you going on some basic tasks.

Recognizing What You See in Outlook

After you start Outlook, you see a screen within a screen. The area along the top edge and left side of the screen offers a collection of menus and icons. These items enable you to control what you see and what you make happen on the other areas of the screen. The different parts of the Outlook screen have names, as shown in Figure 1-1.

Along the left side of the Outlook screen is the *Outlook bar.* It has large, clearly marked icons for each of the Outlook modules: Outlook Today, Inbox, Calendar, Contacts, Tasks, Journal, Notes, and Deleted Items. You can click any icon at any time to switch to a different module and then switch back, just like changing channels on your TV.

The Outlook bar also has three gray separator bars, named Outlook Shortcuts, My Shortcuts, and Other Shortcuts. You can click these separator bars to switch to a different section of the Outlook bar that has a different set of icons. You can add icons to any section of the Outlook bar. You can also add sections to the bar itself by right-clicking the Outlook bar. This action opens the shortcut menu, which enables you to choose the appropriate command.

Icon

Toolbar   Menu bar   Folder banner

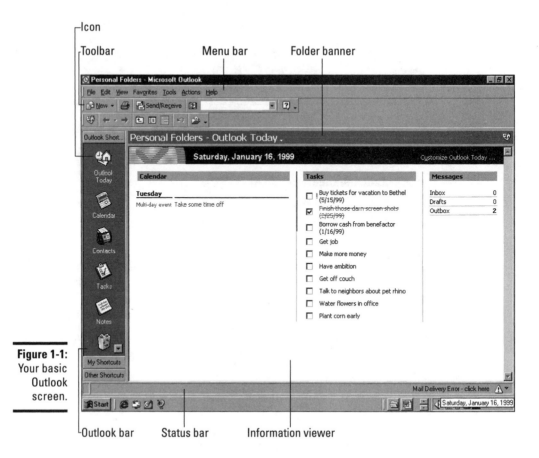

Figure 1-1:
Your basic
Outlook
screen.

Outlook bar   Status bar   Information viewer

✦ **The folder banner:** The folder banner is the name of the area that sits below the toolbars and above the main part of the Outlook screen (known as the information viewer). The name of the folder or module you're using is displayed in large letters at the left end of the Folder Banner. The right end of the banner displays a large icon that is also used by the Outlook bar to represent the module you're using. In addition, clicking the small, downward-pointing triangle next to the name of the module or folder on the left end of the folder banner reveals a copy of the folder list.

✦ **The folder list:** The folder list gives you a quick peek behind the scenes at what's going on in Outlook. To open the folder list, choose View⇨Folder List from the menu bar. Outlook organizes into folders all the information you enter. Each Outlook module has its own folder. Although you usually change modules by clicking the icon for that module on the Outlook bar, you can also switch to a different module by clicking the folder for that module on the folder list. Every Outlook module that has an icon on the Outlook bar has a folder on the folder list, but not every folder on the folder list is represented by an icon on the Outlook bar. Because you can have more folders on the folder list than icons on the Outlook bar, you may have to use the folder list to go to a specific folder rather than click its icon on the Outlook bar.

+ **The information viewer:** The biggest part of the Outlook screen, on the lower-right side, is the information viewer. Whatever you ask Outlook to show you shows up in the information viewer. Dates in your Calendar, messages in your Inbox, and names on your Contact list all appear in the information viewer.

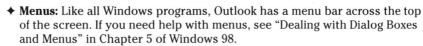

+ **Menus:** Like all Windows programs, Outlook has a menu bar across the top of the screen. If you need help with menus, see "Dealing with Dialog Boxes and Menus" in Chapter 5 of Windows 98.

+ **On-screen forms:** Every time you either open an item or create a new item in Outlook, a form appears. This form either accepts the information you want to enter or contains the information you're viewing — or both. Each module has its own form, and each form has its own menus and toolbars.

+ **Status bar:** The gray bar across the bottom of the Outlook screen is the status bar, which tells you how many items are displayed and a few other pieces of essential information.

+ **Toolbars:** Toolbars offer a quicker way to control Outlook than clicking menus. The Outlook toolbar changes as you switch between different modules or views, to offer you the most useful set of tools for the task you're doing at the moment. If you see a tool button and want to know what it does, let your mouse pointer hover over the button but don't click; a ToolTip box appears, revealing the name of the tool. Outlook 2000 has two toolbars you can choose from on the main screen: the Standard toolbar and the Advanced toolbar. The Advanced toolbar offers a larger selection of tools. You can pick the toolbar you want to use by choosing View⇨Toolbars and clicking the name of the toolbar you want to see.

Adding an Icon to the Outlook Bar

After you get used to using Outlook, you may want to create more icons on the Outlook bar. Because each icon on the Outlook bar is a shortcut to a folder or resource on your computer, you can save some time by adding a few well-chosen icons.

1. **Choose View⇨Folder List.**

2. **Right-click a folder for which you want to add an icon to the Outlook bar.**

The shortcut menu appears, as shown in Figure 1-2.

3. **Choose Add to Outlook Bar from the shortcut menu.**

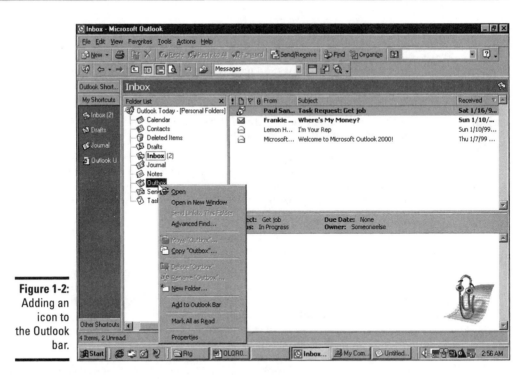

Figure 1-2:
Adding an
icon to
the Outlook
bar.

Adding Specialized Applications

Outlook was designed with expansion in mind. Names, addresses, and files are important things to keep track of. Clever programmers release new modules for Outlook every day. The Microsoft Web site on the Internet offers a collection of sample applications to expand the range of things you can do with Outlook. You can go to the Microsoft Web site directly from Outlook.

Backing up your Outlook work

If you don't mind losing what you do in Outlook, don't bother to back up. However, if you think you would some day regret not backing up, read on. All the items you create with Outlook and all the e-mail you send and receive are stored in one enormous file, called a *message store.* The filename of your message store ends with the letters PST. If you're trying to find your Outlook files so that you can back them up, use the Windows Find utility and search for files named *.PST. The largest file you find by that name is probably your Outlook data file. Copying your MAILBOX.PST file to a floppy disk is not really an option, by the way. The file is usually 10 or 20 times too large to fit on a floppy disk.

You can get these sample applications free from the Microsoft Web site on the Internet. The sample applications include expense report applications, project management programs, and even cute little programs for keeping your recipes or making entries in your diary.

To pick up (or *download,* in tech talk) your free sample applications, follow these steps:

1. **Choose Help➪Office on the Web➪Free Stuff to log on to the Microsoft site on the World Wide Web and see the list of free sample applications available for Outlook.**

2. **Click the name of a sample application you want to use, such as Expense Reports, Project Management, Recipes, or Diary.**

   If your browser is Microsoft Internet Explorer, a dialog box appears (as seen in Figure 1-3), asking whether you want to run the file or save it to disk.

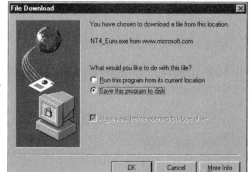

Figure 1-3:
You can download free stuff for Outlook.

3. **Choose Save This Program to Disk.**

   The Save dialog box opens, showing you the name of the folder in which your file will be saved.

   Note the name of the folder in the Save In box; that's where you install the new sample application after downloading the file. If you're not sure about which folder is the best place to save the file you're about to download, click the scroll-down menu (triangle) in the Save In box; then choose Desktop to make your new file go to the Windows desktop.

4. **Click OK and wait for the File Transfer dialog box that shows up to disappear.**

A word of caution: Many of the sample applications you find on the Microsoft Web site are useful only if you're using Outlook on a network that is also running Microsoft Exchange Server. Microsoft sometimes doesn't tell you which applications are useful for stand-alone (non-network) users, so, unfortunately, you're on your own. If you're on a network with Exchange Server, check with your network administrator before adding new applications.

After you download your brand-new sample application, you have to install it. Double-click the icon for the new file and follow the instructions that appear in the dialog boxes.

Some Outlook applications are *version-specific,* which means that they work with only a specific version of the product. For example, an application built for Outlook 97 may not work with Outlook 2000. Be sure to read any information supplied about the application to ensure that it works with your version of Outlook.

Archiving Your Work

You can save a great deal of information in Outlook. After you store enough items, however, Outlook starts to slow down. To keep the program speedy, Outlook periodically sends older items to the archive file. Although the files are still available, Outlook doesn't have to dredge them up every time you start the program.

You can set up Outlook to send items to the archives automatically after the items reach a certain age.

1. **Choose Tools⇨Options to open the Options dialog box.**

2. **Click the Other tab.**

3. **Click the AutoArchive button to open the AutoArchive dialog box (shown in Figure 1-4).**

Figure 1-4:
You can archive a lot of old stuff you don't need.

4. **Click the check box that says AutoArchive Every XX Days and fill in the number of days you want between automatic archive sessions. If the box is already checked and you want AutoArchiving on, leave the box alone.**

5. **Click OK to close the AutoArchive dialog box.**

6. **Click OK again to close the Options dialog box.**

After AutoArchiving is set up, whenever Outlook is ready to send items to the archive, you see a dialog box that asks whether you want the items sent to the archive.

If you choose not to use AutoArchiving, you can always archive items manually by choosing File⇨Archive.

Chapter 2: Getting Going with E-Mail

In This Chapter

✔ **Discovering your Inbox**

✔ **Creating and sending e-mail**

✔ **Checking your spelling**

✔ **Making a mailing list**

*I*f you're like most people, you want to get (and keep) your e-mail up and running without any problems. E-mail may be your lifeline — an indispensable tool for your personal satisfaction or your business needs. Then again, you may simply want to exchange e-mail with your pals, send your opinions to the White House, and seek the wisdom of the Microsoft Product Support Staff. Setting up Outlook 2000 to receive and send your mail is probably high on your priority list, just below eating and sleeping. Chapter 2 intends to help you take care of the necessary chore of preparing for the e-mail barrage that may soon follow your foray into the online world.

The Outlook Inbox

The main Inbox screen enables you to look at a list of your e-mail and helps you manage the messages you send and receive (see Figure 2-1). You can create folders for storing each message according to what the message is about, who sent it to you, or when you got it.

You can change the arrangement of what you see in the Inbox by changing the view. (A *view* is a method of organizing the information you see in Outlook.) Each view has a name, such as Message, AutoPreview, or By Conversation Topic. To change from one view to another, simply choose View⇨Current View and pick the view you want from the list that appears.

Creating and Sending Messages

If you know an e-mail address, you can send a message. You don't even need to have anything to say, although it's usually a good idea to have a thought or two worth sending so that people find your e-mail worth reading.

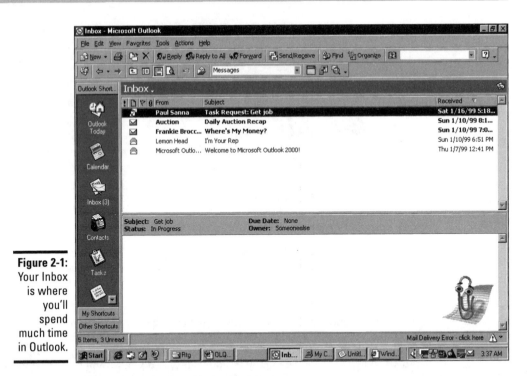

Figure 2-1:
Your Inbox
is where
you'll
spend
much time
in Outlook.

1. **Switch to the Inbox by clicking the Inbox icon on the Outlook bar to show your list of messages.**

2. **Click the New Mail Message button (or press Ctrl+N) to open the New Message form.**

3. **Click the To text box and enter the e-mail address of the person to whom you're sending the message.**

For people whose e-mail addresses you've included on your Contact list (see Chapter 9), just enter the person's name. If Outlook knows the e-mail address of the person whose name you enter, a solid black underline appears under the name.

Another approach is to click the To button to open the Select Name dialog box. Then double-click the name of the person to whom you're sending the message from the list on the left side of the box; click OK to return to your Message form.

4. **Click the Cc text box and enter the e-mail address of the people to whom you want to send a copy of your message.**

5. **Enter the subject of the message in the Subject box.**

6. **Enter the text of your message in the text box.**

7. **Click the Send button (or press Alt+S) to close the Message form and send your message on its way.**

If you send your e-mail over an online service, you also have to press F5 to deliver your message from the Outbox to your online service. If you're on an office network that uses Microsoft Exchange Server, your message goes directly to the recipient when you click Send.

Attaching files to your messages

Whenever you want to send someone a document, a picture, or a spreadsheet that you don't want to include in the message itself, you can add it to the message as an *attachment*. You don't even have to send an actual message; just save the file you're working on and send it along as an attachment.

1. **Switch to the Inbox by clicking the Inbox icon on the Outlook bar.**

2. **Choose File⇨New⇨Mail Message (or press Ctrl+Shift+M) to open the New Message form.**

3. **Click the paper-clip button on the Message form toolbar.**

   The list of files appears, as shown in Figure 2-2. (You may have to click the down arrow of the Look in box in order to scrounge around for the file that you wish to attach.)

4. **Click the name of the file you want to send.**

   The filename is highlighted to show that you've selected it.

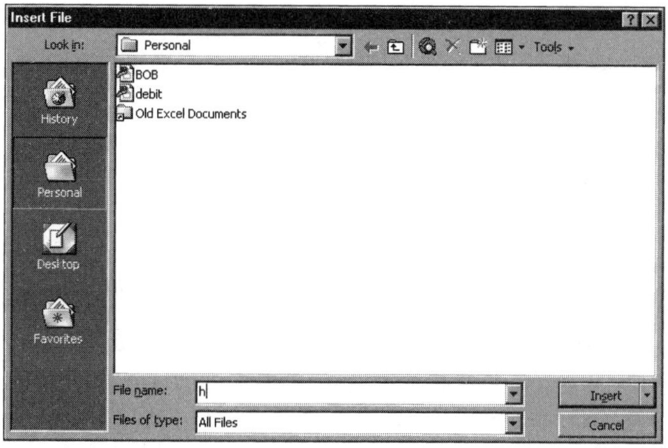

Figure 2-2:
Attach a
file with
the Insert
File
dialog box.

5. **Click OK.**

   The list of files disappears, and an icon representing your file appears in the text box on the Message form.

6. **Enter your message if you have a message to send (you don't have to send a message if you don't have anything to say).**

7. **Get ready to send your message and attachment just as you did with a regular message (as explained in the preceding section).**

If you want to send a document by e-mail while you're creating the document in a Microsoft Office application, you can eliminate most of this procedure by choosing File⇨Send To⇨Mail Recipient.

Formatting message text

You can spice up your messages with text formatting — such as boldface, italics, or different typefaces — whether you use Outlook alone or with Microsoft Office. You can also tell Outlook to use Microsoft Word 2000 as your e-mail editor, which means that every time you open an e-mail message, Microsoft Word steps in and automatically adjusts the appearance of the message. Whenever you create a new message with Word as your e-mail editor, you have the power to add fancy-looking elements to your message, such as tables and special text effects (like flashing text), and you can use all the other powerful features of Word.

To format text in a message without using Microsoft Word as your e-mail editor, use the buttons on the Formatting toolbar on the Message form (see Figure 2-3).

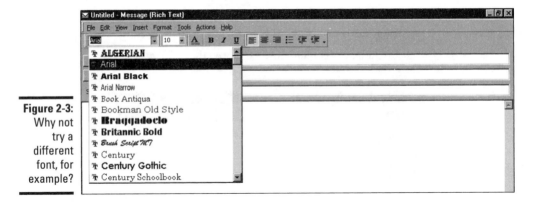

Figure 2-3: Why not try a different font, for example?

If you've ever used a word processor in Windows, the steps you follow to format text in an Outlook message should be familiar to you: Just click the button for the type of formatting you want to add to your text, and then type your text:

✦ **To format text you've already typed:** Hold down the mouse button and drag the mouse over the text to select it. Then click the button for the type of formatting you want to add to your text, such as bold or italics.

✦ **To set the typeface of your text:** Click the scroll-down button at the end of the font menu and choose the name of the font you want to use.

✦ **To set the size of your text:** Click the scroll-down button on the font size menu and highlight the font size you want.

✦ **To set the color of your text:** Click the color button and choose a color. You can choose from only a few colors, but because your choices include teal, fuchsia, and aqua, you can certainly find something to match any décor.

✦ **To make your text bold, italic, or underlined:** Click the Bold, Italic, or Underline button (or press Ctrl+B, Ctrl+I, or Ctrl+U, respectively).

✦ **To align your text to the left, center, or right:** Click the Align Left, Center, or Align Right button.

✦ **To create a bulleted list:** Click the Bullets button. (This is not the button to click when you want to shoot your computer.)

✦ **To indent your text:** click the Increase Indent button. To reduce the amount of space you've indented your text, click the Decrease Indent button.

When you send e-mail to people who don't use Outlook, the formatting you apply in Outlook often gets lost. Although you may enjoy seeing all your messages when you type them in bold fuchsia, many of your readers won't get the same pleasure when they read your messages.

Indicating message importance

Some messages are very important to both you and the person receiving the message. Other messages aren't so important, but you send them as a matter of routine to keep people informed. Outlook enables you to designate the importance of a message to help your recipients make good use of their time. When you open the Message form to create a message, two icons on the Message form toolbar enable you to select the importance of your message:

 ✦ **To assign High importance:** Click the Importance: High button on the Message form toolbar.

 ✦ **To assign Low importance:** Click the Importance: Low button on the Message form toolbar.

An icon corresponding to the importance of the message appears in the first column of the Message List.

Spell Checking

Heaven knows you want to spell everything correctly when you send out an e-mail message. Who knows how many people will see the message or if someone on an archeological dig a million years from now will discover your old messages? Fortunately, you can spell-check all your messages before sending them out:

1. **Choose Tools⟳Spelling (or press F7) to start the spelling checker.**

If everything is perfect, a dialog box opens, saying that the spelling check is complete. If so, you can click OK and get on with your life.

2. **In the highly unlikely event that you've misspelled something, the Spelling dialog box opens and shows you the error (it's probably the computer's fault) along with a list of suggested (that is, correct) spellings. (See Figure 2-4.)**

REAL WORLD

Using stationery

If you get tired if the same, old e-mail day in and day out, try to personalize yours. Stationery is designed to make your messages convey a visual impression about you. You can make your message look uniquely important, businesslike, or just plain fun with the right choice of stationery.

1. **Choose Actions⇨New Mail Message Using⇨More Stationery.**

   The Select a Stationery dialog box appears with a list of each type of stationery you can choose.

2. **Double-click the type of stationery you want to use.**

3. **Fill in your message.**

4. **Click the To button to open the Select Name dialog box.**

5. **Double-click the name of the person to whom you want to send the message. This action copies the name to the Message Recipients list.**

6. **Click OK to close the Select Name dialog box.**

7. **Click Send to close the Message form and send your message along.**

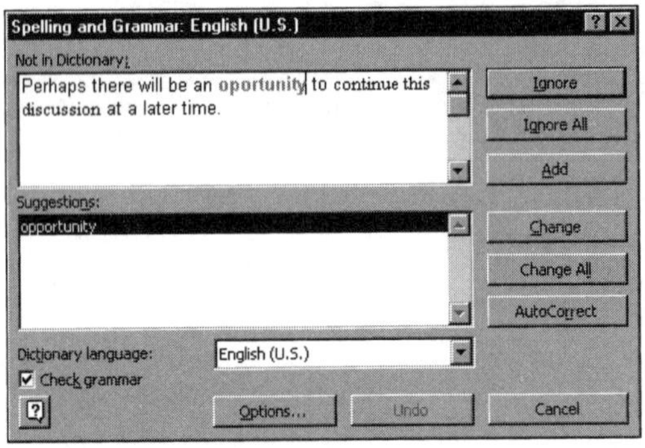

Figure 2-4: Spell checking your messages is a breeze.

3. If one of the suggested spellings is the one you really meant, click the spelling you want. If none of the suggested spellings is quite what you have in mind, enter the spelling you want in the Change To box.

4. Click the Change button.

5. If any other errors are found, repeat Steps 3 and 4 until you've eradicated all misspellings.

Although the spelling checker often thinks that technical terms, like WYSIWYG, and proper names, like Englebert Humperdinck, are misspellings (well, maybe they are), you can increase your spelling checker's vocabulary by clicking the Add button when the spelling checker zeroes in on words like those. You can also click Ignore if the spelling checker stops on a weird word you encounter infrequently.

If you've chosen to use Microsoft Word as your e-mail editor, a wavy red underline appears beneath misspelled words as soon as you type them. When you right-click a misspelled word, a shortcut menu appears with the correct spelling; click the correct spelling and you can go right on entering text.

Creating Personal Distribution Lists and Groups

When you repeatedly send e-mail to the same group of people, you can save lots of time by creating a list that contains the addresses of all the people in the group. Then, when you send your message, rather than enter the name of each person on your list, you only have to enter the name of the list.

Outlook 2000 comes in two different versions: the Corporate version and the Internet Mail Only version. You can tell which one you have by checking the Tools menu. If you have a Tools⇨ Services command, you have the Corporate version and you can create personal distribution lists.

The Internet Mail Only version of Outlook 2000 doesn't have a Tools⇨Services command, and it doesn't have personal distribution lists. However, it does enable you to create *groups,* which are similar to personal distribution lists. You can tell that you have the Internet Mail Only version of Outlook 2000 if you have a Tools⇨Accounts command.

Follow these steps to create a personal distribution list:

1. **Choose Tools⇨Address Book to open the Address Book dialog box.**

2. **Choose File⇨New Entry to open the New Entry dialog box.**

3. **Scroll to the bottom of the Entry Type box and click Personal Distribution List. Make sure that the space at the bottom of the dialog box that says *Put this entry in the* contains the words *Personal Address Book.***

4. **Click OK to open the New Personal Distribution List Properties dialog box (as shown in Figure 2-5).**

5. **Enter in the Name box a name for your new personal distribution list.**

6. **Click Add/Remove Members to open the Edit Members dialog box.**

7. **Double-click the name of each person you want to include on your personal distribution list.**

    As you double-click each name, the names you choose are copied in the Personal Distribution List box on the right side of the Edit Members dialog box.

8. **Click OK after you've finished adding all the names you want to include on your personal distribution list.**

If you have the Internet Mail Only version of Outlook 2000, follow these steps to create groups:

1. **Choose Tools⮕Address Book to open the Address Book dialog box.**

2. **Click the New Group button to open the Group Properties dialog box.**

3. **Enter a name for your new group in the Group Name box.**

4. **Click the Select Members button to open the Select Group Members dialog box.**

5. **Double-click the name of each person you want to include in your group.**

As you double-click each name, the names you choose are copied in the Members box on the right side of the Select Group Members dialog box.

6. **Click OK after you've finished adding all the names you want to include in your group.**

Whenever you want to send a message to everyone in one of your groups or on your personal distribution lists, just type in the To box of your message the name you gave the list in Step 3. You can have as many groups or personal distribution lists as you want.

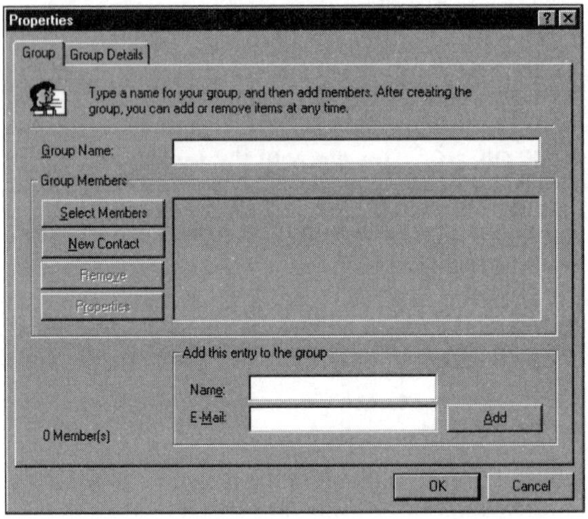

Figure 2-5:
Set up a distribution list to make your life easier.

Chapter 3: Reading and Replying to Your Mail

In This Chapter

- ✔ Taking care of your incoming e-mail
- ✔ Replying to mail
- ✔ Forwarding mail

*I*f you send e-mail, you receive e-mail. It's as simple as that. Heck, you'll probably receive e-mail even if you never send an e-mail message to anyone. That's the funny way that the e-mail world works. And if you don't read your e-mail, you may miss out on something important — like a great joke that you heard long ago but forgot or notification that you can earn lots of money at home working on your computer. Do you want to take a chance?

Of course, if you receive e-mail, you may want to respond (at least to some of it). You may even want to forward some of your e-mail to others so that you aren't the only one to suffer. This chapter coincidentally helps you with your incoming and outgoing e-mail.

Handling Incoming Messages

All your incoming mail piles up unless you do something about it. This section shows you how to read, delete, flag, and do all sorts of things with the e-mail you receive.

Reading your mail

Your Inbox contains your list of incoming e-mail. Even if you've never exchanged e-mail with anybody or even if you don't *know* anybody, you see at least one message in your Inbox the first time you start Outlook — the "Welcome to Microsoft Outlook" message. Isn't that nice of Microsoft?

1. Double-click the title of the message you want to read.

The message is probably in your Inbox unless you've stored it elsewhere. The message opens, using the entire screen so that you can read your message (as shown in Figure 3-1).

Note: Messages in Outlook are displayed on a *form.* A form contains various fields, and these fields store the information about the message you're interested in, such as the text of the message, who sent it, when it was sent, its priority, and more.

2. Press Esc to close the message screen.

The little figures on the Message form toolbar do things that are specific to writing and reading e-mail messages, such as reply, print, or mark as high or low priority, and the up and down arrows enable you to read the next message on your Inbox list.

Previewing messages

Because you can usually get the gist of an incoming e-mail message from the first few lines, Outlook shows you the first few lines of all unread messages, if you want. Although the AutoPreview feature is turned on the first time you use Outlook, you can also turn it off.

1. Switch to the Inbox by clicking the Inbox icon on the Outlook bar.

2. Choose View⇨AutoPreview.

AutoPreview shows you the first few lines of the messages you haven't read yet.

AutoPreview may be the only way you ever want to view your Inbox. If you get a large number of messages, previewing them saves time. You can also take advantage of the preview pane to look at the contents of each message in the lower half of the information viewer while your list of messages appears in the upper half. To turn the preview pane on (or off) choose View⇨Preview Pane.

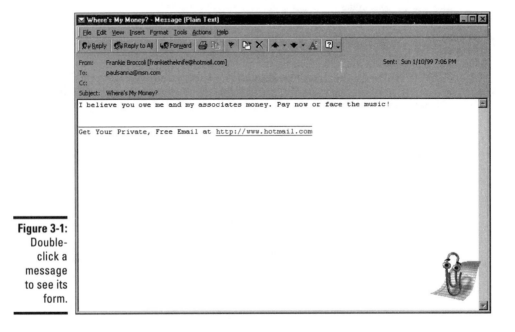

Figure 3-1:
Double-
click a
message
to see its
form.

Deleting a message

If you get mail from the Internet, you can expect lots of junk mail. You may also get lots of e-mail at work. Bill Gates gets scads of e-mail. Maybe that's why deleting messages in Outlook is so easy. Just follow these steps:

1. **Switch to the Inbox by clicking the Inbox icon on the Outlook bar.**

2. **Click the title of the message you want to delete.**

3.  **Click the Delete button on the toolbar or press the Delete key to make your message disappear.**

Flagging your e-mail messages as a reminder

Some people use their incoming e-mail messages as an informal task list. Flagging is designed to make it easier to use your Inbox as a task list by adding individual reminders to each message you get (or even to messages you send).

1. **Switch to the Inbox by clicking the Inbox icon on the Outlook bar.**

2. **Double-click the message you want to flag, and the message reopens.**

3. **Choose Actions⇨Flag for Follow Up (or press Ctrl+Shift+G) to open the Flag for Follow Up dialog box (shown in Figure 3-2).**

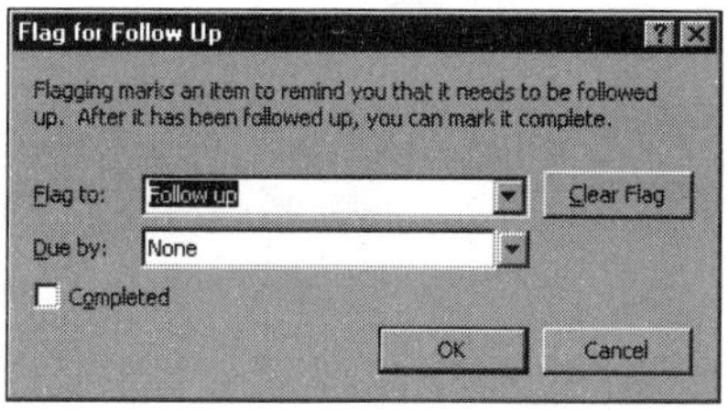

Figure 3-2:
You can
flag the
e-mail that
you
receive.

4. **Click the Flag To text box and enter your reminder, such as** Call headquarters. **You can also click the scroll-down button at the end of the Flag To text box and choose a reminder, such as Follow Up.**

5. **Click the Due By box and type the date on which you want the reminder flag to appear.**

Remember that you can enter dates in plain English by entering something like **Next Wednesday** or **In three weeks** and let Outlook figure out the actual date.

6. **Click OK.**

A little red flag appears next to your message in the Inbox. Another clever way you can take advantage of flagging is to attach a flag to a message when you're sending it to someone else. If you flag a message you're sending to someone else, a reminder pops up on that person's computer at the time you designate.

Saving a message as a file

You may want to save the contents of a message you receive so that you can use the text in another program. For example, you may want to use Microsoft Publisher to add the text to your monthly newsletter or even to your page on the Internet.

1. **Choose File⇨Save As (or press F12) to open the Save As dialog box (shown in Figure 3-3).**

2. **Click the scroll-down button at the end of the Save In box to choose the drive to which you want to save the file.**

3. **Double-click the name of the folder in which you want to save the file to reveal the list of files in the folder.**

4. **Click the File Name text box and type the name you want to give the file.**

5. **If you want to change the type of the file, click the scroll-down button at the end of the Save As Type box and then choose a file type.**

6. **Click Save (or press Enter) to close the Save As dialog box.**

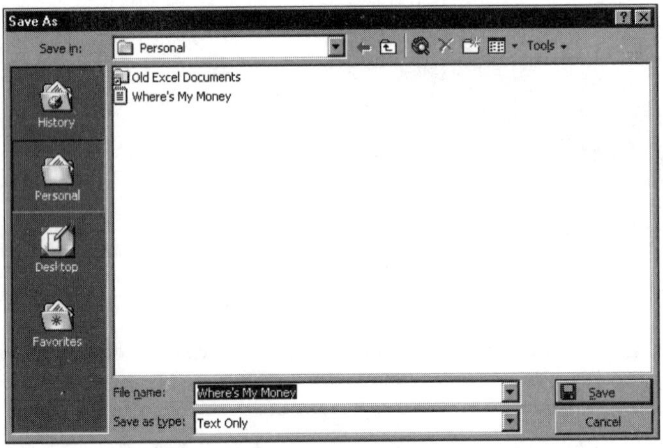

Figure 3-3:
The Save
As dialog
box.

Save As	
Save in:	Personal

Old Excel Documents
Where's My Money

History
Personal
Desktop
Favorites

File name: Where's My Money — Save
Save as type: Text Only — Cancel

Reading attachments

Whenever you receive a message with a file attached, you have to open the attachment before you can read whatever is in the attachment. No problemo:

1. **Double-click the name of the message that has an attachment you want to read.**

The Message form opens. An icon in the body of the message represents each file attached to the message.

2. **Double-click the icon to open the attachment; double-clicking the icon also launches the program that created the message.**

Replying to or Forwarding Messages

The e-mail wagon may not always stop in your Inbox. Often you need to answer the e-mail messages that you receive or even forward them to others.

Sending a reply

Replying to the e-mail that you get is a breeze. To reply to a message, follow these steps:

1. **Switch to the Inbox by clicking the Inbox icon on the Outlook bar.**

2. **Double-click the title of the message to which you want to reply.**

   Doing so shows the text of the message to which you're replying. You don't absolutely have to open a message to send a reply; you can click the name of a message once to select the message to reply to and then click the Reply button.

3. **If you want to reply only to the people who are named on the From line, click the Reply button (or press Alt+R) to open the New Message form.**

4. **If you want to reply to the people who are named on the Cc line in addition to the people named on the From line, click the Reply to All button (or press Alt+L) to open the New Message form (see Figure 3-4).**

5. **Enter your reply in the message box.**

6. **Click the Send button (or press Alt+S) to close the New Message form and send your message on its way.**

The text of the message to which you're replying is automatically included in your reply unless you turn that option off by choosing Tools⇨Options and then selecting your options on the Reading tab.

Forwarding a message

If you get a message you want to pass on to someone else, just forward it. You can send mail without actually having to create it!

1. **Switch to the Inbox by clicking the Inbox icon on the Outlook bar.**

2. **Click the title of the message you want to forward (thus highlighting the message).**

3. **Click the Forward button on the Outlook toolbar (or press Ctrl+F) to open the New Message form.**

4. **Click the To text box and enter the e-mail address of the person to whom you're forwarding the message.**

5. **Click the Cc text box and enter the e-mail addresses of the people to whom you want to forward a copy of your message.**

6. **In the text box, enter any comments you want to add to the message.**

7. **Click the Send button (or press Alt+S) to close the Message form and send your message on its way.**

You can also forward a message as you read it by clicking the Forward button on the Message form toolbar, which is visible when you open a message to read it.

Setting up online services

Before you can use Outlook to exchange e-mail through an online service — such as CompuServe, America Online, or the Microsoft Network — or through an Internet service provider — such as Netcom or AT&T WorldNet — you have to set up Outlook to work with that particular service.

If you work in a large organization that uses Microsoft Exchange Server for its e-mail system, your system administrators will set up the Outlook 2000 Corporate version for you. They probably don't want you setting up online services on the copy of Outlook 2000 on your desktop! You can still send e-mail to people on online services, like CompuServe or AOL, by typing their address in the To box of your message.

If you're using Outlook 2000 somewhere other than on a large corporate network, you should use the Outlook 2000 Internet Mail Only version. The Internet Mail Only version enables you to set up e-mail accounts to work with most online services and Internet service providers. Although the method you use to set up any service is somewhat similar, the exact details differ, and those differences are important. Before beginning to set up Outlook e-mail accounts, it's a good idea to check with the tech-support people from your online service so that you understand the details. After you get the skinny from your online service, follow these steps to set up e-mail accounts on the Outlook 2000 Internet Mail Only version:

1. **Choose Tools⇨Accounts.**

2. **Click the Add button and then choose Mail from the shortcut menu to start the Internet Connection Wizard.**

3. **Follow the prompts in the Internet Connection Wizard and enter the information provided by your online service or Internet service provider.**

Chapter 4: Making Your E-Mail Life Easier

In This Chapter

✔ Using folders to manage e-mail

✔ Automating your Inbox with the Rules Wizard

✔ Changing your Outlook view

*B*ecause all your incoming e-mail lands into your Inbox, you may soon end up with a list of messages whose sheer number makes staying on top of things seem almost impossible. The battle is not yet lost, however! Before you become overwhelmed with e-mail and begin sinking into despair, find out how to manage your mail with folders. Get on familiar terms with your Inbox and take advantage of what it can do for you. You can even automate some tasks so that you can sit back and relax as those e-mail message come flooding in.

This chapter shows you how to take the initiative now so that your e-mail life can indeed be easier later.

Managing Your E-Mail with Folders

Although you can leave all your incoming e-mail messages in your Inbox if you want, filing your messages in another folder makes more sense because you can see at a glance which messages you've already dealt with and classified and which ones have just arrived in your Inbox.

 If you have used Windows 98 for any amount of time, you may already be familiar with the concept of files and folders. (If you want to know about them or need a refresher, see the Windows 98 mini-book included for your convenience in this very book.) Being able to handle your files and folders in Outlook 2000 really helps you stay on top of your e-mail. For one thing, you need to be able to move files around — usually into folders — and then to move folders around — sometimes into other folders! Such an authority over your files and folders pays off when you get going in Outlook.

Creating a folder

Before you can file messages in a new folder, you have to create the folder:

1. **Click the Inbox icon to switch to your Inbox (if you're not already there).**

2. Choose <u>F</u>ile⇨New⇨Fold<u>e</u>r (or press Ctrl+Shift+E) to open the Create New Folder dialog box (shown in Figure 4-1).

3. Click the word *Inbox* on the list of folders at the bottom of the Create New Folder dialog box to highlight it.

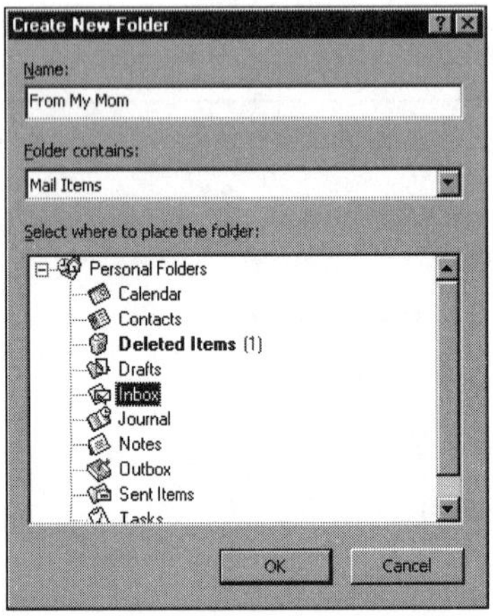

Figure 4-1:
Create folders to store your mail.

Create New Folder	? X

<u>N</u>ame:

From My Mom

<u>F</u>older contains:

Mail Items ▼

<u>S</u>elect where to place the folder:

⊟ 🌐 Personal Folders
   📅 Calendar
   📇 Contacts
   🗑 **Deleted Items** (1)
   📝 Drafts
   📥 Inbox
   📓 Journal
   🗒 Notes
   📤 Outbox
   📨 Sent Items
   📋 Tasks

OK   Cancel

4. In the Name text box, type a name for your new folder.

5. Click OK to close the Create New Folder dialog box.

Although you can create as many folders as you want, you can find things more easily if you minimize the number of folders you have to search.

Moving messages to another folder

After you've created extra folders for sorting and saving your incoming messages, you can move new messages to the different folders when they arrive.

1. Switch to the Inbox by clicking the Inbox icon on the Outlook bar.

2. Click the title of the message you want to move to highlight the message title.

3. Drag the message to the icon on the Outlook bar for the folder in which you want to store it. The name of the file disappears from the list in the Inbox.

The folder to which you want to move the message isn't always visible on the Outlook bar. If the folder to which you want to move your message isn't visible on the Outlook bar, choose <u>E</u>dit⇨<u>M</u>ove to Folder to make a more complete list of folders appear. Then you can click the folder in which you want to file your message and press Enter.

After you've made a habit of moving messages between folders, you can speed up the process by clicking the Move to Folder button. When you click the Move to Folder button, you see a list of the last ten folders to which you've moved items. Click the name of a folder on the list, and your message is zapped directly to the folder of your choice.

Using the Sent Items folder

Outlook stores in the Sent Items folder a copy of every message you send unless you tell it to do otherwise. You can review and reread the messages you've sent by looking in the Sent Items folder. To get there, click the My Shortcuts divider on the Outlook bar and then click the Sent Items icon. The same collection of views is available in the Sent Items folder as is available in the Inbox or any other mail folder (see "Using and Choosing E-Mail Views," later in this chapter).

Using the Rules Wizard

The Rules Wizard reads your incoming and outgoing e-mail and takes an action of your choice. You can make Outlook display a pop-up announcement when important messages arrive or make a rude noise when you get messages from certain people, or it can just file certain types of messages in certain folders.

Wizards are little tools Microsoft adds to all Office programs to guide you through multistep processes and help you make the choices you need to make. The Rules Wizard asks you questions at each step in the process of creating a rule to help you create the rule you want.

You can create literally thousands of different kinds of rules with the Rules Wizard. As you explore this feature, you discover many types of rules that you'll find useful. This one moves a message that arrives from a certain person to a certain folder.

Follow these steps to create a rule:

1. **If you're not in the Inbox, click the Inbox icon on the Outlook bar.**

2. **Choose Tools⇨Rules Wizard to open the Rules Wizard dialog box.**

3. **Click the New button to open a dialog box for creating new rules.**

4. **Choose the type of rule you want to create by clicking the box cleverly named Which Type of Rule Do You Want to Create? Then click Next.**

   The Rules Wizard, shown in Figure 4-2, offers several common types of rules you might want to create, such as Move Messages from Someone, Assign Categories to Sent Messages, or Notify Me When Important Messages Come.

5. **Click the first piece of underlined text in the Rule Description box, which is *people or distribution list.***

   Your address book opens to enable you to choose the name of a person to put into your rule (as shown in Figure 4-3).

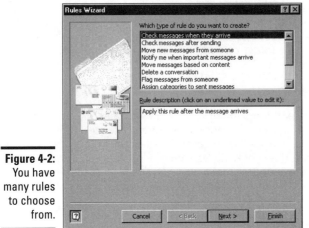

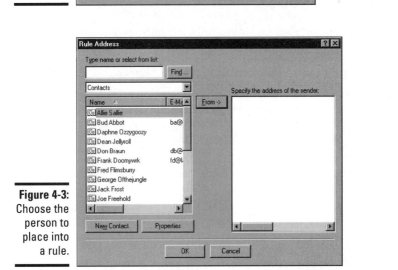

6. **Choose the name of the person whose messages you want to move to a new folder by selecting it and then clicking the From button.**

7. **Click the next piece of underlined text in the Rule Description box — the word specified.**

Another dialog box opens to enable you to choose the folder to which you want to move the message (see Figure 4-4).

8. **Click the name of the folder to which you want to move messages (or create a new folder by clicking New).**

The name of the folder you choose appears in the sentence in the Rule Description box.

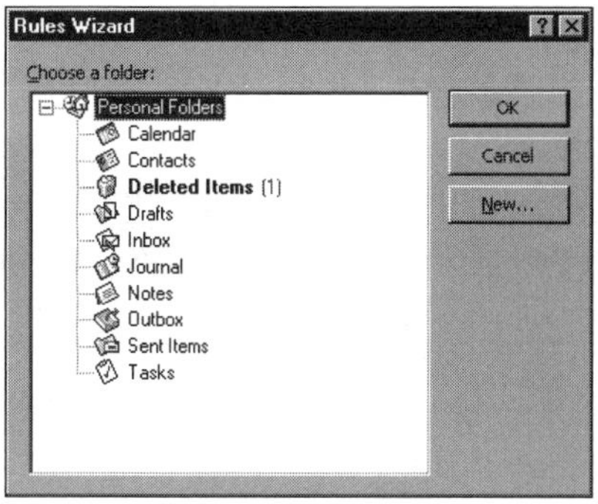

Rules Wizard [?] [X]

Choose a folder:

- Personal Folders
  - Calendar
  - Contacts
  - **Deleted Items** (1)
  - Drafts
  - Inbox
  - Journal
  - Notes
  - Outbox
  - Sent Items
  - Tasks

OK
Cancel
New...

**Outlook
Chapter 4**

**Making Your
E-Mail Life
Easier**

Figure 4-4:
Indicate
where to
move the
message.

9. **Click Finish to complete your rule.**

The first Rules Wizard dialog box appears with a list of all your rules. Each rule has a check box next to it. You can turn rules on and off by clicking the check boxes; if a check mark appears next to a rule, the rule is turned on; otherwise, the rule is turned off.

10. **Click OK to close the Rules Wizard.**

You don't have to limit yourself to making rules for incoming mail. You also can tell the Rules Wizard to act on the messages you send out, such as attaching flags or assigning categories to messages that go to the people you designate or to messages that have certain words on the subject line.

Using and Choosing E-Mail Views

One of the real benefits of Outlook is the variety of ways in which you can sort and arrange your collection of messages, as well as the several different ways you can look at what's in your messages. Your Outlook folders can serve as your filing system as well as your electronic mailbox.

You have many different arrangements you can use to view your e-mail messages. If you don't like the view you have, you can choose View⇨Current View and pick a new view:

- ✦ **Messages view:** A plain-vanilla list of your messages. The titles of unread messages are shown in boldface, whereas messages you've read are shown in a normal typeface.

- ✦ **Messages with AutoPreview:** Shows you the first few lines of all your unread messages.

- ✦ **By Follow-Up Flag:** Shows a list of your messages according to which kind of flag you've assigned to each message (see Figure 4-5).

- ✦ **Last Seven Days:** A list of messages you've received within the past seven days.

- ✦ **Flagged for Next Seven Days:** Shows only flagged messages with due dates scheduled within the next week.

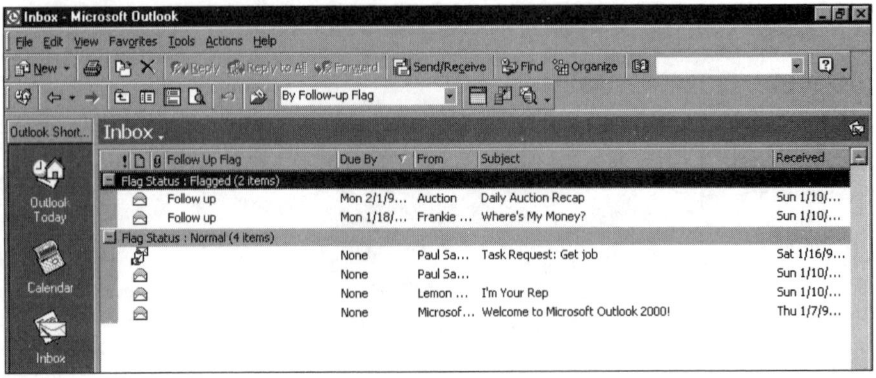

Figure 4-5:
You can
view your
messages
by flag
type.

+ **By Conversation Topic:** Organizes your messages by subject.

+ **By Sender:** Groups your messages according to who sent the message.

+ **Unread Messages:** Shows only unread messages. After you read a message, this view no longer appears.

+ **Sent To:** Sorts messages according to the name of the person it's sent to. In your Inbox, most messages are sent to you, so it makes little sense to use this view in the Inbox. In your Sent Items folder, however, you can use Sent To view to organize your outgoing messages according to the person to whom each message is sent.

+ **Message Timeline:** Shows you a diagram with your messages organized by the time they were sent or received. You can click the icon shown for any message and see that message (see Figure 4-6).

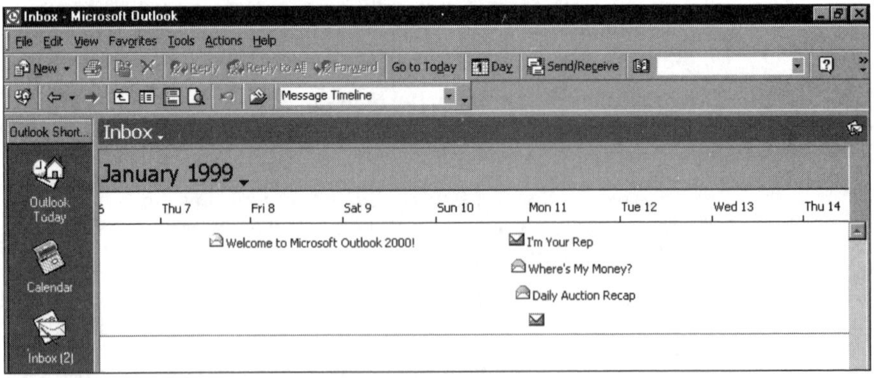

Figure 4-6:
You can
view your
messages
in a
timeline.

Chapter 5: Using the Calendar

In This Chapter

✔ **Getting to know the calendar**

✔ **Scheduling and changing appointments**

✔ **Scheduling an event**

✔ **Printing your calendar**

*Y*ou never have enough time in the day, so why spend precious time trying to figure out what you need to do when? Outlook 2000 is more than simply a convenient way to manage your e-mail. The Outlook calendar can help you with your busy life by organizing appointments, special events, holidays, meetings (ugh), and just about any other task that you must eventually face. You'll never miss your dentist's appointment again, and your brother-in-law may get his birthday card before his birthday from now on. If you really want, you can even use the Outlook calendar to help you *avoid* your commitments! Now that's a deal.

Reviewing the Calendar

You enter appointments in Outlook so that you can remember them later. To use your appointment list in that way, you have to at least look at your list of appointments. Outlook enables you to view your list in dozens of ways (an Outlook view is a way of presenting information in the arrangement you need). Outlook comes with six different views, and you can create your own views. This section describes the views you get the first time you use Outlook.

Basic Calendar views

When you first use Outlook, you have a half-dozen preprogrammed views from which to choose. Although you can add views to your heart's content in any Outlook module, you can go a long way with the views Outlook starts with. Here's the view lineup:

✦ **Day/Week/Month:** Looks like a calendar (as shown in Figure 5-1). It has buttons on the toolbar to enable you to choose between viewing your appointments for one day, a week, or a whole month. You'll probably use this view more often than any other.

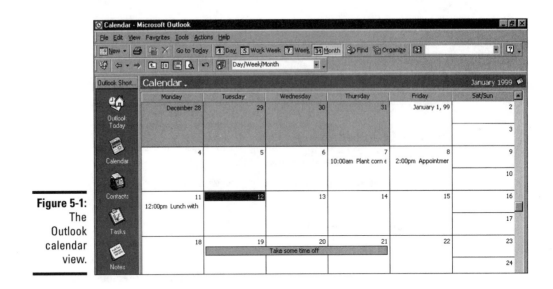

Figure 5-1:
The
Outlook
calendar
view.

♦ **Active Appointments:** This view shows some of the same appointments as Day/Week/Month view, this view also shows you information about each appointment and enables you to sort the list according to the location or subject you entered when you created the appointment.

♦ **Events:** A list that shows you only items you've designated as All Day Events.

♦ **Annual Events:** Shows only the list of events you've made into recurring events that happen yearly. You can enter holidays and anniversaries as annual events.

♦ **Recurring Appointments:** Lists all appointments and events you've set as recurring appointments (see Figure 5-2).

♦ **By Category:** Groups your appointments according to the category you've assigned to each appointment. Grouped views work the same way in all Outlook modules.

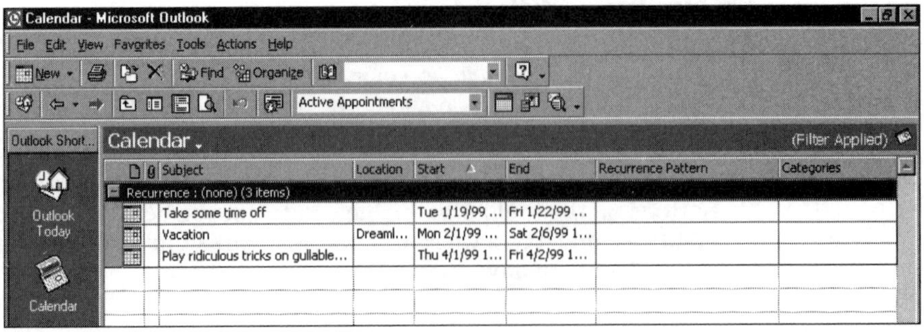

Figure 5-2:
Never
miss an
appointment
again.

Another popular way to view your upcoming appointments is to click the Outlook Today icon on the Outlook bar. As its name suggests, Outlook Today pulls together everything you're doing today — appointments, tasks, and messages — and displays it all on a single page. You can print your Outlook Today page by clicking the Print button on the toolbar or by pressing Ctrl+P.

Changing the amount of time displayed

Outlook enables you to choose from several calendar styles. Some styles show a bigger calendar with fewer dates, and some styles show a smaller calendar with more dates but include no notes about what's scheduled on a certain date. The Date Navigator is a small calendar that enables you to see your schedule for the date of your choice by simply clicking the date with your mouse.

1. **Switch to the Calendar module by clicking the Calendar icon on the Outlook bar to make your calendar appear.**

2. **Choose View⇨Current View⇨Day/Week/Month.**

3. **Click either the Day, Work Week, or Week button on the toolbar.**

The little calendar in the upper-right corner is the Date Navigator. The rest of the screen shows you your appointments for the current week (or the days you've clicked in the Date Navigator). To see what's scheduled for a different date, just click the date on the Date Navigator.

Going to one date

The calendar in Outlook can schedule appointments hundreds or even thousands of years from now. In case you're concerned, Outlook has no problem with the year 2000 (or the year 3000 or 4000, for that matter). Because you have so many years to work with, you need a quick way to make the calendar show the date you're thinking about. These steps show the quick way:

1. **Click the Calendar icon on the Outlook bar, if you're not in the Calendar module.**

When you switch to the Calendar module from another module, Outlook always shows you the current date.

2. **Choose View⇨Current View⇨Day/Week/Month.**

3. **Choose Go⇨Go to Date (or press Ctrl+G).**

4. **Enter the date you want, such as 12/25/2098, or Christmas 2098, or 1 year from now, or even 100 years from now.**

Outlook figures out what you mean.

5. **Click OK to make the calendar display the date you've chosen.**

6. **Click the Go to Today button on the toolbar to return to today's date.**

Scheduling an Appointment

Although Outlook gives you lots of choices for entering details about your appointments, you have to enter only two things: what and when. Everything else is optional. If you want to schedule two appointments at the same time, Outlook subtly warns you with a banner at the top of the form that says *Conflicts with another appointment,* although nothing stops you from scheduling yourself to be in two places at one time. Just to be safe, look at the schedule for the time you are scheduling first:

1. **Click the Calendar icon on the Outlook bar, if you're not in the Calendar module.**

2. **Click the New Appointment button on the toolbar.**

3. **Click in the Subject box and enter something there to help you to remember what the appointment is about. (Refer to Figure 5-3.)**

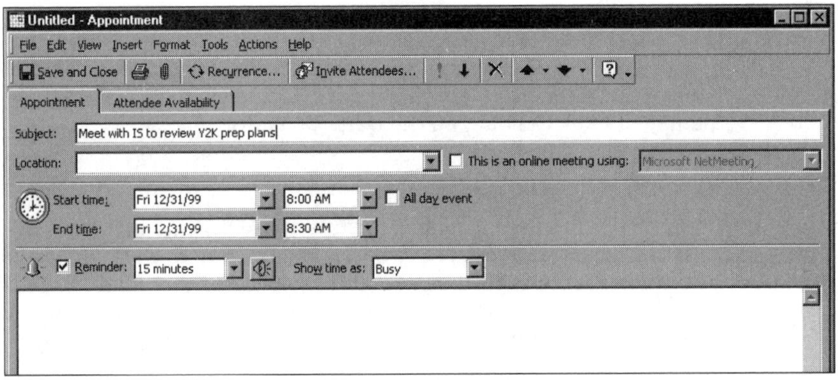

Figure 5-3:
Schedule
an
appointment.

4. **Click in the Location box and enter the location, if you want. If you know the location, enter it there so that you don't forget.**

5. **In the Start Time boxes, enter the date and time when the appointment begins.**

6. **In the End Time boxes, enter the date and time when the appointment ends.**

If you ignore the End Time boxes, Outlook creates a 30-minute appointment.

7. **If you want Outlook to remind you of your appointment, click the Reminder box.**

8. **Enter a category of your choice in the Categories box.**

9. **Click the Save and Close button on the toolbar.**

If you're on a network and don't want others to know about your appointment, click the Private box in the lower-right corner of the dialog box.

Scheduling a Recurring Appointment

Some appointments keep coming back like a bad penny. Your Monday morning staff meeting or Wednesday night bowling league roll around every week unchanged (except for your bowling score), so why enter the appointment over and over? Just call it a *recurring appointment.*

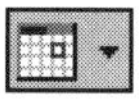

1. **Click the New Appointment button on the left end of the toolbar to open the New Appointment form.**

2. **Click in the Subject box and enter the subject.**

3. **Click in the Location box and enter the location.**

4. **Click the Recurrence button on the toolbar (or press Ctrl+G) to make the Appointment Recurrence box appear (shown in Figure 5-4).**

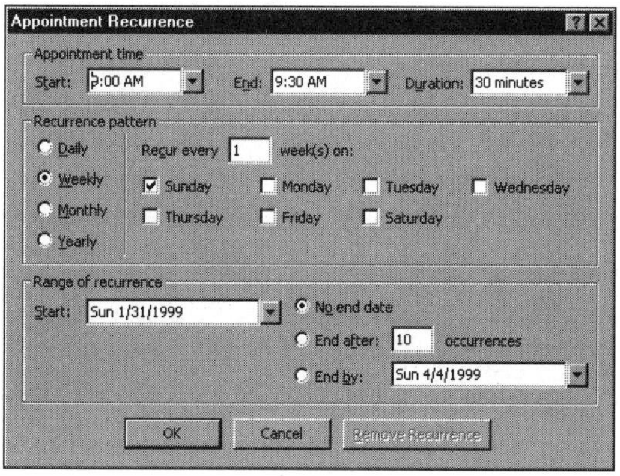

Figure 5-4:
The
Appointment
Recurrence
dialog box.

5. **Click the Start text box and enter the starting time.**

6. **Click the End text box and enter the ending time.**

Don't worry about the Duration box; Outlook calculates the duration for you. On the other hand, you can just enter the duration and let Outlook fill in the missing end time.

7. **In the Recurrence pattern box, click the Daily, Weekly, Monthly, or Yearly option button to select how often the appointment recurs.**

8. **In the next part of the Recurrence pattern box, choose how often the appointment occurs.**

The Recurrence pattern looks different depending on whether you chose Daily, Weekly, Monthly, or Yearly in Step 7.

• If you chose a Yearly pattern, choose something like the first Friday in February.

- If you chose a Weekly recurrence pattern, choose something like every Tuesday.

- If you chose a Daily pattern, choose something like every eighth day.

9. **In the Range of Recurrence box, enter the first occurrence in the Start box.**

10. **Choose when the appointments will end.**

    If you want the appointment to repeat indefinitely, you don't have to do anything; No End Date is checked by default if you don't choose something else.

11. **Click OK, and then click Save and Close (or press Alt+S).**

Changing an Appointment

What? You say that your schedule never changes? You say that you never need to change your schedule? The world's pace is just too fast for anyone's schedule to last for even a short time without modification. Fortunately, Outlook makes its easy to change appointments.

Changing an appointment by using drag-and-drop

Changing the starting time or the date of an appointment is just a matter of using the drag-and-drop technique. Follow these steps to pick up the appointment and slide it to the date or time you want:

1. **Click the appointment in Calendar view (see Figure 5-5).**

2. **Place the mouse pointer over the blue bar; the mouse pointer turns into a little four-headed arrow.**

3. **Press the mouse button, drag the appointment to the new time or date, and release the button.**

Changing the length of an appointment

When you're looking at One-Day view in your calendar, your appointments are shown as boxes of different sizes, depending on the length of the appointment. If you want to shorten or lengthen an appointment, just use your mouse to drag the border of the box that represents the appointment to make the appointment smaller or bigger.

1. **Click the appointment.**

2. **Move the mouse pointer over the line at the bottom of the appointment.**

3. **Drag the bottom line down to make the appointment time longer; drag the bottom line up to make the appointment shorter.**

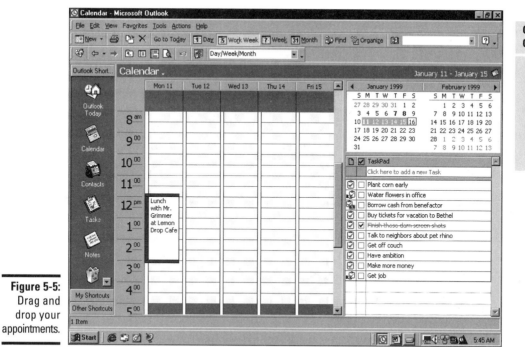

Figure 5-5:
Drag and
drop your
appointments.

Reopening an appointment to change it

Drag-and-drop isn't the ticket for changing appointment times when you can't view enough of the calendar to see both the original date and the rescheduled date. In that case, all you can do is reopen the appointment and change the particulars by following these steps:

1. **Double-click the appointment.**

2. **Click in the first Start Time block and enter the date you want to assign to your appointment.**

3. **Press the Tab key and enter the new appointment time in the text box (if you have a new time).**

4. **If necessary, make any other changes in the appointment by clicking the information you want to change and entering the revised information over it.**

5. **Click Save and Close (or press Alt+S).**

Shortening appointments to less than 30 minutes

When you use the drag-and-drop method to change the length of appointments, you can make appointments begin and end only on the hour and at 30 minutes after the hour. When you have appointments that you need to begin and end at other times, you have to open the appointment and enter the times you want, just as you did when you first created the appointment, like this:

Lengthening your appointments and events

Dragging the box to change the length of an appointment is the easiest way to go if all your appointments begin and end on the hour and half-hour. If your appointments don't start on the hour or half-hour, you can fine-tune the length of an appointment by opening the appointment and typing the starting and ending times you want.

You also can use the drag-and-drop method when you change the length of events. To change the length of an event, click the 31-Day button to switch to Monthly view in your calendar and then just drag the line at the left or right end of the banner that represents an event to make an event longer or shorter.

1. **Double-click the appointment.**

2. **To change the time the appointment begins, click the Start Time box and type the time you want.**

3. **To change the time the appointment ends, click the End Time box and type the time you want.**

You also can change any other details about the appointment while the Appointment form is open.

4. **Click Save and Close (or press Alt+S).**

Remember, when you enter times in Outlook, you don't have to be particular about punctuation. For example, when you type **5p**, Outlook understands it to be 5:00 p.m. and automatically converts the time to the proper format. Dates are even easier to enter; just enter **next Wed**, and Outlook converts it to the date.

Deleting an Item from Your Calendar

Deleting items in Outlook is *intuitive,* which means that you probably can figure out how to do it without reading about it. Here goes anyway:

1. **Click the appointment you want to delete.**

2. **Click the Delete button on the toolbar (or press Delete).**

If you want to delete several appointments at one time, hold down the Ctrl key while clicking each appointment you want to delete. Then press Delete. Selecting items in Outlook is no different than doing it in Windows 98 or in any other Office 2000 application.

Chapter 6: Tasks for Everyone

Throw away all those note pads that you get free from your car insurance company. Take down every sticky note that you have stuck to your computer monitor or on your desk. Tear off those old pages from your *Dos For Dummies* desk calendar. You are no longer under the dominion of little pieces of paper that tell you what to do and when to do it. With Outlook 2000, you can control your list of tasks with a tool that keeps track of your obligations and chores. Now you can fall under the dominion of some software that can tell you what to do and when to do it — but this existence is not nearly as messy, and an Outlook task doesn't fall off your computer monitor the day before a big task is to be performed.

Creating a New Task

Outlook can handle all kinds of high-falutin' information and details about each task you enter. You may find that 90 percent of the time you just need to type a quick note to jog your memory. For the other 10 percent, however, you may need to go whole hog and keep lots of information handy about tasks you must do — things like travel directions and discussion notes.

Creating an abbreviated task quickly

Most times, you may need only a word or two to jog your memory about a task, something like **Call Mom.** Because you don't need much detailed information about how to do that, resort to the fast way:

1. Click the Tasks icon on the Outlook bar to switch to the Tasks module if you aren't already there.

If you don't see anything that says Click Here to Add a New Task, switch to a different view of your task list by choosing View⇨Current View⇨Simple List.

2. **Click the text that says Click Here to Add a New Task.**

   This step makes an insertion point (a flashing vertical bar) appear where the words were.

3. **Type the name of your task (see Figure 6-1).**

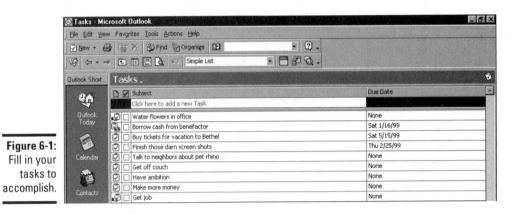

Figure 6-1:
Fill in your
tasks to
accomplish.

4. **Press the Enter key to make your new task drop down to join your list of other tasks.**

   If you're using Calendar, you can use TaskPad, a miniature version of the task list. You can enter tasks in the TaskPad by typing in the box labeled Click Here to Add a New Task.

Creating a detailed task slowly

Suppose that you need to enter more information about your task, such as driving directions, or you want to have Outlook remind you just before the task is due. There is no limit to the information you can add to a task if you go the slow, complete way.

1. **Click the Tasks icon on the Outlook bar to switch to the Tasks module if you're not already there.**

2. **Click the New Task button on the toolbar (or press Ctrl+N) to open a blank New Task form (see Figure 6-2).**

3. **Type the name of the task in the Subject box.**

4. **If you want to assign a due date to the task, click the Due Date button; then click the Due Date box and enter the due date.**

   You don't have to be fussy about how you enter the date; Outlook understands 7/4/98, the first Saturday of July, or 90 days from today — however you like it.

5. **If you want to enter a start date, click the Start Date box and enter a date. Because not all tasks have start dates, you can skip this step if you want.**

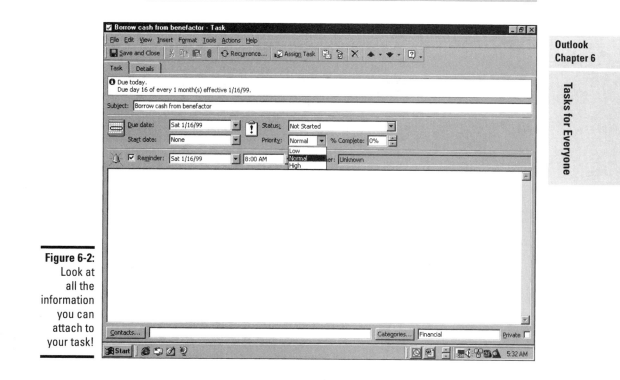

Figure 6-2:
Look at
all the
information
you can
attach to
your task!

6. **If you want to keep track of the status of a task, click the triangle at the right end of the Status box (the scroll-down button).**

   You have to revise your task as the status of the task progresses.

7. **If the task you're entering is unusually important, urgent, or even relatively unimportant, click the scroll-down button at the right end of the Priority box to choose the priority of the task.**

8. **If you want to be reminded before the task is due, click the Reminder check box and then click the date box next to it and enter the date on which you want to be reminded. Enter the time of day when you want to activate the reminder in the time box.**

9. **If you want, enter miscellaneous notes and information about this task in the text box.**

10. **If you want to assign a category to your task, type in the Categories text box the category you want.**

11. **Click the Save and Close button (or press Alt+S) to finish.**

Deleting a Task

Sometimes you change your mind about a task you've assigned yourself and want to delete the task. Deleting tasks is *so* much simpler than getting them done. You'll never know that the task existed.

1. **Select the task by clicking the Task icon in the first column of the list.**

 2. **Click the Delete button on the toolbar (or press Ctrl+D).**

Modifying an Existing Task

The weather changes. Social mores change. The height of hemlines changes. Your task list changes. It's likely that some aspect of an item on your to-do list changed before you even finished entering the task in Outlook.

You can use the same method to change the information in a task that you used to enter the information in the first place.

1. **If you're not already in the Tasks module, go to it by clicking the Tasks icon on the Outlook bar.**

2. **Choose View⇨Current View⇨Simple List.**

3. **To open the Task form, double-click the name of the task you want to change.**

4. **Type the new information or replace and change what you already have entered.**

5. **Click the Save and Close button (or press Alt+S) to finish.**

Creating a Recurring Task

When tasks have to be done over and over on a regular schedule, set them up as *recurring* tasks. You can designate a task as recurring while you're entering the task the first time.

You can also create a recurring task by reopening the task and following these steps:

1. **Double-click the task to open the Task form.**

2. **To open the Task Recurrence dialog box, click the Recurrence button on the toolbar of the Task form (or press Ctrl+G). See Figure 6-3.**

3. **Choose the Daily, Weekly, Monthly, or Yearly option to specify how often the task occurs.**

4. **In the next box to the right, specify how often the appointment occurs, such as every third day or the first Monday of each month.**

5. **In the Range of Recurrence area, enter the first occurrence in the Start box.**

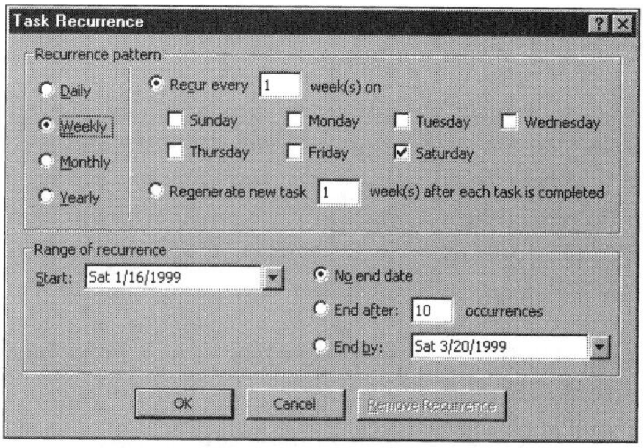

Figure 6-3:
The Task
Recurrence
dialog box.

6. **Choose when the appointments will stop (no end date, after a certain number of occurrences, or at a certain date).**

7. **Click OK to close the Task Recurrence dialog box.**

8. **Click Save and Close (or press Alt+S).**

Recurring tasks can be confusing because the Task Recurrence dialog box changes appearance depending on whether you choose a Daily, Weekly, Monthly, or Yearly recurrence pattern.

Creating a Regenerating Task

Sometimes it doesn't make sense to schedule the next occurrence of a task until you've completed the preceding occurrence. For example, if you get your hair cut every two weeks but you get busy and get one haircut a week late, you still want to wait two weeks for the following haircut. If you use Outlook to schedule your haircuts, set it up as a regenerating task. A regenerating task is "getting a haircut every two weeks," and a recurring task is "getting a haircut every Monday." Follow these steps to create a regenerating task:

1. **Double-click the task to open the Task form.**

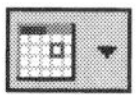

2. **Click the Recurrence button on the toolbar on the Task form (or press Ctrl+G) to open the Task Recurrence dialog box.**

3. **Click the Regenerate New Task option.**

4. **Enter the number of months between regenerating the task.**

5. **Click OK to close the Task Recurrence dialog box.**

6. **Click Save and Close (or press Alt+S).**

Attaching a File to a Task Item

You can include word-processing documents, spreadsheets, or any other type of file in a task by making the document an *attachment*. For example, if you've had a bad day and enter **Update Résumé** as your new task, you can link your résumé to the task to find the résumé faster when you're ready to update it. To link a task to an attachment, follow these steps:

1. **Double-click the task to open the Task form.**

2. **Click the Insert File button on the toolbar to open the Insert File dialog box (see Figure 6-4).**

3. **Choose from the list of files in the Insert File dialog box the file you want to attach.**

You may have to look around for the file that you want to attach, of course; just click the down arrow of the Look in text box and begin rummaging around.

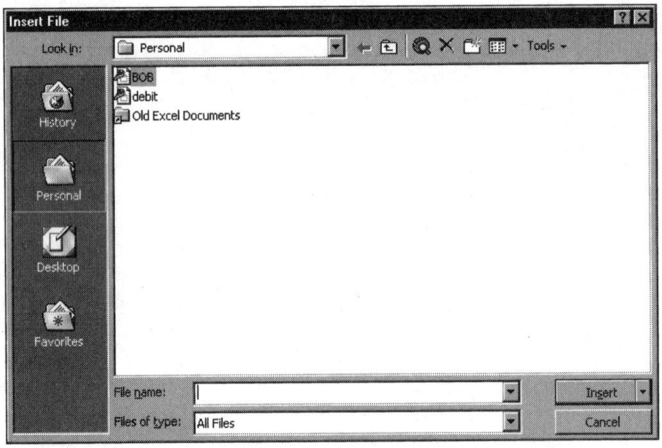

Figure 6-4:
You can
attach a
file to a
task item.

4. **Click Insert to close the dialog box and return to the Task form.**

5. **Click Save and Close (or press Alt+S).**

The process of attaching files to your tasks is much like the process for attaching files to any other Outlook item. When you delete a task that has a file attached, only the task — not the file — is deleted.

Changing the Appearance of Your Task List

Task lists are just that: lists of tasks. You don't typically need fancy layouts when you choose a view. You just need a list that contains the information you want. To switch between views, choose View⇔Current View, and then pick the view you want to use. Here's a list of the views that come with Outlook right out of the box:

✦ **Simple List:** Just the facts — the names you gave each task and the due date you assigned (if you assigned one).

✦ **Detailed List:** A little more . . . uh, detailed than Simple List view. It's really the same information, plus the status of the tasks, the percentage completed of each task, and whatever categories you may have assigned to your tasks.

✦ **Active List:** Shows you only tasks you haven't finished yet.

✦ **Next Seven Days:** Even more focused than Active List view. Next Seven Days view shows only uncompleted tasks scheduled to be done within the next seven days.

✦ **Overdue Tasks:** Shows (oops!) tasks you've let slip past the due date you assigned. You ought to finish these up before the boss finds out.

✦ **By Category:** Breaks up your tasks according to the category you've assigned each task. (See Figure 6-5.)

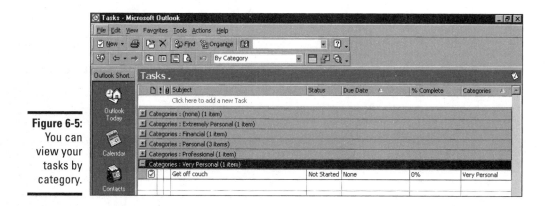

Figure 6-5:
You can view your tasks by category.

✦ **Assignment:** Lists your tasks in order by the name of the person on whom you've dumped each task.

✦ **By Person Responsible:** Contains the same information as Assignment view, except that the list is grouped so that you can see the assignments of only one person at a time.

✦ **Completed Tasks:** Shows (you guessed it) only tasks you've marked as complete.

✦ **Task Timeline:** Draws a picture of when each task is scheduled to begin and end. Seeing a picture of your tasks gives you a better idea of how to fit work into your schedule sensibly. (See Figure 6-6.)

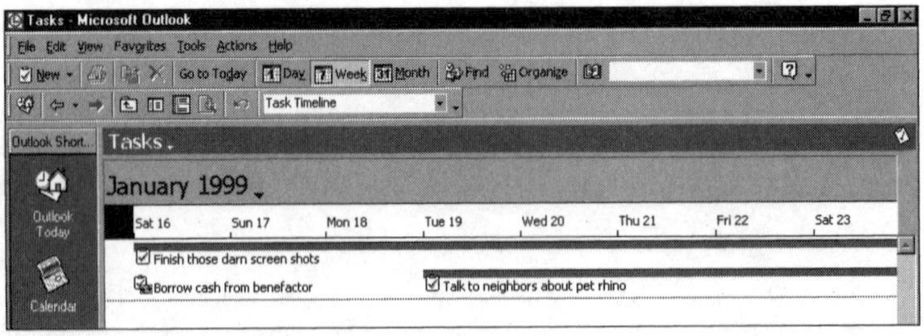

Figure 6-6:
You can
view your
tasks by
timeline.

Marking a Task as Complete

It's satisfying to note your accomplishments for the day. You can do so by marking off each task as you add to the list of tasks you've finished, which you can also view.

1. **If you're not in the Tasks module, switch to it by clicking the Tasks icon on the Outlook bar.**

2. **Choose View⇨Current View⇨Simple List.**

3. **Click the box next to the name of the task you want to mark as complete (as shown in Figure 6-7).**

All the tasks you selected appear with a check mark to show that they're completed. A line appears through the name of the task to drive the point home.

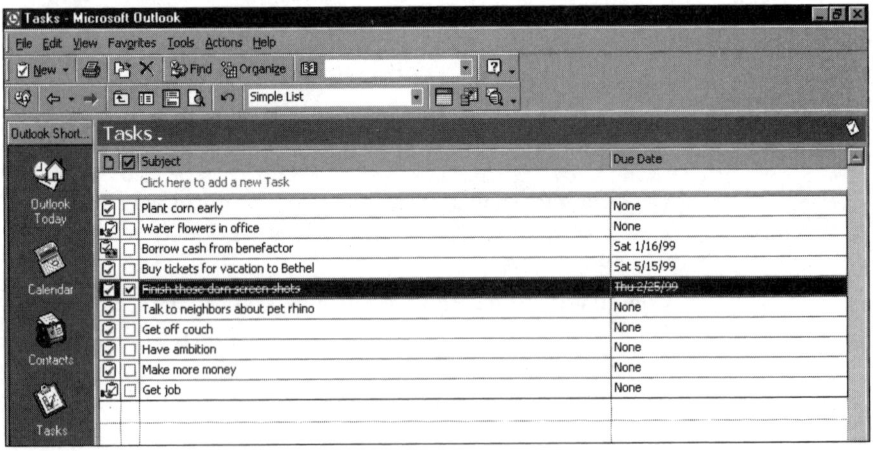

Figure 6-7:
You can
mark a
task as
complete.

Chapter 7: Working with Your Contacts

In This Chapter

✓ Adding a contact

✓ Finding contact information

✓ Displaying and changing contact information

✓ Customizing your contact list

✓ Using a contact to call someone

*I*n Outlookspeak, contacts are people about whom you keep some information (as if you were an FBI agent who was responsible for compiling a dossier on a select group of individuals). You can collect information including addresses, phone numbers, fax numbers, job titles, Web page addresses, and so on. You also have ample room to add free-form information for any contact on your list. Outlook allows you to communicate more easily with your contacts, whether they be friends, acquaintances, co-workers, or foreign spies.

Entering a New Contact

In the Contacts module, you can save and organize nearly any type of information about the people you deal with. You then can find everything again lickety-split. If you want, you can enter quick scraps of information without interrupting the flow of your work. You also can spend the time to enter minutely detailed information every time you create a new contact.

Adding names to your Contact list is as simple as filling out a form. You don't have to fill in everything the form asks for, just the name of the contact you're entering. While you're entering the name, you may as well enter other things you need to know about the person, such as an address, phone number, e-mail address, Web page address, and whatever.

To add a name to your Contact list, follow these steps:

1. **Click the Contacts icon on the Outlook bar, if you're not already in the Contacts module.**

2. **Click the New Contact button on the toolbar to bring up the New Contact form.**

3. **Enter the person's name in the Full Name box.**

When you open the New Contact Form, the insertion point is already in the Full Name text box, so you don't have to click anywhere. Enter the first name and then the last name, such as George Washington.

When you enter a name, such as George Washington, in the Full Name text box and then press Tab or click your mouse in any other box, the name appears again in the File As box — except that now the name appears last name first: Washington, George. The entry in the File As box tells you how Outlook plans to file your contact — in this case, by the last name, in the W section. You also can file a contact according to some other word. For example, George Washington could also be filed under F, for father of our country. More practical examples are filing the name of your plumber under the word *plumber,* your auto mechanic under *mechanic,* and so on.

4. **Click the Address box and enter the person's address.**

Outlook interprets addresses by using the same method it uses to make sense of names. Breaking the address into street, city, state, zip code, and country enables you to use the Outlook Contact list as a source of addresses when you're creating form letters in Microsoft Word. You don't have to do anything to make Outlook perform this interpretation trick (*parsing,* as the techies call it), but you may want to double-check the Outlook interpretation by clicking the Address button. After you click it, the Check Address dialog box appears (shown in Figure 7-1), showing you how Outlook interpreted the address you entered. If the name of the city wound up in the State/Province box or the name of the state wound up in the Zip Code box, you can fix everything in the Check Address dialog box.

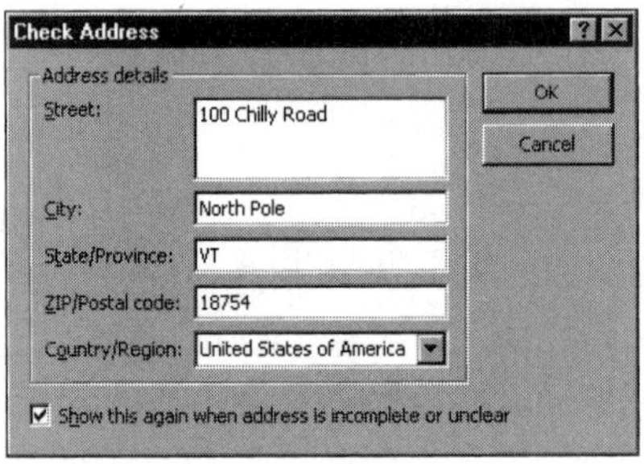

Figure 7-1:
Fix
incorrect
addresses
now rather
than later.

5. **Click the check box labeled This Is the Mailing Address if the address you've just entered is the contact address to which you plan to send mail.**

6. **Click in the other text boxes to enter the contact's business phone number, home phone number, business fax, e-mail address, Web page, and so on.**

7. **Click in the large text box at the bottom of the form and type anything you want.**

8. **Click the Categories button in the bottom-left corner of the screen to assign a category to the contact, if you want.**

9. **Click the name of each category that applies to your contact. If none of the existing categories suits you, click Master Category List in the lower-right corner to see the Master Category list box.**

10. **Type the name of a new category in the Item(s) Belong to These Categories box at the top of the Master Category list box.**

11. **Click Add and then click OK to return to the Categories list.**

12. **Click the name of the category you've just added, which now appears on the Categories list.**

13. **Click OK to close the Categories list and return to the New Contact form.**

14. **Click the Private box in the lower-right corner of the Contact form if you're on a network and don't want others to know about your contacts.**

15. **After you're finished, click Save and Close (or press Alt+S) to close the New Contact form.**

With the help of Outlook, you can easily save and recall a huge list of items about all your contacts. Do as much or little as you want. You always can go back and make changes later.

Finding a Name, Address, or Phone Number

Chances are that you want to find the names of your contacts sometime in the future, if you take the time to enter them in the first place. The quick, simple way to find a contact is simply to look up the name. Sometimes, however, you can't remember the name. You may recall something else about the person that you know you entered — such as the company she works for or the city where he lives. This section shows you several ways you can dig up information about your contacts.

Finding a contact the quick, simple way

The quick, simple way of finding a contact assumes that you remember the last name or the word you used in the File As box. To find a contact by last name, follow these steps:

1. **Choose View⇨Current View⇨Address Cards.**

   Address Cards view looks like a deck of address cards laid out across your screen.

2. **Type the first letter of the contact's last name.**

   The view moves to the part of Address Cards view that contains people whose names begin with that letter.

3. **If you still don't see the person's name, press the right-arrow key to scroll through the list alphabetically.**

If you entered something other than the contact's name in the File As box, such as *plumber* or *dentist,* press the letter *p* for plumber or *d* for dentist.

Finding a contact by using the Advanced Find feature

You can use the Find button on the toolbar to find a contact quickly the same way you find any other Outlook, although the Advanced Find feature can do a more detailed search if that's what you want. Sometimes you can't recall the name of the person you're looking for but you remember some fragment of the information you entered about him or her. For example, you remember that his name ends with *Jr* or you remember that he lives in Omaha. The Find Items feature finds all items that contain the tiniest scrap of information you entered.

1. **Choose Tools⇨Advanced Find (or press Ctrl+Shift+F) to open the Advanced Find dialog box (shown in Figure 7-2).**

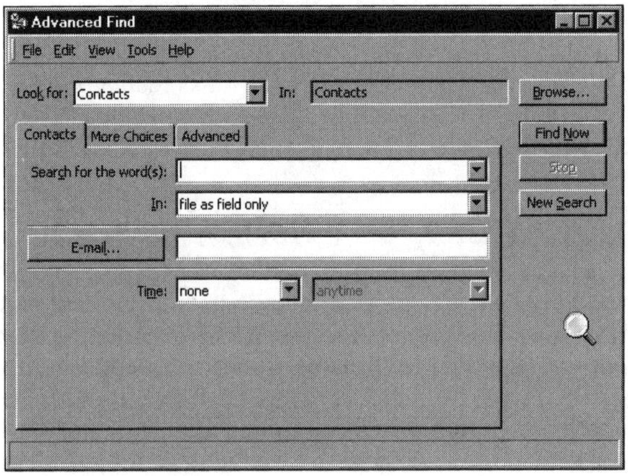

Figure 7-2:
You can conduct an advanced search for a contact.

2. **Click the scroll-down button at the right end of the Look For text box.**

3. **Choose Contacts from the menu. If you start from the Contacts module, the Look For box should already say *Contacts.***

4. **Click the triangle at the right end of the In text box on the Contacts tab to see the list of parts of the Contact list you can search.**

5. **Choose Frequently-Used Text Fields.**

6. **Click the Search for the Word(s) text box and enter the text you want to find.**

7. **Click the Find Now button.**

A little magnifying glass turns in circles while Outlook finds contact items that contain the text you entered. When items are found, their names appear on a list at the bottom of the Advanced Find dialog box (see Figure 7-3).

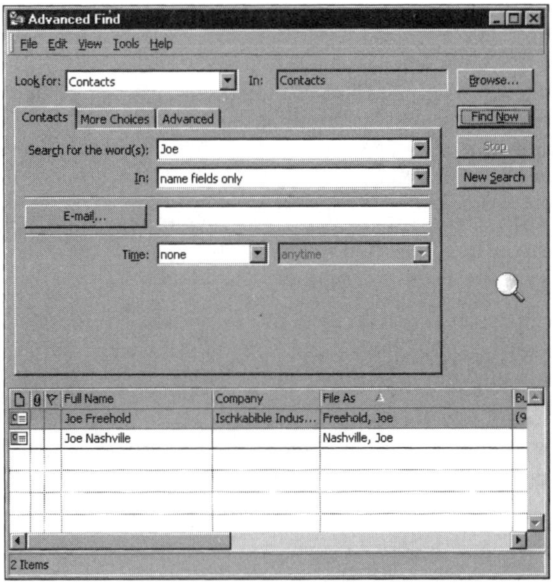

Figure 7-3:
So that's
Joe's last
name!

8. **Double-click the name of a contact on the list at the bottom of the Find Items dialog box to see that person's Contact record.**

Changing Information about a Contact

The main advantage to saving names and addresses with a program like Outlook is that when the information you collect about the people you deal with changes over time, you can easily update your records. Making changes to an item in your Contact list is simple.

1. **Double-click the name of the contact you want to change.**

   The contact item appears.

2. **Click the information you want to change or click in the text box for the information you want to add. Type the new information.**

3. **Click Save and Close (or press Alt+S).**

Customizing the Appearance of the Contact List

You can look at your Contact list in a variety of views, just as you can look at the information in all Outlook modules in a variety of ways. If you spend much time dealing with contacts, you can save a great deal of time using the options for sorting, grouping, and filtering the different items in an Outlook view.

About views

Although Outlook comes with dozens of different views and you can create hundreds more if you want, Outlook has only a handful of basic view types. You can see what the choices are by choosing View➪Current View➪Define Views and then clicking the New button. (After you've finished looking, press Esc twice to return to the screen from where you started.)

You can cook up an endless variety of views, beginning with these five general types. The Create a New View dialog box enables you to choose from among only five basic types of view in any Outlook module:

✦ **Table:** Your plain-vanilla arrangement of rows and columns. Phone List view in the Contacts module, Simple List view in the Tasks module, and Active Appointments view in the Calendar are all examples of table-type views.

✦ **Timeline:** Draws a picture depicting each item in a view, either in order of their due dates or the date when you dealt with them. The Inbox, Tasks, and Journal modules all include Timeline views.

✦ **Card:** Looks like a collection of file cards. Address Cards view and Detailed Address Cards view in your Contacts module are the only examples of card views that are included with Outlook.

✦ **Day/Week/Month:** Calendar-style views designed — you guessed it — for the Calendar module.

✦ **Icons:** Fill the screen with icons representing each item and a title that matches the title of the item. The Notes module uses Icons view.

Choosing a view

Contact views come with Outlook when you first start the program. These views cover things for which most people use the Contact list. You can add as many views as you need, however, so don't feel limited by the initial selection. Here's what you have when you begin:

✦ **Address Cards:** Looks like a screen full of little file cards arranged in alphabetical order (see Figure 7-4).

✦ **Detailed Address Cards:** A more detailed version of Address Cards view. This view shows everything on the first page of the Contact form, including the person's title, company, and the first few lines of text from the text box at the bottom of the Contact form.

✦ **Phone List:** Turns your collection of contacts into a plain-looking list of names, addresses, and phone numbers.

✦ **By Category:** Contacts are clumped together according to the category you've assigned to each of them.

✦ **By Company:** Similar to the By Category view: They are both grouped views (grouped views in Outlook usually have a name that starts with the word *By*).

✦ **By Location:** This view gathers contacts together — in this case, according to the country you've entered for each contact.

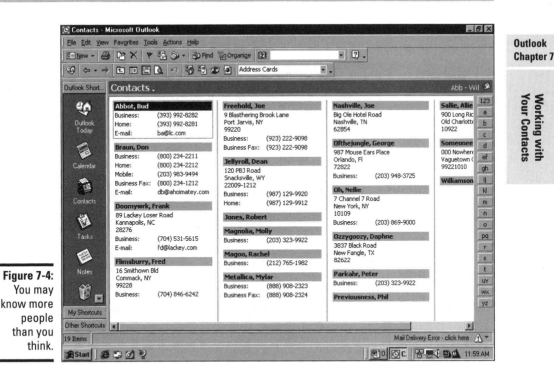

Figure 7-4:
You may
know more
people
than you
think.

✦ **By Follow-Up Flag:** Shows a list of your messages according to which kind of flag you assigned to each message.

Switching between views in any Outlook module is as simple as changing channels on your TV. Choose View⇨Current View and then pick the view you want. If you don't like the new view, just switch back by using the same commands to choose the view you were looking at before.

Filtering views

Filtered views show only items that have certain characteristics, such as a certain job title or a certain date. All views in all Outlook modules can be filtered, and some modules include filtered views. Although the Contacts module doesn't come with any filtered views when you begin using Outlook, you can easily create filtered views of your Contact list. Filtered views are useful if you frequently need to see a list of contacts who work at different companies but have the same job title, such as president or sales manager. You may also want to create a filtered view of contacts who live in your immediate vicinity if you need to call on customers in person. To filter items in a view, follow these steps:

1. **Choose View⇨Current View⇨Customize Current View to open the View Summary dialog box.**

2. **Click the Filter button to open the Filter dialog box.**

3. **Enter the text you want to filter in the box labeled Search for the Word(s).**

For example, if you want to see only the names of people whose job title is president, type the word **president** in the box.

4. **Click the scroll-down button next to the In text box to reveal the list of field types you can choose from.**

5. **Click OK to filter your list.**

The words *Filter Applied* appear on the folder banner (as shown in Figure 7-5), and your list shows only the items that match the text you entered in Step 3.

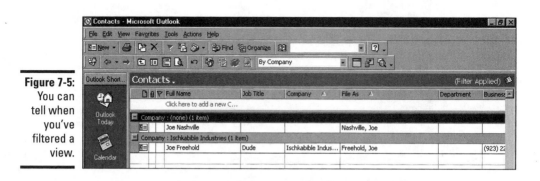

Figure 7-5: You can tell when you've filtered a view.

Putting new fields in a view

Most Outlook views display fewer than a dozen fields, even though items in nearly every Outlook module can store several dozen fields. You can even create your own fields. You can add fields to any Outlook view and use the fields you add to sort, group, or filter your collection of items.

1. **Choose View⇨Current View⇨Customize Current View to open the View Summary dialog box.**

2. **Click the Fields button.**

The Show Fields dialog box opens (see Figure 7-6).

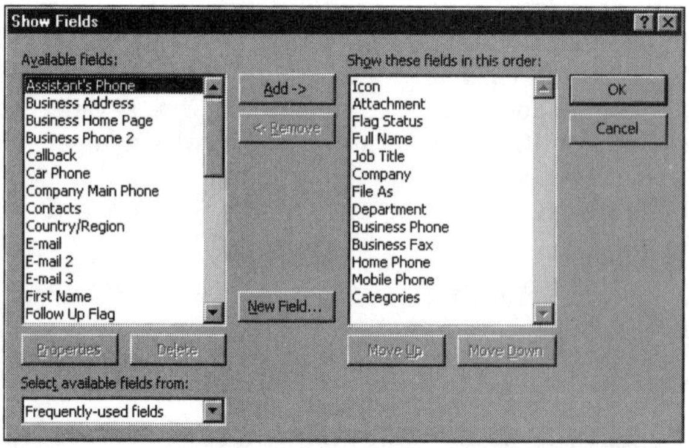

Figure 7-6: Feel free to add new fields to a view.

3. **Click the name of the field you want to add in the Available Fields list box and click Add.**

The field you chose is copied to the bottom of the Show These Fields in This Order box.

4. **Click Move Up to move the field you chose higher on your list.**

Every time you click Move Up, your field moves up one position on the list. The highest items on the list are displayed closest to the top of any Address Cards view and farthest left in any Table view.

5. **Click OK to close the Show Fields dialog box.**

Your new field is displayed in the position you selected.

Sorting a view

Each piece of information you enter about a contact is called a *field*. Each field shows up as a separate column in Phone List view. However, each field shows up as a separate *line* in Address Cards view. When you use this method of sorting your Contact list (or sorting the items in any Outlook module), the Sort dialog box refers to each item as a field (Name field or State field, for example).

1. **Choose View⇨Current View⇨Edit Current View to open the View Summary dialog box.**

2. **Click the Sort button to open the Sort dialog box (see Figure 7-7).**

3. **Click the scroll-down menu under Sort Items By and choose State from the menu.**

The word **State** appears in the Sort Items By box.

4. **Click Ascending if you want your view to begin with contacts from states that begin with the letter *A,* like Alabama and Alaska. Click Descending if you want your view organized in reverse alphabetical order, starting with Wyoming and West Virginia.**

A black spot appears in the circle next to whichever choice you click.

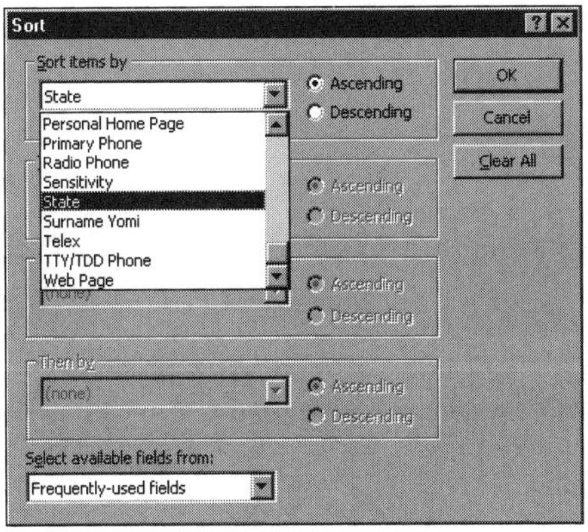

Figure 7-7:
You can
sort a view
by many
different
fields.

5. Click OK to begin sorting your list.

6. Choose Yes if a dialog box appears saying that the field "state" you want to sort by is not shown in the view and asking whether you want to show it.

Calling Someone from Outlook

After you've entered the phone number for a contact, you don't have to settle for just looking up that person's number; you can make Outlook dial the number for you. You must have a modem attached to your computer and a phone attached to the modem and, of course, you must already have the person's phone number entered on the Contact list:

1. Click the Contacts icon on the Outlook bar to make the Contact list appear.

2. Click the name of the contact you want to call.

3. Choose Actions⇨Call Contact and choose which of the contact's phone numbers you want to dial.

The New Call dialog box appears.

4. If the number shown in the New Call dialog box is the number you want to dial, click Start Call (or click the scroll-down button next to the phone number and pick the number you want).

You see the Call Status dialog box, as shown in Figure 7-8.

5. When the Call Status dialog box opens, pick up the phone.

6. When the person you're calling picks up the phone, click the Talk button in the Call Status dialog box to make the Call Status dialog box disappear.

7. After you finish the call, click the End Call button in the New Call dialog box.

The phone hangs up when you click the End Call button.

8. Click the Close button to make the New Call dialog box disappear.

Figure 7-8:
The Call
Status
dialog box.

Chapter 8: Tracking Activities with Journals

In This Chapter

✔ Viewing Journal entries

✔ Viewing a specific date

✔ Finding a Journal entry

✔ Recording automatically your Outlook activities

The Journal is the one part of Outlook 2000 that can be useful to you even if you never look at it. If you don't mess with the Journal at all other than to turn the feature on, you still have a record of every document you create, every e-mail message you send and receive, and a chronology of most of your important interactions with the people on your Contacts list.

Then again, if you actually use your Journal, you can keep track of meetings, phone calls, conversations, and a number of other routine events. Why would you want all this information? Because sometimes it's hard to remember what you named a document that you created or the folder in which you saved a certain spreadsheet. But you may remember when you did what you did — like last Thursday. The Journal comes in handy as a chronological record of all your activities.

Viewing the Journal

You can view your Journal entries in a variety of screen arrangements, called *views*. When you first start Outlook, six views are already set up for you to use with the Journal. You can switch among them by choosing View⇨Current View and picking the name of the view you want. If one view doesn't suit you, switch to another view in the same way. This list describes each of those six built-in views:

◆ **By Type:** Groups your Journal entries on a timeline according to the type of entry, such as e-mail messages, Excel spreadsheets, or Word documents. (See Figure 8-1.) You can scroll forward and back in time to see different slices of your Journal.

◆ **By Contact:** Another grouped timeline view that organizes your Journal entries according to the contact associated with each entry. You cannot print the By Contact view of the Journal.

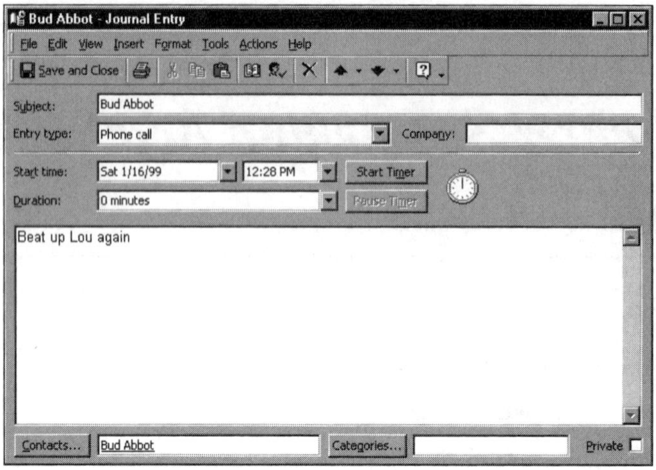

Figure 8-1:
A Journal
entry from
a task.

◆ **By Category:** Looks much like the By Type view except that the entries are grouped according to the category you've assigned each entry. You cannot print the By Category view of the Journal.

◆ **Entry List:** A simple list of all your Journal entries. (See Figure 8-2.) You can sort the Entry List according to any piece of information listed, such as subject, contact, starting time, or duration. You also can select and copy a range of entries from the Entry List. You then can paste the range into an Excel spreadsheet to calculate the total time spent on work for a certain contact or on projects in a certain category.

◆ **Last Seven Days:** Just like the Entry List except that it hides entries that occurred more than seven days ago.

◆ **Phone Calls:** Shows only the phone calls you've entered in your Journal.

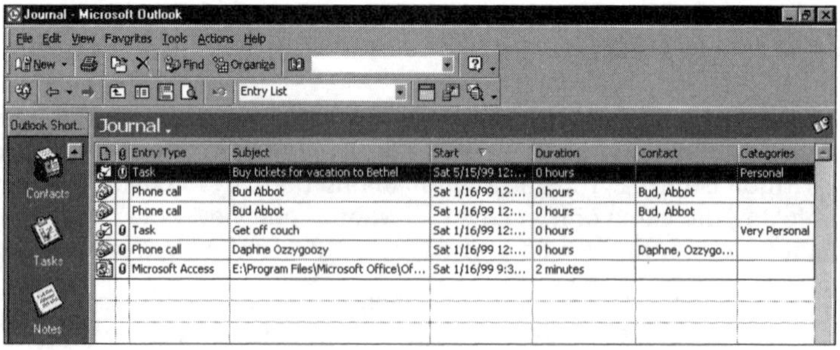

Figure 8-2:
A simple
list of
Journal
entries.

Viewing a Specific Date in Your Journal

If you use the Journal to record your activities, you accumulate lots of information. Sometimes the amount of information is so great that sorting through all the entries becomes difficult. To see only the activities on a certain date, follow these steps:

1. **Click the Journal icon on the Outlook bar. The Journal appears.**

2. **Choose any view that begins with the word *By* (By Type, By Contact, or By Category) by choosing <u>V</u>iew⇨Current <u>V</u>iew and picking the view you want.**

3. **Choose <u>Go</u>⇨Go to Dat<u>e</u> (or press Ctrl+G).**

The Go To Date dialog box opens, as shown in Figure 8-3.

4. **In the Date box, enter the date you want to view, such as December 16, 1998, or type the amount of time since the date you have in mind, such as two weeks ago.**

The display shifts to the date you asked for, and you see a collection of icons representing the Journal entries for the date you specified. If no entries exist, no icons appear.

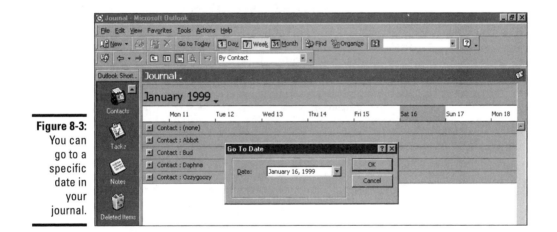

Figure 8-3: You can go to a specific date in your journal.

Creating Journal Entries Manually with Drag-and-Drop

Even though the Cold War is over, you may be skittish about having some computer record all your activities. On the other hand, it's nice to have a record of important things, like phone calls, without exerting too much effort. You can use the manual (drag-and-drop) method to record individual events in your Journal.

1. **Drag to the Journal icon the item you want to record (such as an e-mail message).**

A new Journal Entry form opens.

2. **Fill in any information you want to record.**

3. **Click <u>S</u>ave and Close (or press Alt+S).**

Your e-mail message (or whatever you dragged to the Journal icon) is now immortalized in your Journal. Congratulations!

Creating Journal Entries with the New Journal Item Button

Drag-and-drop isn't the only method of creating new Journal entries. You can make a new Journal entry for any reason at all. Simply go to the Journal and create a new item.

1. **Click the Journal icon on the Outlook bar, if you're not in the Journal module.**

2. **Click the New Journal item button on the toolbar.**

The Journal Entry form opens, as shown in Figure 8-4.

3. **Enter the subject of the Journal entry in the Subject text box.**

4. **Click the scroll-down button in the Entry Type box to pick an entry type.**

5. **If you want to add any other information to the Journal entry, enter it in the appropriate text box.**

6. **Click Save and Close (or press Alt+S).**

Your new Journal entry now appears in your Journal.

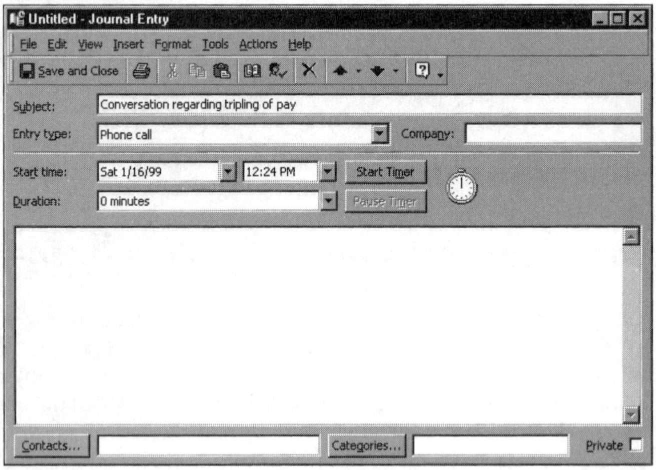

Figure 8-4:
The
Journal
Entry form,
ready for
your input.

Finding a Journal Entry

Although the Journal is time-oriented (it tracks items by time and date), occasionally you may need to find a Journal entry without knowing when the entry was made. To dig up the Journal entry you want, simply use the Find Items button.

1. **Click the Journal icon on the Outlook bar. Your list of Journal entries appears.**

2. **Click the F̲ind button on the toolbar (or press Alt+I).**

   The Find window opens, as shown in Figure 8-5.

3. **Enter in the Look For text box a word or phrase you can find in your Journal.**

4. **If the Journal entry you're looking for turns up, double-click the icon next to the entry to see the item's contents. If the entry you're looking for doesn't show up, try searching for different text.**

5. **Click the F̲ind button again (or press Alt+I) to close the Find window.**

The icon that appears in the text box of your Journal entry is a shortcut to the document itself. You can open the document by double-clicking the shortcut.

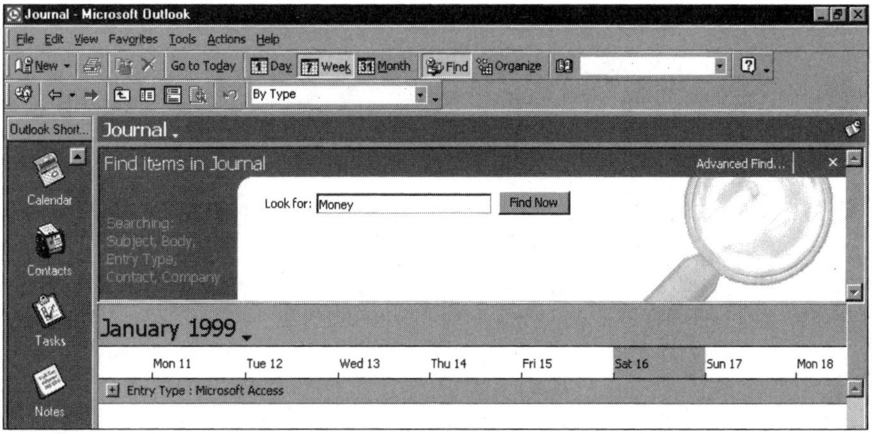

Figure 8-5:
What do
you want
to look for
today?

Activating the Automatic Recording Feature

You wouldn't really be lying if you said that you don't have to do anything to make the Journal work for you. But you would be exaggerating a little. Although you do have to tell the Journal to record everything, you have to tell it only once. To activate the Journal's automatic recording feature, follow these steps:

1. **Choose T̲ools⇨O̲ptions to open the Options dialog box.**

2. Click the Journal Options button to open the Journal Options dialog box (shown in Figure 8-5).

3. Click to place a check in the check box for the items and files you want to record automatically and for the contacts about whom you want the information recorded.

4. Click OK.

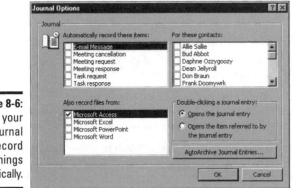

Figure 8-6:
Make your
journal
record
things
automatically.

Printing your journal

Sometimes you just don't get the same picture from a screen that you do from a good ol' piece of paper. It's a good thing you can print the Journal. To print your Journal, follow these steps:

1. **Click the Journal icon on the Outlook bar to see your list of Journal entries.**

2. **Choose from the Current View menu the view in which you want to print.**

3. **Select the entries you want to print (unless you want to print them all).**

4. **Click the Print button on the toolbar (or press Ctrl+P). The Print dialog box opens.**

5. **Choose Table or Memo format.**

6. **Choose All Rows or Only Selected Rows.**

7. **Click OK to print your Journal entries.**

The Print dialog box has a Preview button, which enables you to see what you're about to print before you commit everything to paper. Because a Journal can quickly develop thousands of entries, you would do well to preview what you print before tying up your printer with a document that could be more than a hundred pages long. Check out Appendix B for the complete rundown on printing in Office 2000.

Chapter 9: Managing Outlook Notes

In This Chapter

✔ **Creating and reading notes**

✔ **Finding notes**

✔ **Choosing how to view notes**

✔ **Forwarding notes**

✔ **Deleting notes**

✔ **Manipulating notes**

*J*otting down an important note on a stray piece of paper is easy. You probably do it all the time. Finding those notes again when you really need them is a different matter! Now where did you put that scrap of paper on which you jotted down the plans for your surefire money-making venture? Could someone have thrown away that napkin where you scribbled your important lunchtime thoughts? Unless you enjoy looking under piles of junk or digging through the trash for your important notes, let Outlook 2000 help you organize your note-taking attempts.

Creating Notes

If you can click a mouse, you can create a new note:

1. **If you're not already in the Notes module, click the Notes icon on the Outlook bar.**

2. **Click the New icon on the toolbar (or press Ctrl+N).**

A blank note appears, as seen in Figure 9-1.

3. **Enter what you want to say in your note.**

4. **Press Esc to close and save the note.**

Your new note takes its place in the collection of notes in the Notes module. Creating a note doesn't involve a great deal of fuss; just open, type, and close.

To create a note quickly, you don't even have to switch to the Notes module. Just press Ctrl+Shift+N from any other part of Outlook. A blank note opens, ready for you to fill in. When you've finished writing your note, press Esc to close the note.

Figure 9-1:
A blank
note
awaits you.

Reading (Or Changing) a Note

Opening a note so that you can read it or edit it is as simple as can be. To open a note, follow these steps:

1. **If you're not already in the Notes module, click the Notes icon on the Outlook bar.**

2. **Double-click the title of the note you want to open.**

It opens! You see the note on your screen.

3. **Read the note or make changes as you want.**

4. **Press Esc to close the note.**

Finding a Note

After you see how easily you can create a note, you're likely to add notes at your slightest whim, quickly amassing a large collection of notes. Finding one note among a large collection can be a needle-in-a-haystack proposition, except for the Find Items feature. Thank heavens that it's easy to use. To find items with the Find Items feature, follow these steps:

1. **If you're not already in the Notes module, click the Notes icon on the Outlook bar.**

2. **Click the Find button on the toolbar (or press Alt+I).**

The Find window opens (see Figure 9-2).

3. **In the Look For box, enter the word or phrase you're looking for.**

It doesn't matter how little text you use for your search. If you're looking for the words *George Washington,* for example, the letters geo find any note that contains the words *George Washington.* It also finds *National Geographic* and a reminder to do your geometry homework (assuming that you've written notes about all those things).

4. **Click the Find Now button.**

An hourglass appears as Outlook searches for the text you specified. When Outlook is finished, a list of items that satisfy your search appears.

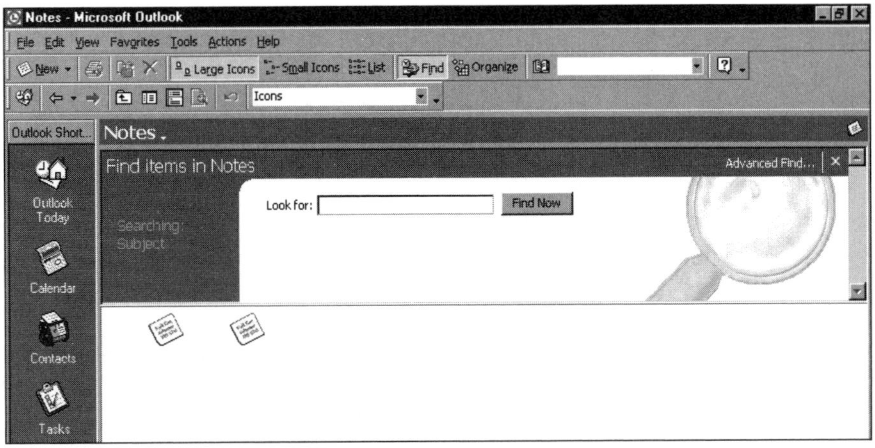

Figure 9-2:
You can
find any
note
you've
created.

5. **If the note you're looking for turns up, double-click the Note icon to read what the note says.**

   If the note you're looking for doesn't show up, try searching for different text.

6. **Click the Find button on the toolbar again (or press Alt+I) to close the Find window.**

A nice, weird thing about finding notes is that you don't have to enter a whole word. The Find feature can find any sequence of characters you type. If you're searching for a note you saved about John Paul Kowznofsky, you can search for **John Paul** or just **Kowz.** It doesn't matter whether you use upper- or lowercase letters; Outlook just looks for the letters you entered.

Viewing Notes

You can make Outlook display your multitude of notes in a variety of ways. Each type of screen style, called a *view,* emphasizes something different about your collection of notes. You can change between different views of your notes by choosing View➪Current View and picking a different view. You can choose from the following views:

   ✦ **Icons:** Splashes your collection of notes in little boxes all over the screen (as seen in Figure 9-3). To open one, just click the box representing the note you want to open.

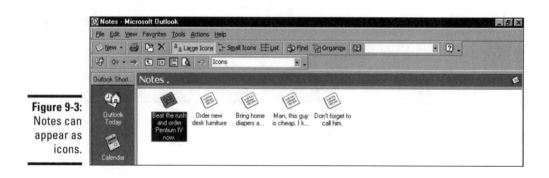

Figure 9-3:
Notes can
appear as
icons.

+ **Notes List:** As its name suggests, presents a two-column list of your notes (see Figure 9-4). One column is for the subject of each note, and the other column is for the date on which you created each note. You can sort the list according to the date you created each note by clicking the word *Created* in the gray box at the top of the column. You also can sort the list in alphabetical order by subject by clicking the word *Subject* in the gray box at the top of the column.

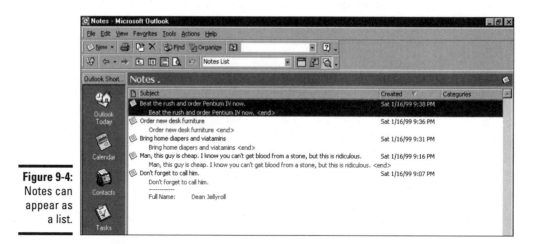

Figure 9-4:
Notes can
appear as
a list.

+ **Last Seven Days:** Shows only notes you've modified within the past seven days. After more than seven days have passed since you changed either the text in a note or its color, size, or category, the note disappears from Last Seven Days view, although you see notes of all ages in all other views.

+ **By Category:** Groups your notes according to the category you've assigned to each one (se Figure 9-5).

+ **By Color:** Groups your notes according to the color you've assigned to each one.

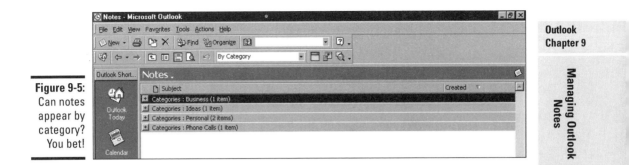

Figure 9-5:
Can notes
appear by
category?
You bet!

Forwarding a Note to Someone Else

After you've accumulated a treasure trove of information in your collection of
notes, you don't need to keep these juicy tidbits to yourself. Forwarding a note
to anybody by e-mail is simple. To forward a note by e-mail, follow these steps:

1. **Click the title of the note you want to forward.**

The title of the note is highlighted.

2. **Choose Actions⊅Forward (or press Ctrl+F).**

The New Message form opens (as shown in Figure 9-6).

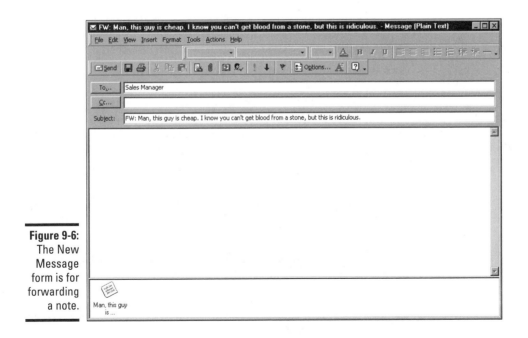

Figure 9-6:
The New
Message
form is for
forwarding
a note.

3. **Click the To text box and enter the e-mail address of the person to whom you're sending your note.**

   If you want to send a copy to a second person, click the Cc text box and then enter the e-mail addresses of the people to whom you want to send a copy of your note.

4. **Enter the subject of the note in the Subject box.**

5. **If you want, enter the text of a message in the text box.**

6. **Click the Send button (or press Alt+S).**

   Your message is on its way to your recipient.

What you're really sending is an e-mail message with a note attached, which is very quick and simple but not terribly magical. For the recipient to be able to read the Outlook note, keep in mind that they also need Outlook.

Deleting a Note

Creating a huge collection of notes is so easy to do that someday you'll need to delete some of them. (Years from now, you probably won't need that same note to yourself to remember to take out the trash or get your haircut.) Deleting notes is even easier than creating them — it's a piece of cake.

1. **If you're not already in the Notes module, click the Notes icon on the Outlook bar.**

2. **Click the title of the note you want to delete.**

   The title is highlighted to show which note you've selected.

 3. **Click the Delete button on the toolbar (or press Delete).**

   The note disappears.

You don't have to limit yourself to deleting one note at a time. If you know how to select multiple items in Windows 98, you can apply this knowledge to any Office 2000 application. You can select a bunch of notes by holding down the Ctrl key while clicking the different notes you want to delete; then click the Delete button. You also can click one note and then hold down the Shift key and click another note farther down the row to select both notes you clicked — as well as all the notes between them. When you click the Delete key, all the notes you selected are deleted.

Using Notes to Your Advantage

You don't have to just accept notes as they are. Find out how you can manipulate them in order to make these little things even more useful. Now you can claim complete control of your life.

Assigning a category to a note

You can assign a category to any note you create in Outlook. Categories may be a little more useful when you're using Notes than when you're using other parts of Outlook, because you can enter any ol' kind of information in a note, which can make it hard to find later. Assigning categories makes the stuff you collect easier to use and understand. To assign a category to a note, follow these steps:

1. **Click the Note icon in the upper-left corner of the note.**

The shortcut menu appears.

2. **Choose Categories in order to get to the Categories dialog box.**

3. **Choose one of the existing categories, if one suits you; then click OK.**

4. **If none of the existing categories suits you, enter a category of your choice in the New Category box.**

5. **Click OK.**

Your note looks the same, but now it has a category.

Changing the size of a note

A note can appear as a teensy little squib, or it can cover your whole screen. The size of the text in the note is the same no matter how large you make the note. When the note is too small, however, much of your text is invisible, so you have to make the note larger:

1. **Click the Notes icon on the Outlook bar, if you're not already in the Notes module.**

2. **Double-click the title of the note whose size you want to change.**

The note opens.

3. **Move your mouse pointer to the bottom-left corner of the note until the mouse pointer changes into a two-headed arrow pointed on a diagonal.**

4. **Drag your mouse until the note is the size you want.**

In most Windows programs, after you enter more text than will fit in a text box, a scroll bar appears on the right side of the screen. If you want to see text that has scrolled off the bottom of the screen, you click the scroll bar to move the text up. Because notes don't have scroll bars, however, if a note has more text than you can see on the screen, you have to click your mouse on the text and press the arrow keys to scroll up and down through the text. Those little note boxes are cuter without scroll bars, but they're surely harder to use.

Setting the default color and size of your notes

Maybe yellow just isn't your color. Maybe you want a little more space when you create a new note. You can set up Outlook to start each note in the color and size you want (within reason). To change the default settings for the color and size of your notes, follow these steps:

1. **Choose Tools⇨Options.**

The Options dialog box opens.

2. **Click the Note Options button.**

The Notes Options dialog box appears (see Figure 9-7).

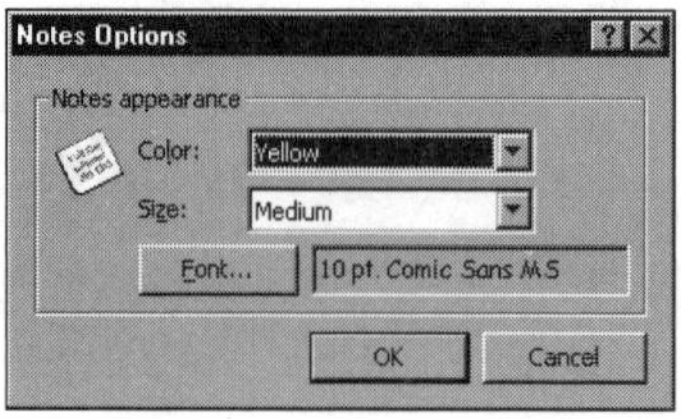

Figure 9-7:
You can
make many
options for
your notes.

Notes Options

Notes appearance

Color: Yellow

Size: Medium

Font... 10 pt. Comic Sans MS

OK   Cancel

3. **Click the scroll-down button at the right end of the Color box.**

4. **Choose a color from the list that appears.**

5. **Click the scroll-down button at the right end of the Size box.**

6. **Click OK.**

Changing the default size and color of your notes has no effect on the notes you've already created. If you want to change the color of a note after you've created it, just open the note and change the color by clicking the Note icon in the top-left corner of the note. When the shortcut menu appears, choose Color. Another menu appears with a list of colors you can choose. Choose from blue, green, pink, yellow, or white.

Printing the contents of a single note

Notes are meant to be read on the screen, but now and then you may want to print the contents of a note. Remember that even though you can change the colors of your notes, the colors don't print on a black-and-white printer.

1. Click the title of the note you want to print.

The title of your note is highlighted to show that it was selected.

2. Click the Print button on the toolbar (or press Ctrl+P) to open the Print dialog box.

3. Choose Memo Style in the Print Style box.

4. Click OK.

Unfortunately, when you print notes, they don't look like the cute little yellow squares you see on the screen; each one looks like an office memorandum.

Index

Book VI

PowerPoint 2000

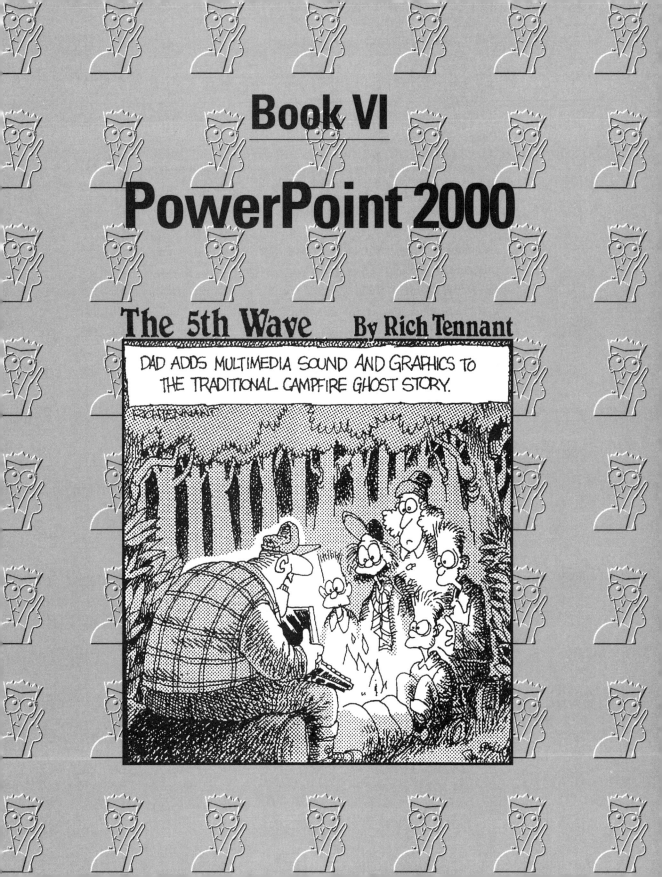

Contents at a Glance

Chapter 1: Getting Started with a PowerPoint Presentation

In This Chapter

✓ Opening a presentation

✓ Making a new presentation

✓ Changing your view

✓ Saving and closing in PowerPoint

At some time you've probably sat through a slick presentation at school or in the office where the presenter has impressed you with expertly timed slides projected on a screen in perfect sequence with lots of nice lettering and colors. And all you ever had for your presentations were pictures glued on that thin, floppy poster board or maybe a handful of hard-to-read overhead transparencies. Don't think that you can't join the growing ranks of great presentation givers! With just a little attention and PowerPoint 2000, you also can make almost any presentation worth sitting through. This chapter gets you started on PowerPoint basics so that you're ready to take advantage of this great presentation program.

Opening a Presentation

PowerPoint 2000 is not going to let you wander aimlessly as you try to make a presentation. You have the choice of several methods with which to create a new presentation. The easiest method, and perhaps best for beginners, is to let a wizard walk you through the process. If you don't want to use a wizard, you can choose to use a template offering a standard group of slides that you personalize according to your needs. Finally, you can start from scratch and build your presentation from the ground up. Whichever method you choose, PowerPoint makes the presentation-creating business a lot easier than ever before.

For the lowdown on how to use the mouse as well as details on cursors and pointers for PowerPoint 2000 (which behaves just like any other Office 2000 application), check out Appendix A. Using dialog boxes and making menu choices is explained in the Windows 98 portion of this book. The basic routines are similar.

After firing up PowerPoint, you see the start-up PowerPoint dialog box (as shown in Figure 1-1).

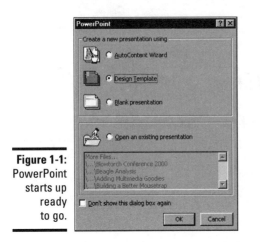

Figure 1-1:
PowerPoint
starts up
ready
to go.

The PowerPoint dialog box provides four choices to begin developing your PowerPoint presentation:

✦ **AutoContent Wizard:** The Wizard yields a nearly complete set of PowerPoint slides. You just need to supply the Wizard some basic lines of text, let the Wizard do its thing, and then you can tweak the final product.

✦ **Design Template:** This option provides you with cool pre-designed layouts that still offer you the flexibility to alter the layout elements.

✦ **Blank presentation:** Gives you blank slides with no color and no artwork, which is great for minimalists and artists. Allows you to build a really barren stack of slides (good for black and white transparencies), or you can create all your artistic elements from scratch.

✦ **Open an existing presentation:** Allows you to go back and work on any presentation that you previously named and saved.

You also have the option of clicking to select the checkbox for Don't show this dialog box again. If you do so, you have to choose File⇔New to open a new presentation each time you run PowerPoint.

Creating a presentation with the wizard

The wizard is a simple program that builds a rudimentary set of PowerPoint slides based on a few tidbits of information you input to the program. The wizard is a good way to get started with PowerPoint, but don't be fooled into thinking that it magically does all the work for you — it doesn't. Just accept the wizard for what it is — a quick and dirty way to generate a basic set of PowerPoint slides.

1. **Start PowerPoint. If you already started PowerPoint, choose New. . . from the Menu bar.**

2. **At the start-up PowerPoint dialog box or New Presentation dialog box, click AutoContent Wizard and click OK.**

The AutoContent Wizard is located under the General tab in the New Presentation dialog box.

3. **Click Next.**

The wizard now asks you a series of questions.

4. **Choose a presentation type from the list and then click Next.**

Your choices consist of All, General, Corporate, Projects, Sales/Marketing, and Carnegie Coach.

5. **Choose a presentation style from the list; then click Next.**

Presentation style choices include On-screen presentation, Web presentation, Black-and-white overheads, Color overheads, or 35mm slides. Choose On-screen presentation if you plan on presenting in front of an audience (face-to-face) or via a computer-networked meeting. Choose Web presentation if you plan to post your slides to the Web for online access. Choose overheads if you want to print transparencies to use with an overhead projector. And choose 35mm slides if you want to show your presentation using a traditional slide carousel.

**PowerPoint
Chapter 1**

Getting Started with
a PowerPoint
Presentation

6. **Complete the presentation options dialog box by typing a Presentation title.**

You can also type a Footer and click in the appropriate checkboxes to have the Date last updated and the Slide number placed on each slide.

7. **Click Next.**

The wizard presents a final wrap-up screen.

8. **Click Finish.**

Your completed presentation appears onscreen in Normal view. (You can read about views later in this chapter.)

Creating a presentation with templates

Choosing Design Template from the PowerPoint dialog box or choosing any non-General tab from the New Presentation dialog box (shown in Figure 1-2) means that you have to shop from a folder full of pretty designs before singling out one that catches your eye. Design Templates and Office Templates (if you have them) offer visually appealing colors and design elements *only,* while Presentations goes one step further by offering suggested content for common presentation themes.

You have Office Templates only if you installed a previous version of PowerPoint before installing PowerPoint 2000.

On all of the templates tabs, clicking on the name of any template yields a thumbnail sketch of how the design appears on your computer screen.

Pick a style that suits your fancy and then click OK to accept it. The New Slide dialog box appears and asks you to choose an AutoLayout for your first slide.

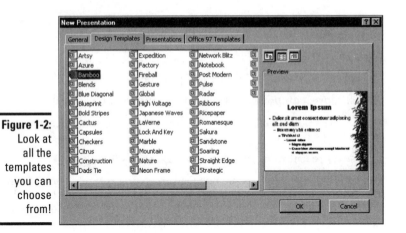

Figure 1-2:
Look at
all the
templates
you can
choose
from!

Creating a blank presentation

Choose Blank Presentation from the PowerPoint dialog box or from the General tab of the New Presentation dialog box to begin with blank slides (no color and no artwork).

Blank presentations can still provide placeholders for adding text and graphic objects, but they are otherwise barren of images, colors or artistic design. Blank presentations are ideal for building complete layouts from scratch or for building simple, text-only presentations.

Opening an existing presentation

PowerPoint offers you the flexibility of saving presentations to — and opening presentations from — a variety of locations. If you're like most users, you may frequently save files to and open files from your own hard drive or possibly a network drive shared by you and your fellow cubicle-dwellers. Open a saved PowerPoint presentation as follows:

1. **Click the Open button on the Standard toolbar, choose File⇨Open from the Menu bar, or press Ctrl+O.**

The Open dialog box appears.

2. **Locate the presentation you want to open in the Places bar or the Look in box.**

The Places bar is located on the left side of the Open dialog box, and contains several folders that may contain the file you seek (History, My Documents, Desktop, Favorites, Web Folders).

3. **Click the presentation you want to open.**

A thumbnail picture of the first slide in the presentation you select appears.

4. **Press the Open button to open the presentation, or press the arrow next to the Open button for special options in opening the presentation.**

Special options include Open Read-only, Open as Copy, and Open in Browser.

Files you have used recently are listed under History on the Places bar.

Beginning a New Presentation

Every time you start the PowerPoint program, a PowerPoint dialog box appears and offers you the option of opening a new presentation. To begin a new presentation, simply click Blank presentation, Design Template, or AutoContent wizard, and then click OK (see Figure 1-3). Clicking Blank presentation opens a new blank presentation in PowerPoint. If you click Design Template or AutoContent wizard, a New Presentation dialog box appears, and you must make some design choices before your new presentation actually opens.

If you already have PowerPoint up and running, you can use either of these methods to start a new presentation:

✦ **Choose File⇨New from the menu bar:** You see a New Presentation dialog box with tabs providing options for generating your presentation. (Don't be surprised that the New Presentation dialog box looks very different than the PowerPoint dialog box.)

✦ **Press Ctrl+N:** PowerPoint automagically creates a new blank presentation and displays the New Slide dialog box.

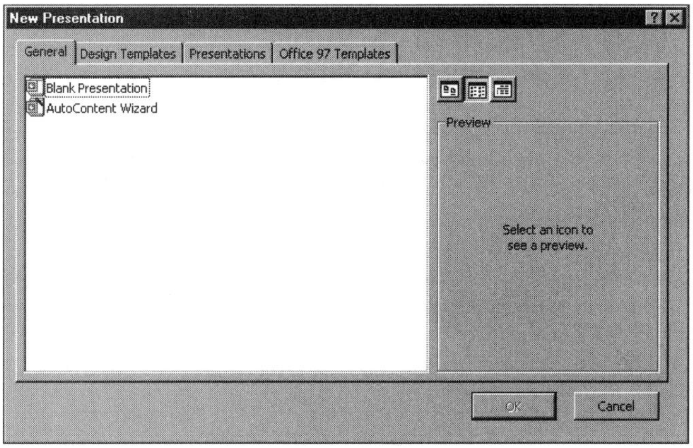

Figure 1-3:
You can always open a new presentation.

Changing Your View

Next to the horizontal scrollbar sits a collection of buttons from which you can choose your view. You can also choose a view by clicking the View menu from the Menu bar. The rest of this book helps you to understand how to use these views, but you just may want to know what is available. You can choose from any of the following views:

+ **Normal view:** A combination of Slide view and outline view. Shows three panes simultaneously — your presentation outline on the left, your slide on the right, and your speaker notes at the bottom.

+ **Slide view:** Shows a single slide under construction. You're able to see all text, colors, pictures, sounds, and movies in the view. This view allows you to create and edit all information and images on your slides.

+ **Outline view:** Shows an ordered list of the text information on your slides. In Outline view, you can examine the entire text content of your presentation all at once. This view allows you to create and edit text information on your slides, but it does not let you add or edit non-text items such as clip art. This view also gives you a cute thumbnail sketch of your slide beside its associated outline position.

+ **Slide Sorter view:** Shows thumbnails of your all your slides simultaneously, neatly presented in orderly rows and columns. Slide Sorter view enables you to quickly change the order of your slides by dragging and dropping them into new positions.

+ **Slide Show:** Presents the completed stack of slides to a viewing audience.

Saving Your Work

While composing an award-winning presentation or lecture, you certainly want to save your work. Save often. If you close your file or exit PowerPoint without saving your slides, consider them gone forever. Saving often also buys you insurance against losing everything in the event you have a power surge or if your computer crashes. Save your goods by clicking the Save button on the Standard toolbar or choosing File⇨Save.

The first time you save a presentation, the Save As dialog box appears for you to type in the name of your newly created file. You may notice that the Save As dialog box includes a Places bar on the left-hand side showing locations where you may want to save your file. Options on the Places bar include History, My Documents, Desktop, Favorites, and Web Folders. You can also click the down-arrow beside the Save in area to locate another folder that you want to save your file to.

Exiting PowerPoint

When it's time to close up shop, kick back for the evening, and bask in a little Microsoft glory, close the PowerPoint files that you're working on by choosing File⇨Close.

PowerPoint doesn't let you quit without asking if you want to save changes. Answer politely to complete the exiting process.

Chapter 2: Sliding into Your Presentation

In This Chapter

- ✔ Getting to know PowerPoint slides
- ✔ Managing your slides
- ✔ Adding, copying, and deleting slides
- ✔ Using Outline View to work with slides

*N*o longer will you always think of slides as being little square things that often get jammed in those noisy carrousel projectors while you attempt to remain awake in a hot, dark room. PowerPoint 2000 has another idea on how to make slides that you can see on the computer screen or project on the wall. And PowerPoint slides don't ever project upside down unless you want them to!

Creating and Working with Slides

Showing PowerPoint slides is also much more exciting than clicking through traditional slides. That's because a PowerPoint presentation can include text, graphics, movies, and audio clips all presented in animated steps to convey your information in a precise, engaging sequence. It can also include television-quality cuts and fades between slides.

So what does a PowerPoint slide actually look like? Basically, a slide looks like anything you want it to look like. Sometimes it looks like a simple piece of text, like your company mission statement. Other times it looks like a list of bulleted items — like ingredients for guacamole — that fly in animated steps, one bullet item at a time, onto the slide. And other times it looks like a graph of product sales forecasts or a labeled diagram of earthworm innards. If you can dream it up, you can probably stick it on a slide and show it to your audience. All the information in your presentation appears either directly on a slide or is attached to a slide as reference material. This section assists you in adding new slides and moving around a collection of slides in a presentation.

Adding a new slide

When you begin a new presentation — except for a presentation created with an AutoContent Wizard — PowerPoint provides you with one spanking-fresh slide to work with. (New presentations created with an AutoContent Wizard may provide you with ten or more slides to contend with.) However, unless you are the most painfully concise human on the planet, you may want more than a single slide in your PowerPoint presentation.

You can add a new slide in any view except Slide Show view. To add a new slide to your presentation, you can click the New Slide button on the Standard toolbar (or choose Insert⇨New Slide from the menu bar). Each time you add a new slide, you're presented with a New Slide dialog box (shown in Figure 2-1).

The New Slide dialog box contains 24 *AutoLayouts,* which are slide layouts that PowerPoint automatically sets up for you. The AutoLayouts offer various combinations of title slides, text bullets, clip art, and other features. If you want to fully customize the slide yourself, choose the Blank slide option.

Each new slide can be created using a different AutoLayout, allowing you to create a presentation with a variety of formats tailored to meet your specific needs.

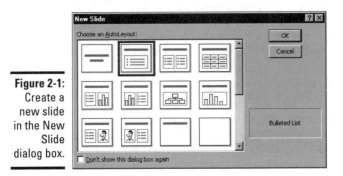

Figure 2-1:
Create a
new slide
in the New
Slide
dialog box.

Typing text on the slide

Each new slide that you create reserves a partitioned zone where you can type your text (except for instances when you choose to create a completely blank slide). These "type here" zones are called *text boxes.* Notice that the placeholders Click to add title, Click to add subtitle, or Click to add text occupy the text boxes until you replace the boxes with your own words. See Figure 2-2.

Moving the cursor into a text box converts the cursor from an arrow to an I-beam, indicating that the text box is ready to accept text. When this happens, click the mouse anywhere in the box (the place you click is your text insertion point) and start typing. Now PowerPoint acts like a word processor. The left and right arrow keys move you around, and the Delete key erases your typing.

Text placeholder   Title placeholder

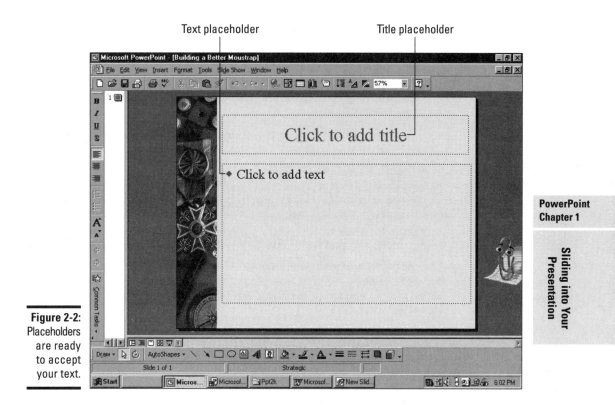

PowerPoint
Chapter 1

Sliding into Your
Presentation

Figure 2-2:
Placeholders
are ready
to accept
your text.

PowerPoint tries to fit any text you type within the boundaries of the text placeholder. If the amount of text you type can't fit in the boundaries comfortably, PowerPoint decreases the point size of the text to create a better fit To turn this feature off, choose Tools⇨Options from the Menu bar to summon the Options dialog box. Click the Edit tab, and then click to clear the Auto-fit text to text placeholder check box.

Pasting clip art onto a new slide

Every so often, you may want to add a relevant picture that "tells the story" to your slides. You may choose to add clip art, photos, drawings, or scanned images to your slides — the possibilities are endless! The simplest way to add a picture to a new slide is to grab one out of the Microsoft Clip Gallery that accompanies PowerPoint. Just follow these steps:

1. **Insert a new slide into your presentation by clicking the New Slide button or pressing Ctrl+M.**

2. **In the New Slide dialog box, select an AutoLayout that includes a clip art placeholder.**

   This doesn't limit you to only adding pictures in the form of clip art — "clip art placeholder" is just an old and beloved name for the type of AutoLayout that includes a picture. You can actually add any image — a photograph, a scanned drawing, a piece of clip art — when using this AutoLayout.

3. **Double-click on the placeholder to open the Microsoft Clip Gallery's catalog of pictures.**

4. **Click a picture category such as Business or Travel and then click a picture in that category.**

5. **Click the Insert Clip button from the pop-up menu that accompanies your selected picture.**

Your chosen image is magically glued to your slide.

Using a color scheme

Color schemes offer you the option of exercising your creative muscle to alter slide background colors, text colors, and accent colors. For each scheme, PowerPoint provides you with eight coordinated colors that complement one another in an aesthetically pleasing combination. The schemes ensure that the colors match and that text readability is maximized relative to the background.

You can get a look at all your color scheme options at any time, in any view except Slide Show view. To look at color scheme option, choose Format⇨ Slide Color Scheme from the Menu bar. This opens the Color Scheme dialog box, shown in Figure 2-3.

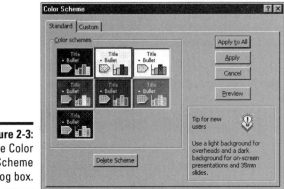

Figure 2-3:
The Color
Scheme
dialog box.

The Color Scheme dialog box has two tabs: Standard and Custom. It also has a Preview button that lets you try on how your Color Scheme choice looks on your very own slides — prior to actually applying the scheme. Each tab offers the following options:

✦ **Standard tab:** This tab offers a selection of premade Color schemes. Click the Color scheme you want for the current slide and press Apply. To apply the selected Color scheme to the entire presentation, press Apply to All.

✦ **Custom tab:** This tab allows you to create your own color scheme. In the Scheme colors area, you can change the individual colors of the following items: Background, Text and lines, Shadows, Title text, Fills, Accent, Accent and hyperlink, and Accent and followed hyperlink. To change an individual color, click the color, select Change Color, and then choose a new color in the dialog box that appears and click OK. After making your changes, click the Apply button to make the changes effective on the current slide only, or click the Apply to All button to make the changes effective on all slides in your presentation.

To save a scheme created within the Custom tab area of the Color Scheme dialog box, press Add as Standard Scheme after making your individual color choices. Your new scheme is added to the Standard tab of the Color Scheme dialog box.

Duplicating a slide

Duplicating a slide is an easy way to reuse the formatting of one slide as a guide for other slides. You may find duplicating particularly useful for churning out slides that have the same title and images with variations only on bullet items.

PowerPoint Chapter 1

Sliding into Your Presentation

To duplicate a slide, use the Edit⇨Duplicate command from the Menu bar, or press Ctrl+D. The currently selected slide is duplicated and placed immediately following its original slide. You are moved to the duplicate slide in the presentation.

If more than one slide is selected, every slide in the selection is duplicated and placed immediately following the last selected slide.

Moving between slides

You can move from slide to slide during the construction of your PowerPoint presentation in several ways:

✦ **In Normal view or Slide view:** Click the slide number you wish to move to in the outline pane. You can also:

   • Click an arrow on the scroll bar at the right side of the slide pane. The up arrow takes you toward your first slide. The down arrow takes you toward your last slide.

   • Use the double arrows to move one slide at a time through your entire set of slides. Dragging the scroll-box up or down between the arrows indicates your current slide position in the stack.

   • Press PgUp or PgDn to move through your stack one slide at a time.

✦ **In Slide Sorter view:** Double-click the slide that you want to move to.

Deleting a slide

Eliminating a slide can be accomplished in any view — but not while you're running a slide show. (It's too late then!) To trash a slide you no longer want, just follow these steps:

1. **Select the slide to be deleted by clicking on it or moving to the slide in Normal view or Slide view.**

   To select multiple slides, move to Outline or Slide Sorter View, hold the shift key down, and click on each slide to be deleted.

> **2.** Delete your selection choosing Edit⇨Cut. You can also press the Backspace or Delete key to delete selected slides.

Working in Outline View

In Outline view, your entire presentation appears as an outline comprised of the titles and body text from each slide. You still see the Slide pane and the Notes pane, but the size of the Outline pane is maximized relative to the other two. Switch to Outline view by clicking the Outline view button, located in the bottom-left corner of the PowerPoint window.

The purpose of Outline view is to concentrate on the text of your slides; you can edit text content, text formatting, and text organization. The benefit of working in Outline view is that it lets you easily see how information progresses from slide to slide. And just so you don't forget, the Slide pane still shows the aesthetics of how each slide looks during the slide show.

You can create a new presentation in Outline view, or you can switch to Outline view to peruse any existing PowerPoint presentation. You can move back and forth among Outline view and all other PowerPoint views at any time as you build and edit your presentations.

How slides and text are organized

In Outline view, as in Normal view, slides are listed vertically, from the first slide to the last. Each slide is designated by a number and a slide marker.

The slide title appears to the right of each slide marker, and body text, indented up to five levels, appears below the slide title. The body text may appear as paragraphs or bullet items, and can be easily moved — rearranged within a slide, or moved to other slides. Some repositioning tasks are accomplished by clicking and dragging the selected slide or text, and others are performed using buttons on the Outlining toolbar.

Outlining toolbar

When working in Outline view or Normal view, you may want to summon an Outlining toolbar containing specialized buttons for working with the outline of your presentation. Call up the Outlining toolbar by choosing View⇨Toolbars from the Menu bar and clicking to place a checkmark by Outlining. (See Figure 2-4.)

Outlining buttons on the toolbar deal primarily with repositioning text so that the text's significance is appropriately conveyed by its position relative to other text. For example, the Outlining buttons let you move text bullets higher or lower on a bulleted list. Outlining buttons also let you move a bulleted item of text to become a major bullet (this is called promoting text) or a minor bullet (this is called demoting text).

Buttons on the Outlining toolbar include the following:

✦ **Promote:** Elevates the position of the selected paragraph or bullet item by moving it up and left one heading level. For example, makes a level two heading become a level one heading.

Promote Collapse ┌Collapse All

Move Up   Summary Slide

Figure 2-4:
The
Outlining
toolbar.

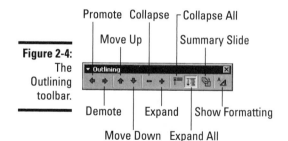

Demote   Expand   Show Formatting

Move Down Expand All

✦ **Demote:** Diminishes the position of the selected paragraph or bullet item by moving it down and right one heading level. For example, makes a level two heading become a level three heading.

✦ **Move Up:** Repositions the selected paragraph or bullet item — and any collapsed subordinate text — up, above the preceding displayed paragraph or bullet item. For example, makes the second bullet item on a list become the first bullet item.

✦ **Move Down:** Repositions the selected paragraph — and any collapsed subordinate text — down, below the following displayed paragraph. For example, makes the second bullet item on a list become the third bullet item.

✦ **Collapse:** Hides body text to show only the title of the selected slide or slides. A slide with collapsed text has a thin gray line underlining its title.

✦ **Expand:** Redisplays collapsed text of selected slides.

✦ **Collapse All:** Collapses the body text of all slides in the presentation.

✦ **Expand All:** Shows the body text of all slides in the presentation.

✦ **Summary Slide:** Builds a new slide from the titles of selected slides. The title of the new slide is Summary Slide, and the summary slide is inserted in front of the first selected slide (serving more as an agenda slide than a summary slide).

✦ **Show Formatting:** Toggles on or off to show or hide text formatting (such as font and point size) in Outline view.

Many of the frequently used Outlining buttons also appear on other toolbars, including the Formatting and the Standard toolbars.

Building a new presentation

Yes, you can build a new presentation in Outline view. To create a new presentation in Outline view, simply follow these steps without wasting any more of your time:

1. **Choose File➪New from the menu bar.**

2. **Choose a presentation type from the New Presentation dialog box. Click OK.**

PowerPoint Chapter 1

Sliding into Your Presentation

3. **Choose an AutoLayout from the New Slide dialog box.**

An empty slide marker for Slide 1 appears.

 4. **Click the Outline view button.**

5. **Type a title for Slide 1, and press Enter.**

6. **Click the Demote button on the Outlining toolbar, or press Enter and Tab to create the first bullet level. Type text for the first bullet and press Enter. Continue typing and pressing Enter to create as many bullet items as you want.**

7. **After the last bullet item, press Ctrl+Enter or press Enter and click the Promote button on the Outlining toolbar to create the next slide.**

8. **Repeat Steps 3 through 7 to create as many slides as you want.**

9. **Choose File⇨Save from the menu bar, or click the Save button on the Standard toolbar. Type a name for your presentation in the Save in area and click Save.**

You can press a different view button at any time to examine how your presentation looks in other views.

Changing the position of a title or paragraph

You can change the position of a slide title or paragraph whenever you want — and you undoubtedly will do this over and over. Follow these two tiny steps:

1. **In Outline view or Normal view, select the title or paragraph you wish to move.**

2. **Drag the selected text to a new position, or click Promote, Demote, Move Up, or Move Down to reposition the selected text.**

Changing the slide order

So you want to move an entire slide to a different position in the outline? It's never too late to fine tune your presentation.

1. **In Outline view or Normal view, click and hold the slide marker representing the slide you want to move.**

The pointer changes to a compass when it moves over the slide marker. The text of the entire slide — title and body text — is now selected.

2. **Drag the selected slide to a new position and let go, or click Move Up or Move Down to reposition the selected text.**

The entire presentation of slides reorders to reflect the repositioning of the moved slide. PowerPoint is just that accommodating!

Chapter 3: Laying the Groundwork with Templates

In This Chapter

- ✔ Discovering templates
- ✔ Applying a template to a new presentation
- ✔ Applying a template to an existing presentation
- ✔ Creating your own templates

*J*ust for the sake of the argument, say that you enjoy doing the same task over and over again. You want to have your name at the top-right of every slide that you show during your presentation. You also want a picture of your cat on every other page. That task is no problem if you enjoy repeating the same actions: entering the text and adding the picture on every slide where you want these things to appear. However, if you are one of those people who would rather save time and avoid errors that occur when you try to do the same thing more than one time, this chapter on templates was custom made for you.

Applying and Creating Templates

PowerPoint comes stocked with tons of premade *templates* — artistic blueprints for constructing your slide presentations quickly and easily. Templates are set up with predefined formatting settings (color schemes, graphic elements, and styled fonts) to minimize the time and effort you spend building slides.

After applying a template, you can tweak it for an individual presentation by modifying the Slide Master and the Title Master (see Chapter 4 for details on masters). If you find that you keep making the same adjustments over and over again, you can also create and save your own template.

Applying a template to a new presentation

If you are just starting a new presentation, and you want the slides to follow a template, just follow these steps:

1. **Click the Template option in the PowerPoint dialog box that appears when you first open PowerPoint.**

2. **In the New Presentation dialog box that appears, choose and click a template from one of the following tabs:**

   • **General tab:** Contains a Blank Presentation template and the AutoContent Wizard template. A Blank Presentation means you'll be working with a template of black text on a white background with no artistic design elements. You can either leave this template as is (a good option if you plan to print your presentation as black and white overhead transparencies) or embellish the template with your own colors and design elements.

   • **Design Templates tab:** Contains 44 ready-to-go templates without content. The styles differ from those in the Presentation folder, and the designs are just gorgeous. Check out Ribbons and Romanesque.

   • **Presentations tab:** Contains 24 content-inclusive templates, such as Communicating Bad News or Motivating A Team. Most of these templates use different colors and layouts. The content text provides suggested talking points for the template you selected. You can use the content or dump it by deleting the text on each slide and typing in your own information.

   • **Office 97 Templates:** Contains 53 templates that may be near and dear to you if you previously used PowerPoint 97. *Note:* This tab exists only if you previously installed PowerPoint 97.

   Click a template once to check out a thumbnail sketch of it.

3. **Click OK to apply the template.**

   If you chose a Design Template or a template from a previous version of Office, the New Slide dialog box now appears. If you chose a Presentation template, a multi-slide presentation of the type you selected now appears in Normal view.

4. **If you're presented with the New Slide dialog box, PowerPoint asks you to choose an AutoLayout for your first slide. Click an AutoLayout and click OK.**

   AutoLayouts provide options for arranging information on your slide. For example, one AutoLayout provides an area for typing title text at the top of the slide and another area for typing bulleted items of text below the title. Another AutoLayout provides an area for typing title text and an organization chart. You can choose from 24 AutoLayouts, including a Blank AutoLayout that lets you add whatever types of text or objects you want to the slide.

Applying a template to an existing presentation

You can easily change templates at any point while creating your presentation. However, before you do so, you need to be aware of the following things:

✦ The template is applied to all slides in the entire presentation. PowerPoint does not allow a mix-and-match approach, so you can't use one template for a few slides and another template for a few others.

✦ Applying a new template obliterates any modifications that you made to the Slide Master for the previously used template. Applying a new template copies the template's background colors, text formatting, decorations — everything — onto your Masters and all slides throughout the presentation.

✦ Changes made to the colors and formatting of non-Master items on individual slides, though, aren't affected by the application of the new template. Any custom-tailoring of non-Master elements on individual slides (except background color) remains safe, as PowerPoint preserves such deviations regardless of changes in the Master. For example, if you add a clip art to a particular slide, the clip art is still there after you apply a new template.

To apply a template to an existing presentation, just follow these steps:

1. **Open the presentation and choose Format⇨Apply Design Template from the Menu bar; or choose Apply Design Template from the Common Tasks drop-down list on the Formatting toolbar or Slide Sorter toolbar. (See Figure 3-1).**

PowerPoint Chapter 3

You can also double-click the name of the template in the status bar at the bottom of the PowerPoint window. The Apply Design Template dialog box appears, and you can search through its folders to select a template.

2. **Choose and click a template from one of these locations in the Apply Design Template dialog box:**

- **Presentation Designs folder:** Contains 44 ready-to-go templates without content — the same stuff you find under Design Templates in the New Presentation dialog box.

- **1033 folder:** Contains 24 content-inclusive templates — the same templates located under the Presentations tab in the New Presentation dialog box.

Figure 3-1:
The Apply Design template.

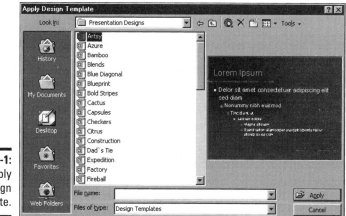

3. Click Apply.

You now see the new template applied to your slides. If you want to tweak the template, see "Editing the Slide Master" in Chapter 4 for further details.

Creating an original template

Don't like any of PowerPoint's templates? Create your own! A template is basically just a set of style elements for your slides, so creating your own is easy. You can create a new template at any time, and save it into the templates folder for application to existing or new presentations. Saving a template is almost identical to saving a presentation — except that the template has no slides, but only Masters.

1. From anywhere within PowerPoint, choose File⇨New.

2. Select any template from the New Presentation dialog box — you're modifying it to suit your needs anyway.

You may want to select a template that most closely resembles the new template that you want to create. Doing so helps reduce the amount of tweaking you have to do to the template. Choosing a Blank template lets you design everything from scratch.

3. Click Cancel in the Add New Slide dialog box.

4. Modify the template by choosing View⇨Master from the Menu bar, and then choosing any or all Masters that you want to change.

You may wish to format text fonts and point sizes, adjust the background color, or add thematic pictures or logos to each Master.

5. Save your newly created template by choosing File⇨Save from the Menu bar.

Store your new template in the same folder as the other PowerPoint templates so that you know where to look when trying to retrieve it. Your PowerPoint templates are probably stored in Program Files⇨Microsoft Office⇨Templates. Choose a subfolder within Templates, or create a new one for your own special creations.

The typical PowerPoint template extension is POT. If you create a new template titled, "Wacky," save it by the name, Wacky.POT in the templates folder. Under Save as Type, select Presentation Template.

The next time you peruse template choices in the Apply Design Template dialog box, you'll see your newly created template appear among the template options.

Chapter 4: Using and Abusing Masters

In PowerPoint 2000, a Master controls the appearance of all the slides in your presentation. And Masters are not optional! Four different types of Master dictate your slide formats, the layout of the presentation's title slide, the look of printed handouts, and finally the format of printed speaker notes. Before you begin to chafe under this oppressive yoke, however, realize that you can rebel and override the formatting of objects for a particular slide. This chapter shows you how to live with Masters and to defy their authority once in a while.

Editing the Slide Master

After applying a template (as explained in Chapter 3), you can make adjustments to it by fiddling with your presentation's Slide Master, which controls all aspects of how slides are constructed: background color; font, size, and color of the text; display of any decorations, borders, or logos; and position of all elements on the slide. If you're creating an original template, you spend lots of time with the Slide Master.

With the exception of the title slide, every slide in your presentation uses the Slide Master format as a layout (unless you specify otherwise). Changing the Slide Master alters every slide in the presentation — adding a polka-dot border to the Master adds a polka-dot border to each and every one of your slides.

Regardless of which fancy colors or decorative elements appear on the Slide Master, every Slide Master contains two text placeholders called the Title Area for AutoLayouts and the Object Area for AutoLayouts. The Title Area for AutoLayouts prescribes how the formatting of slide titles looks, and the Object Area for AutoLayouts prescribes how the formatting of bulleted slide text looks. Any text formatting you apply to these Slide Master text placeholders is applied to text boxes in the same position on slides in the presentation.

If you type specific text in the Title Area or Object Area placeholders, the text doesn't appear on your slides. Placeholder text is shown only as an example of the formatting and placement of text on your slides.

The following list shows you how to modify the Slide Master:

1. **Choose View⇨Master⇨Slide Master from the Menu bar, or press Shift and click the Slide View button to bring up the Slide Master. (See Figure 4-1.)**

2. **Edit the Slide Master as you like.**

   PowerPoint applies text formatting changes to entire paragraphs in the Master — just click anywhere within the paragraph, and your formatting changes apply to the whole shmear. This text formatting on the Master is applied to all paragraphs in the same position on slides throughout your presentation.

3. **Choose View⇨Normal, or click the Normal View button to close the Slide Master and return to Normal view.**

Voilà! Your slides magically morph according to the changes made on the Slide Master.

If the text boxes on your Slide Master are bumping into other Master items (such as clip art), just click each text box and reposition it by dragging it to a new location. Another option is to resize a text box by selecting it (with a single click), and then adjust one of the *handles* that mark the edges of the box. You know you can select a handle when your regular cursor arrow converts to a small double-tipped arrow. After selecting a handle, the double-tipped arrow converts to a small cross (and stays that way) as you resize the box. Adjust the handle by clicking and dragging it to shrink or stretch the text box. To maintain

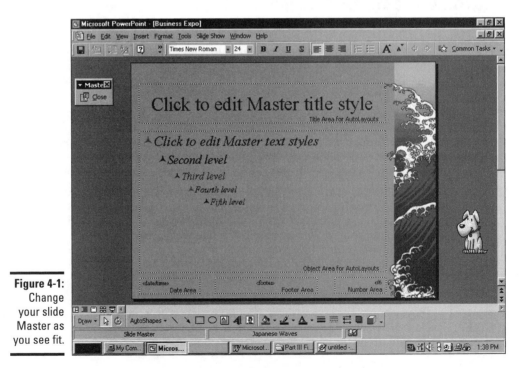

Figure 4-1:
Change your slide Master as you see fit.

the proportions of a text box, hold the shift key down during resizing. (By the way, resizing via the object handles applies not just to text boxes, but to all other objects you add to the Master.)

Inserting headers and footers

PowerPoint gives you an easy method of applying several finishing touches to your presentation in the footer of each slide. The program also allows you to add both headers and footers to notes and handout pages.

1. **From any view, choose View⇨Header and Footer from the Menu bar to bring up the Header and Footer dialog box (shown in Figure 4-2).**

2. **Click either the Slide tab or the Notes and Handouts tab. After working on one tab, you can click the remaining tab to work on it.**

3. **Fill in any of the following boxes:**

- **Date and time:** Displays the date and time. You can choose Update automatically or Fixed. Using Fixed means that whatever date and time you type is used, regardless of what day you actually give the presentation.

- **Slide number (Slide tab only):** Displays the slide number.

- **Page number (Notes and Handouts only):** Displays the page number.

- **Header (Notes and Handouts only):** Displays any recurring text that you want to place at the top of your notes and handouts.

- **Footer:** Displays any other recurring text that you want to place on your slides or notes and handouts.

4. **Click Apply to all to make the changes take effect throughout your presentation.**

On the Slide tab, you can click the checkbox for Don't show on title slide, so that the changes take effect on every slide except the title slide. On the Slide tab you can also click Apply (instead of Apply to all) to make the changes applicable to the current slide only.

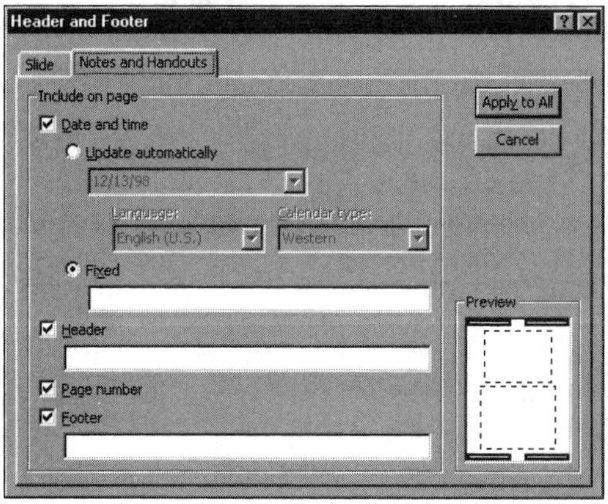

PowerPoint Chapter 4

Using and Abusing Masters

Figure 4-2: The Header and Footer dialog box.

Header and Footer

Slide | Notes and Handouts

Include on page

☑ Date and time
　○ Update automatically
　　12/13/98
　　Language:　Calendar type:
　　English (U.S.)　Western
　⦿ Fixed

☑ Header

☑ Page number
☑ Footer

Apply to All
Cancel

Preview

You can reposition headers and footers anywhere on the slides by switching to the Slide Master, and then dragging the placeholders to new locations. You can also edit the header and footer placeholders directly by displaying the Master, clicking on each placeholder, and typing in your information.

Picking master color schemes

PowerPoint offers incredibly flexible options for tinting your slides. You can fuss with minute details of coloring the masters, but letting PowerPoint serve as your personal designer is a whole lot easier. You can even choose a different color scheme for each master.

1. **Choose View⇨Master from the Menu bar and select the master on which you wish to change the color scheme.**

2. **Choose Format⇨Color Scheme to bring up the Color Scheme dialog box for the selected master.**

3. **Choose an option:**

> **To pick a PowerPoint color scheme:** Click the Standard tab and double-click a scheme you like. You can also single-click a scheme, and then click Preview to decide whether you really want to apply the scheme.

> **To change the colors of individual scheme elements:** Click the Custom tab, double-click any element in the Color Scheme dialog box, and choose a new color.

4. **Click Apply to use the new scheme only on the current slide, notes page, or handout page; or click Apply to All to change all slides, notes pages, or handouts in your entire presentation.**

Shading background colors

You can also change the shading of a slide's background color to obtain a richer feel than you achieve with just plain old brown or plain old orange. How impressed do you think your audience will be? To alter background shading, follow these steps without fail:

1. **From any view except Slide Show view, choose Format⇨Background from the menu bar to summon the Background dialog box.**

2. **Click the color drop-down menu and select Fill Effects to open the Fill Effects dialog box (as shown in Figure 4-3).**

3. **Click the Gradient tab and click one or two colors, along with a Shading style.**

The Shading style allows you to choose how your selected colors blend together on the slide backgrounds: horizontally, vertically, or in some other combination.

The Fill Effects dialog box also has Texture, Pattern, and Picture tabs.

• **Texture:** Try out several of the textures as backgrounds — some of them are absolutely beautiful!

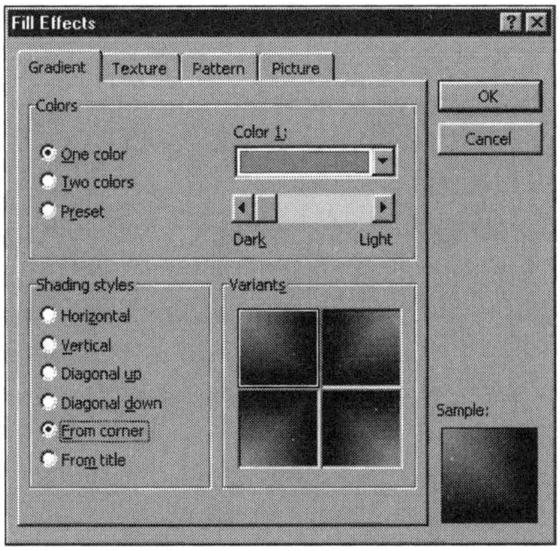

Figure 4-3:
The Fill
Effects
dialog box.

- **Pattern:** As a general rule, you should stay away from using patterns on the background; they make text extremely hard to read.

- **Picture:** Be cautious about using imported pictures, which can also create readability problems. Use background pictures only when they don't compete with text that appears on top of the picture.

Deleting Master components

Deleting an object on the Slide Master is a snap. You can delete thousands and thousands without ever tiring.

1. **Retrieve the Slide Master by choosing View⇨Master⇨Slide Master from the menu bar or press Shift and click the Slide View button.**

2. **Click the object that you want to delete. To wipe out an entire text object, first click anywhere on the text; then click again on the object frame.**

3. **Press the Backspace or Delete key, choose Edit⁄Cut, or click the Cut button on the Standard toolbar.**

You can't move or edit Slide Master elements from the slides themselves. You don't want to waste time trying to delete a theme picture on Slide #7 only to realize (after much frustration) that you can't grab the darn thing because it's not on the slide — it's on the Slide Master.

Editing the Title Master

You can add a Title slide to your presentation by switching to Slide Sorter view and adding a new slide to the left of Slide #1. Choose the Title Slide AutoLayout in the New Slide dialog box. PowerPoint provides you with a separate Title Master for designing title slides. The idea is that you can use it to format your title slide differently than the rest of your slide presentation.

1. **In Slide view or Normal view, move to the first slide in your presentation (assuming that the first slide is the title slide).**

2. **Choose View⇨Master⇨Title Master.**

The Title Master appears (see Figure 4-4).

3. **Alter the Title Master to your heart's content.**

4. **Click the Slide View or Normal View button to return to your first slide — your title slide — and examine how it looks.**

Editing the Handout Master

The Handout Master allows you to lay out the appearance of your presentation as a hard-copy audience handout. You have the following two options for your handouts:

✦ **The presentation outline:** Your handouts show only a collapsed outline of your presentation material.

✦ **Small versions of the presentation slides:** This option shows the full text of your handouts in miniature. You can choose how many slide images appear on the printed page. You have the option of 2, 3, 4, 6, or 9 slides per page.

You also have the option of adding placeholders on the Handout Master for the following items:

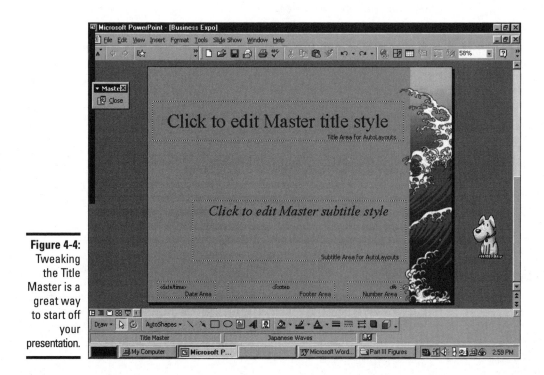

Figure 4-4:
Tweaking the Title Master is a great way to start off your presentation.

✦ **Headers and footers:** Headers are placed at the top of the handouts, and footers are placed at the bottom. You can click on the placeholder for any header or footer to change the font, format, and content of the text contained within that placeholder.

✦ **Date or page number:** These fields are automatically updated.

To format the Handout Master for your presentation, follow these steps:

1. **From any view, Choose View⇨Master⇨Handout Master.**

The Handout Master appears, as shown in Figure 4-5.

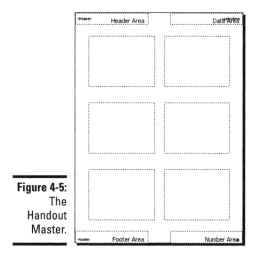

Figure 4-5:
The
Handout
Master.

2. **Right-click the mouse to open the Handout Master Layout dialog box.**

3. **At the Handout Master Layout dialog box, click the selection box for all the placeholders that you want located on the Master.**

Placeholders already in use are deselected and show checkmarks in their checkboxes. Click OK to close the Handout Master Layout dialog box.

4. **At the Handout Master toolbox, click whether you want 2, 3, 4, 6 or 9 slides per page, or the presentation outline shown on the handouts.**

The Handout Master generates dashed outlines showing where the slides or outline are printed. (If you inadvertently close the Handout Master toolbar or it does not otherwise appear onscreen, you can make it rematerialize by choosing View⇨Toolbars⇨Handout Master.)

When you are finished formatting the Handout Master, click on any view button to return to your presentation. You may want to print and peruse your handouts by choosing File⇨Print from the Menu bar.

Editing the Notes Master

Notes pages are printed pages that you — the speaker — create to remind yourself what you want to say about each slide during your presentation. Notes pages are also referred to as Speaker Notes, and are typically used only by the speaker giving the PowerPoint presentation — not for distribution to participating audiences.

Notes can be added to a slide by typing in the notes pane of a slide in Normal view. To add notes in Slide Sorter view, you click the slide where you want to add notes, press the Speaker Notes button on the Slide Sorter toolbar, and type your text in the Speaker Notes dialog box that appears.

Overriding the Master Style on a Single Slide

You can disregard the master format for a particular slide, which allows you to modify individual slides as needed without altering the rest of your presentation. The processes of adding and moving text and objects on an individual slide are the same as those you use to alter the master slides.

Changing the text formatting

Suppose you created 9 slides that lead to a critical, culminating key point, and to ensure that every participant's brain captures and processes this super-important key point, you want to use bright gold, italic, 60-point Impact — but just on this one slide. Use the following steps to make changes to the Master style of text on one particular slide:

1. **Move to the slide where you want to make the change.**

2. **Switch to Normal view or Slide view.**

3. **Click the text box and select (highlight) the text that you want to edit. Use the Formatting toolbar to make your changes.**

Changing the background color

If you want to change the background color on a single slide, just follow these steps:

1. **In any view, move to the slide where you want to use a different background.**

2. **Choose Format⇨Background to bring up the Background dialog box.**

3. **Click the color drop-down arrow to reveal a menu for changing the background color to your preference.**

4. **Click the Apply button to make the changes on the current slide.**

Do *not* click the Apply to all button, or every slide in your presentation is affected. However, clicking the Apply to all button at this stage is a convenient way of editing the Slide Master without opening up the Master itself.

Chapter 5: Adding Text to Your Presentation

In This Chapter

- ✔ Getting to know text boxes
- ✔ Aligning and indenting text
- ✔ Finding and replacing text
- ✔ Spell-checking your text

*U*nless you plan to have a 100 percent visual presentation without diluting your message with that imperfect thing we call text, you've opened to the right chapter. However imperfect our language may be, we need to resort to the written word in order to convey some things that pretty pictures just can't express. In this chapter, you discover how to add text to your presentation in creative and meaningful ways. And if you happen to err once in a while when adding your text, PowerPoint 2000 also has ways to help you.

Who knows? People may stop looking at your pretty pictures long enough to actually read what you've written. In this case, you need to be prepared.

About Text Boxes

All slides — the Slide Master, the Title Master, and all slide AutoLayouts except the Blank slide option — appear with at least one *text box* (a zone reserved for adding text).

You can do with your text just about anything that you can do in a word-processing program such as Office 2000. You may want to check out the Word 2000 section of this book for extra help. This section gives you some of the most common procedures you probably need to do to a PowerPoint slide.

Adding text boxes

You can add as many text boxes to a slide as you like. Each text box can be formatted and moved independently from all the other text boxes. To add a text box, just follow these steps:

1. **In Slide view or Normal view, click the Text Box button on the Drawing toolbar.**

2. **Point the I-beam cursor to the position on your slide where you want the upper-left corner of your new text box.**

3. **Click and hold the mouse as you drag the cursor to position the lower-right corner of your new text box.**

   The cursor appears as a crosshair during the positioning, and you see solid edges appear as the borders of the box.

4. **Release the mouse button after you give the text box the desired proportions.**

The new text box is now complete. Click inside the box to type text, or click the edge of the box to format how text appears inside the box.

Selecting text boxes to modify

Before you can modify a text box (such as moving or resizing it), you have to identify for PowerPoint which text box you want to work on. To select a text box:

1. **In Slide view or Normal view, click the Select Objects button on the Drawing toolbar.**

2. **Point the arrow anywhere along the border of the text box that you want to edit; then click the left mouse button.**

   The text box suddenly sprouts *handles* — dots marking the corners and sides of the box (see Figure 5-1). The appearance of handles indicates that the text box is selected.

Text box

Figure 5-1:
A selected
section of
text.

• 1/2 tomato
• 1/8 clove garlic ———— Side handle
• salt to taste

———— Corner handle

Resizing or moving text boxes

After you select a text box, you're free to resize and move the box as you want. Go wild! And follow these simple guidelines along the way:

✦ **To move a text box:** Click and hold down the mouse button anywhere along the edge of the text box — except on a handle! Drag the box anywhere on the slide and release the mouse button.

✦ **To change the size of a text box while keeping the original proportions:** Click and hold down the mouse button on any of the corner handles, drag the handle to enlarge or shrink the text box proportionally, and then release the mouse button. To keep the center of the box positioned in the same spot during resizing, hold down the Ctrl key while dragging a sizing handle.

✦ **To change the proportions of a text box:** Click and hold down the mouse button on any of the side handles. Drag the top or bottom handle to increase or decrease the text box's height; drag the left or right handle to adjust the width.

Moving around and typing inside a text box

Remember that you type and edit text in a PowerPoint text box in virtually the same way that you use a word processor. But first you have to tell PowerPoint that you want to manipulate the text:

1. **Click the Select Objects button on the Drawing toolbar.**

2. **Click inside the text box.**

A thick border appears around the text box, a solid background color appears behind the text, and the arrow changes to an I-beam inside the text box — all of which indicate that you can now start typing.

**PowerPoint
Chapter 5**

**Adding Text to Your
Presentation**

You need to know the following tips about typing and editing in a text box:

✦ When you reach the end of a line, keep typing — PowerPoint automatically moves to the next line. You press Enter only when you want to begin a new paragraph.

✦ If you attempt to type more text than can fit in your text box, PowerPoint automatically adjusts the point size of the text to fit the box.

✦ Use the ↑, ↓, ←, and → keys on your keyboard to move the cursor up or down one line, or left or right one character.

✦ Move the mouse until the little I-beam is positioned where you want to make an edit, and then click the left mouse button. The I-beam cursor instantly repositions itself to your chosen destination.

✦ To delete text, first highlight the text to be deleted and then press the Backspace key or the Delete key to delete the text.

Aligning Paragraphs of Text

Adjust the way your text lines up by selecting an entire text box or selecting only specific lines of text within a text box. Then choose Format⇨Alignment from the Menu bar or click the appropriate toolbar button to align your selected text. PowerPoint provides you with several ways to align text on your slides:

✦ **Centered:** Multiple slides on the same topic can have the title centered on the first slide and deleted altogether on all subsequent, related slides.

✦ **Left-aligned:** For bulleted body text and short sentences, use left alignment, which lines up text neatly against the left edge of the text box.

✦ **Right-aligned:** For something different, try right alignment, which lines up text neatly down the right-hand side of the text box.

✦ **Justified:** Justified text alignment centers text in the box and also lines up each edge of the text.

Finding and Replacing Text

The Find and Replace commands are helpful when you need to change one piece of text that appears several times throughout your slides — for example, the date on a series of slides from a long-ago presentation that you want to reuse.

1. **Choose Edit⇨Find from the Menu bar or Press Ctrl+F to bring up the Find dialog box (shown in Figure 5-2).**

2. **In the Find area, type the text that you want to locate.**

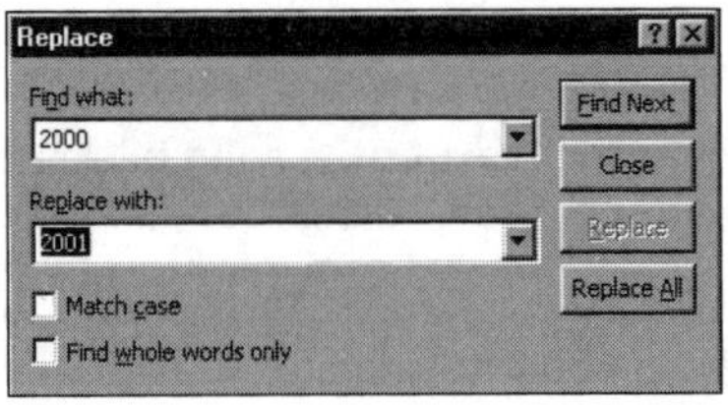

Figure 5-2:
The Find
dialog box.

If you're looking for an exact match of capital and lowercase letters, click the Match case box. If you want to locate only whole words — not pieces of larger words (like cat in catalog) — click the Find whole words only box.

3. **Press Enter to start the search.**

If your chosen text is located anywhere among your slides, the Find command moves to the first slide containing that text. It also highlights your found text so that you can then edit it or continue searching for the next occurrence.

4. **If you want to replace your found text with something else, click the Replace button. A Replace dialog box appears. In the Replace with area, type your replacement text. Then press Replace to replace just the current instance of your found text, or press Replace All to replace every instance of your found text.**

5. **When you're done finding (or replacing) text, click Close to get rid of the Find dialog box.**

If you already know that you want to replace all instances of a given word — like substituting next year's date for this year's date — use the Replace command instead of Find by following these steps:

1. **Choose Edit⇨Replace from the Menu bar to call up the Replace dialog box.**

2. **In the Find what area, type the word or phrase that you want to replace.**

3. **In the Replace with area, type your replacement text.**

4. **Click the Replace All button.**

Every instance of the sought-after text changes to the replacement text.

Spell-Checking

Correct spelling is vital in everything you communicate to your audience. If you're going to go to the effort of creating crisp, professional slides, you may as well make sure your text is spelled correctly. Besides, nothing is more embarrassing than misspelling a word and displaying your error to a roomful of watchful colleagues.

After typing all your text, summon the spell checker to look for spelling mistakes throughout the document by following these steps:

1. Choose Tools⇨Spelling from the Menu bar or click the Spelling button on the Standard toolbar.

When PowerPoint finds an error, the program shows the faulty slide and highlights the potentially misspelled word. PowerPoint also recommends possible corrections for your error (see Figure 5-3).

2. Accept one of PowerPoint's corrections and click the Change button, click Ignore to leave the word as it is, or type in your own correction.

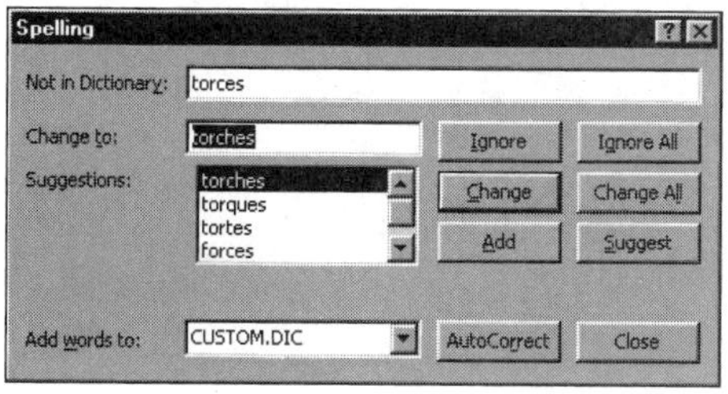

Figure 5-3:
PowerPoint
tries its
best to
help.

If PowerPoint red-flags a word that you know is spelled correctly, click Ignore All to have PowerPoint ignore that word throughout the presentation.

If you know that you misspelled a certain word throughout the presentation, click the Change All button and correct all instances of your error in one fell swoop.

For any red-flagged misspelled word, you can type your own correction into the Change To area and press the Change button. This is a useful option when none of the suggested changes are correct spellings for your word.

3. Repeat Steps 1 and 2 until PowerPoint informs you that the spelling check is complete.

PowerPoint can also perform spell check on-the-fly as does Word 2000. You can actually see your misspellings signaled before your very eyes — which is a very humbling experience. Be sure to check out the spell check on-the-fly function in the Word 2000 minibook.

**PowerPoint
Chapter 5**

**Adding Text to Your
Presentation**

REAL WORLD

Using the Internet to get PowerPoint information

PowerPoint also offers help via the Internet by providing a direct link to Microsoft's Office Update Web site. But you need to have an Internet connection to use this nifty feature! To use online help, choose <u>H</u>elp⇨Office on the <u>W</u>eb from the menu bar. Choosing this help option launches your Web browser and transports you directly to a Web site called Office Update. Many support features are available from the Office Update Web site, but you may find these two areas most worthwhile to visit:

✔ **Search:** This area is a searchable database of technical information about all of Microsoft's programs, PowerPoint included. Office Update Search serves a similar role as PowerPoint's Help feature, but the online information is much more comprehensive and up-to-date.

✔ **Home⇨PowerPoint:** Choosing Home from the Office Update page leads you to a page

where you can get information on any Microsoft program. Choosing PowerPoint from the Home page takes you to the following helpful areas:

✔ **Assistance:** Includes extra clip art, FAQs, and Newsgroups. FAQs are "Frequently Asked Questions" — and answers — most commonly posed regarding PowerPoint. This is a good place to go if you believe you're asking something that many other people have probably asked at some point.

✔ **Newsgroups:** Provides access to Microsoft-sponsored Internet discussion groups about PowerPoint. This area is ideal for asking the quirky questions you believe may require an expert to figure out. Simply post a question to the group, and a few hours (or days) later, someone in the know will respond with an answer.

Chapter 6: Making Your Text Look Presentable

In This Chapter

✔ Formatting text with color, fonts, and more

✔ Making a numbered list

✔ Making a bullet list

So you've added text to a presentation and still nobody bothers to read it? That's because you may have forgotten that people, if they must read, at least like to read text that *looks* good. Fortunately for you, PowerPoint 2000 makes it easy for you to surpass the talents of many 17th-century typesetters who actually had to do this stuff the hard way! You can have your text jazzed up in no time.

Formatting Text

The fastest way to format text for an entire presentation is to format text in the text boxes located on the Slide and Title Masters. Text on all slides in the presentation follows this formatting, eliminating the need for you to format text on a slide-by-slide basis. Individual text boxes on any slide can be reformatted as needed, overriding the formatting prescribed for them by the masters.

Changing the overall look of text

To adjust the way your text looks (the formatting), highlight the text and then choose one of the following methods:

✦ Open the Font dialog box, which offers one-stop shopping for any and all formatting features, by choosing Format⇨Font from the Menu bar or by clicking the right mouse button and then clicking Font on the shortcut menu. (See Figure 6-1.)

✦ Click a button on the Text Formatting toolbar to change a single formatting feature.

✦ Use a keyboard shortcut to change a formatting feature (see Table 6-1).

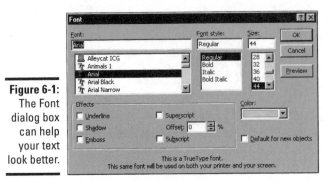

Figure 6-1:
The Font
dialog box
can help
your text
look better.

Table 6-1 **Keyboard Shortcuts to Formatting**

Keyboard Shortcut	Format or Function
Ctrl+B	**Bold**
Ctrl+I	*Italic*
Ctrl+U	Underline
Ctrl+spacebar	Normal (remove formatting)
Ctrl+Shift+F	Font
Ctrl+Shift+P	Highlights the current point size in the Font Size list box on the Standard toolbar. Typing a new number and pressing Enter changes the size of the currently selected text.
Ctrl+Shift+>	Increase point size
Ctrl+Shift+<	Decrease point size

To reset the point size of selected text, click the Font Size area on the Formatting toolbar and type a new point size in the box. Alternatively, you may press the arrow attached to the Font Size area to reveal a drop-down list of point size choices.

Note: Ctrl+spacebar clears font attributes, such as bold and underline, but it doesn't reset the font or point size of your text.

Changing capitalization for blocks of text

To quickly change the capitalization of text — a single character or a block of text — follow these steps:

1. **Highlight the text that you want to capitalize.**

2. **Choose Format⇨Change Case from the Menu bar to summon the Change Case dialog box (shown in Figure 6-2).**

3. **Choose a capitalization option from the Change Case menu and click OK.**

- **Sentence case:** The first letter of the first word in each sentence is capitalized. All other text is changed to lowercase.

Figure 6-2:
The cute
Change
Case
dialog box.

Change Case

- Sentence case.
- lowercase
- UPPERCASE
- Title Case
- tOGGLE cASE

OK

Cancel

- **lowercase:** All text is changed to lowercase.

- **UPPERCASE:** All text is changed to uppercase.

- **Title Case:** The first letter of each word is capitalized except for articles, such as *a* and *the*.

- **tOGGLE cASE:** Uppercase letters are changed to lowercase and vice versa. The toggle case option comes in handy when you discover you've been typing away with the Caps Lock key on.

Color

Change the color of highlighted text by clicking the Font Color button on the Drawing toolbar and clicking a color from the palette that appears.

If the font colors that pop up don't suffice, click on More Font Colors for even more color choices. If these colors don't meet your needs either, click the Custom tab and create the one and only perfect shade that you're searching for by clicking in the spectrum of Colors and pressing OK.

Font

To change the font of highlighted text, click the arrow next to the Font box on the Formatting toolbar and choose a font from the drop-down selection list that appears. You can also select a new font in the Font dialog box by choosing Format⇨Font from the Menu bar. Remember to first mark the text destined for change or to select the text box where the text is located.

PowerPoint places the fonts you use most frequently at the beginning of the font list so that you don't waste time scrolling through the list.

Shadows

Shadowing text adds a touch of class to your slides. It may also improve readability for some slides by making text characters stand out against their PowerPoint background. Apply a shadow to selected text by clicking the Text Shadow button located on the Formatting toolbar.

Size

To change the size of highlighted text, click the Font Size box on the Formatting toolbar; then click a preset point size (sizes range from 8 points to 96 points) or type in the point size you desire.

Numbering Lists

PowerPoint offers a quick and easy way to number items in a list, to change numbering styles from Arabic to Roman numbers, and to change numbers to a lettered outline.

1. **Highlight the lines or paragraphs of text that you want to number.**

Text items must be separated by paragraph returns in ordered to be given separate numbers.

2. **Click the Numbering button on the Formatting toolbar.**

The Numbering button toggles so that clicking it again removes numbering from the text.

To select the type of numbering you want, choose Format➪Bullets and Numbering from the Menu bar to call up the Bullets and Numbering dialog box. In the Bullets and Numbering dialog box, select the Numbered tab and choose the size and color of your numbers, and the starting number. (Clicking None removes numbering from the selected text.)

Numbered lists are automatically renumbered when you change the order of items in the list.

Bulleting Text

A bullet marks the start of a line to indicate a new text item. Bullets come in many styles, including spots, check marks, and arrows — but they're almost never shaped like real-life bullets.

1. **Select the lines or paragraphs of text that you want to bullet.**

Each bullet must be separated by a paragraph return. For example, if you want a bulleted list of three text items, make sure those three items are separated by paragraph returns.

2. **Click the Bullets button.**

The Bullets button operates like an on/off switch (a toggle). Following these steps adds bullets to unbulleted text; repeating the steps removes the bullets.

If you don't like the style of the bullets that appear on-screen, choose Format➪ Bullets and Numbering from the Menu bar to call up the Bullets and Numbering dialog box. In the Bullets and Numbering dialog box, you can select a default bullet character and adjust its font, size and color. (Clicking None "unbullets" the bulleted text.)

Chapter 7: Getting Visual

In This Chapter

✓ Getting to know the Drawing toolbar

✓ Making all sorts of lines

✓ Adding WordArt

✓ Using clip art

You've worked long hours on your new presentation. The lights go out, and your slide presentation has begun. Ten minutes into your presentation, however, you notice that the lights aren't the only things that have been extinguished. Your audience is also out — lost who knows where and obviously not absorbing anything from your presentation. So what if you have the neatest looking text in town (see Chapter 6). Sometimes you have to go even further to keep your audience alert. Get down and get visual!

In this chapter, you find out about the basics of getting your presentation looking better with some graphic elements. Remember, you don't necessarily need to replace your text. You simply need to complement it so that your message stands out even better.

About the Drawing Toolbar

Each button or menu on the Drawing toolbar offers a unique tool to assist you in creating something Picasso-esque.

The Drawing toolbar can be used in both Normal and Slide views. Summon the Drawing toolbar by selecting View⇨Toolbars⇨Drawing from the Menu bar. You can use the buttons in Table 7-1 to create your drawings.

Table 7-1	Drawing Toolbar Buttons
Button	*Name*
Draw ▾	Draw menu button
↖	Select Objects button
↻	Free Rotate button

(continued)

Table 7-1 *(continued)*

Button	Name
AutoShapes ▾	AutoShapes menu button
	Line button
	Arrow button
	Rectangle button
	Oval button
	Text box button
	Insert WordArt button
	Insert Clip Art button
	Fill Color button
	Line Color button
	Font Color button
	Line Style button
	Dash Style button
	Arrow Style button
	Shadow button
	3-D button

Drawing Lines

So you think lines are boring? You should know that PowerPoint allows you to make your mark using a variety of different line styles.

Straight lines: These steps show you how to draw a straight line:

1. **Click the Line button on the Drawing toolbar, or choose AutoShapes⇨Lines, and then click the Line button.**

2. **Click and hold the mouse where you want the line to start.**

3. **Drag the mouse to create a line of the desired length and position, and release the mouse when you reach the end of the line.**

Curved lines: To draw a curved line, just do this:

1. **On the Drawing toolbar, select AutoShapes⇨Lines, and then click the Curve button.**

2. **Click your slide where you want the curve to start; then start drawing.**

3. **Click each time you want to create a turn or bend in your line (you can add as many turns as you want).**

4. **Double-click to end the line.**

Double-clicking in close proximity to your starting point creates a closed figure.

Freehand lines: To draw a freehand (squiggly) line, give this a go:

1. **On the Drawing toolbar, select AutoShapes⇨Lines, and then click the Scribble button.**

2. **Click and drag the mouse to create your line.**

3. **Release the mouse button to end the line.**

Changing line style

After you draw a line, you can change its style — making it thin or thick, solid or dashed, and with or without arrows. To set line style, click the line that you want to change. Then click one of the following buttons on the Drawing toolbar:

✦ **Line Style button:** When you click the Line Style button on the drawing toolbar, a line style menu appears. You can choose a new thickness, or select the More Lines command, which provides you with millions of other choices in a dialog box.

✦ **Dash Style button:** Choose a new dash style if you want to use something other than a solid line. The Dash Style button on the Drawing toolbar opens a menu that lets you select whether your line appear as a series of dots, short dashes, long dashes, or dots alternating with dashes. Sort of like Morse code!

✦ **Arrow Style button:** Choose arrows as end points for your line. Click the Arrow Style button on the Drawing toolbar to call up a menu including a More Arrows command that provides additional arrow options.

Drawing with AutoShapes

Selecting the PowerPoint AutoShapes menu from the Drawing toolbar produces a pop-up list from which you can choose predrawn line styles and common shapes, like hexagons, banners, moons, and flowchart arrows.

1. **Select the AutoShapes menu on the Drawing toolbar.**

A veritable shopping mall of shape selections appears (see Figure 7-1).

Figure 7-1:
You can go
crazy with
AutoShapes.

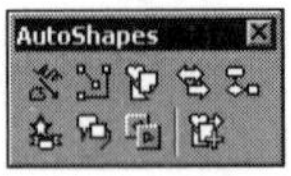

2. **Select the AutoShapes category that you want:**

   • **Lines:** Every type of line from straight to swervy. You can also build closed-line figures here.

   • **Connectors:** Line segments with strangely shaped end points. Commonly used for road maps and electrical circuits.

   • **Basic Shapes:** Hearts, moons, and parallelograms. Get yer Lucky Charms here, laddy!

   • **Block Arrows:** Directions such as north, south, and U-turn.

   • **Flowchart:** Directional signs which track the flow of money from the wallets of your consumers, into the profit pool of your company, and out to the wallets of your shareholders.

   • **Stars and Banners:** For patriots and American history teachers.

   • **Callouts:** You can type text inside these shapes; the text may describe an image the shape is pointing to or represents what the image is saying or thinking.

   • **Action Buttons:** Navigation icons for slide-show and Web-based presentations. Some of these little guys resemble buttons on your VCR.

   • **More AutoShapes:** Summons the Microsoft Clip Gallery where you can obtain additional AutoShapes.

3. **Click a shape featured in the category.**

4. **Create your chosen shape by clicking your slide and dragging the mouse until your AutoShapes clip reaches the desired size.**

   To maintain the same height-to-width proportions when you resize an AutoShapes clip, hold down the Shift key as you drag the mouse.

5. **Release the mouse button to finish creating your AutoShapes clip.**

Adding WordArt

WordArt is a nifty feature that allows you to place fancy, three-dimensional, shadowed text on your slides. The text can even be given a perspective quality, as if you're standing at the H looking toward the rest of the letters in the HOLLYWOOD sign.

Because WordArt clips don't function like editable text, they don't appear in Outline view and they can't be spell-checked.

To add a WordArt clip to a slide, follow these steps:

1. **On the Drawing toolbar, click the WordArt button.**

The WordArt Gallery dialog box appears, as shown in Figure 7-2.

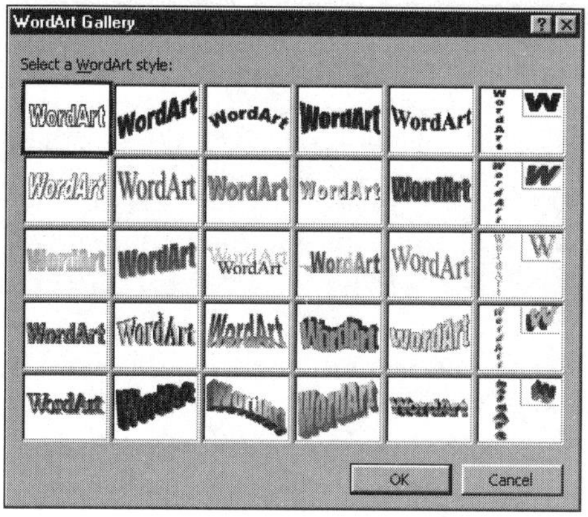

Figure 7-2:
The
WordArt
choices are
overwhelming.

2. **Click the thumbnail representing the WordArt style that you want to use, and click OK.**

An Edit WordArt Text dialog box appears, as shown in Figure 7-3.

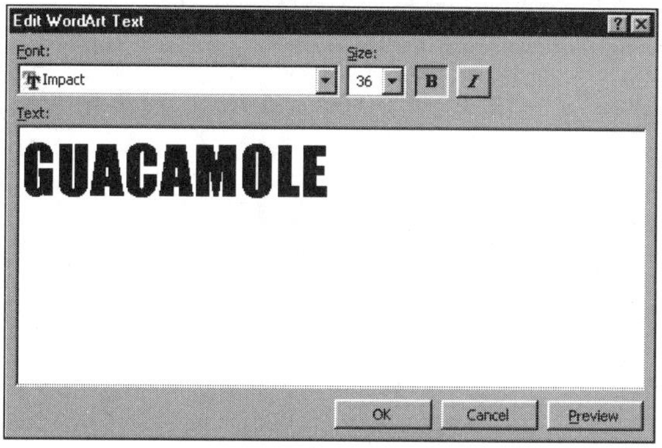

Figure 7-3:
Guacamole
is ready for
manipulation.

3. **In the Edit WordArt Text dialog box, type your text, select a font and point size, and choose bold or italic formatting options. Click OK.**

The WordArt text is placed on your slide.

To edit your WordArt, use the tools on the Drawing toolbar. For additional WordArt editing tools, select <u>V</u>iew⇨<u>T</u>oolbars⇨WordArt from the Menu bar, and the WordArt toolbar appears. The WordArt toolbar offers several tools for editing your WordArt clip.

About Clips

PowerPoint refers to multimedia goodies — things you put on your slides besides text — as multimedia clips, or just clips. Clips can include simple drawings, graphic images (clip art and photos), sounds, or movies — all of which serve to enhance the content and quality of your presentation.

Using clips from the Clip Gallery

The PowerPoint Clip Gallery is a valuable resource, with thousands of free, high-quality pictures, sounds, and movies. It's neatly organized into such categories as Animals, Business, Maps, Photographs, and Transportation, and it provides a helpful little thumbnail sketch of each clip. You can also use the Search for clips feature to look for specific clips. The following steps show you how drop in a clip from the Microsoft Gallery:

1. **Move to the slide where you want to add a clip. If you want your clip to appear on all your slides, move to the Slide Master by choosing View⇨Master⇨Slide Master from the Menu bar.**

2. **Click the Insert Clip Art button on the Drawing toolbar to bring up the Insert Clip Art dialog box (see Figure 7-4).**

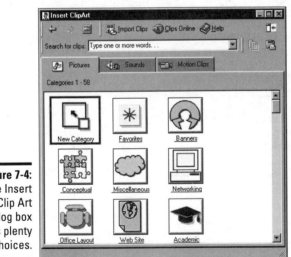

Figure 7-4:
The Insert
Clip Art
dialog box
has plenty
of choices.

3. **Click a tab — pictures, sounds or movies — and scroll through the clips until you locate one you want. Or type in the Search for clips area to look for specific characteristics.**

4. **When you settle on a clip, click it once to select it.**

A border appears around the clip, along with a menu of options pertaining to your selected clip.

Need more clips?

When the Clip Gallery collection becomes dull and passé, PowerPoint offers users a resource called Clip Gallery Live, which includes more free multimedia clips, frequently updated and downloadable off the Internet. To access it, just click the Clips Online button in the Insert ClipArt dialog box. Clip Gallery Live works the same way that the regular Clip Gallery does. And when you click a filename to select a clip, that clip is downloaded from the Internet and added as a permanent resident to your Clip Gallery.

5. **To place the clip on your slide, click the Insert clip button.**

PowerPoint places the clip in the middle of your slide. You may need to move it to a more favorable position. To do so, just click it and drag it to your chosen destination. You may also need to resize the image.

Lining up clips with guides

PowerPoint provides a set of horizontal and vertical crosshairs that aid you in lining up clips on your slides. These guides serve the same helpful purpose as grid lines on a sheet of graph paper. When you drag a clip close to a guide, the clip automatically aligns its edge to fit snuggly against the guide. When you drag a clip close to the intersection of two guides, the clip automatically aligns its center at the guides' point of intersection.

If you're working in Normal view or Slide view, activate the guides by choosing View⇨Guides from the Menu bar. The guides are initially positioned so that they cross at the geometric center of the slide. See Figure 7-5. Each guide may be moved by clicking on it and dragging it to a new position.

You can add a new guide by clicking an existing guide, pressing Ctrl, and dragging the new guide away. You can delete a guide by dragging it toward the edge of the slide: After it reaches the edge, it vanishes.

✦ To automatically align clips with guides, click Draw⇨Snap⇨To Grid on the Drawing toolbar.

✦ To automatically align objects with guides that run through the horizontal and vertical edges of other shapes, click Draw⇨Snap⇨To Shape on the Drawing toolbar.

Moving and resizing clips

PowerPoint adds clips to your slides the same way that the cafeteria worker adds food to your tray in the buffet line: glopped down smack dab in the middle. You may want to move your clip to a more appetizing location, as well as stretch or shrink it to fit nicely on your slide.

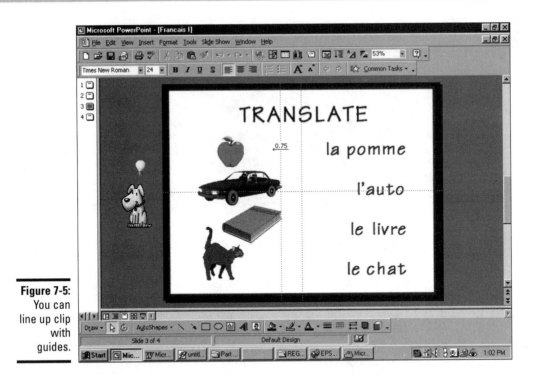

Figure 7-5:
You can
line up clip
with
guides.

When you insert a clip, it appears on your screen as a selected clip — with resizing handles surrounding it like a picture frame. If you click outside the clip, the handles vanish. Click the clip once to make handles reappear. Handles must be visible to move and resize your clip.

+ **Move the clip:** Click it once and drag it to a new spot.

+ **Enlarge the clip:** Click a corner handle and drag the handle outwards from the clip.

+ **Shrink the clip:** Click a corner handle and drag the handle in toward the clip.

+ **Make the clip taller or shorter without changing the width:** Click a top or bottom center handle and drag the handle up or down.

+ **Make the clip wider or narrower without changing the height:** Click a left or right center handle and drag the handle horizontally.

Chapter 8: Manipulating Your Multimedia

In This Chapter

↙ **Getting to know multimedia possibilities**

↙ **Adding images to your presentation**

↙ **Adding sound and movies**

*M*ultimedia is a magic word. Tell someone that your presentation incorporates multimedia elements and you'll perk up some interest. (Tell the same person that your presentation involves a lot of reading black text on a white background and notice the difference in reactions.) Text and pictures are fine, sure, but sounds and even movies are the icing on the cake. Perhaps your lecture on New Zealand cinema can have a few film clips. Or maybe your outlining of the new Human Resources policies at the next staff meeting can have sounds of employees cheering and clapping.

Of course, you don't want to overdo it, but just a little effort with multimedia can place you in the ranks of the great high-tech presenters.

Adding Pictures: Clip Art and Photos

Pictures take the form of either clip art or photos:

✦ **Clip art:** Line drawings are composed of lines, ovals, squares, and all sorts of other shapes. The component shapes of a clip-art image are electronically glued together (in other words, *grouped*) to form the final piece of clip art. A piece of clip art can be broken down into its individual shapes, and each of these shapes can be edited separately.

✦ **Photos:** Images are comprised of rows and columns of colored dots (called *pixels*). Photos cannot be separated into their component elements, except with a photo-editing program, like PhotoShop.

You can find pictures in the Clip Gallery that comes with PowerPoint, the Clip Gallery Live that PowerPoint users can access on the Internet, and clip-art collections that you can buy in stores or find on the Internet. PowerPoint allows you to include a wide selection of graphics file formats in your presentations.

The following steps tell you how to add a piece of clip art or a photo from the Clip Gallery or from a file to your slide:

1. **In Slide or Normal view, move to the slide where you want to add a picture.**

2. **Choose Insert⇨Picture⇨Clip Art from the Menu bar or click the Insert Clip Art button on the Drawing toolbar.**

   To insert something from a file, choose Insert⇨Picture⇨From File from the Menu bar.

   For clip art, an Insert Clip Art dialog box appears with the Pictures tab selected. For other art, an Insert Picture dialog box appears.

3. **Find and click on the picture you want to add and click Insert Clip or click OK.**

4. **(Optional) Resize the picture and reposition it by dragging it to a new location.**

Adding Polygons and Freeform Shapes

For those occasions when a regular ol' square or circle just doesn't cut it, you may want to create a more elaborate polygon or even a wild freeform shape. Create such beasts using the following steps:

1. **On the Drawing toolbar, choose AutoShapes⇨Lines. A palette of line types appears. Click the Freeform button.**

2. **Click your slide at the spot where you want to start drawing your object.**

3. **Release the mouse button and drag the mouse to form a straight line segment, or hold the mouse button down and drag to draw freehand.**

4. **If you want to draw a straight line segment, click the mouse button to create a corner and redirect your line.**

   If you're drawing freehand, release the mouse button to create a corner and redirect your line.

5. **Complete your shape by double-clicking.**

   Double-clicking in close proximity to your starting point forms a closed figure. Otherwise, you form an open figure.

Adding Rectangles, Squares, Ovals, and Circles

PowerPoint lets you create all sorts of rectangles, squares, ovals, and circles like those shown in Figure 8-1. To draw a rectangular (or square) or oval (or circular) shape, follow the steps that are generously provided here.

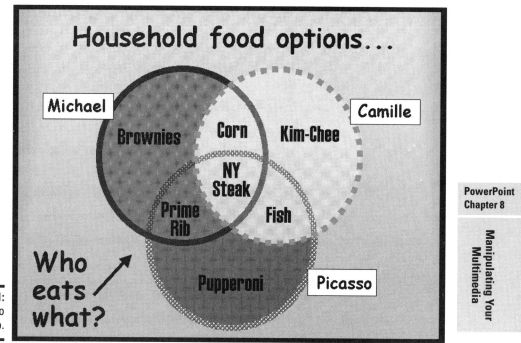

**PowerPoint
Chapter 8**

Manipulating Your
Multimedia

Figure 8-1:
You can do
this, too.

1. Click the appropriate button:

- **Rectangle or square:** Click the Rectangle button. To draw a square, hold down the Shift key in Steps 2 and 3.

- **Oval or circle:** Click the Oval button. To draw a circle, hold down the Shift key in Steps 2 and 3.

2. **Click and hold the spot where you want to position the top-left boundary of the shape.**

3. **Drag to create the shape in the size you choose.**

4. **Release the mouse when your shape attains the desired proportions.**

You can adjust the size and dimensions of your shape by clicking the created shape and then grabbing and dragging one of its resizing handles.

Adding Movies and Motion Clips

PowerPoint offers you the option of adding small movies to slides in your presentation. You can also choose to add a special kind of animated movie called a *motion clip* from PowerPoint's accompanying Clip Gallery.

You can also choose to add a movie from other files that you have available on your hard drive or on disk or other removable media. A movie can be made to play automatically during a slide show, or only when you click on the movie on the slide where it resides.

Adding a motion clip from the Clip Gallery

The following steps tell you how to add a motion clip from the Clip Gallery to your slide. Give them a try and see what you think.

1. **In Slide or Normal view, move to the slide where you want to add a motion clip.**

2. **Choose Insert⇨Movies and Sounds⇨Movie from Gallery.**

   An Insert Movie dialog box appears with the Motion Clips tab selected.

3. **Click a category of clips and then click a motion clip to select it.**

4. **Click Insert Clip.**

   The motion clip is inserted right in the middle of your slide.

5. **(Optional) Resize the motion clip and reposition it by dragging it to a new location.**

   Because a motion clip is both heard *and* seen, you need to give it some room to physically reside on your slide. Be aware that you may need to rearrange slide elements — text boxes, clip art, and other objects — to accommodate an added motion clip.

When not playing, the motion clip shows only the first frame as a placeholder on the slide where it is located. In this sense, the motion clip appears similar to other graphic elements on a slide. Start the slide show and move to the motion clip-embellished slide to see how the motion clip appears while playing.

Adding a movie from a file

So you can't find what you want from the Clip Gallery? No need to despair. The following steps show you how to add a movie from a file to your slide.

1. **In Slide or Normal view, move to the slide where you want to add a movie.**

2. **Choose Insert⇨Movies and Sounds⇨Movie from File from the Menu bar.**

   The Insert Movie dialog box appears.

3. **Find and click on the movie you want to add and click OK.**

   The movie is inserted right in the middle of your slide.

4. **PowerPoint asks whether you want the movie to play automatically in the slide show. Click Yes to make the movie play automatically on the slide or click No to play the movie only when you click on it.**

5. **(Optional) Resize the movie and reposition it by dragging it to a new location.**

When not playing, the movie shows only the first frame as a placeholder on the slide where it is located.

REAL WORLD

Add sound and motion with caution

A movie clip takes up tons of memory and can really drag down the performance of your computer. File sizes are typically 1MB or more, even for a teensy-weensy movie snippet. Sound files also take up a fair amount of disk space. Each second of sound can occupy 10K or more — a small enough space to make use of sound but not so small a space that you can go completely nuts with it. Use sound and motion with care!

**PowerPoint
Chapter 8**

**Manipulating Your
Multimedia**

Playing a movie

You can play many movies in Normal view or Slide view simply by double-clicking on them. Motion clips added from the Clip Gallery, however, won't play in Normal view or Slide view. If you're running the slide show presentation, just single-click the movie to play it. If you've chosen to have the movie play automatically, it begins playing when you reach the slide where it resides.

Adding Sound

Adding music, sound effects, and other audio snippets to your PowerPoint slides electrifies your presentation more than mere text and images alone can. PowerPoint comes with a small library of sound files that you can raid whenever you need a foghorn, phone ring, or rooster. You can find more sounds on the Internet (even beyond Clip Gallery Live), where you can locate Web sites offering sound clips for virtually every sound imaginable.

Adding a sound from the Clip Gallery

Inserting a sound into a PowerPoint presentation is as simple as making your choice and pasting that choice onto a slide. When you run the slide show, you can set up the sounds to play either during slide transitions or at the click of a Sound icon.

1. **Move to the slide that you want to jazz up with sound.**

2. **Choose Insert⇨Movies and Sounds⇨Sound from Gallery.**

The Clip Gallery dialog box appears with the Sounds tab selected.

3. **Scroll through the list of Clip Gallery sounds until you find the one you're looking for; then click the sound to select it.**

4. **Click Insert.**

The sound is pasted on the slide. Notice that a little sound icon appears on the slide to show you that your sound has been added.

Adding a sound from another source

If you want to insert a sound that hasn't been cataloged in the Clip Gallery (such as one you downloaded from the Internet, or one you digitized and stored yourself), follow these steps:

1. **Move to the slide where you want to add a sound.**

2. **Choose Insert⇨Movies and Sounds⇨Sound from File.**

The Insert Sound dialog box appears.

3. **Find and click on the sound you want to add and click OK.**

The sound is inserted as a little sound icon right in the middle of your slide. A dialog box appears, asking whether you want the sound to play automatically (see Figure 8-2).

Figure 8-2:
You make
the call
about your
sound.

Playing an added sound

To play a sound you added as you're working in Slide view, double-click the sound icon.

To play the sound during a slide show presentation, single-click the sound icon whenever it appears on a slide (unless you choose to have the sound play automatically on a slide).

You can also cause sounds to play in between slides (during a slide transition).

Chapter 9: Making a Graph (ical) Presentation

In This Chapter

✔ Using datasheet to start a graph

✔ Making a graph

✔ Inserting a table

Some presentations just don't seem to fly without your having to provide substantial proof of what you're talking about. Multimedia will take you only so far. And what constitutes substantial proof? A well-timed projection of a fancy graph is often a way to quiet a restless crowd. Then while you have your onlookers in your control, finish them off with some nifty tables. PowerPoint 2000 makes convincing presentations even better.

Starting with the Datasheet

Microsoft Graph uses information you supply in the datasheet to construct the graph that ultimately ends up (looking beautiful) on your slide. The datasheet functions as a simple spreadsheet, providing rows and columns where you insert your data (see Figure 9-1). Rows are designated by numbers, and columns are designated by letters. Each data point you enter is cubbyholed in a unique cell of the datasheet. Simply click a cell and type to enter information into the cell.

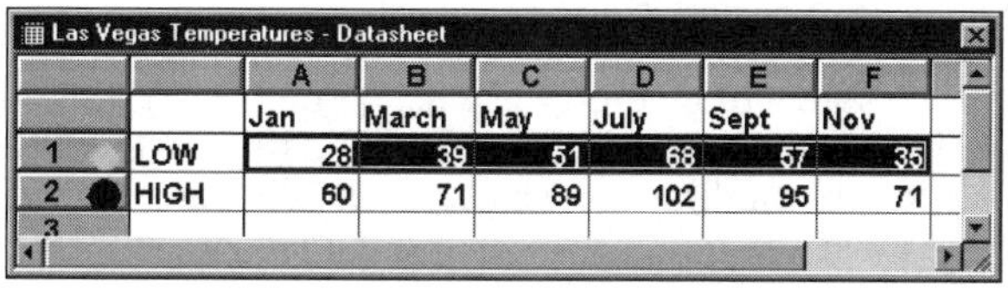

Figure 9-1: The datasheet is a simple spreadsheet.

Las Vegas Temperatures - Datasheet

		A	B	C	D	E	F
		Jan	March	May	July	Sept	Nov
1	LOW	28	39	51	68	57	35
2	HIGH	60	71	89	102	95	71
3							

After filling your datasheet with numbers, you can transform those numbers into a graph suitable for display. Microsoft Graph offers you 14 graph types, from the frequently used (line and scatter) to the weird (bubble, cone, and tube) and the really strange (doughnut and radar). It also offers you a handful of unusual, custom graph types in case none of the standard types suits your needs. To choose a graph type after completing your datasheet:

1. **Double-click the graph on the slide to activate the Microsoft Graph program.**

If you're already working in Microsoft Graph, just single-click the temporary graph you see onscreen to select it.

2. **Choose Chart⇨Chart Type from the Menu bar to open the Chart Type dialog box (see Figure 9-2).**

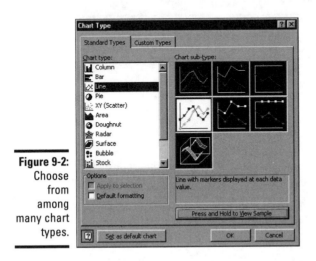

Figure 9-2:
Choose
from
among
many chart
types.

3. **Click either the Standard Types tab or the Custom Types tab.**

4. **Choose a graph by selecting an option in the Chart Type area.**

On the Standard Types tab, you may also click an option in the Chart Subtype area, which offers variations on the Standard theme.

For the Standard Types tab, you can obtain a thumbnail preview of how your data appears in a selected graph type by clicking the Press and Hold to View Sample button.

5. **Click OK to accept your choice.**

You can also use a shortcut method to select a graph type while working in Microsoft Graph. Click the down arrow just to the right of the Chart Type button on the Standard toolbar in Graph. A small palette appears, allowing you to choose from the most commonly used graph types.

Creating Graphs

PowerPoint includes a program called Microsoft Graph that you can use to convert numerical information into pie graphs, bar graphs, and even some exotic things called cone graphs. You don't have to do anything special to access Microsoft Graph — the program starts up immediately whenever you choose to build a graph in PowerPoint.

Adding a slide with a graph placeholder

To create a new slide on which you intend to place a graph, follow these steps:

1. **In Slide Normal or Slide Sorter view, move to the location in your presentation where you want to insert a new slide with a graph.**

2. **Choose Insert⊏>New Slide from the Menu bar, click the New Slide button on the Standard toolbar, or press Ctrl+M.**

   The New Slide dialog box appears.

3. **Select an AutoLayout design that includes a graph and click OK.**

   A new slide appears with a placeholder for a graph.

4. **Double-click the graph placeholder to begin building your graph.**

   Microsoft Graph opens and displays a sample graph accompanied by a sample datasheet.

5. **Input your own data into the datasheet, which works like a spreadsheet.**

   See "Starting with the Datasheet" earlier in this chapter for more details.

6. **Accept your datasheet (close the datasheet) by clicking the X in the upper-right corner of the datasheeet.**

7. **Click outside the graph area to return to the slide.**

   The graph is redrawn with the data you entered in the datasheet.

Adding a graph to an existing slide

To add a graph to a slide already in your presentation:

1. **In Slide or Normal view, move to the slide where you want to add a graph.**

2. **Click the Insert Chart button on the Standard toolbar or choose Insert⊏>Chart from the Menu bar.**

   A sample datasheet and graph appear on the slide.

3. **Replace the data in the sample datasheet with your actual information.**

4. **Accept your datasheet (close the datasheet) by clicking the X in the upper-right corner of the datasheet.**

5. **Click outside the graph area to return to the slide.**

   The graph is redrawn with the data you entered in the datasheet.

Labeling a graph

After you add a graph to your slide, you need to complete the graph by adding labels: a title, labels for the axes, and a deciphering legend. The datasheet only allows you to type in names for column and row labels — you'll have to add the other labels to the graph itself. Add labels to your graph as follows:

PowerPoint
Chapter 9

Making a
Graph(ical)
Presentation

1. **Double-click your graph to activate the Microsoft Graph program.**

If you're already working in Microsoft Graph, just single-click your graph to select it.

2. **Choose Chart⇨Chart Options from the Menu bar to open the Chart Options dialog box (shown in Figure 9-3), which allows you the following options:**

• **Titles:** Add a title for the graph and titles for the axes.

• **Axes:** Hide or show the labels you gave the data on the datasheet.

• **Gridlines:** Activate and deactivate the graph paper-style horizontal and vertical gridlines lines that appear with the graph.

• **Legends:** Click the Show legend checkbox to include a legend on your graph. Also click a radio button to position the legend in the Bottom, Corner, Top, Right, or Left of the Graph.

• **Data Labels:** Display the actual numerical data for each data point in your datasheet on the graph itself.

• **Data Tables:** If you want to show actual data, choose the Data Table option as an accompaniment for your graph.

Close the Chart Options dialog box and click on your slide (outside the graph) to view your completed slide.

While working on your graph, you can double click any element — axes labels, datapoints, gridlines, and so on — to open a dialog box that offers you extensive customizing options for that element. These dialog boxes provide you with complete control over the color, size, and other formatting attributes of every element in your graph.

Moving and resizing a graph

Because Microsoft Graph may or may not position your newly created graph in the appropriate location, you may want to move or resize your graph:

✦ **To move a graph:** Click and drag the graph — not on the sizing handles — to move it to a new destination.

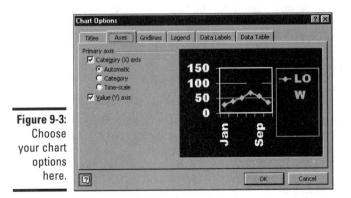

Figure 9-3:
Choose
your chart
options
here.

+ **To resize a graph:** Click the graph and then pull on one of its handles. Holding down the Shift key as you resize the graph maintains the proportions of the graph. Be aware that resizing may alter text readability.

Using Tables

Inserting massive quantities of text on your PowerPoint slides is rarely a good idea. Too many words means you have to use a small text point size to fit everything in, which may make it difficult for audience members to read your slides. If you're forced to present text-intensive information, consider organizing that information into a tidy table.

Inserting a new slide with a table

The easiest way to insert a simple table on a PowerPoint slide is to create a new slide with a table placeholder:

1. **In Slide view, Normal view, or Slide Sorter view, move to the location in your presentation where you want to insert a new slide with a table.**

2. **Choose Insert⇨New Slide from the Menu bar, click the New Slide button on the Standard toolbar, or press Ctrl+M.**

3. **In the New Slide dialog box (shown in Figure 9-4), select the Table AutoLayout and click OK.**

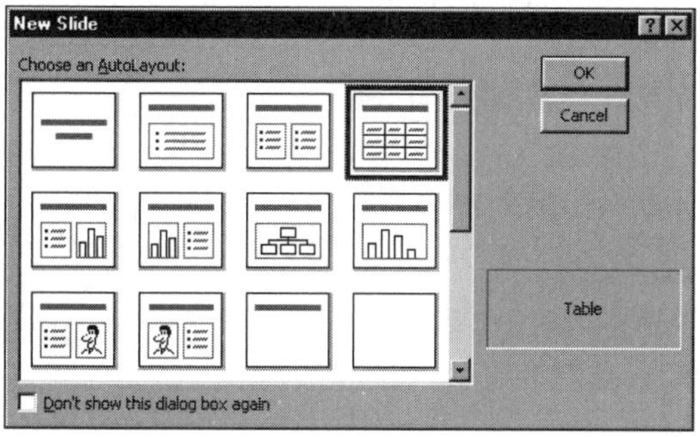

PowerPoint Chapter 9

Making a Graph(ical) Presentation

Figure 9-4: The New Slide dialog box with its choices.

4. **In Slide or Normal view, double click the table placeholder.**

The Insert Table dialog box appears (see Figure 9-5).

5. **Type the desired number of columns and rows in the Insert Table dialog box and then click OK.**

6. **Type and format text in each cell just as you do in a text box.**

7. **Click outside the table to return to your slide.**

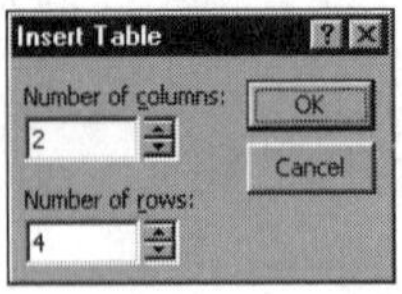

Figure 9-5:
The teensy
Insert
Table
dialog box.

Inserting a simple table on an existing slide

Just like the title of this section promises, you can add a simple table to any existing slide. All you need to do is to follow these steps:

1. **In Slide or Normal view, move to the slide where you want to insert a simple table.**

2. **Click the Insert Table button on the Standard toolbar.**

3. **Hold the mouse button down and drag the mouse to select the number of rows and columns you want. Release the mouse button to accept your chosen dimensions.**

4. **Type and format text in each cell, just as you do in a text box.**

5. **Click outside the table to return to your slide.**

Formatting a simple table

Several tools exist to help you in formatting your simple table (if you are not already editing the table, click the table once to start editing):

✦ **To resize row height or column width:** Click and drag a line that defines the border of the row or column.

✦ **To insert a new row (or column):** Highlight the row (column) where you want to insert the new row (column). Right-click the mouse and choose Insert Rows (Insert Columns). A new row appears above the selected row; a new column appears to the left of the selected column.

✦ **To delete a row (or column):** Select the row (column) to be deleted. Right-click the mouse and choose Delete Rows (Delete Columns).

✦ **To format the borders, fill, text orientation, and other attributes:** Select the cells to be formatted. Right-click the mouse and choose Borders and Fill. The Format Table dialog box appears. The Format Table dialog box offers three tabs — Borders, Fill, and Text Box — that help you adjust table formatting.

Right-click outside the simple table to stop editing and return to the slide. Click and drag your simple table to move it to a new location on the slide. Resize your simple table by pulling on the sizing handles.

Inserting a Word table on an existing slide

If you're already an expert tablemaker using Microsoft Word, you can save yourself a significant amount of effort by building your table in Word. Then you can insert it on a PowerPoint slide.

1. In Slide or Normal view, move to the slide where you want to add a table.

2. On the Standard toolbar, choose Insert⇨Picture⇨Microsoft Word Table.

3. Type a number in the Number of Columns and the Number of Rows areas in the Insert Table dialog box.

   A blank table appears with your chosen number of columns and rows.

4. Fill the table cells and adjust text formatting and cell formatting using standard Word table procedures. You can also right-click the mouse to check out additional table formatting options. (See Figure 9-6.)

5. Click outside the table to complete its creation and return to PowerPoint. Your newly-created table appears on the slide.

   Click and drag your table to move it to reposition where it sits on the slide.

You can edit a completed table at any time by double-clicking the table and using the Word tools and menus to make modifications.

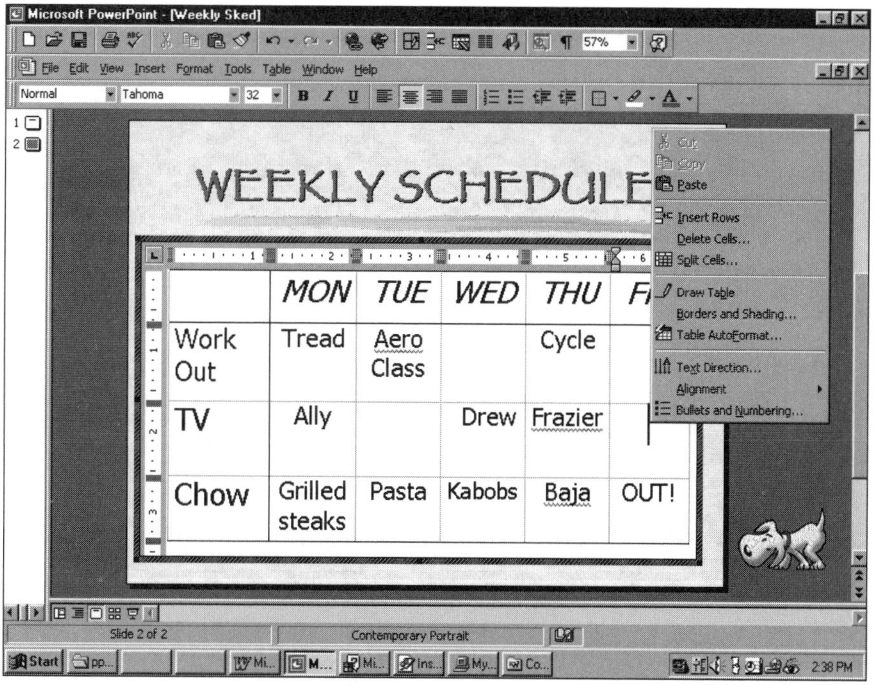

Figure 9-6:
You can
format as
you fill a
table.

Locating a lost file

If your creativity has outlasted your memory, don't give up hope for locating those files you know you have but just can't seem to locate. Choosing File⇨Open allows you to access search criteria that can help you retrieve files.

✔ **File name:** Lets you specify any portion of the filename your brain may selectively recall.

✔ **Files of type:** Allows you to specify the file type for which you are searching. This is a great option when, for example, you know that the file you seek is a Word document or an Excel spreadsheet.

Note: In the Open dialog box, you can also click the arrow beside Tools and select Find to open a Find dialog box with extensive options for locating files.

Chapter 10: Planning the Presentation

In This Chapter

- Using Slide Sorter View
- Making transition between slides
- Animating text and other objects
- Adding buttons to your presentation
- Creating hyperlinks to other slides, presentations, and Web sites

*W*hen you create a presentation, it just doesn't run itself. You control how the slides display and how much time is allowed between them. If you leave a slide on the screen for too short of a period, you risk getting too far ahead of your viewers. If you leave a slide on the screen too long, you risk pushing your viewers to find other forms of entertainment (sleeping, talking to their neighbors, doodling, and so on). You also decide how the text displays on the slides. For example, do you want text to pop up suddenly? Or do you want it to roll on dramatically? And finally you choose the buttons and hyperlinks to other things. Yes, you plan the presentation.

Adding Action Buttons

PowerPoint 2000 offers you some way-cool *action buttons* that you can click during a slide show to perform certain specialized functions. You can use action buttons to perform a range of functions, such as running external programs or moving to certain slides.

The process of adding an action button to a slide involves first creating the button itself, then defining its function. To add an action button to a slide, follow these steps:

1. **In Normal or Slide view, move to the slide where you want to add an action button.**

2. **Choose AutoShapes⇨Action Buttons from the Drawing toolbar to bring up the Action Buttons toolbox (see Figure 10-1).**

Figure 10-1:
The Action
Buttons
toolbox.

3. **In the Action Buttons toolbox, click a button shape.**

   You can choose buttons that represent actions, such as home, forward, backward, document, and movie. You can embellish the blank button with text to customize your choices (see Step 6).

4. **Click your slide to start drawing the button, starting with the upper-left corner of the button. Drag the mouse until the button reaches the size that you want; then release the mouse button.**

   An Action Settings dialog box appears (see Figure 10-2).

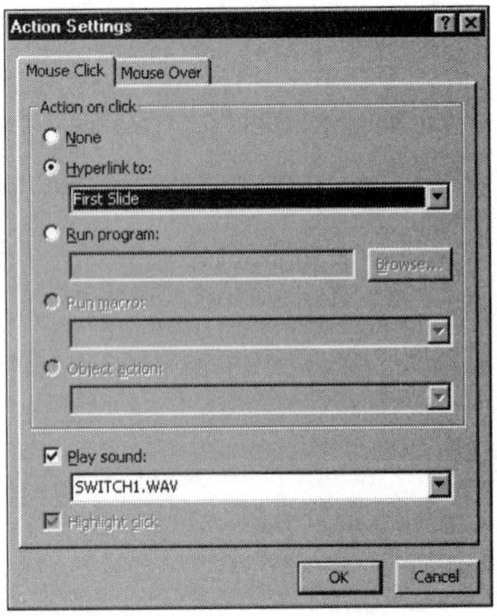

Figure 10-2:
The Action
Settings
dialog box.

5. **In the Action Settings dialog box click the Mouse Click or Mouse Over tab to set up the condition under which you can perform your hyperlink.**

   Choosing Mouse Click requires that you click the button in order to execute its action, while choosing Mouse Over requires only that you move the mouse on top of the button (without clicking) to perform the button action.

6. **Assign an action to your newly created button.**

   Default actions are preset for many buttons. For example, returning to the home slide (the first slide in the presentation) is the default action for the action button that looks like a house.

To find out the default action of a button, consult the Hyperlink to area of the Action Settings dialog box.

You may want to redefine button actions according to your specific needs. Use the following options in the Action Settings dialog box to redefine button actions:

- **None:** No action is taken.

- **Hyperlink to:** Activates a drop-down list indicating everywhere the hyperlink can go.

- **Run program:** Allows you to choose a program that runs when you click the action button. *Note:* If you choose this option, you need to be certain that the program is available on whatever system you run your presentation.

- **Run macro:** Produces a list of all available macros in the presentation.

- **Object action:** Applies to a slide object to which you can assign the action of open, play, or edit. For example, you can assign the play action to a movie clip, or assign the open or edit action to an Excel Chart. To use this option, switch to Slide or Normal view and click the object you want to attach an action to. Right-click the object and choose Action Settings from the menu. On the Mouse Click or Mouse Over tab, click the Object action radio button and choose Open, Play, or Edit from the drop-down list.

- **Play sound:** Plays a sound in conjunction with any other action taken. You can choose from sounds in PowerPoint's Clip Gallery or your own files. A neat idea is to play a cash register sound when you click a button that links to an Excel financial spreadsheet.

- **Highlight click:** Applies to an object other than an action button to which you attach an action. Because Action Buttons highlight when clicked or moused over, checking this option allows other objects — like movies or text boxes — to look as if they too are being click or moused over.

After you have made your selections, click OK to close the Action Settings dialog box.

7. **(Optional) Tweak the button's appearance: Pull the handles to adjust button size and yank on the diamond handle to alter the 3-D effect of the button. Move the entire button by clicking it and dragging it to another place on your slide. Adjust the fill color as you do for any drawing object.**

You can add text to any selected button by right-clicking the action button, choosing Add Text, and then typing at the cursor. After text exists, you simply need to click on the text and start typing or editing. Button text can be formatted using the Formatting toolbar.

If you want to change a button's action setting at a later time, right-click the action button and select the Action Settings command from the menu.

PowerPoint
Chapter 10

Planning the
Presentation

Adding Slide Transitions

Slide transitions dictate how slides enter and exit as you present your on-screen slide show.

You can opt to use one type of transition consistently throughout your entire presentation, or you can choose unique transitions for individual slides. You can also adjust the speed at which a transition occurs — slow, medium, or fast — and even have a sound play as the transition takes place.

PowerPoint provides you more than 40 cool transitions to use in your presentations. You can add transitions to your presentation using either the Slide Transition Effects menu or the Slide Transition dialog box. Creating transitions with the menu is the more expedient process, while creating transitions with the dialog box allows you greater control over transition details like speed and sound.

Adding a transition to a slide dictates how that slide will enter on-screen — not how it will exit. PowerPoint doesn't allow you to set up an exit transition.

Using the Slide Transition Effects menu

To add transitions to your presentation using the Slide Transition Effects menu, follow these steps:

1. **In Slide Sorter view, click on a slide where you want to add a transition.**

To select multiple slides, hold down Shift as you click. To select all slides, choose Edit⇨Select All or press Ctrl+A.

2. **Click the down arrow tab on the Slide Transition Effects menu and select a transition.**

PowerPoint tags each slide with a transition effects marker indicating that a transition has been added.

In Slide Sorter view, clicking a slide's transition effects tag causes a thumbnail preview of the transition to play.

Using the Slide Transition dialog box

To add transitions to your presentation using the Slide Transition dialog box:

1. **In any view except Slide Show view, click on a slide where you want to add a transition.**

To select multiple slides in Slide Sorter view, hold down Shift as you click. To select all slides in either view, choose Edit⇨Select All or press Ctrl+A.

2. **Choose Slide Show⇨Slide Transition from the menu bar.**

The Slide Transition dialog box appears, as shown in Figure 10-3.

3. **In the Effect area of the Slide Transition dialog box, choose a transition from the drop-down menu box. Also choose a transition speed: slow, medium, or fast.**

A thumbnail preview shows how your choices appear in the slide show.

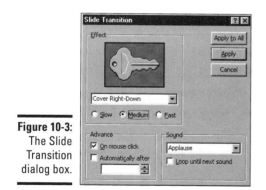

Figure 10-3:
The Slide
Transition
dialog box.

4. **In the Advance area, choose whether you want the transition to occur** **On Mouse Click or Automatically.**

Choosing Automatically allows you to specify the number of seconds before the transition is performed. You have the option of leaving the number of seconds at 0 — the default — which causes each transition to play directly after the previous transition finishes.

5. **If you want a sound to accompany your transition, select a sound from** **the drop-down menu box in the Sound area (choose Other Sound to use** **non-PowerPoint sound files).**

The Loop until next sound option causes the sound to play repeatedly until another sound in the presentation is played.

6. **Click Apply to accept and apply your choices or click Apply to All if you** **want your choices applied to every slide in the presentation.**

PowerPoint allows you to apply any transition to any slide. However, if you want to look like a real PowerPoint pro, pick one transition type and apply it consistently throughout your entire presentation. Don't use any transition with the adjective *random* in its name. Be creative, but don't overdo it, because then your audience pays more attention to your wacky transitions than to the information on your slides. You appear most professional if you choose something elegant, like a straight cut (the No Transition choice), a Fade Through Black or a Dissolve, Cover, Uncover, Wipe, or Strip. Avoid the Blind and Checkerboard effects — they will totally annoy your audience!

REAL WORLD

Copying a slide from one presentation to another

If you have that perfect slide in one presentation but want to use it in another, don't despair! You don't need to recreate that slide; all you have to do is copy it from one presentation to another.

1. **Select the slide you want to insert another slide after.**

2. **Choose Insert⇨Slides from Files.**

3. **In the Slide Finder dialog box, find and select the presentation you want to copy a slide from.**

4. **Select the slide or slides you want to copy, and then click Insert.**

To go crazy and copy an entire presentation, click Insert All. And if you find yourself returning often to a presentation in order to borrow from it, click Add to Favorites to add the presentation currently displayed to your list of favorite presentations.

Chapter 11: Showing Off Your Work

In This Chapter

✔ Using a computer to show your slides

✔ Presenting automatically or manually

*O*ne of the best things about giving a PowerPoint presentation is that you no longer have to get your hands messy drawing on a flip chart or on one of those dry-erase boards. Most important, you can spend less time turning your back on your audience — which is always a dangerous thing, especially on a warm Friday afternoon. If you can turn on a computer, you can give your presentation. (And if you can't turn on a computer, how the heck did you manage to make a PowerPoint presentation?) In any case, this chapter gives you the lowdown on how to give your presentation with a computer — not the only option with PowerPoint, but perhaps the most common.

Showing Your Slides via Computer

After creating your presentation, you're ready to take your message to the world. PowerPoint allows you lots of control over your presentation when you deliver it on your computer.

Preparing your show for presentation

After you create your slides, you have to make some final decisions about how your show will be presented.

1. **Choose Slide Show⇨Set Up Show from the Menu bar.**

   The Set Up Show dialog box appears (see Figure 11-1).

2. **Click one of the following three radio buttons in the Show type section:**

   • **Presented by a speaker:** The speaker controls the pace of the presentation by clicking through slides at his or her own pace.

   • **Browsed by an individual:** Sets up a smaller screen presentation, which appears in its own window with commands for navigating the show and for editing and printing slides. This option is most frequently used by someone who browses the show over a company intranet.

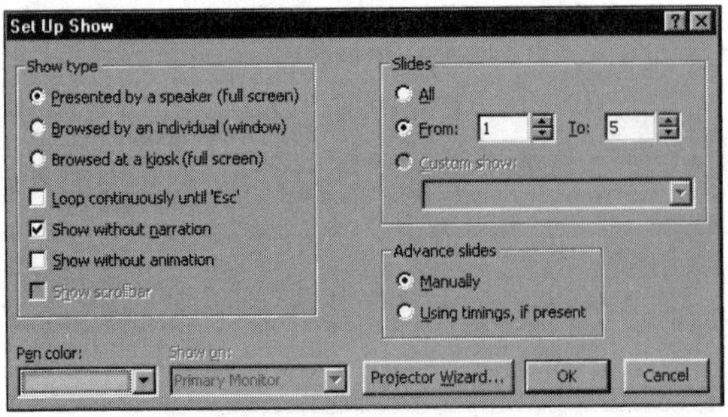

Figure 11-1:
Set up your
show with
the Set Up
Show
dialog box.

Set Up Show dialog box showing Show type options (Presented by a speaker (full screen), Browsed by an individual (window), Browsed at a kiosk (full screen)), check boxes (Loop continuously until 'Esc', Show without narration, Show without animation, Show scrollbar), Slides options (All, From: 1 To: 5, Custom show), Advance slides (Manually, Using timings, if present), Pen color, Show on: Primary Monitor, Projector Wizard, OK, Cancel buttons.

- **Browsed at a kiosk:** Creates a full-screen self-running presentation that is most often used in an unattended display at a convention or a mall. The show restarts after 5 minutes of inactivity. Navigation commands (hyperlinks and action buttons) can be included to give users perusing the show control over how they view the presentation — but users cannot modify the presentation itself.

3. **Click one or more of the three check boxes:**

- **Loop continuously until 'Esc':** Starts over at the first slide after the show finishes, until the presenter or user presses the Esc key.

- **Show without narration:** Checking this option allows you to turn off recorded narration that you record using the Record Narration option on the Slide Show menu. This option allows you to present face-to-face a slide show that's typically presented without a speaker (for example, a self-running show at a kiosk).

- **Show without animation:** Shows each slide in its final form, as if all animations have been performed. Check this option to show an animation-free version of your presentation. Showing your slide show without animations speeds up the presentation. This is an important option to have available when the half-hour of presentation time you were told you'd have has suddenly been reduced to ten minutes.

  If you previously selected Browsed by an individual, you can also check the Show Scrollbar box. This option places a scrollbar on the slide show window to make all parts of the window accessible to the person viewing the show.

4. **Choose to show All the slides in the presentation or specify a range in the From and To boxes.**

5. **Choose whether the presenter or user Manually proceeds from slide to slide or whether the slides should advance Using timings, if present.**

6. **Click OK.**

Clicking the Projector Wizard button brings up a wizard that assists you in setting up the projection system — the computer projection system — for your show. Note that a computer projector is not the same as an overhead projector! A computer projector is a high-tech (and relatively expensive) system that connects to your computer and beams your computer display through a high-powered lens onto a large screen. An overhead projector is the familiar device from high school that your algebra teacher used to show overhead transparencies.

It's always a good idea to choose the Loop continuously until 'Esc' option. If you choose this option, you return to your first slide when you complete your presentation. Without looping back, your audience ends up staring at an ugly old slide construction view (whatever you started the show from — for example, from Slide Sorter view) when you click off your final slide. If you choose the Browsed by an individual option and don't loop back, the viewer sees the words "End of slide show, click to exit" after the last slide.

Presenting slide shows manually

If you choose to run your show manually (see the preceding section for your other options), move to the first slide in your presentation and do one of the following to start the show:

PowerPoint Chapter 11

Showing Off Your Work

+ Choose Slide Show⇨View Show from the Menu bar

+ Click the Slide Show view button from the row of view buttons in the lower-left corner of the PowerPoint window

+ Press F5

Besides speaking eloquently and making eye-contact with your audience members, you spend the majority of your time delivering a manually-run PowerPoint slide show performing the following tasks:

+ **Moving along:** The first slide of your show appears and stays on-screen until you click the left mouse button.

    If you created animation that builds your slide one bullet at a time, only the unanimated objects appear at the start of each slide. Click the mouse button to show the first animation and continue clicking to advance each additional animation. When all animations on a slide are complete, click the mouse button to move to the next slide.

+ **Writing notes on the slides:** Make notes on a slide by picking up the pen and holding down the left mouse button as you write. Release the button to stop writing.

You can use a whole bunch of other shortcuts, but be aware that a handful of other keyboard sequences yield certain bizarre results during your slide show. Don't get too curious about what these other functions may be during a really important presentation to the board of directors.

Automating the slide show with slide timings

Use slide timings whenever you want to create a stand-alone show. This option allows you to designate how long each slide appears on-screen before the next slide appears.

1. **Choose Slide Show⇨Rehearse Timings from the Menu bar.**

The show starts and a small Rehearsal dialog box with a timer appears in the corner of the screen (see Figure 11-2). The Rehearsal dialog box times how long each slide is displayed, as well as the total time for the entire presentation. PowerPoint displays both times in the dialog box.

2. **Display Slide 1 for whatever duration you choose; left-click to advance to the next animation or next slide.**

When you click to Slide 2, PowerPoint records how long you displayed Slide 1. PowerPoint resets the timer to zero to start recording how long Slide 2 is displayed.

If you mess up timing a slide, click the Repeat button in the Rehearsal dialog box and try timing the slide again. Clicking the Pause button in the Rehearsal dialog box pauses the timing process. Resume timing by pressing Pause again.

3. **Continue clicking to advance your slides until you reach the end of the show.**

PowerPoint times how long each slide is displayed. It also times how long the entire show runs from start to finish.

4. **After you time the last slide, PowerPoint informs you of the total time for the show and asks whether you want to record the presentation as timed. Click Yes to accept your timings or No to ditch them.**

Set the show to run with timings by clicking the Using timings, if present radio button in the Set Up Show dialog box (see also "Preparing your show for presentation" earlier in this chapter). Now you can play hooky while PowerPoint does all the work!

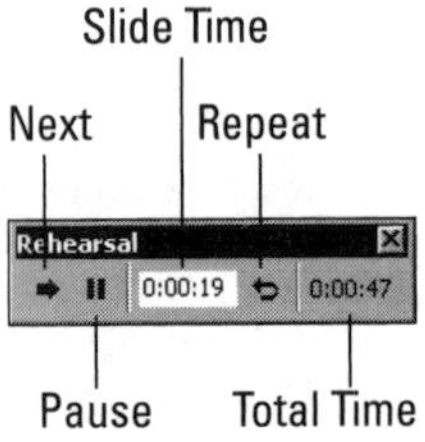

Slide Time

Next | Repeat

Figure 11-2:
Rehearse
with the
Rehearsal
dialog box.

Rehearsal ☒

➡ ‖ 0:00:19 ↻ 0:00:47

Pause | Total Time

Chapter 12: Publishing Your Presentation

In This Chapter

- ✔ **Making handouts for the audience**
- ✔ **Getting your presentation on the Web**

*P*oof! You give your presentation, the lights go on, and your audience scatters. Is that all there is to it? Is your presentation nothing more than a 15-minute splash that is soon to be forgotten? No! If your presentation has any type of enduring quality, why not let PowerPoint 2000 help you publish it? Besides giving your audience something tangible to hang on to, you can also convert your presentation into a Web presence that can carry your message far and wide.

Printing Audience Handouts

Audiences appreciate copies of your slides — handouts make it easier for the audience to follow your presentation, plus they have a permanent record of what you said. Audience handouts show miniatures of your slides, and if you want, you can include on each handout a header, a footer, and even lines where audience members can jot down notes.

1. **Choose File⇨Print from the Menu bar.**

   The Print dialog box appears.

2. **Select Handouts from the drop-down menu in the Print what area of the Print dialog box.**

   This activates the Handouts area of the Print dialog box.

3. **In the Handouts area, select the number of Slides per page you want from the drop-down menu.**

   Your choices consist of 2, 3, 4, 6, or 9 slides per page.

4. **If available, press the radio button indicating whether you want slides ordered Horizontal or Vertical.**

   These radio buttons are available when you choose to print 4, 6, or 9 slides per page.

5. **Click OK to start printing.**

Be sure to check out Appendix B for further printing hints that PowerPoint shares with other Office 2000 applications.

Publishing on the Web

You can give your presentation some longevity and added accessibility by posting it on the Web. Thanks to PowerPoint, you don't need to know how to write HTML code to publish your show online. PowerPoint 2000 offers a quick and easy option for translating your slide shows into the HTML language required for publishing Web pages online.

Saving a presentation as a Web page

To post your PowerPoint presentation to the Web, you must save the file in HTML format — the language of the Web. Saving your presentation in HTML makes it possible to display and view your presentation in a Web browser such as Netscape or Internet Explorer.

Saving your slide show as a Web page also sets the Web page title and the location where the file is stored. The following saving procedure does not automatically make your presentation available for viewing online. You'll have to save it on a Web server for other people to have access to it.

To save your presentation as a Web page:

1. Choose File⇨Save as Web Page from the Menu bar.

The Save As dialog box appears. Any other PowerPoint presentations you save as Web pages are listed here. You may have to browse to see the other presentations that you have saved. (See Figure 12-1.)

Figure 12-1: The Save As dialog box.

2. At the Save As dialog box, click the Publish button.

The Publish as Web Page dialog box appears, shown in Figure 12-2.

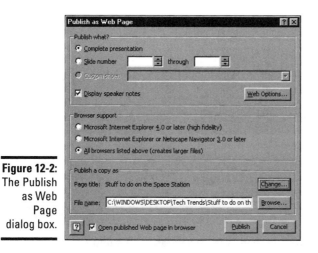

Figure 12-2:
The Publish
as Web
Page
dialog box.

3. **In the Publish as Web Page dialog box, you can make adjustments to the
following attributes that affect how your presentation is saved:**

- **Publish what?:** Choices consist of the Complete presentation; a specific
range of slides selected by typing in start and end slides in the Slide
number area; or a Custom show selected from the drop-down menu. You
can also click the Display speaker notes checkbox to include speaker
notes on the Web page.

   Clicking Web Options summons a Web Options dialog box where you can
   make additional choices about how your presentation is shown in the
   Web browser, and how users navigate the presentation. The Web Options
   dialog box has four tabs: General, Files, Pictures, and Encoding. The
   General tab provides choices regarding the appearance of your presentation in the browser window, including the choice of adding navigation
   controls (and how those controls look); the option of playing or disabling
   animation; and the option of resizing graphics to fit the browser window.
   The Files tab provides options for naming and locating the Web files. The
   Pictures tab offers choices of picture file formats. Encoding offers a large
   selection of options for the browser language in which the presentation
   is saved.

- **Browser support:** Choose which browsers the presentation will be
displayed on. Choosing Microsoft Internet Explorer version 4.0 or later
(high fidelity) ensures that users are able to take advantage of advanced
Web browser features like animations, sounds, and movies. Choosing
Microsoft Internet Explorer or Netscape Navigator version 3.0 or later
expands your accessible audience by allowing users with older browsers
to view your presentation — although they aren't able to experience the
bells and whistles that are present with a more advanced browser.
Choosing the All browsers listed above option creates larger files but
allows for virtually anyone with any kind of browser (including WebTV
users) to access your presentation.

• **Publish a copy as:** Accept the current page title or press the Change button to summon the Set Page Title dialog box and type in the name of your presentation for the browser title bar. Also type a name for your presentation in the File name area, or click Browse to change the location where you want your resulting Web files stored.

• **Open published Web page in browser:** Click this check box to view your presentation as a Web page upon saving it.

4. **Click Publish to accept your choices and save your presentation.**

Saving your file as a Web page organizes all the components of your presentation (like text, graphics, and sound) into a special Web folder. The default name of this folder is the name of the presentation file followed by the word "files".

The very first time you save a presentation as a Web page, PowerPoint converts all graphic images to one of three Web-supported formats: GIF, JPEG, or PNG. The more graphics you include in your presentation, the more time this initial save takes.

Placing a presentation on a Web server

If you want to make your PowerPoint presentations available online, you need access to a Web server where you can save your presentations. Placing a presentation on a Web server can also make it available to colleagues on your company intranet.

To create a Web folder where you can save Web page files on a Web server:

✦ **To create a new Web folder while you're working in PowerPoint:** Choose File⇨Open from the Menu bar and click Web Folders on the Places Bar in the Open dialog box. Click the Create New Folder button and type in the information requested by the Add Web Folder Wizard (as shown in Figure 12-3).

✦ **For a URL already on a Web server:** Choose File⇨Save As to summon the Save As dialog box. Type a Web address (such as http://Camilleserver/ public/) in the File name box and press Save to create a Web folder at that location on the Web. You must have the appropriate access rights to create the folder on the Web server.

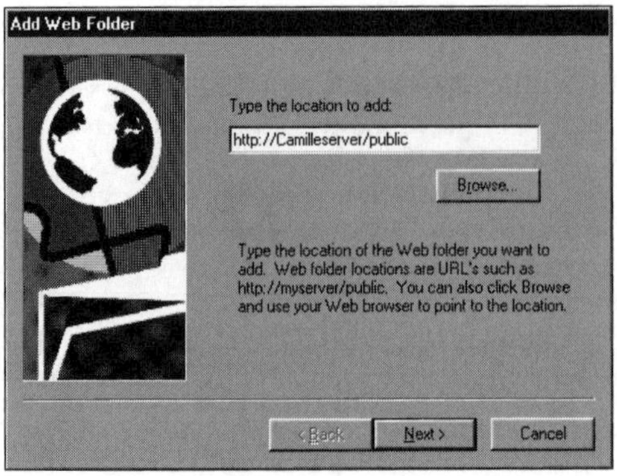

Figure 12-3:
The Add
Web Folder
Wizard
helps you
place your
Web page.

Add Web Folder

Type the location to add:

http://Camilleserver/public

Browse...

Type the location of the Web folder you want to
add. Web folder locations are URL's such as
http://myserver/public. You can also click Browse
and use your Web browser to point to the location.

< Back   Next >   Cancel

Index

Book VII

FrontPage 2000

The 5th Wave   By Rich Tennant

"THE FUNNY THING IS, I NEVER KNEW THEY HAD DESKTOP PUBLISHING
SOFTWARE FOR PAPER SHREDDERS."

Contents at a Glance

Chapter 1: Getting to Know FrontPage 2000

Do you look longingly at those nifty pages that you see on the Web and wonder what genius could have done such work? Have you ever regretted not having finished your computer science degree at MIT (or not having finished your high school keyboarding class) so that you could put things on the Web? Then you've been agonizing in vain. You no longer need to be a whiz-kid to churn out a quality Web page. With FrontPage 2000, you can join the ranks of Web-page designers. FrontPage is a powerful program that enables you to do just about anything you ever wanted to do for a Web page. Your job, however, is to find out how to use FrontPage — and this chapter is your best place to begin.

What Is FrontPage 2000, and What Can I Do with It?

FrontPage 2000 is an all-in-one Web publishing tool that's made for big-time Web publishing companies (such as Yahoo! or ESPN), small companies, and personal users — you not only can create individual Web pages but also can use FrontPage 2000 to publish Web pages to the Internet, generate tracking reports about those Web pages, and effectively administer an entire Web site once it's on the Net . . . all from within the same program.

Of course, you may never want to administer an entire Web site and use all that functionality, and that's okay. If you just want to use FrontPage to build plain old HTML pages on your own and put them up on the Internet the way you've always done, that's fine, too. FrontPage is exceptionally flexible and scalable; it can grow with you as your Web site needs grow.

What's New with FrontPage 2000?

FrontPage 2000 is a complete overhaul of previous versions of FrontPage and represents the largest upgrade of any of the Office 2000 software products.

The addition of FrontPage 2000 to Microsoft Office 2000 marks the largest change to the product. FrontPage 2000 now shares links to those products through the Microsoft OLE and ActiveX controls and an interface that's similar to other Office products. In noncomputer speak, that means that you can do things that were previously impossible, such as embedding an "editable" Excel spreadsheet into a Web page.

Site management is the other major feature upgrade in FrontPage 2000. Although previous versions of FrontPage enabled good site administration, the addition of source control and site reporting make FrontPage 2000 a better tool for companies that need to administer large sites with multiple content creators.

How FrontPage Is Organized

FrontPage 2000 contains a multitude of features, mini-applications, and menus, all wrapped up in one tidy little package. Still, maneuvering around FrontPage 2000 can baffle anyone. So to better orient you, Figure 1-1 shows you a typical

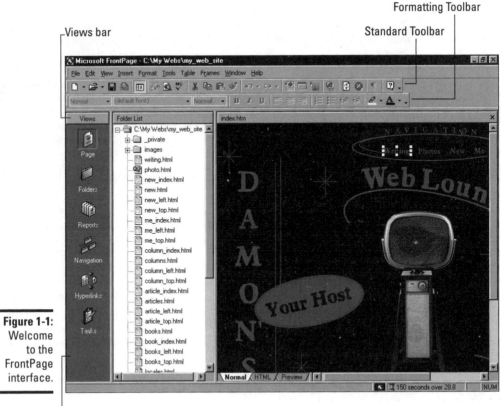

Figure 1-1: Welcome to the FrontPage interface.

FrontPage 2000 interface. You also see figure callouts for a number of features. Pay particular attention to the callouts, because you're no doubt going to find yourself using those features the most.

Why Does This Look Like Microsoft Word?

If you looked at FrontPage 2000 and then turned your head away really quickly, you might think for a moment that you'd just seen a copy of Microsoft Word 2000. That's because FrontPage 2000 closely mimics Microsoft Word 2000, right down to the menus and toolbars. Don't believe me? Check out Figure 1-2.

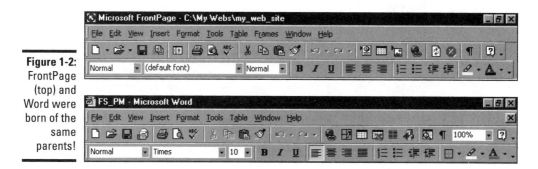

Figure 1-2: FrontPage (top) and Word were born of the same parents!

FrontPage Chapter 1

Getting to Know FrontPage 2000

Microsoft's idea here is that providing a familiar and integrated approach to Office 2000's various product interfaces helps you, the Web builder, have an easier time getting a handle on using the products. And if you need guidance using FrontPage, be sure to check out the many ways you can get help (you can find details in Appendix A).

The Views Bar

It's pretty hard not to notice the Views bar after you fire up FrontPage 2000 for the first time. The Views bar's big menu (shown in Figure 1-3), with all its icons running down the left-hand side of the screen, makes accessing the vast majority of features in FrontPage 2000 easy.

Each Views bar icon represents a different feature in FrontPage 2000. To jump to a FrontPage feature, simply click the icon. The new feature appears in the right three-quarters of the screen, below the menus and toolbars.

If you don't like the Views bar, you can turn it off by right-clicking the bar and choosing Hide Views Bar from the pop-up menu. Presto! The Views Bar disappears. After you turn off the Views bar, you can still toggle your view within FrontPage by choosing one of the six views from the View menu.

If you want to change the size of the icons in the Views bar, right-click the Views bar and select Small Icons from the pop-up menu.

Figure 1-3:
The views
are
stacked
high and
ready for
your
choices.

FrontPage 2000 features six key *views* to represent major components that you may or may not use, depending on your Web project. The following list describes these views:

✦ **Page View:** The Page View (shown in Figure 1-4) is where you build all your Web pages. Within the Page View, you can review a Web page in three different ways. You select the Normal tab to use FrontPage's drag-and-drop

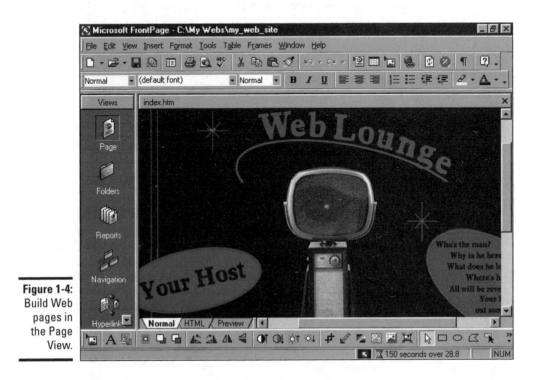

Figure 1-4:
Build Web
pages in
the Page
View.

visual HTML Editor. In addition, you can edit HTML directly through the HTML tab. You can also preview the pages in the Preview tab, which mimics the Internet Explorer Web browser.

✦ **Folders View:** The Folders View (shown in Figure 1-5) is pretty much how it sounds. This view displays a typical Windows 95 Explorer menu, making all your Web project's files and folders easily accessible within FrontPage. From this view, you can also drag and drop files, which makes adding and deleting content easy.

A Folder List also appears in the Folders View. You can access the Folder List in the other FrontPage views by choosing View⇨Folder List.

✦ **Reports View:** If you select the Reports View (shown in Figure 1-6), you get an immediate Site Summary, which gives you a bird's-eye view of what's working (or not working, if, say, you have some broken hyperlinks!) within your Web site. From the Reports View, you can also run a more detailed series of reports that give you immediate information on the status of various aspects of your Web site, such as load times or hyperlink status.

✦ **Navigation View:** The Navigation View (shown in Figure 1-7) provides a visual representation of all the pages on your Web site and the pages' hierarchical order. By dragging around the pages, you can change the relationships of those pages to one another and organize the pages of your site more effectively.

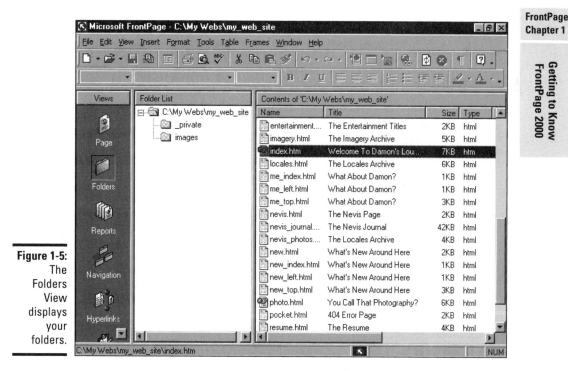

Figure 1-5: The Folders View displays your folders.

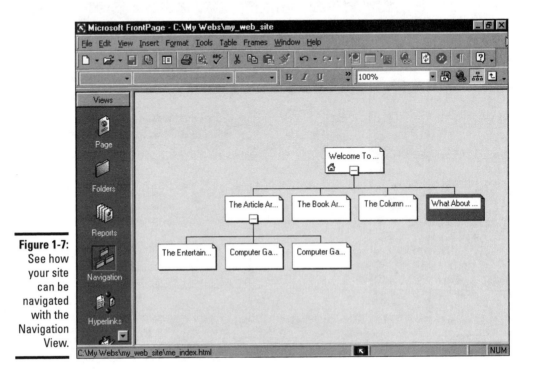

Figure 1-6:
Reports
View lets
you
manage
your site at
a glance.

Figure 1-7:
See how
your site
can be
navigated
with the
Navigation
View.

✦ **Hyperlinks View:** Figuring out how your Web pages connect to one another can be a serious chore. The Hyperlinks View (shown in Figure 1-8) gives you a graphical representation of how every Web page connects to every other page within your Web site. This can be particularly useful if you want to see how your pages are connected to one another. In addition, the Hyperlinks View provides a quick way to see which pages are linked to other sites outside your own.

✦ **Tasks View:** If you're going to be using FrontPage in a multi-user environment, the Tasks View (shown in Figure 1-9) will no doubt be a common site. The Tasks View enables you to assign tasks to individuals on your team, check the status of tasks that are already underway, and manage the workflow and the publishing of new elements to the site.

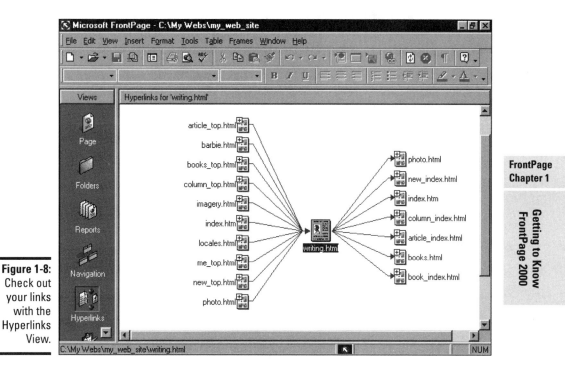

Figure 1-8:
Check out
your links
with the
Hyperlinks
View.

**FrontPage
Chapter 1**

Getting to Know
FrontPage 2000

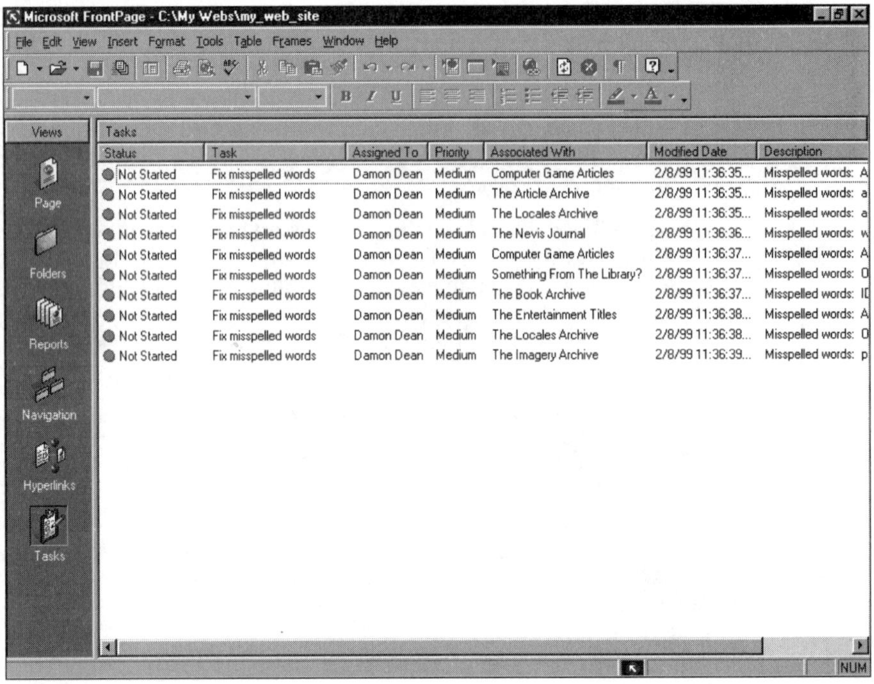

Figure 1-9:
Tasks View
permits
easy use
by multiple
participants.

Introducing the FrontPage Editor

The FrontPage 2000 Editor is the program's built-in tool for creating and viewing Web pages. It's broken into the following three parts:

✦ **Normal Mode:** Normal Mode is FrontPage 2000's visual editor for Web development. In Normal Mode, you can place elements — meaning text, graphics, applets, or whatever — on-screen in any location, and FrontPage automatically generates HTML to account for the location of every object on-screen.

✦ **HTML Mode:** For the purist, HTML Mode enables you to edit raw HTML by hand, just as in the good ol' days.

✦ **Preview Mode:** Preview Mode enables you to see what your pages look like in a Web browser window before you put them up on the Internet. FrontPage 2000's default browser is Internet Explorer.

Chapter 2: Starting Your Webbing

In This Chapter

↙ **Creating a new Web yourself or with a template**

↙ **Creating a Web page yourself or with a template**

↙ **Naming (and renaming) your Web page**

↙ **Opening a file**

↙ **Saving your Web page**

*O*h what a tangled Web you can weave — but FrontPage 2000 makes it easy to get started and to keep track of what you are doing. Whether you plan to create a Web page on your own or to use one of the provided Web templates, this chapter shows you the basics. If you can find out how to open, save, and close your Web pages, you are well on the road to Webmastery.

Creating a New Web

Whenever you start FrontPage 2000, the program creates a default HTML page, `New_page_1.html`, and then opens that page for you. Even though FrontPage does some of this work for you, you will want to create your own Web project. To do so, follow these steps:

1. **Choose File➪New➪Web to open the New dialog box (as shown in Figure 2-1).**

2. **Enter the location for your new Web (either on your local machine or on your local network) in the Options area.**

3. **Select a type of Web from one of the available templates.**

The templates make possible different kinds of Web sites that you may want to build. The default selection — the one that FrontPage loads on startup — is One Page Web.

4. **Click OK or press Enter to create your new Web.**

Note: When you create a Web, you'll notice that FrontPage 2000 creates a few "extra items," including an Images folder and a Private folder. The Images folder is the default location for housing images in your Web. The Private folder is where FrontPage puts the majority of its automatically generated code.

Creating a Web Site from a Template

FrontPage 2000 comes with several Web templates that enable you to design a Web site that you can tailor to your business or personal needs. Table 2-1 highlights the features of each template.

Table 2-1	Web Templates in FrontPage
Template	**Description**
One Page Web	Includes just a single Web page.
Corporate Presence Wizard	Includes pages for products and services, feedback, and a search page, as well as pages for mission statements and contact information.
Customer Support Web	Includes the tools necessary for building a compelling customer support site, including pages for discussion groups, FAQs, bug-list reports, a searchable database, and bulletin board postings.
Discussion Web Wizard	Includes search forms, a discussion area, and user registration.
Empty Web	Includes only the empty default folders.
Import Web Wizard	Walks you through the process of importing an existing Web into a new Web.
Personal Web	Includes a home page, plus pages for a photo album, your personal interests, and your favorite sites on the World Wide Web.
Project Web	Includes such thing as schedules, task status, discussion pages, and team-member information.

Creating Web Pages

Creating new Web pages is perhaps the most common task you perform in FrontPage 2000, especially if you have a good-sized Web site. It's not surprising, then, that FrontPage offers you a plethora of options for generating new Web pages, whether you want to create merely an empty page or something as sophisticated as a page involving frames.

Creating an empty Web page

You can create a new, empty HTML page to add to your Web in several ways, but these may be the easiest:

✦ **From the File menu:** To create a Web page by using the File menu, choose File➪New➪Page. In the New dialog box, select Normal Page and click OK.

✦ **From the Toolbar:** Just below the File menu is the New Page toolbar button. Click this button to create a new Web page.

✦ **From the Folder List:** Anytime the Folder List is active, you can generate a new, blank Web page by right-clicking a blank part of the Folder List and choosing New Page from the pop-up menu.

Creating a separate Web page from a template

FrontPage gives you many more options for creating Web pages than just making an empty page. In fact, FrontPage includes 25 different Web page templates that can make it easy for you to choose a Web page for almost any of your needs. Table 2-2 lists some of these templates. To create a Web page from a template in the Page View, press Ctrl+N or choose File➪New➪Page to open the New dialog box.

FrontPage
Chapter 2

Starting Your
Webbing

Table 2-2	Web Page Templates
Web Page Template	*Features*
Bibliography	Creates a page with entries in the correct form for a bibliography.
Confirmation Form	Creates a customer service reply page for users to submit a query.
Feedback Form	Provides a form for submitting and receiving feedback.
Form Page Wizard	Creates a customized page with a form that Web surfers can submit.
FAQ	Includes a blank table of contents and links to major sections (you get to fill them in, however).
Guestbook	Creates a form that visitors can use to post comments to your Web site.
One-column Body	Creates a page with a column in the middle, a title at the top, and some default text down the middle of the page.
Two-column Body	Creates two text columns and a header at the top.
User Registration	Includes a default set of text fields for registering new visitors to your Web site.
Search Page	Creates a search form with instructions.
Table of Contents	Creates a set of topics and built-in links for your Web pages.
Three-column Body	Creates three columns and a header at the top.

Saving an HTML file as a template

Say that you're working on a Web page and you suddenly realize, "Zoinks! All my other Web pages should have these same basic elements!" With FrontPage 2000, you have the option to save an HTML page as a template, which you can then load like other HTML templates. To save an HTML page as a template, follow these steps:

1. **Choose File⇨Save As.**

   The Save As dialog box appears.

2. **In the Save In drop-down list box, select the FrontPage 2000 Template directory. FrontPage 2000 usually resides in**

C:\Program Files\Microsoft Office\ Templates\1033\Pages, but the actual location of your program files depends on where you installed your version of FrontPage 2000.

3. **Select FrontPage Template (*.tem) from the Save As Type drop-down list.**

4. **Click the Save button.**

After you save your file, you'll be able to see and choose your new template in the New Page dialog box. (See the section "Creating a separate Web page from a template," in this chapter.)

Creating framed Web pages

Ever see a Web page where you can scroll down the page, but the menu at the top never moves and the scrolling page seems to disappear underneath the menu?

A feature known as *frames* controls these nifty tricks — and it's one of the great secrets of HTML.

In FrontPage 2000, creating framed Web pages is easy! Just follow these steps:

1. **In the Page View, choose File⇨New⇨Page from the menu bar. The New dialog box appears.**

2. **Select the Frames Pages tab (shown in Figure 2-2).**

3. **Click the style of framed Web page you want.**

4. **Click OK to generate the framed pages.**

After you select your framed page, you don't automatically see the page the way it's eventually going to look. When you choose a frame page style, FrontPage 2000 creates a control page for the frame style, leaving the selection of the pages in the frame up to you. On-screen, you see borders breaking up the page according to the frame style you selected. Within each framed area on-screen, you find three long buttons. You use these buttons to select the pages for each framed area in the style you selected. Figure 2-3 shows what these buttons look like on-screen after you've created a framed page.

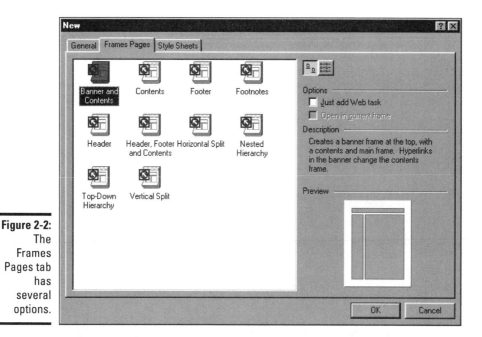

Figure 2-2:
The
Frames
Pages tab
has
several
options.

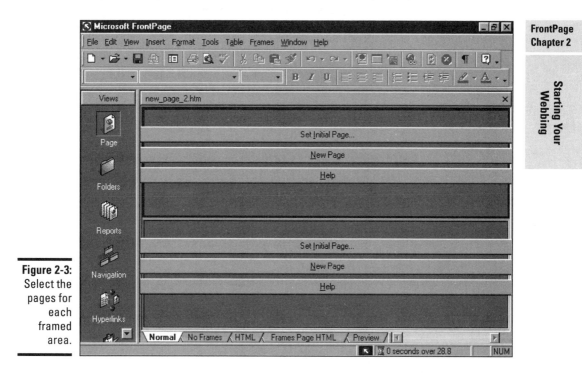

Figure 2-3:
Select the
pages for
each
framed
area.

**FrontPage
Chapter 2**

**Starting Your
Webbing**

Here's what these buttons do:

+ **Set Initial Page:** Click this button to select a page in your Web to be included in for that framed area.

+ **New Page:** Click this button to create a new empty HTML page for that framed area.

+ **Help:** Click this button to access the Microsoft online help for framed pages.

Naming Your Web

If you let FrontPage have its way, it names a new Web simply "My Web." Although this name may seem nice and homey, it isn't particularly effective in helping you remember what your Web contains.

You need to know, too, that, after you name your Web, changing the name can prove a hassle if you decide that you don't like the current name. Naming your Web, therefore, can be one of the more important decisions you make.

You name your Web in the New dialog box (shown back in Figure 2-1). In the Options area, in the Specify the Location of the New Web field (catchy name, isn't it?), FrontPage asks you to specify the location of your Web. In fact — and this is confusing — this field determines both the location *and* the name of your new Web. After you name your new Web and click OK, FrontPage 2000 creates a new folder with the name you chose, and then FrontPage generates the Web contents in that folder.

Changing a Filename

If you're familiar with the way Windows 98 allows you to rename files, then FrontPage 2000 will seem awfully familiar, because it works nearly identically. To change the name of a file, follow these steps for an easy way:

1. **If you don't already have the Folder List open, choose <u>V</u>iew⇨Fold<u>e</u>r List.**

   The Folder List area appears.

2. **Right-click the file in the Folder List that you want to change.**

3. **Choose <u>R</u>ename from the pop-up menu that appears.**

4. **Type the new name for the file.**

5. **Press Enter.**

Whenever you change the name of a Web page, you break the links that connect the page to any other pages in your Web site. Fortunately, FrontPage knows exactly how all your Web pages are linked, so when you change the name of a file, FrontPage asks whether you want to automatically update your other pages as well.

Keep those filenames short

Although you live in the wonderful world of Windows 98/NT, where you can have long filenames that even include spaces between words, keep your Web names short. Many servers out there on the Internet still use the 8.3 filename/extension lengths (that is, those still using DOS and UNIX syntax . . . ack!) for their filenames, so the closer you stay to the 8.3 convention, the fewer problems you'll experience in the long run.

Opening Files

Because FrontPage 2000 is part of Microsoft Office, the program can read and edit a large number of different file formats in addition to HTML. To open a file in FrontPage, follow these steps:

1. **Choose File⇨Open to access the Open File dialog box (shown in Figure 2-4).**

You can also press Ctrl+O to bring up the Open File dialog box.

2. **Select the file type you want from the Files of Type drop-down list box.**

3. **Use the Look In drop-down list box to find the file you need.**

4. **Click the name of the file you want from the list and then click the Open button.**

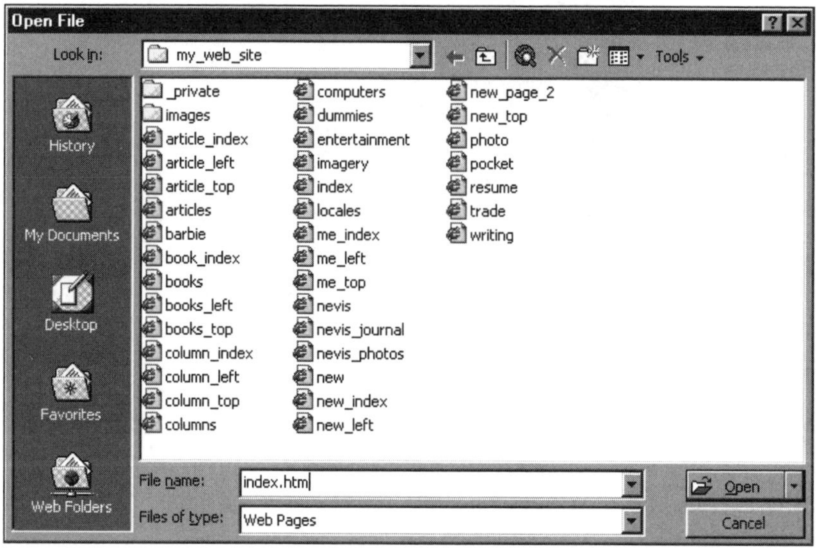

FrontPage Chapter 2

Starting Your Webbing

Open File

Look in: my_web_site

_private   computers   new_page_2
images   dummies   new_top
article_index   entertainment   photo
article_left   imagery   pocket
article_top   index   resume
articles   locales   trade
barbie   me_index   writing
book_index   me_left
books   me_top
books_left   nevis
books_top   nevis_journal
column_index   nevis_photos
column_left   new
column_top   new_index
columns   new_left

History
My Documents
Desktop
Favorites
Web Folders

File name: index.htm
Files of type: Web Pages

Open
Cancel

Figure 2-4:
The Open File dialog box.

Saving Your Web Pages

There's an old saying in software development circles, and it goes a little something like this: "Save and save often." Well, saving and saving often is a great idea in FrontPage, too. The number of times you save a file is directly proportional to how mad you'll get if you lose all the work you just finished. Keeping that in mind, use one of the following three easy ways to save a file in FrontPage 2000:

✦ Choose File➪Save.

✦ Click the Save button on the Standard toolbar.

✦ Press Ctrl+S.

If you haven't yet saved the file, the Save As dialog box appears (as shown in Figure 2-5).

From the Save As dialog box, you can give your file a name and choose where to save it. After you save the file for the first time, you no longer see the Save As dialog box when you use any of the preceding three methods of saving.

Figure 2-5: The Save As dialog box helps you place and then save your file.

Chapter 3: Getting Organized Before It's Too Late

In This Chapter

✔ **Getting to know the FrontPage Editor**

✔ **Setting up your toolbars**

✔ **Dealing with your folders**

✔ **Importing Web elements**

*B*efore you get too far along into churning out Web pages like a well-oiled machine, you should take a step back and set things up in FrontPage to your liking. Get your toolbars just right because you may end up clicking lots of buttons during your Web creating. Organize your file folders so that you can at least remember where you are putting your masterpieces. And don't forget to use some of the Web stuff that you may have already lying around. With a little advanced thought, your future efforts won't seem so hard.

A Quick Guide to the Three Views of the FrontPage Editor

Like most things in FrontPage 2000, you can make the Editor as simple or as complex as you like. The Editor is designed to appeal to HTML editing newbies as well as to HTML masters and purists. It achieves this delicate balance between the new kids on the block and the veterans by enabling users either to use drag-and-drop tools for composing pages or to edit the HTML directly.

The FrontPage Editor is split into three basic views, which you can access by clicking one of the three tabs in the bottom-left corner of the editing window:

✦ **Normal view:** This is the default view for the Editor, and undoubtedly the way Microsoft prefers that you create your Web pages.

In the Normal view (shown in the Figure 3-1), you can create Web page elements on-screen and position them anywhere you like. As you do this, FrontPage autogenerates the necessary HTML to make the page that you've created.

The idea is that FrontPage takes HTML editing out of the HTML creation process and replaces it with menus, toolbars, wizards, and other elements that Office users are accustomed to seeing.

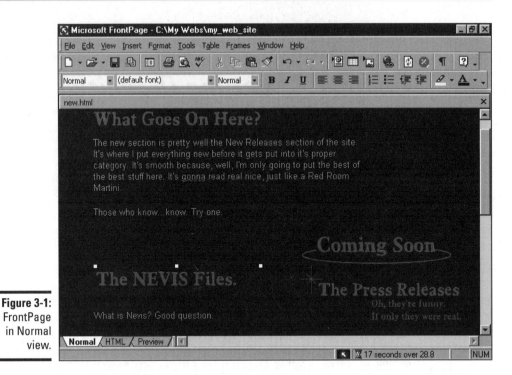

Figure 3-1:
FrontPage
in Normal
view.

✦ **HTML view:** Prefer to do your own HTML editing? You can use the HTML view (shown in Figure 3-2) to edit your HTML directly and bypass all the automated features that the Normal view offers. This view works like a more traditional HTML editor, but it also offers a number of handy features, like HTML coloring and tag viewing, to make the editing process a little more user friendly.

✦ **Preview view:** The Preview view eliminates the need to open up a browser to see what your pages look like. This view gives you an immediate idea of whether a page you've created is working properly, because Preview view works like Internet Explorer emulator.

The Preview view is a good idea . . . almost. The downside is that it emulates Internet Explorer, which means that if you use the Preview view as the only method of previewing your work, you're neglecting the large number of Web users who use some form of Netscape Navigator.

Using FrontPage Toolbars

Now that FrontPage 2000 is included in the Microsoft Office suite, it comes with the requisite Office toolbars, including the Standard and Formatting toolbars. In addition to these two toolbars, FrontPage supports seven other toolbars that you can display and customize. If you get to know these toolbars, your life may be much easier later! Table 3-1 highlights the functions of each toolbar.

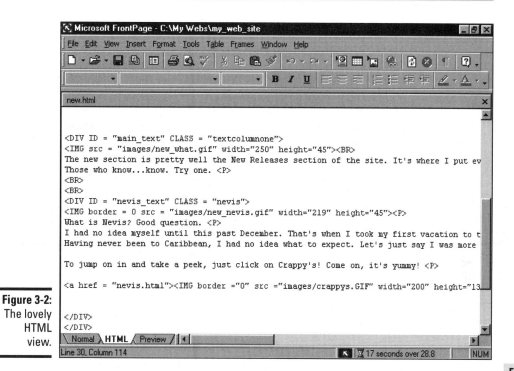

Figure 3-2:
The lovely
HTML
view.

Table 3-1	FrontPage Toolbars
Toolbar	*Features*
Standard	Includes such general Office functions as Open, Save, and Print.
Formatting	Provides font-style and formatting functions.
DHTML Effects	Assigns Dynamic HTML events to things like mouse clicks and rollovers.
Navigation	Lets you control the layout and size of the Navigation view. You can also use this toolbar to add external links.
Picture	Gives you point-and-click access to all the image-editing tools built into FrontPage 2000.
Positioning	Enables you to set locations and move the position of objects on a page.
Reports	Makes all the FrontPage reports accessible through a drop-down list.
Style	Launches the Cascading Style Sheet dialog box.
Table	Generates quick and easy HTML tables.

To display a toolbar, choose <u>V</u>iew⇨<u>T</u>oolbars⇨*Name_of_the_toolbar.* After you choose the toolbar you want, a recessed check mark appears in the menu next to the name of the toolbar, and the toolbar you chose will either float on-screen or sit next to the Standard and Formatting toolbars.

If a toolbar appears to be floating randomly on-screen, you can drag it up to the location of the other toolbars. After you get the toolbar up there, the toolbar area grows to accommodate the new toolbar. You can also double-click the title bar of a floating toolbar to mount it with the other non-floating toolbars.

Creating Folders

FrontPage 2000 offers you two ways to create new folders for a Web project. The easiest way is to go to the Folders view and choose File➪New➪Folder from the menu bar. In this case, FrontPage generates the new folder in the directory that's currently selected in the Folders view.

Switching back over to the Folders view to create a new folder isn't always convenient, however. Fortunately, you can generate new folders in any of the views in which you can bring up the Folder List. Here's how you do it:

1. **If the Folder List is not already open, choose View➪Folder List to activate it.**

2. **Right-click the folder in which you want to place your new folder and then choose New Folder from the pop-up menu that appears.**

   FrontPage creates the new folder and prompts you to enter a name for it.

3. **Enter a name for your new folder in the active text box next to your new folder.**

   The text box appears as a black box with a blinking white cursor at the end of the box.

4. **Press Enter to set the name of your new folder.**

Collapsing and expanding folders

If you use Windows 95, Windows 98, or Windows NT, you may already be used to seeing your folders arranged in a hierarchy that you can collapse and expand. Such an arrangement makes it easy to grasp the overall structure of your folders. FrontPage 2000 also employs the capability to view data through collapsing and expanding folders.

1. **Activate the Folders List by choosing View➪Folder List.**

2. **Click any folder with a plus sign surrounded by a box to expand the folder and view the contents of that folder.**

After you click the plus sign, you'll notice that it changes to a minus sign surrounded by a box.

3. **To collapse the folder, click the minus sign surrounded by a box.**

You can also copy and move files by using the Folders List, just as you can in the Windows Explorer. Simply right-click the file, drag it into the desired folder, and choose either Copy or Move from the pop-up menu.

Deleting Files and Folders

FrontPage 2000 offers a number of ways for you to delete files and folders. To delete any file or folder from your project, choose from any of the following methods:

✦ **Deleting from the Folder List:** Click an item and press Delete. The Confirm Delete dialog box appears to make sure that you're really serious about wanting to delete the file or folder (see Figure 3-3).

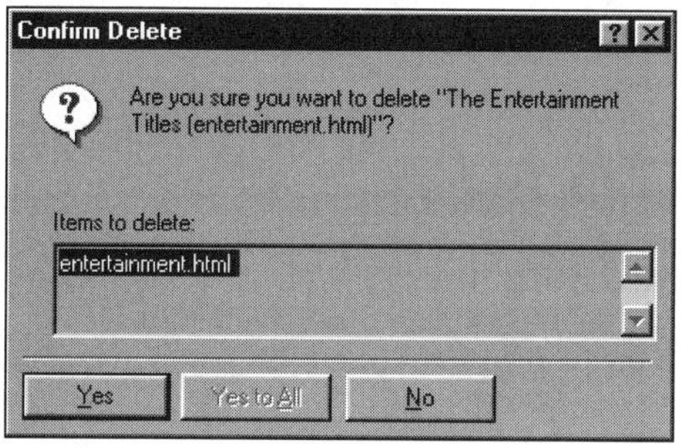

Figure 3-3:
Are you
really sure
you want
to delete?

✦ **Deleting from the Folder view:** This procedure works just like the Folder List option.

✦ **Deleting from the Reports menu:** You can also delete various HTML pages on which you generate reports. Just click the HTML page in a report and press Delete. Again, the Confirm Delete dialog box appears to confirm that you want to delete the HTML page. You can't do this from the Site Summary report, however.

✦ **Deleting from the Navigation view:** Deleting from this view is slightly different. Select the page that you want to delete and then press Delete. The Delete Page dialog box appears, as shown n Figure 3-4. Select the Remove This Page and All the Pages Below It from All Navigation Bars radio button to keep the page in the Web but delete all links to the file, or select the Delete This Page and All the Pages Below It from the Web radio button to eliminate the page entirely.

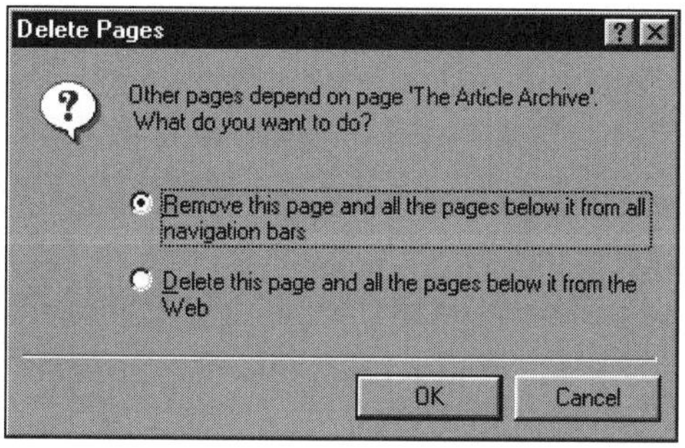

Figure 3-4:
The Delete
Page
dialog box.

**FrontPage
Chapter 3**

**Getting Organized
Before It's Too Late**

✦ **Deleting from the Hyperlinks view:** Select the page that you want to delete and press the Delete key. The Confirm Delete dialog box appears to make sure that you want to delete your selection.

✦ **Deleting from drop-down lists:** This option is available whenever you have a file selected. To delete the selected file, you can either press the Delete key or choose Edit⇨Delete.

After you delete a page from your Web, you can't undo the action. You're always better off eliminating the page from the active Web by stripping the page out of the Navigation view first and then removing the page. This method eliminates the file from use but at least keeps it in the Web. That way, you can check to see whether deleting it had any unintended repercussions. The same rule applies for other kinds of files as well.

Importing Webs and Web Pages

If you're working with a number of different Web sites, you may want to import important Web pages, graphics, and even other Web sites into your current Web site. Fortunately, FrontPage 2000 enables you to import such accessories quite easily.

You always need to specify the destination into which you want to import files first! To do so, first activate the Folder List by choosing View⇨Folder List from the menu bar. Then click the folder into which you want to import the data.

Importing files

To import a file into FrontPage, follow these steps:

1. **Choose File⇨Import to bring up the Import dialog box (as shown in Figure 3-5).**

2. **Click the Add File button. The Add File to Import List dialog box appears.**

3. **In the drop-down list in the Add File to Import List dialog box, select the file(s) that you want to import from either your local drive or the network.**

4. **Click the Open button to add the file(s) to your Import List.**

5. **Click OK in the Import dialog box to import the files into your Web.**

Importing folders

To import a folder into FrontPage, follow these steps:

1. **Choose File⇨Import to bring up the Import dialog box.**

2. **Click the Add Folder button to bring up the Browse for Folder dialog box.**

3. **Select the folder from which you want to add files by searching through the available local and network drives.**

4. **Click OK to add that folder and its contents to the Import List.**

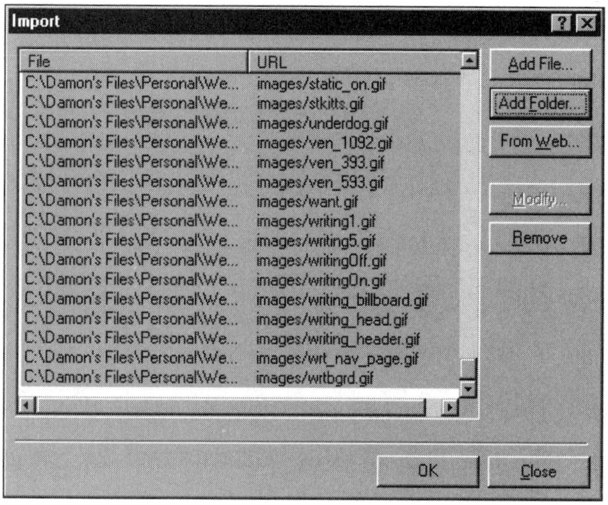

Figure 3-5:
You can
import a
file into
FrontPage.

5. **Click OK in the Import dialog box to import the folder into your Web.**

You don't have to import files and then import folders separately. You can make a collection of files and folders by adding them to the Import List first. Once you've collected all the items you want to import, click OK in the Import dialog box to import the whole collection.

**FrontPage
Chapter 3**

**Getting Organized
Before It's Too Late**

Importing a Web

To import another Web into your existing FrontPage Web, follow these steps:

1. **Choose File⇨Import to bring up the Import dialog box.**

2. **Click the From Web button to bring up the Import Web Wizard.**

3. **Choose the location of the Web you want to import.**

   The wizard provides two simple import options. If you select the From a Source Directory radio button, a browse button appears on-screen. Select that button to search your local and network drives for available Webs. If you choose the From the World Wide Web radio button, the Wizard provides a field for you to enter the URL from which you want to import the Web.

4. **Click Next to bring up the Choose Download Amount dialog box.**

5. **Set the download options for the Web you want to import.**

   You can limit the size of the Web you want to download by choosing from a series of check boxes. These check boxes let you specify the number of layers of the Web you want to import, the size (in kilobytes) that you want to import, and the kinds of files you want to import.

6. **Click Next to bring up the Finish dialog box.**

7. **Click the Finish button to import the Web.**

Chapter 4: Laying the Groundwork for Your Web Pages

In This Chapter

✔ **Giving your Web a theme**

✔ **Editing your theme**

✔ **Determining background images**

✔ **Selecting background colors**

✔ **Choosing page margins**

*I*f you thought you'd just jump right in and start punching keys and buttons to make a Web page, you've probably figured out by now that life isn't quite that easy. To do a thorough job, you need to consider the elements that may seem secondary to you but make a big difference — especially when you try to apply them later and realize that you should have thought of doing these things first! Yes, you need to consider before getting too far along whether you need a theme for your page as well as additional background images and colors. And how about your page margins? Save yourself some grief later by giving your Web some groundwork today.

Applying a Theme to a Web

Themes are compelling graphics and varying text styles that help provide a common look and feel for your Web. FrontPage 2000 comes with more than 60 different themes that you can apply to individual pages, as well as to an entire Web. To add a theme to a Web or Web page, follow these steps:

1. **Choose Format⇨Theme to open the Themes dialog box (see Figure 4-1).**

2. **Click the theme that you want.**

The four check boxes that occupy the bottom-left corner of the Themes dialog box give you the following additional options:

• **Vivid Colors:** Uses more vibrant colors as you create your theme graphics and text.

• **Active Graphics:** Creates more interesting and dynamic-looking graphics for such elements as your banner.

• **Background Picture:** Adds a background image to the pages.

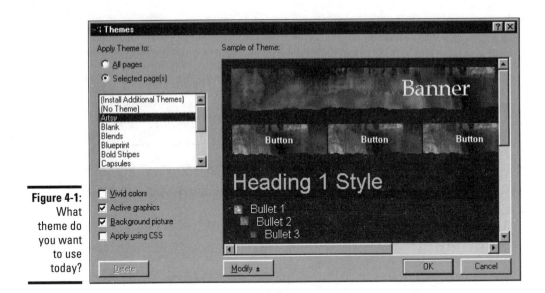

Figure 4-1:
What
theme do
you want
to use
today?

- **Apply Using CSS:** Uses Cascading Style Sheets instead of HTML to create your text and graphics styles.

3. **To choose any of these options, click the check box next to the text that describes the option you want.**

4. **Click OK to apply your chosen theme.**

Editing a Theme

What if you like the look of a theme, but the color just doesn't work for you? Thankfully, FrontPage lets you be as picky as you want. You can almost endlessly modify any of the more than 60 themes in FrontPage, providing hours of fun for the entire family!

1. **Choose Format⇨Theme to open the Themes dialog box.**

2. **Click the theme that you want.**

3. **Click the Modify button.**

   The new level of options that appears gives you the option to change the colors, graphics, and/or text of your theme.

4. **Click the Colors, Graphics, or Text button to edit the color, graphic, and text properties of your theme.**

5. **Click the Save button to save any changes to the theme, or click the Save As button to save your theme under a new name. If you click the Save As button, the Save Theme dialog box appears (see Figure 4-2). Choose a new name for your theme and then click OK to save the new theme.**

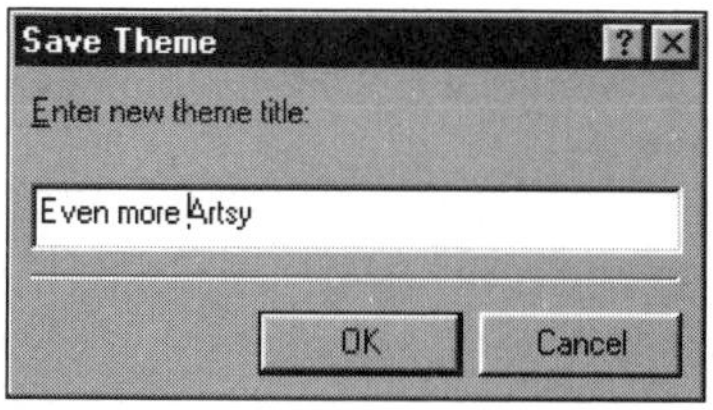

Figure 4-2:
The Save
Theme
dialog box.

Editing Page Properties

Every Web page has a number of individual options that you can modify to fit the needs of the site you're building. These options range from choosing Web page background images to specifying the color of hyperlinks. FrontPage organizes these options in one convenient place so that accessing them is a snap.

In the Normal view, you can right-click in a Web page and choose Page Properties to access a tabbed dialog box, called Page Properties, shown in Figure 4-3.

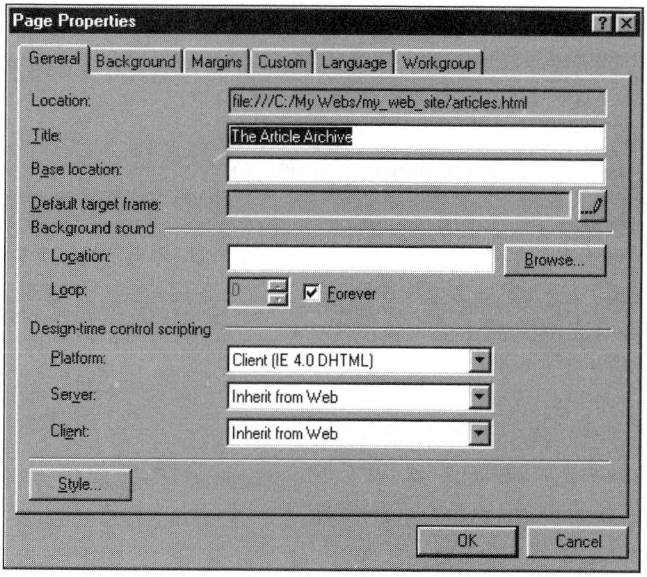

Figure 4-3:
Choose
your page
options
here.

You can do a number of detailed things from the Page Properties dialog box, most of which are described in the following sections. Some of the simpler options that you can easily change include

✦ **Changing a page title:** You can change a page title by inputting a new name in the Title field on the General tab.

◆ **Specifying a default page sound:** Also on the General tab, you can click the Browse button to place a sound in your Web. Unless you leave the Forever box unchecked and insert a value in the Loop field, the sound will loop continuously when the page is loaded.

Sounds are platform-dependent, so if you specify a PC sound file (for example, a .wav file), Macintosh and UNIX Web users won't hear it.

◆ **Specifying the page language:** On the Language tab, you can choose the language for both the page text and the HTML coding.

◆ **Assigning categories to the page:** Categories are used to track a page when it's being worked on in a multi-user environment. On the Workgroup tab, you can specify the categories that a page falls under, as well as the current review status of the page and who's assigned to work on it.

Setting a background image

To set a background image from the Page Properties dialog box (which you access by right-clicking in a Web page in the Normal View and choosing Page Properties — shown in Figure 4-4), follow these steps:

1. **Select the Background tab.**

2. **In the Formatting area, select the Background Picture check box.**

3. **Click the Browse button to locate and select the background image that you want to use.**

When you click this button, the Select Background Picture dialog box appears, as shown in Figure 4-5. Like every other dialog box in FrontPage that requires you to find a file, the Select Background Picture dialog box

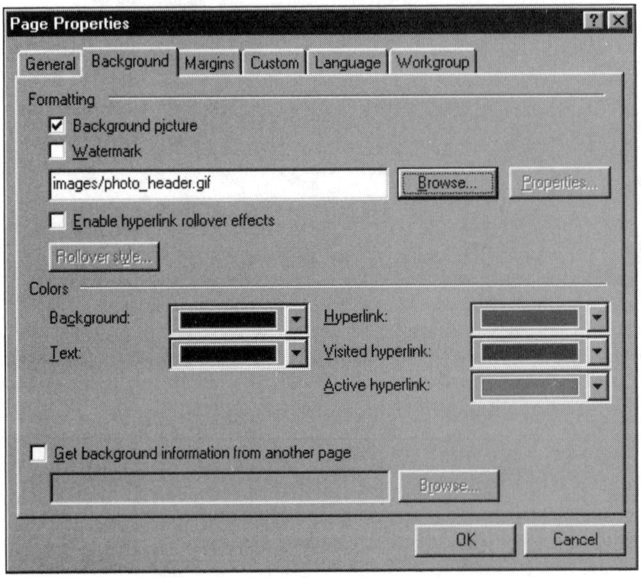

Figure 4-4:
The Page Properties dialog box shows background options.

Page Properties

General | **Background** | Margins | Custom | Language | Workgroup

Formatting

☑ Background picture
☐ Watermark

images/photo_header.gif   [Browse...] [Properties...]

☐ Enable hyperlink rollover effects

[Rollover style...]

Colors

Background: [▼]   Hyperlink: [▼]
Text: [▼]   Visited hyperlink: [▼]
                                 Active hyperlink: [▼]

☐ Get background information from another page

[   ]   [Browse...]

[OK]   [Cancel]

defaults to letting you choose files from your Web only. However, by clicking either the Globe button or the File Folder button, you can look for background images on the Web or elsewhere on your computer as well. You can also click the Clip Art button to bring up the Clip Art Gallery to find an image from there.

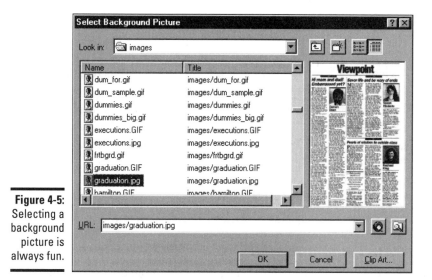

Figure 4-5:
Selecting a background picture is always fun.

4. **Click OK.**

   The image you chose won't be visible until you click OK to close the Page Properties dialog box, too.

If you've already set a background image for another page on your Web site, you can use the same background image for the page you're currently in by importing the page settings. To do so, check the Get Background Information from Another Page box and then click the Browse button to find the page from which you want to import the page settings.

If you choose to import a background image, your background colors and hyperlink colors (see the following section) will also be imported.

If you're using a theme, you'll find that the Background tab in the Page Properties dialog box is missing. That's because you're using a theme, and themes require that all the pages using the theme have the same background settings.

Setting background colors

From the Background tab in the Page Properties dialog box, you can set the background colors and the various hyperlink colors for a Web page. For each option, a drop-down list enables you to choose from a series of default colors, as well as to specify your own Web-safe color through the color picker, shown in Figure 4-6. In total, you have five color options.

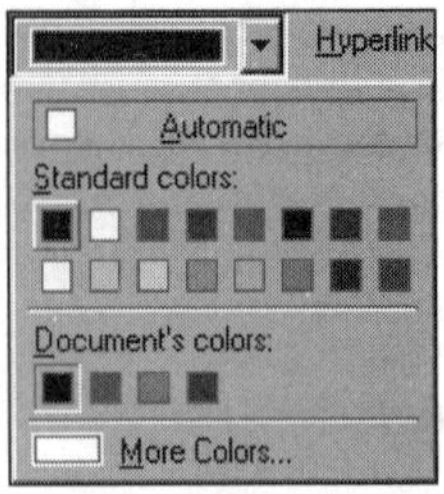

Figure 4-6:
Specify
your
Background
color the
easy way.

✦ **Background:** If you don't have a background image selected, this color appears on the page.

✦ **Text:** This menu sets the default color for text on your Web page.

✦ **Hyperlink:** The hyperlink color is the color that is shown for either text that represents a link or the border around an image that's a link. This color is shown only if the link has never been visited.

✦ **Visited Hyperlink:** Identical to the Hyperlink, except this color is displayed if a link *has* been previously visited.

✦ **Active Hyperlink:** This color appears on a link when a user clicks it.

Setting page margins

Say you want to indent an entire Web page, either from the top or from the left. What might otherwise be a bear of an HTML problem, FrontPage 2000 makes an exceptionally trivial task. Here's how you do it:

1. **From the Page Properties dialog box (which you access by right-clicking a Web page in the Normal view and then choosing Page Properties), select the Margins tab.**

2. **Check the box of the margin that you want to indent. FrontPage lets you indent only the top and left-hand margins.**

3. **In the Pixels fields, type the desired margin size.**

4. **Click OK to see how your new margins look!**

Chapter 5: Getting the Basics on Your Page

In This Chapter

ν Getting your text just right

ν Making and modifying tables

ν Creating and updating hyperlinks

The early Web seemed to have just a few common elements. Of course, there was text on the page — nothing too fancy, but with a little bit of variety (maybe some color, a nice bullet list, and so on). And to help present some of this text in columns and rows, tables soon became the rage. Tables were also a sure-fire way to arrange text on a page. Finally, the Web would not have become the Web without its capability of letting you use hyperlinks — you click here and go there.

These concepts are still the fundamentals of the Web today. What a coincidence it is that you find out how to do all these basic things in this chapter.

Changing Text Attributes

FrontPage 2000, by and large, looks and feels like Microsoft Word when it comes to changing text attributes. In the Normal view, creating text is as simple as placing the cursor where you want it on-screen and then typing away. Editing your newly typed text is merely a matter of selecting the text and then choosing the appropriate text-editing feature.

But the flexibility that the FrontPage offers in changing text attributes does come with a price. In making the FrontPage 2000 text-editing features comparable to Word's, Microsoft has committed itself to the latest browser technology. As a result, a number of the advanced text-editing options beyond boldface, italics, and alignment have absolutely no visual effect on older Web browsers, including even Internet Explorer 3.0 and Netscape Navigator 3.0.

You can change most of the basic attributes of a piece of text by highlighting it and then selecting the appropriate button from the Formatting toolbar, shown in Figure 5-1.

Figure 5-1:
With the
Formatting
toolbar,
formatting
is a click
away.

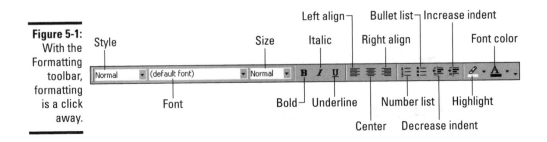

Changing font properties

To change the text attributes for text that you've created in the Normal view, follow these steps:

1. Highlight the text that you want to change.

2. Choose Format⇨Font from the menu bar.

The Font dialog box appears, as seen in Figure 5-2. (You can also get to the Font dialog box by pressing Alt+Enter or by right-clicking the selected text and choosing Font from the pop-up menu.)

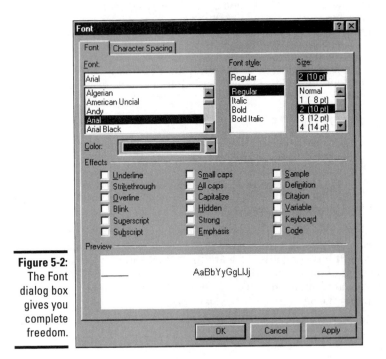

Figure 5-2:
The Font
dialog box
gives you
complete
freedom.

3. **Choose the new attributes for the selected text.**

On the Font and Character spacing tabs, you can change the font type, style, color, and size, as well as modify things like character positioning and spacing. You can also choose from a number of effects, which allow you to modify things like the text's visibility and its emphasis.

One of the biggest problems with Web site development involves fonts. When you change fonts through the Font dialog box, you're changing to fonts that are installed on *your* machine! Those fonts may not be installed on someone else's machine. As a result, what the user sees may be entirely different from what you saw when you created the page. The two safest fonts to use are Arial and Times New Roman.

Many of the items in the Effects category do not work with the older 3.0 browsers.

4. **Click OK to enable your text changes.**

Changing paragraph settings

You change paragraph settings in the same manner as you change font attributes, so if these steps seem familiar, it's because they are the same!

To change the paragraph setting for a chunk of text, follow these steps:

1. **Highlight the text that you want to change.**

2. **Choose Format⇨Paragraph from the menu bar to get to the Paragraph dialog box (see Figure 5-3).**

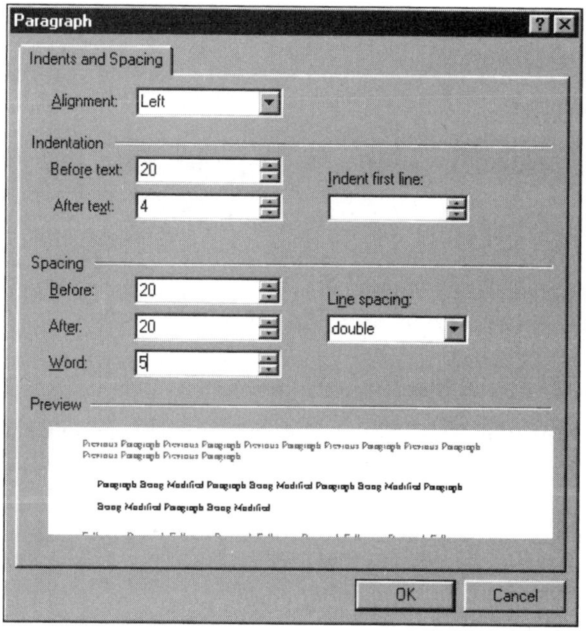

Figure 5-3:
Change
your
paragraph
settings
with a few
deft clicks.

3. **Enter the new paragraph settings in the Paragraph dialog box.**

   You can change the alignment, line spacing, and indentation of the paragraph.

   Like font attributes, paragraph settings use Cascading Style Sheets and newer versions of HTML to set property values, making many of these settings non-functional with the 3.0 and lower versions of Netscape Communicator and Internet Explorer.

4. **Click OK to change the paragraph settings.**

Creating bulleted and numbered lists

Bulleted and numbered lists are a simple yet effective way to communicate an idea or concept with emphasis. And yes, FrontPage 2000 handles them just like the rest of the Microsoft Office programs. To turn a series of text items into a bulleted or numbered list, follow these steps:

1. **Highlight the text that you want to change.**

2. **Choose Format⇨Bullets and Numbering from the menu bar to bring up the Bullets and Numbering dialog box.**

3. **Select the appropriate tab for the kind of list you want.**

   FrontPage provides three basic kinds of lists: picture bulleted, plain bulleted, and numbered.

4. **Select the bullet or number style that you want.**

5. **Click OK to change the text to a bulleted or numbered list.**

Although HTML has had simple list and bullet commands since the early days of the browser, FrontPage uses more complicated HTML. As a result, this feature may not work on some of the older browsers like Netscape Navigator 3.0 and Internet Explorer 3.0.

Changing borders and shading properties

FrontPage 2000 gives you a number of varying text border and shading options. The value in changing these settings is that you can create more emphasis on a particular piece of text by contrasting it with other text elements. Putting emphasis on particular pieces of text is especially useful for important elements that you want visitors to your site to see, such as navigation menus, sidebars, and forms.

1. **Highlight the text that you want to change.**

2. **Choose Format⇨Borders and Shading from the menu bar to call up the Borders and Shading dialog box (see Figure 5-4).**

3. **From the Borders tab, specify the border style that you want for the text box. You have a number of options to choose from:**

   • **Setting:** You can choose from one of three options: no border, a complete border around the text, or a custom border.

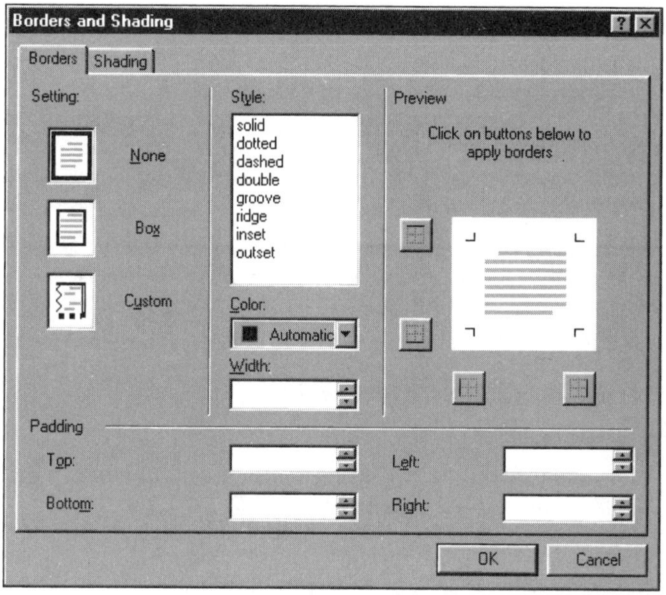

Figure 5-4:
Go wild
with the
Borders
and
Shading
options.

- **Style:** This box lists all the border styles that you can choose from, including solid lines, dashed lines, and groove lines (my favorite) just to name a few.

**FrontPage
Chapter 5**

**Getting the Basics
on Your Page**

- **Color:** Here, you can choose a color for your border from the many Web-safe colors.

- **Width:** In this box, you can specify how wide (in pixels) you want the border to be.

- **Padding:** Here, you can set how much padding (in pixels) you want between all sides of the border and the text inside it.

- **Preview:** In this field, you can see what your borders will look like, as well as add or remove individual sides of the border.

4. Choose your shading options.

From the Shading tab, you can set the foreground and background colors, as well as select an image as the background for the text box. To choose a background image, click the Browse button to find an image on your local drive, a network drive, or the World Wide Web. With each color selection, you have several default choices, but you can also specify any color from the Web palette.

5. Click OK to set your border and shading options.

WARNING!

All the HTML code required to create these effects from HTML 3.2 and Cascading Style Sheets 1.0 or higher. As a result, the older 3.0 browsers do not support most of the border and shading options.

Working with Tables

Tables are the backbone of nearly all Web page development. The notion of a table with rows and columns was one of the first concepts introduced in the very first version of HTML. Even with the advent of Dynamic HTML, Cascading Style Sheets, and a host of plug-ins, tables are still the simplest way of presenting data within a Web browser.

Not surprisingly, FrontPage offers a host of utilities that make generating and maintaining tables a reasonably easy task. It should also come as no surprise that the syntax and methodology for creating tables is very similar to that in the other Office programs.

Creating a new table

To create a table in FrontPage, follow these steps:

1. **Choose Table⇨Insert⇨Table from the menu bar to call up the Insert Table dialog box (shown in Figure 5-5).**

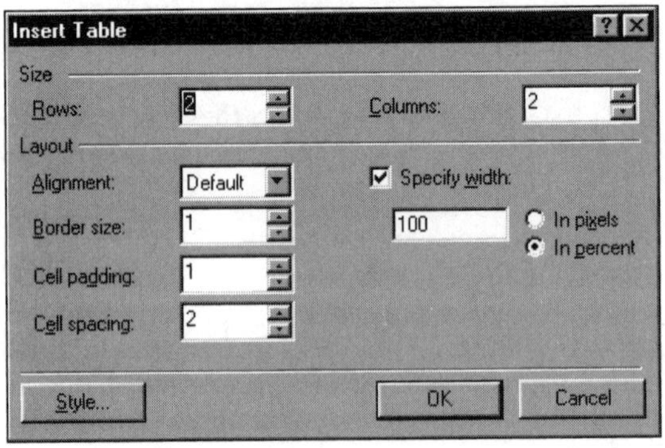

Figure 5-5:
You can
insert
tables into
your page
the easy
way!

2. **Choose the number of Rows and Columns that you want for your table.**

Remember: If you need more rows and columns after you create your table, you can just right-click a cell and choose Insert Row or Insert Column from the pop-up menu.

3. **Set your layout options from the five options in the layout area of the Insert Table dialog box:**

- **Alignment:** Sets how you want the table to be aligned on the page. Choices are left, right, center, and justify.

- **Border Size:** Sets a line border around both the cells and the outside of the table. If you don't want a border, set the value to 0.

- **Cell Padding:** Sets the distance, in pixels, between the borders of a cell and the text within the cell.

- **Cell Spacing:** Sets the distance, in pixels, between cells.

- **Specify Width:** Sets the width of the table. You can specify the width as a percentage of the page or as a set pixel width.

  You can also set the text style for the table by clicking the Style button.

4. **Click OK to insert the new table.**

TIP

Once you've created a table, you can go back and change the properties you just set by placing your cursor in any table cell and then choosing Table➪ Properties➪Table to bring up the Table Properties dialog box (see Figure 5-6).

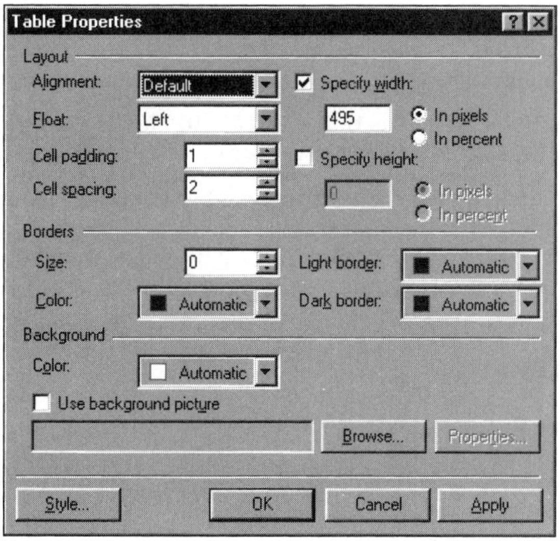

Figure 5-6:
The Table
Properties
dialog box.

You can also choose Table➪Properties➪Cell to change the properties you just set for individual cells. Make your changes in the Cell Properties dialog box that appears.

Modifying tables

In addition to generating tables, FrontPage offers a host of tools for modifying tables after you create them. The following is a list of the ways in which you can modify a table:

+ **Adding cells:** You can add individual cells, rows, or columns. In all cases, first place the cursor where you want to create the new cells, rows, or columns.

  - To insert new cells, choose Table➪Insert➪Cell. FrontPage places a new cell directly to the right of the cell in which you placed the cursor.

  - To insert new rows or columns, choose Table➪Insert➪Rows or Columns. The Insert Rows or Columns dialog box appears (see Figure 5-7). Choose the number of rows or columns that you want to insert, as well as their location, and then click OK to insert them.

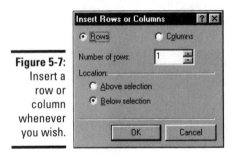

Figure 5-7:
Insert a
row or
column
whenever
you wish.

◆ **Deleting cells:** Select a cell (or group of cells) and then choose Table➪ Delete Cells to eliminate the cell and its contents from the table.

◆ **Merging cells:** Select the cells that you want to merge and then choose Table➪Merge Cells to collapse the two cells and combine their contents.

◆ **Splitting cells:** Select the cells that you want to split and then choose Table➪Split Cells. From the Split Cells dialog box (shown in Figure 5-8), choose whether you want to split into rows or columns and how many rows or columns you want to split the cell(s) into, and then click OK.

Figure 5-8:
Splitting
cells is
never a
chore.

◆ **Distributing cells:** Select rows or columns of uneven size and then choose either Table➪Distribute Rows Evenly or Table➪Distribute Columns Evenly to make the rows or columns equal sizes.

◆ **AutoFit:** AutoFit tries to find the optimal size for the cells in the table based on their contents. This way, there's no wasted space in the table. Oftentimes, this is a good tool to use when you've replaced text or a graphic of a different size within a table cell. Select the cells and choose Table➪AutoFit to set the optimal table.

Creating and Using Hyperlinks

Hyperlinks sounds like such an impressive word . . . very futuristic . . . the kind of thing you'd expect Captain Kirk or Captain Picard to burst out with on any given episode of *Star Trek*. Truthfully, though, hyperlinks are just a way of jumping from location to location within a series of Web pages.

Checking spelling throughout a Web

Don't wait until your pages go before the entire world on the Web! Check your spelling before others find your mistakes! From anywhere inside FrontPage, you can run a Web-wide spell-check to see which pages contain spelling errors. You can also tell FrontPage to fix those spelling errors and track them so that you can see them in the Tasks view. To track spelling errors in FrontPage, follow these steps:

1. **Choose Tools⇨Spelling. The Spelling dialog box appears. (As with other Office products, you can also press F7 to open the Spelling dialog box.)**

2. **Choose whether you want to run a spell-check on the Entire Web or on only Selected Page(s) by selecting one of the two radio buttons in the dialog box.**

3. **Select the Add a Task for Each Page with Misspellings check box to turn those spelling mistakes into tasks.**

4. **Click OK. FrontPage checks through all the files you specified and provides you with a report on the pages that contain spelling errors, as well as the number of spelling errors on those pages.**

Hyperlinks are the navigational building blocks of any Web site. Without hyperlinks, you'd never get off the home page of a Web site. So it should come as no surprise that FrontPage has a vast array of tools for generating and maintaining hyperlinks. To create a hyperlink in a Web page, follow these steps:

1. **Highlight the text or image that you want to turn into a hyperlink. (You can also create a link to a page without highlighting anything at all. In this case, the link uses the title of the page that you're linking to for a text description.)**

2. **Choose Insert⇨Hyperlink from the menu bar to bring up the Create Hyperlink dialog box (see Figure 5-9).**

If you're trying to cut down on using menus, you can click the Hyperlink button shown to the left on the Standard toolbar to access the dialog box.

3. **Enter the link location in the URL field. FrontPage has four options for linking to pages and objects:**

- **Browsing your Web:** FrontPage enables you to browse through your Web by using a pull-down menu and to select a page or an object to link to.

- **Using a Web browser:** If you click the Globe button in the Create Hyperlink dialog box, FrontPage launches your default Web browser. With your browser open, you can search for the Web page that you want to link to and then insert it in the URL field.

- **Browsing your computer:** Clicking the file folder with a spyglass lets you browse your entire computer for files, as opposed to looking for files only within the current Web. When you double-click a file that you want to link to, the pathway to the file is placed in the URL field.

FrontPage Chapter 5

Getting the Basics on Your Page

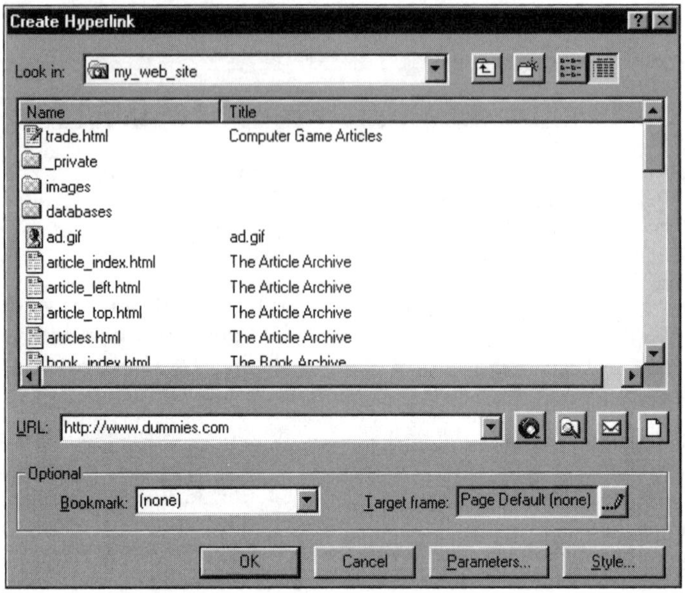

Create Hyperlink

Look in: my_web_site

Name	Title
trade.html	Computer Game Articles
_private	
images	
databases	
ad.gif	ad.gif
article_index.html	The Article Archive
article_left.html	The Article Archive
article_top.html	The Article Archive
articles.html	The Article Archive
book_index.html	The Book Archive

URL: http://www.dummies.com

Optional

Bookmark: (none)   Target frame: Page Default (none)

OK   Cancel   Parameters...   Style...

Figure 5-9:
Hyperlinking
has never
been so
easy.

Although browsing your computer may be a good way to create links to files on an Intranet, where everyone has access to the same files on a network server, it's a very bad way to link to files when publishing to a Web site. FrontPage inserts an absolute pathway to a file that includes the drive letter (C:, D:, and so on). If the files are on your local machine, the link won't work when it's posted to your Web site. The only instance in which this is not the case is when your computer *is* the Web server.

• **Inserting an e-mail address:** If you click the E-Mail button in the Create Hyperlink dialog box, you can enter an e-mail address to serve as the link. In this case, when a user clicks the link, the browser launches the default e-mail client and inserts the specified address in the To: field of a message.

• **Creating a new page and linking to it:** FrontPage 2000 also enables you to create a new page and generate a link to that page. You can accomplish this by clicking the New Page icon to the far right of the Edit Hyperlink dialog box. Doing so brings up the New dialog box, which enables you to create the new page.

4. **Click OK to insert the link into your Web page.**

Working with the Hyperlinks view

One of the nice things about the Hyperlinks view is that you can choose any object in your Web site — including HTML pages and graphics — and see exactly what pages or other objects are linked into that object. You can also see where the object links. With the Folder list open, all you have to do is click an object, and the Hyperlinks view displays all the links to and from that page, as shown in Figure 5-10.

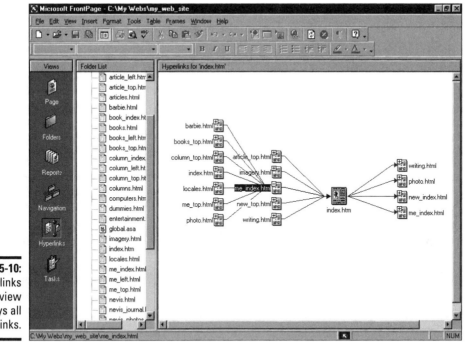

FrontPage Chapter 5

Getting the Basics on Your Page

Figure 5-10: Hyperlinks view displays all your links.

FrontPage 2000 comes with a Web browser built into its editor, but sometimes, you just can't beat the real thing. In FrontPage, you can preview a Web page in any of the browsers installed on your computer.

Recalculating a project's hyperlinks

Through the process of building pages, moving folders around, and generally doing the work that's required in maintaining a Web site, some things are liable to get broken. Hyperlinks are usually the first things to go. To combat this, FrontPage 2000 depends on Hyperlinks view, which enables you to see the links to and from every page and graphic on your site.

Ah, but if it's broken and you can't see it amid the links, how do you know that it's broken? That's where the FrontPage Recalculate Hyperlinks feature comes in handy.

To recalculate hyperlinks, choose Tools➪Recalculate Hyperlinks. FrontPage warns you that recalculating may take a while and asks whether you really want to do it. Select Yes when prompted, and you're off. Although a progress indicator doesn't appear, the bottom-left corner shows you that FrontPage is recalculating your hyperlinks.

So what is your page looking like?

You probably don't like the idea of working on something that you can't see. Well, FrontPage won't keep you in the dark. To preview a Web page from any browser on your desktop, follow these steps:

1. Switch to the Folders view by clicking the Folders icon in the Views bar, or choose View⇨Folder List to open the Folder list from your current view.

2. Click the page that you want to preview in an external Web browser.

3. Choose File⇨Preview in Browser from the menu bar. The Preview in Browser dialog box appears.

4. Select the browser in which you want to preview the page.

5. Designate a window size by selecting one of the radio buttons in the Window Size area.

   FrontPage supports four viewing ranges: the browser Default size, 640 x 480, 800 x 600, and 1024 x 768.

6. Click the Preview button to view your Web page in the specified browser.

Chapter 6: Giving Your Pages Something to Look At

In This Chapter

✔ Adding ad banners, buttons, counters, and marquees

✔ Inserting a page banner

✔ Adding clip art and other graphics

✔ Inserting a navigation bar

*I*f people just wanted to see black text on a white background, they'd probably read a book. A book without pictures or any other fancy stuff. You've probably realized by now that people like to push things, watch things move, and see neat pictures — especially if they are surfing the Web. And when they are at a Web site, they really like to know where exactly they are and where they can go. So why not oblige them? If you want to make your Web page a success, you need to make it visually pleasing, and your "look" can also carry over to navigation aids that you supply.

Inserting Some Extra Effects

You may have admired some Web pages that have those moving messages, animated buttons, hit counters, and the like. These effects are easily within your reach, too, and this section shows you the way.

Adding banner ad

So what is a banner ad, anyway? Well, mostly, it's how companies make their money on the Web — but that's a different story! Actually, a banner is simply a set of similarly sized images, usually appearing either at the top or the bottom of a Web page.

Banners are commonly used as a method of promoting advertising messages as well as key pieces of information that you want users to know. Adding a banner in FrontPage 2000 is exceptionally simple. Just follow these steps:

1. Choose Insert⇨Component⇨Banner Ad Manager from the menu bar.

You see the Banner Ad Manager Properties dialog box (see Figure 6-1), in which you can specify all the different settings for your Ad Banner.

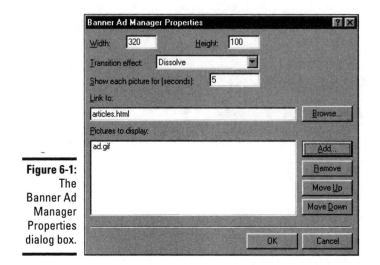

Figure 6-1:
The
Banner Ad
Manager
Properties
dialog box.

2. Choose the settings for your banner ad.

Table 6-1 explains the various settings.

3. Click OK to insert the banner ad into your Web page.

4. Select the Preview view in the FrontPage Editor to preview your banner.

Table 6-1	Banner Ad Settings
Setting	*What It Means*
Width/Height	The size of the banner. If your images are large, FrontPage crops them to fit.
Transition Effects	How the banner ads transition from one to the next. The more complicated the images are, the slower the page downloads.
Show Each Picture For	The duration of time that users can view each image.
Link To	If you want the banner to link to another page or Web site, specify in this field where you want it to link.
Pictures to Display	Using the Add, Remove, Move Up, and Move Down buttons, you can specify from this area the number of images, as well as their viewing order that you want to display.

Banner ads work by adding a Java applet to your Web. The advantage to using Java is that the ad transitions look nicer. However, if you start using a lot of transitions, adding an applet makes your Web page run slower.

Adding a hit counter

A hit counter tracks the number of times a page has been accessed and displays that number of "hits" on the Web page itself. It's a nice way of saying, "Hey, look how popular my Web page is!" That is, unless nobody's visiting your Web site, in which case you probably don't want to include a hit counter.

1. **Choose Insert⇨Component⇨Hit Counter from the menu bar to bring up the Hit Counter Properties dialog box (shown in Figure 6-2).**

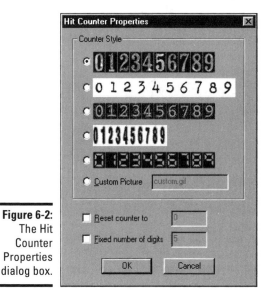

Figure 6-2:
The Hit
Counter
Properties
dialog box.

2. **Specify the style and number of digits you want in your hit counter.**

3. **Click OK to insert the hit counter into your Web page.**

If you're editing an existing hit counter and you want to reset the counter, check the Reset Counter To check box and, in the field next to it, type the number to which you want to the counter to be reset.

Adding a hover button

If you don't have buttons that animate or highlight when you roll your mouse cursor over them, then something's definitely wrong with your Web site — at least that's what the conventional wisdom preaches. There are a number of methods for adding this kind of graphical quality to a Web page, including using JavaScript and Dynamic HTML. Not to be outdone, FrontPage 2000 offers you a way to use Java to create the same effect!

1. **Choose Insert⇨Component⇨Hover Button from the menu bar to bring up the Hover Button Properties dialog box (shown in Figure 6-3).**

2. **Specify the properties for your hover button.**

You can set a number of different options for the button, including the size and color of the button and its highlight state, the *rollover effect* (what happens when the mouse cursor rolls over the button), and the page to which the button links when you click it.

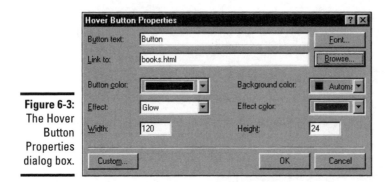

Figure 6-3:
The Hover
Button
Properties
dialog box.

You can also customize your hover button by clicking the Custom button. Here, you can pick rollover and mouse-click sounds and even provide your own rollover graphics.

3. Click OK to insert the hover button into your Web page.

In all honesty, this is not the most efficient way to build animated buttons because it uses Java, which is a memory hog and can slow down even the fastest Web browsers.

Adding a marquee

Have you ever seen the stock listing whoosh by on one of the digital boards or on the bottom of your television screen? Sure you have! Well, those are two examples of marquees, and yes, you can easily embed a marquee in your Web page. To add a marquee to a Web page in FrontPage 2000, follow these steps:

1. Choose Insert⇨Component⇨Marquee from the menu bar to get to the Marquee Properties dialog box (see Figure 6-4).

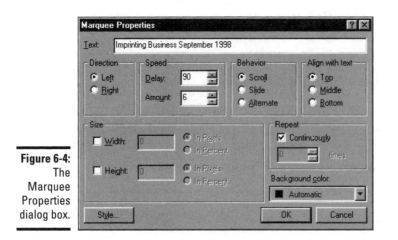

Figure 6-4:
The
Marquee
Properties
dialog box.

2. **Specify the properties for your marquee.**

Table 6-2 explains your options. In addition to these options, you can change the text style associated with the banner. To do so, click the Style button and then either choose from the available styles or select Format to create one.

3. **Click OK to insert the marquee into your Web page.**

Table 6-2	Marquee Settings
Setting	*What It Means*
Direction	Specify the direction in which you want the text to move across the screen.
Speed	Choose the speed at which you want the text to move.
Behavior	Indicate how you want the text to move on-screen.
Align with Text	Specify where you want the banner to be located in relation to the text around it.
Size	Choose the size of the banner.
Repeat	Decide whether the banner repeats continuously or just once.
Background Color	Indicate the background color for the banner.

Inserting a Page Banner

Page banners are a quick and easy way to add titles to your Web pages. To add a page banner, follow these steps:

1. **Place your cursor in the location on the page where you want to insert the banner.**

2. **Choose Insert⇨Page Banner from the menu bar to access the Page Banner Properties dialog box.**

3. **Select whether you want the banner to be treated as plain text (select the Text radio button) or as an image (select the Picture radio button).**

4. **Insert a title for your banner in the Page Banner Text field.**

5. **Click OK to insert the banner.**

Adding Graphics to Web Pages

Now that FrontPage 2000 looks more like Word than anything else, the similarities between adding graphics to a Web page in FrontPage and adding graphics to a document in Word are not surprising. In fact, adding graphics in FrontPage is very similar to adding graphics in Word. However, if you can't adjust your preferences to using the Word-like interface in FrontPage 2000, you can still use the FrontPage HTML capabilities.

FrontPage
Chapter 6

Giving Your Pages
Something to
Look At

Although FrontPage 2000 supports a host of file formats for graphics, older browsers do not support many of the file formats that FrontPage supports. As a result, you're better off making sure that the graphic you want to import is in either .gif or .jpg format before you import it into FrontPage 2000.

Adding graphics through the Normal view

To add a graphic by using the FrontPage graphical user interface, follow these easy steps:

1. **Click the location on the active Web page in the Editor where you want to put your graphic. (If your page is blank, your only choice is to place your cursor in the top-left corner.)**

2. **Choose Insert⇨Picture⇨From File to bring up the Picture dialog box (see Figure 6-5).**

   You can also add graphics to a Web page via the traditional Windows drag-and-drop interface. To do so, go to the folder on your desktop that houses the graphic you want to insert. Click and drag the graphic onto the active Web page and voilà! There it is . . . good to go!

3. **Choose the graphic that you want to insert from the Picture dialog box.**

   From the Picture dialog box, you can browse your Web, the rest of your computer, or the Internet to find the graphic that you want to insert. FrontPage 2000 also provides thumbnail previews for each graphic you click, so you can see what you're adding before you add it. FrontPage 2000 defaults to enabling you to view only the files in your Web. To add graphics from another place, you need to click either the globe with the spyglass (for the Internet) or the folder with a spyglass (for your computer) to choose graphics from files in another location.

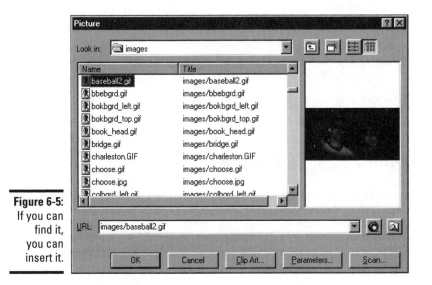

Figure 6-5: If you can find it, you can insert it.

You're always better off adding graphics files to your Web before adding them to a Web page. That way, the files are already contained in your Web, and you'll never have to worry about changing the file pathnames of links in the Web pages.

4. **Click OK to add the graphic to your Web page.**

Adding Clip Art to a Web Page

FrontPage 2000 comes with an extensive Clip Art gallery that helps you easily create buttons and banners, as well as communicate all kinds of different themes and emotions. To add clip art to your Web page, follow these steps:

1. **Choose Insert➪Picture➪Clip.**

   The Clip Art Gallery dialog box appears, as shown in Figure 6-6. Notice that you can add various types of clip art, including graphics, sound files, and video clips.

2. **Select the tab for the kind of clip art that you want to insert into your Web page.**

   Be careful with sound and video clips. Unlike graphics, sound and video clips are specific to the various operating systems, such as Windows 95, Macintosh, and UNIX. So if you choose to insert a .wav file in your Web page, for example, Mac users will probably not be able to hear it.

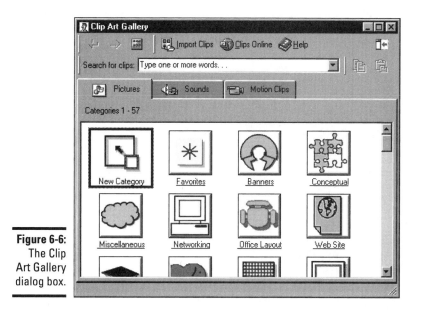

Figure 6-6:
The Clip
Art Gallery
dialog box.

3. **Choose a category of clip art that interests you.**

Notice that in the case of sound and video clips, a number of the categories contain no clips.

4. **Click the image that you want to use in your Web page.**

This action brings up a floating menu that gives you four button choices for that piece of clip art:

- **Insert Clip:** Yep, you guessed it. Selecting this button puts the clip in your Web page.

- **Preview Clip:** Select this button to look at or listen to your clip before inserting it into your Web page.

- **Add Clip to Favorite or Other Category:** If you love this clip so much that you keep using it over and over, you can move it to the favorites or another category to make it easier to get to.

- **Find Similar Clips:** Use this option to find other clips that are similar to the one you've currently selected.

To bypass the floating menu altogether, right-click the clip that you want to insert and choose Insert.

Chapter 7: Image Editing for Everyone

In This Chapter

✔ Using the Picture toolbar

✔ Manipulating and editing your images

✔ Making an image map

*I*f you think that you can simply grab or create an image and then plop it as-is into your Web page, you're not going to take advantage of what a little bit of editing can do. Sure, you may have a great image to use, but think about what else you can do to it. Scale it, flip it, move it, bevel it, brighten it, and more! You may even want to place some text over it or turn the image itself into a hyperlink. Hey, you can even turn different parts of the image into hyperlinks and make a clickable image map. Now aren't you sorry that you were going to settle for less?

Activating the Picture Toolbar

In FrontPage 2000, you can't edit a graphics image without first activating the Picture toolbar. Unlike a number of the other toolbars in FrontPage, the Picture toolbar does not have any corresponding keyboard or menu options. To activate the Picture toolbar, choose View➪Toolbars➪Picture.

Figure 7-1 shows the basic functionality of each button on the Picture toolbar.

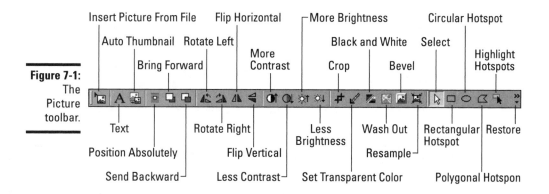

Figure 7-1: The Picture toolbar.

Working with Auto Thumbnails

An *Auto Thumbnail* is a handy tool that enables you to create a mini-version of a picture. This is particularly useful when you want to use an image as a button that then links to a larger version of the picture. To create an Auto Thumbnail, click the Auto Thumbnail button after you select an image.

After you create a thumbnail and go to save the page, FrontPage prompts you to save the new thumbnail image that you created. After you load the page in a browser, you see the thumbnail rather than the original image. Then, when you click the thumbnail, the larger version appears in the Web browser by itself.

Image Manipulation Made Easy

If FrontPage doesn't make image manipulation easy, it at least makes image manipulation easier than ever before. Although image editing in FrontPage is not as powerful as PhotoShop or some of those other popular graphics software, you can't beat the convenience — and the price — of having this editing capability already built into your Web-creation application.

Scaling an image

Scaling, is the process of making an entire image either larger or smaller. There's no cutting away of the image involved here. In fact, there isn't even a button for this one! You can scale an image just by clicking the image.

After you click an image, you see anchor points appear around the border of the image. To scale the image, click and drag one of these anchor points. The image resizes itself according to where you let go of the anchor point.

 To scale an image and keep its proportions intact, choose one of the corner anchor points, and then scale the image. Scaling in this manner keeps the aspect ratio (the height-to-width ratio of an image) consistent as the image gets bigger or smaller.

After you scale your image, you can resample it by clicking the Resample button on the Picture toolbar. The Resample tool analyzes the image that you just scaled. If, for example, the image became bigger, the pixels that make up the image will have been stretched. The Resample tool then breaks up the stretched pixels into smaller pixels to create a crisper, cleaner image. Similarly, if you shrink the image, you end up with more pixels than are really necessary for a smaller image. In this case, using the Resample tool eliminates any unnecessary pixels without sacrificing image quality.

 If you don't like the way your new-scaled image looks, you can click the Restore button to reset the image to its original size.

You can use the Restore button on a number of other Picture toolbar features as well, including the Color, Brightness, Contrast, Rotate, and Flip tools.

Changing brightness and contrast

Changing a graphic's *brightness* makes the graphic appear lighter or darker. Changing a graphic's *contrast* makes the graphic's individual pixels either stand out more or become more muted. Usually, setting a graphic's contrast goes hand in hand with changing the graphic's brightness. So, for example, the brighter a graphic becomes, the more contrast you need to avoid it becoming washed out.

1. **In the Normal view, click the image that you want to modify.**

2. **Click any of the four Contrast or Brightness options on the Picture toolbar:**

- **More Contrast** increases the color distinctions between pixels.

- **Less Contrast** makes the colors blend together.

- **More Brightness** washes the image out.

- **Less Brightness** darkens the image.

Every time you click a button, the brightness or contrast either increases or decreases incrementally. The more times you click the brightness button, for example, the brighter the image gets.

You can undo your work by pressing Ctrl+Z. In fact, FrontPage supports multiple undos, so if you're fiddling with an image and you want to return it to its previous condition, press Ctrl+Z a few times.

Setting an image's transparent color

Gif images support transparency, which means that you can choose to make a particular color on your image invisible. This feature is downright helpful if you have a square graphic and you want to display only the logo in the middle of the image. With FrontPage 2000, setting the transparent color is a cinch! Here's what you do:

1. **Click the graphic that contains the color you want to make transparent.**

2. **Click the Set Transparent Color button on the Picture toolbar.**

3. **Click the color on the image that you want to make transparent.**

After you do so, all instances of that color in the image become invisible, and you can see the Web page background through it.

Choose a color for the transparency that you're not likely to need from the Web palette. Gray, lime green, and hot pink are all good choices for the transparent color. (You choose the transparent color as you edit the image in an image editor.)

If you're using other image types in your Web page — a .jpeg image, for example — FrontPage will try to turn the image into a .gif file when you click the Set Transparent Color button on the Picture Toolbar. In addition, you can set only one transparent color with this tool. If you select the tool again and click another color, that color becomes the transparent color, and the preceding transparent color is no longer transparent.

Beveling an image

Beveling adds both a border and three-dimensional depth to a graphic. More often than not, you bevel an image to create a button effect. Follow these easy steps to bevel an image in FrontPage 2000:

1. **In Normal view, click the image that you want to bevel.**

2. **Click the Bevel button on the Picture toolbar.**

The button adds a bevel to your graphic, as shown in Figure 7-2.

Figure 7-2: An image can have a beveled edge.

3. **If you want to make the bevel darker and add more emphasis to it, click the Bevel button again.**

Cropping an image

Cropping reduces an image in size. Cropping images comes in handy if, say, you've got a picture of you and your mother-in-law and you want to eliminate your mother-in-law from the picture. To be honest, however, the FrontPage cropping features are limited in that you can crop only rectangular areas.

1. **Click the image that you want to crop.**

2. **Click the Crop button on the Picture toolbar.**

After you click the button, a rectangular box appears inside the image's border (see Figure 7-3).

3. **Click the anchor points and move the rectangle around if you want to resize the cropping area. (You can also use the arrow keys to move the cropping area around the image after you've created it.)**

4. **Press Enter to crop the image to the size of the rectangle.**

Figure 7-3: You can crop any part of an image.

Cropping cuts away everything that remains outside the cropping rectangle. If you specify an area, you're specifying the area of the image that you want to keep and not the area that you want to cut.

If you decide that you don't want to crop an image, press the Escape key to disengage the cropping tool.

After you click the Crop button, you can't deselect the tool by clicking the button again. Clicking the Crop button a second time crops the image to the size of the rectangle. You must press the Escape key to deselect the cropping tool.

Flipping and rotating images

FrontPage makes flipping and rotating images easy. Here are the steps:

1. **Click the graphic that you want to flip or rotate.**

2. **Click the Rotate Left, Rotate Right, Flip Horizontal, or Flip Vertical button on the Picture toolbar, depending on the action that you want to initiate.**

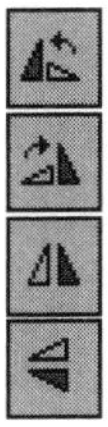

You have the following two options with each button:

• **Rotate Left** rotates the image 90 degrees to the left.

• **Rotate Right** rotates the image 90 degrees to the right.

• **Flip Horizontal** mirrors the image left to right.

• **Flip Vertical** mirrors the image top to bottom.

Placing text over an image

FrontPage 2000 supports a clever little way of placing text in image maps to achieve a nice effect. What do you have to do? Just this:

1. **Click the graphic over which you want to place text.**

2. **Click the Text button on the Picture toolbar.**

Clicking the Text button generates a text box in the middle of your graphic (see Figure 7-4). To resize the text box, drag the box's anchor points with your cursor.

FrontPage Chapter 7

Image Editing for Everyone

Figure 7-4:
You can place text over an image.

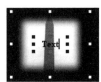

3. **Type the text that you want in the text box.**

4. **Press Escape to deselect the text box.**

To generate another text box on that image, simply click the Text icon again. If you want to move a text box around on the image, click and hold down the mouse button while the cursor is in the middle of the text box and then move the text box to its new location.

Because this graphic is essentially an image map with text, you can also turn these text boxes into hyperlinks. Just press Ctrl+K to open the Edit Hyperlink dialog box after you create a text box on a selected image. Then enter the link location and click OK to add the link to the text on the image.

If you're using other image types in your Web page — a .jpeg image, for example — FrontPage tries to turn the image into a .gif file when you click the Text button on the Picture toolbar. In most cases, this compromises the graphical quality of the image you're adding text to, because converting from a .jpeg to a .gif reduces the number of colors in the image.

Adding a hyperlink to an image

Using images as hyperlinks can add pizzazz and flair to a Web site. Follow these steps to add a hyperlink to an image:

1. **In Normal view, click the image that you want to make a hyperlink.**

2. **Choose Insert➪Hyperlink from the menu bar or press Ctrl+K.**

The Edit Hyperlink dialog box that appears may look familiar; it's the same dialog box that FrontPage uses to create text hyperlinks (see Figure 7-5).

Figure 7-5:
The Edit
Hyperlink
dialog box.

Edit Hyperlink		
Look in: D:\My_Web_Site		
Name	Title	
books_left.html	The Books Archive	
books_top.html	The Book Archive	
column_index.html	The Column Archive	
column_left.html	The Column Archive	
column_top.html	The Columns Archive	
columns.html	The Columns Archive	
computers.html	Computer Game Articles	
default.html	Template	
dummies.html	The Book Archive	
entertainment.html	The Entertainment Titles	
URL: writing.htm		
Optional		
Bookmark: (none)	Target frame: Page Default (none)	
OK	Cancel	Parameters...	Style...

See Chapter 6 for more information about creating text hyperlinks.

3. **Type the URL that you want the image to link to in the URL text box.**

In addition to other Web pages, you can link to other graphics files from a hyperlink. For example, if you have a large picture that you want to show off, you can add a link to a thumbnail image of the picture that loads the larger image. The capability to use thumbnail images as links to larger images keeps your page size down and makes including other elements on the page easier.

4. **Click OK.**

You can now use the image as a hyperlink on your Web page.

Creating Image Maps

Image maps are great navigation tools that you see in many Web sites. You load a Web page, and a big graphic appears smack dab in the middle of the page. On the graphic are a host of hot links to various locations. How did the Web designers create such a helpful tool, you ask? The answer lies in image maps.

You create image maps by specifying regions of a graphic and then setting links for those regions. In the past, you had to create image maps in a separate program and then load the map into your Web page. Times change, however. The following steps show you how to create an image map in FrontPage:

1. **In the Normal view, click the graphic for which you want to create an image map.**

2. **Select one of the Image Map shapes tools from the Picture toolbar.**

   FrontPage provides the following three different shape tools for creating image maps:

FrontPage Chapter 7

Image Editing for Everyone

   - **Rectangular Hotspots** creates squares and rectangles. To create a square or rectangular link, click the image and then drag the mouse while holding down the mouse button. A square image is created from the point at which you first clicked.

   - **Circular Hotspots** creates circles and ovals. You create a circular link precisely like you do a rectangular hotspot.

   - **Polygonal Hotspots** enables you to create multisided polygon areas. Click the image once to create a path, and click again to specify the points for the linked area. You finish creating the polygon by selecting the first path point. Doing so encloses the polygonal image.

3. **Create the shape that you want as a link by using one of the methods given earlier.**

   After you create the shape, the Create Hyperlink dialog box appears.

4. **Type the link in the URL text box. Alternatively, you can use the drop-down list in the Create Hyperlink dialog box to search for other pages within your Web to link to.**

5. **Click OK to set the hyperlink.**

You may want to move your link around on the graphic after you create it. To do so, click the arrow button on the Picture toolbar and then click and hold down on the link. As long as you hold down the mouse button, you can drag the link around on the graphic.

To change the size of the link, click and hold any of the link's *anchor points* — the square dots along the outline of the link area. Then drag the anchor to the desired location, and the link is automatically scaled according to where you moved the anchor point. Letting go of the mouse button changes the link's size.

Chapter 8: Publishing Your Web Pages

In This Chapter

✓ Publishing via HTTP

✓ Publishing via FTP

✓ Connecting to a FrontPage server

The time will eventually come when you need to put all your hard work on the World Wide Web for everyone to see. This process of publishing on the Web may seem like a technological mystery to you, but it just may be one of the easiest things that you've done thus far. In fact, publishing on the Web is a simple process — which explains why so much junk is already out there on the Web. It's time for you to join the fray.

Publishing a Web by Using HTTP

HTTP sounds new and nifty, but if you've ever loaded a Web page, you already know what HTTP does. HTTP, which stands for HyperText Transfer Protocol, is simply a way of transferring data from a server to your Web browser (and vice versa). In fact, HTTP is the preferred way of transferring files in FrontPage 2000.

To use this method of file transfer, your Internet service provider must support the FrontPage server extensions.

Here's how you publish a Web by using HTTP:

1. Choose File⇨Publish Web.

The Publish Web dialog box appears, as shown in Figure 8-1. From this dialog box, you can manage the amount of content you want to publish and specify the Web server on which you want to post it.

2. Click the Options button.

This button reveals other publishing options that you may want to consider. You can choose to publish only those Web pages that change, for example, and you can include other sub-Webs that you include in your site.

3. **Enter the URL where you want to publish your Web content in the Specify the Location to Publish Your Web To text box at the top of the dialog box.**

Click the WPP's button if you're not sure whether your ISP provides the appropriate server extensions to support the FrontPage publishing features. The WPP's button sends you to the Microsoft Web site for the most current list of ISPs that support the extensions.

If you're not sure of the location to which you want to publish your Web, click the Browse button in the Publish Web dialog box to search for FrontPage servers from the Open Web dialog box (yes, that's a bit of a misnomer). You can use the link buttons on the left side of the dialog box or use the drop-down list to look for FrontPage servers on your hard drive, on network drives, or in your Web Folders area.

4. **Click P̲ublish to submit the new Web content.**

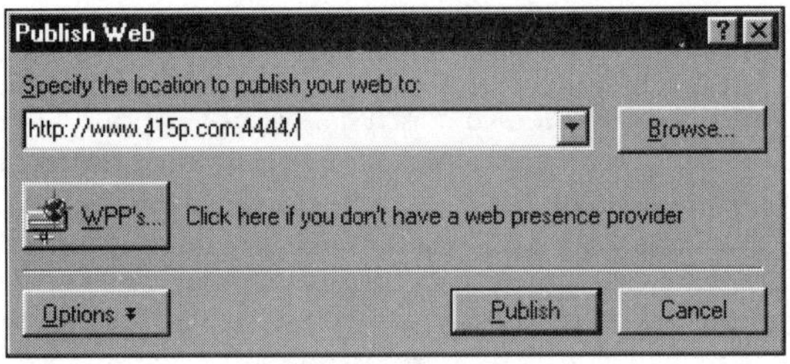

Figure 8-1:
The
Publish
Web dialog
box.

Publish Web	? X
S̲pecify the location to publish your web to:	
http://www.415p.com:4444/ ▼	Browse...
💲 WPP's... Click here if you don't have a web presence provider	
O̲ptions ≢	P̲ublish Cancel

FrontPage tracks the progress of the upload and shows you which pages are being transferred. Once the upload is complete, an alert box appears, telling you that the upload is done. (See Figure 8-2.)

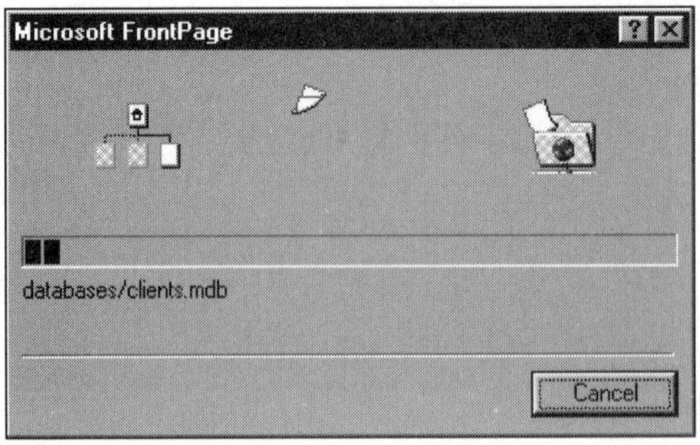

Figure 8-2:
FrontPage
tracks the
progress of
your
upload.

Microsoft FrontPage	? X
databases/clients.mdb	
	Cancel

If you're publishing your Web to a Web server, there's a pretty good chance that it's password-protected. When you first see the Publish Web dialog box, you're more likely than not going to get another dialog box prompting you for your user name and password. This is to prevent people from coming along and posting content on any Web site they want.

Publishing a Web by Using FTP

People were publishing Web sites by using the Internet File Transfer Protocol long before Microsoft came along and tried to make the whole process transparent to the user. Now, with FrontPage 2000, you can finally connect to any server and publish your content on the Internet by using FTP.

There are actually two parts to the process of publishing with FTP. The first is to make your FTP connection, described here. The second is to publish the content.

To set up an FTP connection, follow these steps:

1. **Choose File➪Open Web to bring up the Open Web dialog box.**

   Or, if you prefer, you can do these same steps from the Open File dialog box, which you access by choosing File➪Open.

2. **From the Look In drop-down list, select Add/Modify FTP locations. Doing so brings up the Add/Modify FTP Locations dialog box.**

3. **In the Name of FTP Site text box, enter the name of the FTP site. For example, for the Dummies FTP site, you would type** `ftp.dummies.com`.

4. **In the Log On As area, choose how you want to log on to the FTP site.**

   If you want to log on anonymously, select the Anonymous radio button. If you're a registered user, select the User radio button and then type your name in the text box to the right of that button.

5. **Type your password in the Password text box.**

   When you log on anonymously, most FTP sites either request or require that you use your e-mail address as your logon password.

6. **Click the Add button to add your FTP location to the FTP Sites area.**

   You can also edit a location by clicking it in the FTP Sites area and then clicking the Modify button. Similarly, you can delete a location by selecting it and clicking the Delete button.

7. **Click OK in the Add/Modify FTP Locations dialog box to activate the connection and return to the Open Web dialog box.**

8. **Click Cancel to return to FrontPage 2000.**

To publish your Web content, follow these simple steps.

1. **Choose File➪Publish Web from the menu bar.**

   This brings up the Publish Web dialog box.

2. **Click the Browse button to access the Open Web dialog box.**

3. **From the Look In drop-down list, select an FTP location from beneath the Add/Modify FTP Location indicator.**

   The site you select appears in the Folder Name text box at the bottom of the dialog box.

4. Click Open to return to the Publish Web dialog box.

You see that your FTP location has been entered in the Specify the Location to Publish Your Web To field.

5. Click the Publish button to FTP your content to the server.

Connecting to a FrontPage Server

Here's a simple example to illustrate how the FrontPage server concept works. Say you're working remotely on a Web site. You've been assigned a laptop that has FrontPage 2000 on it but does not have the site on it. The Web site is being hosted on a FrontPage server back at your corporate office. With FrontPage 2000, you can connect directly to the site, as if you were working locally on it, and make changes to the site in real time without ever having to click the Publish button.

1. From the menu bar, choose File⇨Open Web to bring up the Open Web dialog box.

2. Click the Web Folders button in the series of buttons along the left-hand side of the dialog box.

You can also select it from the Look In drop-down list.

3. In the Folder Name text box, enter the name of the FrontPage server to which you want to connect.

4. Click the Open button to connect to the FrontPage server.

FrontPage prompts you for a user name and password when you try to connect. After you enter these, the program displays the parts of the Web to which you have access.

If you aren't connected to the Internet when you try to connect to a FrontPage server, FrontPage 2000 tells you that the FrontPage 2000 server extensions could not be loaded. Though accurate, this message is a bit misleading, so be sure to double-check that connection before you log on.

Index

Book VIII

Publisher 2000

The 5th Wave   By Rich Tennant

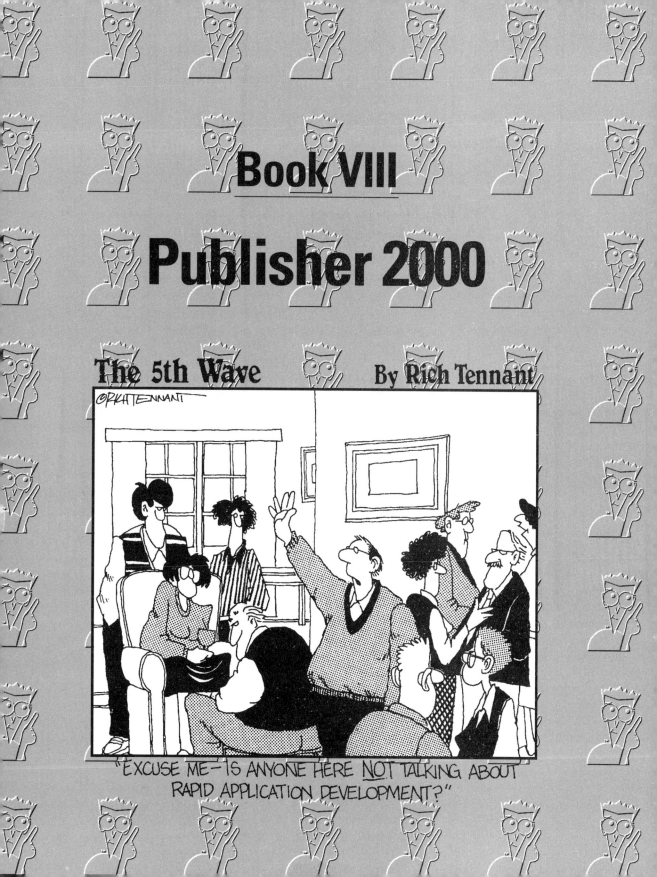

"EXCUSE ME—IS ANYONE HERE NOT TALKING ABOUT RAPID APPLICATION DEVELOPMENT?"

Contents at a Glance

Chapter 1: Publisher 101

In This Chapter

✔ Creating publications on your own

✔ Creating publications with a wizard

✔ Saving your files

*T*his part of the book covers Microsoft Publisher 2000 basics. Here you find out how to do the day-to-day stuff, such as creating publications, using the wizards, and such. If you've been using Publisher 2000 for a while, feel free to skip this section. A word of warning, though, this material is on the test. Okay, so there is no test. Read it anyway, and you may just discover something new!

Creating a Publication

A *publication* is any document that you create using Microsoft Publisher 2000. Publications range from newsletters to flyers to business cards. Even Web sites are publications when you're using Microsoft Publisher 2000. And Microsoft Publisher 2000 gives you several ways to create publications.

Starting Microsoft Publisher 2000 and getting help with any part of the program is similar to any other Office 2000 application. Be sure to check out Appendix A for details.

Starting from scratch

When you first start Microsoft Publisher 2000, you're presented with the Microsoft Publisher Catalog shown in Figure 1-1. If you're one of those do-it-yourself types, click the Blank Publications tab. Figure 1-2 shows the Blank Publications tab of the Catalog with a blank business card selected.

Select a publication type in the Blank Publications pane of the Blank Publications tab of the Microsoft Publisher Catalog. Wow! Try saying that ten times, fast! The pane on the right shows you a preview of the layout you choose. Click the Create button in the lower-left corner of the Catalog to see your blank presentation.

Publisher obligingly opens this wizard. Figure 1-3 shows a blank business card with the Quick Publication Wizard open.

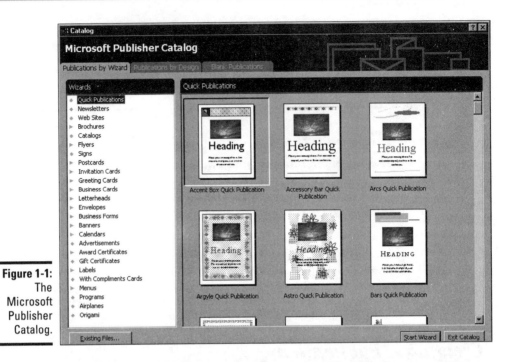

Figure 1-1:
The
Microsoft
Publisher
Catalog.

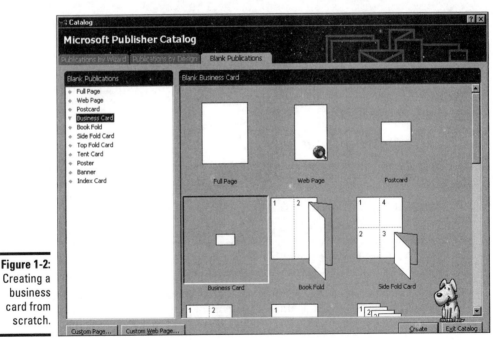

Figure 1-2:
Creating a
business
card from
scratch.

You can use the Quick Publication Wizard to change the design, color scheme, page size, layout, or Personal Information set that your publication uses. If you want more real estate for working on your publication, you can tell the Quick Publication Wizard to go away by clicking the Hide Wizard button. Click the Show Wizard button to bring the wizard back.

Now that you have the blank publication created, you're free to add things such as text frames, picture frames, WordArt frames, tables, and Design Gallery objects. Take a look at Chapter 3 for the up and up on objects and frames.

Those wize and wonderful wizards

So, you want to take the easy way out? Why reinvent the wheel every time you want to create a publication? Publisher's wizards can make quick work of creating just about any type of publication you can imagine. All you have to do is replace the text — and picture, if you want — to make the publication your own.

The first two tabs of the Microsoft Publisher Catalog enable you to create some pretty spectacular-looking publications in minutes. Both the Publications by Wizard tab and the Publications by Design tab let you create the same publications.

The Publications by Wizard tab organizes the publications by type. You can use the Publications by Wizard tab to create sets of publications that have a consistent and professional look and feel. Click Master Sets in the Design Sets pane to see a list of all the available designs. Then just click a design and Publisher,

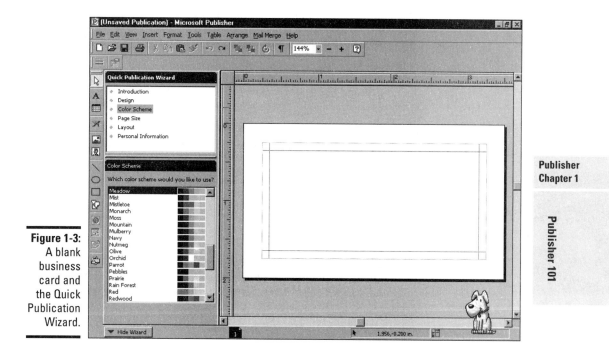

Figure 1-3:
A blank
business
card and
the Quick
Publication
Wizard.

**Publisher
Chapter 1**

Publisher 101

using your selected design, enables you to use any of the wizards to create a publication. Find a design that suits your purposes and use it to create all your business publications.

Here are the types of publications you can create by using this tab:

+ **Quick Publications:** Choose this option and answer four questions — Color Scheme, Page Size, Layout, and Personal Information — to create a quick one-page publication.

+ **Newletters:** Create multi-page, multi-column newsletters in no time.

+ **Web Sites:** Can't spell HTML? No worries, use the Web Sites Wizard.

+ **Brochures:** Professional-looking Informational, Price List, Event, or Fund-raiser brochures in a snap!

+ **Catalogs:** Make your own product catalogs — complete with pictures of your products — to send to your clients.

+ **Flyers:** Need an Informational, Special Offer, Sale, Event, Fund-raiser, or Announcement flyer in a hurry? This wizard can do the job.

+ **Signs:** Choose from a variety of signs for your business. Print a Business Hours sign for the front door, or a We Speak Portuguese sign to let your customers know that you speak their language.

+ **Postcards:** Informational, Special Offer, Sale, Event, Invitation, Holiday Party Invitation, Holiday Greeting, Holiday Thank You, We've Moved, Announcement, Reminder, or Tent Fold. Probably, one of these postcards fits the bill.

+ **Invitation Cards:** Select from Party, Theme Party, Holiday Party, Birthday Party, Housewarming, Shower, Event, Celebration, or Fund-raiser invitation cards.

+ **Greeting Cards:** These include Thank You, We've Moved, Engagement Announcement, Birth Announcement, Reminder, Holiday, Birthday, Special Day, Congratulations, Friendship, Romance, I'm Sorry, Get Well, and Sympathy cards.

+ **Business Cards:** Design business cards that you can print on plain paper or on special paper you purchase from Papers Direct.

+ **Letterheads:** Make your own letterhead and look like a pro! Choose to print your letterhead on plain paper or on special paper that you can purchase from Papers Direct.

+ **Envelopes:** Create envelopes to match your letterhead. Select plain paper or special paper from Papers Direct.

+ **Business Forms:** You can create a professional looking Expense Report, Fax Cover, Inventory List, Invoice, Purchase Order, Quote, Refund, Statement, Time Billing, or Weekly Record form.

+ **Banners:** Informational, Sale, Event, Birthday, Welcome, Congratulations, Holiday, Romance, and Get Well banners are real attention-getters!

+ **Calendars:** Choose between Full Page and Wallet Size calendars. These make great promo items to give to clients.

✦ **Advertisements:** Lay out your own ads.

✦ **Award Certificates:** Recognize your employees with an award certificate. Choose between plain paper and special paper.

✦ **Gift Certificates:** Got a customer who can't decide on a gift purchase? Sell him a gift certificate that you created.

✦ **Labels:** With this wizard, you can create Mailing Address, Shipping, Return Address, Computer Disk, Cassette, Compact Disc, Video, Jar/Product, Binder, Bookplate, and Identification labels. Many of these labels match standard Avery brand labels.

✦ **With Compliments Cards:** You can use these cards when you send gifts or promo items to your clients!

✦ **Menus:** Own a restaurant? Design Regular, Take-Out, Daily Special, or Wine/Dessert menus.

✦ **Programs:** Music, Religious Service, and Theater programs made easy!

✦ **Airplanes:** Not much business use for these, but they sure can make you look good in front of the kids!

✦ **Origami:** Why did Microsoft include an Origami Wizard? Personally, I think one of the programmers must have lost a bet to one of the marketing types.

Saving Your Files

You can spend hours creating the greatest business publications ever to grace the computer screen, but until you save them, they don't really exist.

File-saving formats

You can save your Publisher 2000 publications in any of three different formats: Publisher Files, Publisher Template, and Publisher 98 Files. Publisher Files is the default. This format is how you normally save your publications. The Publisher Template type is useful if you create a publication that you want to save and base other publications on. Save your file as Publisher 98 Files if you intend to give the publication file to someone who has Microsoft Publisher 98 installed.

The other file types save the text from your publication in various and sundry word-processing formats. Most of these file types — except plain text — retain character and paragraph formatting but lose layout and graphics.

File-saving mechanics

 Saving is as easy as clicking the Save button in the Standard toolbar. If you prefer to use the menu, select File⇨Save. Or you can press Ctrl+S. The first time you save a publication, you're presented with the Save As dialog box depicted in Figure 1-4. Type a name for your publication in the File name box, and click Save. That's all there is to it! After you save a publication, you can save any changes you make by choosing your favorite method of issuing the Save command. Publisher saves your publication without bothering your with the Save As dialog box.

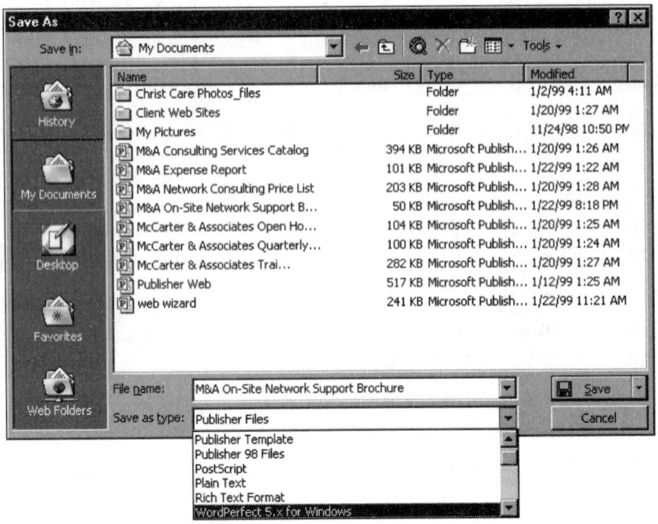

Figure 1-4:
The Save
As dialog
box with
the Save
as Type
box
expanded.

Chapter 2: Working with Pages

In This Chapter

✔ **Moving around in your publication**

✔ **Changing your point of view**

✔ **Using rulers and guides to align objects**

✔ **Using backgrounds for a consistent look**

✔ **Modifying a page layout**

*W*hether you use one of the wizards to create a publication or start with a blank publication, Microsoft Publisher establishes defaults for the number of pages, the page size, margin guides, and so on. If these defaults suit your needs, great! If you need to change things a bit, this chapter is here to help. At any rate, you find out how to add and delete pages, change margins, and more.

Moving from Page to Page

Every publication must have at least one page. In a one-page publication, you have no question which is the current, or active, page. It's the page you're currently working on. In multi-page publications, the active page is determined by the Page Navigation controls located on the Status bar to the right of the Show Wizard button. Figure 2-1 shows the Page Navigation controls with Page 2 as the current page. Notice that Page 2 is highlighted.

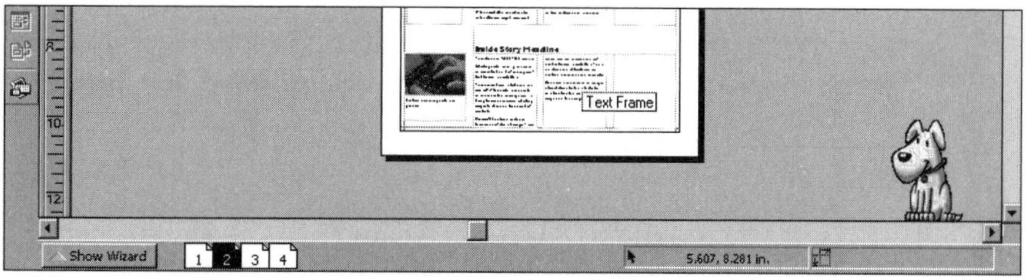

Figure 2-1: The Page Navigation controls with Page 2 as the current page.

If you're in Two-Page Spread view, you may see two pages in the Page Navigation controls highlighted.

Microsoft Publisher 2000 often provides several ways to accomplish a task. Moving among pages is no exception. To move to a different page:

✦ In the Page Navigation controls, click the page that you want to go to. This method is probably the easiest, unless you have more than fifteen or so pages in your publication. If you have a large number of pages, you may have to use the Page Navigation Control scroll arrows — those little, black arrows to the left and right of the pages — to see the page you want to select.

✦ Select View⇨Go To Page, press F5, or press Ctrl+G and then type the number of the page that you want to work on in the Go To Page dialog box, shown in Figure 2-2. Press Enter or click OK to close the Go To Page dialog box and move to the page number you entered.

✦ Press Shift+F5 to move to the next page and Ctrl+F5 to move to the previous page.

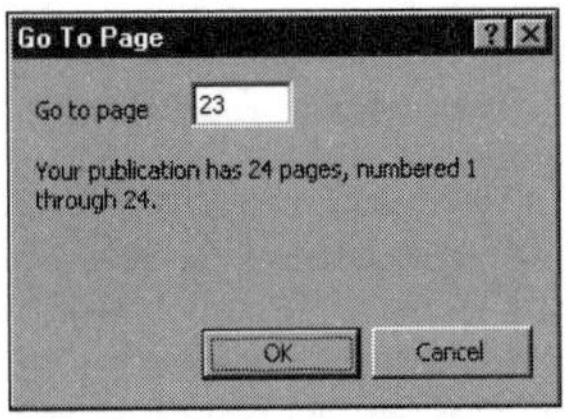

Figure 2-2:
The Go To
Page
dialog box.

Go To Page

Go to page   23

Your publication has 24 pages, numbered 1 through 24.

OK   Cancel

Changing What You See On-Screen

When designing a page layout, being able to change your view of the page is important. When working with text or a graphic, you probably want a magnification that lets you see what you're working on. To see the overall layout of your page, you want a magnification that lets you see an entire page.

Fortunately, Microsoft Publisher 2000 makes changing your view of the page very easy. You can change the apparent size of the page on-screen or change to a view that lets you see two facing pages at once.

Two-page spreads

A two-page spread is simply a pair of facing pages. Select View⇨Two-Page Spread from the menu.

If you're working on a single Page publication, nothing seems to happen. If you're working on Page 1 of a multi-page publication, however, nothing seems to happen. Hey! What's going on? Microsoft Publisher 2000 — and most other Desktop Publishing programs — display odd-numbered pages on the right and even-numbered pages on the right. Just like books and magazines. Page 1 — being an odd-numbered page — displays on the right. Of course, you have no Page 0 to display on the left. Click Page 2 in the Page Navigation controls. That's more like it. You see Page 2 — the even-numbered page — on the left, and Page 3 — the odd-numbered page — on the right. If the last page in your publication is even numbered, you see only that page when you select it in Two-Page Spread view.

The Two-Page Spread command is a toggle. Select View⇨Two-Page Spread a second time to return to single page view.

Whole Page and Page Width views

In addition to Two-Page Spread view, Publisher 2000 offers two views that you might find useful: Whole Page and Page Width views.

+ Choose View⇨Zoom⇨Whole Page. This view comes in handy when you want to see the layout of the entire page.

+ Choose View⇨Zoom⇨Page Width. In this view, you probably have to scroll vertically to see the entire document, but you don't have to scroll horizontally. This view comes in handy when you're working with text or objects that fill the page from left to right.

Lining Things Up

Even the most proficient sometimes encounter difficulty getting things to align just right on the page. Luckily, Microsoft Publisher has a couple of features to help you line things up on the page.

Margin and grid guides

Layout guides create a grid that you can use to organize text and pictures into neat rows and columns to help give your publication a consistent look. Layout guides repeat on each page of your publication. These layout guides appear on the screen as pink and blue lines but don't show up when you print your publication. Use the Publisher 2000 Snap To commands on the Tools menu to automatically align objects with these guides.

Microsoft Publisher 2000 offers two types of layout guides:

+ *Margin guides* show the boundary of your printable area.

+ *Grid guides* let you create a grid with any number of rows and columns.

Every publication has Margin guides. These pink and blue lines help you align text and graphics along the outside edges of your publication. Although you can place objects anywhere you want, placing them outside the Margin guides may cause unpredictable results.

Grid guides help you align objects that you don't want to align with the Margin guides.

Don't be surprised if a publication you created with one of the wizards already has layout guides. The wizard is just trying to be helpful. If you don't like the placement of these guides, change them. To set up or change layout guides, select Arrange⇨Layout Guides. The Layout Guides dialog box, shown in Figure 2-3, appears.

**Publisher
Chapter 2**

Working with Pages

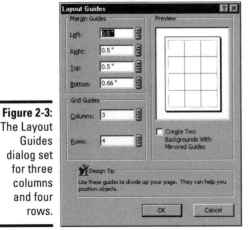

Figure 2-3:
The Layout
Guides
dialog set
for three
columns
and four
rows.

Enter the number of Columns and Rows that you want. Grid guides evenly divide the space contained by the margin guides.

Ruler guides

Grid guides can come in very handy, but they don't give you much flexibility in their placement. Ruler guides let you align objects anywhere on the page. You can create as many ruler guides as you need. One drawback to ruler guides is that they don't automatically show up on every page as the margin and grid guides do. You have to create them separately for each page. Fortunately, that isn't very difficult. Here's how ruler guides work:

✦ To create a vertical guide, press and hold the Shift key and click and drag from the vertical ruler right to the desired position on your layout. Your cursor changes to include the word `adjust`, and a green dotted line appears when you release your mouse button. If you don't hold the Shift key, you drag the ruler.

✦ To create a horizontal guide, hold the Shift key down and click and drag from the horizontal ruler down to the desired position on your layout.

✦ To place a vertical guide in the exact center of your view, choose Arrange➪ Ruler Guides➪Add Vertical Rule Guide.

✦ To place a horizontal guide in the exact center of your view, choose Arrange➪ Ruler Guides➪Add Horizontal Rule Guide.

✦ To move a ruler guide, just click and drag it while holding the Shift key.

✦ To remove a ruler guide, hold the Shift key and drag the ruler off the page.

✦ To remove all ruler guides, choose Arrange➪Ruler Guides➪Clear All Ruler Guides.

Snap to it!

Well, now that you have decorated the page with those pretty pink, blue, and green lines, what do you do with them? You use the Publisher 2000 Snap to Guides command to automatically align objects that you place close to a guide.

The Snap To feature helps you to make sure that objects you drag close to a guide, automatically attach to the guide. This makes lining up several objects with the guide easy, without having to "eyeball" it. You can also make objects snap to the nearest ruler mark (increment) if you like. You can even make objects snap to other objects.

The Snap To commands are toggles. Select them once to turn them on. Snap To commands that are turned on have a check mark next to them on the Tools menu. Select them a second time to turn them off. Here's how:

✦ Choose Tools⇨Snap to Guides (or press Ctrl+W) to align objects with your layout guides.

✦ Choose Tools⇨Snap to Ruler Marks to align objects with your ruler marks.

✦ Choose Tools⇨Snap to Objects to align with selected objects on-screen.

Creating Background Pages

Frequently, when you design a multi-page publication, you need objects to show up on every page. Objects that you want to appear on every page may include page numbers, copyright information, or a company logo, to name a few. The good news is that you don't have to place the objects on each page individually. The bad new is that you have to find out about backgrounds.

So, how do backgrounds work? Each page of your publication consists of two layers. The background layer is like a piece of preprinted letterhead. The company name and logo may appear at the top, and perhaps the company address is located at the bottom of the page. The words that you type on the page are similar to the foreground layer. Every page you print using this letterhead has these same items, even though the text on each page may be different. The Microsoft Publisher 2000 backgrounds work in a similar fashion. Of course, you don't have to call the print shop every time you want to change the background!

Every object on a background repeats on foreground pages throughout the publication. Those *background objects* that aren't obscured by objects above them in the foreground print together with any *foreground objects* present on each foreground page.

Back to the foreground

To move to the background, select View⇨Go to Background or press Ctrl+M.

If you're just starting a blank publication, you may not notice any changes when you switch to the background. One way to tell whether you've moved to the background is to look at the Page Navigation controls at the bottom-left of your screen. If the Page Navigation controls are still there, you're in the foreground. If the Page Navigation controls have been replaced with one or two *background buttons,* as shown in Figure 2-4, you've successfully moved to the background.

Figure 2-4:
The L and
R in the
Page
Navigation
controls
indicate
that you
are in
Background
view.

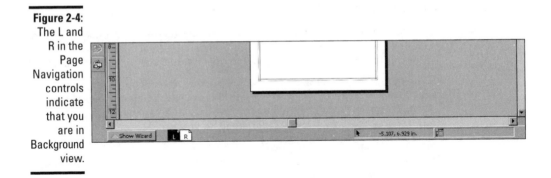

Select View➪Go to Foreground or press Ctrl+M to return to the foreground. You return to the last foreground page that you were in, and the normal Page Navigation controls return.

Working with multiple backgrounds

When you start a publication, Publisher sometimes creates just one background for you and other times creates two, based on the type of publication you create. To determine whether you have one or two backgrounds, move to the background and then observe the area usually occupied by the Page Navigation controls. If you see only one background button, your publication has only one background. If you see two background buttons, your publication has two backgrounds.

When designing a publication with facing pages, creating two backgrounds is often convenient: one for the left-facing pages and another for the right-facing pages. To create a second background, select Arrange➪Layout Guides to open the Layout Guides dialog box. Click to place a check mark in the Create Two Backgrounds With Mirrored Guides check box. When you create mirrored layout guides for left- and right-facing pages, you automatically create a second background.

When you create a second background, three things happen:

◆ The original background becomes the right background.

◆ The new background becomes the left background.

◆ Publisher copies everything on the original (right) background — guides and objects — and places it in mirrored positions on the new (left) background. Figure 2-5 shows an example of what happens when you create mirrored layout guides.

To move between background pages (if you have two of them):

◆ In Single Page view, click the L or R Page Navigation controls to move back and forth from the right to the left background page.

◆ In Two-Page Spread view, you don't have to click any buttons. Both background pages are visible. Just click directly on the page and element or object that you want to work on.

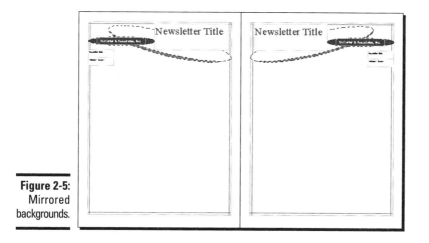

Figure 2-5:
Mirrored
backgrounds.

Two backgrounds are great for creating facing-page publications. Unfortunately, having twice as many backgrounds means twice as much work setting them up, so use only one background if that's all you need.

Adding Background Objects

The procedure for adding objects to backgrounds is the same as adding objects to foreground pages (see Chapter 3). Try to keep your background objects close to the margins. Background objects placed in the middle of the page tend to get covered up. To avoid having to rearrange your foreground objects, set up your background pages first.

Creating Headers and Footers

If you've worked with word processors, you probably know that headers and footers contain text and graphics that repeat along the top and bottom of each page, respectively. Headers and footers may contain logos, page numbers, publication title, current chapter, author's name, company information, and so on. Headers and footers usually repeat on every page. Anyone know a good place to put stuff that repeats on each page? That's right, the background!

The two-background advantage

In addition to providing separate areas for different sets of layout guides, having two backgrounds enables you to set up separate sets of background objects — one set that repeats on left-hand foreground pages, and another set that repeats on right-hand foreground pages. Separate left- and right-hand repeating objects are quite common in facing-page publications.

1. **Select** <u>V</u>iew⊅G<u>o</u> **to Background or press Ctrl+M to go to the background.**

2. **Add an object(s) where you want your header or footer to appear.**

Text frames are probably the most common objects added to headers and footers, but you can add any object that you want to appear at the top bottom of each page.

3. **If appropriate, fill and format the object and then format its contents.**

4. **Select** <u>V</u>iew⊅G<u>o</u> **to Foreground or press Ctrl+M to return to the foreground.**

Headers and footers should line up with the top or bottom margin. Set ruler guides for the bottom of the header and the top of the footer and turn on the Snap To Guides command to make lining them up easier.

Adding and Deleting Pages

Microsoft Publisher 2000 makes inserting and removing pages easy — maybe too easy.

You aren't limited to adding just one or two pages at a time. Publisher enables you to insert up to 999 pages at a shot. Follow these steps to insert multiple pages into your publication:

1. **Choose** <u>I</u>nsert⊅**Page.**

The Insert Page dialog box appears, as shown in Figure 2-6.

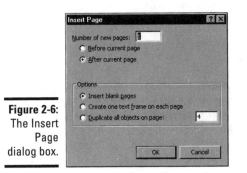

Figure 2-6:
The Insert
Page
dialog box.

2. **In the Number of New Pages text box, type the number of pages that you want to insert.**

Type any number up to 999.

Insert pages in even numbers so that your left-hand pages don't become right-hand pages and vice versa. This process becomes more important as your publication nears completion. Inserting pages in odd numbers can cause you quite a lot of work after your publication is set up.

3. **Click the Before Current Page or After Current Page option to tell Publisher 2000 where to put the pages.**

4. **In the Options area, choose the kind of pages you want to insert:**

   • **Insert Blank Pages:** Inserts pages that are devoid of objects.

   • **Create One Text Frame on Each Page:** Places a blank text frame on each new page that you create. Each text frame matches your publication's margin guides. Keep in mind that this text frame probably covers up your background.

   • **Duplicate All Objects on Page:** Makes a copy of whatever objects already exist on the page number you specify in the option box and places those objects on each of the new pages.

5. **Click OK.**

When you delete a page, all the objects on that page are also deleted. Only objects off the page, on the scratch area, remain untouched. Publisher then automatically renumbers the remaining pages so that you don't end up with pages out of sequence. Follow these steps to delete a page:

1. **Move to the page you want to delete.**

2. **Choose Edit⊅Delete Page.**

   Note that this command is not available if you're currently viewing the background of your publication.

   When you select the Edit⊅Delete Page command in Single page view, Microsoft Publisher 2000 displays a confirmation box asking if you really want to delete the page. Click OK to delete the page. Click Cancel if you're having second thoughts. Use this command with caution. Press Ctrl+Z if you accidentally delete a page.

   When you select the Edit⊅Delete Page command in Two-Page Spread view, Publisher opens the Delete Page dialog box, as shown in Figure 2-7.

Figure 2-7:
The Delete
Page
dialog box
for a two-
page
spread.

Delete Page	? X
Delete	
⊙ Both pages	
○ Left page only	
○ Right page only	
OK	Cancel

3. **Click the option you want: Both Pages, Left Page Only, or Right Page Only.**

4. **Click OK.**

Delete pages in even numbers so that your left- and right-hand pages don't get messed up. If you delete just a left- or right-hand page in the Two-Page Spread view, Publisher opens a dialog box asking if you really want to delete just one page.

Modifying the Page Layout

Although changing the layout of your publication is relatively easy, that doesn't mean that you should. The time you spend deciding on a page layout before you begin designing your publication is time well spent. Changing a layout late in the game can cause you hours of work rearranging objects on your pages.

To change the layout of a publication, Select File⇨Page Setup. The Page Setup dialog box, shown in Figure 2-8, appears.

Publisher gives you five publication layout options:

✦ **Normal:** Creates newsletters, brochures, flyers, and many other layouts.

✦ **Special Fold:** Creates greeting cards, tent cards, and book folds.

✦ **Special Size:** Creates posters, banners, business cards, and index cards.

✦ **Labels:** Creates mailing labels and full-page labels.

✦ **Envelopes:** Creates #10, #6, or custom-sized envelopes.

The options in the bottom half of the Page Setup dialog box change depending on the option you choose in the Choose a Publication Layout section.

Figure 2-8:
The Page
Setup
dialog box
for a
Normal
layout.

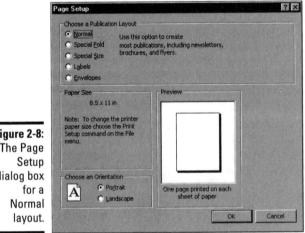

Chapter 3: Objects and Frames

In This Chapter

✔ **Working with frames**

✔ **Working with drawn objects**

✔ **Aligning objects**

✔ **Wrapping text**

*A*n *object* is simply a publication design element. Text or graphic frames, a line, a circle, or other item on a page are all considered to be objects. Objects come in two basic flavors: those that are contained in frames and those that aren't. *Frames* are container objects into which you place the content of your publication. Text and graphics are two common examples of publication elements that require frames. Lines and rectangles and other objects that you draw are examples of publication elements that don't require frames.

Working with Frames

Microsoft Publisher 2000 offers four types of frames:

✦ **Text frames:** Text frames contain — well, text. Text frames can be linked to create what Publisher calls *stories*.

✦ **Table frames:** Table frames contain — well, tables. Are you seeing a pattern here? Tables are handy for display data — both text and numbers — in rows and columns.

✦ **Picture frames:** Publisher requires that you put pictures and other graphics inside picture frames.

✦ **WordArt frames:** WordArt enables you to create many special text effects that are useful in headlines and other places.

Creating frames

Select a tool in the Objects toolbar and then click and drag your layout to create a frame. Figure 3-1 shows you where each tool is located in the Object toolbar. Select the Text Frame tool to create a text frame, select the Table Frame tool to create a table frame. You get the idea.

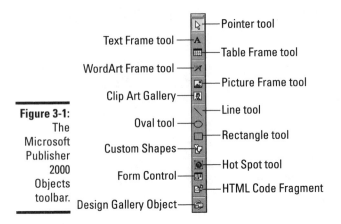

Figure 3-1:
The
Microsoft
Publisher
2000
Objects
toolbar.

When you click a tool and create a frame, the Formatting toolbar appears underneath the 2000 Standard toolbar. The Formatting toolbar contains buttons that let you modify the format of your frame or the objects that you put in it. For the most part, these formatting buttons are duplicates of menu commands. The buttons that appear on the Formatting toolbar vary depending on the type of frame you select. Follow these steps to draw a text or picture frame:

1. **Click the Text Frame tool or Picture Frame tool in the Objects toolbar.**

Your cursor changes to a crosshair.

2. **Move the crosshair over the publication page or scratch area.**

The sliding ruler lines and the status bar's Object Position box show your exact position.

3. **Click and drag to create the outline of your frame.**

As you drag, the program draws a sample to show you the size and shape of your new frame. The status bar's Object Size box indicates the frame's size.

To draw a frame from the center out, hold the Ctrl key as you draw. To draw a perfectly square frame, hold the Shift key. To do both, hold down the Ctrl+Shift keys together as you drag.

4. **Release the mouse button to create the frame.**

Publisher creates your text or picture frame and selects it (makes it active) so that you can work with it further.

Figure 3-2 shows you a selected text frame. Empty picture frames and text frames look the same.

You create a table frame the same way you create a text frame. Click the tool in the Objects toolbar and then click and drag in the publication page. When you create a table frame, Publisher opens the Create Table dialog box, shown in Figure 3-3.

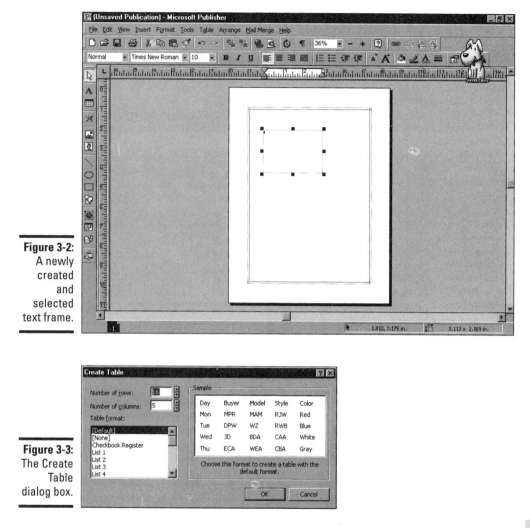

Figure 3-2:
A newly
created
and
selected
text frame.

Figure 3-3:
The Create
Table
dialog box.

1. **Select the Number of Rows and the Number of Columns that you want in your table.**

Publisher lets you have up to 128 rows and 128 columns in your table. If you aren't sure how many rows and columns you want, you can accept the default that Publisher 2000 offers.

2. **Choose a format for your table (optional).**

Publisher offers more than twenty pre-set table formats in the Table Format list box.

3. **Click the OK button.**

Your table frame is now complete. Figure 3-4 shows a selected table frame with the List 2 format.

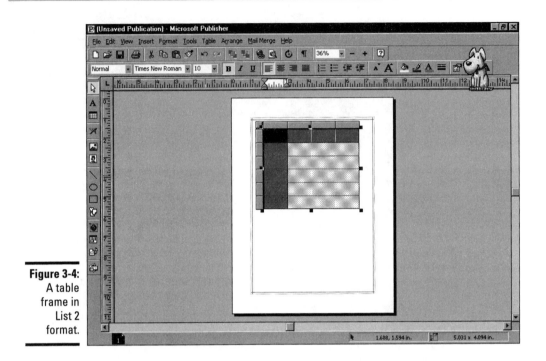

Figure 3-4:
A table
frame in
List 2
format.

When you draw a frame, Publisher automatically deselects the Frame tool and activates the Pointer tool so that you can manipulate your object. If you want to create multiple frames of the same type, you can get a Frame tool to stay selected by pressing the Ctrl key while you click the Frame tool. After you're done drawing frames with that tool, deselect the tool by clicking any other tool in the toolbox, or press the Esc. key These techniques work for any tool in the toolbox (for example, the Line, Box, and Circle tools), not just for frame tools.

To delete a frame — or any other type of object — select it and choose Delete Object from the Edit menu. You can delete any empty frame by selecting it and pressing the Delete key. In the case of a table frame, you have a container with many "drawers"; you can delete the contents of each cell in the table by selecting the contents of that cell and pressing the Delete key.

Moving and resizing frames

To move a frame or object, move your pointer over the border or the shape itself until the pointer turns into a truck with the word *Move* on it. Then click and drag the frame or object to a new location.

As you drag, a dotted outline of the object follows your pointer. When the outline is where you want your object, release your mouse button.

If you want to move an object or set of objects to a different page within your publication, drag the object or set completely off the publication page and onto the scratch area. Then move to the destination page and drag the object or set from the scratch area to that page.

To resize an object, first select it and then place the pointer over one of the eight selection handles. The mouse pointer becomes a resize pointer, and you should see the word *Resize.* After the resize pointer appears, you can click and drag.

Working with Drawn Objects

Publisher 2000 also offers eight additional buttons on the Objects toolbar for creating objects. The following list describes the five drawing tools that are discussed in this section. The other three — the Hot Spot tool, the Form Control, and the HTML Code Fragment buttons — are discussed in Chapter 6. Figure 3-5 points out the drawing tools.

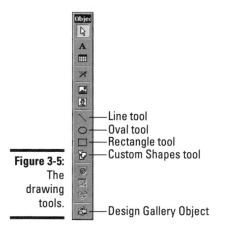

— Line tool
— Oval tool
— Rectangle tool
— Custom Shapes tool

Figure 3-5:
The
drawing
tools.

— Design Gallery Object

✦ **Line tool:** Used to create lines on your layout. Click and drag to draw a line.

✦ **Oval tool:** Used to create an oval. If you want to create a perfect circle, press the Shift key while you click and drag.

✦ **Rectangle tool:** Used to create a rectangle. Press the Shift key while you click and drag to create a square.

✦ **Custom Shapes tool:** Used to create more complex shapes. Figure 3-6 shows you the pop-up menu for the Custom Shapes tool. Click to select the shape that you want from the menu and then drag to create your object on the layout.

✦ **Design Gallery Object tool:** Lets you select from a library of objects. Click the Design Gallery Object tool to open up the Microsoft Publisher Design Gallery, shown in Figure 3-7, that lets you select from a number of objects to insert into your publication.

Figure 3-6:
The
Custom
Shapes
pop-up
menu.
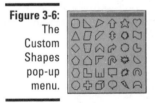

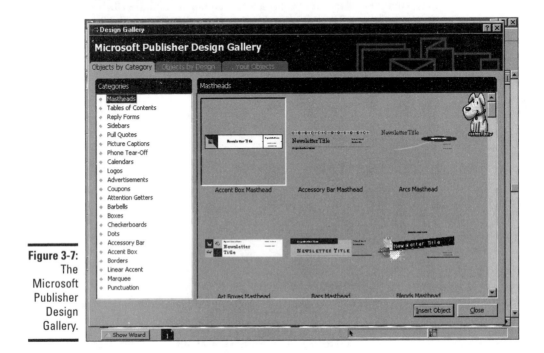

Figure 3-7:
The
Microsoft
Publisher
Design
Gallery.

Aligning and Positioning Objects

The quick and dirty way to position any object is to drag it. Dragging an object is the electronic equivalent of using your finger to slide a playing card across a table. The following commands on the Arrange menu are also used for precise positioning or alignment:

✦ **Align Objects:** This command opens the Align Objects dialog box, shown in Figure 3-8. Selected objects are aligned using the Left to Right and Top to Bottom options that you choose. You can set either or both of these alignment options. The Sample section shows you an example of your choices.

✦ **Nudge:** The Nudge command opens the Nudge dialog box, shown in Figure 3-9. *Nudges* are small movements of an object in one direction.

Click one of the Nudge control arrows. Each time that you click an arrow, your object moves one pixel in that direction.

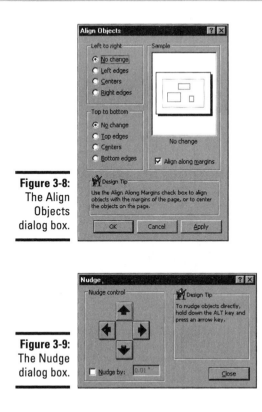

Figure 3-8:
The Align
Objects
dialog box.

Figure 3-9:
The Nudge
dialog box.

+ **Rotate or Flip:** Publisher offers five commands to rotate and flip selected objects: Custom Rotate, Rotate Left, Rotate Right, Flip Horizontal, and Flip Vertical.

Creating Regular Text Wraps

In Publisher, wrapping text is very easy. Just place any type of frame — even another text frame — on top of a text frame, and the text underneath automatically wraps around the frame above.

Sometimes Publisher 2000 wraps text too closely or too loosely around a frame. Closely wrapped text can be difficult to read, whereas loosely wrapped text can waste space and create big gaps on the page. With all frames except table frames, you can easily change the amount of space between the wrapping text and the frame it wraps around by changing the margins of the wrapped-around frame.

To increase the margins of a text frame, click the text frame and then choose Format⇨Text Frame Properties from the menu. Make your selections from the Text Frame Properties dialog box, shown in Figure 3-10. Turn text wrap on and off by checking or unchecking the Wrap Text around Objects check box. The Margins section changes the amount of space between the frame's border and the text.

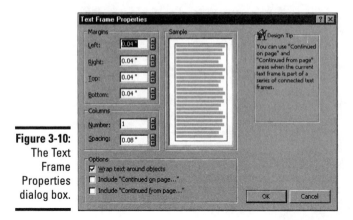

Figure 3-10:
The Text Frame Properties dialog box.

By default, Publisher wraps text in a rectangular pattern around the perimeter of a frame. If you're working with a picture or WordArt frame, however, you can have your text wrap to the actual shape of the graphic within that frame by selecting the Picture Only radio button in the Object Frame Properties dialog box. Figure 3-11 shows you an example of text wrapped around a picture.

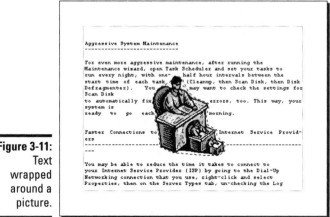

Figure 3-11:
Text wrapped around a picture.

Chapter 4: Getting the Word

In This Chapter

- ✔ **Working with text frames**
- ✔ **Using table frames**
- ✔ **Dealing with table text**

This chapter focuses on two frame types: text frames and table frames. You use *text frames* to place and manage text in your publication. You use *table frames* to hold data in tabular form. The end result is getting text into Microsoft Publisher 2000.

Using Text Frames

Those of you familiar with word-processing software may find it a bit disconcerting that you can't type on the page. At least, not directly. Before you start typing in Publisher, you must create a text frame. This is easy enough to do. Just click the Text Frame tool in the Objects toolbar and then click and drag on the layout to draw a box. That's it! Start typing. After you create a text frame, you can type text directly into the text frame, paste text in from the Clipboard, or import text from your word processor or text file.

Typing text

After you've created a text frame to hold your text, typing text in Publisher is not much different from most word processors, and is very similar to Microsoft Word. In fact, Publisher shares some common features with Word, such as similar menus and toolbars, AutoCorrect, and Spell Check.

As you type, your text begins filling the text frame from left to right, top to bottom. If the text frame isn't large enough to accommodate all your text, you eventually reach the bottom of the frame. When you type more text than can fit into a text frame, the extra text moves into an invisible place called the *overflow area*. The Text in Overflow indicator alerts you to the fact that you have typed more text than can fit into the current frame. (See Figure 4-1.)

Importing text

When you create text in another program, such as Word, and bring it into Publisher, you *import*. Importing text can be a great time saver. If you've entered text in a program, and decide you need that same text in a publication, you don't have to retype it. An easy way to import text into Publisher is simply by copying and pasting. Or you can use the Text File command on the Insert menu to import files saved by other programs. You don't have to have those programs on your computer to import their files.

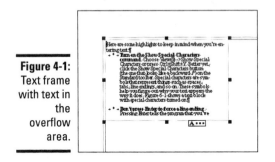

Figure 4-1:
Text frame
with text in
the
overflow
area.

Table Frames

Table frames let you quickly and easily create tables to hold your tabular data. Figure 4-2 shows a newly created, unformatted table frame.

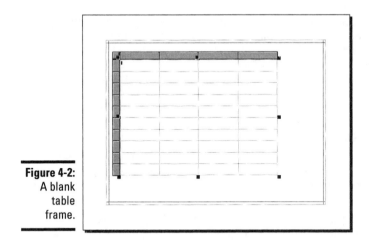

Figure 4-2:
A blank
table
frame.

Creating a table frame

If you have created a text frame in Publisher, creating a table frame won't cause you any trouble. Click the Table Frame tool in the Objects toolbar and then click and drag on the layout to create the table frame. The dialog box, shown in Figure 4-3, appears. You have three selections to make in this dialog box: Number of Rows, Number of Columns, and Table Format.

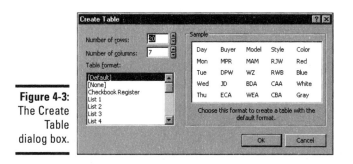

Figure 4-3:
The Create
Table
dialog box.

Tables can have up to 128 rows and columns. Publisher offers you 23 different table formats. As you select a format, the program shows you a sample of the format in the Sample portion of the dialog box. The [Default] and [None] formats usually give you the same thing: a very plain, unformatted table frame. When you click OK in the Create Table dialog box, Publisher creates your table.

Resizing tables, columns, and rows

The structure of a table frame is what really differentiates it from a text frame. Whereas a text frame is one big rectangle into which you type your text, a table frame is divided into a grid of separate text compartments called cells. Like just about everything else in Publisher, table frames are subject to change. You can resize the entire table frame; resize, insert, or delete selected columns and rows; merge multiple cells into one; and split a cell into separate cells. In short, you can restructure a table frame just about any way you want.

To resize a table frame, click and drag any of its selection handles. Publisher automatically adjusts the height of each row to fit each row's contents. If you choose Table⇨Grow to Fit Text, the table's row height expands to accommodate the text that you enter.

To resize a column or row, move your pointer to one of the lines that separates columns or rows in the selection bar at the top or left of the table frame. Your pointer changes to a double-headed arrow with the word Adjust. Then click and drag until the column or row is the size that you want.

Inserting and deleting columns and rows

You can insert and delete all the columns and rows you want. If you run out of table cells when entering data, just press the tab key when you get to the last cell. Publisher adds a new row at the bottom of the table frame and places the insertion point in the first cell of that row. You're now ready to type in that cell. Here's how to add rows or columns to your table:

1. **Place the insertion point in the column or row adjacent to where you want to insert a new column or row.**

2. **Choose Table⇨Insert Rows or Columns.**

Publisher opens the Insert dialog box, as shown in Figure 4-4.

Publisher Chapter 4

Getting the Word

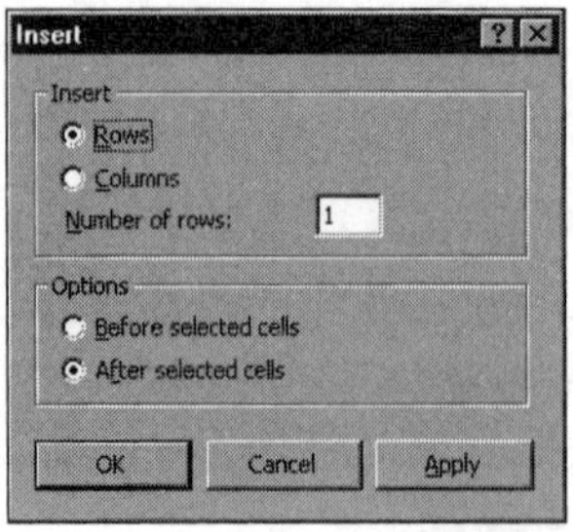

Figure 4-4:
The Insert
dialog box.

3. **Select whether you want Rows or Columns inserted, type in the Number you want to insert, and select whether the new columns or rows go Before Selected Cells or After Selected Cells.**

4. **Click OK to finish inserting your rows or columns.**

   Publisher increases the table frame's size to accommodate the new columns or rows.

Deleting a column or row is just as easy:

1. **Click anywhere in the row or column you want to delete.**

2. **Choose Table⇨Delete Rows or Columns.**

   The Delete dialog box, shown in Figure 4-5, appears.

3. **Click the Current Rows or Current Columns option.**

4. **Click OK to dismiss the Delete dialog box.**

You can't delete an entire table frame using the Delete Rows or Columns command on the Table menu. To delete a table frame, select it, and then choose Edit⇨Delete Object.

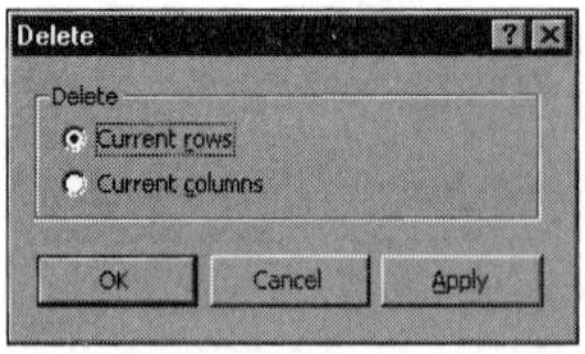

Figure 4-5:
The Delete
dialog box.

Working with Table Text

As with text frames, you can fill a table frame either by typing the text directly into the frame or by importing existing text from somewhere else. With just a couple of exceptions, typing and importing text into both types of frames is pretty darn similar.

Each cell in a table frame works much like a miniature text frame. For example, when you reach the right edge of a cell, Microsoft Publisher 2000 automatically word-wraps your text to a new line within that cell. If the text that you type disappears beyond the right edge of the cell, you have probably locked the table. Choose Table⇨Grow to Fit Text to unlock it. If you want to end a short line within a cell, press Enter. Filling in your table frame row by row is usually easiest; after you finish one cell, just press Tab to move on to the next one.

Importing table frame text

Just as you can with text frames, you can paste or insert a text file into a table frame. Cut or copy the text to the Windows Clipboard; then click the cell that is to be the upper-left cell of the range and choose Edit⇨Paste or press Ctrl+V.

Moving and copying table text

As with text frames, you can use the Clipboard or drag-and-drop text editing to copy and move text within and between table frames. If you like, you can even copy text between text and table frames.

Because of the way in which Publisher overwrites destination cells, rearranging entire columns and rows of text requires some extra steps. First, insert an extra column or row where you want to move the contents of an existing column or row. Then, move the contents. Finally, delete the column or row that you just emptied.

Two commands on the Table menu, Fill Down and Fill Right, enable you to copy the entire contents of one cell into any number of adjacent cells either below or to the right.

Do the following to fill a series of cells in a row or column:

1. **Select the cell containing the text you want to copy and the cells to which you want to copy the text.**

   To use the fill commands, you must select cells adjacent to the cell containing the text to be copied.

2. **Choose Table⇨Fill Down to copy the value in the topmost selected cell to the selected cells in the column below it.**

   Or, choose Table⇨Fill Right to copy the value in the leftmost selected cell to selected cells in the row to the right.

Formatting table text manually

You can use all the character- and paragraph-formatting options that are available for text frame text: fonts, text size, text effects, line spacing, alignment, tab stops, indents, bulleted and numbered lists, and so on. You can even hyphenate table-frame text.

The key difference when applying paragraph formatting in table frames is that Publisher treats each cell as a miniature text frame. Thus, when you align text, the text aligns within just that cell rather than across the entire table frame. And when you indent text, that text indents according to that cell's left and right edges.

To improve the look of cells, you can also change cell margins, thus changing the amount of space between a cell's contents and its edges. To change cell margins, choose Format⇨Table Cell Properties. The resulting dialog box is shown in Figure 4-6.

Enter a new Left, Right, Top, or Bottom margin and click OK.

You can change the margins for multiple cells at the same time. Just select the cells before choosing the Format⇨Table Cell Properties command.

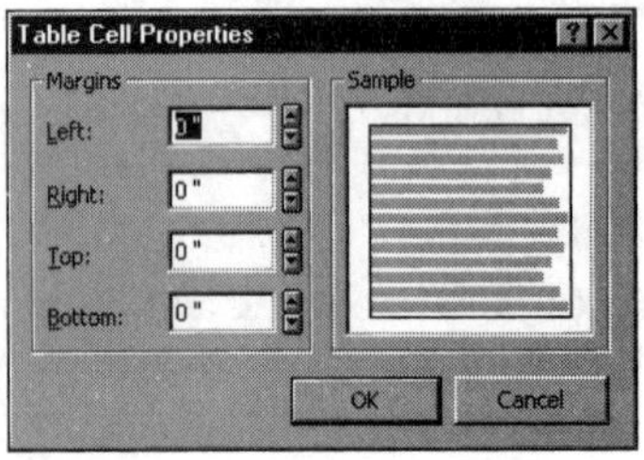

Figure 4-6:
The Table
Cell
Properties
dialog box.

Chapter 5: You Ought to Be in Pictures

In This Chapter

✔ Creating and working with picture frames

✔ Getting pictures in and out of Microsoft Publisher 2000

✔ Resizing and cropping your images

✔ Using BorderArt and the Design Gallery to enhance your publications

Although Microsoft Publisher 2000 really isn't the place to draw complex pictures, it's mighty flexible when it comes to importing pictures created elsewhere. Some desktop publishers rely heavily on collections of electronic clip art and libraries of photographs, whereas others are daring enough to create their own pictures using specialized graphics programs. Whether you're working from a clip art collection or creating your own pictures, this chapter shows you how to get pictures into and out of your publications and how to work with pictures after they're in Publisher.

Understanding More about Picture Frames

Publisher uses picture frames to display graphics on a layout. You don't create graphics inside a picture frame; they must be created elsewhere. You can create picture frames in two ways. You can draw them yourself or have the program create them for you when you insert or import a graphic of some kind. Which method is best depends upon your purpose:

✦ When you need to place a picture frame of a specific size at a specific position in your layout, draw the frame with the Picture tool (in the toolbox) and fill the frame with a picture manually.

✦ When the content and size of the graphic determine the size of the frame, have Publisher create the frame for you as you bring in the picture. You can always adjust the frame's size and position later on.

Getting Yours

Publisher provides five ways to insert or import pictures:

+ Copy a graphic from another Windows program onto the Windows Clipboard and then paste it into a picture frame.

+ Use the Insert➪Object command to fill a picture frame with any OLE object, such as an Excel Chart or a PowerPoint slide.

+ Choose Insert➪Picture➪Clip Art to open the Microsoft Clip Gallery, which provides easy access to the thousands of pieces of clip art that you can install with Publisher.

+ Choose Insert➪Picture➪From File to import any picture that is saved in a format that Publisher can recognize.

+ Choose Insert➪Picture➪From Scanner or Camera to scan a hard copy of an image or capture an image from a digital camera.

No matter how you put a graphic into a picture frame, you can use any of the methods to replace that picture.

Using the Microsoft Clip Gallery

Microsoft Clip Gallery is a program that can contain thousands of pieces of clip art that you can install along with Publisher. To place clip art in your publication, you simply click a miniature version of the picture in the Gallery. To insert a picture using Microsoft Clip Gallery:

1. **If you want to import the picture into a specific picture frame, select that frame.**

Otherwise, make sure that no frame is selected — Publisher creates a frame for you in this case.

2. **Choose Insert➪Picture➪Clip Art.**

The Insert Clip Art dialog box, shown in Figure 5-1, appears.

3. **Click a category of pictures.**

The Clip Gallery displays all the images in the selected category.

4. **Scroll as necessary and then click the picture that you want.**

5. **Click the Insert Clip icon in the pop-up menu that appears.**

If the Clip Gallery completely covers your publication, it appears that nothing happens. Click the close button in the Insert Clip Art dialog box to dismiss the Clip Gallery and return to your publication.

If you selected a picture frame in Step 1, the picture completely fills that frame. Otherwise, Publisher creates a picture frame for you in the center of the current view and places the picture in that new frame.

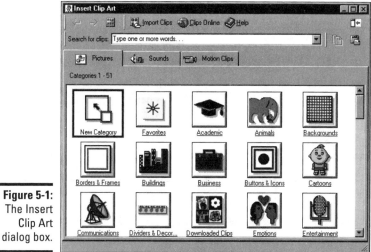

Figure 5-1:
The Insert
Clip Art
dialog box.

If you draw a picture frame before you import a picture from Microsoft Clip Gallery, Publisher automatically resizes the frame to keep the inserted image in proper proportion. After the image has been inserted into the frame, you may resize it to your heart's content.

Replacing the picture from the clip art collection with another picture is very easy. Just double-click the existing picture to reopen the Microsoft Clip Gallery dialog box. Click a different picture and then click the Insert Clip icon.

Inserting picture files

The Insert⇨Picture⇨From File command imports a picture stored on disk into your publication.

1. **If you want to import the picture into a specific picture frame, select that frame.**

   Otherwise, make sure that no frame is selected — Publisher creates the frame as needed.

2. **Select Insert⇨Picture⇨From File.**

   The Insert Picture dialog box appears, as shown in Figure 5-2. Microsoft Publisher builds a preview of the picture for you in the dialog box.

3. **Find the file that you want to insert and click Insert.**

   The picture is inserted into your publication. If you select a picture frame before importing a picture from a file, Publisher changes the frame to maintain the picture's correct proportions. You can always resize the frame later manually or by using the Scale Picture command I describe later in this chapter.

**Publisher
Chapter 5**

**You Ought to Be
in Pictures**

REAL WORLD

Need more clip art?

Chances are that you'll eventually get tired of seeing and using the same clip art images. Why not grab some more? If the clip art and images that come with the Microsoft Publisher 2000 CD aren't enough for you, check out the Microsoft Web site for even more. Just click the Clips Online button in the Insert Clip Art dialog box. There you find additional clip art images, sounds, videos, and photos. Any clips that you select from this Web site are automatically added to the Clip Gallery. Don't forget that you must have an Internet connection to use this feature.

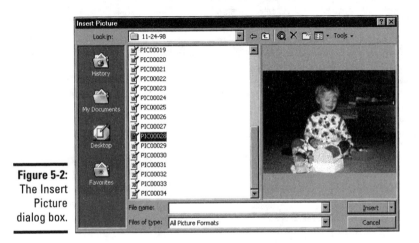

Figure 5-2:
The Insert
Picture
dialog box.

If you import a picture and later decide that you want a different picture, just double-click the existing picture. The Insert Picture dialog box reopens. Click a different filename and then click Insert.

If Publisher doesn't understand the format of the picture that you're trying to import, it whines: `Cannot convert this picture`. If you have access to the program that created that picture, try saving the picture in a different format. Or, if you can open the picture in any other Windows program, try copying the picture to the Windows Clipboard and pasting it into your picture frame.

Modifying Pictures

After you import a picture, you can adjust it in Microsoft Publisher in several ways: You can resize it, chop off parts of it (called cropping), and add some space between the picture and its frame to create a border. These changes apply to the format of the frame and not to the picture itself.

Resizing a picture

To resize a picture, you resize its frame. By default, both the picture and its frame are the same size and proportions. You can resize a picture frame much as you would resize any other frame: by dragging any of its selection handles.

To maintain the proportions of a picture and its frame, hold down the Shift key as you drag a corner selection handle. If Microsoft Publisher 2000 distorted your picture when you imported it, holding down the Shift key as you drag a corner selection handle simply maintains that distortion. To undistort a picture, try using one of the Scale commands described next. (*Scaling* in Publisher is just another term for *resizing*. Scaling in snakes and pipes is another thing entirely.) The Format⇨Scale Picture command is also a way to resize a picture without using the mouse.

Here's how to resize a picture using the menu command:

1. **Select the picture that you want to resize and/or restore.**

2. **Select the Scale Picture command from the Format menu or select Change Picture⇨Scale Picture from the picture's context-sensitive menu.**

The Scale Picture dialog box, shown in Figure 5-3, appears.

Scale Picture		? X
Scale height:	37.62	%
Scale width:	37.62	%
☐ Original size		
OK	Cancel	

3. **Enter numbers in the Scale Height and Scale Width text boxes to set the percentages to which you want to resize your picture.**

These percentages vary according to the picture's original file size. Use the same percentages in the Scale Height and Scale Width boxes to retain the figure's proportions.

**Publisher
Chapter 5**

To see the picture in its original file size, click the Original Size check box.

4. **Click OK.**

Both the picture and its frame resize accordingly.

**You Ought to Be
in Pictures**

Cropping a picture

Publishing professionals who still assemble publications *without* a computer often remove unwanted edges of a picture by lopping off those edges with a pair of scissors. In the publishing world, editing a picture in this way is called *cropping*. Why bother with scissors, though? You can use Publisher to crop a picture *electronically*.

1. **Click the Crop Picture button on the Formatting toolbar.**

2. **Point to one of the picture frame's selection handles.**

Your mouse pointer changes to a *cropper pointer* — two scissors with the word *Crop.*

3. **Drag inward until you exclude the part of the picture that you don't want and then release the mouse.**

Cropping a picture doesn't permanently remove any picture parts; it only hides them from view. To restore a picture part that you've cropped, repeat the preceding steps, but drag outward. Regardless of whether you've cropped or not, you can drag outward on any picture to *reverse crop,* thus adding space between the picture and its frame.

Applying Borders and BorderArt

You can give your picture frame a border by using the Line/Border Style command's dialog box or the pop-up menu of the Line/Border Style button on the Format toolbar. If the picture frame is a regular rectangle, you can also apply BorderArt to it.

1. **Select F̲ormat⇨Line/B̲order Style⇨More S̲tyles.**

The Border Style dialog box appears.

2. **Click the BorderArt tab of the Border Style dialog box.** The BorderArt tab of the Border Style dialog box appears, as shown in Figure 5-4.

3. **Make your selection from the A̲vailable Borders list box, set a B̲order Size and Col̲or (if desired), and click the OK button.**

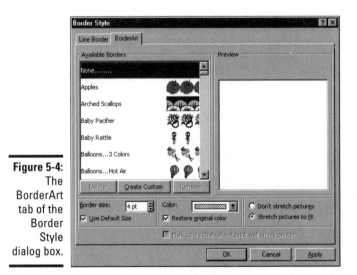

Figure 5-4:
The
BorderArt
tab of the
Border
Style
dialog box.

Chapter 6: Spinning a Web Site

In This Chapter

✔ Using the Web Sites Wizard

✔ Adding text or picture objects

✔ Adding hyperlinks

✔ Adding color and texture to the background

*Y*ou don't know how to write HTML code, but you want to create professional-looking Web pages? Microsoft Publisher 2000 can help. In fact, if you can click a few buttons, you can create some great-looking Web pages in minutes! How? Read on.

Using the Web Sites Wizard

The easiest way to create a publication in Publisher is to use a wizard. Creating a Web site is no exception. Can you create a Web site from scratch using Microsoft Publisher? Sure. Would you want to? Probably not.

1. **To use the Web Sites Wizard, just click Web Sites in the Wizards pane on the Publications by Wizard tab of the Microsoft Publisher Catalog. If the Catalog is not visible, you can get it back by choosing File⇨New.**

    After you click Web Sites in the Wizards pane, Publisher offers you 45 styles of Web sites to choose from in the Web Sites pane.

2. **Select the style of the Web site that you want to create and click the Start Wizard button located at the bottom right of the Microsoft Publisher Catalog.**

    After a few seconds (seems like hours), Publisher creates the first page of your Web site and shows you the Introduction panel of the Web Sites Wizard, as shown in Figure 6-1.

3. **Click Next to select a color scheme from the Color Scheme panel of the Web Sites Wizard.**

    Publisher lets you choose from over 60 color schemes. Microsoft paid big money to have these color schemes designed, so it is hard to go wrong when selecting one. Still, if you can't decide which color scheme looks the best, stick with the default. Figure 6-2 shows the Color Scheme panel of the Web Sites Wizard with the Meadow color scheme selected.

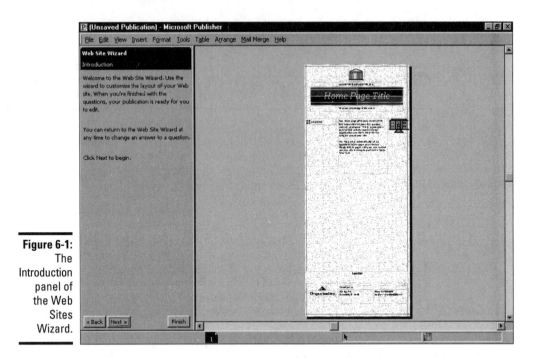

Figure 6-1:
The
Introduction
panel of
the Web
Sites
Wizard.

4. **Click the color scheme of your choice and then click Next.**

The Additional Pages panel of the Web Sites Wizard leaps to the screen. At this point, you have only one page in your Web site: the home page. Here you can choose to add one of six different page types to your Web site. Your choices are Story, Calendar, Event, Special offer, Price list, and Related links.

5. **Click the check box next to the type of page that you want to add.**

You may use any or all the offered types. Click Next without selecting any of the check boxes to continue without adding any pages. You can always return to the wizard to add pages later.

After you click Next, the Form panel of the Web Sites Wizard appears. Forms allow you to receive feedback from visitors to your Web site. Notice that the forms have a radio button; you may select only one.

6. **Select the form that you want to add and click Next.**

Microsoft Publisher displays the Navigation Bar dialog box, asking what kind of navigation bar you would like to link the pages of your Web site. Your choices are Both a Vertical and Horizontal Bar, Just a Vertical Bar, and None.

7. **Unless you're creating a single-page Web site, adding a navigation bar is a good idea. Make your selection and click Next.**

Next, the wizard wants to know if you would like to have a sound played when your home page is opened.

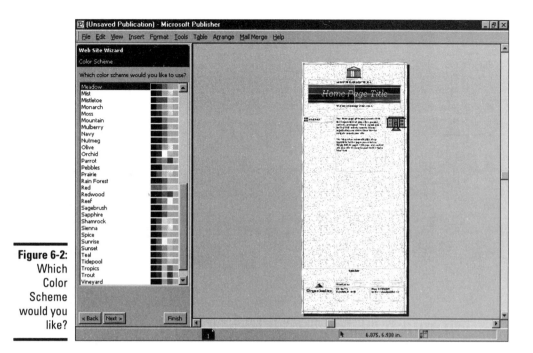

Figure 6-2:
Which
Color
Scheme
would you
like?

8. **Unless you have a very compelling reason to play a sound when your home page is opened, click No.**

Sounds can take a long time to download, especially over slow dial-up connections. Nothing makes most visitors want to move on to another Web site than having to wait for someone's alma mater's fight song to download. After clicking No, click Next.

The Background Texture panel appears.

9. **If you want a texture, click Yes. If not, click No.**

This is a trade-off between legibility and visual impact. Textures can look great, but sometimes they make text difficult to read. Oh, what the heck. Click Yes and then click Next.

The Personal Information panel of the Web Sites Wizard appears (see Figure 6-3), demanding that you choose a Personal Information Set.

10. **Choose an option or accept the default and click Finish.**

You're done! Notice that the Web Sites Wizard is still hanging around the left side of the screen. If you don't like the way that your Web site turned out, use the wizard to change any part of it. Click the Hide Wizard button to free up some on-screen real estate.

Figure 6-4 shows the completed Web site with the Web Sites Wizard visible on the left side of the screen. That's all there is to it. Now you can edit the text and picture frames to personalize your Web site.

**Publisher
Chapter 6**

Spinning a Web Site

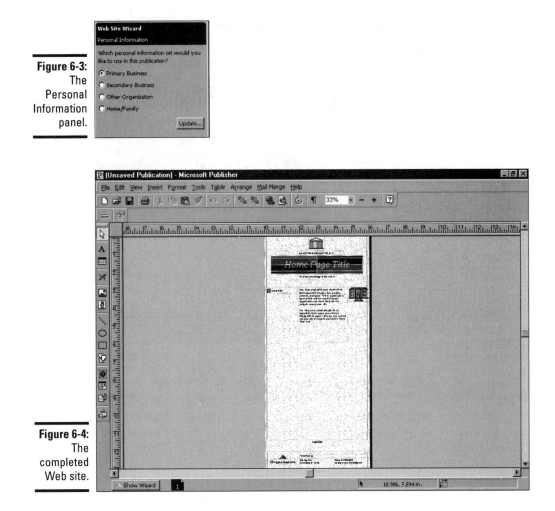

Figure 6-3:
The
Personal
Information
panel.

Figure 6-4:
The
completed
Web site.

Adding Text or Picture Objects

Adding text or pictures to your Web site is pretty simple. In fact, if you have added text or pictures to a Publisher publication, you already know how to add them to your Web site. If you used the Web Sites Wizard to create your Web site, you probably have several text and picture frames in your publication.

Use the Web Sites Wizard to create your Web site. Creating the site using the wizard and changing what you don't like is much easier than creating the Web site from scratch.

Adding text

To change the place holder text that the wizard put in your publication, just highlight the text and start typing.

If you don't have any text frames or don't want to change the text in an existing text frame, just create a new one.

1. **Click the Text Frame tool.**

2. **Draw the text frame.**

3. **Start typing.**

The Web Sites Wizard does a reasonably good job of designing the Web page, but feel free to add, delete, or move objects as you see fit.

Adding a picture

To change a picture on your Web page, follow these steps:

1. **Double-click the picture.**

The Microsoft Clip Gallery appears, and you can select a new picture for your Web page.

2. **Click the Pictures, Sounds, or Motion Clips tab.**

The Picture tab contains (what else?) pictures; the Sounds tab contains — well, sounds; and the Motion Clips tab contains animated GIFs for use in Web pages. Figure 6-5 shows the Clip Gallery with the Motion Clips tab selected.

3. **Select a category.**

The images in the selected category are displayed.

4. **Click the image that you want to insert and then click the Insert Clip button on the pop-up menu that appears.**

The picture that you selected replaces the existing picture in your Web site.

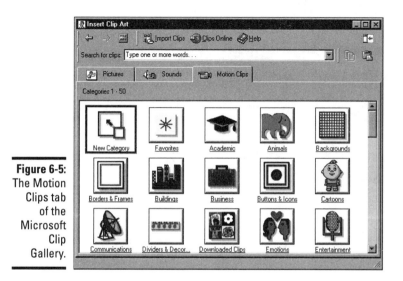

Figure 6-5:
The Motion
Clips tab
of the
Microsoft
Clip
Gallery.

**Publisher
Chapter 6**

Spinning a Web Site

To preview an animated GIF in the Clip Gallery, click the image, and then click
the Play clip button from the pop-up menu.

Adding and Removing Hyperlinks

Hyperlinks allow a visitor to your Web site to click an object (text or a graphic)
and jump to another document on your Web site or elsewhere on the Internet,
and to send an e-mail.

Adding hyperlinks

Several ways are available to add a hyperlink to an object on your Web page.
You add hyperlinks to text, pictures, WordArt, and even the contents of table
frames. To add a hyperlink to text or a table frame, you must first select the
individual text that you want to hyperlink. Selecting just the text frame or table
frame won't work. Follow these steps to create a hyperlink:

1. **Select the object to which you want to add a hyperlink.**

2. **Select Insert⇨Hyperlink, click the Insert Hyperlink button on the
   toolbar, or press Ctrl+K.**

3. **Select the type of hyperlink that you want from the Hyperlink dialog box.**

4. **Fill in the Hyperlink information section of the Hyperlink dialog box
   and click OK.**

As shown in Figure 6-6, you can create four types of hyperlinks:

✦ A document already on the Internet: You need to supply the URL (Uniform
   Resource Locator or address) of the document the hyperlink connects to.

✦ An Internet e-mail address: You need to supply an e-mail address.

✦ Another page in your Web site: Select the appropriate page in your Web site.

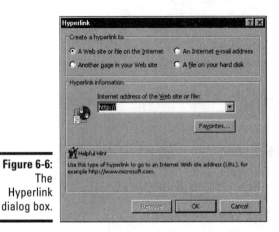

Figure 6-6:
The
Hyperlink
dialog box.

✦ A file on your hard disk: You need to supply the path to the file to which you want to link. This file will be published along with your Web site.

Removing hyperlinks

Removing a hyperlink from an object is a snap:

1. **Select the object from which you want to remove a hyperlink.**

2. **Select Insert⇨Hyperlink, select Hyperlink from the context menu, click the Insert Hyperlink button on the toolbar, or press Ctrl+K.**

3. **Click the Remove button in the Hyperlink dialog box.**

Adding Color and Texture to the Background

You can produce dramatic effects by applying texture and/or color to the page background. The easiest way to do this is to select Yes from the Background Texture panel of the Web Sites Wizard. If you opted not to have a textured background and have now changed your mind, read on.

Adding color to the background

To add or change the color of the background, do the following:

1. **Select Format⇨Color and Background Scheme.**

The Color and Background Scheme dialog box, shown in Figure 6-7, is displayed.

2. **Click the Texture button to remove the check mark.**

Figure 6-7:
The
Standard
tab of the
Color and
Background
Scheme
dialog box.

**Publisher
Chapter 6**

Spinning a Web Site

3. **Click the Custom tab.**

The Custom tab of the Color and Background Scheme dialog box shown in Figure 6-8 is displayed.

4. **Click the down-arrow next to the Solid Color option and select a color.**

5. **Change the Custom Scheme Colors options as desired.**

6. **Click OK.**

You're returned to your Web site publication.

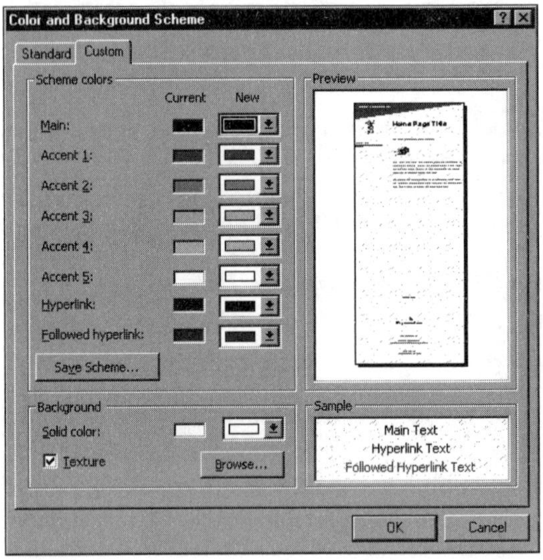

Figure 6-8:
The
Custom tab
of the
Color and
Background
Scheme
dialog box.

Adding texture to the background

To add or change the texture of the background, follow these steps:

1. **Select Format⇨Color and Background Scheme.**

The Color and Background Scheme dialog box, shown back in Figure 6-8, is displayed.

2. **If necessary, click the Texture check box to place a check mark in it.**

3. **Click the Browse button.**

The Web Backgrounds dialog box appears.

4. **Click the name of the file containing the texture that you want to apply.**

Take a look at your selection in the pane of the Web Backgrounds dialog box.

5. **Click Open.**

6. **Click OK to apply the texture and return to editing your Web site.**

Index

Book IX

PhotoDraw 2000

The 5th Wave   **By Rich Tennant**

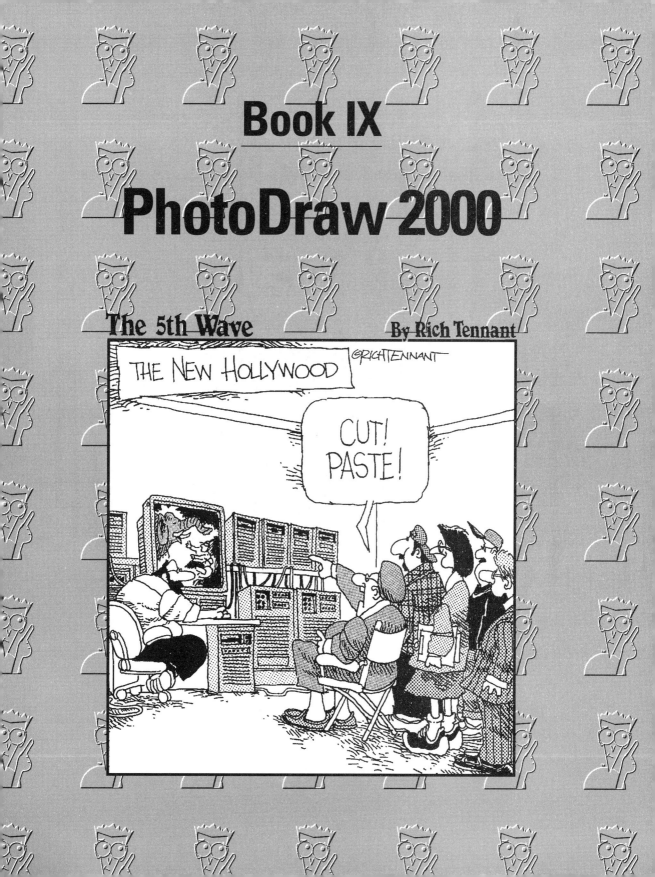

Contents at a Glance

Chapter 1: Your Personal Tour

In This Chapter

✔ **Getting to know PhotoDraw**

✔ **Finding your tools on the toolbar**

✔ **Putting pictures in the Picture list**

✔ **Poking around the drawing area**

✔ **Working in the workpane**

✔ **Checking the Status bar**

Anytime you explore a new program, it's fun to poke around and look at the menus, the buttons, the help files, and anything else that may be different from other programs you use. It not only gives you clues to the features you can find, but it also helps get the creative juices flowing. This is your chance to kick the tires, check the options on the window sticker, and maybe even take a test drive.

Microsoft PhotoDraw has a lot of very neat features that are easy to use and can add some life and zest to your photos. What you'll like about PhotoDraw is the simple interface. None of the features are buried very deep within the menus, dialog boxes, or buttons. But, don't be fooled by the simple interface; there's power under the hood of this baby.

Interface Roadmap

When you start up PhotoDraw, you see a dialog box asking how you want to start working on an image: open a blank one, get one from your scanner or digital camera, or use one of the PhotoDraw templates. Just click Cancel to close this dialog box (which is explained in Chapter 2).

At the top of the screen are the pull-down menus and toolbars. These are the things you have to push, pull, click, and pick to tell PhotoDraw what you want to do.

On the bottom of the window you find the Status bar. The left side shows your picture list. The right side will show the workpane after you start a task. And in the center, the drawing area is where the action takes place. Read on, brave souls, and seek thy knowledge. (See Figure 1-1.)

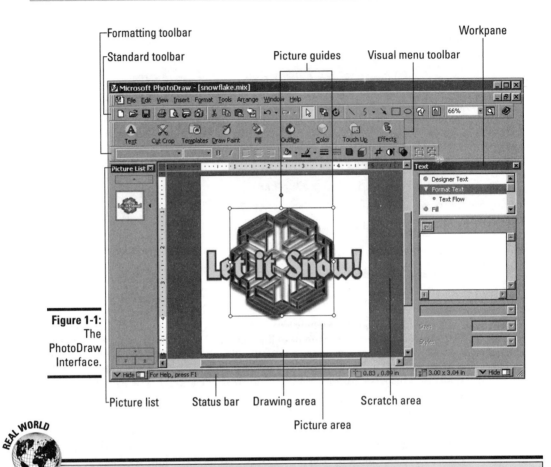

Formatting toolbar

Standard toolbar

Picture guides

Visual menu toolbar

Workpane

Figure 1-1:
The
PhotoDraw
Interface.

Picture list   Status bar   Drawing area   Scratch area

Picture area

Belly up to the toolbars, boys

If you're a button lover, you'll like the plush, pushable puppies in PhotoDraw's few toolbars. Many of the other programs you'll find in the Office 2000 suite carry a lot of overhead in toolbars — some having 10 to 15 different toolbars that pop into the picture when you do certain tasks. Not so with PhotoDraw. Sweet, simple, and easy to digest. Anytime you want to turn a toolbar on or off, you can right-click in the gray area to the right of the toolbars and get a menu with the

three PhotoDraw toolbars listed. The checkmark tells you they are showing. Click once to turn one off; click again to turn it on. Yes, like all the other applications, you have a standard toolbar that allows you to open files, print, save, and the other drab necessary grunt tasks of any application. And, if you get confused, all you have to do is pause your mouse cursor over the button. A little ToolTip opens and explains what the button is.

The Visual Menu Toolbar

You can't miss the jewels on the Visual Menu toolbar. This toolbar sports all the big guns of the program (and big buttons, too!). The Visual Menu works like the drop-down menus. Click a button, and down drops the various choices you can make in that category (see Figure 1-2). Why Microsoft didn't put the little down arrows on each button in this toolbar is a mystery, but you can be sure that if you click, choices will drop.

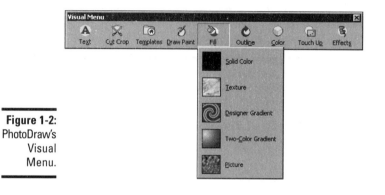

Figure 1-2:
PhotoDraw's
Visual
Menu.

✦ **Text:** Unlike stuffy old Microsoft Word, this text menu lets you not only insert letters, words, and phrases, but it also lets you do some pretty neat effects. Chapter 4 shows you the ooo's, ahhh's, and how's of working with text.

✦ **Cut Crop:** With the Cut Crop tools, you can take the scissors to your work and remove bits and pieces of your picture at will. Your masterpiece is at your mercy. Don't let the power go to your head.

✦ **Templates:** How about some no-brainer setups? Using the templates that come with PhotoDraw, you can not only create all types of greeting cards and invitations, but there are some pretty snazzy photo edges, graphics for the Web or the office, and some pretty nice clip art pieces to help you get started at a quick pace. Excellent for those of us who were in the wrong line when talent for drawing was passed out.

✦ **Draw Paint:** And, for those who got more than their fair share of talent, this button's for you. Pick a tool or shape and knock yourself out. Let those creative juices flow and splatter paint for that next museum piece.

✦ **Fill:** If you have a need, here's the place to fill it. After you select an object or area, you can use one of the endless fill patterns PhotoDraw has to offer. The good ole standby solid fill is here as are gradients, textures, and others. Check out Chapter 4 on how to use your good buddy Fill to his highest extent.

✦ **Outline:** Don't worry. These aren't outlines like you had to do in school for your book reports. These outlines can give objects a harsh or soft look. They can contain, enhance, flatter, buy the little lady some roses. . . . Well, maybe they're not that good. But if you think about your coloring books of days past or look at many cartoon characters, they use outlines to add clarity and definition. Now you can, too.

+ **Color:** This is Fill's cousin, twice removed. You can use the different options here to mute, enhance, alter, and possibly destroy the overall colors in your image. Explore these guys in Chapter 4.

+ **Touch Up:** Okay, so you're an amateur photographer or received some pictures from an amateur. You have some real problems on your hands and don't know whether you can salvage an inept photo or not. Before you go through the roof, these tools can help you correct or compensate for those goofs. Here you'll find tools to remove red eye, scratches, dust, and more. Becoming an expert is as close as Chapter 3.

+ **Effects:** What's the difference between, "That's a nice picture," and "Oh my God! You must have been up all night creating this!"? Quite simply, the Effects tools. Shadows, 3-D, and other quick slight-of-hand and mind-bending feats are waiting for you under this button. Turning ho-hum into wow awaits you in Chapter 4.

The Formatting Toolbar

The format menu places necessary settings and functions at your beck and call. Whether you are dealing with type, objects, or images, a quick click of the mouse gives you power to create and alter. If you don't see this one, try pulling down the View menu and clicking Toolbars⇨Formatting. It'll answer your beck and call to appear.

When using these buttons, you can click them to apply the effect or issue the command. Some function just like the ones that turn on and off the toolbars. Click once and the effect is applied; click again and it is removed. Others, you'll notice, have a little arrow next to them. That means more options are available, and you have to click the little arrow to get to all of them.

The Picture List

Over to the left side of the working area (which is explained shortly), is the Picture list (see Figure 1-3). Here is where you will find thumbnails of the pictures you are working on in any given session. You can consider this like a holding area. Until you close PhotoDraw, each picture, whether you have saved it or not, will take a rest in the Picture list. Anytime you want to work on one of these jewels, all you have to do is click its thumbnail.

With the pictures arranged in a nice little column, you can use the arrows at the top and bottom of the Picture list to scroll up and down your collection of pictures. On top, there is one arrow pointing up. But, at the bottom, you have three different arrows to choose. Clicking the single arrow pointing down scrolls down the list. The upward-pointing double arrows take you to the very top of the Picture list, and the double arrows pointing down take you to the end of the list. Of course, if you haven't over-filled the Picture list, these arrows won't become available.

Figure 1-3:
Uncover
all the
components
of the
image in
your
Picture list.

Beside each picture in your list is yet another arrow that points to the left. A quick click of the mouse on this arrow opens up another row of pictures that show the different elements of that picture's file. There, you can also find the same configuration of arrows as you found in the Picture list, but these arrows help you run through the elements that make up that individual picture.

You'll probably notice the little All button, too. Click that button to select all the picture elements. If you don't want all the elements selected, you can select them one or several at a time.

Just like any Office 2000 application, holding down the Shift key while clicking on the first and last element in the list will select those two elements and everything in between. If you hold down the Control key, you can click any element willy nilly in the list and only the elements you choose are selected in the picture that is sitting in the drawing area.

The Drawing Area

That big gray area in the middle of your screen is called the Drawing area. When you have a picture open, that image sits in the Picture area. Your image can consist of one single, solitary, maybe lonely element, or it could also be a conglomeration of many different elements.

While you are dinking around to achieve your final masterpiece, you can use the gray area that surrounds your image to temporarily hold different elements you may choose to incorporate in the final image. This Twilight Zone is called the Scratch area. Whatever is in the Scratch area does not print or export; whatever sits in the Picture area will print or export. Spooky, huh?

In simple terms, the Drawing area is your desk. The Picture area is your paper. When you have several little clippings that you are going to paste into your picture, you can lay them in the Scratch area. If you have some spare clippings on your desk when you're finished, they stay in the Scratch area. When it comes time to export the picture to use on the Web or in another Office 2000 program, the leftover clippings stay on your desk. They won't be part of your picture.

From Window Panes to Workpanes

Whenever you access one of the tools from the Visual Menu, a window with different options opens to the right side of the drawing area. This is called the *workpane*. Workpanes can be just a series of choices using radio buttons, drop-down menus, and check boxes as you normally see in programs like this, yet others can be like a wizard, taking one step at a time to walk you through the effect and how to apply it.

Sometimes a little floating menu comes out of hiding when the workpane shows up. This floating menu gives you buttons to click to apply different effects, alterations, and more. When you close the workpane, the floating menu also goes away.

Feedback from the Status Bar

For those who have to know where they're at and what's going on all the time, PhotoDraw gives you the Status bar (see Figure 1-4). Here's what you'll find on your status bar:

- ✦ **Show/Hide Picture list:** Click once to turn the Picture list off, click it again to pop it open again. Rather than clicking this button, you can use the F3 key to show or hide the picture list.

- ✦ **Progress bar:** Displays pretty moving color when something is happening in your picture . . . like when you create an effect.

- ✦ **Position information:** Immediate feedback to tell you the coordinates of the top-left corner of a selected component. Coordinates is a fancy term for x, y position: the amount of space down from the top (y) and over from the left side (x) of your overall picture. If you see a negative number, part of your component is off your picture area.

- ✦ **Size information:** Want to find out just how tall and wide a component is? Select the component and look at these numbers. To see how large your overall picture is, look here when nothing is selected.

- ✦ **Show/Hide workpane:** Click it to hide the workpane, then click on it again to show it again. Use the F2 key for a shortcut.

- ✦ **Resize window:** Click and drag this triangular icon to make the PhotoDraw window a custom size on your desktop. If you don't see this little icon in your program window, you are running the PhotoDraw window maximized.

Figure 1-4:
Your
PhotoDraw
feedback
panel, the
Status bar.

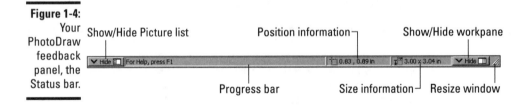

Show/Hide Picture list   Position information ⌐   Show/Hide workpane

Progress bar   Size information ⌐   Resize window

Chapter 2: Getting Pictures into PhotoDraw

In This Chapter

✔ **Opening an existing image file**

✔ **Snagging an image from a scanner**

✔ **Pulling images out of a digital camera**

✔ **Extracting images from your mind**

Surely you don't want to stare at the PhotoDraw interface, just waiting for something to happen. If that's your job and you get paid well for it, there are probably many people wanting to apply for your job when you retire. But for the massive number of readers who are itching to get their feet wet in PhotoDraw, this is where the foot powder begins to get applied.

You have several options when bringing in an image. With the price of scanners, digital cameras, and video cards falling tremendously over the years (and hopefully, in the future), you have so many choices for getting an image — not to mention, you can save most images on the Internet to your disk.

Here's a word of caution: Never use an image that you don't have a right to use. Copyright laws are very straightforward, and lawsuits happen almost daily over these types of infringements. Besides, jail food is not all it's cracked up to be.

Getting Images Already on Your System

When you start up PhotoDraw, you get a dialog box, as shown in Figure 2-1. Not only are you offered the various ways to open an image at the top of the dialog box, but there is a list of the last few images that you worked on in the lower part of the dialog box. Of course, you can choose the option, Open an Existing Picture. You do have the option to make this dialog box disappear the next time you start the program. Just place a check next to the Don't Show This Dialog Box Again checkbox, which you'll find right above the OK button. You may like this dialog box to show when you start PhotoDraw, especially after a long weekend. If you usually forget the last thing you were working on, the list of most recent images may help spur your memory along. Besides, it doesn't take a lot of effort to click the Cancel button and pretend it never came up in the first place.

Opening an existing file is a common procedure for any Office 2000 application: Click the Open icon on the Standard toolbar or press Ctrl+O. In the Open dialog box, select the file, click Open, and you're set to go.

Figure 2-1:
Welcome
to
PhotoDraw.
Now get to
work!

Clipping Art from the CD

Office 2000 comes with a lot of free clip art. Well, almost free. You had to pay for the program one way or another. To bring clip art into PhotoDraw, you can either open them directly from the Office CD, or use Microsoft Clip Art Gallery.

Clip Art Gallery is nice to use because it categorizes the individual pieces of art so you don't have to wade through thousands of files to find just the one you want to use. In order to access the Clip Art Gallery, you have to start with an open or blank picture. Honest. Try to get to the gallery without an open image. Can't do it. Nope, nope, nope.

If you're inserting clip art into an existing picture, you can open that picture as explained in the preceding section and then skip to Step 5. Or, because opening a blank image is not big deal, just follow these steps:

1. **Choose File⇨New.**

You can also click the New button or press Ctrl+N.

2. **When you get the New dialog box, make sure the Pictures tab is showing.**

3. **Find and click the Full Screen icon.**

This step is just for general measures. You can change the image size or scale the clip art to fit in the existing image after you insert it.

4. **Click OK.**

Don't you just hate being second-guessed? If so, you can double-click the Full Screen icon and forego this step. What you end up with is a blank, white space in your Drawing area.

Opening files the visual way

Of course, if you're the picture type of person, you have another more graphic way to open files. PhotoDraw has a Visual Open command that you can reach from the File menu, or just press Ctrl+Shift+O. The Visual Open dialog box opens where you can see thumbnails of your image files. The routine for opening files is about the same, but the options have been moved around a little to make room for the pictures. On the left side of the dialog box, use the Look In drop-down list to find the drive where your images are stored. Underneath that, you click the plus signs and folders until you reach your destination. It's just like wandering around in Windows Explorer. After you find your picture, double-click the thumbnail. PhotoDraw places it in the Picture area, ready for your next move.

5. **Choose Insert⇨Clip Art.**

   Now, if you have everything in order, the Microsoft Clip Gallery dialog box opens, and you can find the clip art you need (see Figure 2-2).

Scanning Your Way Through

Wonderful things, these scanners today. With the click of a couple of buttons, photos, line art, and more can be lifted and transformed into digital art. Once inside the computer, nothing is sacred. Draw moustaches on children, fix tacky complexions, add or remove freckles, or change heads on bodies. Watch what you do; you can make a lot of enemies this way.

PhotoDraw uses the TWAIN driver that was installed when your scanner software got dumped onto your computer. TWAIN is a universal interface for your scanner

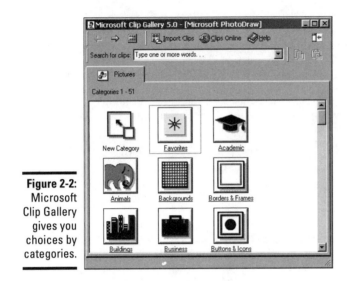

Figure 2-2:
Microsoft
Clip Gallery
gives you
choices by
categories.

and is called upon from many different applications. If you're shopping for a scanner, be sure it is TWAIN-compliant. It makes the job go a lot easier.

Whether you chose to scan right off the bat when you opened PhotoDraw or decided to fire the scanner up after a few image edits, the scanning process begins and ends the same.

1. **You can either choose Scan Picture from the opening dialog box and click OK (refer to Figure 2-1), click on the Scanner button in the Standard toolbar, or go the long way by clicking File⇨Scan picture.**

Any route you choose will bring in the Scan workpane, shown in Figure 2-3.

2. **If you have more than one scanning source, choose it from the drop-down Source list.**

3. **Choose either the Automatic Scan or Your Scanner Software under the Method.**

Selecting the Automatic Scan puts PhotoDraw in the driver's seat. Your picture will be previewed, cropped, and scanned for a final image. Should you choose Your Scanner Software, the software that came with your scanner opens, and you can scan as you would in any other application.

If you choose to use your scanner software, the rest of the options are grayed-out so you can't use them. If your choice is to go on automatic settings, you should choose the resolution for the image using the Resolution drop-down list.

If you're not sure what resolution to scan your picture at, check the manual that came with your scanner or printer. Different printers are capable of different resolutions. For those pictures that you'll be uploading to a Web site, stick with a resolution of 72 or 96 pixels per inch (ppi) and reduce or enlarge the scan so it will be the same size as it will appear on the Internet site.

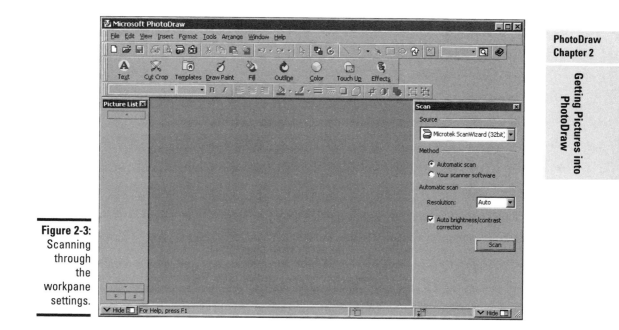

Figure 2-3:
Scanning
through
the
workpane
settings.

4. **Keep the Auto Brightness/Contrast Correction checked.**

    It's a good idea to let the computer do this stuff initially. If the results you get are not quite what you expected, turn this setting off and try again. You can always adjust the brightness and contrast later using the Visual Menu toolbar buttons (discussed in Chapter 3).

5. **Click the Scan button.**

    Watch the Progress Indicator in the Status bar. Using the automatic method of scanning will take PhotoDraw through a preview scan and a final scan. It may take awhile, depending on the speed of your computer and the scanner.

You eventually see your picture dropped into the Drawing area, ready to be manipulated to whatever perverse extent you want. Don't forget to save your image before you start playing with it. Otherwise, you may have to scan once more. It's also a good idea to keep your scanned picture intact by saving it to a separate file so you can recall it whenever you need to start over.

Using a Digital Camera

PhotoDraw can suck the pictures right out of most digital cameras. Once an image is imported, you can have your way with it, using some of the most unusual and fun effects at your disposal.

1. **You can either choose Download from Digital Camera from the opening dialog box and click OK (refer to Figure 2-1), click the Digital Camera button on the Standard toolbar, or choose File➪Digital Camera.**

Whatever route you take to get there, the workpane turns to what you see in Figure 2-4.

2. Choose your camera from the Source drop-down menu.

If you don't have a camera listed here, you'll have to be sure that it is compatible and installed correctly.

3. Click the Download button.

Popping up before your eyes will be the interface that comes with your camera, which may resemble the one in Figure 2-5.

4. Get your image.

Depending on the digital camera and the software interface, your procedure may vary. In brief, you first have to pull in the images from your camera into this interface.

Images through Imagination

If you think you have to possess one ounce of drawing ability to come up with some dynamic graphics, you're dead wrong. Of course, to make your own designs, you have to start with a blank image area.

1. Choose File⇨New.

If you just fired up PhotoDraw, you can select Blank Picture from the opening dialog box (refer to Figure 2-1) and click OK.

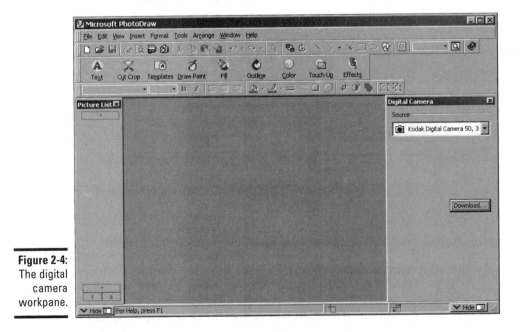

Figure 2-4:
The digital
camera
workpane.

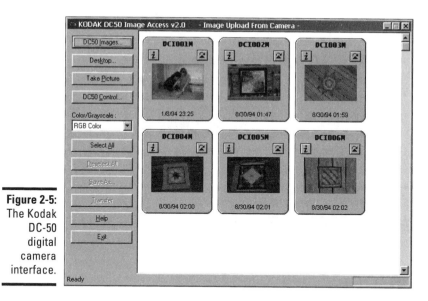

Figure 2-5:
The Kodak
DC-50
digital
camera
interface.

2. **In the New dialog box, double-click Full Screen.**

Assuming that you are just going to start dropping stuff in the drawing area and don't have a specific task in mind, this will do. But, if you have another specific project in mind, like an envelope, banner, or postcard, the other icons in the Pictures tab portion of the dialog box in Figure 2-6 may interest you more.

PhotoDraw opens a blank area for you to work in that is exactly the size of the resolution you have your monitor set at. For example, if you're running your monitor at 800 x 600 pixels, your new blank image is 800 x 600 pixels, too. That's what PhotoDraw means by "Full Screen." You can verify the image size by looking at the rulers along the top and left side of the drawing area, which convert to displaying pixels as the unit of measurement rather than inches. Note that if you select the 100% view size from the Zoom menu, you can see the image at the size it will appear when displayed on any monitor that's using the 800 x 600 resolution, which is helpful for sizing Web graphics.

3. **Click OK.**

If you want to avoid the OK button, you can just double-click the icon. It's the same thing.

4. **Go nuts designing something you'll be proud to post on the fridge or pass this image off as a polar bear in a blizzard.**

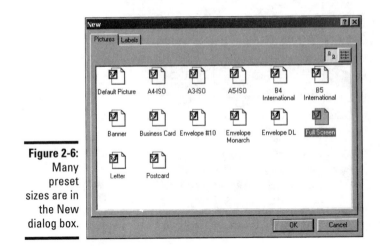

Figure 2-6:
Many
preset
sizes are in
the New
dialog box.

Chapter 3: Fixing Photos

In This Chapter

✓ **Tuning up your color**

✓ **Touching up blemishes and defects**

✓ **Removing the unwanted**

*I*f you're a professional photographer, you can probably bypass this entire chapter. You are the types who take perfect pictures with the correct lighting, color balance, and composition. Some of us, however, do tend to make tiny errors when we shoot our pictures, especially when they are at the family reunion, during summer vacation, or the kids' Christmas pageant.

Coloring Using Slider Controls

When dealing with the individual choices under the Color button on the Visual Menu toolbar, you can think of them as two different types. The first five choices — Brightness and Contrast, Tint, Hue and Saturation, Colorize, and Color Balance — all provide menus with sliders that let you make minute adjustments. Those adjustments can be applied either to the entire image or just parts of the image.

After you make one of the choices from the Color button menu, the top portion of the workpane offers two options: *Correct Selection* and *Correct by Painting*. (See Figure 3-1.)

Choosing Correct Selection applies your settings to the entire picture, or, if your picture is made up of several individual objects, the selected object. If you want to change only parts of a picture or object, choose Correct by Painting. This choice allows you to brush on the settings to certain parts of the picture, leaving the rest of it intact.

Dragging the adjustment sliders changes your picture immediately if you select the Correct Selection method. You have a few other choices to make, however, if you choose to paint on your changes. You need to pick a brush by clicking the arrow to the left of the brush selection (which appears when you choose the Correct by Painting option) and decide where to paint the changes. If you mess up, don't worry. There's a Restore button that you can escape to and start the process all over again. When using the Restore option, all you need do is brush (drag) over the part you want to revert back to the original settings.

Figure 3-1:
You can
correct by
selection
or by
painting.

When you choose to Correct by Painting, there is a small floating menu that allows you to tell PhotoDraw when you are finished with your brush, undo the last action, or Restore what you brush over. If this little feller gets in your way, you can move it around your screen by dragging its title bar.

After you begin color correction, you can change to the different options by using the Effect drop-down menu in the workpane, without having to return to the Color button on the Visual Menu toolbar.

Brightness and contrast

Sometimes you get a picture that is a little muddy looking (like the one in Figure 3-1). By using the Brightness and Contrast controls, you can add a little more definition to your picture.

1. **Click the Color button on the Visual Menu toolbar and choose Brightness and Contrast from the drop-down list.**

Or, you can click the Brightness/Contrast button on the Formatting toolbar. Either way, the workpane becomes a control panel for all the color settings of your image.

2. **Select how you want to apply the settings you choose.**

In the upper part of the workpane, choose either Correct Selection or Correct by Painting.

3. **If you are painting your changes on, choose a brush.**

4. **Adjust the sliders to the desired settings.**

Start out conservatively first and get radical later. As you make changes to the sliders, the image will adjust to those settings.

5. **Drag your cursor over the parts of the picture that you want the setting applied to.**

If you chose to do the entire selection, the changes are made as you slide your sliders.

Tint

Sometimes you get a little too much of a certain color in a picture that you'd like to tone down. Or, if a particular color is weak and you want to beef it up, you can go to the Tint setting. You may also check out the options in Color Balance discussed later. Those tools may serve your purpose much better.

1. **Choose Tint from the Color button on the Visual Menu toolbar.**

2. **Using the Hue slider, choose the color you want to alter.**

3. **Move the Amount slider left or right depending on whether you want more or less of the color.**

When you select the Automatic button, PhotoDraw prompts you to click an area of the picture that is white or light gray. Doing so tells PhotoDraw how to treat the rest of the colors in your picture.

If you want to adjust a certain color on only one part of your picture, click Correct by Painting in the upper option box. Pick a brush and drag over the areas you want changed.

Hue and saturation

If your color is off a bit or you want to create some really bizarre color shift effects, try adjusting the hue and saturation in your image. When you use this adjustment, you shift the red, green and blue levels, but the black and white colors stay intact. Play around with the controls to see what kind of effects you can achieve.

Should you want to adjust only part of the picture, be sure to select the Correct by Painting option and choose a brush. Drag over the portions of your image you want to change.

Colorize

When you colorize something, you replace the color in the image with the color you select in the Settings color box. But when you apply the color you choose, you apply it at the percentage of light and dark that is in your original picture. To see this work to its fullest extent, try it with the Correct by Painting method. When you choose to do the entire picture, you can see replacement of almost all the colors, giving you a duotone look. And if that's the look you're after, by all means, go for it.

1. Click the Color button on the Visual Menu toolbar and choose Colorize.

2. Choose Correct by painting.

3. Pick a color from the Color box in the Settings area.

   If you don't find a color that suits your fancy, click the down arrow and pick another color from the Active palette, True Color palette, or Click More Colors to get the More Colors dialog box. From there, you can pick another Color palette from the drop-down list, import a pre-saved palette, or export the current palette for use later. In addition, you can create a totally new palette and save it for later.

   You can also "lift" a color from your image. Click the little eyedropper button in the workpane and then click in your image on the color you want to use.

4. Using the Amount slider, choose how much color you want to add or remove.

   Moving the slider left decreases the amount of color replaced, resulting in a more vivid color; sliding to the right increases the amount of color replaced, giving you a less saturated, less colorful image.

5. Pick a brush with which to apply the color change to the picture.

   If you start with a shaded brush instead of a solid one, you can apply a little at a time, making some parts lighter than others. You can tell the difference between the brushes because the shaded brushes start out dark in the center and get lighter toward the outside edges.

6. If you have finished with one color and would like to do another, click Finish in the floating Touchup Paint toolbar and repeat Steps 2 through 4.

Anytime that you want to revert back to the way the image looked originally, you can click Restore in the floating toolbar and run your brush over the area you want to change back. No matter whether you applied the effect once or 20 times, you have to brush over it only once to remove it. When you are done, click Finish in the Touchup Paint toolbar.

Color balance

Old photos that you scan, new photos that have improper lighting, and normal photos that you want to make a little weird, can all use some work in the Color Balance arena. To change the color balance of a photo, follow these steps.

1. Choose Color Balance from the Color button on the Visual Menu toolbar.

2. Adjust the individual colors in the sliders.

You can also enter a positive or negative amount in the text boxes to the right of the sliders.

If you want to apply changes to only a certain area of the photo, you can choose Correct by Painting and apply the brush to the area you want to alter.

Two of the Color options are simple to apply. No need to adjust sliders, pick colors, or slop around with a brush. These two jewels are like turning a light on or off.

Negative: The negative selection in the Color menu inverts your picture to its negative equivalent, giving you some pretty eerie-looking results. This is an all or nothing effect.

1. Choose Negative from the Color button on the Visual Menu toolbar.

2. Click the Negative button in the workpane. Too simple. Too easy.

Grayscale: When printing on a black and white printer, sometimes you can get a better image if you convert a color image to grayscale before running it through. When you convert from color to grayscale, you accomplish two things. First, all the colors in your picture are changed to a shade of gray for better black and white reproduction. Second, the file size decreases, making it quicker to print. If you're gonna live in a black-and-white print world, change those color images to grayscale like such.

1. Choose Grayscale from the Color button on the Visual Menu toolbar.

2. Click the Grayscale button in the workpane.

Your color is sucked out of the picture and is reduced to shades of gray.

Touching Up

Everyone needs a little professional help now and then, especially when you're trying to turn a candid snapshot into something printable or sharp enough to upload to your Web site. When you take pictures, especially ones where you can't control the environment like in a professional studio, you're bound to end up with a few goofs. Some of the most popular include red eye, spots, and scratches. Under your capable hands, PhotoDraw can repair these defects.

Fixing red eye

Luckily, automatically fixing red eye in PhotoDraw is a simple procedure. Getting your subject to quit blinking is beyond its scope, however.

1. Choose Fix Red Eye from the Touch Up button in the Visual Menu toolbar.

2. Click when the center of the bulls-eye cursor is centered over the red eye.

Notice that your cursor looks like a circular sight, almost like you'd see on some guns. When you click the afflicted eye, you leave behind the red eye surgical target, as shown in Figure 3-2.

3. In the floating Touchup menu, click Fix.

If you have set your cursor correctly, PhotoDraw corrects the red eye using the color information from the surrounding eye area.

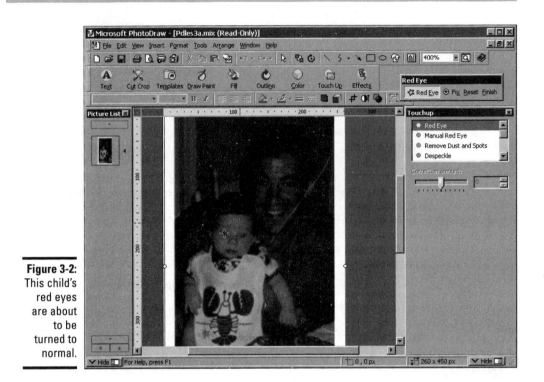

Figure 3-2:
This child's
red eyes
are about
to be
turned to
normal.

Use the Correction Amount slider to alter the effect if PhotoDraw colors too much or too little of the eye area when you click Fix. To apply the new eye color to a larger area, drag the slider to the right. Drag left to color a smaller region.

Removing dust and spots

If you can't keep your scanner clean, or you have a friend whose office resembles a barnyard, you're bound to end up with a picture that has little white spots all over it. That's what dust will do to scanned images. Lucky for you, you have a built in vacuum in PhotoDraw.

1. **Choose Remove Dust and Spots from the Touch Up button in the Visual Menu toolbar.**

Watch your cursor become your personal, digital dust rag as it turns into the bulls-eye circle, similar to the Red Eye filter cursor. Everything else you need is in the floating toolbar.

2. **Click the spots you want removed.**

Watch the Progress bar until you're dizzy and end up with a clean image.

On the downside, Dust and Spots can obliterate image details, so take care where you click. Sometimes you get a blotchy, blocky spot that looks far worse than that original dust speck. For subtle changes, you may want to give the Clone Paint tool a whirl instead.

Despeckling

If your picture is a veritable black sweater flaked with dandruff and it would take a few years to hunt them down and douse them one-by-one, consider the Despeckle tool. With a few adjustments of the slider, PhotoDraw can systematically remove small spots from your image.

1. **Click the Touch Up button on the Visual Menu toolbar and choose Despeckle.**

2. **In the workpane, adjust the Despeckle Amount slider.**

You can tell PhotoDraw how color-sensitive to be with dust and pollen and just how large of a spot to search for. As you adjust the slider to one of the ten settings possible, you'll see your picture take on a smoother, younger look. But you have to be careful because a large setting tends to make your subjects look rather blobish as you lose clarity.

Remove scratches

So the cat got to the only picture of great-grandma that is still in existence. Or, more likely, your negative came back from the photo lab with a scratch. Instead of taking the feline to the taxidermist or the photo technician to court, scan the photo and let PhotoDraw fix it. After the photo is loaded, mend your sentimental image like this.

1. **Click the Touch Up button in the Visual Menu toolbar and choose Remove Scratch.**

2. **Slide the Scratch Width slider to the approximate width of the offending line.**

Because PhotoDraw is going to blend the pixels around the scratch onto the scratch, it's best to adjust this setting as close as possible.

3. **Move your cursor to one end of the scratch and click.**

This sets the beginning of the area that is going to get seamed.

4. **You can set your mending line two different ways. If you hold down the mouse button as you trace over the scratch, a highlighted line will follow your mouse until you reach the end. At any time, you can click to end the line. (See Figure 3-3.) The other option is to click once and set the beginning point, then move your mouse to the ending point. Click again and you end your straight line mend.**

Cloning paint

Now you, too, can be a master at cloning more than sheep. In the non-scientific world of visual image editing, you can copy one part of your image into another part to rid yourself of unwanted subject matter. Imagine that the shepherd sitting on the fence in Figure 3-4 has not signed a release form to grant his permission to be included in this book. You could cut off the entire right side of the picture, but you'd also lose the nice wooden gate you want to keep. The clone paint tool is the ideal tool to knock the man right off the fence. That'll teach him to sign the next release form that comes his way!

Figure 3-3:
Scratches
are best
removed a
little bit at
a time.

Figure 3-4:
A stubborn
shepherd
and his
cooperative
flock.

1. **Click the Touch Up button in the Visual Menu and choose Clone.**

The workpane offers you your weapons of eradication by the way of brushes, and the Touchup Paint floating toolbar pops up at your disposal, as shown in Figure 3-5.

2. **Choose a brush.**

Brushes with soft edges will blend your image copy into a new position; hard edge brushes will do a total replacement.

3. **Choose a spot in your picture where you will be copying from and click the mouse button.**

This action plants an invisible reference point for your brush to pull the image from.

4. **Move your mouse to the area you want to cover and start dragging the brush over the unwanted material.**

As you drag your brush, you are also dragging your invisible planted cursor as if there were a connection between the two. Wherever your invisible planted cursor is, that part of the image is transferred to the brush you are dragging, hence cloning from one area to another.

5. **When you finish cloning an area, click the Finish button in the floating toolbar.**

Your clone paint tool is deactivated, and you can move on to your next task.

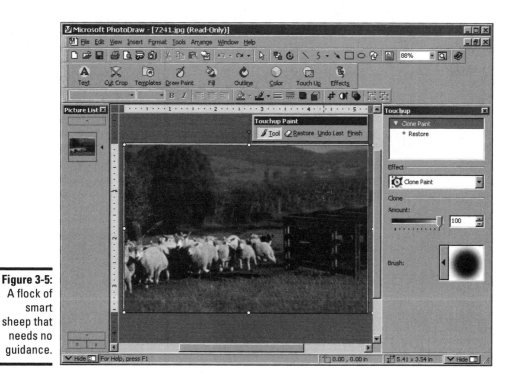

Figure 3-5:
A flock of smart sheep that needs no guidance.

If you are picking up unwanted parts of the photo and want to change the position of the invisible planted cursor, click the Finish button. After you deactivate the tool, click the Tool button in the floating toolbar and replant your cursor.

Using your floating Touchup Paint toolbar, you can restore cloned areas of your picture to their original state by clicking the Restore button and then dragging over the area you want to restore. Or, undo the last swipe of your clone brush by clicking the Undo Last button.

Smudging some paint

Ever wondered how some pictures seem to get a feeling of movement in them? One way that you can accomplish this effect is with the Smudge Paint tool. In Figure 3-6, the top half of the bat stays in its original form. The lower half of our furry friend has had a touch of the Smudge Paint tool.

1. **From the Touch Up button on the Visual Menu toolbar, choose the Smudge tool.**

2. **Choose a brush from the palette.**

   Soft brushes will smear and smudge with softer edges that blend better with the picture background.

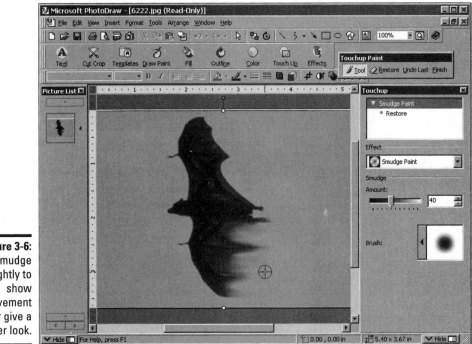

Figure 3-6:
Smudge lightly to show movement or give a softer look.

3. **Adjust the slider to reflect the amount of smudging your brush will do.**

   The higher the number used in the Amount setting, the more of the color under your brush is picked up and smeared.

4. **Click and drag from the starting point of the smudge.**

   Note that if you chose a low Amount value in Step 3, PhotoDraw doesn't smudge your colors for the full length of your drag. You only get smudging over the full length if you set the Amount value to 100.

5. **Release the mouse button to end the smudge.**

The Smudge tool is great for making watercolor effects, or to soften some areas of your image. Because you can apply the effect with a variety of brushes, you can always switch brushes and change the Smudge Amount by clicking Finish in the floating toolbar and reselecting either or both.

Erasing some paint

The Erase tool works exactly like the Smudge Paint tool with one small difference. Instead of picking up color from the picture and smearing it into another part of the picture, the Erase tool removes the color and lets the underlying color come through. In most cases, you wind up revealing the background color of the picture area, which is white by default.

If you want to change the background color of your image, or check to see what it is, choose File➪Picture Setup. In the Picture Setup dialog box, shown in Figure 3-7, be sure that the Active Picture tab is selected. On the far right side of the dialog box, you can select another background color from the Color drop-down menu or just check to see what color is selected. This is the color that will come through when you use the Erase tool unless you are erasing a portion of an object that rests atop another object in your picture. In that case, the underlying object is revealed.

To use the Erase Paint tool on your picture, choose Erase from the Touch Up button in the Visual Menu toolbar. Follow the steps for the Smudge tool to erase parts of your picture. You won't get too confused; even the cursor looks the same. Note that if you set the Amount value to 100 percent, you erase completely; if you choose a lower Amount value, you don't erase clear through the areas you stroke.

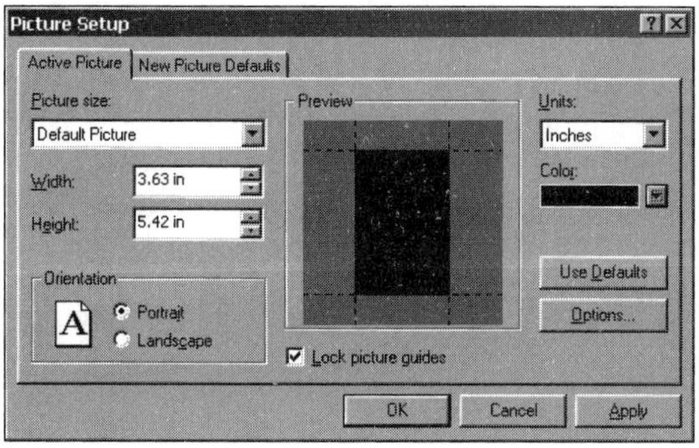

Figure 3-7:
Change the underlying color from the Picture Setup dialog box.

Cropping, Cutting, and Erasing

PhotoDraw offers three different ways to rid you of the refuse in your pictures: Cut Out, Crop, and Erase, all of which can be found under the Cut Crop button in the Visual Menu.

Cropping

When you crop a picture, you tell PhotoDraw what part of the picture you want to keep and what part to throw out like yesterday's trash.

1. **From the Cut Crop button on the Visual Menu toolbar, choose Crop (or click the Crop button on the Formatting toolbar).**

   The workpane pops in on the right side of your window and offers you a gallery of 56 different shapes that you can use to place on your picture. If you want to see all 56 shapes at once, click the Expand Gallery button above the gallery and your list is expanded.

2. **Choose a shape from the gallery.**

   After you select a shape, you see it overlaid onto your picture, complete with selection handles and a rotation handle. The selection handles are the little circles around the perimeter of the shape outline; the rotation handle is the green circle just above the top-center selection handle. Figure 3-8 shows a figure ready to be cropped.

3. **Drag the handles to size or rotate the shape to your desire.**

   If you want the shape to cover as much of your picture as possible, click the Stretch to Fit button, found underneath the gallery in the workpane.

4. **Click the Finish button on the floating toolbar.**

   By clicking Finish, you are telling PhotoDraw to remove the ghosted area of the photo outside the shape and keep the image inside the shape. Plus, clicking Finish now allows you to come back and change size and orientation of your current shape or even select a new one.

If you click the None icon in the workpane (it's the very first crop shape icon, the one with an X through it), you undo your crop. You can then try again with your cropping if you want.

If you click the Lock Crop button, your picture is forever altered and you can't reclaim by clicking the None icon any of the picture that fell outside the crop shape. (You can, however, choose Edit⇨Undo to reverse your cropping decision.)

Cutting out

Just like you learned in kindergarten and first grade, this tool will take digital scissors to your image and leave you with a perfectly cut picture. Plus, if you choose to tell PhotoDraw ahead of time, it will leave your original picture intact and create a new file with just the cut out portion of your picture.

1. **Choose Cut Out from the Cut Crop button on the Visual Menu toolbar.**

Expand Gallery

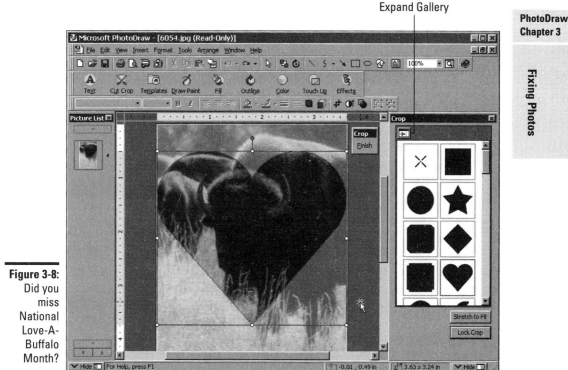

Figure 3-8:
Did you
miss
National
Love-A-
Buffalo
Month?

This action opens up the tools you can use in the workpane. In the upper part of the workpane, you have four different ways to select portions of your picture: By Shape, By Drawing, Edge Finder, and By Color. To get through the steps here, use the By Shape method. (See Figure 3-9.)

2. Pick one of the shapes provided in the list.

You can either use the scroll bar to see more shape options, or click the Expand Gallery button above the list. This arrow expands the windows to show you more shapes.

3. Select the type of edge you want on your picture by sliding the Edge slider.

Soft edges give your image a wispy, faded look. Hard edges take it to the shape outline and cut it straight off.

4. In the Options section, choose Cut Out Opposite area and/or Put in New Picture.

If you choose Cut Out Opposite area, the portion of your picture that is on the outside of the outline will be kept. Keeping this option unchecked will save the inside of the outline. A check in the Put in New Picture options will create a New Picture that contains just your cutout, leaving the original picture as it was.

5. Position your outline.

You should have noticed that your outline sports the same handles that your image does. This means that you can move it around, make it bigger or smaller, or stretch it to whatever proportion you want.

6. Click Finish on the Cut Out floating toolbar.

Be sure to experiment with cutting out things using By Drawing, Edge Finder, and By Color — these options work pretty much like they sound.

Erasing

When you choose the Erase tool, the workpane takes on the same look as the Cut Out tool. As a matter of fact, it works almost exactly the same way. You get the same four methods for selecting part of your picture: By Shape, By Drawing, Edge Finder, and By Color. The By Shape method is described here.

1. From the Cut Crop button on the Visual Menu toolbar, choose Erase.

Watch the workpane very closely because it takes on multiple personalities. This personality is so closely related to the Cut Out psyche.

2. Choose the selection method in the list at the top of the erase workpane.

For instructional purposes, choose By Shape.

3. Pick a shape from the list.

Expand the listing to its greatest stretch by using the left-pointing arrow above the list or scroll down using the scroll bar.

4. Use the Edge slider to indicate a sharp or fuzzy edge.

5. Choose whether to keep the inside or outside of the shape border.

When a shape is placed over your picture, all you need remember is that the portion that looks like waxed paper has been placed over it will be erased. The part that you can see clearly is the keeper. To reverse things, check the Erase Opposite Area check box in the workpane.

6. Stretch and move the border shape.

Use the handles to shape and rotate the border.

7. Click Finish on the Erase floating toolbar to eradicate the area you have selected.

There are a couple of slight differences here that you should notice. Yes, Erase does do pretty much what Cut Out did. Your image is the same size as you started with (unless you chose to create a new picture with the Cut Out tool), but with Erase you've sent part of your picture to digital Never Never Land, never to return after you save the file.

Don't forget that you also have the By Drawing, Edge Finder, and By Color options to fool around with.

Figure 3-9:
You have many cut-out shapes to choose from!

Chapter 4: Adding Text and Dressing Up Photos

In This Chapter

✔ Adding text with style

✔ Templates to make setup easy

✔ Drawing and painting a masterpiece

✔ Filling and outlining objects

✔ Eye-popping special effects

*A*fter a picture is cleaned up just the way you like it, you may want to spice it up a little with some extras that come in PhotoDraw. Sometimes these extras can make the big difference when you're building a Web site, designing an ad for a high-style magazine, or just making that special birthday card for your mom. Master these extras, and you'll make Mom proud!

Adding Text Effects

Anybody behind the keyboard can type text into a PhotoDraw file, but it takes the imagination that only you possess and the tools that PhotoDraw gives you to make it pop and sizzle.

By the way, here's a little secret. You don't have to have a picture open to use these text tools and effects. PhotoDraw is great for creating type with all kinds of special effects that you can use as a picture wherever you would insert an image or piece of clip art.

Inserting text

Done well, text can be just as decorative and jazzy as some pictures. Here's how to start laying those letters on your screen after you have an open spot in the Drawing area. Open up a blank picture as described back in Chapter 2.

1. Click the Text button on the Visual Menu toolbar and choose Insert Text.

You can also use the Insert Text button on the Standard toolbar. Lo and behold, the workpane opens and presents you with your tools. Plus, somewhere in your Drawing area you get a jump start with the phrase, "Your text here" plopped in the middle of the screen.

2. **Type in the text you want in the midsection of the workpane.**

If you feel a little verbose, you can click on the Expand Gallery button above the text entry area to make it a lot larger. When you want to begin a new line, press the Enter key. (See Figure 4-1.)

3. **Choose your typeface, size, and style from the drop-down menus.**

4. **In the upper part of the workpane, choose Text Flow, found underneath the Format Text choice.**

The workpane tools change to let you align your copy however you want.

5. **Pick the horizontal alignment you want from the Align drop-down list (left, right, or centered).**

6. **Choose your text orientation (horizontal or vertical).**

7. **Choose whether you want your text to appear smooth on-screen.**

This setting won't affect the way your text is printed.

Now that the easy part is done, there are still many things you can do with your text. For example, have you noticed that the selection handles are surrounding your text block? You can stretch and rotate your text just as you would an image. Just grab a handle and do-si-do with your words.

Bending text

Were you impressed when Superman bent the barrels of handguns and rifles? Now you can impress your friends and scare your enemies by doing the same thing with your text. PhotoDraw gives you as many presets as you need to run circles around your text.

1. **Select the text that is going to get a twisted personality by clicking on it.**

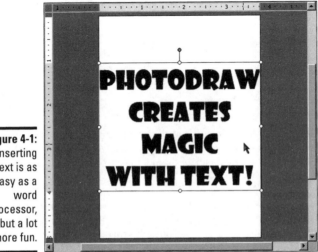

Figure 4-1:
Inserting
text is as
easy as a
word
processor,
but a lot
more fun.

Formatting text after you insert it

Want to change that pithy quote you just added? Double-click the text in the Drawing area to display the selection handles and the Text workpane. To edit the words themselves, click the Format Text option. Then edit your text in the text box as you would in any word processor.

You can also change the font, size, and style on this same panel of the Text workpane and change

any of your choices on the Text Flow panel. But here's a tip: If you have the Formatting toolbar visible, you can use the Font, Type Size, Style, and Align options from the toolbar instead.

Of course, if your writing really stinks, you may want to trash that text altogether. To do so, click the text in the Drawing area and then press Delete.

---

2. **From the Te<u>x</u>t button on the Visual Menu toolbar, choose B<u>e</u>nd Text.**

   Here comes the workpane, porting all the bending tools you need. (If the workpane is already open, just choose Bend Text from the scrolling list at the top of the workpane.) See Figure 4-2.

3. **Choose one of the preset icons in the box, or use the slider to create custom bends.**

   If you opt to use the slider, remember the further left you slide, the more upturned you text becomes. Slide to the right and text runs downward. The more you slide, the more you turn.

Figure 4-2:
Give your text a smile or frown by bending it to your will.

3-D text

Making text jump off the page or screen is an easy job with the 3-D tools that PhotoDraw provides. With the selection of preset dimensions and colors, you can quickly apply an effect that can suit even the pickiest of tastes. If you're a total control freak, however, you can customize every step of the project to get just the right perspective. After you have your text placed and formatted, follow these steps.

1. **From the Visual Menu toolbar, click Te_x_t and choose 3-_D_ Text.**

You can also click on the 3D button in the Formatting toolbar. Either way, the workpane converts to your Designer 3-D playground, and you don't even need special glasses. (See Figure 4-3.)

2. **Choose one of the 25 presets in the Designer 3-D gallery.**

Use the Expand Gallery button to see more at one time, or use the scroll bars to move up and down the listing. After you select a preset, your text is transformed using the same settings as the examples in the Gallery.

To clear the alterations, click on the first item in the gallery with the symbol shaped like an "X".

Designer text

For down and dirty quick text effects, try the Designer Text Gallery. Not only are the fonts already selected, but all the special effects that you see in the examples shown are applied as well. This is also a good way to see how some of the custom settings in the previous menus are used together. All you have to do is visit those menus to view the settings that are given to text when you make one of the Designer Text choices.

1. **After entering your text, select the Text button on the Visual Menu toolbar and choose Designer Text.**

Up pops the different preset effects in a Gallery within the workpane.

2. **Click one of the choices in the Gallery.**

Stand back and wait until you see the effects in the Picture area (as shown in Figure 4-4). Depending on which preset you choose and how much text you are converting, it may take PhotoDraw a while to process the changes and spit them back to the monitor.

Templates

Can you believe it? Custom graphics for just about every conceivable purpose, professionally assembled by you with a helping hand from PhotoDraw. The templates in PhotoDraw can give you thousands of graphics that bear no resemblance to each other. Because PhotoDraw steps you through creating graphics from each of these templates, it's a waste of time to include the instructions here. Instead, click through the options in the workpane to see all the things it's possible to create using the PhotoDraw templates.

Figure 4-3:
Down and
dirty 3-D
effects.

Figure 4-4:
The
Designer
Text
Gallery
gives you
slick and
quick
settings.

To get an idea of how you would use a template to get a graphic that holds up next to those done by highly-paid professionals, here's how they work.

1. **Choose the template type from the Template button on the Visual Menu toolbar.**

You have a choice of Web Graphics, Business Graphics, Cards, Designer Edges, and Designer Clip Art.

2. Click on a category of objects that you want to create in the workpane.

When you click an item in the workpane Gallery, the entire Picture Area lists the items that you can make in that category (see Figure 4-5).

3. Double-click the icon in the Picture Area that you want to build.

You can also just click once on the item and then choose the Next button at the bottom of the workpane.

4. Select a picture item in the layout by clicking it.

Each item is available, just as if you had placed it there yourself. PhotoDraw takes you through replacing pictures first, then the text.

5. Use the Replace, Browse, or Picture Position buttons to edit a picture item.

If you choose Replace, (that little hand icon next to the Browse button in the workpane) you can click on another open image or an item in that image to replace the currently selected one in the template with the one you select. If you do not have the file open that you want to steal . . . er . . . borrow from, you can use the Browse button to locate and open it. If all you want to do is change the position of the element, choose the Picture Position button and you can move the item around on the page.

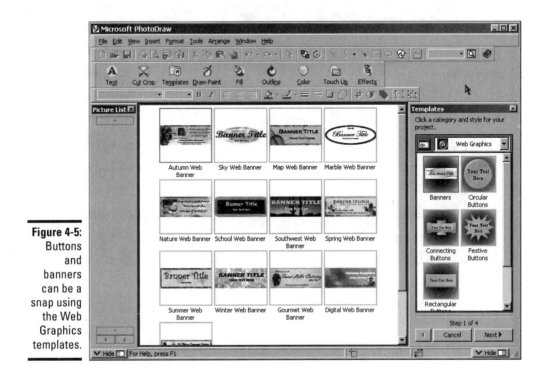

Figure 4-5:
Buttons and banners can be a snap using the Web Graphics templates.

6. **When you're ready to replace text, select the text and click the Next button.**

The workpane changes to let you type in new text, change the font, its size and style. If you have more text to replace, click on that text in the Picture Area and make changes in the same way.

7. **When you're finished editing text and replacing or moving items, click the Next button in the workpane.**

At any time during these steps, you can use the Back button (that's the one with the arrow on it to the left of the Cancel button) to return to the previous step. It won't discard the changes you've made, but it will back up to let you replace graphics or all the way back to change your project in the list of templates.

Drawing and Painting

The drawing and painting tools that PhotoDraw puts at your fingertips let you create new pictures from a blank page or add graphics to your photos. When you pick Draw or Shapes from the Draw Paint menu, the workpane will look essentially the same. You get the same floating toolbar and tool options listed in the workpane. With Paint, however, you lose the ability to create the different shapes, and freehand drawing (or should that be free-mouse drawing) is your only means of applying designs to the drawing area. In all cases, however, you still have the artistic and photo brushes available along with the plain lines.

To create your own picture, you need to start with a blank page in the Picture Area which you can get by clicking on the New button in the Standard toolbar, pressing Ctrl+N, or choose File⇨New to get a preset size from the New dialog box.

Drawing with shapes

Drawing gives you the solid-lines-and-shapes look. And the little extras that PhotoDraw lets you do with the drawing tools helps make your job a little easier.

1. **From the Draw Paint button on the Visual Menu toolbar, select Draw or Shapes.**

Now you get the new workpane with the Draw tools in it and the AutoShapes floating toolbar

2. **Choose one of the tools in the AutoShapes floating toolbar.**

Each button represents a different type of line or shape that you can lay down on your picture. They include: Line, Curve, Arrow, Rectangle, Ellipse, and AutoShapes (shown in Figure 4-6).

3. **Draw the shape.**

You can click one and drop the shape in the Picture area, or drag to create a custom size.

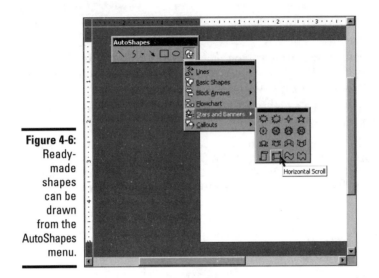

Figure 4-6:
Ready-
made
shapes
can be
drawn
from the
AutoShapes
menu.

4. Edit the Outline.

After you have your shape on the drawing area, you can begin to enhance and change its appearance. The default starting point is with the outline of the object. In the workpane, you can change the type of line using the drop-down menu of line types. Choose either the Plain, Artistic Brushes or Photo Brushes. Choose a line style, color, and width, all of which vary according to the brush you pick. To get the entire story on outlines, check out the section on Outlines, later in this chapter.

5. Choose Settings (Plain) from the workpane menu and edit your outline further.

This submenu of the Outline menu lets you change the color, transparency, and width of the outline. You can even tell PhotoDraw to place the lines on top of or beneath the fill color. If you chose one of the brushes in place of the Plain line, that brush type will appear in the parentheses after Settings.

6. Change the arrowheads on the lines.

Naturally, a closed shape doesn't have any line endings, so the arrowheads aren't available for them. But if you have a line and want it to point to something, you can edit it to add or remove the arrowheads here. To access the arrowhead options, click Arrowheads in the workpane scrolling list.

7. Edit the points.

By points, PhotoDraw is not referring to the arrowhead points, but the individual spots in a line or shape where the line takes a different turn. Look at Figure 4-7 to see small squares that show where the points are in the shape. When you click on a point, it becomes black, meaning it is selected. Once selected, you can use the options in the Point Properties section of the workpane to make changes to the shape of the point, delete

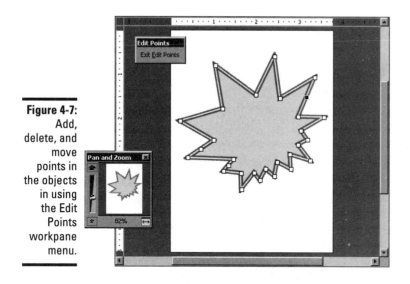

Figure 4-7:
Add, delete, and move points in the objects in using the Edit Points workpane menu.

a point, or add another point to change the shape of the outline. You can also move the points around in the drawing to get a different shape by dragging them with the mouse.

In Line Properties, you can open up a closed object by using the Open Curve button, or close it up.

If the point you've chosen sits on a curve, two small handles will be revealed. Dragging these handles lets you edit the shape of the curve. It may take some practice, but you'll get the hang of it real quickly.

8. Fill the object.

At the bottom of the menus in the workpane, you'll find Fill. Here again you have several options when picking a fill for your object. Look in the next section on the different types of fills that PhotoDraw provides and how to assign them to your object.

Painting

Painting is a bit different than using the drawing tools or shapes in PhotoDraw. This is where your talents as a fine artist come in handy.

1. From the Draw Paint button on the Visual Menu toolbar, choose Paint.

The Artistic Brushes jump into the workpane, and the intimidating Creative Paint floating toolbar drops in.

2. Choose your weapon in the form of a brush.

If you prefer to paint in solid lines, you'll find the Plain lines available in the dropdown menu along with the Photo Brushes.

TIP

If you hover your cursor over the individual brush choices, you'll find they have descriptive names like Watercolor — Paper Wash or Oil — Palette Knife Narrow. This should give you experienced artists an idea of the medium and tools you'll be mimicking.

3. Select a color from the color box.

Don't forget that you can click the eyedropper icon and then click a color in your photo to paint with that same color.

4. Select the width of the brush strokes.

Use the slider and increase or decrease the swash that your brush will lay down.

5. Paint.

Yes, it is a simple, but necessary step. You have to drag the brush on your Picture Area to lay some color down. (See Figure 4-8 for a sample.)

If you're not happy with your last stroke, you can also click the Undo Last button in the floating toolbar and redo it. Point in fact, you can click on this button repeatedly, removing the last brush stroke, one right after the other, until you stop at the point where you're satisfied with what's on screen.

Figure 4-8: This watercolor is certainly not museum quality.

Filling Objects

Turning a drab one- or two-color graphic into an eye-popping, color-rich piece of art is just what PhotoDraw is all about. Not only is your finished image enhanced, but people look at you as quite the accomplished professional, as well.

Solid color

If you think that solid color is boring, you're going to have to rethink. Since there is a transparency option in the solid color fill, you can come up with some interesting effects.

1. **With object selected, click on the Fill button in the Visual Menu then Solid Color.**

If you just got done drawing a closed shape, you can select Fill from the menu in the workpane or click on the Fill button in the Formatting toolbar. Pick a color, any color, from the color box in the workpane. If the colors showing aren't to your liking, click on the down arrow to the right of the box and choose one of the other palettes or the More colors option. Or use the eyedropper to lift a color from your picture.

2. **Adjust the Transparency slider.**

Wherever colors may overlap, you can get some striking effects. If you place an object with a transparent fill on top of another, the object underneath will show through.

Texture

PhotoDraw comes with a nice selection of textures that you can fill an object with. Not only can you fill objects, but text as well.

1. **From the Visual Menu toolbar, choose Fill and then Texture.**

2. **With an object selected, click on one of the texture patterns in the Gallery.**

If you want a better look at the selections, you can click on the Expand Gallery button above the list of fills.

3. **You can change the second color effect in the fill by picking a new color from the color drop-down menu, which shows you the ever-familiar color box.**

You can also use the eyedropper to pick a color out of the existing image. Just click the eyedropper and then click in the image where the color is located.

4. **If you don't want the full effect of the fill, you can tone it down using the Transparency slider.**

Of course, anything underneath the item that you fill will show through the fill.

5. **Adjust the Scaling.**

When the fill texture looks too rough, you can use the scaling option to make the texture shrink the pattern. It will tile seamlessly in the image.

Designer gradient

For a rainbow of fills, try the Designer Gradient variety. PhotoDraw's 61 wonderful flavors of gradient fills can be customized to fit the majority of your needs.

1. **Choose the Fill button on the Visual Menu toolbar and select Designer Gradient.**

If you are getting the idea that whenever you see the term, "Designer" that it means presets, you're right. When the workpane shows you the list of gradient fills that you have available, you may get a little overwhelmed.

2. **Choose a gradient from the Gallery.**

If you want to see more of the possibilities, click on the Expand Gallery button. Once you click on your choice, your object is immediately filled.

3. **Adjust the Transparency slider.**

If you want some of the underlying image to show through, lighten up the gradient with the slider.

4. **Choose a Shape.**

By clicking on the left-pointing arrow, a row of different gradient patterns are displayed. Choose one and continue.

5. **Adjust the Angle.**

This is a good setting to play around with, especially because you get immediate results in the Picture Area. Enter any amount in degrees from –360 to 360. The angle of the gradient will change accordingly. (See Figure 4-9.)

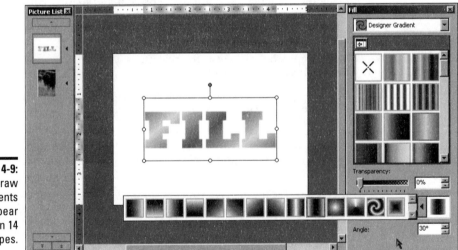

Figure 4-9:
PhotoDraw gradients can appear in 14 shapes.

Two-color gradient

Now you get into a little more control over your gradient fill. With a two-color gradient fill, you get to choose the beginning and ending color, customize the transparency of each color and much more. Your only limitation is you can choose only two colors. Your frustration will be picking out those colors.

1. **You'll find the Two-Color Gradient selection under the Fill button on the Visual Menu toolbar.**

The simple-to-operate controls come into the workpane.

2. **Pick a Start and End color.**

Use the color boxes to pick the colors that will be used in your gradient fill. If you want some or all of the fill to be transparent, make adjustments to the sliders in each color choice section. You can also use the eyedropper tool to pick up a color from an existing image.

3. **Pick a Shape from the available choices in the large Shape flyout.**

4. **Adjust the angle.**

Enter a percentage to give the gradient a slant. You can use any degree increment from –360 to 360.

5. **Change the location of the Center.**

Using the Center slider, you can tell PhotoDraw how much of each color you want in your swirl. The further left you move the slider, the more of the End color is blended into your swirl. Move the slider right to get more of the Start color. See Figure 4-10 for an example of what you can do.

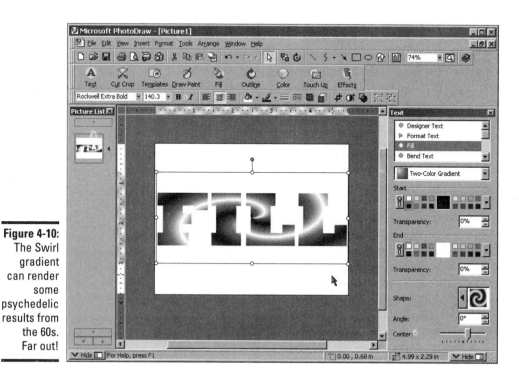

Figure 4-10:
The Swirl gradient can render some psychedelic results from the 60s. Far out!

Picture

Whatever text or object you have selected, you can fill it with a picture that you already have or you can use one out of the list that PhotoDraw provides. Pretty cool effect, wouldn't you say?

1. Click the Fill button on the Visual Menu toolbar and choose Picture.

In the workpane, a Gallery of pictures is shown as well as some other controls that you may have worked with before.

2. Click on an image in the Gallery.

Whatever you have selected in the Picture Area is now filled with that picture. (See Figure 4-11.)

Figure 4-11:
Electrify
your
images
with a
picture fill.

3. To blend another color into the picture, choose a color from the color drop-down list.

When you click on the drop-down list, you get the color box where you can pick one of the colors shown, or choose from one of the palettes below it. If you want a color to match a certain area of a picture you already have, click on the eyedropper and then inside the picture where the desired color resides. In essence, the color you choose will replace the colors in the picture, but you'll retain the highlights and shadows. You end up with a duo-tone look.

4. Adjust the Transparency.

You can move the Transparency slider to let more of the underlying picture show through. If there is not a picture underneath, you are simply lightening the picture fill.

5. **Click the Picture Position button and move the picture inside the image.**

If you want to position a certain part of the fill inside a special spot in the object, clicking on this button will let you drag the fill within the object until it is positioned just the way you like it.

Outline

Outlining in PhotoDraw is more than putting a black line around an object to hold the color in like you see in coloring books. With all the tools at your beck and call, outlining is an art form all in itself. Use it wisely to enhance your images. From the Outline button in the Visual Menu toolbar, select one of the following options and start experimenting.

✦ **Soft Edges:** To give your outline a warm and fuzzy look, you can use Soft Edges to blur the harsh straight lines of your object. Easy concept; easy to do.

✦ **Plain:** Probably a misnomer, the Plain outline setting can be anything but plain. With the choices available to you in the Gallery, your lines can be doubled, dotted, dashed or square-dotted.

✦ **Artistic Brushes:** Even though you may be familiar with Artistic Brushes to paint freehand, you can also use them to outline objects.

✦ **Photo Brushes:** Photo Brushes outline your object with actual pictures. Some of the choices are continuous, like pipe and ivy; others are a series of objects like daisies and pool balls.

Effects

Although most of these effects work best on text or symbol objects, you can use them on photos with great success. These effects are the helpers that make the non-artists look like they have been studying art for years. From the Effects button on the Visual menu toolbar, choose one of the following.

✦ **Shadow:** Casting shadows used to be a tedious job where an artist would airbrush around an object. What used to take hours, now can be done on the computer in just a few clicks of the mouse.

✦ **Transparency:** Have you ever wondered how some of the picture shows through a milky white box with text printed on top of it? For a good example, open up the Designer Business Templates and take a look at the diskette label. You can see through the white box and it makes the text on top a lot easier to read.

✦ **Fade Out:** Fade Out is just an easy way to turn Transparency into a gradient transparency, being denser on one side over the other. (See Figure 4-12.)

✦ **Blur and Sharpen:** Pictures can sometime be made overly blurred or sharp for a reason. Many times, a blurred picture will make reading text on top of it much easier. Or, pictures that have a lot of sharpening to them create a pixilated effect.

Figure 4-12:
The lyrics
of the song
show up
much
better with
the fade-
to-white
underneath
it.

◆ **Distort:** Ever see those pictures where there is a fish eye effect? The picture seems to bulge at the center. Or how about the pictures that look like you are seeing them through waves of water? Those are all distortions that you can reproduce in PhotoDraw.

◆ **3-D:** A favorite of Web designers and science fiction artists, the 3-D effect makes images jump off the page by giving them depth and substance. This particular effect works best with text, symbols, and other line art. When applied to pictures, you get some pretty distorted outlines and your pictures can get totally blown away where they are even unrecognizable.

Designer Effects

A whopping 208 Designer Effects are included with PhotoDraw. Just about every imaginable means of altering pictures can be found in this workpane. If that number of effects is a bit too much to digest at one time, you can use the categories to sort them out.

1. **On the Visual Menu toolbar, select the Effects button then Designer Effects from the list of choices.**

Get ready for the workpane that features the largest number of items in its Gallery.

2. **Choose the category of effects you want to choose from.**

Just above the Gallery, there is a drop-down list of the various category choices you have. Each of the Designer Effects has been placed in one of these categories. If you want to access them all at one time, select All. Otherwise, pick a category that reflects the mood or style you want to assign to your picture.

3. **Pick an effect from the Gallery.**

4. **To change the settings for the effect, click on the Settings menu in the upper part of the workpane.**

Because there are so many choices in Designer Effects, it is futile to try to explain all the various settings that can be made on each of them. Suffice it to say, that you need to play around with these settings to either broaden the effect or make it more fine, change the amount of highlighting, or the intensity of color.

5. **Click the Lock Effect button.**

If you are planning on combining two or more effects, you have to lock one before moving on to the next. If not, when you choose the next effect, it will replace the current one instead of enhancing it.

Chapter 5: Dressed Up and Someplace to Go

In This Chapter

- ✔ Using the wizard to save for the Web-ready graphics
- ✔ Using the wizard to save for Office documents, presentations, and publications
- ✔ Saving without the wizard
- ✔ Special printing options

After you put all that hard work into your creations, you need to know what to do with them. Because PhotoDraw is a pretty versatile program in making high-quality graphics, it only stands to reason that it will output those graphics with style and perfection.

The very first thing you should note is that the native file format for PhotoDraw is .mix. By saving your images in this format before you save to another type of format, you can be sure that every element in your image is 100 percent editable. After saving to some of the other formats, your picture gets flattened. That is, all the elements are essentially glued together and can't be torn apart very easily. And if you want to make changes later, you might just be out of luck. So the first rule of PhotoDraw is always save in the .mix format.

The Wizard that Saves

Enter PhotoDraw and the amazing "Save for Use In" Wizard. All you need do is answer a few questions, pick a spot to save the files, and before you can break a fingernail or leg, you're done. Conjure up the wizard and command it like so.

To get to the wizard, you have to choose File⇨Save for Use In. After that, you are faced with five choices on how to save your file. Because these steps are really important to ensure the best possible image, you can find instructions here for each choice.

Saving as a Web graphic

1. **After you choose File⇨Save for Use In, select On the Web and then click Next.**

This option exports your file to an Internet compatible format that the majority of browsers are capable of viewing. PhotoDraw evaluates your image to see if there are any transparent areas in it.

2. **Choose whether you want your Web page background to show through the transparent area of your picture (see Figure 5-1).**

If you want to see the background through your image, choose Let the Web Page Background Show Through and keep on reading the next subsection. If not, click Fill Them with the Background Color and skip down to the next subsection. Then click Next.

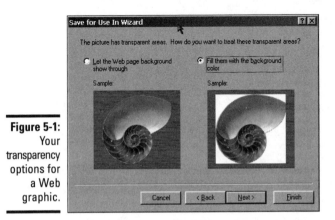

Figure 5-1:
Your
transparency
options for
a Web
graphic.

If you want your Web page to show through the transparent areas:

The next step asks whether the Web page has a solid color background or a tiled image. If you're not sure you can match the background color, select My Web Page's Background is a Tiled Image. If you can match the background color, choose My Web Page's Background is the Following Solid Color and select a color from the Color Box dropdown. Click Next; then review the information on the file and click Save.

The Save for Use In dialog box opens and lets you maneuver around your drives and folders until you find the spot where the file is to be saved. Notice that the file format has already been selected for you and all you have to do is either accept the filename or type in a new one. Click Save.

When saving a transparent Web graphic, you should be warned that the file will be written as a .gif in 256 color format. If your image contains a lot of color and detail, this may not be a wise choice. Your image may look flat, and some color will be lost.

If you want your transparent areas to be filled with the background color:

Pick a color to fill the transparent spots. Using the drop-down list to access the color box, click a color that will be used to replace the transparent areas of your image. Click Next.

Next, pick a file format and quality. Now you get to see the difference in file formats and the way your image is saved. PhotoDraw gives you five choices: .gif, .jpeg Best Quality, .jpeg High Quality, .jpeg Medium Quality, and .jpeg Low Quality. You not only get to see samples of what the image will look like, but you get information on the amount of time is takes for your viewer to download the image in their browser. Use the Connection Speed drop-down to see the amount of time it would take at other speeds.

Because many Internet users are still using a 28.8 modem, you should base your selection on this speed. Maybe in a year or so, homes will be equipped with faster lines and modems.

3. **Select the Next button or go straight to Finish.**

Going one more step in the wizard with the Next button will give you a final look of the image information that includes the file format, the color palette used, what compression is used (if any), transparency settings, and the Web background color.

Making a Web thumbnail

Many times, when you have a lot of images and you don't want them all to load at once, you create a thumbnail or small version of the picture. Then you create a hyperlink so that when viewers click the thumbnail, they will jump to a Web page with the larger version or are able to download the file to their computer. The wizard takes the guess work out of thumbnail creation.

After you choose File⇨Save for Use In, click the On the Web as a Thumbnail radio button. You're on your way to Lilliputian-like images when you click the Next button.

From here, you are presented with the same options as the normal size Web graphic in the preceding section. The only difference is the end result. PhotoDraw produces the same image, but in a smaller size.

Saving for use in a Microsoft Office document

Talk about a quickie. . . this option is like the Texas Two-step because that's exactly how many steps it takes.

1. **After you choose File⇨Save for Use In, choose In a Microsoft Office Document.**

No matter if you're placing this picture in Word 2000, Excel 2000, or Microsoft Publisher, this is the route to go. The only exceptions would be PowerPoint and FrontPage. Those programs would use the on-screen presentation and Web options, respectively.

2. **Click Next.**

3. **Click Save.**

After you give your picture a name, choose a storage location, and click the Save button, your image is saved in the relatively new .png format. It's good for those Office applications just mentioned, but eventually, you'll see it used on the Web more. That is, as soon as more people are using the browsers that support it.

Saving for an on-screen presentation

Here is yet another long set of instructions. Repeat the steps for preparing an image for an Office document in the preceding section.

When PhotoDraw saves the file for an Office document, it assumes it will be printed on a conventional laser or ink jet printer eventually. Therefore, the resolution has to be higher. For an on-screen presentation, the image only has to be about 72 pixels per inch; that's all most monitors are set up to display.

File format for the on-screen presentation image is .png, the same as for the Office document.

Saving for a publication

When PhotoDraw is referring to a publication, it means something that is going to film and will be printed on a press. Normally, these types of documents call for a higher resolution than what you need for laser and ink jet printers. PhotoDraw not only keeps the resolution as high as possible, but it also saves the image in the format most compatible with desktop publishing programs, .tif.

1. **After you choose File⇨Save for Use In, choose In a Publication in the Save for Use In Wizard dialog box.**

2. **Click Next.**

3. **Click Save.**

After you pick a filename and a drive and folder, you're done. One .tif file is ready for the presses.

Saving the Old-Fashioned Way

If you're the "Mother, please, I'd rather do it myself" type of person, you can always bypass the wizard and use the Save As option in the File menu. Here are a few things that will enlighten and entertain you about the file formats you can save in PhotoDraw.

You have 8 possible formats you can save in: PhotoDraw (*.mix), Picture It 2.0-3.0 (*.mix), GIF (*.gif), PC Paintbrush (*.pcx), Portable Network Graphic (*.png), Tagged Image File Format (*.tif), Targa (*.tga), and Windows Bitmaps (*.bmp).

In the Save As dialog box, you can find an Options button. The things you can control through these settings include:

✦ Color conversion

✦ Palette use

✦ Compression type and amount

✦ Exported size and proportion

PhotoDraw Printing Options

You can print your PhotoDraw creations in the same way you print any other Office document, spreadsheet, or report. (See Appendix B for help on printing in Office 2000.) There is, however, one pretty slick feature that some of the other programs don't offer: Print Reprints. This printing wizard steps you through choosing pre-sized and formatted labels, stickers, and more to print duplicates of your pictures. All you do is choose the manufacturer and stock number of the form you are using, and PhotoDraw does the rest.

As an added plus, you aren't limited to just printing multiple copies of one image. You can select any number of images to drag from your Picture list or browse your drives for other pictures to drop into the template that the wizard dishes out. After stepping through the wizard, you are presented with a new picture in the Picture list that you can save for later use.

Index

Numbers

3-D effect, 728
3-D text, 716, 717

A

alignment, text, 714, 715
AutoShapes toolbar, 719, 720

B

bending text, 714–715
blur/sharpen effect, 727
brightness, 698–699

C

clip art, 690–691
Clone Paint tool, 703–706
color balance. *See also*
        touching up
    changing, 700
    grayscale, 701
    negative, 701
coloring
    applying, to entire picture, 697
    applying, to part of
        picture, 697
    brightness, 698–699
    contrast, 698–699
    correcting, by painting, 698
    correcting, by selection
        method, 697
    hue, 699
    saturation, 699
    tint, 699
colorizing, 699–700
colors
    blending, 726
    fill, 723, 724–725
    options, 686
    painting, 722
    two-color gradient, 725
    underlying, 707
contrast, 698–699
copyright laws, 689
Creative Paint toolbar, 721, 722
cropping, 708
Cut Out toolbar, 709, 710, 685
cutting out, 708–710

D

Designer 3-D Gallery, 716
Designer Effects. *See also* effects
    categories, 728
    locking, 729
    settings, 729
Designer Gradient fills, 723–724
Designer Text Gallery, 716, 717
despeckling, 703
digital cameras
    choosing, 694
    Kodak DC-50 interface, 695
    using, 693–694
    workpane, 694
distort effect, 728
drawing
    images, 694–696
    outline, editing, 720
    points, 720–721
    with shapes, 719–721
Drawing area, 687
dust, removing, 702

E

edges, 709, 710
Edit menu, Undo command, 708
effects
    3-D, 728
    blur/sharpen, 727
    Designer, 728–729
    distort, 728
    fade out, 727
    shadow, 727
    transparency, 727
Effects tools, 686
Erase tool, 707, 710

F

fade out effect, 727
File menu
    Digital Camera command, 693
    New command, 690, 694
    Picture Setup command, 707
    Save As command, 734
    Save for Use In command, 731
    Scan Picture command, 692
    Visual Open command, 691

files, opening, 690–691
Fill menu
    Designer Gradient
        command, 724
    Picture command, 726
    Solid Color command, 723
    Texture command, 723
    Two-Color Gradient
        command, 725
fills
    Designer Gradient, 723–724
    object, 722–727
    picture, 726–727
    selecting, 685
    solid color, 723
    texture, 723
    transparency, 723, 724, 726
    two-color gradient, 724–725
formatting text, 714, 715
Formatting toolbar
    3-D button, 716
    Crop button, 708
    Fill button, 723
    opening, 686
Full Screen mode, 695

H

hue/saturation, 699

I

images
    digital camera, retrieving,
        693–694
    drawing, 694–696
    preparing, 689–690
Insert menu, Clip Art
        command, 691
interface, 683, 684–687, 688

M

Microsoft Clip Gallery, 691, 692
Microsoft Office documents,
        saving as, 733
Microsoft PhotoDraw dialog
        box, 689–690
monitor resolution, 695

Book X

Appendixes

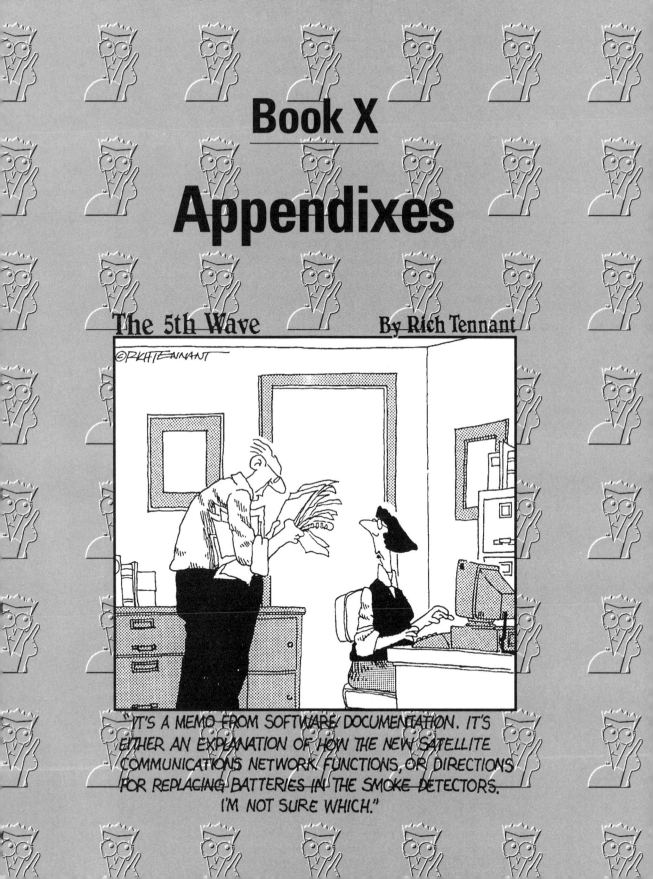

"IT'S A MEMO FROM SOFTWARE DOCUMENTATION. IT'S EITHER AN EXPLANATION OF HOW THE NEW SATELLITE COMMUNICATIONS NETWORK FUNCTIONS, OR DIRECTIONS FOR REPLACING BATTERIES IN THE SMOKE DETECTORS. I'M NOT SURE WHICH."

Contents at a Glance

Appendix A: Starting, Surviving, and Getting Help

In This Appendix

⊯ **Starting an Office 2000 application**

⊯ **Mousing your way through Office 2000 applications**

⊯ **Using the Office 2000 clipboard to cut, copy, and paste**

⊯ **Undoing your mistakes**

⊯ **Getting help**

*O*ffice 2000 may seem to you like a bunch of complicated and mysterious products — and they certainly can be! Fortunately for you, Office 2000 is an integrated group that shares many similar ways of doing things. This appendix shows you some things you do all the time with Office 2000, from starting an application to finding help when you need it.

Starting an Office 2000 Application

Windows almost always gives you more than one way to perform a task, and starting an Office 2000 application is no exception. The most popular way to start is to use the Start button in the taskbar.

1. **Click the Start button on the taskbar (you'll find the Start button in the lower-left corner of your screen).**

2. **Choose Programs on the menu that appears.**

3. **Choose your application (such as Microsoft Word, Microsoft PowerPoint, Microsoft Excel, and so on).**

Here are some other easy ways to get going.

✦ If you have the Microsoft Office shortcut bar, click the Open a Document button on it, choose an existing Office 2000 document, and click the Open button.

✦ Double-click an existing Office 2000 file in Windows Explorer or My Computer. Windows starts the application and opens the document that you double-clicked.

Using the Mouse

Odds are that you can recognize your mouse, even at ten paces. Or perhaps you use a trackball, or another pointing device. The important thing is that you have a mouse (or other pointing device) and know how to use it. Otherwise, an Office 2000 application can be next to impossible to navigate.

Your pointing device controls the cursor and the pointer (see "Cursors and Ponters" later in this appendix). In general, when you are told to click something, you should move the mouse pointer to that thing and then click the left mouse button. Table A-1 shows some common pointing procedures and how to perform them.

Table A-1	Clicking Your Way through Office 2000
Clicking Action	*What It Means or Does*
Click something	Move the pointer to the something and click the left mouse button
Double-click something	Move the pointer to the something and click the left mouse button twice quickly, without moving the pointer even the littlest bit
Right-click something	Move the pointer to the something and click the right mouse button
Click and drag	Move the pointer to the something and click with the left mouse button. Holding the left mouse button down, move the mouse without letting go of the button.
Ctrl+click	Press and hold down the Ctrl key while you click the left mouse button

Cursors and Pointers

Cursors and *pointers* are little symbols that let you know where you are on-screen and what the computer is doing. There are a bunch of different cursors and pointers, but the only ones you really need to know about are listed in Table A-2.

Table A-2		Must-Know Cursors and Pointers
	Cursor/Pointer	*What It Does*
I	Insertion point	Sits in the text and blinks on and off (for example, in Word it is found on the page you are using, in Excel it is in the Formula bar, and so on). All the action takes place at the insertion point: When you start typing, text appears at this point, and when you paste something from the Clipboard, it appears at the insertion point.
I ▵	Mouse cursor	Moves around on-screen when you move your mouse. Jiggle your mouse to see what the mouse cursor is. When this cursor is over something that you can select — a menu item or a button, for example — it turns into an arrow. Click the mouse when it's an arrow to select a menu item or press a button. When the mouse cursor is over text, it looks like a large, egotistical *I*. To enter text in a new place, move the *I*, click, and start typing.

	Cursor/Pointer	What It Does
⧖	 Busy cursor	When an application is very busy, you see an hourglass on-screen. Twiddle your thumbs until the hourglass disappears and you can get back to work.
☞	 Link Select cursor	When you move the pointer over a hyperlink, you see the Link Select cursor, a gloved hand. A *hyperlink* is a link between two documents or a document and a page on the Internet. Click a hyperlink and you travel to another document or a Web page.

Shortcut Keys for Doing It Quickly

Next to some commands on menus are Ctrl+key combinations called *shortcut keys.* If you want to select all the text in a document, for example, you can just press Ctrl+A, the shortcut key equivalent of the Select All command on the Edit menu.

Lots of menu commands have shortcut keys that help you get your work done faster. If you find yourself using a command often, see if it has a shortcut key and start using the shortcut key to save time. Many commands have buttons next to their names as well. Instead of choosing these commands from menus, you can simply click a button on a toolbar.

Cutting, Copying, and Pasting

As in other Windows-based programs, the Cut, Copy, and Paste commands involve the Clipboard. The Office 2000 Clipboard offers many more features than the Windows Clipboard. For example, the Windows Clipboard keeps only the text (or other object) most recently cut or copied; the Office Clipboard can hold as many as 12 items at any given time. Items can be copied and collected from virtually any other program and can remain on the Office Clipboard until you exit all Office programs.

The Office Clipboard is operated with a special Clipboard toolbar that can be summoned by choosing View➪Toolbars➪Clipboard from the Menu bar (see Figure A-1).

Figure A-1:
You can
really fill
up the
Clipboard
now.

The Clipboard toolbar displays all items currently cut or copied to the Clipboard. Click an item and then click the Copy, Paste, Paste All, or Delete button to manipulate the item. To select multiple items, hold down the Ctrl key as you click each item.

Undoing Errors

The Undo command is wonderful because it literally undoes your last action in an Office 2000 application. Cleared text reappears. Moved text goes back to its original location. Undo tracks your 20 most recent actions — but try to fix undo-able errors the minute you notice them. The only thing Undo can't reverse is the passage of time. You can invoke the Undo command in any of three ways:

✦ Choose Edit⇨Undo from the Menu bar.

✦ Click the Undo button on the Standard toolbar.

✦ Press Ctrl+Z

In case you're the finicky sort, Office 2000 also provides a Redo command, which allows you to redo whatever you previously undid. You can use the Redo command as follows:

✦ Choose Edit⇨Redo from the Menu bar.

✦ Click the Redo button on the Standard toolbar.

✦ Press Ctrl+Y

Getting the Help You Need in Office 2000

Office 2000 offers a bunch of different ways to get help, and one or two of them are really useful. Choose your favorite way or mix and match.

Contents and index

The best way to get help is to choose Help⇨Contents and Index. That takes you to a dialog box with three tabs for finding the instructions you need (see Figure A-2 for an example):

✦ **Contents:** A bunch of general topics. Double-click a book icon, and it opens to more topics, each with a question mark beside its name. Click the question mark beside the topic that interests you and click Display, if general topics are your cup of tea.

✦ **Index:** This is the most useful means of getting help. Click the Index tab and type a few letters that describe what puzzles you. The alphabetical list of index topics scrolls down to show you which topics are available. If a topic strikes your fancy, double-click it or click it and choose Display. You'll go straight to an informative instruction box or some other help feature.

✦ **Answer Wizard:** Allows you to ask a question. The help system provides topics for you to choose from.

The Help window also provides some tools that you can use: buttons, links, and windows that pop up when you click particular words or symbols.

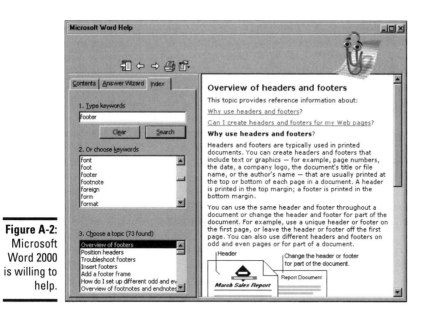

Appendix A

Starting, Surviving, and Getting Help

Figure A-2: Microsoft Word 2000 is willing to help.

The buttons at the top of the Help window are useful for navigating the Help system and working with the help you find (see Figure A-3):

> ✦ **Hide:** Displays the Help pane and hides the pane with the Contents, Answer Wizard, and Index tabs. Click the Show button, which appears in the same position, to redisplay the pane with the Contents, Answer Wizard, and Index tabs.

> ✦ **Back:** Displays the previous Help topic.

> ✦ **Forward:** Displays the next Help topic. This button is only active if you have used the Back button.

> ✦ **Print:** Prints the displayed Help topic.

> ✦ **Options:** Displays a drop-down list of options — things that you can do with Help windows.

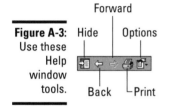

Figure A-3: Use these Help window tools.

Close the Help window by clicking its Close button.

What's this?

Another useful way to get help is to choose Help➪What's This or press Shift+F1.The pointer changes into an arrow with a question mark beside it. Click this quizzical cursor on a part of the screen that you want to know more about. With any luck, you get concise instructions for carrying out the thing you clicked. Figure A-4 shows a mini-Help screen you get when you click text to see how text is formatted in a Word document.

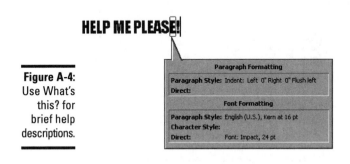

Figure A-4:
Use What's
this? for
brief help
descriptions.

Dialog box help

The upper-right corner of dialog boxes also has Help buttons in the shape of question marks. Click a dialog box Help button and click the part of the dialog box you need help with to get a brief explanation of the thing you clicked.

Help from the Internet

Yet another way to seek help is to find it on the Internet. Choose Help➪Office on the Web to go to the official Microsoft Office Web site, where you can get advice about using each Office product and even submit questions to Microsoft technicians (but don't expect an answer right away).

The Office Assistant

In keeping with its goal of making computers as much fun to use as watching Saturday morning cartoons, Microsoft also offers the Office Assistant. Click the Help button on the Standard toolbar (or press F1) and the Office Assistant appears in a corner of the screen along with a bubble caption into which you can type a question (see Figure A-5). Type your question, click Search, and hope for a sensible answer. Choose Help➪Hide the Office Assistant when you want the Office Assistant to go away.

The Office Assistant provides the following types of help:

♦ It displays a tip of the day when you start the application (optional).

♦ It watches you work and lets you know when there's a more efficient way to perform an operation. A yellow light bulb appears next to the Assistant (or in the Microsoft Help toolbar button) when it has a tip for you. Click the light bulb to read the tip.

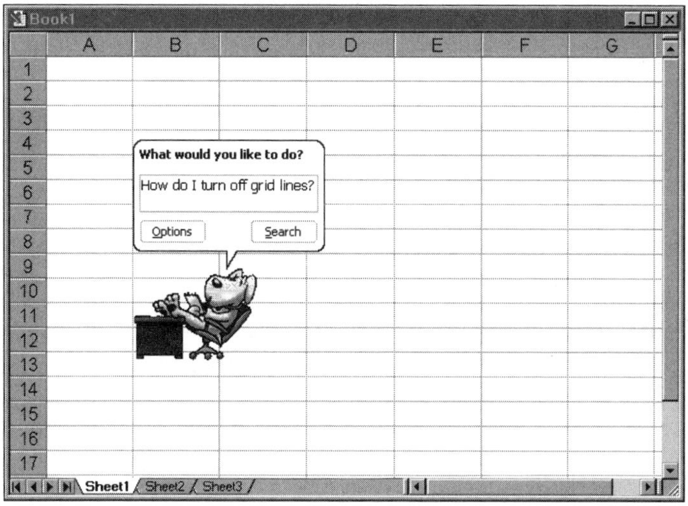

Figure A-5:
The Office
Assistant
in Excel
2000.

In the spreadsheet figure, a speech box reads:

What would you like to do?

How do I turn off grid lines?

Options   Search

+ It provides automatic help with certain tasks. For example, if you're about to create a chart in Excel 2000, the Assistant asks if you need help.

+ It responds to natural language questions. Just type your question in the Assistant's box and click Search.

If you find that the Office Assistant is sometimes too helpful and it gets distracting, customize it to your liking: Right-click the Assistant and choose Options from the shortcut menu. The Office Assistant dialog box appears with the Options tab selected. To turn the Assistant off, clear the checkbox next to the Use the Office Assistant label. To turn the Assistant on, select the Help⇨Show the Office Assistant command.

You can select Help⇨Hide the Office Assistant to hide the Assistant when the Assistant is turned on. Hiding the Assistant is not the same as turning the Assistant off. Hiding the Assistant simply hides the icon from view. If you later click the Microsoft Help button on the toolbar, the Assistant reappears. When you turn the Assistant off and then click the Microsoft Help button, your application displays the Help dialog box but does not show the Assistant.

To hire a different Assistant, follow these steps:

1. **Right-click the Assistant and select Choose Assistant from the pop-up menu.**

An Office Assistant dialog box appears with the Gallery tab selected (see Figure A-6).

2. **Browse the Gallery by clicking Next or Back until you find an Assistant you like.**

3. **Click OK to accept your choice of Assistant.**

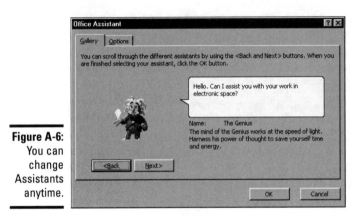

Figure A-6:
You can
change
Assistants
anytime.

Appendix B: Printing an Office 2000 Document

In This Appendix

✓ Previewing before you print

✓ Choosing some options for your printing

✓ Printing a document

✓ Canceling your printing

*P*rinting an Office 2000 document can be as easy as clicking a button or as complicated as going through a bunch of menus and dialog boxes in order to get what you want. Fortunately, most of the printing chores in Office 2000 applications are similar, so you can often go from Excel to Word to Publisher, for example, without missing a beat.

This appendix introduces you to the basics so that you can sit down and print just about anything in Office 2000. If you have some special printing considerations for a particular application (such as printing noncontiguous ranges in Excel, or something fun like that), be sure to check out the application's Help files. You can read all about getting help in Office 2000 simply by flipping back to Appendix A.

Previewing What You Print

Before you print a document, do yourself a big favor by *previewing* it. That way, you can catch errors before you send it through the printer and waste 1, 2, 5, or 20 sheets of paper. For that matter, preview your documents from time to time to make sure that they are laid out correctly.

To preview a document:

1. **Put the document you're about to print on-screen.**

2. **Choose File⇨Print Preview or click the Print Preview button on the toolbar.**

A panoramic picture of your document appears on the Preview screen (see Figure B-1).

Prints document
Shows many pages
Shrinks document
Displays rulers
Enlarges preview screen
Shows one page
Changes size on-screen
Closes preview screen
Zooms in
Gets help

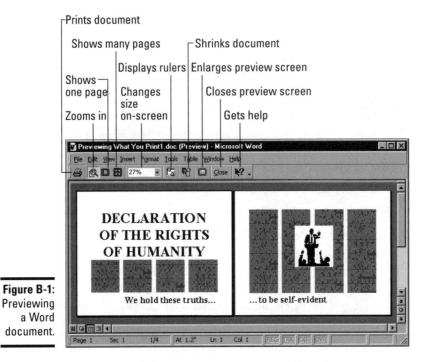

Figure B-1:
Previewing
a Word
document.

3. **Use the buttons and scroll bar on the Preview screen to get a better look at your document:**

- Click part of the document to zoom in and examine closely. The pointer, which previously looked like a magnifying glass with a plus sign in it, now has a minus sign where the plus sign used to be. Click again to zoom out and get back to the Preview screen. If your pointer doesn't look like a magnifying glass, click the Magnifier button on the Print Preview toolbar.

- Click the One Page or Multiple Pages button to view one or several pages at once.

- Click the Zoom Control menu and either enter a percentage and press the Enter key or choose a different percentage from the menu to see more of a page. You can also click the Page Width setting on the Zoom menu to make the page fill the Preview screen.

- Click the Shrink to Fit button, and your document shrinks a bit if it can. Choose this option if the last page has only a few lines of text and you want to save a piece of paper.

- The Full Screen button removes the menu bars and ruler so that you can really get the "big picture" of a page.

4. **Click <u>C</u>lose if you need to go back to the document and make changes; otherwise, click the Print button.**

Choosing Some Page Options

You don't have to print exclusively on standard 8.5 x 11 paper; you can print on legal-size paper and other sizes of paper as well. A Word newsletter with an unusual shape really stands out in a crowd and gets people's attention. Or maybe your Excel spreadsheet begs to fit across a big page. You can also sometimes choose the direction you want to print on the page (portrait or landscape).

Office 2000 applications share many options, but each program also has unique needs and demands. Be sure to explore what each program can do for you.

1. **Choose File⇨Page Setup.**

2. **If you don't see page setup operations right away, click the tab that indicates paper options.**

3. **Pick and choose your paper options.**

Choose a setting from the Paper Size drop-down list (as shown with Access in Figure B2). If none of the settings suits you, you can sometimes indicate a size (as shown with Word in Figure B-3) or perhaps scale your document (Excel). With Publisher, you can choose your layout and your fold (see Figure B-4).

Select either Portrait (tall pages) or Landscape (wide pages).

If you keep legal-size paper in one tray of your printer and standard-size paper in another, for example, find a Paper Source drop-down list or tab in the Page Setup dialog box and change settings there.

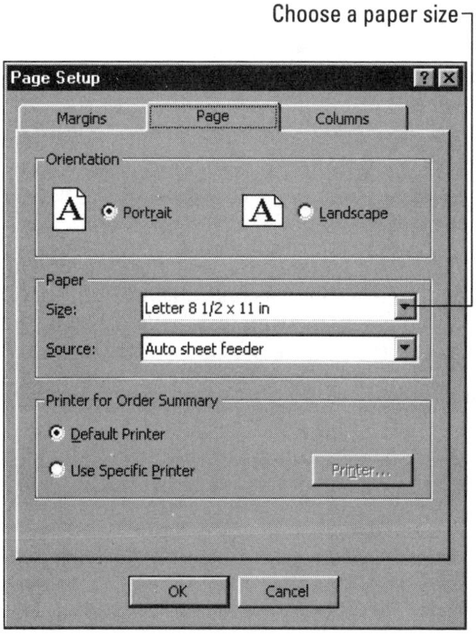

Choose a paper size ⌐

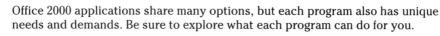

Page Setup   [?][X]

| Margins | Page | Columns |

Orientation

[A] ⦿ Portrait   [A] ⦱ Landscape

Paper
Size: Letter 8 1/2 x 11 in ▼
Source: Auto sheet feeder ▼

Printer for Order Summary
⦿ Default Printer
⦱ Use Specific Printer   Printer...

[OK]   [Cancel]

Figure B-2:
Access
lets you
choose a
paper size.

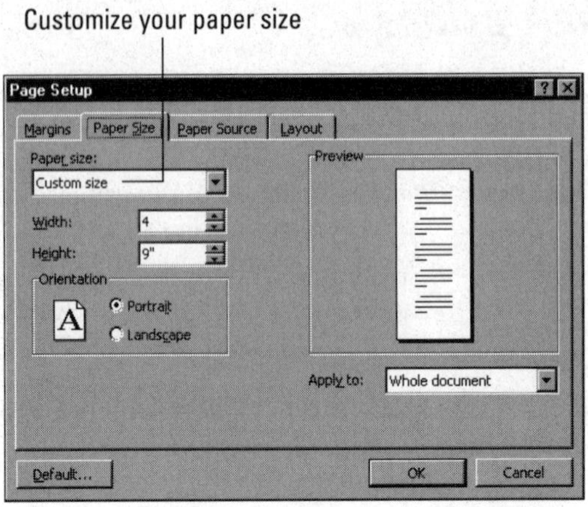

Customize your paper size

Figure B-3:
Word lets
you also
indicate a
custom
size.

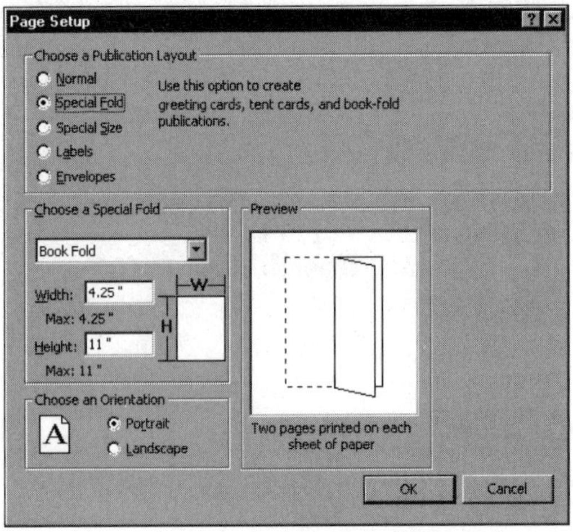

Figure B-4:
Publisher
has some
special
page
considerations.

Some applications also allow you to adjust your margins from the Page Setup dialog box. (A *margin* is the blank space on the side of the printed page. The wider the margins, the less space is available for printing.) For example, in Access you can control all four page margins from Excel. Just look for the Margins tab (see Figure B-5).

4. **Click OK after you're finished playing around with your options.**

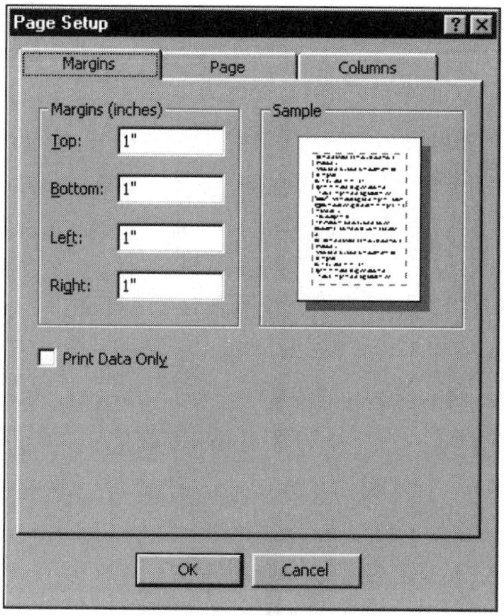

Figure B-5:
You can adjust all four margins in Access.

Printing a Document

The fastest way to print a document is to click the Print button on the Standard toolbar. Go this route if you want to print the entire thing from start to finish.

To print part of a document, selected text in a document, the entire thing, or even unusual things like comments and summary text, follow these steps:

1. **Choose File⇨Print (or press Ctrl+P) to open the Print dialog box (see Figure B-6).**

2. **If you don't see your printer name in the Name file of the Printer section, use the drop-down list to look for it.**

   If you have multiple printers set up and attached to your computer (perhaps through a network), you can choose the Name option in the Print dialog box to tell your application which printer to print to (see Figure B-7).

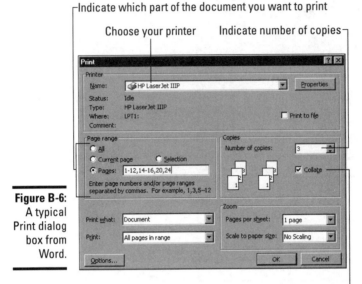

Indicate which part of the document you want to print

Choose your printer   Indicate number of copies

Figure B-6:
A typical
Print dialog
box from
Word.

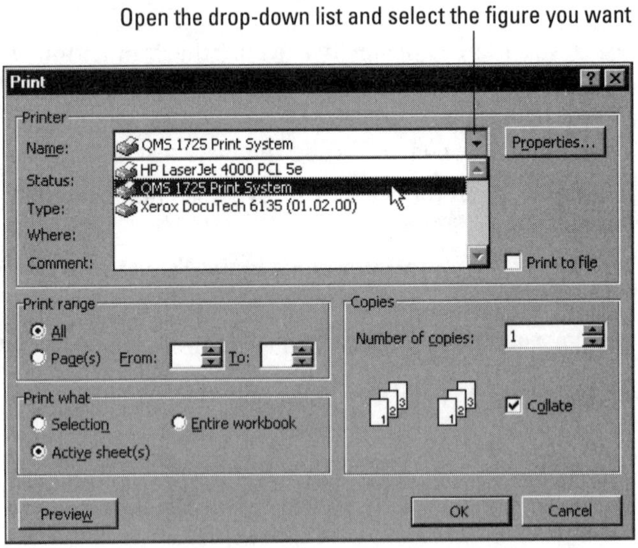

Collate copies

Open the drop-down list and select the figure you want

Figure B-7:
You may
have to go
fishing for
a network
printer, as
shown
here in
Excel.

3. **Enter the number of copies you want in a Number of Copies box
(located in a section of the dialog box aptly named "Copies"), as shown
in Figure B-8.**

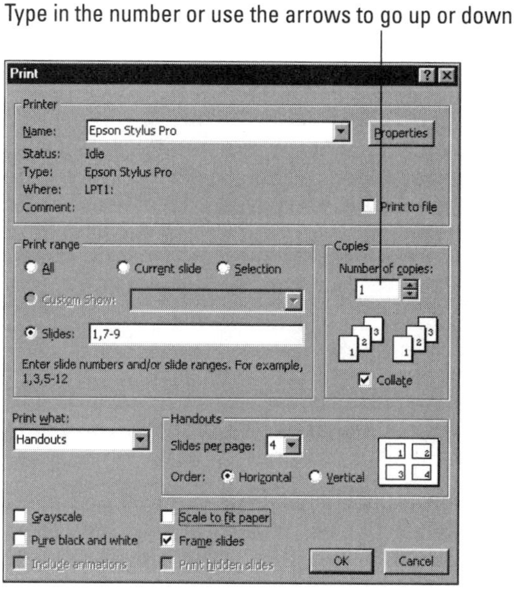

Type in the number or use the arrows to go up or down

Figure B-8: PowerPoint wants to print the number of copies that you want.

4. **Tell the application how much of the document to print (look for a Print Range section in this dialog box).**

Depending on the application, you can indicate possibilities such as all, the current page, the pages you indicate, the portion you have currently selected, and so on. (See Figure B-9.)

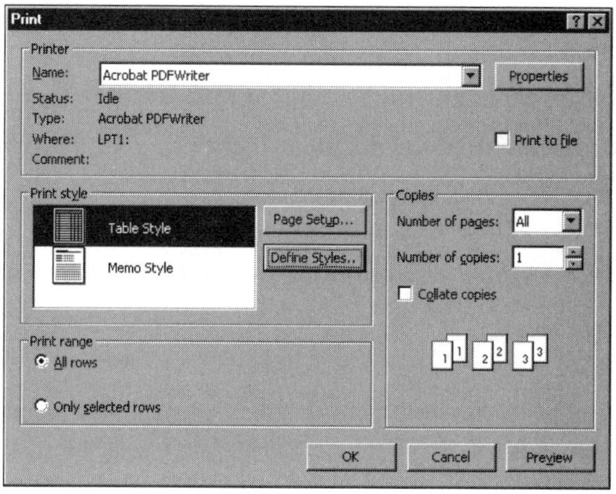

Figure B-9: In Outlook, you can indicate selected rows to print.

5. **Choose Print to File to copy the document to a print file if you plan to take your document to a print shop for printing.**

6. **Click OK.**

A Print dialog box also offers the options to collate. If you're printing more than one copy of a document with many pages and you don't want the copies to be collated, click the Collate box to remove the check mark. If you print three three-page documents, for example, the pages will come out of the printer 111, 222, 333, instead of 123, 123, 123.

Canceling a Print Job

If you have a printer directly connected to your computer, you get two chances to cancel a print job. The first chance is when you see a small dialog box telling you that your table (or report or whatever) is printing. The dialog box includes a Cancel button that you can click to cancel the print job.

The printer doesn't stop printing immediately, and may print out another page or two, but clicking the Cancel button stops the application from sending more information to the printer.

If you want to stop a print job after the dialog box with the Cancel button disappears, you have to resort to the fallback method — using the Windows Printer window. When any document is printing in Windows, a small printer appears in the indicators box in the taskbar. (The *indicators box* usually appears on the right of the taskbar and contains the time.) Double-click that small printer icon to display the Windows Printer window — a window that contains the name of your printer on the title bar and lists current print jobs.

If the printer you use is on a network, you may not be able to use the Printer window to cancel a print job. You should identify your network guru (or someone who knows how to cancel print jobs) to find out how to cancel a print job on your network.

To cancel a print job from the Printer window, follow these steps:

1. **Right-click the name of the document that you want to cancel to display the shortcut menu.**

2. **Choose <u>C</u>ancel Printing from the shortcut menu.**

The printer mercifully stops printing (when it is good and ready).

Appendix C: Binding Office 2000 Documents Together

In This Appendix

- ✔ Creating a new binder
- ✔ Getting documents into your binder
- ✔ Switching between binder sections
- ✔ Opening an existing binder
- ✔ Deleting data from your binder

*I*f your work often consists of using Word, Excel, and PowerPoint together, you probably have files in these applications scattered all over the place in different locations and in different folders. The odds of misplacing a file rise, of course, as your collection of files accumulates. Now where was that cover letter you were working on? And what was the name of that accompanying spreadsheet? If you find yourself asking such questions, you may be a perfect candidate for Microsoft Binder.

A *binder* is a single file that can hold data from several Word, Excel, or PowerPoint files (but not Access or Outlook files) at once. Don't confuse a binder with a folder, however. A folder holds from none to as many different files that you can stuff into it. A binder is a unique file containing data from those Word, Excel, or PowerPoint files.

If you intend to share a binder with someone else, realize that this person must have Microsoft Office 2000 — not just Word, Excel, or PowerPoint — to view or edit the file.

Note: If you have not installed binders, you need to install it from the Microsoft Office 2000 CD.

Creating a New Binder

You have two ways to create a Microsoft Office Binder: through the Office Tools submenu or through the Windows taskbar menu.

Creating a new binder with the Office Tools submenu:

1. **Click the Start button on the taskbar and choose _Programs.**

2. **From the pop-up menu, choose Office Tools and then choose Microsoft Binder.**

   A blank Microsoft Office binder appears (see Figure C-1). This binder is empty, of course, until you insert data from your files.

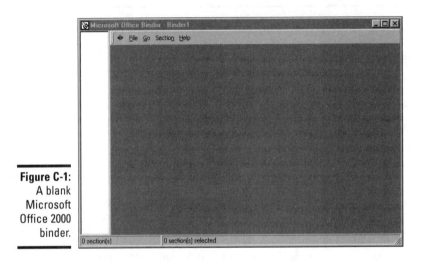

Figure C-1:
A blank
Microsoft
Office 2000
binder.

Creating a new binder from the Windows taskbar menu:

1. **Click the Start button on the taskbar and choose New Office Document.**

   The New Office Document dialog box appears (see Figure C-2).

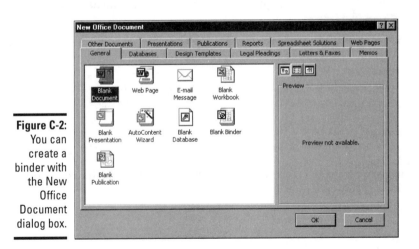

Figure C-2:
You can
create a
binder with
the New
Office
Document
dialog box.

2. Select Blank Binder and click OK.

A blank Microsoft Office binder appears (refer to Figure C-1).

Note: Don't forget to save your binder just as you save any Office 2000 application. To save a binder, choose File⇨Save Binder.

Putting Documents into a Binder

Although a binder is a unique file, a binder consists of one or more *sections*. Each section consists of a single Word document, Excel spreadsheet, or PowerPoint presentation.

Adding a new document (section) into a binder

If you are planning ahead and want to add a blank Word document, Excel spreadsheet, or PowerPoint presentation into a binder, follow these steps (but don't forget to have a new or existing binder open).

1. Choose Section⇨Add.

The Add Section dialog box appears, as shown in Figure C-3.

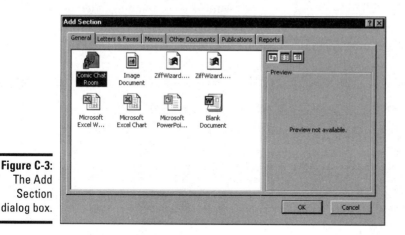

Figure C-3:
The Add
Section
dialog box.

2. Select the type of blank document that you want to put into your binder.

- Microsoft Excel Chart
- Microsoft Excel Worksheet
- Microsoft PowerPoint Presentation
- Blank Document (Word)

3. Click OK.

An icon that represents your choice suddenly appears in the left pane of the binder (as shown in Figure C-4).

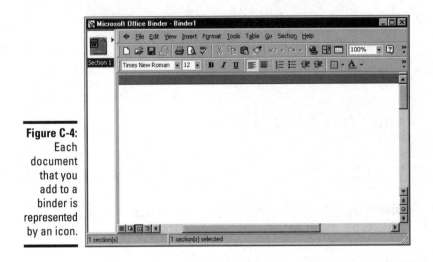

Figure C-4:
Each
document
that you
add to a
binder is
represented
by an icon.

Putting an existing file into a binder

Maybe you've had the great idea to use Binder after having created some Word, Excel, or PowerPoint files. It's not too late! To put an existing Word, Excel, or PowerPoint file into a binder, follow these steps (with a binder already open, of course!).

1. **Choose Section➪Add from File.**

The Add from File dialog box appears, as shown in Figure C-5.

Figure C-5:
The Add
from File
dialog box.

2. **Click the Files of Type list box and choose the type of document that you want to add to your binder.**

3. **Select the file that you want to add to your binder.**

4. Click A*dd*.

Microsoft Office 2000 proudly displays your added file icon in the pane to the left of your binder.

When you add an existing Word, PowerPoint, or Excel file to a binder, you have two copies of the file. One copy is stored in your binder, and the original is still a separate file on your disk. Because these two copies are separate, changes in one file are not going to be reflected in the other file. You may want to delete the original file to avoid having two copies of the same data confusing you.

Switching between Sections in Your Binder

The left pane of a binder shows you all the sections (documents) that make up your binder and lets you switch between these sections.

A binder displays the data of only one section at a time. For example, you can't view a Word document at the same time that you view an Excel spreadsheet. You need to switch between your sections. To switch between sections in the same binder, simply click the icon representing the section you want to see.

If you have too many section icons, you can hide one or more of these icons from view. Just select the section icon that you want to hide and choose Section⇨Hide. To bring a hidden section back into view, choose Section⇨Unhide. In the Unhide Sections dialog box, select the section that you want to view again and click OK.

To hide (or unhide) the entire left pane of a binder, click the Show/Hide Left Pane button on the Standard toolbar.

Opening an Existing Binder

You don't create and fill up a binder just for fun, do you? To open a binder so that you can work on it, you get to choose two different methods: through the Office Tools submenu or through the Windows taskbar menu.

Opening a binder through the Office Tools submenu:

1. Click the Start button on the taskbar and choose *P*rograms.

2. From the pop-up menu, choose Office Tools and then choose Microsoft Binder.

3. From the blank Microsoft Office binder that appears, choose *F*ile⇨*O*pen or press Ctrl+O.

The Open Binder dialog box appears, as shown in Figure C-6.

4. Select the binder that you want to open and then click *O*pen.

Appendix C

Binding Office 2000 Documents Together

Figure C-6:
The Open
Binder
dialog box
lets you
open an
existing
binder.

Opening a binder through the Windows taskbar:

1. **Click the Start button on the taskbar and choose Open Office Document.**

2. **When the Open Office Document dialog box appears, find the binder that you want and select it.**

3. **Click Open.**

Deleting a Binder Section

Not every binder section that you create is going to be a keeper! You may feel the need to delete a section once in awhile. To delete a binder section, follow these steps:

1. **In the left pane, select the section icon that you want to obliterate.**

2. **Choose Section⇨Delete.**

A dialog box appears, asking whether you really want to delete the chosen section.

3. **Click OK to make that section disappear forever.**

Index

IDG BOOKS WORLDWIDE BOOK REGISTRATION

We want to hear from you!

Register This Book and Win!

™

...FOR DUMMIES

BESTSELLING BOOK SERIES